emperor michael palaeologus and the west

eMPeROR
michael palaeologus
and the west

1258 - 1282

a study in
Byzantine-latin Relations

BY

DENO JOHN GEANAKOPLOS

ARCHON BOOKS

1973

Library of Congress Cataloging in Publication Data

Geanakoplos, Deno John.
   Emperor Michael Palaeologus and the West, 1258-1282.

   Bibliography: p.
   1. Michael III Palaeologus. Emperor of the East,
1234-1282. 2. Byzantine Empire—Foreign relations. I.
Title.
[DF635.G4   1973]   949.5   72-11525
ISBN 0-208-01310-5

©1959 by the President and Fellows of Harvard College
Reprinted 1973 with permission in an unaltered
and unabridged edition as an Archon Book by
The Shoe String Press, Inc., Hamden, Connecticut 06514
Printed in the United States of America

TO MY WIFE

ACKNOWLEDGMENTS

Among the many who have helped during the long years of preparing this book for publication, my thanks go first to Professor R. L. Wolff of Harvard, who guided the work in its early phase and later gave valuable advice on a large number of problems. I am grateful also to Professors F. Dvornik and M. Anastos of Dumbarton Oaks and Harvard University and A. C. Krey of the University of Minnesota for their encouragement during various stages, as well as to Professors Alexander Turyn of the University of Illinois and George H. Williams, Giles Constable, and Cedric Whitman of Harvard for useful counsel on historical and palaeographical considerations. To my assistant at the University of Illinois, Catherine Ridder, I am indebted for wearisome hours spent on the manuscript. To many other friends here and abroad, who have read sections and advised on specific questions but are too numerous to mention, I can only make collective but grateful reference. Finally, to my wife for her unfailing assistance, patience and endurance, the dedication is a small sign of appreciation.

I am indebted to the Dumbarton Oaks Research Library (under whose auspices this work was initiated), the Harvard History Department, the American Council of Learned Societies, and the Research Board of the University of Illinois, all of which provided generous financial aid or grants enabling me to carry on research in this country and in Europe.

Acknowledgment is made to the following publications for permission to quote from several articles of mine which originally appeared therein and which I have drawn on, in revised form, for the present book: *Traditio* for "The Nicene Revolution of 1258 and the Usurpation of Michael VIII Palaeologus," IX (1953) 420–430; *Dumbarton Oaks Papers* for "Greco-Latin Relations on the Eve of the Byzantine Restoration: The Battle of Pelagonia (1259)," VII (1953) 99–141; *Harvard Theological Review* for "Michael VIII

ACKNOWLEDGMENTS

Palaeologus and the Union of Lyons (1274)," XLVI (1953) 79–89; *Greek Orthodox Theological Review* for "On the Schism of the Greek and Roman Churches: A Confidential Papal Directive for the Implementation of Union (1278)," I (1954) 16–24. Thanks are also due to the following publishers and individuals for permission to reproduce maps or photographs: Professor J. Hussey and the Hutchinson University Library for "Map of the Aegean World ca. 1214–1254," from J. Hussey, *The Byzantine World* (London, 1956); Cambridge University Press for maps of "The Environs of Constantinople," and "The City of Constantinople," from *Cambridge Medieval History*, vol. IV, maps 47B and 47A, and of "Italy under Charles of Anjou," from the same work, vol. VI, map 60; John Murray Ltd. for map "Greece in 1278," from W. Miller, *The Latins in the Levant* (London, 1908) 151; Velhagen and Klasing for maps "The Byzantine Empire in 1265" and "The Mediterranean Lands after 1204" from *Shepherd's Historical Atlas*; and, finally, Alinari for a photograph of a statue of Charles of Anjou.

Urbana, Illinois   D. G.
1957

contents

CONTENTS

ıllustRatıons

Greek and Western portraits of the Emperor Michael VIII Palaeologus. Two miniatures from fourteenth century manuscripts. Page 194.

Bayerische Staatsbibliothek, Munich, Cod. Graec. 442, fol. 174r; Biblioteca Marciana, Venice, Cod. Lat. 393, fol. 76.

Statue of Charles of Anjou in the Palazzo dei Conservatori, Rome. Page 195.

Alinari.

Record concerning a loan for the defense of the Latin Empire of Constantinople (Appendix B, no. 1). Page 378.

Biblioteca Marciana, Venice, Lat. class. 14, no. 37, fol. 20r–v.

Three epigrams in political verse, eulogizing Michael — VIII or IX? (Appendix B, no. 6). Page 379.

Biblioteca Marciana, Venice, greco 464, fol. 1r.

MAPS

The Aegean world ca. 1214–1254: the Latin and Nicene Empires and the Despotate of Epirus. Page 12.

From J. Hussey, The Byzantine World *(London, 1956).*

The environs of Constantinople. Page 98.

From Cambridge Medieval History, *IV, map 47b.*

The city of Constantinople. Page 128.

From Cambridge Medieval History, *IV, map 47a.*

The Byzantine Empire in 1265, shortly after Michael VIII's recovery of Constantinople from the Latins. Page 172.

From Shepherd's Historical Atlas, *no. 89.*

Italy under Charles of Anjou, ca. 1270. Page 247.

From Cambridge Medieval History, *VI, map. 60.*

The Mediterranean lands after 1204, background of the conflict between Michael and Charles. Page 281.

From Shepherd's Historical Atlas, *no. 73.*

Greece in 1278. Page 327.

From W. Miller, The Latins in the Levant *(London, 1908).*

emperor michael palaeologus and the west

Introduction

THE ISSUES AND THE SOURCES

On Easter Monday, 1282,[1] the bells of Santo Spirito summoned the faithful of Palermo to Vespers. But what began as a call to worship ended in revolution for the Sicilians, victory for Aragon, and the collapse of a vast coalition to restore Western rule over Constantinople. Byzantium was saved from a second occupation by the Latins.

This book examines the relations between Greeks and Latins,[2] Eastern and Western Christendom, during the reign of the Byzantine Emperor Michael VIII Palaeologus (1258–1282). The investigation focuses on the career of the Emperor from the years immediately preceding his recovery of Constantinople from the Latins in 1261 to the climax of his struggle against the West in the celebrated Sicilian Vespers of 1282. Virtually every facet of Byzantine-Western relations in the later Middle Ages is reflected in Michael's reign, for, as will be seen, restoration of Greek rule after a half-century of alien occupation did not arrest the penetration of Latin influence within the Empire. And, externally, it excited the hostility of an aggressive West, eager to reassert its authority in Byzantium. Michael was therefore faced with a succession of diverse problems demanding almost immediate solution at his hands. It was his ability to cope with these difficulties, when failure would have resulted not only in Western political domination but, possibly, even in realization of the basic Byzantine fear — Latinization

[1] On the date see Chapter 14, note 101.
[2] The term "Latins" refers to the peoples of the West — French, Germans, Castilians, Aragonese, and above all Italians and Sicilians, as well as to persons of Western origin residing in the Greek East.

3

of the Greek people[3] — that marks his reign as crucial for the subsequent history of East and West.

Central to Michael's diplomacy was his aim of appeasing the papacy, still near the pinnacle of its power, which alone could save the Greek Empire from Western designs. Thus was signed at Lyons the controversial ecclesiastical union with Rome, which resulted in the establishment of a kind of papal protectorate over Constantinople and, in effect, the tying of Byzantium to the Western political system.

A vast array of issues confronted the Emperor: the continual rivalry of Genoa and Venice for commercial supremacy in his territories; the papal aim to subordinate the Greek church to Rome and, with Greek aid, to launch a new crusade to the Holy Land; the politics and ambitions of Manfred, Baldwin, Louis IX, and the rulers of Castile, Aragon, Pisa, and Montferrat. Most consequential was the consuming ambition to conquer Byzantium of Michael's arch-foe Charles of Anjou, who at last succeeded in organizing a huge coalition not only of the Latin West but of practically all the Slavic and Eastern states encircling Constantinople. The dramatic duel between Charles and Michael, to which the last part of the book is devoted, is one of the most fascinating in all medieval history, and its delineation, it is hoped, will help to fill the lacuna of a history of Charles's reign.[4]

Still another problem of Empire was the Turkish peril in the East, which, though outside the main scope of this book, has been taken into consideration as it affected policy toward the West. As is shown, the charge frequently levied against Michael of virtually unqualified neglect of his Asiatic frontiers[5] must, to a certain de-

[3] On the fear of Latinization see especially Chapter 11, section 2. Culturally, it may be noted, Latin domination might have inhibited, if not prevented, the development of the so-called Palaeologan Renaissance of the thirteenth to fifteenth century, so important in certain respects for its influence on the Renaissance of Italy.

[4] The important work of E. Jordan, *Les origines de la domination Angevine en Italie* (Paris, 1909), extends only to his enthronement and victory at Tagliacozzo in 1268.

[5] See P. Wittek, *Das Furstentum Mentesche* (Istanbul, 1934) 16ff., 24ff.; cf. G. Arnakis, Οἱ Πρῶτοι 'Οθωμανοί (Athens, 1947) 37ff.; G. Ostrogorsky, *History of the Byzantine State*, trans. J. Hussey (Cambridge, 1956) 438; and A. Vasiliev, *History of the Byzantine Empire* (1952) 599, 603.

gree at least, be modified in the light of his bold plan of using Latin crusading armies to restore Anatolia to Byzantine rule.

In view of the complexity of Michael's career, I have deemed it advisable to follow a fairly regular chronological order rather than to discuss relations with the Latins according to broad subject divisions covering his entire reign. Nonetheless, within each chapter I have tried to preserve a certain topical arrangement (e.g., ecclesiastical negotiations with Rome, political and economic relations with Venice and Genoa, conflict in the Morea, etc.). Thus the reader may at once see the interaction of each aspect of Michael's tortuous diplomacy within the total context of developing events — in the last analysis the only satisfactory way to judge the success of a policy projected on such an ecumenical scale.

The long career of this soldier-Emperor — possibly the most subtle, Machiavellian diplomat ever produced by Byzantium — has been divided into three major sections. Part I deals with the Nicene period of Michael's life, presenting an extensive account of his early career leading to his usurpation of the Nicene throne and subsequent victory at Pelagonia, and crowned by the capture of Constantinople. Part II concerns the establishment and critical early years of the restored Empire, with attention directed to the questions immediately facing the Emperor, especially the threat of Venetian reprisals and the treatment to be accorded Western minorities residing within the capital. With the Greek restoration the scope of the narrative is broadened to include the struggle between Manfred and the papacy, both engaged in negotiations with the expelled Latin Emperor.

Part III constitutes the most challenging phase of Michael's reign, the fifteen year conflict with Charles of Anjou, newly enthroned as King of Sicily. Charles's ambition to conquer Byzantium and the desperate resistance of Michael involved almost the entire Mediterranean area as various powers aligned themselves on either side. It was to save his state from the Angevin danger that Michael committed the Greek people to ecclesiastical union. Negotiations with successive popes, culminating in 1274 in the agreement of Lyons and continuing until the rupture of union in

1281, are discussed from the viewpoint of the Greek clergy and people as well as Emperor and pope. The book concludes with the collapse of Angevin designs in the famous but controversial Sicilian Vespers, presenting for the first time a fully documented account of the role played by Michael Palaeologus. Though diplomatic negotiations and military encounters necessarily hold the center of the stage, careful consideration has also been given — and insofar as possible without disturbing the flow of narrative — to social aspects of Greco-Latin relations,[6] such as the reasons for the Greek populace's refusal to accept religious union with Rome, in spite of the fate apparently awaiting Constantinople if such an accord were rejected.

Despite anti-Latin sentiment among the Greeks, Michael, as will be shown, was able successfully to use Westerners in the imperial administration as interpreters, secret envoys, and commanders of fleets and armies. Some were even named to the imperial nobility and, in a conflation of Latin and Greek feudal practice, given jurisdiction over certain Byzantine territories. But the intensification of Latin penetration during the period under discussion did not, it will be noted, lessen the feeling of the Greeks that they were basically different from the Latins. This attitude was shared by the West, whose memory of the continuing Greek disavowal of the Lyons union was in no small measure to be responsible for subsequent Western failures to provide Byzantium with effective aid against the Turks. It is this fundamental Greco-Latin cleavage, a tragedy for Medieval Christendom and one insufficiently studied from a combined East-West point of view, that is the underlying theme of this book.

BIBLIOGRAPHICAL NOTE

There is no work in English on any Emperor of the Palaeologan dynasty (1258–1453), and only a single, pioneer monograph, that of C. Chapman, *Michele Paléologue restaurateur de l'empire*

---

[6] See Chapter 1, text and notes 23–34a; Chapter 2, notes 57 and 61; Chapter 6, *passim*; Chapter 10, section 3; Chapter 11, section 2.

byzantin (*1261–1282*) (Paris, 1926), exists on the reign of the founder and most important representative of the house, Michael VIII Palaeologus.[7] In spite of its lack of critical evaluation of sources and analysis of events,[8] and, of course, inability to profit by advances in Byzantine scholarship during the subsequent thirty years,[9] Chapman's slim volume (177 pages of text) is of aid in providing a basis for further investigation. Of greater usefulness is W. Norden's valuable survey of Greco-papal relations, *Das Papsttum und Byzanz* (Berlin, 1903), extending from 1054 to 1453.[10] I have re-examined the entire corpus of material on imperial-papal negotiations for the period under consideration, however, not only to verify the presentation of Norden but also to fill in certain gaps in his work, e.g., the inadequacy of his treatment of the opposition of the Greek people and clergy to union, his neglect of Michael's project for a joint Greco-Latin crusade to recover Asia Minor for the Greeks, the meagre discussion of the period from Lyons to the disruption of union (1274–1281), and especially his failure to examine the involvement of Michael and the papacy in events leading to the Sicilian Vespers.

A third book, valuable primarily for its bibliographical data, is the study of E. Dade, *Versuche zur Wiedererrichtung der lateinischen Herrschaft in Konstantinopel* (Jena, 1938). A résumé of Western diplomatic attempts to organize a crusade to reconquer Constantinople from the Greeks, Dade's work makes useful contributions but is all too brief (65 pages on Michael's reign) and neglects such important considerations, indispensable for an un-

[7] In a recent review in *Jl. of Theol. Studies*, VI (1955) 310, J. Hussey refers to "the badly needed book on the Palaeologus."

[8] On Chapman's use of sources see L. Previale, "Un Panegyrico inedito per Michele VIII Paleologo," *Byz. Zeit.*, XLII (1942) 3: "Chapman's bibliography is far greater than that actually used by him." (Previale finds it "incredible," for example, that Chapman ignores Michael's important *prostagma* of 12 November 1272.) Cf. judgment of Vasiliev, *History*, 583: "brief and superficial"; also Ostrogorsky, *Byzantine State* (1956) 401, 429.

[9] Including works of S. Borsari, G. Bratianu, P. Charanis, F. Dölger, R. Guilland, V. Laurent, J. Longnon, R. Lopez, G. Ostrogorsky, R. Wolff, D. Zakythinos, etc. (see Bibliography).

[10] For a detailed review, if unduly harsh, see J. Haller, in *Hist. Zeit.*, XCIX (1907) 1ff. But cf. Vasiliev's history, French ed. (Paris, 1932): "très important"; and Ostrogorsky, *Byzantine State*, 405: ". . . excellent comments in Norden."

derstanding of Michael's policy, as the continuous Greco-Latin campaigns in Achaia and the religious and social factors involved in union.[11] Particularly helpful has been the unpublished thesis of R. L. Wolff, "The Latin Empire of Constantinople" (Harvard, 1947). Though chiefly concerned, as the title indicates, with the period preceding the present work, it has, nevertheless, been a source of inspiration and exemplar of painstaking scholarship.

As to original sources for the period, relatively few Greek documents have survived, notably those edited by Tafel and Thomas, Miklosich and Müller, and Troitskiĭ, in addition to the hardly used orations of Holobolos [12] and various polemics and encomia. Of fundamental significance, of course, are the Greek historians: among contemporaries, the Grand Logothete George Acropolites and the ecclesiastical officials George Pachymeres and (lesser in importance) Theodore Scutariotes; in the fourteenth century, Nikephoros Gregoras. Through the use of this material, in particular the voluminous account of Pachymeres (many passages of which have been surprisingly overlooked or neglected by scholars), I have attempted to revise or elaborate previous explanations and, in a number of instances, to offer new interpretations.

A mass of Western sources is at the historian's disposal. To begin with, there are available five large collections of documents — first, the papal registers edited by members of the Écoles françaises d'Athènes et de Rome, in addition to Mansi, Raynaldus, Martène, Wadding, and, very recently, Tautu. Second, the reservoir of Hohenstaufen-Angevin diplomas and rescripts, the originals of which, now destroyed, are accessible in editions of Capasso, Minieri-Riccio, del Giudice, Carabellese, Durrieu, De Lellis, and, currently, in the reprinting of the Angevin corpus by the Neapolitan archivist R. Filangieri (only a part of which has yet ap-

[11] See J. La Monte's review, *Speculum*, XIV (1939) 233–235: "Dade treats the idea [of a crusade] as if it occurred in something of a vacuum as far as the East itself is concerned . . . the history of the Frankish states in Greece is almost entirely ignored; the effect of western politics is stressed, but the events in the East are virtually disregarded."

[12] I am indebted to Professor F. Dölger for suggesting to me the use of Holobolos (see Bibliography).

peared).[13] Third, Venetian archival sources as edited by Tafel and Thomas. Fourth, Genoese documents published by Manfroni, Belgrano, Bertolotto, Bratianu, and Sauli. Fifth, material from the Aragonese archives edited by Carini and Saint-Priest. There are also the less important Tuscan documents in the collections of Müller and Ferretto.[14]

Among the large number of Western narrative sources, of first importance is the *Istoria del Regno di Romania* of the Venetian, Marino Sanudo (Torsello). This work, composed in the early fourteenth century on the basis of official documents and reports of eyewitnesses, contains a wealth of information, much of it completely unused. The more important Latin or Western vernacular accounts that I have utilized are the Genoese *Annales Ianuenses*, the Venetians Martino da Canale and Andrea Dandolo, the north Italian *Chronicon Marchiae, Tarvisinae, et Lombardiae* (otherwise known as *Annales S. Justinae Patavini*), the papal Saba Malaspina, the Dominican Ptolemy of Lucca, the Franciscan Salimbene of Parma, the Sicilian Bartolomeo of Neocastro, the Florentine Giovanni Villani, and the Ghibelline *Annales* of Piacenza. I have also drawn material from the French chronicles of the Primate, Joinville, and Guillaume de Nangis, as well as the Catalan accounts of D'Esclot and Muntaner. Not to be overlooked, lastly, is the fourteenth century *Chronicle of Morea*, particularly in its Greek and French versions, which, however biased it may be, frequently provides information of value.

It seems unnecessary at this point to provide a detailed analysis and comparison of the literary accounts, since I have throughout sought to note prejudices of the sources in connection with discussion of specific events and have in addition provided an annotated bibliography. It may be said, however, that the Western writers, with the probable exception of Sanudo and Bartolomeo of

[13] Entitled *I registri della cancelleria angioina* (Naples, 1950ff.), this reprinting is intended to include all available Angevin documents culled from earlier scattered editions. Thus I have thought it necessary to cite the Filangieri ed. only in the relatively rare cases where new material is provided or a meaningful change in text adopted.

[14] For all these see Bibliography.

Neocastro, are generally anti-Greek in sentiment, and the Greek, correspondingly anti-Latin. As for the attitudes of the Byzantine historians to Michael Palaeologus in particular, Acropolites is markedly partisan, Pachymeres, our most important Greek source, relatively free of bias (except where the problem of union is immediately concerned), and Gregoras on occasion critical of Palaeologus.

In conclusion, I have appended to this volume six of a number of unpublished manuscripts and documents that I found while working in European archives at various times during the period 1951–1954. Two of the documents are directly concerned with Greco-Latin relations during the period of the Byzantine restoration (the material from one being incorporated into the text in Chapter 4). Three illustrate Greco-Latin-Jewish relations in Venetian-dominated Crete. And the last consists of three Greek epigrams addressed to the Emperor Michael (or possibly his grandson Michael IX), hitherto wrongly assumed to be an autograph of the famous Byzantine scholar, Demetrios Triklinios.[15]

With the source material so vast and diverse and yet at the same time necessarily incomplete, one cannot hope to say the final word on every aspect of a subject so complex as that undertaken in these pages.[16] Thus, while essaying to delineate in broad outline the drama of East and West, my more modest purpose has been to provide a clearer portrayal of the man Michael Palaeologus as he confronted the West, aspirant to, then occupant of, the throne of a newly reconstituted Byzantium.

[15] For these see Appendix B.

[16] Considerations of space prevent inclusion of a special chapter on Byzantine-Latin cultural relations; I expect to publish the results of my research as a separate study. Throughout this book, however, I have tried to stress the attitudes of Greeks and Latins to each other.

PART I

the empire of nicaea and michael palaeologus

1224-1261

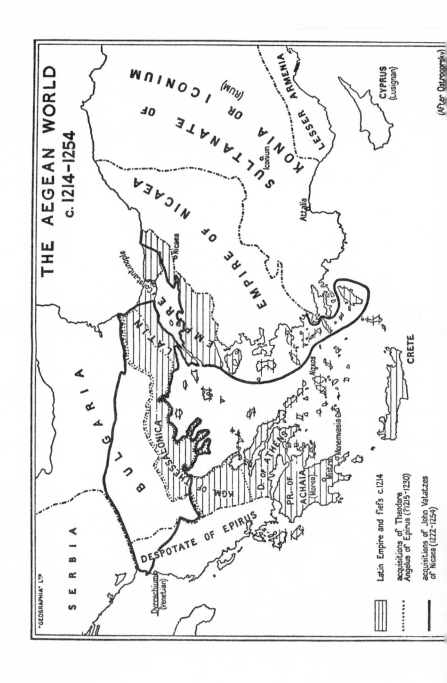

THE AEGEAN WORLD
c. 1214–1254

"GEOGRAPHIA" LTD

SERBIA

BULGARIA

DESPOTATE OF EPIRUS

Durcachiumo
(Venetian)

KGM. OF THESSALONICA

LATIN EMPIRE OF

EMPIRE OF NICAEA

Constantinople

Nicaea

SULTANATE OF
KONIA OR ICONIUM
(Rum)

o Iconium

LESSER ARMENIA

Attalia

D. OF ATHENS

PR. OF
ACHAIA
(Morea)

Mistra

Monemvasia

Naxos

CRETE

CYPRUS
(Lusignan)

(After Ostrogorsky)

Latin Empire and fiefs c.1214

acquisitions of Theodore
Angelus of Epirus (?1215–1230)

acquisitions of John Valatzes
of Nicaea (1222–1254)

Prologue

THE BYZANTINE EAST AFTER THE FOURTH CRUSADE

(1204)

Any discussion of Byzantine-Western relations in the later Middle Ages must take as its point of departure the Latin conquest of Constantinople in 1204. This event brought to a dramatic climax the centuries-old antagonism between Greek and Latin Christendom — a gradually developing estrangement based not only on political, ecclesiastical, and commercial rivalries but on diverse cultural traditions and mental attitudes. Nevertheless, despite unmistakable indications of widening cleavage, such as schism between the churches, the differences between East and West before 1204 had not yet become insuperable. It was the notorious assault on Constantinople by the Western armies of the Fourth Crusade, with the ruthless sack of the capital, the carving up of Byzantine territories, and the enforced conversion of the Greek population to the Roman faith, that thereafter rendered impossible any genuine Greco-Latin rapprochement.

After the Fourth Crusade the map of the Byzantine East was entirely redrawn. Constantinople now became the seat of a Latin Empire under the rule of Baldwin of Flanders, while Venice, whose fleet had been the mainstay of the crusaders' victory, acquired three-eighths of the capital (including the cathedral of Hagia Sophia) and such strategic, commercial points as Negropont (Euboea), Crete,[1] Gallipoli, and islands of the Aegean Sea. The territory around the city of Thessalonica was soon formed into a Latin kingdom by Boniface of Montferrat, with the remainder of what constitutes modern Greece divided into a number of small

[1] Actually Crete was originally granted to Boniface of Montferrat.

13

Frankish states. Most important of these were the Duchy of Athens-Thebes, under a Burgundian dynasty, and the principality of Achaia or Morea (the ancient Peloponnese), which shortly afterwards passed to the suzerainty of the Villehardouin family.[2]

Disintegration of the Byzantine Empire, however, did not crush the Greek spirit. For alongside the more numerous Latin possessions there emerged several political organisms which, as virtual governments-in-exile, were able to cherish the aim of a Greek recovery of the capital. Already in Trebizond, on the southeast shore of the Black Sea, descendants of the famous Byzantine dynasty of the Comnenoi had created an empire which was to survive until past the middle of the fifteenth century. In western Greece and modern Albania, and extending from Naupactus in the south to Durazzo (Dyrrachium) in the north, the Despotate of Epirus was founded by Michael I, bastard son of the imperial Angeloi family. Meantime, in northwest Asia Minor, an empire centering around the famous city of Nicaea was established by Theodore I Lascaris, son-in-law of the last reigning Byzantine Emperor before the Latin conquest, who, in 1208, was crowned "Basileus of the Romans." Thus, apart from Trebizond, which was to remain outside the main course of events, two Greek centers of resistance to Latin domination — Epirus and Nicaea — emerged to preserve the continuity of the Byzantine tradition.

In the intense rivalry for recovery of the old capital — possession of which alone could provide the seal of legitimacy — it at first appeared that the west Greeks would prevail. Indeed, the Despot Theodore I of Epirus, after acquiring Serres, Berroia, and a number of other important towns, in 1224 seized Latin-held Thessalonica and shortly thereafter had himself crowned Emperor. But when, finally, he was in position to make an attempt on Constantinople, a fatal blow was dealt to Epirot ambitions by the rising power of the Bulgars, themselves with aspirations to Constantinople.

[2] On the division of Byzantine territories see esp. "Partitio regni Graeci," in G. Tafel and G. Thomas, *Urkunden zur älteren Handels- und Staatsgeschichte der Republik Venedig* (Vienna, 1856–1857) I, 452–501 (cited hereafter as T.-Th.).

A more solid foundation was being laid in the East for the ul-imate triumph of Nicaea. The son-in-law and successor of Theo-lore Lascaris, John III Vatatzes, besides controlling almost all of vestern Asia Minor, reconquered from the fragile Latin Empire the Aegean islands of Samos, Chios, Lesbos, and Cos and exercised au-thority over Rhodes. In precarious partnership with the Bulgars, he even made a great assault on Constantinople (1236), but a falling-out of the allies permitted longer life to the dismembered Latin Empire.

Nonetheless, the Nicene state continued to gain strength, seiz-ing Thessalonica from its Epirot prince in 1246 and a large part of Macedonia from the Bulgars, and creating an alliance with the neighboring Seldjuk Turks of Iconium (Asia Minor). The Despot Michael II Angelos of Epirus was himself forced to recognize Ni-cene suzerainty and had to cede various fortresses of Macedonia and Albania. Under the wise leadership of Vatatzes, Nicaea thus successfully assumed, for the Anatolian Greeks at least, the mantle of the lost Byzantium, carrying on its old practices and providing the main rallying point for hopes to expel the foreign usurper from the capital. A rich, prosperous, economically balanced state, Nicaea had at last eliminated Epirus and the Bulgars from the con-test for Empire and practically encircled Constantinople with its territory. All that remained was the actual recovery of the Queen City. This was to be the achievement of the Nicene Emperor Mi-chael Palaeologus,[3] and it is to the early years of his life and ca-reer that we now turn.

[3] As to the orthography of Greek names, in general I follow the original, except where such spellings would do undue violence to established English usage (e.g., Alexios and Angeloi, but Palaeologus instead of Palaiologos or the inconsistent Palaeologos).

1

THE FORMATIVE YEARS OF
MICHAEL PALAEOLOGUS

CHILDHOOD AND YOUTH

*t*he early life of Michael Palaeologus, particularly his childhood and youth, is very little known to us because of the meagerness of the sources. Sporadic remarks of the Byzantine historians together with a few statements in Michael's so-called Autobiography [1] provide virtually our only guide. But however scanty and fragmentary this information may be, it deserves attention, for it offers glimpses into the character development of a person who was to become a supreme opportunist and a master of political intrigue.

[1] *Imperatoris Michaelis Palaeologi de vita sua opusculum necnon regulae quam ipse monasterio S. Demetrii praescripsit fragmentum* (St. Petersburg, 1885). This work, cited hereafter as Autobiography, is actually a *typikon* or monastic rule, written presumably by Michael himself for the Constantinopolitan monastery of St. Demetrios, which he planned to endow. The first and principal section consists of a recital of Michael's life and deeds: hence the title Autobiography, assigned by its editor J. Troitskiĭ, who has published the Greek text with a Russian translation; cf. the not always accurate French version of C. Chapman, in *Michel Paléologue restaurateur de l'empire byzantin* (Paris, 1926) 167ff. For a few additional remarks on Michael's early life see another *typikon*, composed by the Emperor for the monastery of St. Michael (published in A. Dmitrievskiĭ, *Opisanie liturgičeskih rukopisej*, I, pt. 1, Τυπικά [Kiev, 1895] 769–794). In the *Typikon for St. Michael*, as in the Autobiography, Michael makes a kind of apologia for his life and career — a fact which must, of course, be kept in mind when one draws on the information provided. See also F. Dölger, *Regesten der Kaiserurkunden des oströmischen Reiches*, pt. 3, Series A, *Corpus der griechischen Urkunden des Mittelalters und der neueren Zeit* (Munich-Berlin, 1932), nos. 2061 and 2065.

Michael Dukas Angelos Comnenos Palaeologus, to cite his full name,[2] was born in the year 1224 or 1225,[3] very probably in some city of the Nicene Empire.[4] By birth he seemed destined for the throne, as his lineage, which can be traced back to the eleventh century, reveals descent from all three imperial houses which ruled Byzantium before the Latin conquest of 1204.[5] Shortly be-

[2] For Michael's imperial autograph with these names see documents listed *passim* in Dölger, *Regesten*, and, for a specific document, T.-Th., III, 77. Each of Palaeologus' names had special significance: Angelos denoted relationship to the imperial family ruling immediately before the Latin conquest of 1204, and Ducas referred to the dynasty of the latter half of the eleventh century. Most important was Comnenos, indicating descent from the house whose period of rule (1081–1185) was considered most glorious; thus George Acropolites in his *Historia* (*Opera*, ed. A. Heisenberg [Leipzig, 1903] vol. I) 161, l. 10, calls Michael simply "Michael Comnenos." Palaeologus, finally, was his family name proper.

[3] Calculated from Acrop., 98, l. 16, who says that Michael was twenty-seven years of age during his trial before Vatatzes (in 1252; see note 23); and George Pachymeres, *De Michaele et Andronico Palaeologis*, vol. I, ed. I. Bekker (Bonn, 1835) 531, l. 19, who writes that he was fifty-eight when he died (1282). Cf. George Sphrantzes [= Phrantzes, Bonn ed.], *Chronicon* (Bonn, 1838) 24, ll. 8–9, who records, evidently wrongly, that at Michael's death he was sixty-eight, and had ruled for thirty-five years. On Michael's age see also A. Papadopulos, *Versuch einer Genealogie der Palaiologen 1259–1453* (Munich, 1938) 3, and diagram attached at end.

[4] The exact place is unclear from the sources, but as his family seems generally to have been connected with the court, it was perhaps at Nicaea or possibly even at Nymphaeum, which in effect replaced Nicaea as capital of the Nicene Empire. (The Emperor John III Vatatzes, during his reign, 1222–1254, transferred the court to Nymphaeum on account of its superior climate and location near the cities of Smyrna, Magnesia, and Sardis — Nicaea, however, being retained as patriarchal seat and place of coronation.) Had Michael been born at Constantinople, he very probably would have made use of this fact later in seeking to legitimize his usurpation of the throne. Cf. the encomium of Gregory of Cyprus, *Laudatio Michaelis Palaeologi*, in Migne, *PG*, vol. 142, col. 349 (and observations of L. Previale, "Un panegyrico inedito per Michele VIII Paleologo," *Byz. Zeit.*, XLII [1942] 2, note 4), who, in vague rhetorical style, refers to Constantinople as Michael's homeland (τὴν σὴν πατρίδα), but a few lines later, and evidently more accurately, terms Constantinople his ancestral city (σὴν ἐκ προγόνων πόλιν). Constantinople was, of course, under Latin rule at the time of Michael's birth.

[5] On Michael's ancestry see Papadopulos, *Genealogie*, 1–2. More analytical is V. Laurent, "La généalogie des premiers Paléologues," *Byzantion*, VIII (1933) 125ff., who dismisses the view that Michael was descended from a Serb family, and especially the theory — of particular interest for the present work — of Michael's alleged descent from an Italian family of the city of Viterbo, Italy. Evidence I have found for the latter theory includes (1) a (spurious) letter (see Dölger, *Regesten*, no. 1906) supposedly sent by Michael to Pope Urban IV in 1262 congratulating him on his enthronement and referring to Michael's own Viterban descent (for the letter see F. Bussi, *Istoria della città di Viterbo*, II

17

fore the occupation his maternal grandmother Irene, eldest daugh ter of the then Emperor Alexios III Angelos, and her husband Alexios Palaeologus, had been designated for the imperial succes sion by the Emperor, who was without male issue. But the deatl of Irene's husband prevented the realization of this design. Sub sequently, the couple's only daughter, Theodora, married another Palaeologus, the Grand Domestic Andronikos, highest ranking military official of Byzantium,[6] and it was from this union that Michael was born.[7] Descended from Palaeologoi on both side of his family, Michael was aptly called *Diplopalaiologos*.[8]

Michael's mother does not seem to have exercised a great in fluence on his early life: at least there is no mention of her in the sources after the birth of Michael's youngest brother Constantine, himself but a few years younger than Michael.[9] Moreover, we

[Rome, 1743] 409, no. 20); (2) a wall painting in the Palazzo Comunale of Viterbo purporting to be a portrait of the Emperor Michael "Viterbiensis"; (3) the (improbable) derivation of the name Palaeologus (παλαιὸς λόγος) from *vetus verbum* (hence "Viterbo"); and (4) a genealogical chart drawn up by a sixteenth century Paduan monk who traces his own descent back to Michael and Viterbo. For secondary works referring to Michael's purported Italian ancestry see W. Miller, *Cambridge Medieval History*, IV (1936) 503; G. Typaldos, "Οἱ ἀπόγονοι τῶν Παλαιολόγων μετὰ τὴν "Ἅλωσιν," Δελτίον τῆς Ἱστορικῆς καὶ Ἐθνολογικῆς ἑταιρείας τῆς Ἑλλάδος, VIII (1923) 129ff., esp. 156–157; and esp. the recent study of F. Rodriguez, "Origine, cronologia e successione degli imperatori Paleologi," in *Rivista di araldica e genealogia*, I (Naples, 1933) fasc. 4–5. Rodriguez seems convincingly to dispose of Michael's putative Italian descent by attributing responsibility for the theory to Palaeologan descendants of the Renaissance period in Italy, who, through claims to relationship with the Byzantine Emperor, hoped to gain financial assistance from the Viterban and papal governments. Finally, regarding Palaeologus' connection with Viterbo, see Chapman, who, in a genealogical table on Michael and his family, p. 178, lists "N. Paléologue de Viterbe," but without explanation; and cf. the old but still useful work of C. Ducange, *Familiae Augustae Byzantinae* (Venice, 1729) 188ff.

[6] On Byzantine military officials of the period see L. Bréhier, *Les institutions de l'empire byzantin* (Paris, 1949) 396–397.

[7] On all these details see Acrop., 9; Nikephoros Gregoras, *Bizantina historia*, vol. I, ed. L. Schopen and I. Bekker (Bonn, 1830) 69; *Typikon for St. Michael*, 787; Sphrantzes, 6–7; and cf. Papadopulos, *Genealogie*, 2.

[8] Greg., 69, ll. 13–14; cf. Sphrantzes, 7, l. 2.

[9] Papadopulos, *Genealogie*, 4–6. The only significant information I can find about Michael's mother Michael himself provides in his *Typikon for St. Michael*, 787, where it is related that just before her death (no date given) she became a nun under the name of Theodosia. Michael's father, too, before his death in 1247, became a monk, under the name Arsenios. See Papadopulos, *Genealogie*, 2, and also (for a hitherto neglected source on Andronikos) S. G. Mercati, "Sulla vita e

are told that Michael, for a time at any rate, was brought up by his elder sister, Martha, wife of the Grand Domestic Nikephoros Tarchaneiotes.[10] Another sister, Eulogia, evidently also had some part in caring for him, for a curious story of Pachymeres relates that when as a baby Michael could not be induced by his nurse to sleep, Eulogia would quiet him by singing how he would someday become Emperor and enter Constantinople through the Golden Gate.[11] Authentic or not, such stories about his imperial destiny were not uncommon [12] and suggest what might well have constituted the early fantasies of the child Michael.

During his boyhood, as Michael himself informs us, he attracted the attention of the great Emperor John III Vatatzes, who called him to the palace and brought him up "as if he were his son." [13] There is no evidence that the lad was educated with Vatatzes' own son of almost the same age, Theodore Lascaris,[14] who was to become one of the most learned of Byzantine emperors. But whatever their association, it is certain that Michael, nurtured in the culture of the Byzantine tradition, had at least the typical education of a thirteenth century Nicene noble.[15]

Later when Michael was able to bear arms (so he writes in

sulle opere di Giacomo di Bulgaria," *Actes du IVe congrès international des études byzantines*, IX (Sofia, 1935) 170–175.

[10] Pach., 127, l. 17. According to the sources (see Papadopulos, *Genealogie*, 13 and 18) Michael's two sisters were only about ten and six years older than he. Their original names were Maria and Irene, which were changed to Martha and Eulogia on their assuming the monastic habit.

[11] Pach., 128, ll. 10–15.

[12] Cf., e.g., Pach., 28, ll. 15–17.

[13] Autobiography, 3: ἄρτι μὲν γὰρ οὔπω καθαρῶς τὴν βρεφικὴν παρήμειβον ἡλικίαν καί με ὁ θεῖος (Ἰωάννης) ἐν τοῖς βασιλείοις ἀνελόμενος . . . ἐπιμελῶς ὅσα καὶ αὐτοῦ γνήσιον ἔτρεφε καὶ ἀνῆγε. Cf. *Typikon for St. Michael*, 790.

[14] In the large collection of his letters edited by N. Festa (*Theodori Ducae Lascaris Epistulae CCXVII* [Florence, 1898] 130, l. 71), Theodore (who later, as we shall see, intensely disliked Michael) mentions Michael only once and then merely *obiter*. Theodore's teachers were the celebrated Nikephoros Vlemmydes and, later, the historian George Acropolites.

[15] Note the rhetorical excellence of the Autobiography; also the editor's opinion (p. 44) on Michael's learning; and, finally, the remark of Michael's contemporary George Metochites (*Historia dogmatica*, in A. Mai, *Patrum nova bibliotheca*, VIII [Rome, 1871] Bk. I, ch. 80, 106) that Michael, toward the end of his life, busied himself with letters: περί που δὲ τὰ τελευταῖα τῆς βιωτῆς παρακλητηρίους ὑπὲρ αὐτοῦ κανόνας ἄριστα ἐμμελεῖς πρὸς τοὺς τῶν μαρτύρων ἐξόχους συντεθεικώς.

his Autobiography, probably not without exaggeration), he was selected by Vatatzes in preference to older and more experienced men and sent to command in the western campaigns of the Empire, in Macedonia and Epirus.[16] It was at this time presumably that he had his first taste of warfare with the Latins, against whom almost his entire life was to be spent in conflict. Such were his early successes that they surpassed even the expectations of Vatatzes, who, we are told, came to look upon the youth with increasing favor.[17]

To this period may perhaps be assigned a provocative passage in Michael's Autobiography which mentions forays against the environs of Latin-held Constantinople. It reads:

I established camp on the Asiatic side opposite the city . . . everywhere I hindered their [the Latin] sorties, repulsed their attacks, and cut their lines of supply. . . I cannot say that with God's help I did not drive them to the last extremity. And this occurred while he [Vatatzes] was still among the living and we were advancing from glory to glory.[18]

Now the only large-scale operations against Constantinople recorded for the reign of Vatatzes are those of the celebrated Greco-Bulgar expedition of 1236.[19] At the time, however, Michael was still too young to command, being only eleven or twelve years of age. Nor could the passage refer to Michael's later assault on Galata in 1260, since this was not launched from the Asiatic shore and, in fact, did not even occur in the reign of Vatatzes. We

[16] Autobiography, 4: ἐγὼ δὲ ὡς εἰς μείρακας ἤδη πρώτως παρήγγελον καὶ ὅπλα φέρειν ἦν ἱκανός. Cf. Typikon for St. Michael, 790, where Michael says he was eighteen (τὸν ὀκτωκαιδέκατον χρόνον) when he was first put in command of a large army.

[17] Autobiography, 4, IV.

[18] Ibid., V: καὶ τὴν ἀντιπέραν τῆς πόλεως 'Ασίαν ἔχων στρατόπεδον, οὐκ ἔχω εἰπεῖν ὡς οὐκ εἰς τοὔσχατον ἀπορίας αὐτοὺς ὑπὸ θεῷ συμμαχοῦντι συνήλασα, ἀπανταχόθεν αὐτῶν εἴργων τὰς ἀποβάσεις, καὶ τὰς ὁρμὰς ἀναστέλλων, . . . ἀλλὰ ταῦτα μὲν ἦν ἕως ἐκεῖνος ἦν ἐν τοῖς ζῶσι. Unless otherwise specified, all translations of passages quoted in this book are my own.

[19] On this siege see especially A. Meliarakes, 'Ιστορία τοῦ Βασιλείου τῆς Νικαίας καὶ τοῦ Δεσποτάτου τῆς 'Ηπείρου (Athens, 1898) 271–273 (hereafter cited as Nicaea). The harrying tactics against Constantinople of Vatatzes and the Bulgar John Asen just before 1236 are to be considered part of the same expedition.

are forced therefore to believe that, if such attacks by Michael on Constantinople or, more probably, its environs did indeed take place, they were of minor importance, since they have escaped the specific notice of both Greek and Western historians.[20]

TRIAL FOR TREASON

Michael participated in other military campaigns during this period,[21] but it is not until 1246 that he emerges more clearly into the light of history as the youthful governor of the Thracian towns of Melnik and Serres under the command of his father, the Grand Domestic Andronikos Palaeologus, whose headquarters were at Thessalonica.[22] During Michael's governorship a remarkable incident occurred which reveals the discipline of an already strong character and which has become a *locus classicus* for the comparative study of Byzantine and Western legal institutions.

In the fall of 1253 Michael was accused before the Emperor John Vatatzes of plotting against the throne. The charge was based on a hearsay account of a rather vague, trivial conversation between two citizens of Melnik. They had been discussing the unseemly grief of their governor, Michael, on the death of Demetrios Tornikes, private councilor to the Emperor and relative of Michael.[23] It was insinuated during the conversation that Michael's grief was caused by political disappointment rather than

[20] For a possible reference to these operations-mentioned in the Autobiography see note 44, last part.

[21] Autobiography, 4, v.

[22] Acrop., 83 and 84, ll. 1–4. Thessalonica, captured in 1246 by Vatatzes, had been placed under the governorship of Michael's father, a famous general, who in 1233 had conquered Rhodes. On Andronikos see Acrop., 45–56, and Mercati, 'Giacomo di Bulgaria," 165–176, a lament on his death.

[23] Acrop., 93; Greg., 49, ll. 7ff. Tornikes had married a first cousin of the Grand Domestic and was therefore Michael's second cousin. Acrop., 93, l. 20, says that he held the office of οἰκονόμος τῶν κοινῶν (administrator of public affairs), on which office see C. Diehl, R. Guilland, etc., *L'Europe orientale de 1081 à 1453* (Paris, 1945) 190. On the date of the accusation against Michael see G. Czebe, "Studien zum Hochverratsprozesse des M. Paläologos im Jahr 1252," *Byzantinisch-neugriechische Jahrbücher*, VIII (1931) 59ff., who places it in 1252, as does A. Siatos, Μία ποινικὴ δίκη κατὰ Μιχαὴλ Παλαιολόγου μὲ θεοκρισίαν (Athens, 1938) 9. But cf. Heisenberg's authoritative, careful edition of Acrop., 92ff., which includes it under the year 1253.

genuine sorrow over the death of his kinsman. Moreover, mention was also made that peace would be maintained in the area as Michael (presumably without imperial consent) might wed the daughter of their dangerous enemy, the Bulgar Lord Kalomanos.[24] The tenor of this curious exchange with its hint of treason was subsequently reported to an important official of Melnik, Manglabites by name, who in turn carried the story to the Emperor.[25] The motives of those who betrayed the conversation are not disclosed.

The Emperor John was sufficiently disturbed by the report to arraign before him the two citizens and their governor. On being questioned, both townsmen persisted in their stories, one insisting that Michael was inculpated and the other equally maintaining that he was not. In a manner apparently borrowed from Western feudal usage,[26] a military trial by battle between the two citizens was then arranged, and in the encounter the partisan of Michael was defeated. Just before the vanquished combatant was to be executed, he was re-interrogated, but, persisting once more in his story, he was remanded to prison.[27]

---

[24] Acrop., 94, ll. 10–11. Implied, of course, are secret negotiations between Michael and the Bulgars. See below, note 41a.

[25] Acrop., 94, ll. 15–16. A. Gardner, *The Lascarids of Nicaea* (London, 1912) 189, suggests that perhaps Michael had violated the conditions of a Golden Bull awarded previously to Melnik citizens (under the leadership of Manglabites) in return for the surrender to Vatatzes of their city, then held by the Bulgars. Cf. Acrop., 77, ll. 14–16.

[26] This is the thesis of Czebe, "Studien zum Hochverratsprozesse des M Paläologos," 88ff., who believes that the judicial duel was borrowed by the Byzantines from the Frankish Assizes of Jerusalem via Cyprus, where the Assizes had been anonymously translated in the 12th century into vulgar Greek, whence the code was disseminated to the Greek East. Czebe, however, overlooks more obvious means of transmission: the previous close contacts between Greeks and Latins during the late 11th and 12th centuries (Anna Comnena, e.g., in her *Alexiade*, ed. B Leib, I [Paris, 1937] 98, even mentions witnessing a Western judicial duel) and also the presence of the Latin mercenary troops, in Nicaea itself, which Palaeologus himself commanded. On the judicial duel and its probable Western provenience see my study, "Greco-Latin Cultural Relations in the Mid-Thirteenth Century: Ordeal by Fire and Judicial Duel," Appendix A of my doctoral dissertation, "The Emperor Michael VIII Palaeologos and the Latins: A Study in Greco-Latin Relations" (Harvard, 1953), various materials from which have been incorporated in revised form into the present book.

[27] Acrop., 94, ll. 15ff.

At this point, by order of the Emperor, Michael was informed hat to prove his innocence he himself would have to undergo the rdeal of the red-hot iron — a method of proof alien, of course, to he principles of Byzantine (i.e., Roman) law, and of which the rovenience in this particular case — though again probably West- rn — has been debated by scholars.[28] Michael replied that if any- ne were to accuse him of a definite charge he would gladly meet im in single combat, but that since no such accuser had appeared, e failed to see the need for the ordeal.

am not such a one as to perform miracles . . . [he asserted]. If a ed-hot iron should fall upon the hand of a living man, I do not doubt hat it would burn him, unless he be sculpted from stone by Phidias or 'raxiteles, or made of bronze.[29]

The Emperor, however, insisted that it was because of the very ack of a specific charge that he would have to undergo the trial: would clear his reputation and reveal the truth. To this the wenty-seven-year-old Michael replied with the astuteness that as to characterize his later career as Emperor. Insisting that he

[28] Those who support the theory of the derivation of this practice from the atins include H. C. Lea, Superstition and Force (Philadelphia, 1892) 299; Gard- er, Lascarids, 192 ("there is no doubt that in its developed form this ordeal was troduced from the West and was despised on the same ground as other Western stitutions"); Meliarakes, Nicaea, 406; also (apparently) Zachariä von Lingen- al, Geschichte des griechische-römischen Rechts (Berlin, 1892) 407, note 1500; e rather popular article of A. Siatos, Μία ποινική δίκη κατὰ Μιχαὴλ Παλαιολόγου, θεοκρισίαν (Athens, 1938) 29; and again Czebe, "Studien." On the other hand, Koukoules, citing Sophocles, Antigone, vv. 264–265, champions its provenience om the ancient Greeks (Βυζαντινῶν Βίος καὶ Πολιτισμός, III [Athens, 1949] 356– 57), while C. Sathas attempts (and fails) to show its derivation from Albanians Macedonia: La tradition hellénique et la legende de Phidias de Praxitèle et de fille d'Hippocrate au Moyen Age (Paris, 1883) 23ff. Finally, L. Bréhier believes at it was "empruntée à l'Occident et aux peuples barbares voisins de Byzance" Institutions, 243). For a full discussion of the transmission of the ordeal by fire d the reasons for its remarkable appearance at the trial of Palaeologus, see my arvard dissertation, pp. 389ff.

[29] Acrop., 95–96. For the curious mention of Phidias and Praxiteles see Sathas, a tradition hellénique, 23ff. Sathas believes that Michael here was recalling a pular Byzantine tradition according to which the two sculptors were super- atural beings made of marble and bronze who could safely undergo any kind of ial or ordeal. (Sathas' thesis has been sharply attacked by N. Polites, Λαογραφικὰ ύμμεικτα, II [Athens, 1921] 7ff.) For the bearing of this story (and a similar one rrent in medieval Rome) on this trial, see my dissertation, 392ff.

was a sinful man and could not perform miracles, he said that :
the Holy Metropolitan Phokas of Philadelphia (who evidentl
had seconded the proposal of the Emperor) would invest himse
with his ecclesiastical panoply, take with his own hands the hc
iron from the altar, and then place it into those of Michael, h
would gladly receive it in the faith that all his sins would be re
moved and the truth revealed. But that worthy prelate decline
the honor, affirming:

This is not a part of our Roman institutions, nor even of our ecclesia
tical tradition. . . The practice is barbarous and unknown to us, an
is performed only by imperial command.[30]

Michael thereupon added rather contemptuously that if he wer
of barbarian race he would gladly be tried according to ba
baric law, but as he was "a Roman born of Romans," his trial shoul
be conducted in accordance with Roman law and written trad
tion.[31]

According to the partisan testimony of Acropolites, the Em
peror at this time was himself actively seeking condemnation
Michael. But the lack of a definite charge, the resoluteness
Michael's defense, and, not least, his great popularity with th
army, senate, and people all militated against conviction.[32] Indee
most of those present, including even the judges (of whom Acr
polites was one), favored Michael's cause. Particularly partial
Michael, it should be noted, were the Latin mercenary troop
who, as Acropolites records, "are accustomed to speak more free
[than the Greeks] to their lords."[33] In the face of such favorab

[30] Acrop., 97–98. See also a similar passage in Demetrios Chomatianos, the ne
contemporary canonist of Epirus, in *Analecta sacra Spicilegio*, ed. J. Pitra, \
(Paris-Rome, 1891) cols. 389–390: "It [the practice] is entirely unknown not o
to ecclesiastical but to civil practice . . . it has come from a barbaric people, a
. . . it is not looked upon with a good eye." Also cf. Sphrantzes, 9.

[31] Acrop., 98.

[32] Acrop., 99, 1. 10. Cf. Greg., 68, ll. 12–13.

[33] Acrop., 99, ll. 3–9. On the Latin mercenaries of Nicaea, see Chapter 2, n
57. These were probably the same Latins Michael was later to command as Gra
Constable. According to Pach., 21, ll. 3–5, Michael already held that position
this time, but Pachymeres' chronology appears confused here.

ʒntiment the charge was dropped. Nevertheless, Vatatzes took
ιe precaution of extracting from Michael a solemn oath of al-
ᵉgiance to the throne.[34]

The significance of this fascinating incident lies not only in its
ᵊvelation of the youthful Michael's self-assurance and resource-
ιlness but also in the fact that it constitutes a striking commen-
ιry on the differences between the medieval Greek and Latin
ttitudes to law. Whereas Vatatzes, in order to determine the
ᵊuth through divine judgment, made appeal to such Western
ιethods of proof as trial by battle and ordeal by fire (although the
ιtter, according to certain authorities, is not necessarily Western
ι origin),[34a] Michael, as a "Roman," could justifiably invoke his
ght of a trial conducted according to the traditional judicial
rocesses of Byzantium.

Probably as a gesture of conciliation the Emperor then gave
ɔ Michael in marriage Theodora, granddaughter of Vatatzes'
rother Isaac Dukas.[35] A more exalted union had apparently been
ɔntemplated by Vatatzes, who had previously intended to marry
lichael to his own grandchild, the daughter of his son Theodore.[36]
ʹhe alteration in plans may be evidence of lingering imperial sus-
icions, for a marriage to his own granddaughter would have
rought Michael uncomfortably close to the throne.

On the basis of the relatively meagre information before us,
ow may we evaluate the charges of treasonable negotiations
rought against Palaeologus? While it would seem that the ac-
usations should not be accepted in their entirety, the fact that
ll the Greek historians, despite Michael's acquittal, emphasize
ιperial mistrust of Michael and frequent demands for oaths of
ɔyalty,[37] the sudden and inadequately explained shift in Vatatzes'
ttitude toward Michael, and, above all, the circumstance that

---

[34] Acrop., 100–101.

[34a] See note 28.

[35] Acrop., 101, ll. 6–10.

[36] Autobiography, 4: τὴν αὐτανεψιὰν καὶ ἴσα θυγατρὶ στεργομένην κατεγγυήσας
ɔι. It is noteworthy that in this work Michael mentions nothing of the ordeal nor
Vatatzes' change in attitude towards him. On the contrary, he probably exag-
ᵊrates the Emperor's regard for him (4, ιv).

[37] See, e.g., first part of note 58.

Michael actually did subsequently usurp the throne — all sug gest that the suspicions of treason may well have had some basi: in fact.[38]

FLIGHT TO THE TURKS

After his acquittal Michael recovered all of his former honor: except the governorship of Melnik and Serres.[39] Moreover, some time between the date of the trial (latter part of 1253) and No vember of 1254,[40] the Emperor appointed him Grand Constable that is, commander of the Latin mercenary troops of the Em pire.[41] In naming Michael to this office, Vatatzes perhaps con sidered it a means of keeping Michael near the court, thus re moving him from an exposed command near Epirus.[41a] In any case, it is noteworthy that the office of Grand Constable now fo the first time appeared in Byzantium, apparently borrowed by John Vatatzes from the Normans of Sicily, with whose ruler, the famous Hohenstaufen Frederick II, the Emperor was in clos relation.[42]

The campaigns of Vatatzes against Epirus and the Bulgar

[38] For further information on Michael's character see Acrop., 99, ll. 15–18, wh writes: "For to the young he was sweet and kind in speaking, joyful in words, an skillful in practices; while to the old men he seemed old in word and understand ing, and was always welcomed by them." Also Sphrantzes, 7, ll. 4–11: "Micha stood out among the other great nobles, being very pleasant in features, affabl polite, elegant in manner, and generous to others. Because of these virtues an graces many loved him, and he easily attracted to himself all the generals, lowe officers, plebs, and many of the Senate." Note Michael's own words (Autobio raphy, 4, v, and *Typikon for St. Michael*, 790), which stress the jealousy of th nobles toward him — a factor which, though probably exaggerated by him, shou not be overlooked in attempting to explain the anti-Palaeologan attitude of certa nobles, and particularly of Theodore II.

[39] His father had died in 1247, that is, before the trial (see Papadopulo *Genealogie*, 2, and Mercati, "Giacomo di Bulgaria," 174–175).

[40] The date of Vatatzes' death.

[41] Acrop., 134, ll. 10–12. Cf. Pach., 21, ll. 4–5.

[41a] According to Pachymeres' account of Michael's trial (which differs from th of Acropolites, whom I have in the main followed because he was present at th proceedings), Michael was accused of treasonous negotiations with the Despot Epirus, Michael II (21, ll. 11–17).

[42] On this see Bréhier, *Institutions*, 397 and R. Guilland, "Le Grand Conn table," *Byzantion*, XIX (1949) 104.

ontinued, while he patiently awaited a favorable opportunity to
eize Constantinople. But this prized objective was never to be
ealized, for suddenly the great Emperor had an epileptic attack,
nd on 3 November 1254 he died. His untimely death after an
eventful reign of thirty-two years left Nicaea in flourishing condi-
ion, lacking only the city of Constantinople itself to complete the
apture of almost the entire Latin Empire.[43] This was to be the
ask of his two successors.

Vatatzes was succeeded by his son Theodore II Lascaris,
vhose reign was from the very beginning disturbed by external
lifficulties. At the news of Vatatzes' death the Bulgars attacked
Thrace and Macedonia, while in the West the Epirots also pre-
ared to invade Nicene territory. Theodore personally marched
against the Bulgars, leaving behind as regent the Grand Domestic
George Muzalon, and appointing Michael Palaeologus to the im-
ortant governorship of Nicaea.[44] Theodore was able to secure a
emporary peace with Epirus by giving his daughter, Maria, in
narriage to Michael II's son, Nikephoros, upon whom Theodore
hen bestowed the title of Despot.[45] But when in September of
256 Nikephoros and his mother came to Thessalonica for the
vedding, Theodore treacherously seized them and, in exchange

[43] For encomiums on Vatatzes see Acropolites' tribute, *Opera*, II, 12; also Pach.,
9; Scutariotes, 509; and M. Andreeva, "A propos de l'éloge de l'empereur Jean
II Batatzes," *Seminarium Kondakovianum*, X (1938) 133ff.
[44] Acrop., 133–134; Greg., 57, ll. 21–23. Cf. Pach., 24: τοῦ Παλαιολόγου εἰς
εφαλὴν τεταγμένου Μεσοθυνίας καὶ αὐτῶν ὀπτιμάτων . . . καὶ τὰ πολλὰ κατ' Ἰταλῶν
ράττοντος. The precise location of Mesothynia is not easily determinable, but it
vould seem to be the region to the north of Nicaea in Asia Minor. See the opinion
f Possinus, who did the glossary of Pach., 581, placing it between the River
Aesopos and the Propontis; of J. Cantacuzene, *Historia* (Bonn) I, 341, ll. 10ff.,
ocating it near Pelecanon, itself situated slightly south of Chalcedon; and the re-
nark of Pach., 310, l. 7, that the Paphlagonian military corps consisted mainly of
nen of Halyzon who were vulgarly called Mesothynians (the term Halyzon is de-
ived from Aleve, a city of Pontus). As Pach., 24, l. 17, affirms that Michael ac-
omplished much against the Italians while governor of Mesothynia, it is perhaps
ossible that Michael's operations against Constantinople from Asia, as mentioned
n his Autobiography (see above, text for notes 18–20), might instead have oc-
urred at this time.
[45] Acrop., 134, ll. 3–6. Actually the marriage had been arranged seven years be-
ore by Vatatzes, at which time Nicephoros had originally been named Despot.
See Acrop., 88–89; Greg., 48–49.

for their return, extorted from Michael II the cities of Dyrrachium and Servia.[46]

It was while the Emperor Theodore was at Thessalonica that he received from his guards in Bithynia the disquieting news that their governor Michael Palaeologus had fled to the Turks.[47] Alarmed lest Palaeologus' flight might be for the purpose of securing Turkish aid to deprive him of his throne, Theodore summoned the Grand Logothete George Acropolites and questioned him as to his knowledge of Palaeologus' intentions.[48] The Logothete, evidently already in Michael's confidence, explained that Michael wished to escape the blinding and other punishment that Theodore in the past had often threatened to inflict upon him and therefore was now merely seeking guarantees for his personal safety.[49]

In truth Michael had been in an insecure, perhaps precarious position. For Theodore, extremely excitable by nature, was becoming increasingly subject to epileptic fits [50] and unable to control his sudden impulses. Along with other nobles, consequently, Michael, possibly from boyhood an object of Theodore's dislike and perhaps still viewed with suspicion as a result of his trial, had been repeatedly threatened with severe chastisements.

[46] Acrop., 133, ll. 1–18.
[47] Acrop., 134, ll. 13–14; and Greg., 57, ll. 19–21. Cf. Sphrantzes, 11, ll. 15–16. There were precedents for this flight. In 1190 Michael I of Epirus, tax-collector in Caria for the Emperor Alexios III, had deserted to the Sultan, under whom he subsequently held a governorship; indeed, Alexios III himself (who reigned during the Fourth Crusade), after being released by his captor, the Latin Boniface, also fled to the Sultan of Iconium. See Acrop., 14–15; cf. R. L. Wolff, "The Latin Empire of Constantinople" (unpublished Harvard Ph.D. thesis, 1947) 1079.
[48] Acrop., 134. The Greek historians' accounts of Michael's flight to the Turks differ in minor respects, Though biased, Acropolites, as practically an eye-witness, is probably most reliable. However, Pachymeres, who may have heard certain oral reports (cf. Czebe, "Studien," 66), again provides information unknown to the others but probably worthy of belief, since it supplements and does not contradict Acropolites.
[49] Acropolites' outspokenness contrasts sharply with his reticence a few years before (on account of which he had been bastinadoed by Theodore) — a fact suggesting that Acropolites already was a confidant of Michael. Witness the Grand Logothete's reply to the Emperor when asked the motives for Michael's flight: "observing his mentality and thoughts I know him to be a 'philo-Roman'" (Acrop., 134, ll. 22–24).
[50] See letter 48, pp. 64–65, of the Festa collection, and below, note 61. Michael

28

According to Pachymeres, Michael was warned of imminent danger by a certain Kotys of the palace, who advised immediate flight to the Turks. Recalling his difficulties with Vatatzes and mindful in addition of the fate which had befallen one of his uncles,[51] Michael followed the advice and with a few close friends crossed the Sangarios River separating Nicaea from the Turkish territory of Roum. After a hazardous journey he reached Iconium, the Turkish capital of the Seldjuk Sultan, 'Izz al-Dīn Kaika'us II, who received him honorably.[52] The Sultan, threatened by a Mongol invasion, had need of a capable general and therefore entrusted to Michael the command of his numerous Christian mercenaries. With these forces Michael subsequently distinguished himself in combat against the Mongols.[53]

In the meantime, not wishing to burn his bridges behind him, Michael had dispatched letters to the troops formerly under his command in Bithynia on the Turkish border. He exhorted them to persevere in guarding the area, explaining that he had undertaken flight only to avoid personal danger. As was probably intended, the letters served to diminish Theodore's anxiety over Michael's motives.[54]

---

autobiography, 4, v, attributes his flight to the enmity of Theodore's noble advisers. See also Greg., 58; and Sphrantzes, 10.

[51] His uncle had been imprisoned for asserting that one destined to rule is blameless for his acts (Pach., 25, ll. 4ff.).

[52] According to Acrop., 136ff., Michael first was captured by the Turcomans a nomadic Turkish people), and only after they had stolen all his possessions was he able to escape to Iconium. Also see Marino Sanudo (Torsello), *Istoria del Regno di Romania*, 135, in C. Hopf, *Chroniques gréco-romanes* (Berlin, 1873).

[53] Acrop., 137, ll. 11ff.; Pach., 25: σημαίαις βασιλικαῖς παραταξάμενος. Greg., 58, l. 19ff., and Sphrantzes, 11, ll. 7–11. Cf. *Typikon for St. Michael*, 791, where Michael says that he led Turkish troops: μοῖραν φέρων Περσῶν (Turks were often termed Persians in the Byzantine accounts). That Michael led Christian troops for the Turks is not extraordinary, since the Seldjuk Sultans were often aided by Christian mercenaries, both Latin and Greek, attracted to their service by the high rate of pay. Vincent of Beauvais, *Speculum historiale*, bk. XXX, ch. 144, in *Bibliotheca mundi* (Douai, 1624) IV, 1282, notes that in 1237 there were one thousand Latins in Seldjuk service. He also informs us that the Emperor Vatatzes supplied troops regularly to the Seldjuk armies. On this see C. Cahen, "Les Turcomans de Rum au moment de l'invasion mongole," *Byzantion*, XIV (1939) 131ff.; G. Sorranzo, *Il papato, l'Europa cristiana e i Tartari* (Milan, 1930); and A. Vasiliev, "The Foundation of the Empire of Trebizond," *Speculum*, XI (1936) 31 and note 3.

[54] Acrop., 135, ll. 20ff., alone records this. However, as Acropolites notes, he was with Theodore when the letters were received from Nicaea.

Not long afterwards circumstances combined to bring about Palaeologus' recall. In the first place he himself was doubtless growing apprehensive over the situation at Iconium, which had markedly deteriorated as a result of recent Turkish defeats at the hands of the Mongols.[55] Moreover, the Emperor Theodore apparently no longer opposed his return, either because he needed a competent general for his western campaigns[56] or because he still feared collusion between Palaeologus and the Sultan. In any event, when at the beginning of 1258 the Emperor went to Sardis to confer with the Sultan about an alliance against the Mongols — now rapidly becoming a threat also to Nicaea[56a] — Michael's recall was arranged through the mediation of the Greek Bishop of Iconium.[57] Before the fugitive was permitted to return, however, he was required to take stringent oaths never to aspire to the throne and always to be faithful to the Emperor and his young son John. In exchange the Emperor guaranteed Michael's safety with an oath of his own.[58]

In spite of Theodore's assurances, Michael, if we are to believe the testimony of Pachymeres, was once more to incur Theodore's enmity.[59] On his return from Iconium, Michael was grudgingly provided by Theodore with a few mediocre troops and dis-

---

[55] See Autobiography, 5, v, where Michael himself says that he was nostalgic to return.

[56] This reason is proposed by Chapman, 28. Michael's Autobiography, 5, implies that Theodore made the advances for Michael's return by appealing to his patriotism: πρὸς τὸ γένος καὶ τὴν πατρίδα παρακαλοῦντα.

[56a] The Sultan received only a small force from Theodore but in exchange surrendered Laodicea and several other places. According to Scutariotes, 531, Laodicea was soon afterwards recovered by the Turks. Also see Acrop., 144, ll. 10ff.

[57] Pach., 26, ll. 3–4.

[58] Pach., 26, l. 5; Acrop., 144, ll. 20–23; Greg., 59, ll. 11–14; and Sphrantzes 12, ll. 2–9. Greg., 59, ll. 24ff., explicitly records that Michael was renamed Grand Constable at this time.

[59] Pachymeres alone mentions this new incident, except for the Arab historian Abû'l Faraj (commonly called Bar Hebraeus): Chronography of Gregory Abû' Faraj, trans. E. Budge (Oxford, 1932) 427. Acropolites, while noting Michael restored command in the west, says nothing of his disgrace, but Acropolites, for at least part of this time, was a prisoner of Michael II in Epirus. Yet it is difficult to believe that Acropolites did not soon learn of Michael's disgrace. Chapman (30, note 1) doubts that this affair involving Chadenos should be considered a new incident.

patched against Michael II. After defeating and killing a son of
the Despot, Palaeologus was able to advance to Dyrrachium on
the Adriatic coast, but the final result, owing especially to defeats
suffered by other Nicene generals, was the loss of most of western
Macedonia.[60]

For reasons not clearly set forth — Pachymeres alone records
that because of the increasing severity of his illness, Theodore began to attribute his malady to evil spells cast upon him by various
persons, and especially by Palaeologus [61] — the Emperor then
ordered Michael's arrest. Though evidently forewarned, Michael
did not this time attempt to flee, but instead surrendered to Chadenos, Count of the Imperial Horse, who had been sent to Thessalonica to arrest him. Michael's tractability is attributed by Pachymeres to the influence of the Bishops of Dyrrachium and Thessalonica, whom Michael had solicited for advice. Interpreting a mys-
terious prophecy pronounced during religious services as an indication of divine favor and a prognostication of Michael's elevation to the throne, the prelates counseled his surrender and return to Nymphaeum.[62]

The question, nevertheless, remains why a person of Michael's
character, without more realistic assurances of safety, would permit himself to be taken prisoner, possibly thereby to suffer death
at the hands of Theodore. How to reconcile such docility with the
resourcefulness of his flight to the Turks and his youthful bravado
before Vatatzes during his trial for treason? Expediency has been

[60] See Pach., 26, ll. 9ff., where Theodore, the slain son of the Despot, is called
Manuel, and Acrop., 145–149. The passage which follows in the text is drawn
from Pachymeres.

[61] In a letter to the philosopher Nikephoros Vlemmydes (probably written
shortly before his death), Theodore discusses his malady: "The suffering I ex-
perience is insupportable ($\overset{\circ}{\alpha}\sigma\tau\epsilon\kappa\tau o\nu$) . . . and even worse is the torpor and im-
mobility; . . . the doctors do nothing and prate only nonsense ($\overset{\circ}{\alpha}\nu o\eta\tau\alpha\acute{\iota}\nu o\upsilon\sigma\iota$)"
(Festa ed., letter 48, p. 65). Regarding his suspicions of sorcery on Michael's
part, see Pach., 35, l. 13, where another story is related about Michael's sister
Martha and her daughter, who, likewise accused of sorcery, was thrown nude
into a sack with some cats in order to induce a confession (Pach., 34, ll. 21ff.).
On other accused persons who purged themselves through the ordeal by hot-iron,
see the interesting description in Pach., 33.

[62] Pach., 28, esp. l. 16. This curious passage, among others, reveals Pachymeres' belief in prophecies.

suggested as the motive for his acquiescence.[63] And indeed it would not be surprising if Michael, together with other discontented nobles who realized the critical state of the Emperor's malady, had organized a conspiracy against the throne. Flight now, moreover, just after the loss of much of Macedonia, would probably have put him in a bad light in the eyes of the people and the army, whose good opinion he was always most careful to cultivate.[64] Thus Michael may have reasoned that the time was ripe for his return.

When Michael was brought before the Emperor, the familiar scene was again enacted, but now for the last time. Michael was cast into prison without trial or definite charges,[65] then freed after taking the usual oath of fidelity. But this time Theodore, while informing Michael that his escape from punishment was attributable only to imperial grace (*sympatheia*), commended his children to the care of Michael.[66] There can be little doubt that Theodore's change of attitude was the result not of a suddenly benevolent feeling toward Michael, but of preoccupation over the security of his children. The Emperor must have recognized that with Michael's growing influence over the army, senate, and people [67] it was only prudent to enlist his support for the peaceful succession of his young son John in the event of his own death, which now may have seemed imminent.

[63] Gardner, *Lascarids*, 229.

[64] Pach., 29–30, relates that Michael evoked even the solicitude and respect of Chadenos.

[65] Pach., 31, ll. 9ff.

[66] Pach., 35, ll. 15–20.

[67] Note particularly Greg., 68, ll. 12–14, who emphasizes Michael's efforts to ingratiate himself with all ranks of the military, from generals down to simple soldiers. Cf. above, note 38.

2

REVOLUTION AND USURPATION

(1258)

In August of 1258, after a reign of less than four years, the Emperor Theodore II Lascaris died.[1] One of Theodore's final acts had been to draw up his testament, naming his boyhood favorite, the Protovestiarios George Muzalon,[2] regent of the Empire and guardian[3] of his eight-year-old son and heir, John IV Lascaris.[4] This presumptuous disposition of the Empire, in

[1] The Greek historians, despite unanimous praise for Theodore's intellectual attainments, differ in their judgments of his character and reign. Acropolites, though he was Theodore's boyhood teacher and later chief minister, slurs over his accomplishments in comparison with those of Palaeologus. Pachymeres, too, is rather unfavorable, while Scutariotes, a close friend to Theodore, praises him lavishly (cf. J. Pappadopoulos, *Théodore II Lascaris, Empereur de Nicée* [Paris 1908], which is probably unduly favorable to Theodore). In general, however, Theodore, though precipitous in implementing his aims, seems to have had Nicaea's best interests at heart.

[2] Note, in *Theodori Ducae Lascaris Epistulae CCXVII*, ed. N. Festa (Florence, 1898) 214, no. 1, the extremely affectionate salutation of Theodore's letter to George Muzalon: Γλυκύτατέ μοι Μουζάλων, ποθεινέ μοι υἱέ, τῶν ὀφθαλμῶν μου τὸ γλύκιον. Cf. Greg., 62, ll. 12–16.

[3] Pach., 39, l. 13 and Acrop., 154, ll. 15–16. Both Greg., 62, ll. 19ff. and Sphrantzes, 12, ll. 13–15, record that the Patriarch Arsenios was named with Muzalon as guardian of John. This seems logical since the cloak of religion would lend an air of legitimacy to the regency. It is to be noted, however, that neither Gregoras nor Sphrantzes is contemporary with these events.

[4] Acrop., 154, l. 13, says John was eight, but Greg., 62, l. 22 and Sphrantzes, 12, l. 17, record six; and Pach., 35, l. 23, nine.

33

particular the assignment of the regency to a man of humble birth, was, of course, extremely unpopular with the great Nicene nobles. But their attitude had already been anticipated by Theodore, who, shortly before his death, had taken measures for the confirmation of his testament by whatever nobles were on hand at the time.[5]

The bitterness of the nobles toward Muzalon was to a considerable extent based on antipathy toward Theodore himself. For, following the policy of his father, John III Vatatzes, but in more ruthless fashion, Theodore had tried to curb the influence of the hereditary Anatolian magnates whose power tended to diminish the authority of the central government. Thus in order to counteract the influence of the nobility and at the same time to establish a class of civil servants faithful to him personally, Theodore had elevated and attached to himself many men of low birth, but with tastes similar to his own.[6] Chief among those raised to high office were the brothers Muzalon.[7] As Protovestiarios, George, the eldest, became Theodore's most powerful official and closest confidant, while his two brothers were named Grand Domestic and Protokynegos.[8] Under these circumstances it is easy to understand how resentment and jealousy would have been aroused in an ambitious young nobleman such as Michael Palaeologus. Despite an illustrious descent as great-grand-son of Alexios III Angelos-Comnenos, and notwithstanding a distinguished military career, Michael was now inferior in rank not only to the low-born George Muzalon but even to his brother the Grand Domestic, whose tenure of high army office seems to have added nothing to the lustre of Byzantine military annals.

The Protovestiarios was particularly hated by the nobles because of his association with Theodore in the often arbitrary pun-

---

[5] Acrop., 154, l. 20, and Greg., 62, ll. 12–13.

[6] Acrop., 124, l. 10, expresses the nobles' attitude to Theodore's low-born appointees by calling them "little men not worth three obols." In a curious passage revealing his anti-Theodorian attitude, Acrop., 154, l. 13, says that Theodore actually named Muzalon regent more for the latter's benefit than for that of his own son.

[7] Greg., 62, esp. l. 4.

[8] Acrop., 155, ll. 16–19, and Greg., 66, ll. 1–2.

shment of many of them.[9] It was even rumored that, having induced the sickness and death of Theodore by sorcery, Muzalon was planning to overthrow the Lascarid dynasty and seize the throne for himself.[10] That Muzalon seriously contemplated usurpation is to be doubted, however, for according to our sources all classes were antagonistic toward him and he would have had few supporters in such an undertaking.[11]

Besides the nobility, the clergy too were anti-Muzalon as a result of Theodore's high-handed, independent manner towards the Church.[12] And even the people, recalling the glory and prosperity of Vatatzes' recent reign, naturally supported the legitimate heir whose rights they now believed threatened. Last, the military forces scorned the Muzalons because of their lack of military prestige, and on account of the Protovestiarios' identification with Theodore in an unfavorable policy towards them. Of all these classes, the support of the military was most important, and without it any coup was doomed to failure.

With Nicaea surrounded by hostile forces and in need of a strong and faithful army, Theodore had desired to adopt a revolutionary military policy. He had, for perhaps the first time in Byzantine history, sought to recruit the army exclusively from among the Greeks.[13] This meant, presumably, that Latin and other foreign troops were eventually to be dismissed and Greeks were to replace them. The policy seems never to have been carefully im-

[9] See Acrop., 154ff., where the malcontents are listed. Among these is the Grand Logothete and historian George Acropolites, who, at Theodore's order, had been flogged before his own troops for supposed impertinence. Acropolites at this time was still the prisoner of the Despot Michael II of Epirus. This fact, together with Acropolites' pro-Palaeologan bias, makes his account of the subsequent revolution short.

[10] Pach., 54, ll. 11–13.

[11] On this see Pach., 53–54; also Greg., 63, l. 24, and 64, ll. 3–4. Cf. the opinion of Meliarakes, Nicaea, 493.

[12] For an appraisal of Theodore's attitude to the Church, see Gardner, Lascarids, 202 and 208.

[13] On this plan see, in Festa, Epistulae, 58, no. 44, a letter to Nikephoros Vlemmydes, in which Theodore writes that he is amassing the country's gold to build an army, not of Turkish, Italian, Bulgar, or Serb soldiers, but a Greek one, which alone could be depended upon. Note the extraordinary use here — one of the very first in the Byzantine period — of the word Ἑλληνικόν instead of Ῥωμαῖον to apply to the Greeks.

plemented, however, for we find Latin mercenary troops ofter mentioned in the sources throughout his reign. Failure to adop the scheme was doubtless due to the scarcity of Greek troops a well as to the common Greek aversion for war. Nevertheless, ever if the plan was not publicly enunciated (we know of it, in fact only through the letters of Theodore himself),[14] rumors of th intention probably filtered through the military forces, and it ma well have been an important cause of the alienation of the Latir troops. More concretely, it seems that Theodore and his ministe Muzalon had neglected to pay the Latin mercenaries their stipend and donatives, despite a well-stocked treasury.[15] Thus the Latir troops, "this blond and bellicose race," as Pachymeres calls them "were deeply resentful and ready to slaughter them [the Muza lons] if only someone might incite them to it." [16]

Realizing the precariousness of his position,[17] the Protovestia rios convoked an assembly of the senate, military commanders and nobility, including especially the Lascarid princes.[18] In ar eloquent peroration intended to dispel the fears of the nobles a to his motives, he offered to resign the regency in favor of whom ever the assembly would select in his place.[19] To this offer, a spokesman for the nobility, Michael Palaeologus responded witl a speech, which, according to Pachymeres, was subtly designec to allay Muzalon's suspicions and at the same time to encourag his opponents. Michael addressed Muzalon:

If you were honored by the Emperor, his friendship for you was no for nothing; everyone is convinced of that. On the contrary, thes honors are due to those inestimable qualities in which you are withou

[14] *Ibid.*

[15] Pach., 54, ll. 17–19 and 68, ll. 6–7. Also 54, ll. 19–20, where he says th Italians complained ὡς καταφρονοῖντο ἐφ' οἷς ἐδικαίουν ἑαυτοὺς τετιμῆσθαι.

[16] Pach., 55, ll. 1–3.

[17] Greg., 64, ll. 7–8. Pach., 54, l. 9, writes that George Muzalon was not awar of all this hatred. This, however, seems difficult to believe. Cf. Pach., 40, ll. 17ff.

[18] Pach., 41, ll. 5–8 and Greg., 64, l. 11. Acropolites does not mention this as sembly. Sphrantzes, 12, ll. 17–18, writes that Arsenios convoked and addressed th senate. Cf. Meliarakes, *Nicaea*, 494, note 1.

[19] Pach., 40–48, alone quotes the speech of Muzalon directly. Though probabl not an exact record of it, his account seems faithfully to represent what was said Cf. Greg., 64.

qual. We all know your judgment and ability as administrator. Some-
ne has to govern; we cannot all rule. Who is more worthy to do so
1an you? Take the regency and affairs of the Roman state in your
ands. We will obey you.[20]

'his sentiment, so fulsome in praise, was applauded and ap-
roved by all the nobles "as if by agreement."[21] At their insistence
Muzalon was prevailed upon to continue the direction of state
ffairs. But he took the precaution of insisting that all the nobles
ake an oath of loyalty to himself as well as to the young Emper-
r.[22]

In the face of the almost universal resentment of the Protoves-
iarios, the general acclamation of the nobles on this occasion can
e satisfactorily explained only by collusion. Indeed there are in-
lications that in the meantime a great conspiracy was being
ormed with the aim of destroying Muzalon.[23] In a plot of this
:ind involving a large number of persons, there must, of course,
ave been a leader, and the evidence, largely circumstantial to be
ure, points to Michael Palaeologus. Spokesman for the nobility
n a palpably deceitful speech, extremely popular and influential
vith the clergy, common people, and especially the army, sus-
ected several times of treason toward the Lascarid dynasty (no
ess than six times had he been required to swear loyalty to the
egime)[24] and, finally, accused more or less outspokenly by the
estimony of the contemporary Pachymeres[25] — Michael can
vith reasonable certitude be termed the chief instigator of the
lot to murder the Protovestiarios and overthrow his regime.

Consideration of other sources discloses nothing to refute the
heory of Michael's responsibility: Acropolites, friend and later
hief minister of Michael, is understandably silent on the latter's

[20] For the entire speech see Pach., 49–52. The summary quoted is taken from
Chapman, 31.
[21] Greg., 64, ll. 15–17. Pach., 48–49, terms the nobles' approval of Muzalon
lissimulation.
[22] Greg., 65, ll. 1–5.
[23] Greg., 65, ll. 9–12, informs us that certain nobles incited the army to murder
Muzalon. Cf. Pach., 55, ll. 1–3.
[24] See Chapter 1, text and notes 34, 37, 58, and 66.
[25] See note 29, below.

part in the conspiracy, while both Gregoras and Sphrantzes, writ
ers of the fourteenth and fifteenth centuries respectively, stres
only Michael's ambition and astute preparation for his selectio
as regent.[26] As for the testimony of Michael himself as revealed b
his so-called Autobiography, there is, as might be expected, noth
ing whatever said about his role. Michael simply and piously at
tributes his elevation to supreme power to the will of God and th
people.[27]

To carry out their plans Palaeologus and his fellow-conspira
tors found the assassins they needed in the discontented forces o
the army, especially among the Latin troops, whose grievance
have already been noted and of whom Michael himself, as Gran
Constable, was commander.[28] In this connection a statement o
Pachymeres is of considerable significance: "It was popular belie
that their commander . . . incited them [the Latin mercenaries
to commit the murders . . . when they would have the oppor
tunity." [29]

It may be wondered how Latin mercenaries — foreigners, ir
many cases recent arrivals, and above all, members of a hate
race — had the audacity to attempt the murder of one who, thoug
detested, was nevertheless the official head of the state. The
must, it would seem, have been impelled to their act by guar
antees of immunity from punishment on the part of their ow
commander, whose enmity coincided so well with their own.[30]
This suspicion is substantiated by the striking but overlooke
fact that Palaeologus took no measures — either as regent or late
as Emperor — to punish the Latin assassin of the regent.[31]

[26] See Greg., 68–70 and Sphrantzes, 14, ll. 3ff.
[27] Autobiography, 5–6: ἀναλαμβάνομαι εἰς βασιλέα τοῦ σοῦ λαοῦ παρὰ σοῦ . . .
δεξιά σου ὕψωσέ με· καὶ κύριος κατέστην τῶν ὅλων, οὐ πείσας ἀλλὰ πεισθεὶς καὶ βιασθε
αὐτός.
[28] Pach., 54, l. 15 and Acrop., 134, ll. 10–12.
[29] Pach., 55, ll. 4–7: ὁ τῶν πολλῶν λόγος ἔχει, ὁ τούτων τῆς φάλαγγος ἐξηγούμενος
ὃς καὶ πάλαι μὲν ὡρμημένους αὐτούς, τότε δ'ἐξαφθέντας πλέον ἀνεθέντας τοῦ φόβου κα
δρασείοντας τὰ ἀνήκεστα ἐξ ἑτοίμου ἠρέθισε τὸν φόνον ἐπιτολμῆσαι καιρὸν ἔχοντας.
[30] Pach., 55, ll. 8–11.
[31] See an unnoticed passage in Pach., 284, ll. 19–20, where this same assassi
(Charles) is mentioned a few years later, still alive and unpunished. Cf. note 65
below.

THE MURDER OF MUZALON AND THE ACCESSION OF
MICHAEL PALAEOLOGUS TO THE THRONE

The opportunity for destroying the Muzalon family soon arrived. In early September, 1258, only a few days after Theodore's death, members of the nobility, soldiery, and clergy assembled at the church of the monastery of Sosandra in Magnesia to attend a memorial service for the Emperor, who was buried there beside his father.[32] On the arrival of the Muzalon brothers and their retinue the rites of the service began.[33]

Outside the church the soldiers, in particular the Latin contingent, began to create a commotion by shouting for the young Emperor John to appear.[34] At their repeated cries the guard surrounding the boy brought him forth, whereupon the soldiers began to clamor even more loudly. The young Emperor, presumably to quiet them, made a gesture with his hand, but the soldiers (as Pachymeres relates) took it as a sign to authorize their action and rushed toward the church, ostensibly to defend the boy's honor, actually to carry out their murderous purpose. Joining them was the rabble outside, easily swayed and eager for vengeance.[35]

In the meantime the Muzalon family [36] was warned of danger but failed to take precautions [37] other than to send a secretary of the Protovestiarios named Theophylact to investigate the disturbance. Mistaken for his master, Theophylact was killed immediately by the rabble, who pierced him repeatedly with swords until finally the error in identity was discovered from his black shoes.[38] Then the mob and the soldiers, the latter advancing with

[32] The sources differ on the exact date when the service occurred. On this see Pach., 55; Acrop., 154; Greg., 65; Sphrantzes, 13. Cf. Meliarakes, Nicaea, 164.
[33] See Acrop., 154–155; Greg., 65; Pach., 55.
[34] Pach., 55, esp. l. 21. Also Greg., 65; Acrop., 154, l. 23; Sphrantzes, 13.
[35] Pach., 56, l. 6, and 57. Also Acrop., 155, ll. 10–14.
[36] Acrop., 155, ll. 16–19 and Greg., 65, ll. 25ff., mention the three brothers. Pach., 60, ll. 6–11, states that two Muzalons were present with their brother-in-law.
[37] Pach., ll. 3ff. and 59, ll. 7–8.
[38] Black shoes signified no particular rank, while those of the Protovestiarios were green. See Ph. Koukoules, Βυζαντινῶν Βίος καὶ Πολιτισμός, IV (Athens, 1951)

swords in hand, pressed into the church. The psalmody ceased.[39] Thereupon there ensued a scene somewhat suggestive of another over two centuries later in 1478, when Lorenzo the Magnificent and his brother were attacked by conspirators before the altar in the cathedral of Florence. While the officiating Nicene clergy quickly disappeared, the Muzalons fled to save themselves into the dark recesses of the church. The Protovestiarios slipped under the altar and hid himself by standing in a narrow opening between two columns. The Grand Domestic ran behind a door which he drew tightly shut behind him, and the third brother concealed himself in a corner near the imperial tomb.[40]

The crazed mob began to look for them in every corner of the church, even in the most sacred places. A certain Charles,[41] one of the Latin mercenaries, soon found the Protovestiarios. Searching around the altar, he espied the protruding knees of his victim and dragged him forth. Muzalon offered to purchase his life, but the Latin, disregarding his entreaties, dispatched him with his sword.[42] At once the mob pounced upon the body, treating it with the utmost brutality as many, muttering imprecations, stabbed it with their swords. So great was the crowd's fury that the body was hacked into pieces, which later had to be collected and thrown into a sack for burial.[43] With this barbaric exhibition of cruelty, respect for law and religion seems completely to have vanished.[44]

The mob, its appetite still unsated, now rushed to sack the

402–404. Pach., 59, ll. 13ff., records that Theophylact was his relative; thus Pachymeres probably had a personal interest in the event. Since his account of the Muzalon murders and Michael's usurpation is the most voluminous, yet in agreement with the others in all salient points, I have elected in the main to follow it.

[39] Pach., 60, ll. 3–5. Cf. Greg., 65, ll. 22–23, who writes that Muzalon was murdered at the altar while the hymnody still continued.

[40] Pach., 60, ll. 6–14.

[41] Pach., 61, l. 8. A sinister prognostication of Palaeologus' later conflict with Charles of Anjou! (Cf. Pach., 284, l. 20.)

[42] Pach., 61, ll. 8, 14–16.

[43] Pach., 61, ll. 16–20 and Acrop., 156, ll. 5–6.

[44] See Greg., 65, ll. 12–15, who attributes the troubles of the state to the broken oaths. Compare this desecration of a Greek altar with that occurring during the Latin sack of Constantinople in 1204; see Niketas Choniates, *Historia*, ed. I. Bekker (Bonn, 1835) 759.

houses of its victims. The wife of the Protovestiarios, meanwhile, ran to Palaeologus clamoring for her husband, but she was told by him to be quiet lest she suffer a similar fate.[45] This circumstance seems to reveal that Michael was near at hand during the uprising. Probably he was at the church with the rest of the nobles and was something more than a disinterested onlooker at the proceedings. In all of this, however, he carefully managed to remain in the background.

With Muzalon now out of the way, Michael's first aim was to secure the guardianship of the young Emperor. But he had to act warily, for other nobles, basing their claims on Lascarid kinship or prestige, were striving for the same objective.[46] Probably fearing a coup by another noble, Michael in his capacity as Grand Constable directed his brothers John and Constantine to take the young Emperor under their personal protection.[47] Such solicitude permitted the Palaeologoi to pose as the defenders of the legitimate heir.

So apprehensive did certain nobles become over the uprising that they made provisions for their safety in the event the situation should get completely out of hand; but the violence soon began to diminish and order to prevail. That a strong man had to be appointed to guide "the ship of state"[48] was evident: otherwise the Empire might fall an easy victim to its menacing external enemies, the Mongols, the Latin Empire, and particularly the powerful coalition of Sicily, Epirus, and Achaia, recently organized by the Despot of Epirus for the conquest of Nicaea.[49] In view of this critical situation, a forceful leader was required who could command the allegiance of all classes in the state, and, above all, the respect and devotion of the military forces.

At this juncture, records Acropolites, "the eyes of all turned to

[45] Pach., 62, ll. 17–21.
[46] Pach., 64, ll. 5ff.
[47] Pach., 63, ll. 19ff.
[48] The Byzantine historians habitually use this phrase, e.g., Acrop., 157, l. 5 and Greg., 70, l. 14.
[49] Michael II of Epirus is often referred to in the Greek sources as "the apostate," that is, as a Greek renegade from the Nicene Empire, whose people considered themselves the continuators of the old Roman Empire.

Michael Comnenos [Palaeologus]." [50] An assembly of nobles was convoked,[51] probably at the direction of the Patriarch Arsenios, who had been summoned from Nicaea as the most important legally-constituted authority remaining.[52] The assembly proceeded to select Michael as regent and guardian of the young Emperor. Because of his great prestige, nobility of birth, and variety of military experience (as is once more emphasized by the sources), Michael was best qualified for the position.[53] Before his selection, however, a kind of referendum had been held to ascertain the choice of the people and military forces.

First the Greeks had been asked their preference, all responding with one accord that they preferred Michael. Then the Latins were interrogated and, in the words of Acropolites, "they needed little time to reflect and asked forthwith for Michael Palaeologus as leader of all." [54] Finally, the Cuman auxiliaries were questioned and they, too, spoke out for Michael.[55] Allowing for Acropolites' evident desire to justify Palaeologus' subsequent usurpation of the throne, such consideration for the wishes of foreign mercenaries in selecting the head of the government seems remarkable. Doubtless it reflects the importance of the Latin and Cuman troops in the eyes of the Greeks, in particular the realization that at this critical time the security of the state demanded unquestioned loyalty on the part of the troops to any leader selected.

[50] Acrop., 158, ll. 7–8. Cf. Greg., 70, ll. 16–17.

[51] According to Pach., 66, l. 7, the nobles alone seem to have been present.

[52] Pach., 66, l. 10. As mentioned above, Gregoras and Sphrantzes write that Arsenios was co-guardian of the boy, John.

[53] Pach., 66, ll. 13ff. and Greg., 70, ll. 8ff.

[54] Acrop., 158, l. 16. He doubtless refers here to the Latin mercenary troops, for, as will be noted, the next to be consulted were the Cuman troops, who of course were mercenaries. Scutariotes, 538, makes a brief reference to this referendum.

[55] On the Cumans, a Turkish people, called Scythians in many Greek sources, see D. Rasovskii, "Poloytsy," *Seminarium Kondakovianum*, VII (1935) 245, and later issues. It is of interest to note that Acrop., 158, l. 19, records that in this referendum the Cumans responded in Greek. Very possibly the Latins replied in Greek also, since as a group they had been in Byzantium for a long time. On the other hand, replacements were constantly being recruited from the West, and thus perhaps many did not know Greek. Cf. Codinus, *De officialibus palatii Constantinopolitani et de officiis magnae ecclesiae liber*, ed. I. Bekker (Bonn, 1839) 57, who notes that as late as the fourteenth century the Varangian troops (see below) saluted every newly proclaimed Emperor in English.

42

In order to invest the new regent with a title more befitting his position, Palaeologus was named Megas Dukas (Grand Duke).[56] Moreover, the imperial treasury at Magnesia, a very substantial one, was given over to his charge. Of this he soon made profitable use for his own ends. The sums at Magnesia were guarded by troops called by Pachymeres "axe-bearing Kelts," presumably members of the famous Varangian guard which seems to have been reconstituted at Nicaea after the Latin occupation of Constantinople.[57] Though nominally master of the treasury, the regent apparently first had to persuade its Latin guardians of the

[56] Pach., 79, ll. 13–14. Though the Grand Duke nominally was commander of the imperial naval forces, Michael does not seem to have exercised effective command of the fleet. See R. Guilland, "Etudes de Titulature et de Prosopographie byzantines," *Byz. Zeit.*, 44 (1951) 231.

[57] The custom of using Latins, especially Englishmen, as imperial guards originated with Alexios I Comnenos. During the great Norman threat to Constantinople in the eleventh century, Alexios had entrusted to the Varangians, recently come from England after the Norman Conquest, the safeguard of his person, family, and treasure. The Kelts of Nicaea were perhaps also Varangians; at least, like the Varangians in Alexios' era, they carried axes (Pach., 71, l. 10: πελεκυφόρον).

The only specific mention of the word "Varangians" that I am able to find in the sources to confirm the thesis that the Varangian guard was re-established at Nicaea after 1204 is one in the Greek *Chron. of Morea*, ed. Kalonaros (Athens, 1940) l. 4319, which states that after the battle of Pelagonia (1259) the Varangians of Michael Palaeologus took the Prince of Achaia away to prison (οἱ Βάραγγοι . . . τὸν πρίγκιπα . . . τὸν ἐδιαβάσασιν στὴν φυλακήν). R. Dawkins, "The Later History of the Varangian Guard: Some Notes," *Jl. of Roman Studies*, XXXVII (1947) 44, while affirming that the guard was re-established at Nicaea after 1204, adduces no evidence for this belief except the above passage. Quite possibly, however, the *Chronicle of Morea*, written c. 1300, may have confused the later re-establishment of the Varangian Guard at Constantinople with its presumed establishment earlier at Nicaea. In this connection, in fact, the *Chronicle* mistakenly refers to Palaeologus as already Emperor of Constantinople (l. 3104): στὸν βασιλέα εἰς τὴν Κωνσταντινόπολιν . . . στὸν Μέγαν Παλαιολόγον.

A double mention of the term "Varangian" is also to be found in a *prostagma* of Palaeologus, but this is dated November 1272, that is, *after* the Greek recapture of Constantinople: see A. Heisenberg, "Aus der Geschichte und Literatur der Palaiologenzeit," *Sitzungsb. d. bayerischen Akademie der Wiss., Phil.-hist. Kl.* (1920) no. 10, 39, l. 30: ἵνα ἔχοις βαράγγους and l. 49: οἱ τῶν ἀμφοτέρων ἐγκλινοβάραγγοι. I have found a third use of the word Varangian in the "Testamentum" of the Patriarch Arsenios, who died in 1273: Migne, *PG* 140, 956B, ἄλλοτε δὲ βαράγγους . . . ἀπέστειλε φυλάττοντάς με. These three apparently unused or overlooked references thus substantiate the view expressed by Dawkins and by M. Dendias ("Οἱ Βάραγγοι καὶ τὸ Βυζάντιον," in Δελτίον τῆς Ἱστορικῆς καὶ Ἐθνολογικῆς Ἑταιρείας τῆς Ἑλλάδος, IX [1926] 193) that the Varangians as a group were restored in Constantinople after 1261. However, whether the Latin troops, in particular the axe-bearing Kelts serving in the Greek armies at the time of the

43

legitimacy of his financial demands.[58] Michael soon succeeded, albeit under false pretenses (at least according to Pachymeres), in withdrawing large sums from the treasury, which he judiciously distributed to those able to aid his ambitions — to the army and plebs, and to demagogues who could stir up the people to demand higher office for him.[59]

His chief blandishments, however, Michael directed toward the clergy. Realizing that in a matter of this kind he could secure the most telling support from the prelates, he sent them numerous gifts by night.[60] Thus, testifies Pachymeres, even the Patriarch Arsenios, despite a rather suspicious nature, was impressed by Michael's apparent respect for the Church, his generosity and modest demeanor. When it was reported, for example, that the Patriarch was approaching, the Grand Duke Michael would rush to meet Arsenios, and, in a performance probably inspired by Latin practice (it is, indeed, strikingly reminiscent of the dramatic meeting between the Western Emperor Frederick Barbarossa and Pope Alexander III in Venice in 1177), grasp the bridle of his mule and lead him personally to the palace.[61] So successful was Michael

Nicene Empire, are definitely to be regarded as forming a reconstituted Varangian guard at Nicaea, is yet to be conclusively demonstrated.

[58] As the imperial bodyguard was famous for its support of the legitimate ruler, it may well be that this part of the Latin troops looked upon Michael as a threat to the rights of young John.

[59] Pach., 71.

[60] Pach., 72–73. It will be recalled that Theodore II, in contrast, had neglected the clergy.

[61] Pach., 72, ll. 13ff.: καὶ ὃς αὐτίκα μαθὼν πρὸ τῶν ἄλλων αὐτὸς ὑπαντᾷ μακρόθεν, τιμὴν τὴν μεγίστην ἀφοσιούμενος τῷ πατριάρχῃ καὶ παντὶ τῷ ἱερῷ πληρώματι, πεζῇ τε βαδίζων καὶ τὰς τῆς ἡμιόνου τοῦ ἱερέως χαλινοὺς κατέχων ἕως καὶ αὐτῶν ἐντὸς τῶν ἀνακτόρων προηγούμενος καθιστᾷ. This performance of Palaeologus probably represents a conflation of two elements: (1) Christ's entrance on an ass into Jerusalem on Palm Sunday and (2) the Western practice (first appearing in an interpolated passage in the Donation of Constantine) according to which the Emperor, holding the bridle of the papal mule, led it while the Pope rode. In the present case at Nicaea, however, the circumstances were not the same. Michael at the time was regent and not Emperor; moreover, Pachymeres' passage says nothing of Palm Sunday, stating only that Michael made the gesture "when the Patriarch came to Nicaea." Despite these differences it is quite possible that Palaeologus, having heard of the custom from the Latins at Nicaea or even from papal emissaries who were sent there during the reign of Vatatzes, adopted the practice, hitherto unknown in Byzantium, merely to flatter the Patriarch and secure his support. Significantly, we hear nothing of such a performance on the part of Palaeologus after

in cultivating clerical good will that it was the prelates themselves who first proposed Michael's promotion to the high rank of Despot.[62] They argued that this alone would insure tranquillity in the state, that Michael would not be a complete stranger to the office since his grandfather Alexios had been Despot before him, and, finally, that the dignity of the state required the highest possible rank after that of Emperor for one who had to receive foreign ambassadors.[63] Despite the vigorous opposition of Lascarid relatives, this proposal of the clergy was adopted with the aid of Michael's friends, including the numerous malcontents of Theodore's reign.[64]

Once named Despot, Michael was quick to reward his followers, to punish his rivals, especially the Lascarid adherents,[65] and to lay the groundwork for his accession to the throne. Artfully stressing that without absolute power for Palaeologus the Empire would disintegrate before John reached his majority, Michael's followers again won the support of Arsenios and the higher clergy. Then, when it was felt that public opinion was appropriately influenced, Michael was raised aloft on a shield at Magnesia and proclaimed Emperor.[66] Finally, a few weeks subsequent to this

---

his accession to the throne. On the practice in general see E. Kantorowicz, "The 'King's Advent' and the Enigmatic Panels in the doors of Santa Sabina," *Art Bulletin*, XXVI (1944) 207ff., 230; and esp. G. Ostrogorsky, "Zum Stratordienst der Herrschers in der byzantinisch-slavischen Welt," *Seminarium Kondakovianum*, VII (1935) 193ff.

[62] Pach., 74, ll. 6ff.

[63] According to Pach., 75, ll. 1–3, Alexios, while holding this rank, had defeated the Italians.

[64] See Pach., 79; Acrop., 154; Greg., 72.

[65] In particular the Tzamantouroi, as Pach., 80, l. 16, records. It should be noted that according to Acrop., 159, ll. 19–24, Karyanites, the Protovestiarites, was responsible for the murder of the Muzalons. He was thrown into prison by Michael, and later escaped to the Turks. Since this is mentioned by no other source, and since Acropolites is generally partisan to Michael, one cannot avoid the suspicion that Michael (or possibly Acropolites in his history) might have made Karyanites the scapegoat for the murders.

[66] Acrop., 159, ll. 15–17 and Pach., 81, ll. 16–18. According to Greg., 78ff., the nobles raised Michael on a shield at Magnesia on the Kalends of December and proclaimed him Emperor. Thereupon the Patriarch Arsenios threatened to excommunicate those involved, but later judged it best to crown Michael after securing oaths from him that he would abdicate when young John reached his majority. Cf. the similar account of Sphrantzes, 16. As has been mentioned, Michael's Autobiography, 5, l. 25, attributes his accession to the will of God, not to his own actions; but this insistence that he secured the throne through no efforts of his own

event, probably at Christmas (1258), he was crowned Emperor at Nicaea.[67]

At the coronation ceremony the Latin soldiers — doubtless the Varangians — once again played an important role on his behalf. When several of the prelates, especially the Bishop of Thessalonica, bitterly contested the plan to crown Palaeologus first and young John Lascaris afterwards or perhaps not at all, the sight of the Latin soldiery brandishing their battle-axes quickly silenced all opposition.[68] Thereupon Michael and his wife Theodora were crowned first, with imperial diadems of precious stones, while John, too young probably to realize exactly what was happening, had to content himself with a narrow band of pearls.

There are numerous discrepancies in the sources concerning the details of Michael's accession to the throne and his coronation, especially with respect to the attitude of the Patriarch Arsenios, who, though protector of young Lascaris, seems at first to have been almost completely taken in by Michael. Whatever the minor differences in the accounts as regards the steps of his ascent, the significant fact is that within the remarkably short time of less than four months Michael advanced from the dignity of Grand Constable to the supreme rank of Basileus. With the attainment of the Empire, there now remained for Michael the important task of legitimizing his usurpation, an objective which could most effectively be accomplished by recovering from the Latins the ancient capital of Constantinople.

---

is somewhat suspect. Acrop., 159, ll. 10–11, reflects Michael's sentiment, saying that Michael, willy-nilly, was forced by the nobles to become Emperor.

[67] Dölger, Regesten, III, 30 (see also his "Die dynastische Familienpolitik des Kaisers Michael Palaiologos," Festschrift E. Eichmann [Paderborn, 1940] 180), following Greg., 78, says Michael was raised on the shield on 1 December 1258 and that his first coronation (the second taking place later at Constantinople) occurred at the end of December of that year (quite probably at Christmas). Cf. V. Laurent, "La date du premier couronnement de Michel VIII Paléologue," Echos d'Orient, XXXVI (1937) 167, however, who follows Pach., 81 and 96, and supports 1 January 1259 as the date of his accession. Concerning this disputed question Ostrogorsky, Byzantine State (1956) 397, note 2, summarizes: "The exact date of Michael's accession to the imperial throne cannot be conclusively determined" (cf. ibid., 516).

[68] On the ceremony and the Latin soldiery, see Pach., 101–104.

3

THE BATTLE OF PELAGONIA

(1259)

THE ANTI-NICENE COALITION OF MICHAEL OF EPIRUS,
MANFRED OF SICILY, AND WILLIAM OF ACHAIA

In the period immediately preceding the Nicene reconquest of Constantinople in 1261 no event was of greater importance than Michael Palaeologus' victory at Pelagonia in the middle or perhaps latter part of 1259. This battle crushed the powerful triple coalition organized against Palaeologus by his arch-rival the Despot Michael II of Epirus and the latter's Latin allies, King Manfred of Sicily and Prince William of Achaia. It thereby enabled Palaeologus, now freed from the menace of a Western attack, to devote all his energies to the recovery of the imperial city, possession of which was essential for any real claim to the mantle of the Byzantine Empire.

As we have seen, Nicaea and Epirus, rival Greek states established after the Latin conquest of Constantinople in 1204, were both striving to recover Constantinople. While the Nicene Emperors John III Vatatzes and Theodore II Lascaris had stripped the Latin Empire of most of its Asiatic and European possessions, Michael of Epirus, by 1258, had occupied former European territories of the Byzantine Empire which today constitute western Greece and Albania. The stage was thus set for a decisive encounter.

The Despot's Latin allies, Manfred, whose Norman ancestor had nourished designs against Byzantium, and William, whose family had played a leading role in the conquest of 1204 and wh himself now aimed at conquering the rest of Byzantine Greece were rulers of states long antagonistic to Epirus. What forces ha now brought all three rulers together in this unnatural Latin Epirot alliance?[1] It is the purpose of this chapter to discuss, first the political and diplomatic factors conducing to the formation o the alliance and, secondly, the circumstances which led to its col lapse at the battle of Pelagonia.

To understand these developments it is necessary briefly t describe prior circumstances. In opposition to papal interests Frederick II (d. 1250), Western Emperor and father of Man fred, and the Emperor John Vatatzes of Nicaea had formed a alliance, which was sealed by the marriage of Vatatzes to the daughter of Frederick.[2] Despite the fact that no important mili tary aid seems to have been exchanged,[3] the moral and politica value of the association was considerable and did not fail t evoke papal fulminations against its two heretical opponents. With the accession and brief reign of Frederick's son and suc cessor Conrad (1250–1254), there was apparently no significan change in Nicene-Hohenstaufen relations, despite Conrad's dis

---

[1] K. Hopf, *Geschichte Griechenlands im Mittelalter und in der Neuzeit*, I (Leipzig, 1867) 283, calls it an "unnatürliche Bundesbrüderschaft."

[2] For this marriage of the sexagenarian Vatatzes with the young Constance called Anna by the Greeks, see Acrop., 110; Greg., 45; Scutariotes, 405; and Matthew Paris, *Chronica Majora*, ed. H. Luard (London, 1877) Rolls Series, IV 299, 357. Also cf. Norden, 321–329; Gardner, *Lascarids*, 168ff.; Meliarakes *Nicaea*, 359ff., and recently S. Borsari, "Federico II e l'Oriente bizantino," *Riv stor. it.*, LXIII (1951) 279ff.

[3] See N. Festa, "Le lettere greche di Federigo II," *Arch. stor. it.*, XIII (1894 18, where the aid of Pergamene soldiers for Frederick is mentioned. Also *Annale Placentini Gibellini*, MGH SS, XVIII (1863) 479, where troops sent by Vatatze are mentioned as participating in the siege of Brescia in 1238.

[4] C. Héfelé-Leclercq, *Histoire des conciles*, V² (Paris, 1913) 1678; Matthev Paris, *Chronica Majora*, 453. See also the Greek letters of Frederick to Vatatze extolling the Greek church for its "happy" immunity from papal interferenc (Festa ed., 1–34, and A. Huillard-Bréholles, *Historia diplomatica Friderici Secundi* VI, pt. II [Paris, 1861] 684–686). Borsari, 284, notes that Vatatzes sent financia aid to Frederick, evidence for which is P. Collenuccio, *Compendio de le istori del Regno di Napoli*, ed. Saviotti, I (Bari, 1929) 141.

patch of an envoy to Vatatzes in 1253 to protest the granting of asylum to relatives of his brother Manfred, his vicar in Sicily.[5]

Meanwhile Nicaea, following the reigns of Vatatzes and Theodore II, was undergoing the revolution of 1258 which brought Michael Palaeologus to the throne. This event, so disturbing internally, afforded an opportunity for Michael II to seize the European provinces of Nicaea and to extend Epirot territory almost to Thessalonica.[6] But the Despot knew that Palaeologus was a resourceful opponent, who would seek reprisals once his power was established.[7] Eager to crush Palaeologus before he could consolidate his position, the Despot accordingly sought to create a powerful alliance with states sharing similar aims against Nicaea.[8]

For this he looked to the rulers of Sicily and Achaia. Manfred, after the death of Conrad, had completed his hegemony over Sicily in defiance of papal wishes. Soon thereafter, probably at the beginning of 1258, while Michael of Epirus was battling the Nicene troops in Macedonia, Manfred took a step which was to have far-reaching effects on the relations between Latins and Byzantines in Greece: he took possession of certain former Norman possessions of Epirus along the Adriatic coast. Evidence for this is a Greek notarial document of Dyrrachium (the modern Durazzo) dated 23 February 1258, attesting that it was already Manfred's first year of seigneury over territories surrounding Dyrrachium and Avlona.[9]

[5] On this see my article "Greco-Latin Relations on the Eve of the Byzantine Restoration: The Battle of Pelagonia" (hereafter cited as Geanakoplos, "Pelagonia"), *Dumbarton Oaks Papers No. 7* (Cambridge, Mass., 1953) 102, note 6.

[6] I.e., up to the Vardar River. See Pach., 82, l. 1; Greg., 71, l. 10; and Acrop., 139–150. Michael II's success was in part due to the favorable disposition of the European Greek population which was partial to Epirus and looked upon Asiatic Nicaea as an interloper. On this see Geanakoplos, "Pelagonia," 103, note 7.

[7] Acrop., 145. Pach., 21, describes accusations made against Palaeologus some years before for allegedly intriguing with the same Despot.

[8] Meliarakes, *Nicaea*, 510, and E. Bertaux, "Les Français d'outre mer au temps des Hohenstaufen d'Italie," *Revue historique*, LXXXV (1904) 240.

[9] Document in F. Miklosich and J. Müller, *Acta et diplomata res graecas italasque illustrantia*, III (Vienna, 1865) 239ff. (hereafter M.-M.). For text and other editions see Geanakoplos, "Pelagonia," 103, note 11. The territories mentioned in the document are Dyrrachium, Bellegrada, Avlona, the Sphinariza mountains, and

On 2 June 1259,[10] at the time of the marriage of Manfred to Michael of Epirus' daughter Helen, it appears that the Despot not only legitimized this occupation of his lands but even made grants of additional territories as well. Lacking adequate data, we can only speculate on reasons for this action. It would seem justifiable, however, to assume that Michael II, contemplating an offensive against Nicaea and observing that Manfred already possessed the territories by right of conquest, turned a *fait accompli* to his own ends by officially granting to Manfred these territories along with others as the dowry of Helen.[11] In this manner the Despot could avoid hostilities and at the same time gain a useful ally.

In view of the former alliance between Vatatzes and Frederick II, the reversal of Sicilian policy toward Nicaea seems at first glance surprising.[12] One must consider, however, that conquest of the Byzantine Empire had been a traditional Norman aim for almost two centuries,[13] and that Manfred was now in a strong enough position in Italy to discard his father's alliance and to look to anyone who could assist him in his ambitions for Balkan domination.

The sources afford meagre detail with respect to the creation of the Sicilian-Epirot alliance.[14] Both Greek and Latin writers

---

the surrounding area. On this see J. Buchon, *Recherches historiques sur la principauté française de Morée et ces hautes baronnies*, I (Paris, 1845) 103–104; and esp. M. Dendias, " Ἑλένη Ἀγγελῖνα Δούκαινα βασίλισσα Σικελίας καὶ Νεαπόλεως," Ἠπειρωτικὰ Χρονικά, I (1926) 223 (hereafter cited as *Helen*). For a point of Dendias' on which the writer disagrees see Geanakoplos, "Pelagonia," 103, note 11.

[10] On this date see note 14.

[11] For documentation of this controversial problem of dating Helen's dowry, and especially its connection with the creation of the alliance, see Geanakoplos "Pelagonia," 104, note 13.

[12] On this see F. Schneider, "Eine Quelle für Manfreds Orientpolitik," *Queller und Forschungen aus italienischen Archiven und Bibliotheken*, XXIV (1932–33) 112. Cf. E. Jordan, *Les origines de la domination angevine en Italie* (Paris, 1909) 381.

[13] Robert Guiscard, Bohemond, Roger II, and Henry VI had all pursued such a policy; and in 1185 William II had actually sacked Thessalonica.

[14] The source for the date and place of the marriage is the chronicle of the contemporary Anonymous of Trani. Discovered by F. Davanzati, it was first published in his *Dissertazione sulla seconda moglie del re Manfredi e su' loro figliuoli*

rovide hardly more than the simple facts of Manfred's marriage
) Helen, eldest daughter of the Despot.[15] Yet it would be of
iterest to know who took the initiative in promoting the mar-
.age alliance, and, more important, whether Manfred's Epirot
ossessions were secured from Michael of Epirus actually as a
esult of conquest or as a dowry. For these questions there is no
efinite evidence, and we must content ourselves with hypoth-
ses based on the few hints the sources offer concerning the
iotives and ambitions of each member of the coalition.

THE MOTIVES OF MICHAEL OF EPIRUS

If one examines the dotal territories of Manfred, both those
·hose previous possession was now confirmed and those added
y Michael II,[16] it is obvious that they constituted certain of the
iost strategic areas of the Despotate of Epirus, a kind of exten-
ion of the Kingdom of Sicily on the Albanian coast. Clearly the
iaster of these would be in position to begin the conquest of
ie Balkan peninsula.[17] For such concessions it is logical to as-
ime that Michael II expected to draw substantial profit from
ie alliance. Now the only territories surpassing these in value

---

Naples, 1791) 11ff. Though J. Ficker, "Manfreds zweite Heirath und der Anony-
us von Trani," *Mitteil. des Inst. für oesterreichische Geschichtsf.*, III (1882)
58–368, considers the chronicle a forgery of Davanzati, it is regarded as authentic
y others including Dendias, del Giudice, Meliarakes, and the present writer. For
a answer to Ficker's argument, see Dendias, *Helen*, 237ff.

[15] Manfred's marriage seems to have preceded that of William of Achaia to
nna, another daughter of Michael II. See Geanakoplos, "Pelagonia," 105.

[16] For evidence that Michael II added other territories to the dowry see my
ticle, "Pelagonia," 105, note 18. The fundamental question here, however, is:
hy should Michael II relinquish to Manfred, ruler of a realm traditionally inimical
» Epirus, lands which were obviously among the most important parts of his
ossessions (i.e., Corfu, Dyrrachium, Avlona, Butrinto, Kanina)? The most reason-
ble answer, I believe, is that he needed Manfred's aid in order to carry out his
esigns against Nicaea and Constantinople. If one admits that the Despot added
irther territories to the dowry, it seems clear that one must also concede that
lanfred already possessed areas in Epirus before his marriage.

[17] Dyrrachium (the medieval name for Durazzo) was the key to the Byzantine
mpire in the west, for that city and Avlona were the Adriatic termini of the
ia Egnatia which led directly to Thessalonica. On Norman policy to gain control
: this route see G. Tafel, *De via Romanorum militari Egnatia* (Tuebingen, 1842)
issim.

were Thessalonica and Constantinople, and there is good reaso
to believe that the Despot hoped, with the help of his allies, t
carry out designs against these cities. Direct reference to this
Pachymeres' statement that it was the plan of the Despot

to gather together as many troops as possible to attack and try to car
ture it [Constantinople], and then to be proclaimed Emperor of th
Romans, for there was no one [thought the Despot], either of Lascari
or any other family, worthier of the Empire than the Angeloi.[18]

Pachymeres re-emphasizes this point with the remark tha
Michael II,

after assembling the men of his allies and as many of his own men as h
could, planned first to attack the generals of Nicaea and then . . . t
assault Thessalonica and overrun the west, after which to make an a
tempt on Constantinople itself.[19]

If Michael of Epirus' ultimate aim was the capture of Cor
stantinople, a more immediate one was Thessalonica, wester
center of the Nicene Empire. This was a realizable and legitimat
objective, as Epirot territory now extended to its very gates, an
especially since Thessalonica had been the capital of an ephem
eral Empire established in 1224–1225 by the Despot's uncle, th
self-styled Emperor Theodore Dukas Angelos.[20] Supported by h
allies and fortified by claims to his uncle's inheritance, the Despo
then, had reason to believe that Thessalonica would soon be hi
  Particularly important in Michael II's plans for conquest wa
the military aid of William of Achaia's Frankish chivalry, th
fame of whose prowess had spread even to France.[21] But ho

---

[18] Pach., 82, ll. 16–20.
[19] Pach., 83, ll. 14–19. See a probable reference to the same objectives
Acrop., 164, l. 7, who notes that the Epirot "meditated grandiose ideas and talke
of excessive gains." For another, modern view of the Despot's aims see Geam
koplos, "Pelagonia," 106.
[20] Theodore had captured Thessalonica from the Latins in 1224, a date gene
ally cited wrongly as 1222 or 1223. See J. Longnon, "La reprise de Salonique p
les Grecs en 1224," *Actes du VIe congrès intern. d'études byz.*, I (Paris, 195(
141ff. and B. Sinogowitz, "Zur Eroberung Thessalonikes im Herbst 1224," *B*y
Zeit., XLV (1952) 28.
[21] On the prestige of the Achaian knighthood in general, see W. Miller, *Th
Latins in the Levant* (London, 1908) 109.

Michael intended to rid himself of this formidable ally after reaping the benefits of his aid is not disclosed.

THE MOTIVES OF MANFRED

As noted, Manfred possessed almost the entire littoral of Albanian Epirus even before his marriage. One indication of his keen interest in this territory and his desire to play a larger role in Balkan affairs is a document of 17 June 1258, revealing that he had sent a strong fleet of one hundred galleys under his Admiral Chinardo "ad partes Romaniae . . . ad provinciam Macedoniae" to support Michael of Epirus against the Nicenes.[22] Although no evidence survives to prove that a battle occurred at this time, it is nevertheless clear that an expedition of this sort would have accorded well with Manfred's Balkan aspirations.[23]

The suggestion is to be questioned that Manfred, content with his Epirot fortresses, furnished aid to his father-in-law merely at the request of his wife.[24] It seems more realistic to suppose that, in imitation of his Norman predecessors, Manfred contemplated using Epirus as a springboard for further conquest. Thus, according to Gregoras, the objective of Manfred and William was the seizure "of all Greek territories from the Ionian Sea to Constantinople without effort."[25] Norden, in fact, supposes that Manfred was seeking a kingdom on the Adriatic, in return for which he would have permitted his father-in-law to have Constantinople;[26] and in this connection Buchon and Dendias believe that Manfred expected and was promised Epirot territory for his aid.[27] Still another theory is offered by Dendias, who sug-

[22] B. Capasso, *Historia diplomatica regni Siciliae* (Naples, 1874) 145–146.
[23] For a denial that such an elaborate expedition took place, see F. Schneider, "Eine Quelle für Manfreds Orientpolitik," *Quellen und Forschungen,* XXIV (1932–33) 112–123. For further discussion see Geanakoplos, "Pelagonia," 107–108.
[24] Dendias, *Helen,* 224.
[25] Greg., 72, ll. 5–6.
[26] Norden, 333–334. Cf. G. Valenti, "Vestigia di Manfredi di Hohenstaufen Re di Sicilia e Signore di 'Romania,'" *Numismatica* (1939) 65, who cites as evidence of Manfred's aspirations to Byzantine territory two coins inscribed "Manfridus R. Siciliae . . . et Dominus Romaniae."
[27] Dendias, *Helen,* 277; J. Buchon, *Recherches historiques sur la principauté française de Morée* (Paris, 1845) 279. On this point the sources are not specific.

53

gests that Manfred sought the Epirot territories of his dowry as a refuge in case of defeat by the Pope. But Manfred's ascendancy in Italy at this time renders this view improbable.[28] The aims of Manfred, at least for the present, very probably included aid for Michael II in capturing Constantinople, or perhaps even a joint occupation of that city. According to Pachymeres, its capture on land would be rendered easier by the use of Manfred's excellent German troops, eager to combat papal forces as previously they had done under his father Frederick.[29] Evidence that Hohenstaufen naval aid was contemplated is lacking, but in view of the importance of the Venetian fleet for the defense of Constantinople, it seems certain that the Sicilian marine must have loomed large in any plans of Manfred for conquest in the Balkans.

It is important, finally, that consideration of Manfred's motives in entering the coalition be related to his basic and permanent aims — papal recognition of his Sicilian hegemony and Hohenstaufen domination of all Italy. Unquestionably a successful Greek policy on his part could exert considerable influence on Italian affairs, and particularly on the papacy, the real protector of the Latin states of Greece.[30]

THE MOTIVES OF WILLIAM OF ACHAIA. THE ROLE OF THE LATIN EMPEROR BALDWIN

Reasons for adherence to the coalition are more complex and hypothetical in the case of the third confederate, William II Villehardouin, Prince of Achaia.[31] Only one statement, in fact, is

[28] *Helen*, 235. Manfred, moreover, was not such a defeatist as to be expecting expulsion from Italy. Only fairly recently has the true character of Manfred, that of a bold, handsome, extremely capable ruler, been rehabilitated from the calumny cast upon it by his fanatical Guelf opponents. See Dendias, *Helen*, 229ff., and *Cambridge Medieval History*, VI (1929) 184. For Manfred's career in general see A. Karst, *Geschichte Manfreds* (Berlin, 1897); F. Schirrmacher, *Die letzten Hohenstaufen* (Göttingen, 1871) 69–298; K. Hampe, *Urban IV. und Manfred* (Heidelberg, 1905), and the same author's *Geschichte Konradins von Hohenstaufen*, 3rd ed. (Leipzig, 1942).

[29] Pach., 83, ll. 19ff.

[30] Norden, 333–334.

[31] William's uncle had helped to found the principality of Achaia shortly after

to be found in the contemporary historians regarding his aims, namely that of Acropolites, who writes vaguely that William could expect to gain considerably from the alliance.[32] It is likely that William supposed that with Michael II's support he could completely surround and subdue the recalcitrant Frankish barons of Middle Greece.[33] At the very least he could strengthen the allegiance of his Greek archons of Achaia (as in fact was manifested by their willing cooperation at the subsequent battle of Pelagonia), since they would naturally favor an alliance with fellow-Greeks of Epirus.[34] Further, he could gain important allies against Palaeologus, whose intention, it was becoming increasingly clear, was the restoration of former Byzantine territories at the expense of Frankish Greece.[35]

Marino Sanudo, the fourteenth-century Venetian chronicler, while emphasizing the Prince's aspirations ("Who can judge the limits of this Villehardouin's ambition?"), believes that he wished to conquer Constantinople on land and to displace the Venetians of that city in revenge for their support of the rebellious triarchs of Negropont.[36] Norden accepts this statement with the additional implication that William planned to become high suzerain

---

the Latin conquest in 1204. On the terms "Peloponnesus," "Morea," and "Achaia," used apparently interchangeably in the sources, see my article, "Pelagonia," 109, note 44.

[32] 165: καὶ πολλὰ ἐκ τούτου προσγενήσεσθαι αὐτῷ προσδοκῶν.

[33] Hopf, Geschichte, 280. For William's conflicts with the Dukes of Athens and the triarchs of Negropont over his claim to part of that island see J. B. Bury, "The Lombards and Venetians in Euboia (1205–1303)," Jl. of Hellenic Studies, VII (1886) 309ff. Worth noting is a statement of J. Longnon, L'Empire latin de Constantinople (Paris, 1949) 221, who cites a passage from Andrea Dandolo, RISS, XII (1941) 363–364, as signifying the existence already of an accord between William and Michael II (which although wrongly reads Michael Palaeologus in Dandolo, says Longnon) against the Venetian lords of Negropont.

[34] Miller, Latins in Levant, 109.

[35] See Pach., 87–88 and 206, l. 18. Note the Chronicon Marchiae Tarvisinae et Lombardiae, RISS, VIII (1916) pt. 3, 47 (= Annales S. Justinae Patavini, MGH SS, XIX [1866] 181), which records that Michael Palaeologus believed "Constantinopoli acquisita, omnes maris insulas et civitates in terra firma constitutas, a Latinis et Venetis maxime iure belli possessas, se breviter habiturum."

[36] Sanudo, Istoria del Regno di Romania (hereafter Istoria), in K. Hopf, Chroniques gréco-romanes (Berlin, 1873) 107, esp.: "credo andasse per assaltar li Veneziani che erano ivi [in Constantinople], e vendicarsi di loro, che li tenivan Negroponte."

over all of Latin Greece.[37] But the latter assumption seems unlikely, as William would first have had to dispossess the Latin Emperor of Constantinople, Baldwin, whose vassal he was.[38] Such a *démarche*, of course, would also involve William in serious difficulties with Baldwin's protector, the papacy. Besides this, William was apparently not on unfriendly terms with Baldwin, as is revealed by their association on the crusade to Damietta in 1250.[39] In sum, though Sanudo may be correct in reporting that William wished to harass, perhaps even to dispossess, his hated rivals the Venetians, it seems unwarranted to accept the view that William planned to replace Baldwin on the throne of Constantinople.[40]

A much more feasible objective on William's part would have been the acquisition of Thessalonica. An ephemeral Lombard Kingdom had been established at Thessalonica during the Latin conquest, and William may well have aspired to revive that realm with himself as its ruler.[41]

Since, in the final analysis, the fate of Constantinople was involved in the alliance against Nicaea, one wonders what role (if any) the Latin Emperor Baldwin may have played in the affairs under discussion. No source, it is true, mentions his participation in the coalition, but it would appear unlikely that the allies failed to consider the advantages to be gained (especially

---

[37] Norden, 332.

[38] Sanudo, *Istoria*, 107: "potria esser, che andasse per servir all' Imperator Latino, a cui era obbligato di Fedeltà e dal qual reconoscea le Terre della Morea che aveva." Hopf, *Geschichte*, 282, finds it difficult to believe that William planned to dispossess Baldwin.

[39] Geoffrey Villehardouin, William's brother, had dispatched aid to Latin Constantinople in 1236 at the time it was besieged by Vatatzes and Asen, the Bulgar ruler. See Philippe Mouskes, *Chronique rimée*, ed. de Reiffenberg (Brussels, 1836–1838) II, 620. On the crusade to Damietta see Joinville, *Histoire de Saint Louis*, ed. N. de Wailly (Paris, 1874) no. 427.

[40] Sanudo's Venetian bias might, of course, have caused him to attribute exaggerated designs to her enemy.

[41] On William's aspirations to Thessalonica see the Greek *Chronicle of Morea*, ed. Kalonaros (Athens, 1940) 1. 3653, which records that William and the Despot planned νὰ ἐπάρωμεν τὰ μέρη Σαλονίκης. Cf. the Aragonese version, *Libro de los Fechos*, ed. A. Morel-Fatio (Geneva, 1885) par. 250; and Miller, *Latins in Levant*, 109.

56

of having a closer base for attacking Nicaea)[42] if Baldwin could be drawn to their side. Indeed, del Giudice suggests, but without adding evidence, that at the time of William's marriage to Anna,[43] sister to Helen and second daughter of Michael of Epirus, an alliance was probably signed by Manfred, William, Michael II, and Baldwin.[44]

Such a statement seems rather improbable. In the first place, for Baldwin to admit the allied army into his territory might have endangered his already enfeebled position [45] and permitted the coalition forces, if they so desired, to take his possessions without undue effort. Moreover, even granted an allied conquest of Constantinople, it would have been difficult for the allies to agree on a satisfactory division of Baldwin's territories.

In view of these considerations — which could not but have been apparent to Baldwin — it would seem that his best course of action would be to remain aloof, or at least benevolently neutral, with respect to coalition affairs. In the meantime Baldwin himself could take advantage of the unfavorable situation of Michael Palaeologus (Michael's external problems were then complicated by internal disturbances)[46] to seek concessions from Nicaea. Thus, according to Acropolites, Baldwin dispatched ambassadors to Michael demanding the return of certain territories. The envoys asked successively for the areas extending from Thessalonica, Serres, and Voleros eastward to Constantinople, each time reducing their demands. Palaeologus, however, boldly refused all,

[42] Constantinople was only some forty miles distant from Nicaea.
[43] For a detailed discussion of the dotal territories received from Michael II by William on his marriage to Anna, see Geanakoplos, "Pelagonia," 111–112 and notes thereto.
[44] G. del Giudice, "La famiglia di re Manfredi," Arch. stor. prov. nap., III (1878) 17 (second edition unavailable to me).
[45] With Baldwin's Empire reduced practically to the city of Constantinople and surrounding territory, he had to make frequent journeys to the West to seek aid personally and even to raise funds by selling the lead from the roofs of palaces of Constantinople. On this see Marino Sanudo's so-called Fragmentum, in Hopf, Chroniques gréco-romanes, 170: "vendidit et distribuit quasi totum quod habebat in Constantinopoli, discoperiendo palatia plumbea et vendendo." (For a new ed. of the Fragmentum see Chapter 5, note 10.)
[46] The supporters of young John Lascaris, whose imperial rights Michael had usurped, were a constant menace to him. See Chapter 5, note 8.

even countering with a demand for half the customs duties of Constantinople plus half the revenue from the gold mint.[47] This embassy of Baldwin has been termed strange, even absurd,[48] by some scholars, but in the context in which we have placed it, it would appear to be only a logical attempt on the part of Baldwin to take advantage of Palaeologus' situation and perhaps thereby to establish a buffer area between Constantinople and the territory of the coalition.[49]

Besides the differences already noted among the allies, there were others, less obvious but of underlying importance. All three rulers were of different religious faiths.[50] All three belonged, so to speak, to different races, and all, finally, were products of entirely different milieux: Michael of Epirus was an astute, calculating Byzantine; William, the brave and crafty epitome of French chivalry transplanted to Greek soil;[51] and Manfred, a product of the Sicilian kingdom's mélange of diverse cultures.[52] Such considerations must have been in the mind of Gregoras when he wrote that "it would not be difficult to plant discord among the three allies since William and Manfred were different in race from Michael Angelos."[53]

[47] Acrop., 161–163. For the location of these towns see Geanakoplos, "Pelagonia," 114, notes 70–71.

[48] Acropolites himself, 162, l. 1, terms the demands absurd and exaggerated, but he may have exaggerated his account in order to display his hero, Palaeologus, in a good light. Cf. Gardner, *Lascarids*, 246: "The story has a bombastic ring to it." Guilland, in Diehl *et al.*, *L'Europe orientale de 1081 à 1453* (Paris, 1945) 183, observes that Baldwin made his demands "dans sa naiveté." So also W. Miller, in *Cambridge Medieval History*, IV, 509.

[49] Chapman, 39, dates this embassy of Baldwin *after* the battle of Pelagonia. But I see no reason to change the order of Acropolites, who introduces it just before that battle and along with Palaeologus' embassies to Manfred, Michael II, and Villehardouin (see below, notes 56–59). See my article, "Pelagonia," 114, note 75, for discussion of a possible secret alliance between Baldwin and Manfred directed against the Despot and William.

[50] William belonged to the Roman church, the Despot to the Greek Patriarchate of Ochrida (not Nicaea), and Manfred was excommunicated from the Roman Church.

[51] William, born in the Morea, spoke Greek. See the Greek *Chron. of Morea*, l. 4130. Frederick II had spoken fluent Greek, which he learned in Sicily, and the same is probably true of his son Manfred.

[52] I.e., Norman, Arabic, and Greek.

[53] Greg., 74, ll. 4–7.

Considering the differences in race and character, and particularly the conflict in aims over Constantinople and Thessalonica, it is remarkable that the three rulers could have overcome their mutual suspicions to achieve even a temporary agreement. Perhaps the explanation lies in a statement of Gregoras that the allies, certain of victory but presumably unable to agree on a division of future spoils, drew lots for their share of the loot even before undertaking their campaign.[54]

The foregoing analysis,[55] lengthy as it may be, is vital for its indication that the ambitions of the coalition members were from the very outset sharply conflicting, indeed almost irreconcilable. This fact is admirably revealed by the sources themselves, whose very discrepancies regarding the ambitions of the protagonists serve to emphasize even more sharply the frailty of the alliance. The conclusions that have been reached, though in part hypothetical, seem reasonable, given the condition of the sources. It now remains to consider how long this coalition, beset by such fundamental differences in race, character, and ambition, could survive.

THE BATTLE AND VICTORY OF MICHAEL PALAEOLOGUS
AT PELAGONIA

Michael Palaeologus, having only recently attained the imperial rank by a *coup d'état*, was, understandably, not eager to risk his throne on the battlefield against this powerful alliance. Accordingly, soon after his coronation (probably 25 December 1258) he made a calculated attempt to dissolve the coalition by the dispatch of an embassy to each of the principals, offering

---

[54] Greg., 72, ll. 6–8. The phrase "to draw lots" is probably figurative, since there is no evidence that Manfred was in Greece at this time. On the other hand, it should be noted that Gregoras wrongly reported that Manfred participated in person at the battle of Pelagonia. Cf. with this passage Nicetas Choniates, *Historia* (Bonn, 1835) 787, ll. 10–18, relating that the Latin conquerors, after Constantinople's conquest in 1204, cast lots for territories, some not yet in their possession.

[55] For an extensive discussion of the hypothesis of a secret agreement between Michael II and Manfred against William of Achaia, see my article, "Pelagonia," 116–118.

concessions and presumably playing upon their conflicting aims. To Manfred he sent Nikephoros Alyattes,[56] probably to propose renewal of the old Nicene-Sicilian alliance, perhaps together with the release of Manfred's sister Constance, widow of Vatatzes, at that time held practically a prisoner in Nicaea. But Manfred, as we are told, "persuaded by the fantasy of greater gain," rejected the overtures and cast the envoy into prison where he was to remain for two years.[57]

Equally futile was the embassy to Achaia, since the ambitious William also anticipated benefits from the alliance.[58] As for Michael II, we learn from Acropolites that he replied insultingly and "talked of immoderate things" to the blind envoy, Theodore Philes, when the latter offered territorial concessions.[59]

Palaeologus' most skillful move was the dispatch of an embassy to the Papacy, perhaps the only power then able to prevent the destruction of his Empire. Not only did the Holy See wield vast moral and political power as protector of the Latin states of Greece; it was the implacable enemy of the Hohenstaufen as well, and thus would not hesitate to restrain Manfred from extending his hegemony, particularly over Thessalonica and Constantinople. It is likely, moreover, that Palaeologus nurtured

---

[56] Acrop., 165, ll. 4–6. For the disputed date of Michael VIII's coronation, and the embassies, see Dölger, Regesten, nos. 1857 and 1861–1864; and see Chapter 2, note 67.

[57] Acrop., 165, ll. 6–7. Alyattes (whom Hopf, Griechenland, 282, erroneously calls Manuel) had had his tongue removed by Theodore II as punishment for some unknown transgression. Imprisoned by Manfred, he was released, it seems reasonable to believe, sometime after Constantinople's recapture in July of 1261, when Palaeologus returned Constance to Manfred in exchange for the captured Alexios Strategopulos. This would be about two years after Alyattes' original imprisonment and would correspond, therefore, to Acropolites' statement that he remained in prison for two years.

[58] Acrop., 165, l. 10. Cf. Dendias, Helen, 225.

[59] Acrop., 163, l. 18. The "insulting and immoderate things" were, no doubt, threats to punish Palaeologus for his claim to, and usurpation of, the imperial throne. Acropolites, it may be noted, is the only historian (besides Scutariotes, who followed his account) to mention Palaeologus' embassies to the allies. As for Philes, he too, for some unknown reason, had been blinded by Theodore II. Though it is difficult to judge Palaeologus' motives in sending maimed envoys to the allies, understanding as we do the realistic temper of Palaeologus' character, we may assume that his use of them was deliberate.

still another design with regard to the Papacy. By offering to the Curia union of the Greek and Latin churches (thus renewing the nearly consummated negotiations of some years before between John Vatatzes and Pope Innocent IV),[60] he could demand recognition of his usurpation of the Nicene throne. Success in this would be an achievement indeed, as besides menacing with papal censure any Western aggressor of his own Empire, it could hasten the collapse of the Latin Empire now tottering slowly to its ruin.

The Registers of Alexander IV contain no papal reply to Michael's embassy. It is permissible therefore to infer that, unless documents have been lost, the Curia considered the price of union too high. It was well aware that recognition of Michael's claims to the Nicene throne (that is, to hegemony of the Roman Empire as styled by the Asiatic Greeks) would mean virtual abandonment of the claims of Baldwin and probable restoration of Constantinople to the Greeks. Furthermore, with the rapid change in Nicene political conditions, it was perhaps too soon to gauge accurately the motives of the usurper and the strength of his ascendancy in Nicaea. Finally, it must have been obvious that Michael's offer of union was based exclusively on fear of Nicene destruction by the coalition. Union based on such flimsy foundations, as 1204 and subsequent events had amply demonstrated, would be lacking sincerity and doomed to failure. On this basis it would be better, the Curia may have felt, not to follow up the proposal but to adopt a policy of watchful waiting.[61]

[60] See F. Schillman, "Zur byzantinischen Politik Alexanders IV," *Römische Quartalschrift*, XXII (1908) 108ff. Cf. Wolff, "The Latin Empire of Constantinople," 643ff.

[61] The basis for the belief that such an embassy took place is a letter sent by Palaeologus to Pope Clement IV. Dated January or February 1267, it contains a passage reading: "When I took in my hands the helm of the Empire, I immediately sent an embassy to Pope Alexander of blessed memory in order to discuss the union with him" (printed in N. Festa, "Lettera inedita dell' imperatore Michele Paleologo al Pontefice Clemente IV," *Bessarione*, VI [1899–1900] 48ff.; and cf. in the same volume, 529ff., "Ancora la lettera di Michele Paleologo a Clemente IV"). Both letter and embassy have been the subject of controversy. Festa, forgetting Palaeologus' first coronation at Nicaea, mistakenly believes Michael's statement to refer to events subsequent to the capture of Constantinople in 1261, that is to two years *after* Pelagonia. Norden, 382, and apparently Dölger, *Regesten*, no. 1864, accept the letter as genuine and applicable to events occurring *before* the battle of Pela-

61

Despite the abortiveness of his attempt to secure papal intervention, Michael's embassy was of signal importance. For it marks the first appearance of the pattern of diplomacy that he was to follow during his entire reign, namely, the offer to submit the Greek church to Rome, in exchange for papal interference in designs of Latin princes coveting Greek territory.

Michael was not disheartened by his diplomatic failure. Indeed he seized the military offensive in order to crush Michael of Epirus before aid could be mobilized by his allies.[62] At once Palaeologus dispatched word to his army already wintering in Macedonia (the troops evidently had left Nicaea soon after 21 September 1258),[63] ordering the commanders, his brother John, now promoted to the rank of Sebastokrator, and the Grand Domestic Alexios Strategopoulos to open a sudden attack on the Despot.[64] Palaeologus himself remained in Nicaea.

Augmented by the garrison forces of Thrace and Macedonia,

---

gonia. They do not, however, fully analyze its significance. Most other authorities overlook the letter completely, as for example Gardner, *Lascarids*, and Chapman. Despite the fact that the Byzantine sources mention no such embassy at this time, I believe that the passage in question indicates that an embassy actually was sent to the papacy, because (1) Michael was too able a diplomat to neglect an appeal to the pope at this critical time; (2) a unionist proposal was nothing new; and (3) contrary to the belief of some historians, the letter itself is not unique since other correspondence had passed between Michael and the papacy before Constantinople's recapture in July of 1261. For example, a papal letter of 28 April 1261 requests Michael to set free two merchants of Lucca that had been seized at Adramyttion in Asia Minor. They were subsequently released, as we are informed by the *Liber jurium reipublicae genuensis*, I, in *Historiae patriae monumenta*, VII (Turin, 1854) cols. 1345 and 1397.

[62] Chapman, 35, believes that by dispatching legates to the allies Palaeologus sought to gain time to reorganize his army. If the *Chronicle of Morea* is correct in reporting that he sent messengers to request the aid of Germans, Hungarians, and Serbs, time, of course, would have been an important factor. See Greek version, ll. 3591–3599; and French version, ed. Longnon (Paris, 1911) par. 268 and 270.

[63] And probably not 1259, as shown by D. Nicol, "The Date of the Battle of Pelagonia," *Byz. Zeit.*, XLIX (1956) 69, based on Greg., 72: μικρὸν μετὰ τροπὰς θερινάς and ἄρτι τὸ δεσποτικὸν περιεζωσμένος ἀξίωμα. On the date of the subsequent battle itself at Pelagonia, no definite conclusions can be derived from the sources, but Nicol, on the basis of certain rather persuasive indications in Acrop. and Pach. (see below, note 69), dates it "perhaps in early summer (?July) of 1259," rather than in the fall or possibly even late fall of that year, as I had determined in "Pelagonia," 120, note 98, in agreement with Dölger, *Regesten*, no. 1882, Buchon, Hopf, Romanos, Dendias, etc.

[64] Acrop., 161 and 165, ll. 17–19.

the Nicene army, marching with remarkable swiftness along the Via Egnatia, soon reached Ochrida and Deavolis.[65] Then, moving quickly north by the pass of Vodena, it altogether surprised Michael II and his army, encamped at Kastoria in Macedonia. The Epirot forces, caught off guard, retreated so hastily that many men were killed at night in the precipitous passes.[66] The Despot himself withdrew behind the Pyrenaea (Pindus) mountains [67] and encamped near Avlona, then in the possession of Manfred. From there he dispatched envoys to summon aid from his two allies.[68] Meanwhile, in the course of a spring campaign (1259), the forces of John Palaeologus captured Ochrida and Deavolis and in lightning succession took many other cities in Macedonia and Epirus. The Despot had now lost a major part of his territories.[69]

But aid for Michael II soon came, and with it his allies sought to implement the plans of conquest meditated since the formation of the coalition.[70] Manfred's aid consisted of a picked force of four hundred superbly mounted and completely armed German cavalry.[71] Gregoras and Matteo Spinelli, a contemporary

[65] The Via Egnatia (the old Roman road extending from Avlona-Dyrrachium through Thessalonica to Constantinople) is not explicitly mentioned in the sources, but it was undoubtedly used by both armies, since almost all the toponymics mentioned are situated on or near it.

[66] Acrop., 165–166. On the topography see K. Miller, *Itineraria Romana* (Stuttgart, 1916) 521.

[67] On these terms and topography see also my "Pelagonia," 121, note 101; and J. von Hahn, *Albanesische Studien* (Jena, 1854), esp. map, 347.

[68] According to Greg., 73, ll. 9–11, the Despot fled to Epirus, where he besieged the lofty citadel of Bellegrada (modern Berat) with the intention of rushing down from its heights to attack the Nicenes. But Bellegrada seems then to have been in the possession of Manfred, the ally of Michael II. See Meliarakes, *Nicaea*, 526, and cf. Nicol, "The Date of the Battle of Pelagonia," 70.

[69] Acrop., 167, ll. 23–24. Cf. Michael's Autobiography, 6, VII. See also Nicol, "The Date of the Battle of Pelagonia," 69.

[70] Greg., 72, ll. 2–6: "They came not so much to aid the Despot as to enlarge their own territories and occupy alien cities. For they hoped that all the Roman [Nicene] territory from the Ionian [Adriatic] directly to Byzantium would fall to them without effort." Similarly, Palaeologus writes in his Autobiography, 4, VII: "They came to aid not because of the alliance, but to enrich themselves and become masters, so they believed, of our country." On certain discrepancies in the sources at this point see my "Pelagonia," note 104.

[71] Acrop., 168 and Scutariotes, 545. Cf. Pach., 83, l. 4, who writes of 3,000 German cavalry. Sanudo, *Istoria*, 107, says that Manfred sent 400 German men-at-

Italian chronicler, would have us believe that Manfred came personally to lead his troops,[72] but this statement has been disproved by modern scholarship.[73]

Unlike Manfred, who was occupied with a campaign against the Guelphs in the Italian Romagna, Prince William came himself to aid the Despot with an army which included a large number of Franks and Greeks of Achaia. A general feudal levy seems to have been imposed in March 1259 [73a] on all his vassals, for in the French and Greek versions of the *Chronicle of Morea* and the Autobiography of Michael Palaeologus we read that William's forces included troops from Negropont, the Archipelago, and Athens, and that many feudal lords personally accompanied him, including those of Salona, Boudonitza, Naxos, and Athens.[74]

Along with Michael II and his Epirot troops [75] came two of his sons, Nikephoros the elder, and the bastard son John. The latter, as Pachymeres and Sanudo inform us, commanded numerous forces of Vlachs from Great Vlachia in Thessaly, the daughter of whose chieftain, Taron, he had married.[76]

---

arms: "avuti dal Rè Manfredi 400 huomini d'armi Tedeschi." Palaeologus' Autobiography, 6, mentions German and Sicilian troops as if they were separate units.

[72] Greg., 75: ὁ δὲ τῆς Σικελίας ῥὴξ διέδρα λαθὼν σὺν ὀλίγοις πάνυ τῶν ἑαυτοῦ. Spinelli, *Diurnali* (ed. G. Del Re, *Cronisti e scrittori sincroni napoletani*, II [Naples, 1868]) 641: "Lo Settembre detto anno, Re Manfredo andao in Romagnia." This passage is listed under the year 1260 in the Vigo-Dura edition (*Annali di Matteo Spinello* [sic] *da Giovenazzo* [Naples, 1872]), which Dendias — see next note — apparently did not use.

[73] By M. Dendias, "Le Roi Manfred de Sicile et la battaile de Pelagonie," *Mélanges Charles Diehl*, I (Paris, 1930) 55ff. This article and E. Darkó, *Byzantinisch-ungarische Beziehungen in der zweiten Hälfte des 13. Jahrhunderts* (Weimar, 1933) 10ff., include a discussion of the battle proper. While Darkó focuses mainly on the presence and importance of Hungarian troops, Dendias is concerned exclusively with the absence of Manfred and does not touch upon the many problems concerning the battle and its background. For a discussion of Dendias' views and those of other sources pertinent to the problem of Manfred's presence at Pelagonia see my "Pelagonia," note 108.

[73a] Greek *Chron. Morea*, ll. 3515–3516 and 3618–3619.

[74] Acrop., 168, ll. 10–16. Pach., 83, ll. 5–6; cf. Greg., 71, l. 20. Also Greek *Chron. Morea*, ll. 3625 and 3632ff.; French *Chron.*, par. 262. Cf. Autobiography, VII, 4.

[75] Acrop., 168, l. 4, and Greg., 71.

[76] Pach., 83, ll. 6–9. Pachymeres is the only Byzantine source specifically to mention the troop contingent of the Bastard. Sanudo, *Istoria*, 107, corroborates Pachymeres: "era Signor de la Parte [Neopatras] d'Odrich [Lidorichi] e final-

Meanwhile the Nicene army was advancing to meet the allied troops. It is difficult to ascertain the size and composition of the imperial forces, since the Greek sources are not specific and the statements of the *Chronicle of Morea* are often exaggerated, obviously seeking to excuse the ensuing Frankish defeat by over-emphasizing the strength of the enemy. According to the Greek and French versions of the *Chronicle*, the Nicene army included Hungarian and German mercenaries from the West, and Serb and Bulgar horsemen,[77] in addition to Turkish and Cuman cavalry and Greek archers.[78] This was, of course, aside from the garrison forces of Macedonia and Thrace. It is noteworthy that no contemporary source mentions regular Latin troops fighting on the Nicene side — probably an omission, as they had been prominent in the armies of Palaeologus' Nicene predecessors and there is no reason to believe that he had discharged them.[79]

Despite the lack of accurate information,[80] one gets a distinct impression from the sources that the allied forces surpassed those of Nicaea in size.[81] Hence, it is plain that if the numerically in-

---

mente della Blachia [Grand Vlachia]." On the places of assembly for the allies see my "Pelagonia," note 115.

[77] The exact figures are 300 German, 1500 Hungarian, 600 Serb, and a detachment of Bulgar cavalry (see Greek *Chron.*, ll. 3591ff., 3706ff., and 3608 with note; also French *Chron.*, par. 270, 279). For a detailed analysis, with documentation, of the problem of the aid of foreign troops for Michael at Pelagonia see Geanakoplos, "Pelagonia," 124–125, notes 116–117.

[78] The presence of Cumans is verified by all the Greek sources. On the Cumans see D. Rasovskii, "Polovtsy," *Seminarium Kondakovianum*, VII (1935) 245–262, and later issues. Like the Nicenes, the Latins too had an alliance with the Cumans, which dated from 1237. It is interesting that at Pelagonia both sides — at least according to the *Chronicle of Morea* — employed Turkish soldiers.

[79] See Pach., 54ff. The Greek *Chron.*, ll. 4319–4321, is the only source to mention Latin (Varangian) troops in any respect. It relates that when William was captured at Pelagonia, he was taken before Palaeologus at Constantinople. (Actually Palaeologus had not yet taken that city, though R. Dawkins, "The Later History of the Varangian Guard," *Jl. of Roman Studies*, XXXVII [1947] 44, quotes this account as correct, forgetting the falseness of the chronology.) William defied his conqueror, whereupon the Emperor ordered the Varangians to return him to prison.

[80] According to the Greek *Chron.*, l. 3711, the Nicene army included twenty-seven *allangia*. The exact size of an *allangion*, a detachment of troops nominally of the imperial bodyguard, is unknown. Cf. Acrop., 122, l. 3, and Greek *Chron.*, ll. 3696–3711.

[81] Acrop., 168, says of the allied forces: παμπληθὴς στρατιά. Michael Palaeologus wrote in his Autobiography, VII, 5: ὧν πολὺ μὲν τὸ πλῆθος καὶ κρεῖττον ἢ ἀριθμεῖν

ferior Nicenes were to achieve victory, they would have to forego hope of a purely military success and employ strategy aimed at weak links in the allied organization. Significant among such weaknesses would be any disunity resulting from a divided command, the heterogeneity of troops, and especially the antagonism of the Greek and Latin contingents – to a lesser degree, of Manfred's Germans and the Franks as well. The attitude of the Greeks toward the Latins was still strongly affected by the hatred induced by the conquest of 1204, and by the racial and especially religious discrimination which they had endured during the years of occupation.[82] As in antiquity, the Greeks still considered themselves superior to the Latins, and on the whole tended to look upon the latter as supercilious, contemptible, and heretical.[83] Latin opinion of the Greeks, on the other hand, was even less complimentary. In general the Greeks were regarded as devoid of moral scruples, cowards, and schismatics.[84] An alliance between members of two groups so mutually antagonistic would

---

ῥᾳδίως. French *Chron.*, par. 273–274: "Si amassa toute sa gent de la Morée"; and "tant de gent que c'estoit merveilles a veoir." For actual size of certain allied troops see Aragonese *Chron. Morea*, par. 256: William had 20,000 armed men and Michael II, 26,000.

[82] See Chapter 6, text and note 30a; Chapter 11, text and notes 54–58; and my article, "Pelagonia," note 121.

[83] Latin superciliousness was the quality most detested by the Greeks, to judge from the freqency with which it is mentioned in the sources. Greg., 96, speaks of τὴν Λατινικὴν ὀφρῦν. Michael Palaeologus, in his *Typikon for St. Michael*, 794, mentions "the stubborn and unbending neck" of the Latins: τὸν σιδηροῦν αὐτῶν καὶ ἀκαμπῆ τράχηλον. Manuel Holobolos, *Orationes* (Potsdam, 1906) 39, refers to the Latin nobles as τὴν ὀφρῦν γυροῦντες . . . περιφρονοῦντες τὴν γῆν. The acme in Greek vituperation was reached by an anonymous author in describing the Latin conquest of 1204, when he called the Latins "excrement of mucous" (A. Mai, *Scriptores Veterum Nova Collectio*, II [Rome, 1826] p. xxxv). And Matthew Panaretos, a contemporary of Palaeologus, wrote of the "evil dogma of the Latins" (in A. Demetracopoulos, *Graecia orthodoxa* [Athens, 1872] 50).

[84] The *Chronicon Marchiae Tarvisinae et Lombardiae*, 48 (= *Annales S. Justinae Patavini*, 182), says of the Greeks: "morum probitate . . . denudati." A letter of Pope Clement IV dated 9 June 1267 refers to the frauds and lies of the Greeks: "eorum . . . fraudibus et mendaciis" (in T. Ripoll, *Bullarium Praedicatorum*, I [Rome, 1729] 485). The Primate, a French monk writing shortly after Pelagonia, calls the Greeks "moulz de leur nature et paoureus avec" (Bouquet, *Recueil des historiens des Gaules et de la France*, XXIII [Paris, 1876] 73). Finally, the "Annales Parmenses Maiores," in *MGH, SS*, XVIII (Hanover, 1863), refer to "certis articulis fidei, in quibus errabant."

hardly be firmly cemented. Such a situation was ripe for the manipulations of Michael Palaeologus.

The sources differ with regard to the outset of the battle. According to Acropolites Michael Palaeologus had advised his brother John (presumably by dispatch) to avoid a head-on collision with the enemy and by frequent and unexpected skirmishes to attempt to exploit their lack of unity.[85] In accordance with this instruction, John, as he approached the enemy troops in western Macedonia, skillfully distributed his forces. To his heavy-armed troops (*cataphracts*) he assigned the task of occupying the strong positions in the surrounding hills, while he deployed his lighter-armed and more mobile Cuman, Turk, and Greek archers in harassing the enemy on the plains with sudden attacks and withdrawals.

The vanguards of both armies met at a place called Vorilla Longos. According to plan, the light-armed Nicene troops skirmished continually with the enemy, allowing no respite by day or night. They attacked their foes' horses while they were being watered and plundered their supply trains. Thus the confederate cavalry, constantly assailed on terrain with which it was unfamiliar, was gradually decimated, and allied supplies began rapidly to diminish. The army of Michael of Epirus in particular lost its morale entirely and fled, eventually to reach Prilap.[86]

It was just before the flight of Michael II, according to Gregoras, that John Palaeologus made an attempt to cause a rupture among the allies. Encamping near the enemy, he secretly sent to Michael II at night a man pretending to be a deserter (αὐτόμολος δῆθεν). The man informed the Despot that his allies had made secret representations to the Nicene commander to betray the Despot for certain sums of money, and that the latter's only hope of salvation lay in flight. Persuaded, the Despot fled before dawn with as many of his troops as could immediately be mustered. The rest of his men drifted away during the night

---

[85] Acrop., 168, l. 19. Cf. the orations of Holobolos (*Manuelis Holoboli Orationes*, ed. M. Treu [Potsdam, 1906] 40), which state that the Emperor sent dispatches to his brother before the battle: διὰ γραμμάτων . . . θάρρους ἐνεπίμπλης. Also Hopf, *Geschichte*, 283.

[86] Acrop., 168–169.

after learning of his departure. In the morning the Latins of Manfred and William, discovering his flight and believing themselves betrayed, also sought to flee, but not before the Nicenes had suddenly fallen upon them. Most of the Latins were killed; the remainder were captured except for a few who managed to escape.[87]

The account of Acropolites differs in that it makes no mention of treason. It records simply that the allied army was so decimated by the Nicene tactics that it lost all hope of victory, and that Michael II and Nikephoros, despairing, fled at night with the Epirot army. Thereupon the remaining Greek forces of the allies, with their leaders and the Bastard John, went over to the enemy and took an oath of allegiance to the Nicene Emperor. Acropolites says that Manfred's four hundred Germans surrendered to only four Nicenes, an unlikely story unless one of the four, as in fact was the case, was a top-ranking officer, the Grand Domestic Alexios Strategopoulos.[88] William and his troops scattered, but the Prince was captured at Kastoria, hidden under a pile of hay and recognized only by his protruding front teeth. Ansel de Toucy, Geoffrey of Karitana, and the other Frankish barons, totaling about thirty,[89] were taken nearby. They were all bound and then led to the Emperor at Lampsakos.[90]

Strikingly different is the version of Pachymeres. He writes of discord arising among the allies before the battle and compares it to that which sprang up among the three goddesses contending for the golden apple.[91] In the present case, dissension arose as a result of erotic glances cast at the beautiful Vlach wife of John

---

[87] Greg., 74, ll. 3–7. Cf. Hopf, *Geschichte*, 283.

[88] Acrop., 170, ll. 5–8 and 19–23. Cf. Dendias, "Le Roi Manfred de Sicile," 56.

[89] The figure thirty is drawn from the hitherto overlooked contemporary source, the encomium cited of Manuel Holobolos, 42: ὁ τούτων πρίγκιψ καὶ οἱ λοιποὶ στρατηγοὶ καὶ βαρῶνες . . . ἄχρι καὶ τριάκοντα ἀριθμούμενοι. The figure seems reasonable, since we know that all or practically all the Frankish lords were captured; cf. Aragonese *Chron. Morea*, par. 256, mentioning 20 nobles, also prelates, etc.

[90] Acrop., 170. Cf. Palaeologus' Autobiography, 6, which says that all without exception were captured.

[91] Pachymeres, a great archaizer, often interpolates Homeric stories and grammatical forms.

the Bastard by knights from the army of Prince William of Achaia. Indignant at the insult to his honor, John threatened revenge; whereupon, in the words of the historian, "matters were inflamed to war and those summoned to fight as allies were drawn up against each other." The strife soon came to the attention of William. Angered and unable (or perhaps unwilling) to punish his own men, he taunted the Bastard for his illegitimacy, reproaching him that he was not of free birth like his brother Nikephoros, but "baseborn like a slave." [92]

Furious at the insult, John plotted revenge. Like another Achilles, says Pachymeres, he would emphasize his importance to the allied army by showing that whichever side he supported would prevail. Thereupon dispatching a secret communication at night to John Palaeologus, he informed the latter that he would desert the coalition and join in an assault on the "stupid and effeminate Italians" and "especially on the men of the Prince . . . if only an attack would be made upon them."

At the request of the Bastard, however, John Palaeologus solemnly pledged that no harm would befall his father the Despot or his brother Nikephoros. Accordingly, just before the battle the Bastard persuaded them to withdraw. Then suddenly the Nicene troops fell upon the Latins, attacking from the front while the forces of John the Bastard assaulted them from the rear. Great carnage resulted.[93] Realizing their predicament, the Latins attempted flight but were unable to escape, and many were killed or captured by the swift Cumans and Turks. William himself, discovered hiding behind a shrub, was taken prisoner.[94] Strangely

[92] Pach., 84–85, esp.: εἰs γένοs ὡs νόθοs, λίαν λαμπρῶs ὀνειδίσαι. Cf. C. Lebeau, *Histoire du Bas-Empire*, XVIII (Paris, 1835) 67, who mistakenly asserts that it was the Despot who taunted his own son John with these words.

[93] Pach., 85, ll. 6–22. What gives Pachymeres' story credibility is: (1) the uniqueness of the story, which makes it difficult to believe it a fabrication; and (2) the retreat of John the Bastard with John Palaeologus *after* the battle, a fact confirmed by all the Greek sources. If some such insult had not taken place, there would have been no motive for the Bastard to abandon his father. From the Bastard's subsequent desertion of John Palaeologus and return to his father, it is evident that his original defection was only a temporary expedient to take revenge on William.

[94] Pach., 85. Cf. Acrop., 170, l. 10, according to whom William was found under a pile of hay.

enough, Pachymeres does not recount the fate of Manfred's forces, which, by his own testimony, totaled three thousand men. A contemporary Byzantine source for the battle, hitherto neglected, is the speeches of Manuel Holobolos, court orator to Michael Palaeologus. Though highly rhetorical and therefore to be used with caution, the orations provide vivid expression of Nicene exultation at the humbling of the Epirot and especially the Latin adversaries. In bold colors Holobolos describes the scene of the bloody battlefield littered with thousands of Latin corpses, and skillfully depicts the plight of the thirty once haughty Latin nobles as they are marched in chains to Thessalonica.[95]

Space prevents presentation of the various versions of the *Chronicle of Morea* which agree in the main with the accounts described but differ in certain details. Critics often discount the *Chronicle of Morea* as a historical source, regarding it as mere fantasy.[96] But if its material can be controlled by Byzantine or Latin sources — especially in the case of the Morea itself, about whose affairs the authors were presumably well-informed, there seems no valid reason to disregard its information.

The testimony of another source, already mentioned, must at this point be considered — that of the *Istoria del Regno di Romania* of Marino Sanudo. Though doubtless Venetian in viewpoint, it is regarded as more accurate than the *Chronicle of Morea*. Sanudo's account is of particular significance because it confirms Pachymeres' story of a Latin insult to the Bastard before the battle, an offense, according to the *Istoria*, leading directly to the Greek betrayal of the Latins.[97]

---

[95] *Orationes*, 39 and 41–42; Geanakoplos, "Pelagonia," notes 148–150, gives the Greek quotations.

[96] For a comparison of the versions see my "Pelagonia," 130–131. On the trustworthiness of the *Chronicle* see Longnon ed., *Chronique de Morée*, p. xix; also Hopf, *Geschichte*, 228, note 95, who remarks that though events in the *Chronicle* are often false, they are "doch nicht ohne Geschick und einen Anstrich von Wahrscheinlichkeit."

[97] Sanudo, *Istoria*, 107: "li Greci lo tradirono, e trà li altri suo Cognato Sevastc Cratora per offesa, che avea riceputo da Latini." (Although John the Bastard i here called Sebastokrator, he actually was given this rank later by Palaeologus.) On the relative accuracy of the *Istoria* and *Chronicle of Morea* see Longnon ed. *Chron. Mor.*, xix.

70

In view of the differences of the various accounts, a comparison must be made in order to establish the real cause of the collapse of the coalition. All sources without exception report the use of a stratagem by the imperial army to deceive its enemies. Both Greek and French versions of the *Chronicle of Morea* agree with Gregoras that a spy, sent to the Epirot leader, brought about his desertion by persuading him of the numerical superiority of the imperial forces or the supposed perfidy of his allies. Acropolites, however, who seems here less informed,[98] writes merely that the Despot's army, decimated by the Nicene tactics, fled, and that the Greek forces — meaning probably the remaining Epirots — and the Bastard deserted to the enemy.[99] None of these accounts in any important respect contradicts the version of Pachymeres; they are merely less complete. Acropolites, who is of course anti-Latin and an apologist for Michael Palaeologus as well, may have sought to exalt the victory of his Emperor and homeland without sullying it by the mention of treachery.[100] On the other hand, it seems strange that the Despot should apparently have been so easily duped by the Nicene commander and induced to flee. The motives for his flight are not difficult to understand, however, if we combine the account of Gregoras with that of Pachymeres, whose version is corroborated by Sanudo. Suspicious of his allies from the beginning and fearing the loss of his own territory, the Despot probably became even more distrustful when he saw the arrival of the many powerful Frankish troops commanded by William. Even with the aid of Manfred's German forces (if the thesis is correct that the Despot and Manfred had made a secret agreement), plus the Vlach contingents of his son John, it was not certain that he could control the forces of William in case of a falling out.[101] A serious conflict had in fact now arisen

---

[98] Acropolites at this time was a prisoner of the Despot at Arta in Epirus, and was therefore not present at the battle. See Acrop., 164.

[99] Acrop., 170, ll. 5–8.

[100] For other examples of Acropolitan bias see Chapter 2, text and notes 26–27; and Chapter 4, text for notes 18–19.

[101] That the Despot's army was weaker than that of his allies seems evident from Greg., 71, ll. 20–21.

between his bastard son John and William, which did not portend at all well for allied success. Moreover, even if the allies should win the battle, it would not be difficult for William, with the aid of the Frankish lords accompanying him (and possibly also of Baldwin), to deprive him of the spoils of victory and to strip him even of Epirus. On the other hand, should the allies be defeated, as was quite possible after the defection of the Bastard's forces to Palaeologus, he knew very well what his fate would be. He could not cope with William now, and the antipathy of the Latin and Greek troops, already overtly expressed, made questionable the gaining of further advantages from the association. It would be more judicious therefore to flee, to carry on the struggle against Nicaea from his own territories, and, if possible, to secure additional aid from Manfred.

Thus Michael II withdrew at night with Nikephoros and as many Epirot troops as could be aroused without stirring the Latins. But with the fall to the Nicene forces even of Arta, the heart of his Despotate, Michael with his family eventually had to retreat to the Ionian isle of Leukas, and then to that of Kephalonia.[102]

The morning after his escape, the combined attack of John Palaeologus and the Bastard crushed Prince William and the remaining Latins. Afterwards the Bastard, remaining on the side of the Nicenes, marched with them to the sack of Latin Thebes. But there, repentant, he once again deserted, to return to his father Michael II.[103] The arrival of his son reinvigorated the dis-heartened Despot, and with the Bastard's help, the unyielding sup-port of the loyal population of his homeland Old Epirus, and re-newed military aid from Manfred, he quickly began to recoup his shattered fortunes, now fallen to their lowest point. As for Man-fred, whether he was angered at the Despot for his betrayal of

---

[102] Acrop., 172, ll. 10–11. Situated off the coast of old Epirus, Leukas (Santa Maura) was still part of the Despotate, while Kephalonia belonged to the Orsini Counts, relatives of the Despot and vassals of Manfred. See Γρατιανὸς Ζώρζης Αὐθέντης Λευκάδος, trans. from the German of K. Hopf by J. Romanos (Corfu 1870) 143.

[103] Acrop., 172, ll. 2–5. Cf. Palaeologus, Autobiography, 6, vii.

the allied cause and the loss of the Sicilian troops is not recorded. But if so, it was not for long, for not once but twice more within approximately a year and a half Manfred provided him with troops. Thus the two maintained their alliance and their aspirations.[104]

On the basis of the above analysis it is clear that the immediate cause of the allied debacle at Pelagonia was the defection of Michael II and John the Bastard. The underlying cause, however, which rendered a rupture almost inevitable, was, it would appear, the mistrust and suspicion existing between the Greek and Latin leaders, manifested in a Latin insult to the Bastard and in the Despot's willingness to believe that his Latin allies were about to play him false. Vivid evidence of Greco-Latin antipathy at this time is provided by Michael Palaeologus himself, who, in describing the battle, declares: ". . . greater than the number [of the Latins] was their insolence and audacious disdain, but surpassing even this was their hostility and hatred for us." [105] In view of such pronounced antagonism, it is little wonder that the coalition collapsed!

Pelagonia was one of the most important battles of the thirteenth century, possibly of the entire period of later Byzantine history.[106] Had the Latins and west Greeks been victorious and maintained their coalition, it could easily have meant the end of Nicaea, and thus a long postponement of a Greek recovery of Constantinople. William and the Frankish feudatories could presumably have turned successfully on the weaker Michael of Epirus and defeated him. They might then have taken Con-

---

[104] Pach., 89, ll. 9–11 and 137. See del Giudice, "La famiglia di re Manfredi," 34. For a discussion of further aid of Manfred to the Despot, involving testimony of the disputed *Annali* of Spinelli (whose authenticity I support) and the subsequent victory of Michael II and Manfred's troops over forces of Michael Palaelogus at Trikoryphos (1260), see Geanakoplos, "Pelagonia," note 165.
[105] Autobiography, 5, VII.
[106] Gardner, *Lascarids*, 248, writes, "It is the larger result of the battle that entitles it to rank as a decisive one in the history of Western Europe." See also *Chronicon Marchiae Tarvisinae et Lombardiae*, 47 (= *Annales S. Justinae Patavini*, 181); Sanudo, *Istoria*, 114; and Odoricus Raynaldus, *Annales ecclesiastici*, II, a. 1260, § LIV (Lucca, 1748) 68.

stantinople from Baldwin, or, as is more likely, have supported him and thereby breathed new life into the Latin Empire. But the unnaturalness of the alliance and the deep-seated antipathy between Greek and Latin did not permit this. Instead at the crucial moment these feelings came to the fore and the Greeks deserted their rivals.

The resulting defeat of the allies had grave consequences for Greco-Latin relations. It marked the beginning of the decline of Latin supremacy in Greece, by giving Nicaea a firm foothold in the Morea.[107] It brought to the brink of ruin Epirus, Nicaea's bitter rival for hegemony over the Greeks. Most important, Pelagonia paved the way for a Nicene restoration of the Byzantine Empire by removing the menace of a Latin attack from the west, thus helping to free the hands of Michael Palaeologus for the task of recovering Constantinople.

[107] See Chapter 7, notes 72–77, for discussion of the settlement after Pelagonia.

4

MILITARY AND DIPLOMATIC PREPARATIONS
FOR THE RECOVERY OF CONSTANTINOPLE

(1260–1261)

THE SIEGE OF GALATA

Michael at Pelagonia had won a brilliant victory, but he realized that in the eyes of the Greeks only one event could remove the stigma of usurpation and establish him firmly on the imperial throne — the recovery of Constantinople itself. To this end he now directed his diplomatic and military efforts.

Michael's strategy, already mapped out by his two Nicene predecessors, was to complete the isolation of the capital by conquering the surrounding territory and forming alliances with its neighbors.[1] As a result of this policy of encirclement the Latin Empire had been steadily declining in strength. So serious had its position become, both financial and military, that the Latin Emperor Baldwin II of Courtenay was forced to make frequent journeys to the West to appeal personally for aid.[2] But the Western powers, absorbed in their own problems, were unable to pro-

---

[1] On Michael's policy see Pach., 110, ll. 3–5. Vatatzes and Theodore II had already conquered most of Thrace, Macedonia, and the territory on both sides of the Hellespont.

[2] On Baldwin's journeys to, and long absences in, the West, see R. L. Wolff, "The Latin Empire of Constantinople," 560.

75

vide effective assistance.[3] The papacy in particular was engaged in conflict with the Italian Ghibellines. And even Baldwin's partner and the mainstay of the Latin Empire, Venice, locked in bitter struggle with Genoa, could not devote full attention to her endangered colony.[4]

Spurred by the Latin Empire's weakened condition, Michael in the early part of 1260 determined to make an attempt on Constantinople.[5] According to Acropolites this was not to be a full-scale investiture, as he lacked sufficient troops, siege engines, and especially a fleet.[6] A large force was unnecessary, moreover, because he hoped to take the city through the treachery of a Latin noble, known to us from Acropolites simply as "Asel," who, captured at Pelagonia, had been granted his freedom in exchange for his promise to open a gate of the city to the army of Palaeologus.[7]

Entering Thrace, Michael first seized Selymbria, then occupied the remaining approaches to the capital except for the strong fort of Aphameia, situated outside the Golden Gate.[8] In order to dispel Latin suspicions of collusion with "Asel," continues Acropolites, Michael encamped near the suburb of Galata and pretended to lay siege to it. In the meantime he secretly sent word to "Asel" that he was awaiting the implementation of the

[3] France especially, homeland of most barons of the Latin Empire, focused its interest, under Louis IX, on a crusade to the Holy Land. Furthermore, Louis himself was not disposed to combat Christians, not even Greek schismatics. See E. Dade, *Versuche zur Wiedererrichtung der lateinischen Herrschaft in Konstantinopel* (Jena, 1938) 11–12, and E. Jordan, *Les origines de la domination angevine en Italie*, 376. As for Manfred of Sicily, he regarded the Latin Empire as an instrument of the Papacy, with which he was, needless to say, on the worst of terms.

[4] See W. Heyd, *Histoire du commerce du Levant au Moyen Age*, I (Leipzig 1885) 344–351; and R. Lopez, *Storia delle colonie genovesi nel Mediterraneo* (Bologna, 1938) 194ff. Note especially a remark in the *Fragmentum* of Marin Sanudo (*Chroniques gréco-romanes*, ed. Hopf), 170, that the Venetians were hard put to sustain Constantinople. Quoted below, Chapter 5, note 10.

[5] On the date see Acrop., 173: ἔαρος ἐπιλάμψαντος. Cf. Scutariotes, 546: ἐ τῷ ᾽Ιανουαρίῳ μηνί.

[6] Acrop., 174: οὐδὲ γὰρ ἦγεν ἀξιόμαχον στρατιὰν εἰς τοιαύτης πόλεως πολιόρκησι

[7] On the probable identification of "Asel" with Ansel de Toucy, see Geanakoplos "Pelagonia," Appendix B, 137–141, "Ansel de Toucy or Ansel de Cayeux? A Attempt to Identify Acropolites' Disputed 'Asel'."

[8] Pach., 110, ll. 8–10. Selymbria was sixty kilometres west of Constantinople.

latter's promise. "Asel," however, kept delaying his answer. At length Michael ordered his men, under cover of night, to approach the walls near "Asel's" house and to question him regarding his pledge. But the Latin declared that he could not carry out the agreement because the ruler of the city (presumably Baldwin) had become suspicious and taken from him the keys to the gate.[9]

Although Acropolites emphasizes at this point that Michael was duped (*exepatemenos*) by the Latin,[10] there is reason to believe that Michael, perhaps questioning the dependability of "Asel," had come prepared with an alternative plan. If "Asel" could not, or would not, carry out his promise, Michael would attempt to seize Galata, situated directly across the Golden Horn from Constantinople.

Evidence for such a theory is the account of Pachymeres. His recital, agreeing in general outline with that of Gregoras,[11] differs so much from that of Acropolites that it has even been considered to refer to a second attempt on Galata.[12] According to Pachymeres, Michael, in the express hope of taking Constantinople, marshaled a great number of troops and siege engines for a full-scale assault on Galata. The Emperor himself watched the operation from an elevation, taking care to be easily observable to the enemy, whom (we are told) he wished to alarm by the sight of him. Investing the settlement, his troops began to sap the wall, assisted by expert Bithynian archers who shot at any Latin appearing on the ramparts. The situation seemed well in hand when succor arrived for the besieged: young Constantinopolitan Latins crossed the Golden Horn daily in fishing boats and penetrated the sea-

---

[9] Acrop., 174–175, esp.: καὶ τὸ μὲν δοκεῖν τὸ τοῦ Γαλατᾶ ἐμάχετο φρούριον.
[10] Acrop., 174, l. 5.
[11] Greg., 81, ll. 3–8ff., describes it as a real siege and adds that the Latins were driven to such straits that they had to destroy the best homes of Constantinople to secure firewood.
[12] E.g., by Meliarakes, *Nicaea*, 552 and 563–564. S. Romanin, *Storia documentata di Venezia*, II (Venice, 1925) 268, speaks of an "assalto" on Galata. Chapman, 40, Gardner, *Lascarids*, 251ff., and R. Guilland, in *L'Europe orientale*, 184, all combine the two incidents, utilizing much of Acropolites' information but disregarding most of Pachymeres' account.

gate of the suburb to join forces with the Galatans. Thus encouraged, and fortified by the realization that they were fighting for their homes, the Galatans put up strong opposition. Their resistance, together with a rumor that reinforcements were approaching,[13] finally induced Palaeologus to withdraw.[14] (It should be noted that in the version of Acropolites Michael's withdrawal was preceded by the signing of a truce of one year between Michael and Baldwin, to last until August of 1261.[15]

Since no other contemporary sources — Western or Greek — confirm the report of a siege of Galata at this time,[16] Pachymeres might be suspected of exaggeration or even fabrication. But Western sources for the period are inadequate,[17] and no convincing motive for falsification can be ascribed to Pachymeres. More probably, therefore, it is Acropolites who has presented a distorted version. As an active propagandist on Michael's behalf, seeking always to portray the Emperor in a favorable light, he might well, through deliberate omission, have concealed the circumstances of Michael's rebuff.[18] The strategic position of Galata, situated directly across the narrow Horn from Constantinople, is of course readily apparent to a military eye, and it seems highly improbable that Palaeologus would not have made at least one attempt to take Constantinople through an attack upon it.[19] Thus we may believe

---

[13] Pach., 124: καὶ ἅμα φήμης διαχεθείσης ὡς ἐξ ἀποστολῆς ἐπέστησαν ἄλλοι πλεῖστοι καὶ ἰσχυροί. The Bonn ed. (1835), translates ἐξ ἀποστολῆς as "from the papacy."

[14] For the entire passage on the assault see Pach., 118, ll. 3–6; 119, ll. 8–11; and 122–124.

[15] Acrop., 175, ll. 16–19; but Pach., 124, l. 11, says Michael departed without making peace terms. Guilland, in L'Europe orientale, 184, asserts that the treaty was for two years.

[16] A contemporary Italian chronicler, Thomas Tuscus (Gesta Imperatorum e Pontificum, MGH SS, XXII [Hanover, 1872] 518), however, mentions that Constantinople was captured through the treachery of a certain Anselm: "proditione cuiusdam nobilis Gallici nomine Anselmi." But his account has apparently confused "Asel's" projected treason with the actual capture of the city later by Palaeologus. On this see my article, "Pelagonia," 141, note 32.

[17] The principal Western sources for the period end about 1241.

[18] On Acropolites' prejudice in behalf of Michael, see Chapter 3, note 100.

[19] See Greg., 80, l. 24, who says that possession of Galata would enable Michael easily to take Constantinople. On Galata's fortifications see A. M. Schneider and M. Is. Nomides, Galata topographisch-archäologischer Plan (Istanbul, 1944) passim.

that both versions regarding Galata, that of Pachymeres-Gregoras on the one hand, and that of Acropolites on the other, are probably concerned with the same event. But the details expounded by the former are dismissed by Acropolites, who presents the entire matter as incidental to a major plan focused on "Asel." In this way Acropolites is able to preserve the reputation of his Emperor's invincibility while rendering Michael's failure with "Asel" excusable through emphasis on Latin duplicity.

LATIN PREPARATIONS FOR CONSTANTINOPLE'S DEFENSE AND THE STRATEGY OF PALAEOLOGUS

While Michael proceeded to concentrate on diplomatic measures that might prove more effective in capturing the capital, the Latin Emperor Baldwin and the Constantinopolitan Venetians were also not idle. Aware that the ring around them was being drawn tighter, and doubtless aroused by Palaeologus' siege of Galata, they made greater efforts to strengthen the capital's defenses. The principal drawback was a lack of trained soldiers to garrison the massive lines of land walls.[20] To Baldwin, upon whom devolved the responsibility for paying such guards, the cost was almost prohibitive. Indeed he had now fallen into such desperate financial straits that to raise money he had to strip the lead from the city palaces and even to mortgage his son Philip to a Venetian firm.[21] Further complicating the problem of defense was the ap-

---

[20] The land walls, built mainly by Theodosios II back in the fifth century, were an enormous triple row of fortifications extending from the Sea of Marmora to the Golden Horn. They were flanked by 192 towers, each about 175 feet apart and requiring a considerable number of troops as guards. See A. Van Millingen, *Byzantine Constantinople: The Walls of the City and Adjoining Historical Sites* London, 1899) 46ff.

[21] On Baldwin's penury see a document published (in part) in Romanin, *Storia di Venezia*, II, 454, no. 16, a record of a loan made to Baldwin and his son in 1258 by St. Louis. Also Sanudo, *Istoria*, 115 and note 1; and Sanudo, *Fragmentum* (ed. Hopf) 171. For a recent article on how Baldwin had even to put up his own son Philip as security for loans (and for the entire document above cited of Romanin), see R. L. Wolff, "Mortgage and Redemption of an Emperor's Son: Castile and the Latin Empire of Constantinople," *Speculum*, XXIX (1954) 5ff.

parent reluctance of Venice to interest herself in anything but her fleet. The only records we have of Venetian solicitude at this time concern a few loans she ordered her Podestà to float in Constantinople for the Empire's defense.[22] One of these consists of an unpublished document recounting the episode of a Venetian who lent money to the government and twice later tried unsuccessfully to collect it.[23]

Venice's apparent lack of deep concern over the fate of so important a colony is difficult to explain adequately. It may perhaps be attributed to the recent Venetian triumph over her rival Genoa and to her alliance with Pisa,[24] developments which may have lulled her into complacency. Or it may have been due, as a modern scholar believes, to a sharp decline in Venetian trade in Constantinople during the last years of the Empire,[25] a condition resulting in great part from the Nicene encirclement of the city. At any rate, whether the siege of Galata or other considerations were responsible, Venice seems at last to have realized the necessity of taking a more active interest in the capital's defense. Thus she appears to have persuaded the proud and independent lords of Frankish Greece that their fortunes were tied to Constantinople and that its fall to the Greeks would gravely jeopardize their own position. In May of 1260, therefore, the Doge of Venice authorized the *Bailli* of Negropont — next to the Podestà of Constantinople the principal Venetian official in Greece — to make agreements with the Latin barons of Achaia, Crete, Negropont, Lemnos, the Archipelago, Athens, and Kephalonia, with the aim of providing, at common cost, a permanent garrison of one thousand

---

[22] See T.-Th., *Urkunden*, III, 24, no. 338, dated 1259: "comittimus. . . Potestati Constantinopoli. . . potestatem. . . accipiendi. . . usque ad illam quantitatem pecunie, que ascendat ad summam trium millium yperperorum, pro negocii nostri communis (et) utiliter in dictis partibus."

[23] For the document, discovered by the author in the Venetian archives, se Appendix B, document no. 1, at end of this work.

[24] On the Pisan alliance see Heyd, *Histoire*, I, 346 and 349ff.

[25] See Wolff, "The Latin Empire of Constantinople," 562 and note 1. By com paring some twenty-five surviving commercial documents for the period of th Latin Empire and noting that almost all belong to the period preceding the fin years of its existence, Wolff deduces a sharp decline in Venetian trade during th Empire's last miserable years.

ιen for the defense of Constantinople.[26] Despite the logic of this
lan, there is no record that it was ever carried out. Nevertheless,
ιe scheme had real merit, as it marked a new and considered
ιolicy in which for the first time all the Latin lords of Greece were
ɔ cooperate in the capital's defense.

Various diplomatic measures were being taken in the mean-
me by Palaeologus. In the first place, during December of 1260
·e sent his Grand Logothete Acropolites on a secret mission to
ἰonstantine Tich, Tsar of the Bulgars, in order to secure his friend-
ɣ neutrality. Even though Michael had recently deprived the
'sar's wife's young brother, John IV Lascaris, of his imperial
ιghts, it would seem that Acropolites was at least partly success-
ιl in his mission.[27]

To render his Asiatic frontiers safe while he pursued his de-
ιgns, Michael also gave refuge to the Seldjuk Sultan of Iconium,
ἰaika'us II, who a short time previously had fled to Nicaea be-
ɔre the Mongol menace. Simultaneously, Michael, in typical By-
antine fashion, secretly reached an agreement with the advanc-
ιg Mongols, according to which he promised, in exchange for
·Iongol neutrality, to "retain" the Seldjuk Sultan at his court.[28]

GRECO-GENOESE NEGOTIATIONS PRECEDING THE
TREATY OF NYMPHAEUM

Assured of peace on both Bulgar and Anatolian frontiers, Pa-
ιeologus now contemplated a much more significant step, the
·reation of an alliance with a Latin naval power. Such a measure

---

[26] Document contained in the unpublished Venetian *Pacta Ferrariae*, I, 62, and
ιdated, though Norden's dating of May, 1260 seems logical. Printed in W. Nor-
·en, *Das Papsttum und Byzanz* (Berlin, 1903), appendix no. 13, 759, the docu-
ιent reads in part: "potestatem. . . tractandi, faciendi, et firmandi. . . societa-
·m. . . pro manutenimento totius imperii ad hoc ut. . . mille homines ponantur
ι Constantinopoli et retineantur ibidem continuo per totum tempus." Despite its
ιportance the document (cited by Hopf, *Geschichte*, 256–257; Romanin, *Storia di
·enezia*, II, 268; and Wolff, "Latin Empire," 655) has been overlooked by Chap-
ιan, Longnon (*L'Empire Latin*), and others.
[27] On the embassy see Acrop., 175, ll. 26ff.; also cf. Gardner, *Lascarids*, 253,
ιd Guilland, *L'Europe orientale*, 184.
[28] Pach., 129–136 and Greg., 81, ll. 14ff. On the Sultan see *Encyclopedia of*

was necessitated by the fact that Constantinople, surrounded k water on three sides and a massive system of fortifications on tl fourth, was almost impregnable on land. Proof of this was tl failure of the great assault in 1236 by 100,000 troops of the allie rulers John Vatatzes and the Bulgar John Asen, and, of cours Michael's own recent siege of Galata, on either of which occasion possession of a strong fleet might have spelled the difference b tween victory and defeat.[29]

The Emperor John III Vatatzes, to be sure, had already a tempted to develop a fleet, as is evidenced by Acropolites' me tion of a Nicene flotilla dispatched against Rhodes in 1249.[30] B Vatatzes' naval aspirations, as well as those of his son Theodor seem never to have materialized.[31] Thus what Palaeologus no needed was the aid of a fleet strong enough to match the pow of Venice.[31a] And since the decline of Pisa and Amalfi only or state possessed such a navy — Venice's great rival, Genoa.

The seeds of Veneto-Genoese rivalry had been sown at lea as early as the year 1204, with the establishment of Venetian cor mercial supremacy in Constantinople. More recently, the rival between the two powers had erupted into a fierce colonial w over the lucrative trade of Syria, which in 1258 resulted in tl expulsion of the Genoese from Acre.[32] It was only natural, ther

---

Islam, IV (Leyden, 1934) 211. Michael's friendship with the Turks dated fr his flight to the same Sultan a few years before (Acrop., 134ff.). Note that Micha permitted the Sultan to assume the imperial prerogative of wearing purple busk (Pach., 132). Cf. now V. Laurent, "Une famille turque au service de Byzanc Les Mélikès," *Byz. Zeit.*, XLIX (1956) 349ff.

[29] Guilland, *L'Europe orientale*, 157, attributes the failure in 1236 to "l'énergiq intervention de la flotte latine."

[30] See Acrop., 36, ll. 9–12 and 87, ll. 14ff. Nikephoros Blemmydes, *Curricult vitae et carmina*, ed. Heisenberg (Leipzig, 1896), 62, ll. 18–19, also mentions fleet of Vatatzes.

[31] Vatatzes seems especially to have lacked capable admirals. See L. Bréhi *Les institutions de l'empire byzantin* (Paris, 1949) 425.

[31a] A Venetian fleet seems to have been stationed at Constantinople since least 1258. See Andrea Dandolo, *Chronica*, in *RISS*, XII (Bologna, 1939) 3("pro tutela Constantinopolitani imperii, Latinorum viribus debilitatis dux Iacob Quirino suarum galearum capitaneus mictens."

[32] On Veneto-Genoese relations in Syria see Heyd, *Histoire*, 344ff. and Lop *Storia delle colonie genovesi*, 194ff. On Genoa's role in 1204 see J. Fotheringha "Genoa and the Fourth Crusade," *Eng. Hist. Review*, XXV (1910) 20–57.

fore, that the humiliated Genoese should look for support to Palaeologus, now coveting Constantinople, the heart of Venetian commercial interests in the East.[33] And if Genoa could be of use to the Emperor, would it not be reasonable to assume that she would acquire the Venetian monopoly of Constantinopolitan trade? What revenge could be sweeter and more profitable!

The grave risk to be assumed by Genoa, of course, would be papal excommunication. For as protector of the Latin Empire, the Holy See would justifiably feel that an attack on Constantinople would be a direct blow at its own prestige. A Greek restoration would, in addition, impede papal attempts to bring about ecclesiastical union, since Constantinople, the Holy See's chief bargaining point, would then be lost. Finally, Genoa would be violating the convention of 1258 which explicitly forbade an alliance between Genoa or Venice and the Greeks except by mutual consent of the two Italian powers.[34]

Some scholars are of the opinion that Palaeologus' greater need led him to take the initiative in establishing an alliance with Genoa.[35] Re-examination of the sources, however, reveals that more likely the reverse is true. Michael's position, despite his recent rebuff at Galata, was certainly not critical. He had already stripped the Latin Empire of much of its territory and thus to a considerable extent isolated Constantinople. The internal situation of Genoa, on the other hand, was much more serious. The Commune's defeats in Syria, plus its decreasing portion of Constantinopolitan trade, were severely damaging to its economic life and prestige.[36] Nor was there any Western power to which Genoa

[33] In 1225 Venice had apparently even considered moving her seat of government to Constantinople. See Romanin, *Storia di Venezia*, II, 208; and L. Sauli, *Della colonia dei Genovesi in Galata* (Turin, 1831) I, 40.

[34] *Ann. Ian.*, III, 42, and *Chronicon Marchiae Tarvisinae et Lombardiae*, 48 (= *Annali S. Iustinae Patavini*, 182). See also R. Caddeo, *Storia marittima dell' Italia*, I (Milan, 1942) 431.

[35] Chapman, 42, seems to imply this, as does Gardner, *Lascarids*, 254-255: "It was a most important achievement on the part of Palaeologus to secure the alliance and the active help of Genoa for the Greeks." G. Serra, *La storia della antica Liguria e di Genova* (Turin, 1834) II, 122, writes: "Allora Michele Paleologo ricorse a' Genovesi." See also J. Longnon, *L'Empire Latin*, 226: "(Paléologue) envoye à cet effet à Gênes des ambassadeurs."

[36] See G. Caro, *Genua und die Mächte am Mittelmeer* (Halle, 1895) I, 66-76.

could turn for aid against Venice: Sicily under Manfred was carefully neutral; Pisa had declined in strength; and the papacy, of course, could be of little help.[37] Thus Nicaea alone remained. An alliance with the Greeks, moreover, would not be a completely new departure for Genoese policy. Already in the twelfth century the Commune had secured an accord with the Emperors Manuel I and John II Comnenos, who had granted it commercial privileges and a quarter in Constantinople.[38] There were even precedents for pourparlers with Nicaea. Some years before (1231 and 1239), on the initiative of Genoa, negotiations had been conducted by the Emperor Vatatzes and the commune with a view to signing a treaty against Venice.[39] But the attempts at alliance had failed, probably owing to Genoese enmity toward Vatatzes' ally Frederick II of Sicily, as well as to Vatatzes' own opposition to Latin commercial competition in his Empire.[40]

Since then, however, Genoa's position with respect to Venice had become intolerable. Without assistance she might in fact be reduced to a second-rate power. And with the deaths of both Frederick and Vatatzes there seemed no longer any obstacle to an alliance with Nicaea.[41] Thus cooperation with Palaeologus had become almost inevitable.[42]

With regard to the opening of negotiations the chief Genoese source, the *Annales Ianuenses*, records:

The Genoese, recalling the injuries inflicted upon them by the Venetians and their allies in the areas beyond the seas, turned their atten

[37] See C. Manfroni, *Storia della marina italiana dalle invasioni barbariche ɑ trattato di Ninfeo* (Livorno, 1899) 440.
[38] On the Genoese quarter see C. Desimoni, "I Genovesi ed i loro quartieri ɔ Costantinopoli nel secolo XIII," *Giornale ligustico*, III (1876) 217ff. Also th outdated but still valuable work of L. Sauli, *Della colonia dei Genovesi in Galaɫ* (Turin, 1831) II, 181ff., who prints a number of important documents unavailabᵈ elsewhere.
[39] *Ann. Ian.*, III, 57.
[40] See C. Manfroni, "Le relazioni fra Genova, l'impero bizantino e i Turchᵌ *Atti soc. ligure st. patria*, XXVIII (1898) 654. Greg., 43, 1. 20, speaks of Vatatzᵉ "nationalistic" attitude in proscribing cloth woven by Italian hands (χεῖρες Ἰταλῶ Cf. Meliarakes, *Nicaea*, 284, and Heyd, *Histoire*, I, 306.
[41] Lopez, *Colonie*, 207.
[42] See G. Bratianu, *Recherches sur le commerce génois dans la Mer Noire* ɑ *XIII⁰ siècle* (Paris, 1929) 81, and Manfroni, "Relazioni," 655–656.

84

tion to any way in which they could inflict injury upon them. Therefore, after due deliberation, a solemn embassy was ordered to be sent to the most serene lord Palaeologus, Emperor of the Greeks, who was at war with the Venetians, in order to create an alliance with him against the Venetians.[43]

Astonishingly enough, the chief contemporary Greek sources — Acropolites, Scutariotes, and Pachymeres — make no reference whatever to the formation of the alliance (very probably to avoid reducing the credit due their Nicene countrymen for recovering Constantinople).[44] But two other contemporary sources, one Western and one Greek, provide material on the creation of the pact. The chronicle of the Venetian Martino da Canale reports that,

the Genoese . . . driven to revenge themselves against Venice, which had inflicted such great damage upon them . . . sent their envoys to Romania to a man called Messer Palaeologus . . . who was an enemy of the Venetians.[45]

The other source, an encomium by the Byzantine orator Manuel Holobolos, affirms that "Genoese nobles crossed the wide seas and sought out the Emperor." [46] To be sure, both writers may be biased: Canale, anti-Genoese, and Holobolos, interested in glorifying his Emperor, as was the duty of a court encomiast. Yet it is significant that three completely unrelated sources, Genoese, Venetian, and Greek, record that the Genoese made the initial overtures for creating the alliance.

Negotiations on the part of Genoa seem to have been undertaken on the sole responsibility of Guglielmo Boccanegra, Captain of the People and virtual dictator of the Commune.[47] Very prob-

[43] Ann. Ian., IV, 41–42.
[44] For a survey of all sources mentioning the alliance see Meliarakes, Nicaea, 654ff. As might be expected, Michael's Autobiography fails to mention the alliance.
[45] Cronique des Veniciens, Arch. st. it., VIII (1845) 480: "Il envoierent leur mesaies en Romanie a un prudome que l'en apeloit Mesire Palialog." Canale (d. ca. 1275), though probably not Venetian by birth, was one by choice. He lived for a long time in Venice, working for the Dogana Marittima and his chronicle was written in French according to the custom of the time. See Enciclopedia italiana, VIII (Milan, 1930) 664.
[46] "Μανουὴλ 'Ολοβώλου, 'Εγκώμιον εἰς Μιχαὴλ Η' Παλαιολόγον," ed. Siderides, Επετηρὶς 'Ετ. Βυζαντινῶν Σπουδῶν, III (1926) 186.
[47] C. Imperiale, Jacopo d'Oria e i suoi Annali (Venice, 1930), 92; Lopez, Colonie, 208.

ably in the last months of 1260 he secretly sent two envoys to Palaeologus, Guglielmo Visconti and Guarnerio Giudice.[48] The fruit of the negotiations was a convention signed on 13 March 1261 at Nymphaeum,[49] the then Nicene capital where Palaeologus was apparently spending part of the winter. On April 28, an appendix to the treaty was also signed in which Michael granted full powers to three legates he was about to send to Genoa, authorizing them to act in his behalf, and if necessary to borrow money from the Genoese, which he himself pledged to repay.[50] Important and trusted officials, the envoys were Isaac Dukas Murtzuphlos, uncle and Parakoimomenos to the Emperor; Theodore Kriviziotes, the Pansevastos; and Leo, Archdeacon of Hagia Sophia.[51]

About two and one-half months later, on 10 July 1261, the treaty, with certain minor changes initiated by the Greek envoys, was solemnly ratified in Genoa by a representative assembly of the Genoese citizenry.[52] Immediately thereafter the Genoese government dispatched to Palaeologus a fleet of sixteen galleys under the command of Marino Boccanegra, brother of the Captain of the People. With these ships sailed the Greek envoys except for Dukas, who had died during the negotiations and was buried in the Genoese cathedral of San Lorenzo.[53]

The speed with which the flotilla was prepared indicates that

---

[48] Manfroni, "Relazioni," 656, note 1, dates the instructions for this embassy in the last part of 1260 (despite the *Annales*, which date it 1261), because the name of the podestà cited is anterior to 1261. (See Lopez, *Colonie*, 208, and cf. Heyd, *Histoire*, I, 428). For the full names of the envoys see the treaty in Manfroni, "Relazioni," 792. In the meantime, to lull Venetian suspicions Boccanegra signed an accord with Venice to end the Syrian war and exchange prisoners. See Lopez, *Colonie*, 208.

[49] Manfroni, "Relazioni," 801. On the date see preceding note (48). Also Serra, *Storia della antica Liguria*, II, 127.

[50] Manfroni, "Relazioni," 802, and *Liber jurium reipublicae genuensis*, I, nos. 1345-1346. Michael promised to pay "secundum formam et tractatum atque ordinamentum lucri sortis et termini quod cum ipsis nostris nunciis sive ipsorum altero pactum fecerint."

[51] On the envoys, see Dölger, *Regesten*, no. 1892. For Isaac Ducas in particular see Acrop., 92, l. 5, where he is named as an envoy of Vatatzes in 1252-1253, and for Krivitziotes see F. Dölger, "Chronologisches und Prosopographisches zur byzantinischen Geschichte des 13. Jahrhunderts," *Byz. Zeit.*, XXVII (1927) 310.

[52] *Ann. Ian.*, IV, 42. Also Manfroni, "Relazioni," 802.

[53] *Ann. Ian.*, IV, 42-43.

it was probably readied beforehand. More noteworthy is the fact that it numbered only sixteen vessels, not the maximum of fifty authorized by the treaty. The reason for this, according to one scholar, is that Palaeologus could ill afford a greater number, obligated as he was by the treaty to pay for the equipment of the vessels and wages of the mariners.[54] That Michael was troubled financially may, of course, be true, but one cannot but recall the large sums amassed by Vatatzes and Theodore II, to which Michael had recently fallen heir.[55] A supplementary explanation, therefore, may also be offered — that Michael and Genoa did not at the moment wish to arouse Venetian suspicions so as to alarm the Doge into sending a greater fleet to protect Constantinople. It is even possible that in the view of the allies sixteen Genoese vessels, together with those at Michael's disposal, were considered sufficient to cope with the Venetian galleys then under command of the Podestà at Constantinople.

PROVISIONS OF THE NYMPHAEUM CONVENTION

The important articles of this celebrated treaty, which opened a new chapter in East-West relations, are the following:[56]

(1) A permanent alliance was signed by the Emperor and Genoa for the purpose of making war on Venice. (2) A Genoese squadron of up to fifty ships was to be put at the disposition of Palaeologus, to be dispatched at the Emperor's request and provisioned at his expense. (3) Genoese merchants were granted the right to trade, free of duty, in all parts of the Byzantine Empire,[57]

---

[54] Serra, *Storia della antica Liguria*, II, 132.

[55] See Pach., 71, ll. 15–20.

[56] The articles of this treaty have been carefully studied by C. Manfroni, "Relazioni," 658ff. and 791–809, and thus only a few pertinent comments or additions will be made here. Also see Dölger, *Regesten*, no. 1890; and the article of E. Skržinskaja, "The Genoese in Constantinople in the 14th Century" (in Russian), *Vizantiskii Vremennik*, I (XXVI) (1947) 221ff. A faulty edition of the treaty of Nymphaeum is printed in the *Liber jurium*, I, 284. Two Latin versions, dated 1267 and 1285, survive, but no Greek one.

[57] Manfroni, "Relazioni," 792, esp.: "ianuenses sint franchi liberi et immunes in toto predicto imperio." According to Skržinskaja, "Genoese in Constantinople," 221ff., Michael here seems to have renounced the imperial grain monopoly. The

such territories to include those already in Michael's possession as well as those to be conquered in the future. In return, Greek merchants in Genoa would be exempt from duties.[57a] (4) A *loggia*, *palazzo*, church, bath, and houses were to be assigned to Genoese merchants in Constantinople, Thessalonica, Aenos, Cassandria, Smyrna, Adramyttion, and the islands of Crete, Negropont, Chios, and Lesbos.[58] In each locality the Genoese would be governed by their own consuls with administrative and judicial authority, civil as well as criminal.[59] These officials would guarantee that traitors to Palaeologus would undergo the same punishment as those unfaithful to Genoa. (5) Michael was to exclude from Greeks waters and markets (including the Black Sea) the warships and merchants of Genoese enemies, except for the Pisans, "the faithful subjects of our imperial majesty." [60] (6) Once Constantinople was taken, the Genoese were to receive back all their former possessions in the city, in addition to such Venetian property as the church of Santa Maria, loggias, cemetery, and the Venetian fortified palace. But this provision regarding Venetian possessions was to be implemented only on condition that Genoa provide immediate aid in taking the capital.[61] (7) The Greek city of Smyrna would be handed over to the Genoese in absolute possession with the proviso that the rights of its ecclesiastics and nobles be respected.[62] (8) Genoa pledged to permit the export to the Greeks

---

Genoese were also required to register all merchandise transferred by them from non-Genoese territories.

[57a] A minor concession since Greek trade there was apparently negligible.

[58] Note the mention of Constantinople and even of Venetian-held Crete and Negropont.

[59] This concession of living quarters in the various cities is similar to those already granted to the Italian commercial colonies in the Holy Land during the twelfth and thirteenth centuries.

[60] An important article, because its full implementation would have completely destroyed Venetian commerce in the Greek Empire. Evidently the Pisans, traditional enemies of Genoa and here named "fideles nostri imperii," were already on friendly terms (even probably allied) with Palaeologus. See S. Borsari, "I rap porti tra Pisa e gli stati di Romania nel Duecento," *Riv. st. it.*, LXVII (1955) 48

[61] "Si dictum comune instanter et efficaciter ad dictam civitatem capiendam succursum miserit galearum" (Manfroni, "Relazioni," 795).

[62] *Ibid.*, 795, esp.: "salvis juribus episcopatus et ecclesiarum ipsius civitatis eorum militum qui sunt privilegiati. . . in hereditate ab imperio nostro." Cf. *An*

of arms and horses; to prevent the arming of warships against Michael in Genoese waters; to allow Genoese to enter Greek military service (for which the Commune would supply arms and horses and the Emperor the pay); to instruct Genoese subjects resident in Greek territories to aid in defending such areas in case of attack; and, finally, to require the captains of Genoese vessels in Greek waters during wartime to place themselves under imperial orders.[63] (9) Michael would present an annual donative of 500 *hyperpyra* and a pallium to the Archbishop of Genoa.[64] (10) It was forbidden for a Genoese to become a Greek subject.[65]

A glance at the above articles, numerous as they are, is sufficient to reveal that the benefits were heavily weighted on the side of Genoa. The only real advantage to Palaeologus was the pledge of a Genoese flotilla of fifty ships, even the expenses of which had to be borne by him. Considering the fact that Genoa was already involved in conflict with Venice and that the ships could, in effect, be used only against that power, even this concession appears small. The privilege accorded to the Genoese of complete exemption from duties (thus favoring them above Greek merchants, who were themselves required to pay certain imposts), the grant of what practically amounted to extraterritoriality in Constantinople and other key cities, the bestowal of virtually absolute possession of the important port of Smyrna, and the closing of the Black Sea to all foreigners except Genoa and Pisa — how can these vast concessions on the part of Palaeologus be explained?

Manfroni attributes Palaeologus' generosity to the fact that Genoa had to distribute her naval forces in such far-flung areas as the waters of Italy, Syria, and Egypt, in addition to providing ves-

---

Ian., IV, 42, which says that Michael bestowed Smyrna on Genoa so that the Commune's merchants and mariners would have a port which they could consider their own.

[63] On the pay to be received by Genoese in Michael's service see Manfroni, *Storia della marina italiana*, 442.

[64] The encomium of Holobolos cited in note 46 refers to the practice of bestowing a pallium.

[65] This had occasionally occurred in the past; see Manfroni, "Relazioni," 659.

sels for neutralizing the Venetian fleet during Constantinople's projected recapture. He believes, moreover, that papal attempts to mediate between Venice and Genoa also induced Michael to grant huge concessions in order that the Veneto-Genoese hostility might be perpetuated.[66] Valid though Manfroni's reasoning may in part be, a more penetrating analysis seems to be that of Imperiale, in whose opinion the concessions are to be explained chiefly through an understanding of the internal situation at Genoa.

At this time the position of Guglielmo Boccanegra, the Ghibelline Captain of the People, brought to power in Genoa by a veritable popular revolution against the nobility, was not secure. There was sharp opposition to him and his Greek policy from the nobles, bankers, and merchant class — in brief from the pro-papal Guelph party, which could readily oppose an alliance with the schismatic Palaeologus by the cogent argument of papal excommunication. Moreover, the Guelphs could contend that an adverse outcome of the projected alliance would destroy the remaining Genoese markets in Syria and Asia Minor, increase the opposition of the merchants and bankers of the Holy Land (who would see in the alliance only a risky war ruinous to their present profits), and, worst of all, so intensify the conflict with Venice that it might well last for years at enormous cost in both men and capital.[67] This line of argument, according to Imperiale, was carefully explained to the Emperor by Boccanegra's emissaries, and Palaeologus must then have realized that to overcome such opposition he would have to make his concessions as far-reaching and attractive as possible.

Granted the plausibility of this reasoning as well, a simpler explanation, more in keeping with the character of Palaeologus, may also be offered. Michael may have calculated that once he had recovered Constantinople, at whatever the immediate cost, it would later be possible, in view of the pressures that would be

---

[66] Manfroni, "Relazioni," 665. On the papal efforts at mediation see the document published in Sauli, *Della colonia dei Genovesi in Galata*, II, 190–204.

[67] Imperiale, *Jacopo d'Oria*, 92–93.

exerted on Genoa to secede from the alliance, to rid himself of his ally or even to play her off against Venice. As we shall see, this is precisely what happened only two years later, when, with the excuse afforded by the suspected treason of a Genoese official at Constantinople, Michael dismissed the Genoese fleet, practically abrogated the alliance, and turned instead to Venice.[68]

[68] *Ann. Ian.*, IV, 65, and Imperiale, *Jacopo d'Oria*, 126. See Chapter 8, section 2.

5

THE GREEK RECOVERY OF CONSTANTINOPLE
AND THE COLLAPSE OF THE LATIN EMPIRE

(1261)

T he great event, so long awaited by the Byzantine world (and for which the way had been carefully prepared by Michael's Nicene predecessors), at last took place on 25 July 1261, with the fall of Constantinople into Greek hands after fifty-seven years of alien occupation. Certain sources for the period, Western as well as Byzantine, which cast further light or provide additional detail on the event but have been overlooked or inadequately examined by scholars [1] are utilized in the account which follows.

In the early part of 1261 the Despot Michael II of Epirus, now recovered from his crushing defeat at Pelagonia, was once again encroaching on the European territory of Nicaea. To counter this threat Michael Palaeologus sent an army to his endangered western possessions under the command of his brother, the Despot John. At the same time the Emperor entrusted about eight hundred Greek and Cuman troops [2] to another high-ranking officer,

[1] See R. Guilland, in Diehl, et al., L'Europe orientale, 186, note 107, who explains the historians' neglect of the Western sources: "Quant au recit de sources occidentales, il n'est pas trés clair." Unused Greek sources (and one Arabic) are noted below.

[2] According to Darkó, Byzantinisch-ungarische Beziehungen, 21ff., these Cu-

the Caesar Alexios Strategopoulos, instructing him to advance to Thrace to quiet the Bulgars and, on the way, to approach Latin held Constantinople "in order to terrify the Latins by shaking the sword at them." Alexios was to attempt nothing more. So run the accounts of Pachymeres and Gregoras.[3]

In substantial agreement is Acropolites, whose version states simply that Alexios, dispatched to the west against enemies of the Empire, was "on the way to rush upon Constantinople and approach its gates so that the Latins within would be seized by terror."[4] All three accounts, it may be observed, agree that Alexios' march to Constantinople was to be only incidental, and that the purpose of the diversion was not to make an attempt on the city but merely to alarm or harass the Latins.[5]

---

mans were mercenary troops from Hungary, which had been sent to Michael two years before by his ally the King of Hungary and had already greatly aided Michael at Pelagonia in 1259. This view, however, has been subject to criticism. See Ostrogorsky, *Byzantine State*, 398, note 1; my article, "Pelagonia," 124, note 116; and P. Charanis, "On the Ethnic Composition of Byzantine Asia Minor," Προσφορὰ εἰς Στίλπωνα Κυριακίδην (Thessalonica, 1953) 144f., who shows that Cumans had already settled in Byzantium as soldiers.

[3] For this whole passage see Pach., 137–138; also Greg., 83, ll. 18–19, esp.: μικρὸν ὑπὲρ τοὺς ὀκτακοσίους. While Pachymeres specifies no date for dispatch of these troops, Meliarakes, *Nicaea*, 589, surmises the beginning of 1261, while Guilland, *L'Europe orientale*, 186, gives June of that year. The troops had to march from Nicaea to the straits, cross to Gallipoli by boat, and thence move by land to Constantinople.

[4] Acrop., 181, ll. 6–9, esp.: ἔφοδόν τινα . . . ποιήσασθαι, which Allatius, in an earlier edition of Acropolites (Bonn, 1837) 190, translates as "in eam irrumpere." Acropolites, Michael's closest political confidant, reached the capital in Palaeologus' company shortly after its conquest. See Acrop., 185–189, and cf. preface to Heisenberg ed., p. xi.

[5] There is a similar interpretation in another contemporary but unused source, the orations of Manuel Holobolos, Michael's official court orator; see *Manuelis Holoboli Orationes*, 66: γράμμα δὲ σὸν βασιλεῦ, . . . τούτοις ἐτίθει τὰ τοῦ σκοποῦ καὶ βραχὺ μὲν παρῶσαι τὰ πρὸς δυσμάς, τὴν δὲ Κωνσταντίνου περιελθεῖν καί, τοῖς ἐν αὐτῇ δεῖμόν τε φόβον τε καὶ θροῦν αἰφνιδίως ὑποβαλεῖν. These lengthy and encomiastic orations were delivered by Holobolos before the imperial court on 25 December 1261, according to F. Dölger, "Die dynastische Familienpolitik des Kaisers Michael Palaiologos," *Festschrift E. Eichmann* (Paderborn, 1940) 187, in the express purpose of eulogizing Michael and Constantinople. I thank Professor Dölger for drawing my attention to the importance of these orations and for permitting me the use of his own copy. (On the orations see also Previale, "Un panegyrico inedito per Michele VIII Paleologo," 1ff.; and Siderides, "Μανουὴλ Ὁλοβώλου Ἐγκώμιον εἰς Μιχαὴλ Η' Παλαιολόγον," 168ff., which deals mainly with Michael's relations with Genoa.)

It has been suggested, nonetheless, that Palaeologus may actually have intended at this time to attack Constantinople.[5a] Such a hypothesis of course gives rise to the question why he dispatched so few troops with Alexios.[6] In answer it might be argued that Palaeologus did not wish unduly to arouse Latin suspicions of his motives, since, were the Caesar to appear before the walls of the capital with a large army, it would have been the surest way to mobilize its entire defenses, secure more effective aid from the West, and thereby jeopardize the success of any subsequent attempt.

Leo Allatius, the seventeenth century Greek *bibliothecarius* of the Vatican library, maintains, however, that had Michael secretly intended to seize Constantinople, he would have gone personally to capitalize on the glory of its recovery.[7] And, indeed, there can be little doubt that as a result of such a success the usurper's position on the throne would have been immeasurably enhanced in the eyes of his subjects. For, as one who had only recently attained the throne through demagoguery and murder, he must have been deeply concerned about the legitimacy of his rule and the establishment of an imperial dynasty.[8]

[5a] See Gardner, *Lascarids*, 255: "How far the result was due to fortune and how far to skillful prearrangement is difficult to say." Also see my Harvard dissertation, "Emperor Michael VIII Palaeologos and the Latins," ch. 5, where I tried to prove that the city's fall was the result of a clever stratagem on Michael's part.

[6] On the size of Alexios' forces see Pach., 137, esp. l. 20: τὸ Σκυθικὸν παραδοὺς σὺν οὐ πολλοῖς ἄλλοις. Acrop., 184, ll. 18–19, cites no specific figure, though he reports Michael himself as saying that he sent few troops against Constantinople. See also the *Orationes* of Holobolos, 67, who describes the army of Alexios as στράτευμα βραχὺ μὲν ὄν. Cf., however, a contemporary letter of Pope Urban IV (*Les registres d'Urbain IV*, ed. J. Guiraud, II [Paris, 1901] no. 131, p. 47A), who writes (not surprisingly) that Michael's army was very numerous: "exercitu copioso." (On Holobolos see further A. Heisenberg, "Aus der Geschichte und Literatur der Palaiologenzeit," *Sitzungsb. d. bayerischen Akad. der Wissens. zu München*, 10. Abhandlung [1920] 112ff.)

[7] See notes to Acropolites' history, entitled *Annales* (Bonn, 1837) 274.

[8] On this see Pach., 188, l. 20, who says that Michael lavishly bestowed gifts upon many Greeks because he could not otherwise retain the power he had usurped. Also see the important article of Dölger, "Die dynastische Familienpolitik des. . . Palaiologos," 179ff. Dölger shows that for Palaeologus the attitude of the Greeks toward his usurpation was a cause of real anxiety, and that at his coronation in Hagia Sophia very shortly after the conquest, Michael sought to found a dynasty by crowning his little son, Andronikos, co-emperor in violation

94

During this period the environs of Constantinople, from the Propontis to the Black Sea, were inhabited by a people, Greek in origin, called by Pachymeres "Voluntaries" (*Thelematarioi*),[9] whose name was derived from a propensity to shift allegiance at will to either Greeks or Latins. Actually their friendship was cultivated by both sides. The Latins indulged them because Constantinople's provisioning depended largely upon their cultivation of fields inside and outside the walls [10] and because the shortage of manpower necessitated their help in the defense of the ramparts. ("To expel them," says Pachymeres, "would have brought the risk of destitution.") The Nicenes, on the other hand, apart from a community of race with the Voluntaries, fostered their friendship because the Voluntaries' daily communication with Constantinople would provide accurate information on conditions within the city.[11]

Regarding the origin of the Voluntaries, it has been suggested that they were sons of soldiers of the Byzantine armies dissolved after the Latin conquest of 1204.[12] Quite possibly they may have been, at least in part, Greek cultivators deprived of their lands by the *Partitio Romanie* of 1204,[13] who once again, by purchase or ap-

---

of the rights of the boy-Emperor, John IV Lascaris. It might be noted that not long afterwards, following Palaeologus' blinding of John IV, a violent pro-Lascarid revolt broke out in Nicaea (see Pach., 192–201).

[9] Pach., 110, l. 17.

[10] According to the so-called *Fragmentum* attributed to Marino Sanudo (Torsello) (in Hopf, *Chroniques gréco-romanes*, 171), the Venetians were hard put to provision Constantinople: "gravati in plurimis expensis ad substinendum civitatem Constantinopolitanam." Cf. the new edition of the *Fragmentum*, of R. L. Wolff, "Hopf's So-Called 'Fragmentum' of Marino Sanudo Torsello," *The Joshua Starr Memorial Volume* (New York, 1953) 149ff. Wolff shows that the document, most probably written by Sanudo (as Hopf had conjectured), is not a *fragmentum* but complete in itself and was actually composed as a supplement to Ville-hardouin's *Conquête de Constantinople*.

[11] For the entire passage see Pach., 110, ll. 3ff. Cf. a similar use of the word θεληματάροι [sic] in the Greek *Chronicle of Morea*, ed. P. Kalonaros (Athens, 1940) and ed. J. Schmitt (London, 1904) ll. 604 and 6935, which refer, however, to Frankish and German troops. Schmitt, 608, translates the word as "wilful, undisciplined."

[12] N. Kalomenopoulos in Μεγάλη 'Ελληνικὴ 'Εγκυκλοπαιδεία, XII (Athens, 1931) 487.

[13] For the *Partitio Romanie* see T.-Th., I, 464ff.

propriation, had recovered their possessions, abandoned by the Latins on account of the Greek and Bulgar threats to the capital. In any event, it is of signal importance that, despite their ostensible neutrality, the Voluntaries were sympathetic to the Greeks of Nicaea.

The existence of Greeks living on the doorstep of Constantinople who were permitted to pass in and out of the city at will — a kind of Trojan horse, as it were [14] — could hardly have been overlooked by Palaeologus, who was diligently seeking a means of penetrating the city. Since his capture of Selymbria and of all territory extending from Rhegium to Constantinople (except for Aphameia), there no longer remained a barrier of any kind between his forces and the Voluntaries. For the first time they were in direct contact, and, we are told, they associated with each other on good terms, "treating one another with affection, neither side taking advantage of the other." [15]

Aside from the Voluntaries, there were, of course, numerous other Greeks living in the capital, most of whom were undoubtedly pro-Greek in sentiment. Nevertheless, some for one reason or another were collaborating with the Latins, certain ones even being in the employ of the Latin Emperor Baldwin II.[16]

There is an extraordinary and apparently completely neglected passage in Pachymeres describing an embassy sent by the Emperor Baldwin to Michael Palaeologus sometime before the expedition of the Caesar. The ambassadors, significantly enough, were Greeks from Constantinople. Receiving them warmly, Pachymeres informs us, Michael was able to learn of conditions in the capital (doubtless the state of the walls, garrison, and fleet)

---

[14] The contemporary *Chronicon Marchiae Tarvisinae et Lombardiae*, 48 (= *Annales S. Justinae Patavini*, 182) compares these events before Michael's conquest of Constantinople to those of Troy: "sicut patres eorum famosissimam Troiam . . . succenderunt."

[15] Pach., 110, ll. 19–20 and 111, ll. 3–5.

[16] For example, John Phylax (on whom see below, text and note 62, and Pach., 147, l. 1). Even the father of Acropolites had at one time been in the employ of the Latins; however, he had sent his young son George (born 1217) at an early age to the court of the Greek Emperor, John III Vatatzes, at Nicaea. See Acrop., 46, ll. 12–14.

and even succeeded in winning them to his side, promising them "whatever they would desire to have in Constantinople if he should take the city." Michael's pledges were formally guaranteed by the grant of golden bulls inscribed with his concessions.[17] The importance of this incident, to be sure, may easily be exaggerated. Yet even if there is no indication of collusion for the betrayal of the city at a specific time,[18] the incident plainly demonstrates that Michael had now succeeded in establishing contact with sympathetic elements within Constantinople who might well cooperate should an opportune moment present itself to take the city.

THE VENETIAN EXPEDITION TO DAPHNUSIA

The hypothesis that Michael planned the capture of Constantinople at this particular time would seem strengthened by the fact that at the very moment of Alexios' appearance before the walls, the Venetian fleet, the chief protection of the Latin Empire, was away besieging Daphnusia, a small island in the Black Sea.[19] Now not only was Daphnusia Nicene territory (a fact students of the period tend to forget), but an expedition against it would be a violation of the not yet terminated treaty of one year concluded in September of 1260 between Michael and the Latin Emperor Baldwin.[20]

[17] Pach., 106: μηδὲν ἔχων ἐν τῇ πόλει ζητούντων ἐδίδου εἰ ἕξει, καὶ χρυσοβουλλείοις λόγοις κατησφαλίζετο τὰ διδόμενα.
[18] Pachymeres gives no specific date for this incident involving the envoys, noting only that it occurred after Palaeologus' coronation at Nicaea. On the coronation date (25 December 1258, or 1 January 1259), see Dölger, Regesten, no. 1860. Cf. Ostrogorsky, Byzantine State (1956) 397, note 2.
[19] Acrop., 182ff.; Pach., 139, ll. 1–2; Greg., 85, ll. 5–8. Daphnusia, situated about seventy miles east of the mouth of the Bosporus, was actually a town located on a little island. Deserted today, it is called Kefhen Adassi, according to W. Ramsay, Historical Geography of Asia Minor (London, 1890) 182. See also Greg., 89, ll. 7–8.
[20] On the treaty see Acrop., 175, ll. 16–19. Also cf. Dade, Versuche, 5, who says that the Latin commander, Marco Gradenigo, attacked Daphnusia confident that the truce still had a month to run. Cf. C. Ducange, Histoire de l'empire de Constantinople, ed. Buchon (Paris, 1826) 346, who believes it improbable the Latins would then have broken a treaty with the Greeks by besieging a place belonging to them.

97

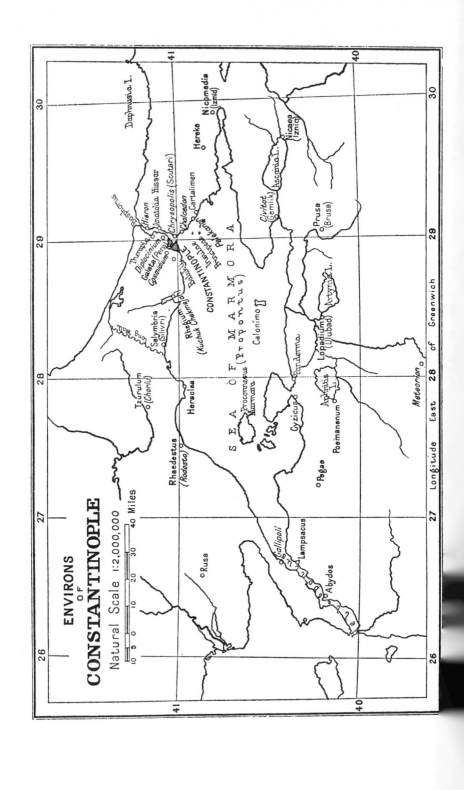

ENVIRONS
OF
CONSTANTINOPLE

Natural Scale 1:2,000,000

10 5 0   10   20   30   40 Miles

Izurulum
o (Chorlu)

Rusa o

Rhaedestus
(Rodosto)

Heraclea

Selymbria
(Silivri)

Long Wall

Gallipoli

Lampsacus

Abydos

Rhegium
(Kuchuk Chekmejä)

CONSTANTINOPLE

Bosphorus

Diplocinium
Galata Pera
Cosmidium

Therapea
Hieron
Anatolia Hissar
Chrysopolis (Scutari)

Daphnusa I.

Hereke

Nicomedia
o (Izmid)

Chalcedon

Cartalimen

Panyeias
Pelekanum

Drakon

Civitot
(Gemlik)

Ascania L.

Nicaea
(Iznik)

Pruse
(Bruse)

Artynia I.

SEA OF MARMORA

(Propontus)

Calonimo

Procconesus
Marmora

Panderma

Lopadium
(Ulubad)

Cyzicus o

Aphtinis
I.

Poemanenum

Pegae o

Meteorion o

Longitude   East   28   of   Greenwich

Several theories have been offered in explanation of the Latin expedition to Daphnusia, a campaign which stripped Constantinople of its defenses by removing the entire fleet of thirty Venetian ships (and one Sicilian), together with practically all the city's able-bodied fighting men.[21] According to Acropolites, it was the aim of the expedition's commander, the fairly recently appointed Venetian Podestà, Marco Gradenigo, to encourage the Constantinopolitan Latins by a more vigorous policy against the Greeks.[22] A modern historian, on the other hand, believes that Venice sought to capture the island because it controlled the mouth of the Black Sea and was the only harbor from the Bosporus to Pontic Heraclea.[23] Still another scholar suggests that Venice coveted Daphnusia as a port of refuge for Venetian ships pursued by Genoese and cut off by adverse winds from entering the Bosporus.[24]

Although each of these theories may contain an element of truth, another explanation, according with the theory of premeditation, may also be adduced: that Baldwin and Gradenigo were lured by Palaeologus *himself* into attacking Daphnusia as a diversion to Alexios' attack on Constantinople. In the so-called *Fragmentum* attributed to Marino Sanudo Torsello it is stated that

the Podestà of the Venetians, Lord Marco Gradenigo by name, had left the place [Constantinople] with a fleet of galleys in order to go and inflict damage on the enemy Greeks and to accept a certain territory which had been promised to be given to him; however, he found himself deceived because, whereas the said Podestà was a very upright man, traitors who were in Constantinople, finding it opportune that the

[21] According to Acrop., 181, ll. 22ff., only women, children, the wall guards, and Baldwin's bodyguard remained (κεκένωται οὖν ἡ πόλις ἀνδρῶν). The wretched state of Constantinople at this time is indicated by Greg., 81, ll. 8ff., who writes that the Latins were driven to such need that they had to destroy the city's best homes to secure firewood. For evidence also that the Latins stripped the capital's palaces and churches see Chapter 3, note 45, and esp. Chapter 6, note 26.
[22] Acrop., 181, ll. 13–22. For evidence of Gradenigo's experience in the Greek East as Bail of Negropont see T.-Th., III, 1–16. Additional bibliographical material on him is given in R. L. Wolff, "A New Document from the Period of the Latin Empire of Constantinople: The Oath of the Venetian Podestà," *Annuaire inst. phil. et d'hist. or.-sl.* (*Mél. Grégoire*), XII (1952) 564, note 2.
[23] Meliarakes, *Nicaea*, 592, note 1.
[24] G. Finlay, *History of Greece* (Oxford, 1877) III, pt. 2, 342.

99

city was emptied of men, handed over the place to the Emperor Kyr Michael Palaeologus.[25]

This passage of the famous fourteenth century Venetian diplomat and crusader propagandist is of considerable importance, not only because it has been generally overlooked, but because Sanudo was on the whole remarkably well-informed on Greek affairs. Living at various times in Negropont (Euboea) and in Constantinople itself, he may well have heard oral reports concerning this event or possibly even have had access to documents now lost.[26]

Careful scrutiny of the source, however, discloses that, tempting as it would be to attribute to Michael the offer of Daphnusia ("a certain territory promised to be given to him") and directly to relate this to the traitorous conduct of Constantinopolitan Greeks, no such causal connection is here actually made. Indeed, as it stands, the *Fragmentum* indicates only that, as a result of the absence of the Latin forces, an opportunity was thereupon afforded for a betrayal of the capital.[26a]

Providing even less ground for a theory of premeditation of this kind is another passage, from the same author's famous *Istoria del regno di Romania*, which reads that

Marco Gradenigo . . . , who had gone to Constantinople as Podestà of the Venetians, decided to undertake a naval expedition against territory of the Greeks, his enemies, and when he was absent from Constan-

<hr/>

[25] *Fragmentum* (ed. Hopf, in *Chron. gréco-rom.*, 172): "Potestas vero Venetorum, nomine dominus Marcus Gradonico, egressus erat terram cum exercitu galearum ut iret et dampnificaret inimicos Grecos et acciperet quamdam terram que ei fuerat promissa dari; verum se invenit deceptum; quia cum dictus Potestas esset vir probissimus, proditores qui erant in Constantinopoli dextrum habentes quomodo terra erat evacuata gentibus, dederunt ipsam terram imperatori Chyer Micali Palealogo. . . " Cf. Wolff ed. (in his article, "Hopf's So-Called 'Fragmentum,'" 151), which, in this particular passage, differs only in minor spellings. Cf. above, note 10.

[26] On Sanudo see esp. Hopf, *Chron. gr.-rom.*, p. xix; Wolff, *op. cit.*, 149ff.; *Enciclopedia italiana*, XXX (1936) 801–802; and above all A. Magnocavallo, *Marin Sanudo il Vecchio e il suo projetto di crociata* (Bergamo, 1901) esp. 24, 36. Finally, see Sanudo's friendly letters to Michael's son and successor, the Emperor Andronikos II, in *Epistulae*, nos. 7, 11, and 12, published in J. Bongars' *Gesta Dei per Francos* (Hanover, 1611) II, 299, 302, 303.

[26a] One may, of course, raise the question why Sanudo is so defensive regarding Gradenigo's integrity. Was the Podestà suspected of collusion with the Greeks?

tinople with this armada, the Emperor Sir Michael Palaeologus negotiated with some citizens of Constantinople so that they might open the gates and hand over the territory, and thus he was received.[27]

A third (unused) source must also be considered in this connection — Bar Hebraeus (Abû'l Faraj), the contemporary Arab Bishop and historian of Melitene in Asia Minor,[28] who writes:

And Michael himself perpetrated another fraud, and he told one of his men who was the commander of a fortress, to show signs of rebellion and send a message to Bodwin [sic] saying that he must send an army and that he would transfer that fortress to him. And the captain of the fortress did so, and he flattered Bodwin and led him into error. And when Bodwin sent the little army which he had with him, Michael swiftly made ready and went and encamped against it. And Michael himself also flattered certain of the citizens and one night they opened to him an old gate which had never been opened since the time of Constantine the Conqueror.[29]

Now while it is true that Bar Hebraeus (the provenience of whose information it would be very interesting to know)[30] might seem

[27] *Istoria del Regno di Romania*, in Hopf, *Chron. gr.-rom.*, 114: "Al Miser Marco Gradonico . . . ch' era andato Podestà à Costantinopoli per i Veneziani parse far un' Armata di Galee e Navilii per corsizar contra la Terra de Greci inimici suoi, ed essendosi esso partito de Costantinopoli con questa Armata, l'Imperator Sir Michiel Paleologo tratto con alquanti Borghesi di Costantinopoli che li dovessero aprir le Porte, e darli la Terra, e cosi fu ricevuto." Sanudo's *Istoria*, it should be emphasized, survives only in a late Italian version and this text may possibly be altered from that of Sanudo's original Latin. As for Sanudo's major work, *Secreta fidelium crucis* (in Bongars, *Gesta*, II, 1ff.), it contains nothing significant on the Greek recovery of Constantinople.

[28] On Bar, note the opinion of his editor, Budge, *Chronography*, I, xlviii: "[Bar Hebraeus] was tolerant in his religious opinions and . . . on the whole a fair-minded and truthful historian." Cf. T. Nöldeke, *Sketches from Eastern History*, trans. J. Black (London, 1892) 255: "Bar Hebraeus' history . . . contains much that is not to be found elsewhere, and is an important authority for the author's own period." Also the very full account of B. Spuler, *Die Mongolen in Iran* (Leipzig, 1939) 12, who describes him as "einer der wichtigsten und interessantesten Gewährsmanner, die wir für diese Zeit besitzen."

[29] *Chronography*, I, 428.

[30] His source might well have been Michael's illegitimate daughter Despoina Maria, who in 1265 was married to Abagha, Khan of the Mongols. Bar tells us that he (Bar) obtained from Maria the services of a Greek painter brought by her from Constantinople, and we know that Bar made frequent visits to the Mongol court at Tabriz (see Budge, *Chronography*, I, xxiii–xxvii). Actually, Maria was originally to have married Abagha's father Hulagu, with whom Michael had formed an alliance. See Pach., 174–175; cf. Dölger, *Regesten*, III, nos. 1900,

more explicitly than Sanudo to corroborate the possibility of Michael's diversion of the Venetian fleet, there is, once again, no express mention made of a pre-arranged plan to open a city gate during the absence of the fleet at Daphnusia. Moreover, it must also be noted that Hebraeus even errs in placing Michael personally at the capture of the capital.[30a]

That Michael, on the other hand, actually did carry on secret negotiations with Greeks within the city, whether Voluntaries or otherwise, is emphatically adduced by an important Western account, the *Chronicon Marchiae Tarvisinae et Lombardiae* (also known as *Annales S. Justinae Patavini*). A contemporary work most probably composed by a resident of Verona or Padua (cities both situated near Venice),[31] its precision in the details it provides leads to the belief that its author has not falsified the general tenor of his story. What lends the account particular credibility is the circumstance, hitherto unappreciated, that its information was very probably drawn from Venetian refugees who escaped from Constantinople to the West at the very time of the capital's fall.[32] It reads:

Through suitable persons, by means of money and fraudulent promises, Palaeologus corrupted certain impious men living in Constantinople, who firmly promised to betray the city to him at an opportune

1901, and 1932; and for a good summary, Spuler, *Mongolen*, 65; also Budge, p. xxvii. It is noteworthy that the Mongols were tolerant to Christianity. Thus Despoina could continue to practice the Greek faith, and even Abagha is said to have been baptized at the time of his marriage. See Nöldeke, *Sketches*, 252; and cf. Spuler, *Mongolen*, 181, note 8. Also "The History of the Nation of the Archers (The Mongols)," by Grigor of Akank, trans. R. Blake and R. Frye, in *Harvard Jl. of Asiatic Studies*, XII (1949) 341.

[30a] And yet Hebraeus (*Chronography*, I, 427) records certain striking information, e.g., that Michael, in his youth, was returned in chains to Constantinople by a certain Chadenos (omitted by Acrop. and Greg. but mentioned in almost identical detail by Pach., 29–31). Hebraeus, 428, also reports that in 1258 Michael had incited Frankish mercenaries to murder the Nicene regent (omitted again by Acrop., but cf. Pach., 54–55). It seems unlikely that Bar Hebraeus (d. 1286) copied the work of Pachymeres (d. ca. 1310), especially since, according to Nöldeke, *Sketches*, 227, Hebraeus had no knowledge of Greek. Cf. Budge, *Chronography*, I, xlvi.

[31] See the commentary to the most recent and best edition of this work, that of L. Botteghi, in *RISS*, VIII, pt. 3 (1916) pp. x–xiv. Cf. previous edition in *MGH SS*, XIX (1866) 148ff., entitled *Annales S. Justinae Patavini*.

[32] On these refugees see below, text and notes 75, 76.

time. And when all this had been secretly arranged between Palaeologus and the traitors, the Podestà of the Venetians with imperial
consent ascended his warships with a great number of soldiers and
sailed to the Black Sea to inflict damage on the enemy. Then the very
heartless betrayers of their country, seeing their opportunity about the
middle of the night on the seventh day before the end of July, after
killing the guards of a gate, provided an entrance to the glorious city
for the soldiers of Palaeologus.[33]

To complete the evidence from pertinent sources recounting
this event, we may take note of still another contemporary work,
that of the Venetian chronicler Martino da Canale, which states
that "because of inadequate guarding, a Greek . . . with a great
company of Greeks stole at night into Constantinople when the
Podestà had gone to the east with a large force of Venetians." [34]
And, in conclusion, we may cite the Greek and French versions of

[33] ". . . per idoneas personas mediante pecunia et promissionibus fraudolentis
corrupuit quosdam impios homines in urbe constantinopolitana habitantes; qui
firmiter promiserunt ei tempore opportuno tradere civitatem. Cum igitur hec omnia
essent inter Paleologum at proditores secretissime ordinata, potestas Venetorum de
imperatorio consensu cum multitudine bellatorum bellicas naves ascendit, et ad
damnificandum hostes versus Mare ponticum navigavit. Tunc patrie crudelissimi
proditores, videntes urbem defensoribus spoliatam, habita opportunitate, circa
mediam noctem die septimo exeunte iulio unius porte occisis custodibus, militibus
Paleologi gloriose urbis aditum prebuerunt . . ." (ed. Botteghi, *RISS*, VIII, 47).
Less explicit regarding Michael's actions but still clearly supporting the thesis of
treachery is a passage from a letter of Pope Urban IV: "[Paleologus,] congregato
. . . exercitu copioso, et civitatis Constantinopolitane finibus appropinquans, civitatem eandem cum non posset illam violenter capere, proditionaliter occupavit"
(from ed. J. Guiraud, *Les registres de Urbain IV*, II [Paris, 1901] no. 131, p. 47A;
it is undated, but Dölger, *Regesten*, no. 1895, assigns it to May, 1262). Urban first
heard the news of Constantinople's fall (according to Andrea Dandolo, *Chronica*,
in *RISS*, XII, 311), from Venetian envoys, who should have had pretty accurate
knowledge of the event. Cf. also a curious passage in the chronicle of another contemporary, Thomas Tuscus, *Gesta Imperatorum et Pontificum*, 518, who says that
Michael took Constantinople through the treachery of a Frankish noble named
Anselm. Tuscus has probably confused this event with Michael's previously attempted collusion with Ansel de Toucy, on which see Chapter 4, text and notes
7–10, esp. appendix listed in note 7. No attempt is made here to list all the
Western sources which make brief, general mention of Constantinople's fall to the
Greeks.

[34] ". . . por mavese garde, . . . un Gres . . . a grant compagnie de Gres,
ublerent par nuit Costantinople, lors quant la Poestes estoit ales en ost, et avoit
veuc lui grant compagnie des Veneciens" (*Chronique des Veniciens*, in *Arch.
or. it.*, VIII [1845] 480). Canale (d. ca. 1275) was employed in Venice's Dogana
Marittima and may well have had access to official sources; see *Encic. ital.*, VIII
(936) 664.

the *Chronicle of Morea* (early fourteenth century). Though affirming — correctly — that Palaeologus' troops entered the city as a result of collusion with its Greek inhabitants, their value is limited not only because of a confused chronology but because of an all too obvious partiality for the Latins which leads one naturally to expect an accusation of Greek perfidy.[35]

In the light of the evidence and reasoning presented, it would appear, then, that the absence of the Latin naval and military forces at the very moment of Alexios' appearance before the walls of the capital was sheer accident — coincidence — and that it was in fact the "lucky" absence of the fleet which spurred Alexios to attempt the city's capture. One must therefore abandon, however reluctantly, the hypothesis of premeditation so compatible with the characteristic resourcefulness exhibited by Michael throughout his entire career. Which is not, of course, to say that Michael, in the meantime, had overlooked the possibility of taking the city by ruse, as mention of his collusion with "Asel" and the negotiations described by Pachymeres and Western writers plainly attest.[36] Even if none of the sources seems clearly to support the theory of the fleet's diversion to Daphnusia, the usual interpretation of the fortuitous circumstances attending the event must at least be modified to take greater cognizance of the calculations of Michael Palaeologus and his intrigues with the Greek population of Constantinople.

THE PENETRATION OF THE WALLS

The three principal Greek sources are in essential agreement on the preliminaries leading to the entrance of the Nicene troops through the walls and into the city. According to Acropolite Alexios learned about the condition of the city's defenses from

---

[35] Greek *Chronicle*, ed. Kalonaros, ll. 1293–1294: οἱ Ῥωμαῖοι ὅπου ἦσαν εἰς τὴ πόλιν ἐσυμβιβάστησαν μετὰ τὸν Παλαιολόγον. French version, ed. Longnon, par. 84 "li Grec qui estoient habité dedens la cité . . . si s'accorderent avec l'emperer grec, et le firent entrer dedens la cité." For bias in these versions see Longnon ed pp. xliiiff.

[36] See Chapter 4, text and notes 7–10, and this chapter, text and notes 17, 25, 2

certain men of the city [the Voluntaries] who informed him of an opening in the walls through which an armed man could pass into the city.
Immediately then he began his task. One man entered, then another,
until fifteen and more had made their way inside . . . Some of the soldiers climbed the walls, seized the guards, and threw them outside
the city. Others with their axes smashed the bolts of the gates, thus
providing an entrance . . . for the troops. In this manner the Caesar
and his Greek and Cuman forces . . . entered the capital.[37]

The account of Gregoras, in substantial agreement, records that
the Caesar, while encamped at Rhegium ("through inscrutable
providence which does not operate through armies"), came upon
some men of the market place, Greeks from Constantinople, who
labored in the fields outside the city. From them he learned of the
weakness of the city's defenses and the absence of the fleet at
Daphnusia. These men, tired of Latin domination, made an agreement with Alexios to betray the city in exchange for valuable
gifts. They declared that aided by their friends they could easily
admit the army into the capital, since they knew of a secret subterranean passage close to the gate opposite the Church of the
Monastery of the Fountain through which fifty men easily might
enter. A few days later, just before dawn, the Caesar entered the
city.[38]

The third version, that of Pachymeres, is far more detailed.
He recounts that Alexios, reconnoitering the area to ascertain the
state of the defenses and contact the Voluntaries "about what he
had in mind regarding the city," was able to learn (from the
Voluntaries) of the absence of the Venetian fleet. Whereupon,
wishing to take advantage of the favorable situation, he offered
them liberal rewards if they would cooperate in seizing the city.[39]
Significantly, Alexios himself became wary when he considered
the magnitude of the task and the failure of far greater forces to
succeed in the past. Discussing the matter in council, however, he

---

[37] Acrop., 182, ll. 8–21, esp.: ὁπήν τινα εἶναι περὶ τὸ τεῖχος. This opening is con-
strued by W. Miller, *Cambridge Med. Hist.*, IV, 592, to be an underground aque-
uct.
[38] Greg., 83, l. 19 to 85, l. 20, and esp. 85: παλαιός τις ὑπόνομος.
[39] Pach., 138: ὑποτείνων κἀκείνοις ἐλπίδας, εἰ συνεργοῖεν, τὰς μείζους.

was encouraged by his nephew, Alexios Koutrizakes by name, the most important of the Voluntary leaders, who demonstrated his support by forming the Voluntaries into a company to aid the Caesar.

The particulars of the plan agreed upon were as follows. On the night selected, the Caesar and his troops were to conceal themselves at the Monastery of the Fountain, located a short distance outside the walls. At the same time, within the city, the Voluntaries were to apply ladders to a section of the wall opposite the Monastery — that is, at the Gate of the Fountain — and, after ascending, were to kill whatever guards were on duty there. During the operation the surrounding area was to be carefully guarded lest the Latin sentries detect anything unusual, for, as the historian emphasizes, "the Voluntaries, too, would incur a great risk if they should be caught." [40]

The operation began. Within the city the Voluntaries applied their ladders, climbed up, and approached the sleeping guards ("They were, of course, Italians!" says Pachymeres scornfully),[41] whom they dispatched and threw over the walls. Certain of the sentries, however, hearing the commotion, took to flight and had to be overtaken and slain. Then the Voluntaries, hurrying to the Gate of the Fountain, smashed it with rocks (it had been walled up for security, evidently because of the shortage of guards)[42] and opened it to admit the waiting forces of the Caesar. Alexios himself, who had been growing apprehensive, even suspicious of Koutrizakes because of the time that had elapsed,[43] immediately rushed with his troops from the monastery to the gate at the first sound of the signal agreed upon, the proclamation of the Em

[40] For this entire passage see Pach., 138, l. 17 to 141, l. 6.

[41] Pach., 142, ll. 1–2.

[42] Opinion of P. Déthier, *Monumenta Hungariae Historica*, XXI, pt. 1 (Buda pest, n.d.) 535. On the Monastery of the Fountain see M. Nomides, Ἡ Ζωοδόχ Πηγή (Istanbul, 1937) *passim* and esp. 166. This monastery, still in existence, situated about 500 metres from the Gate of the Fountain. This Gate is located between the twenty-sixth and twenty-seventh towers north of the Golden Gate. Se also B. Meyer-Plath and A. M. Schneider, *Die Landmauer von Konstantinop* (Berlin, 1943); and R. Janin, *Constantinople byzantine* (Paris, 1950) 257.

[43] Pach., 141, l. 11. Alexios was perhaps afraid that the Voluntaries might betray him and he would be trapped by a Latin army approaching from the outsid

106

peror's name from the battlements. The signal, it so happened, was given by a Greek priest, a Voluntary named Lakeras.[44]

No less than six Byzantine sources provide information on the penetration of the walls. But which account is most worthy of credence? A comparison of the six reveals that five, those of Acropolites, Scutariotes, Gregoras, an Anonymous Poem of the fourteenth century,[45] and the fifteenth century Sphrantzes [46] are very similar, and that one only, that of Pachymeres, differs to any appreciable extent. But this general concurrence is not surprising when we consider that Scutariotes' version is based directly on Acropolites, and that Gregoras (who wrote almost a century later) is likewise considered to have drawn the material for this part of his work from Acropolites.[47] It is clear, then, from this chain of dependence that only the accounts of Acropolites and Pachymeres are worthy of serious consideration. (Both historians were living at the time of this event, Acropolites being already a mature person and Pachymeres — who actually wrote several decades afterwards — a young man of nineteen.)[48]

Examining the two more closely we see that the chief difference, aside from Pachymeres' voluminousness, is Acropolites' greater stress on the providential and fortuitous. For this there is

[44] Pach., 142, l. 12 to 143, l. 4. Note Pachymeres' amusing account of Lakeras' terror as he climbed the wall.

[45] Which provides no new information except (l. 571) the fact that the Voluntaries assembled by Koutrizakes to aid Alexios numbered five hundred men. Published by J. Müller in "Byzantinische Analekten," *Sitz.-Ber. Akad. Wien. Phil.-hist. Kl.*, IX (1852) 366–389. Earlier ed. in J. Buchon, *Nouvelles recherches historiques sur la principauté française de Morée*, II (Paris, 1845) 335ff. Also see P. Charanis, "An Important Short Chronicle of the Fourteenth Century," *Byzantion*, XIII (1938) 337, note 1.

[46] Sphrantzes, *Chronicon* (Bonn) 18, says that an old man led the army in through an underground aqueduct he had often used in the past. (For important criticism on the authenticity of Sphrantzes' [or Phrantzes'] historical work see esp. R. Loenertz, "Autour du Chronicon Maius attribué à Georges Phrantzes," *Misc. G. Mercati*, III [1946] 273ff.) Cf. the similar account of T. Spandugnino, *De la origine degli imperatori ottomani, ordini de la corte, etc.*," in C. Sathas, *Documents inédits relatifs à l'histoire de la Grèce au Moyen Age*, IX (Paris, 1890) 141: "uno luoco aperto nelle mura."

[47] G. Moravcsik, *Byzantinoturcica: Die byzantinischen Quellen der Geschichte der Türkvölker* (Budapest, 1942) II, 330, 276.

[48] See K. Krumbacher, *Geschichte der byzantinischen Litteratur* (Munich, 1897) 288.

probably good reason: Acropolites, former teacher, Grand Logothete (prime minister), and even relative of Michael, was, as already observed, the Emperor's devoted partisan.[49] Like Michael himself he must have been deeply concerned with the task of legitimizing Michael's recent usurpation.[50] How effectively it would silence the partisans of Lascarid legitimacy were it to appear that Divine Power had gratuitously granted Constantinople to Palaeologus! That he was probably thinking along these lines — or may at least have sought to exaggerate what might indeed have appeared to him an indication of God's favor — can be observed from his emphasis on, and repetition of, such phrases as "the event occurred through the operation of Divine Providence"; "Constantinople again fell under the sceptre of the Roman Emperor through the Providence of God"; and "Christ granted you [Palaeologus] Constantinople."[51]

On the other hand, Pachymeres, no apologist for Michael — he was, in fact, later to oppose Michael's policy of religious union with Rome[52] — may well have left us a less biased picture. He describes, for example, in considerable detail Michael's preparations and diplomatic maneuvers before the capture, considerations, it must be noted, almost completely omitted by Acropolites.

With all but the two fundamental accounts eliminated, one may justifiably inquire which is more worthy of belief as to the method of penetrating the city — that of Acropolites-Gregoras about an underground passage,[52a] or that of Pachymeres, which

---

[49] On this see Heisenberg's edition of Acropolites, introduction, p. xiv. Also S. Kougeas, "Ὁ Γεώργιος Ἀκροπολίτης Κτήτωρ τοῦ Παρισινοῦ Κώδικος τοῦ Σουΐδα," *Byzantina Metabyzantina*, I (1949) 71–73, who shows conclusively that Acropolites was related through marriage to the Emperor.

[50] See Acrop., 188, ll. 25ff., where Acropolites writes that shortly after the city's recovery he urged Michael to proclaim his little son co-Emperor and thus to found a dynasty.

[51] Acrop., 181, l. 9; 183, ll. 3, 18–19; 184, l. 13; 186, l. 3.

[52] For Michael's unionist policy see esp. D. Geanakoplos, "Michael VIII Palaeologus and the Union of Lyons (1274)," *Harvard Theological Review*, XLV (1953) 79ff.

[52a] The Anonymous Poem, l. 550, also mentions a water conduit (ἐκ τῶν ὑδραγωγέων [sic]). The fourteenth century chronographer, Ephraem, *Chronographi* (Bonn, 1840) ll. 9494–9495, mentions a hole in the wall. Both, however, follow Acropolites.

describes the application of ladders to the city walls from within. At first glance, the recital of Pachymeres seems more credible, since it contains nothing extraordinary, no suddenly discovered secret passages. It states simply that the Voluntaries, having made an agreement with Alexios to betray the city, at an opportune time put up ladders from inside, killed the guards, and opened the gate. Moreover, in support of Pachymeres, it may be observed that none of the Western sources mentions an entrance into the city via a subterranean passage. Nevertheless, it must not be overlooked that an account such as that of Acropolites is not unique in the annals of Byzantine history. There may be cited, for example, Procopios' famous passage on the Greek capture of Naples in 536 by the troops of Belisarius, who penetrated the city by means of an underground passage.[53] The chronicles of Theophanes and Nikephoros afford additional instances of such entrance into Constantinople itself by Emperor Justinian II in 704.[54] Finally, the *Strategemata* of Polyaenus, a second century A.D. manual of warfare, tells how troops took the fortified town of Sestos by creeping through water-conduits of the city.[55] In view of these prece-

---

[53] *Procopii Caesariensis Opera Omnia, De Bello Gothico*, ed. J. Haury, II (Leipzig, 1905) 50–53.
[54] *Theophanis Chronographia*, ed. de Boor (Leipzig, 1883) 374; and *Nicephori Archiepiscopi Constantinopolitani Opuscula Historica*, ed. de Boor (Leipzig, 1880) 42. Perhaps further corroboration for Acropolites' account is the existence still today in Constantinople of an old underground passage, which begins on the grounds of the Monastery of the Fountain (about one hundred yards from the monastery building) and extends toward the city walls. This was shown to me in the summer of 1951 by the Abbot of the Monastery. In a stooped position I was able to advance into the passage for perhaps one hundred yards until I came to a point where the passage was blocked by water. I was assured, however, by the monks that the passage extended much further under the walls, indeed as far as Hagia Sophia itself. The importance of this discovery, of course, can easily be overemphasized because of the uncertainty over the length of the passage and its date of origin. Nevertheless, its existence might possibly lend a certain support to the theory that at least some of Palaeologus' men entered by means of an underground passage. In this connection, finally, see the twelfth century account of the French monk Odo of Deuil, *De profectione Ludovici VII in Orientem*, ed. V. Berry (New York, 1948) 64–65, who says that "from the outside of Constantinople underground conduits flow in bringing the city an abundance of sweet water" ("a foris subterranei conductus influunt, qui aquas dulces civitati largiter tribuunt").
[55] Ed. I. Melber (Leipzig, 1887) 38.

dents the possibility must not be overlooked that Acropolites (and through him those who based their works on his) might deliberately have imitated these accounts in the belief that such an entrance would further stress the supernatural action of Divine Providence.[56]

Thus the question whether the Nicene troops entered by means of an underground passage or simply through the opened Gate of the Fountain cannot be determined with finality. At any rate, neither interpretation vitiates the thesis established of collusion between Michael Palaeologus and the Greek inhabitants of the capital.

THE FALL OF CONSTANTINOPLE

With the passing of the Greek troops through the walls, the problem was to secure control of the city before the return of the Latin fleet. An experienced soldier but prone to anxieties, Alexios decided to advance cautiously until the coming of day would permit a more accurate appraisal of enemy strength. Once during his march through the streets he almost retreated at the appearance of armed Latins who seemed eager to defend the city; but he was supported by the Voluntaries who rushed quickly to his aid. Fearful of their fate should Alexios' attempt fail, the Voluntaries joined actively in street fights and aided the Greek troops to put to flight whatever Latins were encountered.[57]

The tumult, in the meantime, had awakened the Latin Emperor Baldwin, asleep in the Blachernae Palace at the other end of the Golden Horn. Baldwin is depicted by Pachymeres as so panic-stricken that he could think only of flight.[58] Gregoras, on the other

---

[56] Michael's Autobiography (written near the end of his life), 5-6, omits any mention of the means of penetrating the city and attributes its recovery to God's aid (δι᾽ ἡμῶν . . . διδόντος θεοῦ). The *Typikon for St. Michael*, 771, expresses the same sentiment, as do several other encomia: see S. G. Mercati, "Giambi di ringraziamento per la conquista di Costantinopoli (1261)," *Byz. Zeit.*, XXXVI (1936) 289ff.; and Gregory of Cyprus in Migne, *PG*, vol. 142, col. 377. On these see Previale, "Un panegyrico inedito per Michele VIII Paleologo," 1-3.

[57] Pach., 144, ll. 4-11.

[58] Pach., 144, ll. 11-13. Cf. an unused rhetorical passage from Holobolos (ed. Treu, 68) describing how "Baldwin, now a pitiful little fellow (ἀνδράριόν τι βρα-

hand, relates that Baldwin at once sought to assemble his body-guard, but soon, concluding that resistance was impossible, decided to entrust his safety to the protection of the sea.[59] In the hope of finding a boat he ran to the Great Palace, situated next to the Harbor of the Bukoleon on the Sea of Marmora. So precipitous was his flight that he left behind both crown and sword, the symbols of his rule.[60] These were soon found by Greek soldiers who came seeking him and who probably did not hesitate to show them to Baldwin's subjects in order to impress upon them the futility of further resistance.

What the Caesar most feared now happened — the return of the Venetian fleet. News of the Caesar's coup had been carried on the same day to the Podestà and his fleet at Daphnusia, and the Latins, immediately lifting the siege, hurried homeward.[61] At the same time the Caesar, in apprehension of their return and fearful of the result of a battle between his little army and the Latin forces, adopted the shrewd advice of John Phylax, a Greek in the service of Baldwin.[62] It was Phylax' plan to set fire to the houses of the Latins situated along the shore (presumably along the Golden Horn), first to those of the Venetians [63] and then of the other Western peoples. In this manner the returning Latins would forget the enemy, preoccupied as they would be with sav-

---

χύτατον), though formerly very swollen with pride and exalted in his high imperial rank, fled like a sorry knave, a thief fleeing in the shackles of slaves, a fugitive so to speak from the club and skin of Heracles."

[59] Greg., 86, ll. 5–10.

[60] Pach., 144, ll. 13–18; Greg., 86, ll. 10–13; Acrop., 183, ll. 15–17; 185, ll. 25–28; 186, ll. 1–2. Although the harbor of the Bukoleon is not specified in the Greek sources, Baldwin must have fled there because it was situated next to the Great Palace. See French *Chron. Mor.*, par. 84: "Bauduin . . . reduisi dedens le viel palais . . . dou Lion." Cf. A. Van Millingen, *Byzantine Constantinople* (London, 1899) 269. Gregoras' statement, 85, l. 24, that the Monastery of the Pantocrator was the palace of the Latins probably does not refer to Baldwin's residence, but to the headquarters of the Venetians. Cf. T.-Th., II, 284.

[61] Acrop., 182, l. 28 and 183, ll. 1–3, says that the Latin fleet, unsuccessful in its mission, was returning to the capital when Alexios entered. But Pach., 145, ll. 8–13 and Greg., 186, l. 14, say they were still besieging Daphnusia.

[62] Pach., 146, l. 1. Meliarakes, *Nicaea*, 595, note 1, believes Phylax to be a descriptive rather than a proper name.

[63] Acrop., 183, l. 12, who calls them κάμπους, a name still used in Venice to refer to the city squares.

ing their wives and children. The proposal, once implemented, resulted exactly as foreseen. On arrival the Latins saw their homes burning and their families standing on the quay imploring succor.[64] Hastening at once to save their loved ones, they had to forego all thought of a counter-attack. Thus the Greek troops were able to maintain their position in the city.[65]

In spite of the success of this tactic, Alexios was still apprehensive over a possible action of the Latin forces. He appealed for assistance, therefore, to the Greek inhabitants of the city, many of whom must have been eager to aid their compatriots.[66] Genoese residents, imbued with hatred for the rival Venetians, may also have come to his support, although it is not certain that they had yet learned of the Nymphaeum pact, secretly signed some weeks before by their home city and Palaeologus.[67]

The rapid crossing of the Nicene troops through the entire expanse of the city, from the Gate of the Fountain to the Golden Horn and Bosporus, seems at first glance rather remarkable. But it is less surprising when it is recalled that many areas of the capital, deserted for many years, had become desolate during the Latin occupation.

The scenes of excitement and destruction, of terror and burning which now took place, are vividly described in the Greek accounts. Even Acropolites, abandoning for a moment the usual stark simplicity of his style, eloquently relates how the Latin inhabitants, terror-stricken by the unexpectedness of the event, sought to save themselves, some fleeing to monasteries and adopt-

[64] Pach., 146, ll. 12–17. But according to Greg., 85, l. 22 and Sphrantzes, 18, l. 19, the Greeks set fire to the city shortly after entering, that is, some time before the return of the Latin fleet. Cf. *Chronicon Marchiae Tarvisinae et Lombardiae* 48: "urbem regiam protinus succenderunt."

[65] According to Pach., 147, l. 1, the Latins were aided by the crew of a huge Sicilian ship lying in the harbor. This ship was large enough to hold all the Latin wishing to flee. Cf. note 74.

[66] Pach., 145, l. 19. These Greeks at the same time probably feared Latin re prisals if the coup failed.

[67] Lopez, *Colonie*, 210, argues convincingly that had Gradenigo known of th Nymphaeum pact, he would not have attacked Daphnusia, leaving Constantinopl without defenders. In any event, only about two weeks had elapsed between th official Genoese ratification of the pact, and the capital's fall on July 25, too brie a time for the news to have arrived in Constantinople from Genoa.

ing monkish garb, others hiding in the recesses of walls, in dark stoas, or, if we may believe the neglected encomium of Manuel Holobolos, even concealing themselves in sewers.[68] To these descriptions Pachymeres adds in his rhetorical manner that women and children ("modest women and young maidens scantily clad as they were or wearing only a torn chiton") ran out of their burning houses like smoked-out bees and stood on the shore tearfully stretching out their hands for rescue to their menfolk on the ships.[69]

In view of the dramatization of the sources, it seems surprising that nothing is mentioned of a massacre of the Latins or at least reprisals against them by the Greek population.[70] Indeed, according to one account, the Latins could not have been pressed too hard, for they even managed to carry away part of their wealth with them.[71] That the Latins realized they might never return is suggested by Gregoras, who writes rhetorically that as they sailed away in the morning they voiced a long farewell to their adopted country.[72]

It would be instructive to know the number of the Latin refugees. According to the *Chronicle of Morea* there were three thousand,[73] a figure which may be fairly accurate, since presumably all thirty Venetian ships, including a huge Sicilian vessel at anchor in the harbor, were used in the evacuation.[74] Moreover, we are told that the ships were so crowded that many of the

---

[68] Acrop., 182, ll. 21–27. For Holobolos' encomium see above, note 5. In the same passage (Treu ed., 67) Holobolos also describes the "half-barbarian cries" of the Latins: τὰς μιξοβαρβάρους βοάς . . . τὰς ἐν ὑπονόμοις αὐτῶν καταδύσεις.

[69] Pach., 146–148.

[70] The occasional statements of Greek and Latin writers about bloodshed during the capture are to be attributed only to the relatively minor street clashes which occurred when the troops entered. The Greek attitude toward the Latins seems well expressed by Pach., 148, l. 3, who says that the latter paid the penalty for their treatment of the Greeks in 1204.

[71] Pach., 147, l. 14: συνάμα καὶ τοῖς περιοῦσι πράγμασιν. G. Finlay, *History of Greece*, III, pt. 2, 344, believes that a truce was probably concluded to permit the Latins to depart.

[72] Greg., 86, ll. 20–21.

[73] Greek version, l. 1305, French version, par. 85.

[74] Holobolos (ed. Treu, 67) probably refers to the Sicilian ship with these words: ὧν [the Latin vessels] μία καὶ ὑπὲρ τὰς ἐεικοσόρους, τεράστιόν τι χρῆμα ἰδεῖν.

Latins — men, women and children — died of hunger before reaching their destination, the Latin-held Aegean island of Negropont.[75] Noteworthy is the fact that some of the most prominent refugees and their families settled in Venice, where, as members of the Grand Council,[76] they were able to exert pressure on the government for the reconquest of their former homeland. To return to the Emperor Baldwin, whom we left at the harbor of the Bukoleon: wounded in one arm and on the point of being captured,[77] he was taken aboard a Venetian vessel.[78] Together with the Podestà Marco Gradenigo, numerous Venetians and other Latins, he then sailed to Negropont,[79] from which he was subsequently to begin his long and unremitting search for Western allies to aid in the recovery of his lost Empire.

Thus, with the departure of the Latin Emperor and the spectacular occupation of the capital by Greek troops on 25 July 1261, Michael VIII Palaeologus was at last in a position to realize his most cherished ambition, that of being crowned Basileus in Hagia

[75] *Chronicon Marchiae Tarvisinae, etc.*, 48: "multi utriusque sexiis oppressi dire famis angustia, in navibus antequam partum attinguerent, perierunt." Cf. Sanudo, *Fragmenutm* (ed. Hopf), 172: "Balduinus . . . fuit egressus . . . cum multo populo tam Veneto quam aliis gentium generationibus masculis, feminis, et parvulis, qui cum eo se reduxerunt in navigiis Venetorum" (ed. Wolff, "Hopf's So-Called 'Fragmentum,'" 151).

[76] See S. Romanin, *Storia documentata di Venezia*, II, 270, who cites the chronicle of Stefano Magno, but evidently had access to documents other than those included in "Estratti degli Annali Veneti di Stefano Magno" (in Hopf, *Chron. gréco-rom.*, 179ff.).

[77] Sanudo, *Istoria*, 115: "fù ferito in una mano." Acrop., 183, ll. 16–17: ἐν χρῷ τῆς ζωγρείας γενόμενον.

[78] According to Hopf's ed. of Sanudo, *Fragmentum*, 172, Baldwin was rescued and sailed away on ships belonging to the Venetian firm of Ca Pesaro ("Balduinus . . . fuit egressus cum navibus de Ca-Pesaro civitatis Venetiarum"). Cf. Wolff ed., 151, which makes only general mention of Venetian ships ("egressus, cum navibus comunitatis Venetiarum").

[79] *Fragmentum* (ed. Hopf, 172; Wolff, 151): "[Balduinus] qui venit de Constantinopoli Nigrepontem." Also see sentence quoted in note 75. Cf. Sanudo *Istoria*, 115: "a Negroponte." The Latin Patriarch Pantaleone Giustiniani also escaped, though evidently not with Baldwin. On Giustiniani see L. Santifaller *Beiträge zur Geschichte des lateinischen Patriarchats von Konstantinopel* (Weimar 1938) 42–45; L. de Mas-Latrie, "Patriarches latins de Constantinople," *Revue d l'Orient latin*, III (1895) 435–436; and more recently, R. L. Wolff, "Politics in the Latin Patriarchate of Constantinople," *Dumbarton Oaks Papers No. 8* (Cambridge, Mass., 1954) 294.

Sophia. And for the accomplishment of this aim he was ready to seize upon every advantage that the "Divine gift" of the Queen City could bestow, for he realized only too clearly that in Byzantium a usurper must legitimize his position or perish.

the first years of the restored byzantine empire

1261 - 1266

6

THE "NEW CONSTANTINE" AND HIS CAPITAL

THE ENTRANCE OF MICHAEL PALAEOLOGUS INTO THE CITY

news of Constantinople's recovery came quickly to Meteorion where the Emperor was encamped.[1] First to hear of it was his sister, Eulogia, who at dawn awakened the sleeping Michael. According to the sources, Michael was unconvinced of the truth of the report until the arrival of a messenger from the Caesar bearing the captured crown and sword of the Latin Emperor.[2]

If this was in fact Michael's attitude, it would of course seem irreconcilable with the concept of prior planning on his part. Indeed, the account of Acropolites and the more highly dramatized and precious recital of Pachymeres take great pains to stress the absence of Michael's hand in the capture, emphasizing instead the intervention of God. Thus Eulogia, supposedly unwilling to shock her sleeping brother by a sudden revelation of the great event, is portrayed as tickling his toes in order to awaken him gently.[3] "Oh Emperor," she said, "you are master of Constantinople." "How can I be," he replied, "when I am in Meteorion?" Then changing her tone she affirmed, "Christ has granted you

---

[1] Acrop., 183, 1. 24. Pach., 149, 1. 20, says Michael was at Nymphaeum; Greg., 86, 1. 22, says he was at Nicaea. Acropolites is probably correct, however, since he was evidently with the Emperor at the time, or certainly shortly thereafter when they entered the capital.

[2] Pach., 152, 11. 15–19. Acrop., 185, 11. 25ff. Cf. Greg., 86–87.

[3] Pach., 150–151.

Constantinople." Whereupon, piously throwing his arms toward heaven, Michael exclaimed, "Now . . . I accept it!" [4]

As after the murder of Muzalon, the Emperor's first act was to address an assembly of his people. It was his intention to draw personal profit from the capital's recovery by picturing it as a miraculous expression of divine favor toward his reign — a favor which also inspired the hope of recovering the lost provinces of the Empire. This was a prognostication of the policy he was to follow toward the Latins throughout the entire period of his rule. According to Pachymeres he said to the assemblage:

Although many attempts have hitherto been made to retake Constantinople, none has succeeded. If we have just retaken the city in spite of the resistance of those who defended it, and if we have maintained it despite the efforts of the Latins . . . it is only as a result of the Divine Power which, on the one hand, renders impregnable (when it so desires) those cities which seem the most feeble, and which, on the other, enfeebles those which appear the most invincible. We have undergone so many failures to take Constantinople with no result (although we were greater in number than the defenders) because God wished us to know that the possession of this city was a grace dependent upon his bounty. He has reserved for our reign this grace, which obliges us to eternal appreciation, and in according it to us he has given us hope to retake the provinces which we lost with it.[5]

While Palaeologus was making plans for his entrance into Constantinople, the Caesar Alexios was assiduously preparing the capital to receive him. In view of the continuing danger of a Latin naval attack, the Caesar's task was rendered difficult by the fewness of his troops. He could, to be sure, depend upon the support of the Greek population, but he had constantly to be on guard against treachery or an uprising of the remaining Latins.[6] The

[4] Acrop., 184. See the similar (unused) account of the imperial rhetor Manuel Holobolos, in *Manuelis Holoboli Orationes*, 68–69, esp. 69, ll. 17–22, where Michael, significantly, says to Eulogia, "If you think this achievement [recovering Constantinople] is the product of my mind and hand, you are far from the truth and my purpose. This indeed is my excuse, that I did not try to accomplish it, for how could I have conquered it myself so quickly — such a great and celebrated achievement as this?"

[5] See Pach., 153, l. 9, to 155, l. 12, who alone records his words or at least the substance of his remarks. The passages quoted are only part of the long speech.

[6] Pach., 158–159, esp. 159: Ῥωμαίοις μὲν πιστεύων, Ἰταλοὺς δ' ὑποπτεύων.

Caesar therefore forbade gatherings during the day and ordered the streets and public places to be guarded at night lest the expelled Latins enter through the breaches in the walls still everywhere unrepaired.[7]

Three weeks later, on 15 August 1261, Michael VIII Palaeologus, the "New Constantine"[8] and second founder of Constantinople, as he styled himself, entered the capital. Realizing the enormous moral significance of the occasion for the Greeks, Michael proposed to make the event one of thanksgiving to God. Accordingly, he made his entrance not as a triumphant conqueror but as a suppliant.[9] Ceremoniously entering the Golden Gate, he and his entourage paused to hear prayers of thanksgiving composed by the Grand Logothete, George Acropolites.[10] Then, traversing the entire breadth of the city on foot, with Constantinople's palladium, the holy icon of the Virgin Hodegetria at the head,[11] the procession finally reached Hagia Sophia, where divine services were held. Shortly thereafter Michael and his wife Theodora were crowned *Basileis*; and his baby son, Andronikos, was proclaimed heir-presumptive to the throne, in complete disregard of the rights of the legitimate Emperor, young John IV Lascaris,

---

[7] Pach., 159, ll. 9ff.

[8] See the Genoese source, *Annali Genovesi di Caffaro e de' suoi continuatori* (= *Annales Ianuenses*), ed. C. Imperiale and L. Belgrano (Genoa-Rome, 1890–1929), IV, 45: "ab eo tempore citra idem imperator se appellavit . . . novus Constantinus." Also T.-Th., III, 134. Michael seems to have used this title in documents for home consumption and when addressing the Genoese and Venetians, but apparently not in letters to the papacy. It appears surprising that Michael did not immediately rush to the capital, but evidently he wanted to make a permanent move with much of his entourage.

[9] Acrop., 186, ll. 6–12.

[10] Acrop., ll. 13ff.

[11] On the Hodegetria, an ancient, miracle-working icon of the Virgin, painted, according to tradition, by St. Luke, and kept usually in the Constantinopolitan Monastery of the Hodegon, see R. L. Wolff, "Footnote to an Incident of the Latin Occupation of Constantinople: The Church and the Icon of the Hodegetria," *Traditio*, VI (1948) 319; and, more recently, R. Janin, *La géographie ecclésiastique de l'empire byzantin*, pt. 1, vol. III: *Les églises et les monastères* (Paris, 1953) 208–216. The Caesar Alexios was, for his services, given a triumph, and Michael ordered that his name be mentioned, along with his own, in the public prayers for one year (Greg., 89, ll. 3–13). Pach., 173, ll. 19ff., mentions the prayers but not the triumph.

who had been left behind in Asia Minor.[12] The goal for which Michael had long and carefully labored was now attained.

The Emperor chose as his residence the Great Palace on the Bosporus. The newer palace of the Blachernae overlooking the Golden Horn, though occupied by the Angeloi and more recently by the Latin emperors, was deemed unsuitable because, as Pachymeres scornfully informs us, "it was filled with thick smoke and Italian fire, which the servants of the uncouth Baldwin had allowed to permeate the palace." [13]

The celebration for the recovery of the capital lasted throughout the day and night. All Constantinople rang with joy as jubilant throngs went to give thanks in the churches once again become Greek. So elated were the monks and nuns, we are told, that groups moved from place to place festively adorning the monasteries and convents.[14] The Emperor himself, however, had little time to share in the festivities, for he was at once confronted by a number of pressing problems (which have not as yet been subjected to full scrutiny by scholars).[14a] Most important of these were the defense of Constantinople from an expected Latin attack, the restoration and repopulation of the semi-ruined capital, and the disposition of the Latins remaining in the city.[15]

THE RESTORATION OF CONSTANTINOPLE: REPOPULATION AND RECONSTRUCTION

The removal of the court from Nicaea to Constantinople was not a simple matter. Unlike smaller ambulatory Western courts,

[12] On Andronikos (about whom the sources are not clear) see Acrop., 188–189; Pach., 167, ll. 3–7, and 173, ll. 15–19; also Greg., 87, ll. 11–14. Cf. esp. F. Dölger, "Die dynastische Familienpolitik des Kaisers Michael Palaiologos," *Festschrift E. Eichmann* (Paderborn, 1940) 179ff.

[13] Pach., 161, ll. 7–11. Cf. Greg., 87, ll. 20–23.

[14] *Typikon for St. Michael*, 771: σεμνεῖα καὶ ἀσκητήρια μοναζόντων καὶ μοναζουσῶν περικοσμοῦσι χοροί. Cf. also Pach., 161, ll. 13–14, and 162, ll. 1–3.

[14a] Except for the discussion of Constantinople's population in 1261 in P. Charanis, "A note on the Population and Cities of the Byzantine Empire in the Thirteenth Century," *J. Starr Memorial Volume* (1953) 140.

[15] Pach., 162, ll. 5–9; 163, ll. 18ff.; and Greg., 88–89. A fourth task was the healing of the schism which had arisen in the church over Arsenios' refusal to perform his patriarchal duties following Michael's usurpation. Michael later prevailed upon Arsenios to return to his throne. See Pach., 165, and Greg., 88, ll. 16ff.

that of Byzantium was stationary and needed considerable space to house its officials and nobility, all of whom were encouraged by the Emperor to move to the Bosporus.[16] During the three week period prior to his own arrival, Michael repeatedly dispatched messengers to the Caesar with instructions to select residences for the nobles and courtiers in accordance with their rank.[17] Wherever possible, the noble families were to be permitted to resume possession of their ancestral homes. It must have been difficult, however, to carry out this order, since fire and the passing of fifty-seven years had resulted in the destruction or alteration of many dwellings.[18] Indeed, large areas of the city had been almost completely devastated. Thus Gregoras (doubtless with a certain exaggeration) writes that

Constantinople was then an enormous desolate city, full of ruins and stones, of houses razed to the ground, and of the few remains of the great fire. . . Enslaved it had received no care from the Latins, except destruction of every kind day and night.[19]

Undaunted, the Greeks set about eagerly to repair their beloved capital. But in order to restore its previous proud condition, Michael had first to look to its repopulation, as only a small number of its former residents remained.[20] Thus he recalled the Greek inhabitants who had fled during the occupation to dwell along the Bosporus.[21] At this time or shortly thereafter he also brought in Tzakones, Greeks from the southeastern part of the Morea, newly taken (as we shall see) from Prince William of Achaia. To these colonists Michael assigned as residence a special section of the city.[22]

Most of the property within Constantinople, whether Greek

---

[16] Pach., 160, ll. 3–4.

[17] Pach., 156. See also S. Kougeas, "Ὁ Γεώργιος Ἀκροπολίτης Κτήτωρ τοῦ Παρισινοῦ Κώδικος τοῦ Σουΐδα," *Byzantina Metabyzantina*, I (1949) 61ff.

[18] See Greg., 81, ll. 8ff., who says that some of the best homes were used for firewood during the latter part of Baldwin's reign. The fires of 1204 and 1261 doubtless destroyed many others.

[19] Greg., 87, l. 23 and 88, ll. 1–7.

[20] Greg., 88, ll. 12–16.

[21] Pach., 163, ll. 18–19 and 164, l. 1.

[22] Pach., 188, ll. 2–8 and 164, ll. 9–10.

or Latin, was arrogated by right of conquest to the imperial government for disposition.[23] Solely excepted was that of the nobles, which was returned to them because Palaeologus feared their power and needed their cooperation.[24] It is significant that some of the best lands both within and outside the walls were awarded to the Voluntaries, who had played such an important role in the reconquest.[25]

From the beginning Michael devoted special attention to the condition of the churches. They had fared badly under the Latins, who had stripped the lead from their roofs in order to provide money for the defense of the city and expenses of the court.[26] As has not hitherto been noticed, the Greek historian Scutariotes remarks that during the occupation the Emperor John Vatatzes of Nicaea had even sent money to the Latins to "buy them off" (exonesamenos) from despoiling the Constantinopolitan churches [27] — an extraordinary gesture probably reflecting his hope of soon recovering the capital.

Many churches were repaired or rebuilt at this time.[28] For some Michael provided roofs, and others, particularly Hagia Sophia, he adorned with magnificent treasures, including much-needed holy vessels for their sanctuaries.[29] No less care was lavished on the monasteries, which Michael sought to restore to their previous condition by the award of financial aid and fertile

---

[23] Pach., 391, ll. 3–5.

[24] Pach., 158, ll. 13–17 and 164, ll. 1–2.

[25] Pach., 164, ll. 2–5. This is evidently conclusive proof of Voluntary collusion with Michael's forces in taking the capital.

[26] Scutariotes, 508–509: τῶν τότε αὐτῆς ἀρχόντων ᾿Ιταλῶν πολλὰς τῶν ἐν αὐτῇ ἐκκλησιῶν βουλευσαμένων καταστρέψαι πρὸς θεραπείαν τῆς ἐνούσης ἐνδείας αὐτοῖς. Also Wolff, "Politics," 278, text and note 142, who cites a letter of Pope Honorius III, saying specifically that the Latin Patriarch Matthaeus had stripped the capital's churches. See also above, Chapter 3, note 45, for mention, in Sanudo's so-called Fragmentum, of Baldwin's stripping of lead from the palace roofs. On the basis of these various passages from Sanudo, Scutariotes, and Pope Honorius, it may well be that a division is suggested here: Latin laymen stripped secular buildings, ecclesiastics, the churches.

[27] Scutariotes, 509: αὐτὸς χρήμασιν ἐξωνησάμενος, σῴους διαμένειν περιεποιήσατο.

[28] Greg., 88, ll. 14–15, and Gregory of Cyprus, Laudatio Michaelis Palaeologi, Migne, PG, vol. 142, col. 377: θείων ναῶν ἀπανταχοῦ τῆς ῾Ρωμαίων ἀνοικοδομαί.

[29] Pach., 172, ll. 17–19, and 173, ll. 1–3.

124

lands within and outside the city.[30] Such attention to the welfare of ecclesiastical establishments helped to win clerical support for imperial policies and, needless to say, to heighten still further the patriotism of the Greek people, for whom the most meaningful evidence of the restoration was reestablishment of the Greek church. So bitterly had the Greeks resented the enforced Latinization of their church during the occupation that they had been accustomed to purify their altars and rebaptize their children after each performance of the Latin rite.[31]

Michael's program of reconstruction was ambitious. With labor provided by his light-armed troops he constructed or rebuilt many public buildings: agoras, stoas, law-courts, theaters, even homes for the aged.[32] Finally, and in commemoration of the city's recovery, the Emperor erected, on a column before the Church of the Holy Apostles, a bronze statue of his namesake, the Archangel Michael. At the foot of the statue stood another figure, representing the Emperor himself, holding in his hands a likeness of the city which he offered to the Archangel.[33] It would be difficult indeed for the Greeks to forget that divine favor had sanctioned the reign of Michael Palaeologus!

THE BUILDING OF A FLEET

Most pressing of the problems facing the Emperor was, of course, defense of the city against an expected attack of the Venetian fleet. Realizing his lack of a strong navy, Palaeologus chose to insure Genoese assistance by scrupulously implementing the provisions of the Nymphaeum pact, despite the hitherto

[30] Pach., 164, ll. 5–12.

[31] See the canon on this of the Fourth Lateran Council (1215), in Héfelé-Leclercq, *Histoire des conciles* (Paris, 1914) V, pt. 2, 1333.

[32] Pach., 188, ll. 2–16. Also see Holobolos' encomium (ed. Treu), 58, perhaps the finest remaining testimony (though perhaps exaggerated) to Michael's restoration of Constantinople: ὡραϊσμοί . . . δημοσίων κατασκευῶν· ἱππόδρομοι, θαῦμα ἰδεῖν· ἀγορὰ πλήθουσα· θέατρα· δικαστήρια· στενωποί· κάλλη στοῶν· ἀφθονία λουτρῶν . . . γηροτροφεῖα πανταχοῦ. Cf. Gregory of Cyprus, *Laudatio*, 377: ξένων καταγωγαί, νοσούντων ἐπιμέλειαι, ἀσθενῶν ἰατρεῖαι, etc.

[33] Greg., 202, ll. 10–13 and Pach., vol. II, 234, ll. 16–22.

merely nominal aid of his ally.[34] In accordance with the terms of
the treaty, one of his first acts was to transfer to the Genoese the
former palace of the Venetians in Constantinople.[35]

But Michael did not rely entirely on the Genoese. He knew the
precariousness of a Latin alliance — the pressures that would be
brought to bear on Genoa to abandon him and the instability of
the attitudes of the Genoese and Greeks toward each other.
Therefore, while utilizing the naval power of Genoa, he at the
same time set about to develop his own strength by constructing
a strong imperial fleet as well as by reinforcing the city walls,
especially those on the seaward side. Michael's high opinion of
naval power is emphasized by Pachymeres, who quotes him as
saying that the Greeks could never hope to hold Constantinople
without complete control of the surrounding seas.[36]

It was mainly to provide the manpower for his new fleet that
the Emperor, through the distribution of largesses, transported to
Constantinople a colony of Tzakones and their families from Laconia and the area around Monemvasia.[37] Thus the territories of
the Tzakones [38] and Monemvasiotes (formally ceded to Michael in
1262 by the Prince of Achaia) soon became of cardinal importance
as a military recruiting ground. In this respect they partially replaced Asia Minor, much of which had fallen under Turkish
domination, and the inhabitants of which were in great part still
loyal to the Lascarid dynasty.[39]

The Tzakones were used in the navy as light-armed troops [40]

[34] Greg., 97, ll. 20–21.
[35] *Ann. Ian.*, IV, 45. Cf. below, Chapter 7, text and note 49.
[36] Pach., 309–310: οὐ γὰρ ἦν ἀσφαλῶς κατέχειν τὴν πόλιν τοὺς Ῥωμαίους, ὡς
αὐτὸς ἔλεγε, μὴ τὸ πᾶν θαλασσοκρατοῦντας.
[37] Pach., 309, ll. 16–19, and 188, ll. 2–8. Pachymeres' use of Tzakones and
Monemvasiotes is not always clearly differentiated.
[38] On the much-debated etymology of the word "Tzakones" see C. Sathas,
Documents inédits, IV, pp. lxx–lxxii. For the most recent and convincing theory
(that the word is derived from ἔξω Λάκωνες) see K. Amantos, "Σάλωνα-Τσάκωνες,"
Ἑλληνικά, X (Athens, 1938) 211. Also cf. C. Lehman-Haupt, "Τζάκωνες," Εἰς
μνήμην Σπυρίδωνος Λάμπρου (Athens, 1935) 353, who thinks that the word derives
directly from Λάκωνες.
[39] See Pach., 194–201.
[40] Pach., 188, ll. 2–8. Greg., 98, l. 11, calls them a naval army: στρατὸς ἐν τοῖς
ὅπλοις θαλάττιος. Cf. Pach., 309, ll. 2–5. Also see an implicit reference to them in

along with Gasmuloi of the capital, who also served as rowers.[41] Offspring of Latin fathers and Greek mothers, the Gasmuloi,[42] according to popular belief, combined the prudence and discipline of the Greeks with the daring and courage of the Italians.[43] Though the sources are not very informative as to how many Gasmuloi resided in the city, one may believe that their number was considerable; Westerners had lived there almost continuously since at least the eleventh or twelfth centuries, and inter-marriage between Greeks and Latins, even during the recent occupation, was not uncommon.[44]

That the construction of a strong Greek navy was not the work of a day is evident from the fact that only in 1263 do we hear of a campaign undertaken by the imperial fleet.[45] Thereafter, however, the Greek marine was to play a vital role in Michael's relations with the West.

Palaeologus' Autobiography, 7: καὶ τὰ λείψανα πείθω τὴν θάλασσαν ἀνελέσθαι εἰς οἰκίαν. The Greek *Chronicle of Morea*, ll. 4571ff., informs us that a short time later Michael issued to his generals imperial bulls with spaces left blank for inserting the names of Tzakones, who, in exchange for military service, would frequently receive the noble title of Sebastos.

[41] Pach., 188, ll. 8–11, and 164, ll. 15–16. Greg., 98, ll. 6–8.

[42] Pach., 309: ἐκ 'Ρωμαίων γυναικῶν γεννηθέντες τοῖς 'Ιταλοῖς. Cf. Greg., 98, ll. 8–10. Clear proof of fraternization and intermarriage between Greeks and Latins during the occupation. On the word "Gasmuloi" see Sathas, *Documents inédits*, IV, p. lxxff., and especially D. Kambourouglou, Πρακτικὰ τῆς 'Ακαδημίας 'Αθηνῶν, IV (Athens, 1929) 24, who is of the opinion that βασμοῦλος (more correct, he believes, would be γασμοῦλος) is derived (as is *bâtard*) from *bât* (a stupid person) and from μοῦλος, which in Moreot Greek meant bastard. Cf. Bréhier, *Institutions*, 425 and esp. W. Barthold, *Zwölf Vorlesungen über die Geschichte der türken Mittelasiens* (Berlin, 1935), who says the name is derived from Bosmigli, a mixed Turkish people of Central Asia. Barthold, however, does not explain the transmission of the term to the Greeks and Latins.

[43] Pach., 188, ll. 11–12, and Greg., 98, ll. 8–10.

[44] According to O. Tafrali, *Thessalonique au quatorzième siècle* (Paris, 1913) 44, in the early fourteenth century the Gasmuloi, though essentially Greek in feeling, would pass as Latins if it suited their interest at the moment.

[45] Greg., 98, ll. 13–17; Pach., 209, ll. 5–12. Also cf. *Chronicon Marchiae Tarvisinae et Lombardiae*, 48, which records (with a certain bias) that the Venetian fleet was so strong that, had it not been for Genoese aid, Palaeologus would have lost all Greek territory in the Ionian and Aegean seas to Venice: "tamen tanta erat tunc in mari potentia Venetorum, quod, nisi Ianuenses Grecis auxilium prebuissent, non sine magno tremore in mare Ionio vel Egeo Venetorum exercitui tota Grecia occurrisset." See also Bréhier, *Institutions*, 425–426.

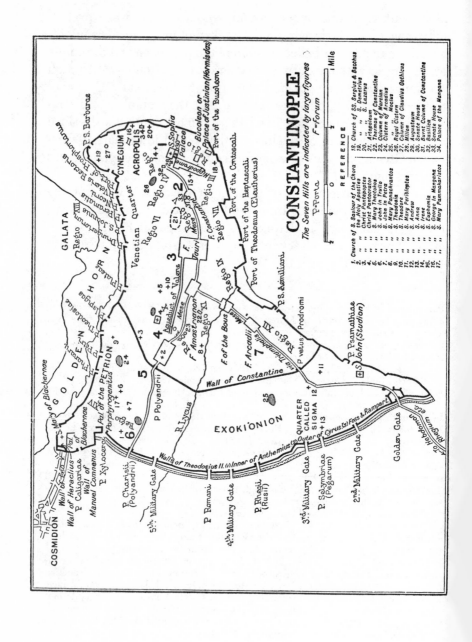

CONSTANTINOPLE

The Seven Hills are indicated by large figures

F=Forum   P=Porta

REFERENCE

1. Church of S. Saviour of the Chora
2.   "   "   the Holy Apostles
3.   "   "   Christ Pantepoptes
4.   "   "   Christ Pantocrator
5.   "   "   S. Mary Theotokos
6.   "   "   S. John in Trullo
7.   "   "   S. John in Petra
8.   "   "   S. Mary Panachrantos
9.   "   "   Theodosia
10. "   "   S. Theodore
11. "   "   S. Mary Peribleptos
12. "   "   S. Andrew
13. "   "   S. Anna
14. "   "   S. Irene
15. "   "   S. Euphemia
16. "   "   S. George Mangana
17. "   "   S. Mary Pammakaristos
18. Church of SS. Sergius & Bacchus
19. "   "   S. Demetrius
20. "   "   S. Lazarus
21. Artopoleum
22. Thermae of Constantine
23. Column of Marcian
24. Column of Arcadius
25. Cistern of Mocius
26. Royal Cistern
27. Column of Claudius Gothicus
28. Milion
29. Augusteum
30. Senate House
31. Burnt Column of Constantine
32. Basilica
33. Senate House
34. Palace of the Mangana

THE RESTORATION OF THE WALLS

Special attention was also directed to the city's fortifications.[46] Although Michael took care to repair the land walls,[47] his chief concern was improvement of those along the sea, which, after long subjection to earthquakes and exposure to the corrosion of moisture and storms, were then in a very unsatisfactory condition.[48] From the Byzantine Acropolis (the Turkish Seraglio Point) to the south end of the land walls on the Sea of Marmora, the seaward fortifications constituted a single, five mile stretch of wall, reinforced by a great number of towers [49] and built close to the shore so that invading troops could be landed only with difficulty. It may be recalled that during the invasion of 1204, Latin ships, bypassing this area to sail through the Bosporus and into the Golden Horn, had there, from their high towers, deposited troops directly onto the walls.[50] Fearing a repetition of this tactic, Michael at this time or shortly afterwards took care to increase the height of the fortifications on the Horn. Since lime and stone were difficult to secure, he was at first content to erect on the summit of the walls great wooden screens seven feet high, which were covered with hides to make them fire-proof.[51] But some years later (probably in 1269–1270, under the threat of invasion by Charles of Anjou), he had the sea walls, somewhat like those on land, made into a double line of fortresses. The capital was thus completely surrounded with fortifications.[52]

[46] See Van Millingen, *Byzantine Constantinople*, 188.

[47] Pach., 186, ll. 11–12, and 159, ll. 12–13. On the land walls see esp. B. Meyer-Plath and A. Schneider, *Die Landmauer von Konstantinopel* (Berlin, 1943).

[48] Pach., 186, ll. 5ff. (Note that Pachymeres stresses the Greek fear of a surprise Latin sea attack: δέος γὰρ μὴ ἀφανῶς ἐπιθοῖντο, ὅπως δὲ φυλαχθείη 'Ρωμαίοις). See also Van Millingen, 188.

[49] On the history of these walls see Van Millingen, *Byzantine Constantinople*, 178–188, 248. Also the review of C. Mango of recent Turkish works on the city's walls, in *Speculum*, XXX (1955) 271.

[50] Niketas Choniates (Bonn) 753–754.

[51] Pach., 186, ll. 15–16; 187, ll. 15–17; 188, l. 1.

[52] Pach., 364, ll. 17–19: ἐδιδύμου . . . τὸ πρὸς θάλασσαν. Greg., 124, ll. 12–14: περιέφραττε πανταχόθεν τὴν βασιλεύουσαν. See Van Millingen, *Byzantine Constantinople*, 189, note 2, for his opinion on the statement of A. Paspates, Βυζαντινὰ 'Ανάκτορα (Athens, 1885) 208–209, that the land walls of what is today the Seraglio enclosure were the work of Michael.

Light-armed soldiers, mainly Tzakones, were employed to defend the walls.[53] For the sustenance of these troops and the population in case of siege, huge quantities of provisions were gathered in storehouses. Large herds of cows were pastured within the city, and great amounts of salted meat, cheese, and hay for horses were set aside. Finally, to render Constantinople as self-sufficient as possible, Michael ordered the cultivation of arable lands within the city.[54]

The walls on the Bosporus and Golden Horn were more vulnerable than those on the Sea of Marmora, as a fleet attacking from the south would be confronted by dangerous currents.[55] For this reason Michael transferred the principal dockyard of his navy from the less defensible Blachernae area to the Kontoscalion on the Sea of Marmora.[56] Some years later, again under threat of Western attack, Palaeologus dredged and deepened the Kontoscalion harbor and surrounded it with immense blocks enclosed with iron gates and protected by a mole.[57] And to complete his sea defenses, he may well have reinstalled the chain stretching from the Tower of Galata to the wall of the Acropolis in Constantinople. This chain, which served to close off to enemy fleets the entrance to the Golden Horn, had been broken by the Venetians during the Latin conquest.[58]

[53] Pach., 187, ll. 1–3, and 188, ll. 2–4. On the reputation of the Tzakones as guards in the thirteenth and fourteenth centuries, see D. Zakythinos, "La population de la Morée byzantine," L'Hellénisme contemporain, III (1949) 24.

[54] Pach., 187, ll. 6–14.

[55] Van Millingen, Byzantine Constantinople, 178–180. Cf. Ville-hardouin, Conquête de Constantinople (ed. N. de Wailly) 138, according to which the Marmora currents in 1204 deterred the Venetian fleet from attacking in that area.

[56] Pach., 365, ll. 4ff. Van Millingen, Byzantine Constantinople, 313, says that the Kontoscalion was located in front of today's Koum Kapoussi. Cf. Pach., 365: τὸ πρὸς τὸν Βλάγκα Κοντοσκέλιον, and Greg., vol. II, 854, ll. 8–9. The latest and best work on this is R. Guilland, "Les ports de Byzance sur la Propontide," Byzantion, XXIII (1953) 196ff.; 227ff.

[57] See Pach., 365–366, who reports in an obscure passage, that Michael inserted liquid silver (quicksilver?) into the area: ἄργυρον ὑγρὸν χυτὸν ἐμβαλόντα. See editor's note, in Pach., 660. Also cf. Guilland, "Les ports de Byzance," 228.

[58] See Ville-hardouin, 88. Niketas Choniates, Historia (Bonn, 1835) 268, ll. 19–23, relates that in the 12th century Manuel I, in order to close the Bosporus from the south, planned to suspend another chain across the straits, to extend from Chrysopolis (Asia) to the Monastery of Mangana (Europe). There is no evidence,

IMPERIAL POLICY TOWARD THE LATIN
POPULATION OF CONSTANTINOPLE

Another task facing the Emperor was the formulation of policy toward the Latins who had remained and those who would inevitably come to the city for purposes of trade. Here the Emperor was confronted by a dilemma. It was clear that Constantinople, grand entrepôt that it was, could not truly flourish without the presence of Latin merchants. They were more enterprising than the Greeks, who were more rooted in antiquated methods of business; and all too frequently the Latins had at their disposal larger amounts of liquid capital.[59] On the other hand, Palaeologus had good reason to be wary of their superior commercial talents. As in the past, Westerners could readily provide severe competition for his own people,[60] and, even worse, Latin inhabitants might at a favorable opportunity be tempted to betray the capital in much the same manner the Greeks had recently done. There was also, of course, the sentiment of the Greek population itself to consider. Years of occupation had sharpened their antipathy toward the Latins,[61] who, in the words of Pachymeres, "had in their stupidity become puffed up with vain conceit and contempt for the Greeks." [62] Factors which probably somewhat mitigated the an-

---

however, that the scheme was ever carried out. Perhaps the engineering problems were too difficult. If it were possible to achieve, it seems probable that Michael would have executed the plan, as in his time the danger of attack by sea was extreme. Cf. R. Guilland's recent "La chaîne de la Corne d'Or," Ἐπ. Ἑτ. Βυζ. Σπουδῶν, XV (1955) 102.

[59] See G. Ostrogorsky, "Agrarian conditions in the Byzantine Empire in the Middle Ages," *Cambridge Economic History*, I (1941) 204; S. Runciman, "Byzantine Trade and Industry," *ibid.*, II, 117, 97. Constantinople had contained a large, principally merchant, population of Latins for several centuries. Cf. the well known statement of William of Tyre that in his day (last half of the twelfth century) there were 20,000 Venetians in Constantinople, and that of his near-contemporary, Eustathius of Thessalonica, that in his time the city had 60,000 Latins. See Manfroni, "Relazioni," 624.

[60] See Lopez, *Colonie*, 207.

[61] Pach., 163, l. 9, says that now the Greeks particularly reviled the Genoese. Cf. *Typikon for St. Michael*, 790, on the haughtiness of the Latin masters of Constantinople: τοὺς τῆς Κωνσταντίνου κατατυραννοῦντας ὑψαύχενας Λατίνους. See also Gregory of Cyprus, *Laudatio Michaelis Palaeologi*, Migne, *PG*, vol. 142, col. 377.

[62] Pach., 161, l. 19.

tagonism of the two races, however, were the influx of new inhabitants into the city, the departure of many Venetians, hitherto the most hated of the Westerners,[63] and the intermarriage of Latins and Greeks, of which Gasmuloi were the offspring. For Michael to alienate the Gasmuloi who manned his ships by exiling their fathers or other Latin relatives would be to strike a blow at subjects whose loyalty might otherwise be encouraged. What, furthermore, would be the criterion for determining the degree of consanguinity constituting Latinity? The whole problem was a thorny one.

A solution of ejecting all the remaining Latins and henceforth permitting no others to enter the city would probably not even have met the approval of all Greeks. For despite the development of a more intense patriotism, anti-Latin sentiment, once Constantinople was recovered, does not seem to have reached excessive lengths. We hear, for example, no report of a massacre or mass transfer of the Latin population. There is, it is true, a reference to the imprisonment of a Latin cleric of Hagia Sophia,[64] but this seems to have been an isolated case and was in all likelihood the result of personal transgression against the Orthodox religion, to which the Greeks were extremely sensitive. Somewhat surprising at first glance is the fact that the populace apparently indulged in no reprisals against Greek collaborators, even the most flagrant. Michael seems, in fact, to have adopted a lenient, almost benevolent attitude toward collaborators, making use of them for his own purposes. Thus he retained in his service two undersecretaries of Baldwin, Nikephoritzes and Alubardes, both of whom, soon after the reconquest, he sent on an embassy to the papacy.[65]

---

[63] *Ann. Ian.*, IV, 42 (which of course may exaggerate) says, regarding the Nymphaeum negotiations, that Palaeologus "Venetos intimo cordis exosos habebat." Heyd, *Histoire*, I, 431, note 1, says that the Venetian officials and great merchants had fled and that only their petty merchants and laborers remained.

[64] *Les registres d'Urbain IV*, ed. J. Guiraud, (Paris, 1904) III, 230, no. 1564, on the cleric Rainaldo, who, after Constantinople's recovery, was held by the Greeks in prison for a time.

[65] Pach., 168, ll. 15–18. Nikephoritzes is presumably a diminutive form, and Alubardes is probably Italian, perhaps from "Lombard" with the addition of a

The policy adopted by Michael toward the Latin population may be described as generous but nonetheless realistic. In general he permitted all who had stayed behind — particularly Genoese, Pisans, and the now relatively few Venetians — to reside in the capital and even to take possession of their old quarters on the Golden Horn.[66] With these three peoples the Emperor sought to secure an understanding on the grounds that their example "would quiet the others even if the latter did not wish to remain tranquil." (Pachymeres notes that he spent a whole day negotiating with the three groups, skillfully drawing them away from their compatriots "by a liberal application of favors and promises.")[67] Other Latins, of considerably lesser number in Constantinople at this time,[68] very likely included Amalfitans (among the first Westerners to carry on an extensive trade in Byzantium),[69] Anconitans,[70] Catalans,[71] and possibly even a few Provençals and Germans.[72]

The specific provisions of Michael's settlement with the Constantinopolitan Latins, according to Pachymeres, were as follows: (1) Each Latin people would be permitted to live undisturbed in a strictly defined area of the city. (2) Each Latin colony would be subject to its own laws and customs under an officer dispatched

---

prosthetic "a." Though Alubardes is called Greek, he may have been a Gasmule. Cf. Dölger, Regesten, no. 1899, and below, Chapter 7, note 7.

[66] Pach., 162–163; Greg., 97, ll. 10ff.

[67] See Pach., 162: ἂν αὐτῶν ὑποποιηθέντων . . . τοὺς ἄλλους καὶ μὴ θέλοντας ἠρεμεῖν — and also: τὰς ὁρμὰς σφίσι σοφῶς ταῖς χάρισιν ὑπετέμνετο.

[68] A fact evident from Pachymeres' statement, 162, ll. 7–10, that Michael's consultations with the leaders of the Italian peoples (τοῖς δοκοῦσι τῶν 'Ιταλικῶν γενῶν) — i.e., Genoese, Venetians, and Pisans — "would influence the others, willy-nilly, to remain quiet." On the Latins of Constantinople see also R. Janin, "Les sanctuaires des colonies latines à Constantinople," Revue des études byzantines, IV (1946) 163ff., who discusses the Latin churches in the capital in this period.

[69] Ibid., 166; Heyd, Histoire, I, 100ff. and 475.

[70] Their colony had probably first been established under Manuel I Comnenos. See Janin, op. cit., 176.

[71] C. Marinesco, "Notes sur les Catalans dans l'Empire Byzantin," Mélanges F. Lot (Paris, 1925) 502. Marinesco believes that Catalan merchants frequented Constantinople from at least 1261. For an interesting document concerning a man from Perpignan (southern France) in Michael's service, see below, Chapter 9, note 83.

[72] Janin, "Les sanctuaires des colonies latines," 175–176.

by the home city,[73] the chief Genoese official being termed podestà, the Pisan, consul, and the Venetian, *bailli*.[74] (3) Genoese and even Venetian merchants were to pay no duties and would be permitted to continue their commercial activities in accordance with their former practices.[75]

With respect to the Venetians in particular, it appears that Michael, while shutting his eyes to the presence of petty merchants and laborers, forbade the influx of the greater Venetian merchants and officials.[76] Moreover, though the treaty of Nymphaeum expressly stipulated the exclusion of all Genoese enemies from Greek harbors and markets,[77] Michael does not seem to have strictly implemented this provision in the case of Venice. The Pisans, specifically exempted from the restriction by the same pact,[78] undoubtedly had little trouble coming to the city. But the most numerous of the Latin newcomers were the Genoese, who at once flocked in great numbers to the Bosporus in order to take advantage of the very liberal provisions of the Nymphaeum treaty.[79]

Ostensibly seeking good relations with all the Latins, Michael nevertheless did not cease to distrust them. By taking pains to reach a separate accord with each people and by establishing contacts with the home governments (we are told that he sent gifts to various officials in Italy) he hoped to prevent a union of

---

[73] Pach., 162: αἱ δ᾽ ἦσαν ἐν καλῷ τε τῆς πόλεως κατοικεῖν ἀνέδην, τόσον τοῦ τόπου λαβόντας. Also see Heyd, *Histoire*, 430, note 3, and Pach., 162, ll. 18–19.

[74] Greg., 97, ll. 22–24, and Pach., 163, ll. 1–5. Before 1261 the Venetian governor had been called podestà (e.g., Gradenigo; see Chapter 5, text and notes 22ff.). Certainly by 1265 at the latest, the Venetian official, by (Greco-Venetian) treaty and evidently at the insistence of Michael, was renamed *bailli* (see T.-Th. III, 83). We have an important example in 1264 of the Genoese, Guercio, being called podestà (see below, Chapter 8, text and notes 31–41). In the Greek text *bailli* is written παϊοῦλος; consul, ἐπίτροπος; and podestà, ἐξουσιαστής (see Pach. 163).

[75] Pach., 162, l. 19, and 163, ll. 1–2.

[76] Heyd, *Histoire*, I, 431, note 1. Cf. *Ann. Ian.*, IV, 47.

[77] See Manfroni, "Relazioni," 794.

[78] In the treaty the Pisans were called "fideles nostri imperii" by Michael. See Chapter 4, note 60 for the probable existence of a Greco-Pisan alliance at this time.

[79] See note 82.

all, and in particular the formation of an anti-Byzantine alliance with Baldwin.[80]

It may be argued in retrospect that Palaeologus' conciliatory attitude toward the Latins, especially the Venetians, was in certain respects fraught with grave danger. To grant to recent enemies, indeed forces of occupation, not only the privilege of residing within the city under their own governor and laws but also exemption from imperial taxation, was no doubt a tremendous concession.[81] Yet it seems probable that, in the Emperor's view, with the maintenance of vigilant control and with careful separation of the Latin peoples, he would in the end see his liberality rewarded. Constantinople needed the trade of the Latins, who, at this difficult time in Greek affairs, could also be used as contacts with, or sources of information on, Byzantium's Western enemies. Moreover, it is very probable that in granting concessions even to the Venetians (and to a lesser extent the Pisans), Michael envisaged their use as a counterpoise to the Genoese, toward whom his mistrust increased as their influence rapidly began to grow to major proportions.[82]

Michael's work of reconstruction, though in many respects rapid and fruitful, did not succeed in restoring Constantinople to its former appearance. The ravages of two terrible fires and Latin neglect were obstacles too great for even so energetic a ruler to overcome in a brief period. A few years later Gregoras, commenting on Michael's difficulty in resisting attack from the West, could still affirm, however rhetorically: "Constantinople in many places was yet in ruins, barely rebuilt and, so to say, restored to life from death only a short time before." Elsewhere the same historian notes "the weakened condition of the city,

---

[80] Pach., 163, l. 10 (τὸ δ' οὖν διαιρεῖν τὰ γένη) and ll. 11–13.

[81] Note that there was a certain precedent for this in the concessions granted to individual Latin peoples already in the twelfth century.

[82] Pach., 163, l. 9 and l. 6: πλὴν τοῖς μὲν Γεννουίταις οὐκ εἶχε πιστεύειν ἐντὸς περικεκλεισμένοις τοῦ ἄστεος, πολλοῖς γε οὖσι. The otherwise excellent survey of Manfroni, "Relazioni," 667ff., makes no mention whatever of these dispositions of Palaeologus immediately after the city's recovery. Nor has any other work discussed them with any thoroughness.

135

torn in many places and broken and in need of much time to be rebuilt."[83]

The repair and construction of churches, public buildings, palaces, sea walls, a navy, and, not least, the distribution of largesses to the Tzakones and even to Latins (especially churchmen) in far-off Italy required the expenditure of enormous sums.[84] The treasury amassed so diligently by Vatatzes and Theodore II Lascaris, lavishly spent by Michael after his usurpation at Nicaea and now further depleted by financial excesses, was not sufficient for all needs.[85] In order to increase his revenues, therefore, Palaeologus took advantage of the favorable Greek sentiment toward his regime to order a systematic recoinage of gold currency, which resulted in a depreciation of the Byzantine *hyperpyron*.[86] Some pieces in particular were struck which *in verso* represented the Virgin protecting the walls of the reconquered capital.[87]

Although Constantinople was, to quote Gregoras once again, "little more than a shadow of its former self," [88] it was in the eyes of its people still their incomparable capital. Something of this Greek feeling is expressed in an encomium by the contemporary Gregory of Cyprus, containing an apostrophe addressed by the city itself to Palaeologus:

---

[83] Greg., 126, ll. 21–23; also 123, ll. 18–20.

[84] Pach., 190: ἀπέστελλε δὲ καὶ πρὸς τοὺς ἐπιδόξους τῆς Ἰταλίας καὶ μᾶλλον τοὺς τῆς ἐκκλησίας, φίλους ἐκείνους καὶ μακρόθεν κτώμενος. Cf. Pach., vol. II, 494, ll. 3–4.

[85] According to Pach., 188, ll. 20ff., Michael was forced by necessity to be so liberal; otherwise he could not have retained the power he had usurped. On the status of the treasury under Vatatzes and Theodore see Chapter 2, text and notes 57–59.

[86] The gold content of the *hyperpyron* in Michael's reign was 15 carats, ⅝ of its nominal value, according to Ostrogorsky, *Byzantine State*, 38 and 430. On Michael's policy see esp. Pach., vol. II, 494; and cf. G. Bratianu, "L'hyperpère byzantin et la monnaie d'or des républiques italiennes," *Mélanges C. Diehl*, I (Paris, 1930) 43; also cf. F. Dölger, *Byz. Zeit.*, XLIX (1956) 429. It should be noted, however, that an inflationary policy had already been instituted at Nicaea by Vatatzes. See Pach., II, 493–494. Also D. Zakythinos, "Crise monétaire et crise économique à Byzance du XIIIᵉ au XVᵉ siècle," *L'Hellénisme contemporain*, I (1947) 8ff.

[87] On other coins issued by Palaeologus depicting himself holding young John Lascaris in his arms, see Sanudo, *Istoria*, 114: "li Liperi [*hyperpyra*] d'oro se batte vano con la sua effige con il Puttino in brazzo." Also cf. T. Bertelè, *L'imperator alato nella numismatica bizantina* (Rome, 1951) 47–51.

[88] Greg., 126, ll. 19ff.

136

Because of you I am once again a city, since I have taken on a more joyous appearance than that which I lost, and have had restored to my head the crown which time and the hands of the evil-doers had hurled to earth.[89]

And Michael himself could write exultantly about the restoration and disdainfully of the Latins:

Then Constantinople, the Megalopolis, the Queen City, . . . the new Jerusalem, could be seen, glorious and proud as of old . . . no longer hearing the confused tongue of a half-barbarian people, but that of the Greek population, now spoken correctly by all.[90]

[89] *Laudatio*, Migne, *PG*, vol. 142, col. 377.
[90] *Typikon for St. Michael*, 771.

7

PALAEOLOGAN DIPLOMACY

(1261–1263)

CHARACTERISTICS OF PALAEOLOGAN DIPLOMACY

While Michael's entrance into Constantinople served to legitimize his reign for the mass of Greek subjects, it resulted at the same time in intensifying the enmity of the West, whose objective it now became to restore the Latin Empire. Michael's weapon against Western designs [1] — except for military campaigns, to which he generally had recourse only when all else failed — was diplomacy. Indeed the finesse of his statecraft, though verging frequently on sheer intrigue, is remarkable even in the annals of Byzantine history. Hence, a word about his aims and methods may be useful.

Michael's fundamental objectives were, first and foremost, preservation of his throne and newly conquered capital, and, second, restoration of the Byzantine boundaries as they existed before 1204.[2] From these goals his diplomacy never deviated. But however firm his basic aims, the execution of policy imple-

---

[1] For a brief summary of Latin diplomacy from 1261–1282, see E. Dade, *Versuche zur Wiedererrichtung der lateinischen Herrschaft in Konstantinopel im Rahmen der abendländischen Politik* (Jena, 1938). Cf. Norden, 387ff., which focuses, however, on Greco-papal relations.

[2] See Pach., 206, l. 18, and 207, ll. 12–13: "[The Emperor] was not content with ruling part of the island [the Peloponnese] but wanted all of it." Cf. Canale, 488, the speech of a Genoese admiral to Palaeologus, which undoubtedly reflects the imperial attitude: "or est venus li terme que vos poes estre sire de Romanie et de tot l'enpire."

menting them had to be highly flexible, conditioned by the capabilities of numerous opponents and a constantly shifting political scene. Characteristic of his technique, in particular, was a keen sensitivity to change in the realities of each situation, every new pressure from the Latin side being met by a corresponding counterpoise. Thus his policy may in brief be described as a perpetual effort to maintain a favorable balance of power against a diversity of enemies.

To keep abreast of Western developments Michael had at his disposal an efficient intelligence service. Whether this was formally organized into an office of state cannot be affirmed with certainty. But it is clear that a vital role in securing and disseminating information was played by Latin agents, residents of Constantinople (especially Galata) or of the West itself, who not infrequently served in the capacity of trusted imperial envoys.[3]

As Michael for the most part had only Genoa as a Western ally, it would seem that a combination of Latin states with powerful fleets and armies at its command could have seized Constantinople with not too great difficulty. Michael, however, knew how to extract every advantage from the rivalries of the Latins and thereby to prevent the achievement of that preponderance of power which could have numbered the days of his Empire. It is to his relations with the more important of the Western states — the papacy and Sicily, Venice and Genoa — and his attempts to manipulate their differences that we must now direct our attention.

POPE URBAN IV, KING MANFRED OF SICILY, AND THE EMPEROR MICHAEL

When Pope Urban IV heard of Constantinople's capture [4] he

---

[3] E.g., see *Ann. Ian.*, IV, 45, where the Genoese are informed of Constantinople's fall by a Florentine dispatched by Palaeologus; L. Belgrano, "Cinque documenti genovesi-orientali," *Atti soc. lig. st. pat.*, XVII (1885) 227, the Emperor sends as envoys to Genoa what probably are a Latin and Greek respectively, Obertus Doceanus and John Rominos; and Canale, 496, the Venetian Henry Trevisano is sent by Palaeologus as ambassador to his homeland.

[4] The city fell during a papal interregnum, Urban being proclaimed Pope on 29

was, to quote the sources, "stupefied" by the news.[5] His immediate concern was preservation of the remaining Latin possessions in Achaia, Negropont, and the Greek islands.[6] At the same time he also began to consider means of detaching Genoese support from Palaeologus.

With the fall of Constantinople, the papacy suffered not only a loss of political prestige but severe damage to its spiritual authority as well. For the Greeks had now effectively reasserted their right to a church divorced from Rome. Thus it became the task of each of the six successive popes of Michael's reign to accomplish the return of the schismatics to the Roman fold. Nevertheless Urban IV, well aware that the union imposed by the crusade of 1204 had proved a complete failure, was receptive to any convincing suggestion of peaceful reconciliation emanating from the Emperor.

On his part Michael, realizing that any influence on papal policy, whether achieved through spiritual or political means, would enable him to exert pressure on Western politics, took care to maintain cordial relations with the Curia. As he had done after his usurpation at Nicaea, now again after the capture of Constantinople he at once dispatched an embassy to the Holy See. The ambassadors were Greeks, Nikephoritzes and Alubardes, former sub-secretaries of the Latin Emperor Baldwin. The envoys carried gifts with which to propitiate the expected papal wrath. But their reception was far worse than they anticipated. Upon their arrival in Italy they were seized by Italians angered over the loss of Constantinople. Nikephoritzes, if we may believe

---

August 1261. See Chapter 1, note 5, for the probably spurious letter of Palaeologus congratulating Urban on his enthronement and mentioning that his own ancestors had come from Italy many centuries before.

[5] See Raynaldus, a. 1262, § 40, Urban's letter to St. Louis of 5 June 1261: "stupidos sensimus sensus nostros." Cf. J. Guiraud, *Les registres d'Urbain IV* (Paris, 1901–1904) II, 75, no. 187. According to Dandolo, XII (1941) 311, Urban (who heard the news from Venetian envoys) was "merore stupefactus."

[6] See "La Complainte de Constantinople," *Onze poèmes de Rutebeuf*, ed. Basti and Faral (Paris, 1946) 36, where the French troubador Rutebeuf probably reflects Western fears in prophesying that with Constantinople's fall the Morea too would soon be lost.

Pachymeres, was flayed alive, while Alubardes succeeded in making his escape.[7]

Corroboration of Michael's dispatch of an embassy of good will to the papacy is provided by a passage in a letter contained in the Registers of Urban IV. Addressed to Palaeologus and dated 18 July 1263, the message mentions certain epistles transmitted by Michael to the Pope immediately after Constantinople's fall.[8] Referring also to a subsequent embassy of Michael's to the papacy, it enumerates among the imperial envoys one "Maximus Alufardus" (sic), who is probably to be identified with the escaped companion of Nikephoritzes.[9] There is no evidence to indicate that Michael at this time broached to Urban the subject of religious union. No doubt it was too soon after the fall of the Latin Empire for the pope to be influenced by Greeks bearing gifts! And Michael perhaps reasoned that for the present a policy of waiting and a mild courting of the Pope, along with gifts of gold to the Curia, would suffice.[10]

During the first year of his pontificate Urban took many steps to secure Western aid for Baldwin. The latter, whose career as titular Emperor was, till his death in 1273, to be occupied by long and unsuccessful peregrinations throughout the West to obtain aid for his lost Empire, finally came to the papal court. Already after his flight from Constantinople he had briefly visited Negropont, Monemvasia, Athens, Bari, and Venice, the last named of which now sent its ambassadors to accompany Baldwin to the Curia.[11] Their combined pleas at length influenced Urban, who

[7] For this incident see Pach., 168–169. Cf. Dölger, Regesten, no. 1899, who says the embassy did not reach its goal. But S. Borsari, "La politica bizantina di Carlo d'Angiò dal 1266 al 1271," Arch. st. prov. nap., n.s. XXXV (1956) 324, says Urban received the embassy. Cf. also M. Roncaglia, Les frères mineurs et l'église grecque (1231–1274) (Cairo, 1954) 121ff., esp. 122, note 3, who says the circumstances in question are impossible to prove.

[8] Guiraud, Reg. Urbain, II, no. 295, 135: "statim capta Constantinopolitana urbe, alias nobis epistolares litteras miseris" (A. Tautu, Acta Urbani IV, etc. [Vatican, 1953] no. 6, 15).

[9] Cf. Dölger, Regesten, nos. 1899 and 1911.

[10] See Pach., 190, ll. 13–15 (quoted above, Chapter 6, note 84). Cf. Norden, 392.

[11] On these visits see Canale, 502; Sanudo, Fragmentum, 172–173; Dandolo, 311; Capasso, op. cit., 233–234; Corpus chronicorum Bononensium, ed. A. Sorbelli,

instituted a series of measures to aid them. Besides commanding the preaching of a crusade for Constantinople's recovery in France, Poland, and Aragon,[12] Urban wrote to Louis IX of France for support, insisting to the pious king that if the Greeks seized all of Romania, the way to Jerusalem would be barred. Furthermore, he decreed a three-year tax on all members of the clergy not already resident in their lands for at least six months. For this purpose he dispatched collectors to France, Castile, and England.[13] The taxes of the French clergy in particular were permitted to be distributed to nobles who would promise to undertake the crusade, and the Latin bishops of Greece were authorized to provide ecclesiastical revenues for the defense of Romania.[14] Lastly, at the insistence of Venice (who guaranteed free passage for the crusaders),[15] Urban struck directly at Michael by ordering the Archbishop of Genoa to demand from the Commune, under pain of excommunication and interdiction, the withdrawal within one month of naval aid to the Greek Emperor.[16]

Despite these vigorous measures, papal efforts to aid Baldwin remained largely ineffectual. Actually the mood of the West at this time was unfavorable for an expedition against Byzantium. King Louis IX of France (who, it may be recalled, had not especially aided the Latin Empire even during its ephemeral existence) would make no binding promises despite personal sympathy for Baldwin. He was still not disposed to fight a Christian Emperor, not even a schismatic, and believed that all military efforts should be directed against the Muslims of the Holy Land.[17] Germany, on her part, was undergoing an interregnum;[18] Eng-

---

in *RISS* (1913) II, 1, p. 159; and K. Hopf, *Griechenland*, 261.

[12] Guiraud, *Reg. Urbain*, II, no. 131. Cf. Norden, 403.

[13] Guiraud, II, nos. 131, 133–135, 231, pp. 46–49, 103.

[14] *Ibid.*, nos. 131–137, 46–49. Norden, 403.

[15] Canale, 502; Guiraud, *Reg. Urbain*, II, no. 131, 47B, and Raynaldus, a. 1262, § 37–43. Cf. Norden, 404.

[16] Guiraud, *op. cit.*, no. 182, 72–73; nos. 228–230, 98–102; nos. 719–721, 341–343 (Tautu, *Acta*, no. 3, 3 etc.). Cf. *Ann. Ian.*, IV, 44. Pachymeres does not specifically mention these papal efforts to aid Baldwin.

[17] Chapman, 52, R. Sternfeld, *Ludwigs des Heiligen Kreuzzug nach Tunis 1270* (Berlin, 1896) 308. Cf. Dade, 11.

[18] Following the death of Frederick II in 1250.

land was too distant; and the ambitions of Aragon seemed to extend only to Sicily. More important, the crusading zeal of the twelfth century seems generally to have diminished. Even the Catholic clergy of the Western lands displayed no more enthusiasm than laymen in contributing to the success of the undertaking, as is evidenced by the frequent dispatch of papal directives prodding them for delays in the raising of revenues.[19]

But the principal deterrent to a Constantinopolitan crusade was the preoccupation of the papacy itself with its struggle against the Hohenstaufen Manfred of Sicily. At bottom this conflict was the real determinant of all important papal policy,[20] and it did not fail vitally to affect papal relations with Palaeologus. A papal conflict with Michael without the aid of Manfred might well lead to no decisive result, since the naval power of Venice would be offset by that of Genoa. It must have been evident, therefore, that the addition of Manfred's strength to that of the papacy and Venice would almost guarantee victory over Byzantium and Genoa. But Urban, inheriting the animus of Innocent IV toward the Hohenstaufen, did not wish under any circumstances to owe to that dynasty the return of Roman Catholicism to Constantinople. Furthermore, the development of a situation which might leave the Greek ruler defenseless before Manfred and his allies could be even more dangerous for the papacy, since Manfred himself, as we have seen, had ambitions with respect to Byzantium.[21] This was the dilemma confronting the papacy.

The advantages of Hohenstaufen aid to the Holy See were certainly apparent to Manfred, who thought that in exchange for aid he could achieve his primary aim, papal recognition of his Sicilian crown. Accordingly Manfred, together with Baldwin (who was, of course, no less eager to recover his own throne), exerted every effort to bring about a rapprochement between the papacy and Sicily. But though Baldwin went personally to the

[19] E.g., see Guiraud, *Reg. Urbain*, II, no. 187, 74–76, letter of 25 January 1263 to the French Archbishop of Berry, complaining that he is late with his subsidy and does not lament Constantinople's fall.

[20] Norden, 431.

[21] See Chapter 3, text and notes 22–30.

Curia for the purpose of mediation, Urban refused even to consider the proposition.[22] Baldwin then wrote a letter (2 July 1263) to Manfred, strongly urging an appeal to the influential King Louis IX of France.[23] Baldwin's dispatch, however, was intercepted and handed over to Urban, who became so incensed at this evidence of intrigue on Manfred's behalf that in a subsequent letter to Louis he referred sharply to Baldwin as *fautor Manfredi*, the most execrable epithet possible for the Curia to employ at the time.[24] With the failure of this attempt at mediation, Baldwin, and the cause of the Latin Empire, fell — temporarily — from papal grace.

The possibility of a papal-Hohenstaufen alliance of course greatly affected Michael Palaeologus. Since before the battle of Pelagonia he had tried unsuccessfully to counter the Sicilian drive to the East by seeking an accord with Manfred. Now, however, in the belief that the similarity of their present positions in papal eyes might serve to draw them together, Michael adopted new tactics. Manfred's sister, Anna, widow of the Greek Emperor John III Vatatzes,[25] was living at the Greek court in semi-captivity. In the hope no doubt that a marriage with the attractive young Anna would be the prelude to a political alliance with Manfred, Michael, in the summer of 1262, offered to divorce his wife Theodora and marry Anna. Pachymeres would have us believe that

---

[22] The only important source for negotiations between Manfred and the papacy seems to be Canale, 498ff. Cf. Sanudo, *Fragmentum*, 172. Also see Dade, 8, and esp. R. L. Wolff, "Mortgage and Redemption of an Emperor's Son: Castile and the Latin Empire of Constantinople," *Speculum*, XXIX (1954) 65–68.

[23] E. Martène and U. Durand, *Thesaurus novus anecdotorum*, II (Paris, 1717) col. 25B.

[24] See *ibid.*, col. 354f., no. 312, another letter of Pope Clement IV (dated May or June 1266) to Baldwin referring to Baldwin's relations with Manfred as "cum hoste pestifero." On all this cf. J. Haller's (overly severe) criticism of Norden in *Hist. Zeit.*, XCIX (1907) 12–13; and Wolff, "Mortgage and Redemption," 67.

[25] Pach., 181, ll. 9ff. On Anna (called Constance by the Latins) see C. Marinesco, "Du nouveau sur Constance de Hohenstaufen," *Byzantion*, I (1924) 451ff.; G. Schlumberger, "Le tombeau d'une impératrice byzantine à Valence en Espagne," *Byzance et croisades* (Paris, 1927) 57ff.; J. Miret y Sans, "La princesa Griega Lascaris," *Revue hispanique*, X (1903) 455ff.; and, by the same author, "Tres princesas griegas," *ibid.*, XV (1906) 668ff.; and "Nuevos documentos de la tres princesas Griegas," *ibid.*, XIX (1908) 112ff. Also C. Diehl, *Figures byzantine.* (Paris, 1908) II, 207ff.

Michael's proposal was motivated by "burning love and especially the fact that he had been spurned by Anna." [26] But this seems to be an exaggeration, for no such sentiment is even vaguely suggested by Gregoras. Nor indeed do the sources elsewhere provide evidence of romantic inclinations on the part of Michael.[27]

What militates most strongly against Pachymeres' statement, however, is the question why Michael, merely for love of Anna, would be willing to risk almost certain excommunication by the Patriarch Arsenios without the gaining of an important political benefit. (Arsenios, it is to be noted, was already deeply incensed over Michael's brutal treatment of his young ward, John IV Lascaris, whom Michael, soon after entering Constantinople, had caused to be blinded.)[27a] Such a benefit in this case could be only an alliance with Manfred.[28] But this was not to be realized. For in the face of Anna's refusal to marry him, the anger of his own wife Theodora, and the threat of ecclesiastical censure by Arsenios,[29] Michael dropped the proposal. Instead he sent Anna back to her brother with a magnificent equipage, presumably in the belief that Manfred's ill-will might thereby be lessened. In exchange for Anna, Michael secured the release of the Caesar Alexios Strategopoulos, who had been captured by the Despot Michael of Epirus and handed over to Manfred at the latter's request.[30]

Failure to secure a Sicilian alliance did not frustrate Palaeologus. Instead the Emperor agilely turned to Manfred's opponent,

[26] Pach., 183: ἔπειθε γὰρ ὁ ἐκκαίων ἔρως, καὶ μᾶλλον παρὰ τῆς δεσποίνης Ἄννης περιφρονούμενος.

[27] It is true that Michael had two illegitimate daughters, but aside from a bare statement to this effect no account provides any information on extra-marital affairs. In view of the violent opposition to him after the Council of Lyons, such irregularities might well have been mentioned.

[27a] On 25 December 1261. See Pach., 191–192; Greg., 93.

[28] Further support for our theory is the remark in Pach., 183, ll. 3ff., regarding the grave danger then threatening Constantinople from all sides "and especially from the relatives of Anna" (κύκλῳ γοῦν τῶν ἐχθρῶν παρακινουμένων . . . ἰδίως δὲ δεδιέναι καὶ τοὺς τῆς βασιλίδος Ἄννης οἰκείους). It is notable also that even Arsenios was surprised at Michael's proposal, "having believed him incapable of such conduct" (αὐτὸς τοιοῦτος μὴ νομιζόμενος πρότερον) (Pach., 184).

[29] Pach., 184.

[30] Pach., 185, ll. 1–5. Cf. Greg., 91, ll. 22ff., and 92, ll. 1–11.

145

the papacy. It is probably to the period immediately following the affair with Anna that another embassy from Michael to the Curia should be assigned. Imperial ambassadors, arriving in the summer of 1262, bore a skillfully worded letter, the theme of which was Christian charity.[31] Speaking of the love which should inspire all Christians, both Greek and Latin, Michael inquired why the Pope sought to hinder an accord between Greeks and Genoese by excommunication of the latter. In his epistle the Emperor skirted the problem of union and carefully avoided definite mention of dogma and rites, declaring that such questions could easily be settled once secular peace was established.[32] He closed, significantly, with a cryptic reference to the papal conflict with Manfred, affirming that if the Greek Emperor returned to church unity, no prince would dare to defy the Pope.

Urban, who saw in the letter at once the possibility of a return of Constantinople to Catholicism and a potential counterweight against Manfred, was very pleased. Particularly gratifying was Michael's indication that all cases of dispute between himself and the Latins should be submitted to papal judgment.[33] Urban's approval, nonetheless, was not unmixed with distrust, as he realized that Michael had not in the meantime ceased his aggressions in Latin Greece.[34]

Following up Michael's bid, the Pope in the summer of 1262 [35] dispatched a reply, addressing him as "Michael Palaeologus, Illustrious Emperor of the Greeks." [36] This was in sharp contrast

---

[31] The letter is summarized in Urban's reply of 18 July 1263. See Guiraud, *Reg. Urbain*, II, no. 295, 135 (Tautu, *Acta*, no. 6, 14). Cf. Norden, 411.

[32] Guiraud, *Reg. Urbain*, no. 295, 135: "de dogmatibus fidei . . . et . . ritibus ecclesiasticis nullum."

[33] *Ibid.*, 140, esp.: "habere. . . Imperium cum Latinis, nullum alium judicem nisi solum Romanum pontificem."

[34] *Ibid.*, 136: "rumores . . . de persecutionibus. . .Villarduino . . . ejusqu terris et insulis ac Latinis morantibus in eisdem."

[35] Norden, 412 (also A. Potthast, *Regesta*, no. 18399), dates this letter July August of 1262 (quoted in L. Wadding, *Annales Minorum*, IV, 203-204; omitte from Guiraud). Chapman, 59, note 1, dating it 1263, evidently has confused with letter of 18 July 1263 (no. 295 of Guiraud).

[36] Wadding, *Ann. Min.*, IV, 203: "Paleologo imperatori Graecorum illustri The title of Emperor of Constantinople or Romania was reserved by the Pope fe Baldwin. On the date of this letter cf. Haller, *Hist. Zeit.*, XCIX (1907) 12.

to previous communications to Latin princes in which Michael had been characterized as "the usurper who calls himself Emperor of the Greeks."[37] Later, in an ably worded letter of 18 July 1263, Urban proceeded to express his happiness that Michael had anticipated him in requesting union. He revealed his readiness to render justice to Michael and his Empire, to send envoys to Constantinople as soon as possible, and even to recognize Michael as legitimate Emperor.[38] Expatiating on the advantages of religious unity, he emphasized matters of special concern to illegitimate rulers such as the effectiveness of papal mediation between Catholic monarchs and the protection that could be afforded minor heirs from the designs of their enemies. In like manner, he wrote pointedly, the church would defend the heirs of Michael.[39] One condition only Urban imposed, that Michael meanwhile "conduct himself in such a manner as to be praiseworthy in the sight of Divine Majesty and in the eyes of men."[40] This, of course, meant that Michael should abstain from attacking the Latins in Greece. Urban's offer to Michael was attractive, but the price — union and the abandonment of imperial aims on Latin Romania — was high.

VENICE, GENOA, AND MICHAEL PALAEOLOGUS

Of all the Western powers, Venice suffered most from the Greek restoration,[41] and it was her diplomacy therefore that served to bind together Latin projects to retake the capital.[42] Particularly humiliating was Michael's scrupulous implementation of the treaty of Nymphaeum.[43] Besides forfeiting to Genoa the

[37] "Qui Grecorum imperatorem vocari se facit." Guiraud, II, no. 131, 46.
[38] How this would affect Baldwin's claim to Constantinople is not explained.
[39] Guiraud, Reg. Urbain, II, no. 295, 138: "statim eadem ecclesia in medias . . . prosiliens . . . per auctoritatem . . . gerit regimen et tutelam; eorum hereditates et regna . . . in tua tuorumque heredum defensione."
[40] Wadding, IV, no. 182, 204.
[41] Except of course for Baldwin.
[42] For Greco-Venetian relations after 1261 the chief source is the chronicle of the Venetian Martino da Canale, who wrote in French, in the custom of the time.
[43] Canale, 480: "mout fu corocies Monsignor li Dus de cele aventure et de cele

147

monopoly of Constantinopolitan and Black Sea trade, Venice now also incurred the danger of losing to the Greco-Genoese alliance her possessions of Crete, Negropont, the Cyclades, Cyprus, and even Coron and Modon.[44]

Immediately after the fall of the Latin Empire, Venice began a feverish diplomatic activity. She set herself two tasks: to obtain Western aid and to split the Genoese from the Greeks by the threat of papal excommunication. As was to be expected, she formed an alliance with Baldwin,[45] whose past weakness she had reason to remember, but whose imperial title could still be of use to her.

Nor was Genoa in the meantime inactive.[46] According to the *Annales Ianuenses,* news of Constantinople's fall was received at Genoa only on 5 May 1262.[47] But this evidently refers to Genoa's first official notification of the event from Michael Palaeologus. For the same passage relates that the bearer of the news (a Florentine who arrived on a ship belonging to the Genoese Ansaldo d'Oria) had been sent by the Greek Emperor.[48] The envoy reported that the Emperor had transferred to the Genoese inhabitants of Constantinople the great palace formerly in Venetian possession. He further described (as the *Annales* note with obvious satisfaction) how the palace had immediately been torn down to the sound of musical instruments and how stones from

parte." Cf. Sanudo, *Fragmentum,* 173: "Dux et commune Venetiarum . . . doluerunt multum et vehementer habiti sunt."

[44] Manfroni, *Marina italiana,* I, 4.

[45] See *Ann. Ian.,* IV, 50, where the papal excommunication against Genoa is mentioned, launched "ad peticionem ambaxatorum Veneciarum et imperatoris Balduini." Note that the *Annales* call Baldwin "the former Emperor," an indication of a deliberate Genoese effort to avoid terminology recognizing the legitimacy of Latin sovereignty over Constantinople. Accordingly, Palaeologus is termed "illustrissimus imperator Grecorum" (*Ann. Ian.,* IV, 107, etc.).

[46] The chief source for Greco-Genoese relations is, of course, the *Annale Ianuenses,* anonymously written up to the year 1265, at which time they were continued by a commission named by the podestà. Genoese and Venetian state archives for the period are scanty, though many notarial documents still await reading.

[47] *Ann. Ian.,* IV, 45: "Die quinta madii . . . nova venerunt quod dictus imperator civitatem Constantinopolitanam a Venetis et Latinis abstulerat."

[48] *Ibid.,* IV, 45: "quedam navis Ansaldi Aurie in qua detullit quendam nuncium dicti imperatoris natione Florentinum."

the building were being transported to Genoa as symbols of the Venetian disgrace.[49]

Already in 1261 Urban ordered the Genoese to send envoys forthwith to the papal court at Viterbo to answer charges of allying with Michael "to the prejudice of Christianity and the Roman church." The envoys were dispatched, but their adamant adherence to Palaeologus drew down upon the Genoese papal excommunication and interdiction of their city.[50] An interesting commentary on the Western attitude of the time is the fact that not a single contemporary chronicler lamented the sentence imposed!

Meanwhile, surprisingly enough, from July of 1261 to the summer of 1262 neither Venice nor Genoa took any decisive action. Venice made no attempt on Constantinople, nor did Genoa make effective use of her initial advantage of surprise to attack Venetian possessions. At the news of Constantinople's fall, Venice, to be sure, had at once dispatched eighteen ships to the East under Marco Michele.[51] The relative inactivity of this fleet, however, requires some explanation. Possibly Venice had too much respect for Palaeologus' resourcefulness and believed that the Greek population, now swept by an outburst of patriotism, would fanatically resist attack. Or, more probably, Venice considered these ships too few [52] for an assault on Constantinople, since the Genoese fleet then in Byzantine waters seems to have consisted of at least forty-six vessels.[53] It is more than likely that Venice

---

[49] *Ibid.*, 45. The Venetian palace, which the Venetians had used as their headquarters, was actually the old Byzantine monastery of the Pantokrator, and was now handed over in accordance with the Nymphaeum treaty. Some of the stones taken to Genoa were later incorporated in the famous Bank of St. George. See *Il banco di San Giorgio* (Genoa, 1911) 294 and 328 (as cited in *Ann. Ian.*, IV, 45, note 2).

[50] *Ann. Ian.*, IV, 44.

[51] Canale, 480: "Dus envoia por garder Romanie. . . Mesire Marc Michel, et li dona 18 galies bien armees." Michael's instructions, according to Canale, were not to make an attempt on Constantinople, but only to defend Venetian possessions (also Dandolo, 311). Cf. Manfroni, *Marina italiana*, II, 444.

[52] See Dandolo, 311, who says that the Podestà Gradenigo, Emperor Baldwin, Giustiniani, and the fleet already in Constantinople, had sailed to Negropont after the city's fall.

[53] Canale, 480: "Et a celui tens meesmes, s'en ala 30 galies des Ienoes en Cous-

believed Urban's excommunication of Genoa would soon mobilize Christian Europe to her aid, while in the meantime she could gather her own strength. Unfortunately, the evidence is too meagre to permit definition of Venetian motivations with any degree of certainty.

As for Genoa, on the other hand, it would seem that by uniting her forces to those of the Greeks, she might have taken Venetian territory in the Levant. Yet there is no important encounter between Venice and Genoa in the East recorded for 1261. For this inactivity Genoa's internal condition was probably a basic cause. Interior ferment is, in fact, revealed by the expulsion, in May of 1261, of Guglielmo Boccanegra, Genoese Captain of the People, who had been responsible for the recent diplomatic triumph over Venice. In his place a coalition of disaffected Guelph and certain Ghibelline nobles, opposed to Boccanegra's dictatorial methods and frightened by papal fulminations, proceeded to re-establish the old government, headed by a podestà and council of nobles.[54] Even after Boccanegra's removal, however, relations with Palaeologus were not broken: the financial profits were too great, and apparently more than counterbalanced the disadvantages of excommunication. To recast a famous phrase, Constantinople was indeed worth more than a mass!

The new Genoese government in 1262 also replaced Guglielmo's brother, Marino Boccanegra, as commander of the fleet dispatched to Constantinople just prior to the fall of the city. The command was finally entrusted to six admirals, each the representative of a group of nobles.[55] This division of authority with

---

tantinople." These 30 were in addition to the 16 Genoese vessels sent East after signing of the Nymphaeum Treaty. See Chapter 4, text and note 53.

[54] Ann. Ian., IV, 45–47. Cf. Lopez, Colonie, 212.

[55] See Ann. Ian., IV, 47, note 4. The editor, Imperiale, cites an unpublished document dated 17 May 1262 referring to Marino's recall: "ordinaverunt dominum Ottonem Ventum presentem et recipientem armiratum et dominum tocius exercitus Ianuensis qui nunc est in partibus Romanie . . . in servitio sacri imperii Grecorum . . . et ipsum Marinum a dicta armiragia removent." See also Lopez, Colonie, 213, and C. Manfroni, "Sulla battaglia dei Sette Pozzi e le sue consequenze," Rivista marittima (Rome, 1900), 232, and note 3, in which Manfroni says that a marginal note of the Annales (perhaps a later revision) mentions Genoese galleys sent to the East. Whether this refers to new ones or those already dispatched is not clear.

the attendant rivalries that it provoked was, as we shall see, to prove disastrous.

Genoese inertia was particularly evident in the summer of 1262. At that time Venice ordered thirty-seven galleys under Giacopo Dolfin to Romania "to search for Genoese ships . . . which had gone to that area in large numbers at the expense of Messer Palaeologus, Signor of the Greeks." In the waters around Thessalonica Dolfin came upon a Greco-Genoese fleet of sixty vessels.[56] According to Canale's somewhat obscure description, the Genoese vessels were shielded by a barricade of four large ships — on which parapets had been constructed — and which, evidently, had been pulled into position by small boats. Although scholars are not in agreement on all aspects of the encounter,[57] the significant fact is that, protected by their barricade, the Genoese refused battle and no action took place.[58]

While the Veneto-Genoese war dragged on without important results, the Lombard nobles of Negropont, on 15–16 May 1262, joined in an alliance with their former enemy, Venice, against the common danger, Palaeologus.[59] The Negropontine lords fitted out three pirate vessels which proceeded to roam the Aegean and the Sea of Marmora and advanced boldly even to Constantinople. But there the corsairs encountered a Greco-Genoese fleet, and, after a sharp struggle, were forced to surrender.[60] This was not to be the last marauding venture of the island nobles against the Emperor.

[56] Canale, 480–482: "il estoient a Salonic LX galies mult bien armees de Ienoes et de Gres." Cf. Manfroni, *Marina italiana*, I, 6, note 2.

[57] Canale, 482: "IIII grans nes armees des Ienoies, que avoient faites les bertresches de sor les nes, et les liches en eive tres devant lor galies." See Manfroni, "Battaglia dei Sette Pozzi," 233, who believes that the Venetian fleet was larger than the allied. Manfroni claims that a scribe may have mistaken the figure of XL ships in Canale for LX. But note Dandolo, 311 (under the year 1261, however) who reports that 37 Venetian vessels encountered 60 Greco-Genoese ships off Thessalonica and that "Veneti nichil dampni inferre potuerunt." Unfortunately medieval accounts too often use figures very loosely.

[58] Canale, 482: "li Ienoes estoient ensi ceres de gros fust, que nul domaie ne lor poroient doner."

[59] See T.–Th., III, 46–55. Also for alliance of William and Venice see *Chronicon Marchiae Tarvisinae*, 48.

[60] Canale, 484.

The island of Negropont, strategically located off the coast of the Duchy of Athens-Thebes, possessed great value in the eyes of the Curia, as is attested by papal letters. More than once when Pope Urban wrote to Genoa ordering the recall of her ships from Romania he added, "especially those from Negropont." And he specifically admonished the Genoese against providing further transit to the island for Greek troops.[61]

That Genoa, however, continued to be active in Romanian waters is indicated by a letter received in 1263 from Palaeologus. In this message he requested the Genoese to spy on Venetian movements in order to provide him with information, and, in accordance with their pact, constantly to maintain the Genoese fleet in Romania on a parity with that of Venice. Reinforcements were to be dispatched only at such times as the Venetian fleet was increased.[62]

Although no major naval engagements had thus far taken place between the two great Italian rivals, isolated encounters between merchantmen and individual warships did, of course, occur. The Venetian historian Andrea Dandolo reports, for example, that in 1261 three Venetian galleys sailed from Negropont to the region near Constantinople, where their crews did much damage and killed many Greeks. When subsequently the ships were apprehended by a superior Genoese force, many of the Venetians were put to death, the rest being haled before Palaeologus, at whose order their eyes were plucked out.[63]

Dandolo's recital should be compared with two other accounts. The first, the *Annales Ianuenses*, relates that a Venetian merchant ship and three galleys, carrying Venetian merchants who were in the Black Sea area at the time of Constantinople's capture, were seized by a Greco-Genoese squadron. The Venetians aboard were handed over to the Emperor, who blinded and cut off the noses of all "except certain ones who were spared at the request of the Genoese"![64] A second passage, from the

[61] See Guiraud, *Reg. Urbain*, no. 228, 101A, dated 7 May 1263.
[62] Belgrano, "Cinque documenti, " 228–229.
[63] Dandolo, 311. Cf. Canale, 484.
[64] *Ann. Ian.*, IV, 48–49. Cf. Heyd, *Histoire*, II, 156.

chronicle of another Venetian, Martino da Canale, recounts that fifty captured Venetians (termed by the Genoese "robbers of the sea") were brought before Palaeologus, who blinded them with hot irons.[65] In spite of the bias probably pervading these three accounts (the last two of which may refer to the same incident), they are important for their clear indication of the bitterness existing between Venetians and Greeks in the years immediately following the Greek restoration.

The relative calm prevailing in the naval war between Venice and the allied powers was abruptly broken by the important battle of Settepozzi. Between May and July of 1263 [66] a Genoese fleet moving southward along the eastern Peloponnesian coast-line towards the Greek-held port of Monemvasia encountered, near the little island of Settepozzi (Spetsai), a Venetian fleet sailing north to Negropont.[67] The allied fleet of thirty-eight galleys and ten *saettie* (cutters), commanded by three Genoese and a Greek admiral,[68] opposed a numerically inferior Venetian fleet of thirty-two galleys under a single admiral, Guiberto Dandolo. According to the *Annales Ianuenses*, when the Genoese ships were ordered to attack, only fourteen obeyed, the others remaining inert then suddenly fleeing.[69] The account of the Venetian Canale seems to indicate, on the other hand, that it was the Venetian fleet which attacked first, while the Genoese were engaged in an attempt to ambush their opponents. In any event, a battle this time ensued in which many Genoese, including an admiral, were killed before the allied fleet could make its escape.[70]

---

[65] Canale, 486: "quant Palialog oi ce que Ienoes distrent que il estoient robeors de mer, si les fist gaster as fers chaus les siaus."

[66] On the date see Manfroni, "Battaglia dei Sette Pozzi," 237, the sole article to deal with this battle.

[67] *Ann. Ian.*, IV, 51: "navigarent ad Malvaxiam ex precepto imperatoris . . . ad insulam. . . Septem Puteos." On the location of the battle see also D. Zakythinos, *Le Despotat grec de Morée* (Paris, 1932) I, 32 and note 3, who says the battle took place in the gulf of Nauplia near the island of Hydra. Cf. Canale, 732, note 202.

[68] *Ann. Ian.*, IV, 51. Cf. Canale, 488 and 490, who reports 39. Also Lopez, *Colonie*, 213–214.

[69] *Ann. Ian.*, IV, 51.

[70] Canale, 490–492. He notes, exaggeratedly perhaps, that 1,000 Genoese were

The material loss to Genoa was not great, but her failure at Settepozzi, as we shall observe, gravely damaged her prestige in the eyes of Palaeologus. As for the cause of the defeat, the chief factor was without doubt the disunity resulting from a divided command. This in turn was contingent on the fact that the Genoese squadron was not eager to incur losses for its capitalist masters, who had a great financial stake involved. (For though according to the terms of Nymphaeum it was the Emperor's responsibility to provide wages for the ships' crews, Genoese citizens themselves had to bear the expense of the ships, their rigging, and arms.) And it was unfortunately these capitalists whose money was involved who controlled the naming of the admirals. Thus the defeat of the Genoese at Settepozzi may in the last analysis be attributed to the self-aggrandizement of the Genoese noble and capitalist class, which was in sharp contrast to the civic solidarity of the commercial aristocracy that governed Venice.[71]

THE WAR IN ACHAIA AND THE ARCHIPELAGO: THE BYZANTINE REVIVAL IN GREECE (1261–1263)

In accordance with Michael's intention of re-establishing the old Byzantine frontiers, he had also, during most of this period, been waging almost continuous war against Prince William in the Morea and the Despot Michael II in Epirus and northern Greece. It was, in fact, the capture of William at Pelagonia (1259) that became the means of restoring Greek rule in the Morea. In exchange for the cession of Achaia, Michael offered William his liberty and money with which to buy substitute territories in France. The Emperor's proposal at that time was peremptorily refused, and it was only after Michael's recovery of Constantinople and three years of captivity [72] that the weary Prince accepted a modified demand for the cession of the Moreot for-

killed or captured, compared to only 420 Venetian casualties, and that one of the admirals who fled was a Greek ("un des Amirail que s'en ala fuiant, fu gres").

[71] See C. Imperiale di Sant' Angelo, *Jacopo d'Oria e i suoi Annali* (Venice, 1930) 119–120, and Manfroni, "Battaglia dei Sette Pozzi," 240.

[72] French *Chron. Morea,* par. 326.

tresses of Monemvasia, Mistra, Maina, Geraki, and the district of Kinsterna.[73]

With the ratification of this settlement in 1262,[74] William was released. But before gaining his freedom he and Michael took solemn oaths of alliance (each according to the custom of his people, says Pachymeres) never again to wage war against each other. This agreement was sealed by a Greek baptismal ceremony in which William became godfather to a son of Michael.[75] Michael, finally, in a combination of Byzantine practice and Latin feudal usage, bestowed upon the Prince the Byzantine rank of Grand Domestic as symbol of vassalage to the Empire.[76]

The establishment of a Byzantine province in the southeast part of the Morea, based on the ceded territories, was a severe blow to Frankish domination. Each of the forts was important, especially the almost impregnable Mistra, situated near ancient Sparta, and Monemvasia, which provided a good naval base and port of debarkation for imperial troops operating in the Morea. With the loss of these fortresses the decline of Latin power and the revival of Byzantine authority in Greece may be said to have begun.[77]

[73] For a careful analysis of the treaty of Constantinople see D. Zakythinos, *Despotat*, I, 15–25. Zakythinos shows that despite the omission of Kinsterna in the *Chronicle of Morea* and other accounts, Pach., 88, correctly includes it.

[74] By the so-called "Ladies' Parliament" of Nikli in Achaia. Almost all the great Frankish lords had been captured or slain.

[75] A source (evidently overlooked by Zakythinos) corroborating Pachymeres' statement of hearing on good authority that William baptized a son of Palaeologus is to be found (out of context) in the Greek *Chron. Morea*, l. 5542, where a Greek prisoner tells William καὶ σύντεκνον σὲ ἔποικεν νὰ στερεωθῇ ἡ φιλία σας. In modern Greek σύντεκνον may signify a relative through baptism. A curious remark of Pachymeres, 87, ll. 14–19, also reveals that both men fortified their oaths "by the Italian custom of extinguishing lighted tapers, which they held before them as they uttered imprecations against anyone who would be guilty of breaking his oath." (This, however, was also a liturgical practice of the Greek church in anathematization.) It was probably Michael's second son, Constantine, born shortly after 1260 (see A. Papadopulos, *Genealogie*, chart at end), who was baptized at this time.

[76] Pach., 88: δοῦλον κεκλῆσθαι Ῥωμαίων. Also μέγας δομέστικος Ῥωμανίας. This title, according to Zakythinos, *Despotat*, I, 18, corresponds to that of Grand Seneschal of Romania, which William had borne during the existence of the Latin Empire.

[77] Pach., 20–21.

Despite the solemn promises exchanged by Michael and William, it could not seriously be expected that they would remain at peace with each other. It was, as noted, the Emperor's avowed objective to recover all of Latin Greece,[78] while William, who fully realized the import of the Greek foothold in the Morea, could hardly remain aloof from Western efforts to retake Constantinople.

Upon whom the chief responsibility should rest for the outbreak of hostilities in the Morea is not clear from the sources. Even if the blame should be attributed to Michael, as asserted by both the *Chronicle of Morea* [79] and Sanudo,[80] his actions do not seem altogether unjustified in the light of the menacing diplomatic measures adopted by the Latins. On 16 May 1262, the signing of a treaty at Thebes between William and the Venetians of Negropont marked the start of collaboration against the Greeks.[81] Then in July of the same year, at a meeting held at Viterbo, Pope Urban IV, the Emperor Baldwin, Venice, and the Moreot barons and prelates decided to undertake joint, active measures against Michael. The Pope not only released William from his pledges to the "Greek schismatics," [82] but sent letters to France and England appealing for aid and a circular directive to the Moreot prelates ordering them to assist William's military preparations by gifts of ecclesiastical revenues.[83]

---

[78] Note the remark of the captured imperial general Kaballarios to William: "The Morea . . . is the rightful heritage [*droit heritaiges*] of the holy Emperor" (Longnon, French *Chron. Morea*, par. 382).

[79] Note the conversation between Kaballarios and William over responsibility for the Moreot war. See French *Chron.*, par. 382–384 and Greek *Chron.*, ll. 5489ff., and l. 5577, where, however, the blame is laid on the Monemvasiotes. Cf. a letter of Pope Urban (ed. Guiraud, II, no. 231, 103), implying that Michael first attacked William: "terram hostiliter impetere . . . presumsit."

[80] Sanudo, *Istoria,* 116: "Imperator commincò a molestar la Morea con Gente e con Turchi."

[81] See T.-Th., III, 46–55; and Guiraud, *Reg. Urbain,* II, 47–48. See Zakythinos, *Despotat,* I, 27–28.

[82] *Ibid.*; Guiraud, *loc. cit.*, and cf. 292–293; Dandolo, 306 (out of context). Pach., 88, says that Urban was pushed to this action by the "King" (Baldwin?): παροξυνθείς . . . πρὸς τοῦ ῥηγός. It should be noted that Urban's relations with Baldwin had not yet been strained as a result of Baldwin's adherence to Manfred. See above, text and note 24.

[83] *Flores Historiarum* (ed. Luard, London, 1891) 478–479; Guiraud, *Reg Urbain,* II, no. 231, 102–103, dated 27 April 1263.

Finally, on 18 July 1263, Urban dispatched an epistle to the Greek Emperor himself, complaining that rumors had reached his ears of the latter's "persecution and oppression of William Villehardouin, Prince of Achaia, devoted son of the mother church and of the lands, islands, and Latins living there." [84] In effect, he asked Michael to refrain from attacking Achaia as the price of papal good will. This letter was in response to another previously dispatched by Michael in the summer of 1262 (already mentioned above), in which the Emperor had offered to submit all differences between himself and the Latins to papal arbitration.[84a] Whether or not the imperial communication followed on the failure of Michael's first attempt to take Achaia is difficult to say with certitude. But whatever the case, Palaeologus probably calculated that in the event of a Greek defeat in the Morea the Pope would protect him against reprisals. On the other hand, if the imperial forces triumphed, the Pope might well be prevailed upon, for the concession of church union, to restore to him the remainder of Latin Greece.[85] After all, had not Popes Innocent IV and Alexander IV been willing for the sake of union to deliver Constantinople itself to the Emperor John Vatatzes while it was still in Latin possession? [85a]

The hostilities in the Morea to which the Pope referred had broken out shortly after William's return from captivity. Probably toward the end of 1262 William had gone to Laconia at the head of a detachment, ostensibly to visit his territories.[86] The Byzantines of nearby Mistra, however, observing his movements with suspicion, notified the imperial governor, Michael Cantacuzene, at Monemvasia, who in turn informed the Emperor of the situation and requested immediate aid.[87] With extraordinary celerity

[84] Guiraud, *Reg. Urbain*, II, no. 295, 136.
[84a] See above, text and note 33.
[85] Cf. Chapman, 66.
[85a] See P. Schillman, "Zur byzantinischen Politik Alexanders IV," *Römische Quartalschrift*, XXII (1908) 108ff.
[86] French *Chron. Morea*, par. 329, and Greek *Chron.*, ll. 4515–4524. Chapman, 59, inaccurately states that William visited Mistra, a fortress which actually now belonged to Palaeologus.
[87] Greek *Chron.*, ll. 4527ff., and French *Chron.*, pars. 330–331, which notes that Michael believed William false to his oaths: "li princes eust faussé son serement."

the Emperor organized an expedition under his brother, the Sebastokrator Constantine, with the Parakoimomenos Makrenos and the Grand Domestic Alexios Philes as subordinate commanders.[88]

In the early part of 1263 the imperial army, composed of Turkish mercenaries and Greeks from Asia Minor (but without Latin troops which Michael deemed it advisable to send to Epirus instead),[89] was transported by Genoese ships to Monemvasia.[90] Simultaneously, in a supporting action, the newly constructed Greek fleet under the Protostrator Philanthropenos, after sacking the Aegean isles of Paros, Naxos, and Cos, and the Negropontine towns of Karystos and Oreos, sailed to the Peloponnese and seized the southern coast of Laconia.[91]

The Sebastokrator Constantine, having first brought to submission the Slavic population of Mount Taygetos, built fortresses at strong points and then laid siege to Lacedaemon.[92] While the Byzantine commander was ravaging the country, William went to Corinth to seek aid from other Frankish barons of Greece. He was handicapped, however, by the refusal of several lords to aid him, and also, it is interesting to observe, by the disloyalty of many of his Greek subjects who deserted to their fellow countrymen.[93] William's predicament proved advantageous to his opponent, Constantine, who now lifted the siege of Lacedaemon and marched directly on the Achaian capital of Andravida in the northwestern part of the Morea.[94] The capture of all Achaia seemed imminent, when suddenly the fortunes of both sides were reversed.

While Prince William was at Corinth, he had left behind as

---

[88] The accounts disagree here on details, but Zakythinos, *Despotat*, I, 33, note 3, believes Pach., 205–206 to be most credible. Cf. Zakythinos, II, 337, note 6, for evidence supporting a somewhat later date for Makrenos' arrival in the Morea.

[89] Pach., 205: τὸ γὰρ Ἰταλικὸν μὴ ἁρμόζον πρὸς μάχην Ἰταλικήν. These were probably the Varangians.

[90] The usual procedure. Cf. Canale, 494: "doner vitaille a Malveisie."

[91] See Pach., 205, ll. 2–5; 206, l. 4; and 209, ll. 6–12.

[92] Called La Crémonie by the Franks.

[93] On all this see Sanudo, *Istoria*, 116; and Greek *Chron. Morea*, ll. 4675–4677.

[94] French *Chron. Morea*, par. 337; Greek *Chron.*, ll. 4664ff., and Sanudo, *Istoria*, 116.

bailli at Andravida John Katavas, a valiant man but old and suffering from the gout.[95] At the sudden approach of the imperial army of fifteen thousand men, Katavas (so runs the remarkable account of the *Chronicle of Morea*) assembled his tiny force of some three hundred Franks and marched to a narrow defile called Agridi Kounoupitza.[96] Learning that the Greek army was unprepared for an attack — scouts reported that the Greeks were playing, eating and drinking[97] — Katavas delivered a ringing exhortation to his men, then ordered a surprise onslaught. In the encounter the Greek troops were badly mauled; many were massacred, the survivors fleeing with difficulty to the forests nearby.[98] The Sebastokrator Constantine himself was barely able to escape to Mistra. While Katavas and his little army prudently retired, Constantine remained idle at Mistra, torn between fear of brotherly censure and apprehension of even sterner reproaches in the event of another defeat.[99] That this astounding debacle of vastly superior Greek forces at Prinitza — as the battle is generally referred to — actually occurred is confirmed by the historian Marino Sanudo.[100] But the details of the encounter as provided by the *Chronicle of Morea* have been sharply questioned by modern authorities.[101]

The period of approximately two years between the recapture of Constantinople and the battle of Settepozzi, so auspiciously begun for Michael with the restoration of the Empire, ended with decisive imperial defeats on both land and sea. While Settepozzi broke Genoese naval power for several years, Prinitza set back the Emperor's timetable for the conquest of the Morea. But events were to demonstrate that Michael's diplomacy — especially his

---

[95] French *Chron. Morea*, 338B; Greek, ll. 4689ff.

[96] Greek *Chron.*, l. 4709; cf. French *Chron.*, par. 338C.

[97] Reported only by the Aragonese *Chron. Morea* (*Libro de los Fechos*, ed. Morel-Fatio [Geneva, 1885] 78–79), but accepted by Zakythinos, *Despotat*, I, 36, note 3, because the ensuing French triumph is otherwise impossible to explain.

[98] On the entire battle see Greek *Chron.*, ll. 4706–4855. Also French *Chron.*, pars. 338D–G.

[99] Cf. Chapman, 61.

[100] *Istoria*, 118ff.; he terms it "Brenizza."

[101] Esp. by Zakythinos, *Despotat*, I, 37–38.

manipulation of the papal-Sicilian and Veneto-Genoese rivalries — could enable him successfully to recuperate from his military setbacks.

8

SETTEPOZZI TO BENEVENTO

(1263–1266)

RELATIONS OF MICHAEL PALAEOLOGUS WITH GENOA, THE
PAPACY, MANFRED, AND VENICE

he disastrous outcome of the battle of Settepozzi indicated to Michael that he was mistaken in tying his fortune so closely to Genoa. With the aid of the Genoese he had, to be sure, successfully maintained Constantinople against the threat of Latin invasion, and in the face of what must have been a considerable Greek protest he had faithfully implemented his obligations of the Nymphaeum pact. But instead of reaping the rewards he expected, he was now gradually draining his treasury to meet the expense of Genoese galleys that coursed far and wide but engaged in no battles of consequence before Settepozzi.[1]

The Basileus had other causes for grievance.[2] Genoese admirals were often loath to attack Venetian war-ships, and refused

[1] In agreement with Norden, 414 (cf. G. Caro, *Genua und die Mächte am Mittelmeer* [Halle, 1895] I, 129), I see evidence of Michael's desire to attack the Venetian fleet, as well as dissatisfaction with Genoese tactics, attested in his letter of 1262 to Genoa: see L. Belgrano, "Cinque documenti genovesi-orientali," *Atti soc. lig. st. pat.*, XVII (1885) 228–229: "De venetis vero sperat imperium meum in Deo quod in brevi bona nova denunciet vobis. . . Si vero predicti veneti non debent armare sufficientes sunt presentes galee . . . illos impugnare et vincere et non alias preparare et consumere thesauros nostros in vanum."

[2] Caro, *Genua,* I, 137, believes that Michael's anger against the Genoese stemmed from their refusal to combat William of Achaia. But note that the Nymphaeum treaty explicitly exempted Genoa from warring against William. See Manfroni, "Relazioni," 803.

or inadequately carried out imperial orders for the provisioning of the Moreot port of Monemvasia,[3] wasting their time instead in preying on Venetian merchant shipping. This was for the Genoese a less dangerous activity and at the same time provided valuable booty. For Palaeologus, however, it brought no benefits and only exhausted his finances.[4]

Most vexatious perhaps to the Greeks was the increasingly important position of the Genoese population in the capital. With the expulsion of most of the Venetians and the vastly enlarged opportunities offered for trade and imperial service, Genoese were flocking in great numbers to the Byzantine Empire. They became masters of the Black Sea and not only far surpassed the Venetians in commercial activities but, what was more serious, they almost completely eliminated Greek merchants from commercial competition. Even Constantinople itself was to a great extent dependent on Genoese shipping for its subsistence. The pride and arrogance of the Genoese grew in accordance with their increased power, and thus they soon aroused the jealousy and enmity not only of the Greeks but of the Latins as well.[5] Little wonder that Palaeologus was eager to rid himself of an embarrassing ally!

The differences between Michael and the Genoese are set forth in the *Annales Ianuenses*. They note that in the year 1263, just after Settepozzi, Michael dismissed from his service about sixty Genoese galleys and ordered them to return home.[6] Their discharge is attributed by the *Annales* to "the great number of admirals and other inconveniences," and to the fact that the Emperor, "after many and various conferences, was not able to accord with them nor they with him."[7] Significant too is the

---

[3] Canale, 494: "il devoient doner vitaille a Malveisie. . . . Il ne le dona pas."

[4] Canale, 494: "[Ienoes] porterent il li CXX mariniers que il pristrent es tarites," and 496: "[Palialog] pensa . . . que il n'osent neis regarder les Veneciens en mi lors vis, il despendroit trestos son avoir, et ne gaagnera nule riens."

[5] See Pach., 167, ll. 15–19, and Greg., 97, ll. 10ff. On the growth of Genoese power see Bratianu, *Recherches*, 61–155, and Heyd, *Histoire*, I, 427ff.

[6] Technically the Emperor was within his rights, as he was not obliged to make use of the ships.

[7] *Ann. Ian.*, IV, 52: "propter multitudinem armiragiorum et propter alia inconvenientia que gerebant, idem imperator post multos et varios tractatus habitos

Annales' account of the board of inquiry established by the
Genoese to fix responsibility for the defeat at Settepozzi.[8] As a
result of the investigation, the admirals, pilots, and counsellors
who had participated in the battle were condemned and fined "for
their excesses . . . and malfeasance in the areas of Romania." [9]
Regrettable as is our ignorance of the precise reference of "inconveniences," "expenses," and "malfeasance," it is nevertheless
a significant indication of guilt that such terms could be used
by the more or less official chronicle of the Commune.

Although Michael's dismissal of the Genoese fleet was unexpected, the Genoese could not have been altogether unaware
of his dissatisfaction. An incident recorded by the Venetian
chronicler Martino da Canale, though perhaps somewhat colored
for effect, provides a revealing glimpse into the Emperor's attitude. Summoning the "Sire" of the Genoese in Constantinople
(probably the Podestà), Michael pointed to his treasury and
angrily exclaimed: "You promised to give me all of Romania
easily and to eject the Venetians. I have spent a mountain of money
such as this but gained nothing at all from you." Canale then
attributes an imprecation to the Emperor: "May God confound
your prowess and your arrogance!" [10] Further evidence of Michael's concern over the mounting cost of the alliance is an
imperial letter to the Commune, dated as early as 1262, in which
its citizens were warned "not to prepare other vessels and to con-
sume our treasure in vain." [11]

Still, Palaeologus' abrupt dismissal of the Genoese fleet did

---

cum eisdem, nec cum eo poterant vel ipse cum eis concordari; idem imperator
exercitum predictum galearum que erant numero LX vel circa, licenciavit eas."

[8] One of the examiners was Ansaldus d'Oria, whom Michael had sent as his
envoy to Genoa (see *Ann. Ian.*, 45, 53); d'Oria's knowledge of Greek affairs insured a thorough inquiry.

[9] *Ibid.*, 53: "pro suis excessibus"; and 52–53: "omnia malefacta . . . in partibus
Romanie." For the Venetian attitude toward the Greco-Genoese naval defeats, see
a poem of the Venetian troubadour, Bertolome Zorzi, in G. Bertoni, *I trovatori
d'Italia* (Modena, 1915) 447.

[10] Canale, 496.

[11] See note 1, last part. For criticism of Belgrano's textual editions see E.
Byrne, *Genoese Shipping in the Twelfth and Thirteenth Centuries* (Cambridge,
1930) 3.

not constitute a complete rupture. More probably it was a dramatic gesture to emphasize his discontent with their services, for soon afterwards he accepted new galleys which the Genoese had just dispatched. Nevertheless, he now seemed reluctant to pay their crews punctually, and the Genoese, on their side, were uneasy before him, as he appeared so explicitly to mistrust them.[12] It seems likely, to judge from a document of 21 September 1263 for the raising of a loan in Genoa "super negociis Romanie," that the Genoese had in any case finally learned a lesson and, to some extent, realized that in the future they would have to exert themselves further and bear a greater share of the expenses of the war in Romania.[13]

Michael's dissatisfaction with the alliance must have been aggravated by the political situation in Italy, which was meanwhile becoming more favorable for the Greeks. By the latter half of 1263, the confusion and instability of the earlier half century were gradually coming to an end, and the shifting forces of the Italian political scene had begun to align themselves into two sharply opposed camps — that of the Ghibellines, championed by the Hohenstaufen Manfred of Sicily, and that of the Guelphs, headed by Pope Urban IV (and later, as we shall see, by Charles of Anjou).[14] While adherents of both parties were to be found at Venice as well as Genoa, it was the Ghibellines who finally triumphed at Genoa and the Guelphs at Venice.[15]

Michael, well-informed as always regarding Italian politics, did not hesitate to profit from this situation. Perceiving Pope Urban's intense absorption in his conflict with Manfred — actually a bitter struggle for the control of Italy inherited from the days of Emperor Frederick II, he considered it an opportune time to extract concessions. By offering to the papacy ecclesiastical un-

---

[12] Lopez, *Colonie*, 214. By contrast Michael, in 1262, had addressed the Commune as "dilectam fraternitatem imperii mei" (Belgrano, "Cinque documenti," 228).

[13] See Belgrano, *op. cit.*, 229.

[14] Urban had announced already in 1262 that Charles of Anjou would replace Manfred on the Sicilian throne. See Raynaldus, III, a. 1262, § 20.

[15] See E. Jordan, *Les origines de la domination Angevine en Italie* (Paris 1909) *passim*; and Chapman, 64–65.

ion and perhaps the suggestion of an alliance against the detested Hohenstaufen, Michael might hope to recover the remainder of Latin Greece.

Similar thoughts were coursing through the mind of Pope Urban, who did not underestimate the advantages at this critical time of a successful unionist policy. Besides increasing the Holy See's prestige in Italy, it could enable him to use against Manfred the preparations hitherto made by Western Europe to aid Latin Greece.[16] Moreover, it would free the papacy once and for all from the chimera of a Hohenstaufen on the Bosporus, able to mobilize the resources of Byzantium as well as Sicily.[17] Once relieved of cares with respect to the East, Urban could devote all his energies to the Ghibellines in Italy, whose power had now become a matter of immense concern.[18]

Urban was anxious not only over the fate of Latin Greece proper but also over the Greco-Genoese threat to the Latin-held Greek islands, especially Negropont, Crete, and Cyprus. This is particularly manifest in the case of Cyprus, from a letter he addressed to its *bailli* and barons warning them against the "insidious" plots of Palaeologus to take the island by intriguing with its "unsuspecting" officials.[19]

In a letter to Michael of 18 July 1263 (in which the Greek Empire was termed "a noble member of the church"),[20] Urban, in response to a communication from Michael, promised at once to send nuncios to effect the union.[20a] As envoys he proposed to dispatch four Minorites selected by the famous Franciscan

---

[16] See above, note 14, papal letter of 1262 proclaiming that Manfred's replacement by Charles would rescue Latin Romania (cf. Norden, 417).

[17] According to Norden, 411, Manfred believed himself strong enough to vanquish both Rome and Constantinople simultaneously.

[18] Norden, 420. Manfred was intriguing in the towns of the Patrimony, even in Rome itself. See Jordan, *Origines*, 456–458.

[19] See Raynaldus, III, a. 1263, § 18 (summarized in Guiraud, *Reg. Urbain*, II, no. 188, 76): "caverent a Paleologi insidiis, ne illis se irretiri atque occupari paterentur."

[20] Guiraud, *Reg. Urbain*, II, no. 295, 137B. Cf. Wadding, *Annales Minorum*, IV, 225.

[20a] Cf. on the chronology S. Borsari, "La politica bizantina di Carlo d'Angiò dal 1266 al 1271," *Arch. st. prov. nap.*, n.s. XXXV (1956) 325, and F. Dölger, in *Byz. Zeit.* (1955) 474.

Minister-general Bonaventura. Certain special instructions issued to the envoys for their voyage to Constantinople are worthy of note: the nuncios were empowered to absolve from excommunication the people of Greek territories who wished to return to unity, and to restore clerical privileges to Greek ecclesiastics who publicly declared their obedience to the papacy.[21]

In August of the same year Urban wrote a letter to William of Achaia informing him, somewhat disparagingly, of the forthcoming papal attempt "to lead to unity, if possible, Michael Palaeologus, who considers himself Emperor of the Greeks." Apprising William of the envoys he had chosen, the Pope requested him, meanwhile, to cease hostilities against Michael, as he had likewise requested the Emperor to desist from attacking Achaia. Urban hastened to assure William that in this affair Achaia's interests would remain paramount.[22] Letters asking safe conduct for the papal envoys were also sent to the Doge of Venice and, strikingly enough, to the Greek Despot of Epirus, both of whom were in turn assured that their interests would not be forgotten.[23]

Assembled and instructed, the four Franciscan envoys finally set out for Constantinople in August of 1263.[24] Though Palaeologus' letters fail to disclose mention of their arrival even by the spring of 1264,[25] their departure from the Curia is corroborated in Urban's reply to Michael's letter, dated 22 June 1263. Affirming that his envoys had set out long before, Urban notes that he has not yet heard of their arrival at the Byzantine court.[26]

Poor communications, the cause of many a misunderstanding in the Middle Ages, now complicated matters. Believing that

[21] Guiraud, *Reg. Urbain*, II, no. 322, 150.
[22] *Ibid.*, II, no. 325, 151, esp.: "similiter . . . interim ab ipsius Paleologi impugnatione desistas."
[23] See *ibid.*, II, no. 326, 151; and letter of 28 July 1263, printed in J. Sbaralea, *Bullarium Franciscanum* (Rome, 1759) II, 495, in which Michael II is addressed as "princeps Thessalonicensis." Cf. Norden, 425.
[24] See Norden, 426.
[25] Hopf, *Geschichte*, 297, provides no basis for his statement that they arrived in Constantinople at the end of 1263. Cf. Norden, 426, note 3. The journey from Italy to Constantinople was long and arduous, usually extending down the Adriatic to Epirus, and thence across Greece to Constantinople.
[26] Cf. Norden, 426, note 3.

Urban had rejected his overtures or was perhaps deliberately being difficult, Michael reopened hostilities in the Morea. On his part, the Pope, thinking Michael faithless, began once again to stir up the West against Palaeologus. Thus on 20 October 1263 Urban angrily wrote to Genoa's Archbishop Turritano directing him to inform the Commune that if within six months it did not withdraw from the alliance with Michael and recall all its vessels and troops from Greek territories, it would be deprived of its archbishopric and denounced to the nations of Europe as an enemy of Christendom. Moreover, both its citizens and goods, wherever they might be found, would be subject to seizure.[27] This was the severest of a number of papal letters hitherto directed to Genoa, all of which sought to dissolve the alliance with the "schismatic" Greek Emperor.[28]

But the Genoese, still garnering abundant profit, did not find it to their interest to sever their connection with Michael, and therefore responded evasively to the Pope.[29] Suddenly, however, with the unexpected return of the Genoese fleet from the East, it seemed as if the Greco-Genoese alliance was broken, and for this Urban believed his own fulminations responsible. Thus, on 11 February 1263, he wrote to the Archbishop of Genoa:

They [the Genoese], after receiving our letter and reading it and also hearing the warnings of our dear brother, the Archbishop Turritano . . . (although they did not show with words that they would obey our precepts in this respect) . . . afterwards revealed [their obedience] more clearly by deeds . . . , since they are said to have recalled all their galleys and ships from the service of the tyrant. For this we have decided that they, their industry, and circumspection deserve worthy praises in the Lord, [and] the sentence of interdict pronounced against the city . . . we take care to relax.[30]

[27] Giraud, *Reg. Urbain*, II, no. 719, 341, dated 20 October 1263: "denuntiabimus ac personas et bona eorumdem civium, ubicumque inventa fuerint, exponemus libere ipsis aliisque Christi fidelibus occupanda."
[28] In an earlier letter, *ibid.*, II, no. 228, 98 and esp. 101, dated 7 May 1263, Genoa had been ordered specifically to recall her vessels from Negropont.
[29] For example, *ibid.*, no. 228, 100: "[The Genoese] dixerunt quod, cum nichil de talibus fuisset eis a vobis [the Pope] injunctum."
[30] *Ibid.*, II, no. 756, 361–362, esp.: "omnes galeas et naves ipsorum, que in predicti tyrampni servitiis morabantur, ad prefatam civitatem revocasse dicantur."

Little did Urban realize at the time that not he but the Greek Emperor was responsible for his newly found satisfaction with the Genoese. Despite Urban's expressions of good will toward Genoa, the Commune still refused to break completely with Michael. Its loyalty, however, was soon to prove useless.

THE PLOT OF THE GENOESE PODESTÀ GUERCIO TO BETRAY CONSTANTINOPLE TO MANFRED (1264)

What finally persuaded Michael to rid himself completely of his turbulent ally was his discovery, shortly after the fleet's dismissal, of an alleged plot on the part of the Genoese Podestà, Guglielmo Guercio, to betray Constantinople to King Manfred of Sicily.[31] Details of the conspiracy are lacking; mention of it is made only in the *Annales Ianuenses* (under the year 1264), while both Greek and Venetian sources overlook it entirely.[32] Nor is anything definite known of the role of Manfred, in particular how the city was to be handed over to him. It may be that Guercio intended to foment a sudden revolt of the numerous Genoese and possibly other Latins within Constantinople, who were to seize the capital for the King of Sicily. But while Manfred may have intended to keep the city for himself, it seems a more plausible assumption, in view of the increasing severity of his conflict with the papacy and Baldwin's unsuccessful attempts at mediation (Urban by now had almost completed negotiations with Charles of Anjou for the latter's invasion of Italy to dethrone Manfred),[33] that once Manfred had gained possession of the city, he would ostentatiously offer it to the Pope as a restoration of the Latin Empire.[34] For this great service to Christendom

[31] *Ann. Ian.*, IV, 65: "Guillermus Guercius . . . accusatus fuit ipsi imperatori quod civitatem Constantinopolim traditurus erat in manibus Latinorum, et quod habuerat de hoc tractatum cum nunciis domini Manfredi."

[32] Cf. Canale, 496, who attributes the rupture to Genoese malfeasance. See above, notes 3 and 4. Cf., however, Pach., 167f., who may possibly be making vague reference to the plot.

[33] See Jordan, *Origines*, 459.

[34] A precedent for such an act could have been the example of his father, Frederick II, who, though excommunicated, had restored Jerusalem to Christendom in the hope of overcoming papal hostility.

Manfred might well force Urban (who unequivocally refused to have anything to do with him) to relax the papal excommunication and recognize him as King of Sicily. After all, had not Urban already promised the indulgences of a crusade to all who would support Baldwin in his efforts to restore the Latin Empire? [35]

Even more speculative are the motivations of Guercio. In his capacity of supreme Genoese official in Romania, it might reasonably be assumed that he was acting under superior orders. And indeed the Genoese government, seeing the handwriting on the wall and anticipating abrogation of the Greek alliance, might well have reached an agreement with Manfred to assign political control to Sicily and retain commercial supremacy for itself.[36] Unfortunately, there is not the slightest bit of testimony to support such a theory, plausible as it may be. In fact, the sole evidence that might suggest Genoese foreknowledge of Guercio's conduct is the circumstance that after the collapse of the conspiracy Guercio, though he had gravely jeopardized Genoese interests in the East, was merely banished from Genoa and thus was able to go quietly to Achaia.[37]

As for Michael Palaeologus, he believed, or professed to believe, that without the connivance of the Genoese government, Guercio would not have dared to become involved in such a

[35] Imperiale, *Jacopo d'Oria*, 124. See also Guiraud, *Reg. Urbain*, II, no. 577, 293. Manfroni, *Marina italiana*, pt. I, 12, believes that Manfred may have intended, through Guercio, to help the Despot of Epirus to depose Palaeologus. (On the possibility of a continuing alliance between Manfred and the Despot see Geanakoplos, "Pelagonia," 116–117.)

[36] Not only was there a strong Ghibelline party at Genoa, but it is known also that Manfred and Genoa, until the first months of Guglielmo Boccanegra's government, were allied in a pact of friendship and commerce against Venice. See Lopez, *Colonie*, 215. By no means to be overlooked, however, is the possibility of a role in the Guercio affair for Baldwin, since, as late as July 1263, he had been in close contact with Manfred. See above, Chapter 7, notes 22–24.

[37] *Ann. Ian.*, IV, 66, and see diploma of Charles of Anjou, dated 1276, in F. Carabellese, *Carlo d'Angiò nei rapporti politici e commerciali con Venezia e l'Oriente* (Bari, 1911) 30, note 3, referring to "Guillelminum Guercium amiratum G. principis Achaye." A possible reference to the treasonous conduct of Guercio may also be found in the subsequent treaty of 1275 between Genoa and Palaeologus, in which the latter insisted that Genoa henceforth appoint as podestà "homo talis juxta temporis qualitatem talis qui sit honor domini Imperatoris et comunis Ianue" (G. Bertolotto, "Nuova serie di documenti sulle relazioni di Genova coll'impero bizantino," *Atti. soc. lig. st. pat.*, XXVIII [1898] 502).

serious conspiracy.[38] As soon as he had discovered the plot (how is not told us), Michael summoned Guercio and, in the presence of Genoese and others, confronted him with the evidence. According to the *Annales*, Guercio made no effort to deny the accusation, but confessed "with his own tongue." [39] Michael then made a protocol of the affair and dispatched it to the Commune.[40] Whereupon, as the same source informs us, he "banished all of the Genoese and the rest of the Latins from the imperial city of Constantinople." [41]

That all Westerners were at this time actually ejected from the capital seems doubtful. Some were, of course, married to Greek women, and others had become Greek subjects by taking an oath of allegiance to the Emperor.[42] Nor do the Byzantine sources report expulsion of the non-Genoese Latins. Pachymeres, in fact, informs us only that the Genoese, the largest group in Constantinople,[43] were relegated by the Emperor to Thracian Heraclea, situated some forty miles west of the capital on the Sea of Marmora.[44] Details of the Genoese establishment at Heraclea are unknown to us, however, for not a single Latin or Greek document casts light on that period of exile.

Realizing the damage they had suffered in the banishment of their colony, the Genoese dispatched two embassies in quick succession to Palaeologus, the first consisting of Egidio de Nigro and the second of Benedetto Zaccaria and Symoneto de Camilla.[45]

---

[38] Lopez, *Colonie*, 216, believes that Guercio had secured Genoese approval. Cf. Caro, *Genua*, I, 167, who suggests that he may have been seeking, through the conspiracy, to secure the return of family properties taken from him by Michael (*ibid.*, 167, note 2, where it is shown that Guercio was descended from a "liege-man" of Manuel I Comnenos).

[39] *Ann. Ian.*, IV, 65: "fuit propria lingua confessus."

[40] *Ibid.*, according to which the Emperor sent the protocol to Genoa "in order to retain their friendship" ("comunis Ianue amiciciam retinere").

[41] *Ibid.*: "fuerunt omnes Ianuenses et ceteri Latini licenciati . . . de imperiali civitate Constantinopolis." Cf. also Pach., 167, ll. 15ff., and Greg., 97, ll. 10ff.

[42] See, e.g., Sanudo, *Istoria*, 146: "e dando [Michael] ad alcuni di loro Moglie delle sue Donne Greche." Also see below, Chapter 9, text and notes 71ff. But cf. the Nymphaeum treaty, Chapter 4, text and note 65.

[43] Pach., 167, ll. 16–17, and 168, l. 5.

[44] Pach., 168, l. 2, and *Ann. Ian.*, IV, 65.

[45] On Zaccaria, who was later to perform valuable service for Palaeologus, see

The envoys asked the return of the Genoese colony to Constantinople or at least permission for its settlement in Pera (another name for Galata), across the Golden Horn from the capital.[46] But despite persistent Genoese requests, Michael was inflexible. He had in mind, it appears, plans for an alliance with another power.[47] Thus the events under discussion almost dissolved the Greco-Genoese alliance. They did not lead to a permanent rupture, for both parties still had use for each other.[48]

THE WAR IN ACHAIA (1263–1266)

During these involvements with Genoa, Michael, believing that the Pope had failed to respond to his advances, resumed the war in Achaia. His brother Constantine had carried on no hostilities during the winter following the battle of Prinitza, preferring to remain idle at Mistra. But Prince William was able to draw from the victory of his *bailli*, Katavas, a double advantage: assembling his feudatories, he organized the defense of Andravida, and at the beginning of 1264 he received subsidies from Pope Urban.[49] That Urban could dispatch aid despite his own needs vis-à-vis Manfred is evidence both of a lack of trust in Michael's unionist proposals and of the importance of the Morea in the eyes of the papacy.[50]

In 1264, with the return of spring, operations were resumed. The Sebastokrator Constantine, reassembling his troops on the plain of Sapikos, now pressed forward, still intending to conquer the principality by seizing its capital, Andravida. Accordingly, he marched through enemy territory to Sergiana, finally encamping with his large army at a place called St. Nicholas of Mesikli.[51]

R. Lopez, *Genova marinara nel duecento: Benedetto Zaccaria* (Messina-Milan, 1933) 11.

[46] *Ann. Ian.*, IV, 66: "vel saltim in quodam loco nomine Peyro."

[47] See below, text and notes 88ff.

[48] Note esp. *Ann. Ian.*, IV, 65: "imperator volens comunis Ianue amiciciam retinere."

[49] See T.-Th., III, 57; Chapman, 70.

[50] Cf. above, Chapter 7, section 2, and Chapter 8, text and notes 22–30.

[51] Greek *Chron. Morea*, ll. 5016–5052; Zakythinos, *Despotat*, I, 38.

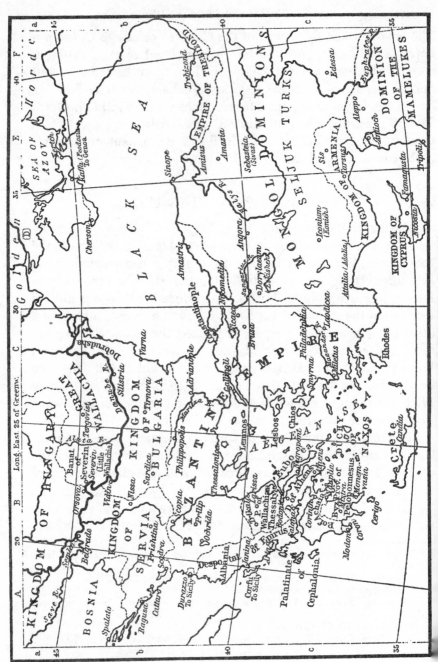

THE BYZANTINE EMPIRE IN 1265

Meanwhile, William, advised of the Sebastokrator's approach, appeared in the area with his troops drawn up in battle array. Only a skirmish took place, but the Latins succeeded in killing the Grand Constable, Michael Cantacuzene, perhaps the bravest of the Greek officers.[52] At the unexpected slaughter of his lieutenant, Constantine became disheartened and withdrew with his troops to Nikli, to which he then laid siege.[53]

It was during the investment of Nikli that a grave event occurred which led to a pulverizing defeat of the Byzantine forces. The mercenary Turkish troops of the Sebastokrator had not been paid for six months, and their chieftains Melik and Salik protested to the Greek commander. On receiving an unfavorable response from the Sebastokrator, who was both short of funds and irritated that he had profited little from their services, the Turkish leaders became angry, and deserted to the Prince of Achaia at Andravida with most if not all of their troops.[54] William, of course, was at first suspicious of his new allies and charged his kinsman Ansel de Toucy (whom we last saw as a prisoner of Palaeologus after the battle of Pelagonia) to negotiate with the Turks.[55] Satisfied finally as to their motives, the Prince engaged them in his service. Then, strengthened by the addition of these troops, William decided to take the offensive.

The desertion of the Turks deeply affected the morale of the Byzantine army. It was perhaps on this account that the Sebastokrator lifted the siege of Nikli (his excuse being sickness) and departed for Constantinople, entrusting the command to the Grand Domestic Philes and the Parakoimomenos Makrenos.[56] As

[52] Of the various versions describing Cantacuzene's death, Zakythinos, *Despotat*, I, 39, prefers that of the Aragonese *Chronicle*, 76. It states that the Constable's horse stumbled during a reconnaissance before the Latin troops, who promptly killed him. Cf. French *Chron.*, par. 343.

[53] French *Chron.*, par. 345; Greek, ll. 5084–5098.

[54] Greek *Chron.*, ll. 5117ff., and French *Chron.*, esp. par. 360. Cf. Sanudo, *Istoria*, 118, who places this incident before the battle of Prinitza (i.e., Agridi Kounoupitza).

[55] On Toucy see Geanakoplos, "Pelagonia," Appendix B, 137–141.

[56] Pach., 207, ll. 17–18. According to the Aragonese version of the *Chron. Morea*, par. 372, Constantine remained in the Morea, for in the ensuing battle he was captured by the Turks. Cf. T.-Th., III, 231–232; and Sanudo, *Istoria*, 118.

for William, with an army superior to that of his enemy, he now prepared to launch an attack on the Byzantine possessions in the southern Peloponnese. Over its difficult mountainous terrain, the expert aid of his newly acquired troops would be invaluable. Sure enough, the Turks, under the command of Ansel de Toucy, succeeded in drawing the Greek troops to Makryplagi, a hazardous pass probably situated between Messinia and the central Peloponnese. In the first encounter the Greeks prevailed, but ultimate victory rested with Toucy and his Turks, before whose fierce attacks the terrified Greeks completely gave way.[57]

After this overwhelming victory William returned to Veligosti, where he found a great number of Greek prisoners, including the generals Makrenos, Philes, and Kaballarios, in addition to many *archontes* (members of the Byzantine nobility).[58] At this time an interesting conversation, indicative of the Greek and Latin attitudes toward aggression in the Morea, occurred between the imperial general Alexios Philes and William. To the claim of the Prince that "God has finally punished Palaeologus for violating his oaths," Philes audaciously replied: "The Morea belongs to the Empire of Romania and is the proper heritage of the Emperor. It is instead you who have broken your oath to your lord." [59]

William's next move was to send an army to surprise the fortress of Mistra, the defense of which was considerably weak-

---

Also see Zakythinos, *Despotat,* I, 39–43, and esp. II, 337, note 6, where a new source (*Manuelis Philae carmina,* ed. E. Miller [Paris, 1855] 123) is adduced, with additional comments of Zakythinos.

[57] The main source for this battle of Makryplagi is the *Chron. Morea* (Greek, ll. 5372ff., and French, pars. 364ff.), though Pach., 208, also attests to a Byzantine defeat at this time.

[58] Greek *Chron.,* ll. 5457–5465; French *Chron.,* pars. 378–380. Philes died in prison, Kaballarios was apparently liberated, and Makrenos was exchanged for a Latin prisoner, probably Philip de Toucy. On his return to Constantinople, however, Makrenos was accused of treason and blinded as a result of the accusations of Eulogia, sister to the Emperor and mother-in-law of Philes. She charged Makrenos with favoring a Greek defeat at Makryplagi in the hope of securing a rapprochement with the Latins so that he could marry Eudocia, daughter of Theodore II Lascaris and widow of the Latin Mathieu de Walincourt (Eudocia was then living in the Morea). See Pach., 208–209 and Zakythinos, *Despotat,* I, 40.

[59] Greek *Chron.,* ll. 5498–5531; French *Chron.,* pars. 380–384.

ened by the capture of the Greek generals. The maneuver failed, however, and the Frankish troops, after pillaging the surrounding Byzantine territory as far as the walls of Monemvasia, withdrew to Nikli.[60]

From the enfeebled military position to which William was reduced after his return from captivity,[61] he had experienced such a reversal of fortune that he was now able to carry the war to the Greek fortresses in the southern Morea. But in the meantime his own principality was undergoing serious hardship: the war, continuous for a long period, had attained such intensity and bitterness that the Morea was gradually becoming depopulated and the fields completely devastated. If we can believe Sanudo, one woman (whether Greek or Latin is not told us) lost seven successive husbands on the battlefields! [62]

Because of the severity of the conflict, hostilities were suspended for a time, while negotiations were conducted to end the war through the marriage of William's daughter and heir, Isabella, to the eldest son of Palaeologus, Andronikos. The plan, in the opinion of Sanudo, was broached by the Greeks as a means of securing the entire Morea, which was to pass in dowry to Andronikos at the death of William. But the proposal was abandoned, apparently owing less to the opposition of Prince William than to the violent objections of his own Latin vassal barons, who feared, probably justifiably, dispossession of their Moreot fiefs.[63]

UNIONIST NEGOTIATIONS BETWEEN PALAEOLOGUS AND POPE URBAN IV

His disastrous defeat at Makryplagi and the realization that the entire Moreot campaign had been a fiasco induced Michael to

---

[60] Greek *Chron.*, ll. 5607ff. and 5621.

[61] See Sanudo, *Istoria*, 118: "era quasi per soccomber del tutto a Greci."

[62] *Ibid.* See also, on the Achaian war, a vehement letter of Urban IV (unused by Zakythinos) in Guiraud, *Reg. Urbain*, II, no. 577, 293: "So much did they [the Greeks] exhaust those who are left by the aforesaid and other afflictions that scarcely any confidence or hope remains."

[63] Sanudo, *Istoria*, 118: "che'l Principe tolesse presso di se il Primogenito dell' Imperator Greco e li dasse per Moglie sua Figliola, il qual morto il Principe, avesse a succedere nel Principato. . . Li Baroni adunque Greci e Conseglieri dell' Imperadore Greco, vedendo che non potevano cazzar li Latini fuori della Morea . . . nà li Baroni Latini non assentirono." No doubt Latin pride also played a role!

renew unionist efforts with the papacy. But now, in addition to a religious accord, he offered Pope Urban aid for a crusade to the Holy Land. This was an astute maneuver, since Urban was himself then promoting the preaching of a crusade against the Greeks. On 13 May 1264, the Pope had written to the Bishop of Utrecht (Holland):

We have turned our attention to the restoration of the Constantinopolitan Empire . . . and we promise to all who personally go to its aid . . . remission of sins . . . , that immunity . . . which is granted in general council to those aiding the Holy Land.[64]

By thus officially stamping the Achaian war a crusade, Urban was able to bring to bear against Michael the most effective weapon of the papal arsenal.

To counter this tactic was no easy matter. Michael had to persuade the Pope not only that he was interested primarily in ecclesiastical union, but that he was sincere in offering aid for a crusade to the Holy Land and, by implication, in asking for favorable papal intercession in the Morea. Michael's carefully worded epistle deserves quotation:[65]

To the venerable father of fathers, most blessed Pope of old Rome, father of our Majesty, Lord Urban, sacrosanct and supreme pontiff of the Apostolic See. . . In the past legates and nuncios were often sent back and forth to bring about peace . . . but these nuncios [papal

[64] Guiraud, *Reg. Urbain*, II, no. 577, 292–293, esp.: "peccaminum . . . veniam indulgemus." Cf. no. 578, 293, a similar directive to the Bishop of Coron. Also a letter of the same date to Hugh IV, Duke of Burgundy, no. 579, 293, granting him absolution from his sins for taking the Cross to aid Achaia. Baldwin, after failing in his attempts to secure aid from the great princes of the West, now turned to lesser lords, among them the Duke of Burgundy. Thus in January of 1266 Baldwin and Hugh IV of Burgundy signed a treaty ceding to the Duke, among other things, the rights to the Kingdom of Thessalonica, formerly in the possession of Boniface of Montferrat. Document in Ducange (Buchon ed.) *Histoire de Constantinople*, I, 455; on the date cf. Dade, 18, and see Norden, 428.

[65] In Guiraud, *Reg. Urbain*, II, no. 748, 356, undated. Cf. S. Borsari, "La politica bizantina di Carlo I d'Angiò dal 1266 al 1271," *Arch. st. prov. nap.*, XXXV (1956) 325, who dates it in 1263; while Dölger, *Regesten*, no. 1923, assigns it to 1264. Cf. Dölger, *Byz. Zeit.*, XLVIII (1955) 474, with date 1263 and also P. Sambin, *Il vescovo Cotronese Niccolò da Durazzo e un inventario di suoi codici latini e greci (1276)* (Rome, 1954) 9–10 (inaccessible to me). But cf. A. Tautu, *Acta Urbani IV, Clementis IV, Gregorii X, etc.* (Vatican, 1953) 38–40 no. 10a, who also dates the letter 1264.

as well as Greek] in the first place did not know how to speak to each other, and, since they conversed through interpreters (who were insufficiently versed . . . or unable to understand the minds of both sides and could not correctly explain the dogmas of both churches . . .), they seldom arrived at the real truth and precepts of the true faith. Thus a constantly increasing hatred between brothers, an extinction of love . . . , and a covering over of the true faith [developed. . . But] a voice from the West . . . adorned with the dogmas of both churches touched our heart . . . [and] there betook himself to our Empire, Nicholas, the venerable Bishop of Croton, . . . to whom, in the third year of our reign we addressed a letter . . . asking him . . . to come secretly to our presence, in order that we might hear directly from his mouth the truth of the faith which the holy and catholic Roman church of God confesses. . .[66] And he revealed to us all things, one after another, of the true faith. . . We found the holy Roman church of God not different from ours in the divine dogma of its faith, but feeling and chanting these things almost with us.

We therefore venerate, believe in, and hold the sacraments of this Roman church. . .[67] We ask you, holy Father, as head of all priests and universal head of all doctors of the Catholic church, that henceforth you may persistently and urgently strive for the reunion of the church. . . To the mother of our church in all things . . . all peoples, patriarchal sees . . . , and all nations in devotion, obedience, and love of this church shall be subjected by the power of our Serene Highness.[68] Therefore we send to your holy Reverend Paternity this Bishop with the present letter of our Catholic faith, not insincere but arising from good conscience and mind, which have been imbued with the love of God. . . We beseech you to return him to us with other discreet and holy men, legates of your holiness and the Apostolic church . . . , who . . . may be able to carry out the infallible work of reuniting the

[66] On the Bishop of Croton see A. Dondaine, "Nicolas de Cotrone et les sources du 'Contra errores Graecorum' de Saint Thomas," *Divus Thomas*, XXVIII (1950) 313–340 (unavailable to me). Cf. *Byz. Zeit.*, XLIII (1950) 457. Also J. Dräseke, "Theodoros Laskaris," *Byz. Zeit.*, III (1894) 511. Cf. letter in *Registres de Innocent IV*, dated 4 September 1254, mentioning the Bishop. Both the Emperors John III Vatatzes and Theodore II Lascaris had had contacts with the Bishop (Theodore in fact dedicated to him a treatise on the procession of the Holy Spirit). On the same prelate, finally, see below, Chapter 11, note 38a.

[67] Guiraud, *Reg. Urbain*, II, 356: "invenimus sanctam Dei ecclesiam romanam non alienatam a nobis in divinis sue fidei dogmatibus, sed ea fere nobiscum sentientem et concantantem . . . nec non et omnia sacramenta ejusdem Ecclesie Romane veneramur."

[68] *Ibid.*, 357, esp.: "Ipsi matri nostre ecclesie . . . omnes gentes et patriarchales sedes . . . ac omnes nationes ad devotionem, obedientiam, et amorem ejusdem ecclesie nostri tranquilli Imperii potentia subjugabitur."

church. . . Let, therefore, this whole matter remain at the discretion of your most pious Serenity so that no accusation may be directed at Our Majesty in the sight of God.[69]

This letter, though essentially a confession of faith, reveals the degree of Michael's finesse. While emphasizing spiritual considerations and obedience to the Pope in all things, Michael indicates his readiness to subject all the Eastern patriarchates to Rome. In view of this attitude, rather vaguely expressed, it is true, it seems reasonable to assume that in exchange he would expect favorable papal intervention in the Moreot war. Such a letter could hardly fail to receive a cordial reception. But its success should not be entirely attributed to its skillful wording, to its appeal to Urban's vanity, or even to what was probably an oblique allusion to the Holy Land.[70] No less important, it should once more be emphasized, was the uncertainty of the papal struggle against Manfred. For with Hohenstaufen strength increasing even in the papal territories, there can be little doubt that Urban believed that peace in the East would aid his cause in the West. To defend himself Urban had been compelled to declare a crusade against Manfred and had appealed to Charles of Anjou quickly to accept the offer of Manfred's Sicilian throne.[71] And Urban's apprehensions may have been further heightened by reports of the Hohenstaufen-Guercio conspiracy to seize Constantinople, the success of which might have opened the way to Rome itself.[72]

As requested in Palaeologus' letter, Urban promptly sent back to Constantinople the Bishop of Croton with other legates to carry out the union and to put an end to the Moreot war. Thus he wrote to Michael on 23 May 1264:

[69] *Ibid.*

[70] *Ibid.*, esp. "patriarchales sedes." Urban had formerly been Latin Patriarch of Jerusalem. Cf. comments of Chapman, 72.

[71] But Charles, supported by his brother King Louis IX of France, did not press himself to accept the papal conditions. See Jordan, *Origines*, 482–485.

[72] In a manifesto to the people of Rome, dated 24 May 1265, Manfred boasted of his Balkan territories as the greater part of Romania ("maiori parti Romanie") See B. Capasso, *Historia diplomatica Regni Siciliae 1250–1266* (Naples, 1874) no 274.

To Palaeologus, Illustrious Emperor [!] of the Greeks. . . The epistle of Your Imperial Excellency, which our venerable brother Nicholas, Bishop of Croton, presented to us . . . was received and read . . . and we were filled with great joy. . . For we see that you . . . , humbly recognizing us with filial reverence, have called us, unworthy as we are and small in merit . . . , father of fathers and highest pontiff of the Apostolic throne. . .

In response to imperial expressions of this sort, Urban expatiated on the growth of malice, hate, and schism, the clash of arms and outpouring of blood, which were all due to the misunderstanding of the dogma of each church, fostered in turn by the inadequacy of interpreters. Then he added:

The Bishop [of Croton] revealed to you and yours all the precepts of the true faith. . . You have found the Holy Roman Church of God not different from yours in its divine dogmas of the faith, but feeling almost with you toward them. . . You confess in your letter that you have undertaken this matter with very sincere faith, that you honor, believe, and hold . . . the sacraments of this Roman Church.[73]

Urban's letter included a long paean of rejoicing that "the Emperor of such a power and so great an Empire declares that he is ready to offer himself for the propagation of the Catholic faith." [74] Urban stated further that although he had previously sent to Palaeologus four Franciscan brothers, he was now, at Michael's request, dispatching the Bishop of Croton, together with the Franciscans, Gerard of Prato and Raynerius of Sens. It was Urban's instruction that the previous papal apocrisiarii, if still in Constantinople, should participate in the negotiations for union. As a final word, the Pope advised Michael to complete the union as quickly as possible "since delay is always harmful to those prepared and because in any case such an important work ought not to be deferred." [75]

The papal embassy arrived at the Golden Horn in the summer

[73] Guiraud, *Reg. Urbain*, II, no. 848, 405–408, esp.: "in ipsa epistola contendo, quod ea fide sincerissima suscipis, honoras, credis, et tenes; et . . . sacramenta ejusdem Romane ecclesie, veneraris."
[74] *Ibid.*: "Imperator tantae potentie et qui tam magni imperii moderatur, abenas, promptum se exponit et offert ad fidem catholicam propagandam."
[75] *Ibid.*, 408.

of 1264. The most important result of the ensuing negotiations (known from a letter sent to Michael by Urban's successor, Clement IV)[76] was an agreement for the convocation of a council to settle the temporal and ecclesiastical questions at issue. This, a major concession on the part of Urban, clearly reveals how dangerous politically the papal position must have been. But before further progress could be made, Urban died, on 2 October, 1264.

Even had Urban lived, however, a successful consummation of union at the time would have been unlikely. To both sides union was simply an instrument: for Michael it was only a means of warding off the danger of a Latin attack and providing a respite from his Moreot defeats; to Urban it was primarily a way of preventing the realization of his gravest fear — a Hohenstaufen Constantinople. Clearly, religious accord was secondary in importance to political aims.

PALAEOLOGUS AND THE BALKANS.
IMPERIAL NEGOTIATIONS WITH VENICE

As Michael expected, the warm papal-Byzantine exchanges had repercussions in other spheres. In the first place William of Achaia now seems to have agreed to a truce with Michael.[77] Unionist negotiations, moreover, led, indirectly at least, to the amelioration of conditions in Epirus, which had again become a source of disquietude for Palaeologus. The Despot Michael II, deprived of further military support from his preoccupied son-in-law Manfred,[78] was forced to sue for peace, and at a meeting with the Emperor's brother, John Palaeologus, the Despot took oaths of obedience and submission to the Basileus.[79] This, how

---

[76] See Wadding, *Ann. Min.*, IV, 302: "Ceterum Fratres ipsi aliquandim in tu Curia commorati, . . . volentes tandem obtinere quod poterant, in quandam tecum . . . convenere scripturam, certos articulos continentem" (cited wrongly i Norden, 432, note 2). Cf. new ed., Tautu, *Acta*, 63.

[77] It was apparently at this time that the proposal was made for the union of the Palaeologan and Villehardouin houses through marriage. See above, note 63.

[78] Pach., 215: τὰ πολλὰ πρὸ τοῦ τῷ Ἰταλικῷ στρατεύματι φρυαττόμενος· διὰ . . τὸν Μαμφρέ . . . ἀφεὶς τὸ ἐπ' ἐκείνοις θαρρεῖν.

[79] Pach., 215, ll. 6–14.

ever, was the only bright spot in an otherwise precarious Balkan situation.

Stephen Uroš I, ruler of Serbia, for some time had been making incursions into Greek territory, while far more serious trouble was being stirred up by the Bulgar Tsar Constantine Tich.[80] At the instigation of the latter's Tsarina, Irene, who had never forgotten Michael's blinding of her young brother John Lascaris,[31] Tich within a four-year period had twice invaded the Greek Empire. However, he had lost certain towns to Michael, including the Black Sea ports of Mesembria and Anchialos.[82] In order to recover these territories Tich negotiated for aid both with the Sultan of Iconium 'Izz-al-Dīn, a disaffected refugee living at the court in Constantinople,[83] and with Mangu, Khan of the Tatars of south Russia.

In the spring of 1265 Mangu sent to the Bulgar Tsar a large force under the command of his general Nogai, who proceeded to ravage Thrace as he marched toward Constantinople. It was precisely at this juncture that Michael Palaeologus, returning with only a few troops from Thessaly to Thrace, was ambushed by the savage Tatars and Bulgars (the latter having been informed of Michael's movements by the Sultan). The situation was of the utmost gravity. Not only had Palaeologus just dismissed most of his troops because of the cessation of hostilities in western Greece, but the barbarian armies were only one half day's march from the capital itself. Even Michael's own officers deserted, Pachymeres relates, each rushing away to save himself, when confronted by the approach of the dreaded Tatars and Bulgars.[84] Michael, almost alone,[85] was able to escape only by crossing the Ganos

[80] On this see C. Jireček, *Geschichte der Bulgaren* (Prague, 1876) 271.

[81] Greg., 99, ll. 21ff.

[82] Pach., 211, l. 1. Cf. also G. Balaschev, *The Emperor Michael VIII Palaeologus and the Establishment of the Turk-Oguz on the Black Sea*, Rumanian tran. from Russian by N. Banescu (Jassi, 1940) (inaccessible to me).

[83] See Pach., 229, l. 18.

[84] Most were apprehended and slaughtered by the Tatars. On this entire campaign see Pach., 229–234, and Greg., 99–100.

[85] According to Greg., 100, l. 18, he was completely alone. Cf. Pach., 235, ll. –11.

mountains and reaching the Marmora coast, where by extreme good fortune he came upon two Latin vessels. Quickly embarking, he arrived the second day afterwards at Constantinople.[86] Fortunately, the Bulgaro-Tatar armies did not then choose to attack the capital, now almost denuded of troops.[87] Thus did Michael survive one of the narrowest escapes of his career.

Soon after expelling the Genoese from Constantinople, Michael entered a new phase in his diplomacy: he opened negotiations with his old enemy Venice with a view to an accord. No doubt the Genoese naval defeats at the hands of the Venetians made him realize that Genoa was now of less use to him than before, and that he should instead seek a rapprochement with the power whose enmity he had chief cause to dread. Of Michael's fear of an attack by sea there can be no doubt. Nor was the possibility of an alliance between Venice and Charles, should the latter prove victorious over Manfred, to be cast aside lightly.

In order to inform the Doge of his desire to negotiate, Michael secretly sent to Venice Arrigo Trevisano, a noble Venetian who had been languishing in a Byzantine prison. The then Doge Rainerio Zeno subsequently returned Trevisano to Constantinople with Benedetto Grillone.[88] These two envoys were themselves replaced by Jacopo Delphino and Jacopo Contareno, and on 18 June 1265 a treaty — more accurately a truce to hostilities — was drawn up between the two powers. The principal stipulations follow: [89]

(1) Quarters were promised to Venetian colonists in Constantinople, Thessalonica, and other important centers of the Greek Empire, with the chief official of the colonists to be called *bajulus* (*bailli*).[90] (2) Venetian merchants were to be immune

[86] Greg., 100, ll. 20ff.: τριήρεσιν ἐνέτυχε δύο Λατινικαῖς. The ships were perhaps Genoese, since Heraclea was not far away.

[87] See Pach., 236ff.

[88] See Canale (who seems to date this 1264), 496–498.

[89] Canale, 582–584 and T.-Th., III, 78. For the treaty in both Latin and Greek versions see T.-Th., III, 66–89 and, in Greek, F. Miklosich and J. Müller, *Act et diplomata*, III, 76–84. Cf. Dölger, *Regesten*, no. 1934, who carefully discusse the treaty's date.

[90] Name changed therefore (evidently at Michael's insistence) from podest: *Bajulus* is Latin, *bailli* the French form often used in English.

from duties in Byzantium.[91] (3) The Genoese were to be expelled from the Empire, and Michael promised to conclude no treaty with Genoa except with the consent of Venice.[92] (4) The Venetians pledged to remain at peace with Michael even should a power friendly to Venice attack Constantinople. Those named as potential enemies of Palaeologus were the papacy, France, Sicily, Castile, Aragon, England, Charles of Anjou, Pisa, and Ancona.[93] (5) In the event of a Genoese attack on Constantinople, Venice was to aid Michael with ships equal in number to the Genoese. (6) Venice was to retain possession of Modon, Coron (the Republic's "two eyes" in southern Greece), and Crete. (7) Michael was to be permitted to attack the Latin lords of Negropont, and the Venetians on the island (whose position was guaranteed) were forbidden to aid the lords with provisions. (8) To Michael would be surrendered the Latin possessions in the Aegean Sea belonging to the Greek Empire at the time of the Latin conquest, and those enfeoffed to the Prince of Achaia.[94]

The above stipulations, though not nearly so one-sided as in the case of Nymphaeum, nevertheless awarded to Venice substantial concessions; indeed, she would secure almost the same commercial position in Constantinople that she had had before 1261. In spite of this, the Doge did not ratify the document. Perhaps the overtures of Michael seemed evidence of weakness on his part. Moreover, although the convention expressly guaranteed

[91] From two later documents in T.-Th., III, 144 and 171, it would appear that Michael at this time opened up the Black Sea to Venetian merchants.

[92] T.-Th., III, 71 and 82. Although Michael had already made the Genoese move from Constantinople to Heraclea, he was still exchanging ambassadors with the Commune, as is seen from the anonymous account of the squire of the Genoese envoy, Frexone Malocello, sent to Constantinople "propter ardua negotia comunis Iane et imperatoris Constantinopolitani." While in the capital the squire stole a Greek relic and carried it to Genoa! (Note that the embassy is dated "verso 1265.") On this incident see P. Riant, Exuviae Sacrae Constantinopolitanae, II (Geneva, 1878) 671.

[93] Note especially the inclusion of Charles of Anjou, the papacy, and even of Pisa (T.-Th., III, 67 and 79). Probably Michael was already uneasy at the prospect of a war with Charles.

[94] T.-Th., III, 68–69 and 80–81. For an analysis of the term "scala" mentioned in the treaty see H. Kahane, "Italo-byzantinische Etymologien, Scala," Byz.-neugriechische Jahrb., XVI (1939–40) 42ff.

Venetian island possessions, Michael's intentions against Negropont and the Archipelago isles were too obvious for a mere treaty to insure his disinterest.[95] Hardly three years before, in 1262, Michael had in fact sent an expedition to Crete, which, with the cooperation of the island's Greek population, had nearly wrested it from Venetian control.[96] Very possibly, also, the recent expulsion of the Genoese from Constantinople may have been a warning of a similar fate awaiting a Venetian restoration under Greek tutelage.

But the chief reason for Venice's failure to ratify the document (besides the possibility of securing even more favorable concessions from Michael) was no doubt the hope of regaining her old predominance in Byzantium under Latin auspices. It is not impossible that Venice might already have entered into negotiations with Charles (he was then on his way to Naples) for Angevin cooperation to restore the Latin Empire.[97] Support for such a theory may perhaps be found in the inclusion in the rejected treaty of Charles's name among potential Greek enemies, and especially in Pope Urban's announcement that Charles, after the defeat of Manfred, would aid in the re-establishment of the Latin Empire.[98] A further reason for avoiding commitment must

[95] In the treaty (T.-Th., 68 and 80), e.g., Michael referred to the Latin islands "quae erant Imperii mei, et Principatus, quando Latini eas tenebant a Constantinopoli . . . quod sint Imperii mei." Michael promised to Venice territory in Halmyros on the mainland of Greece opposite Negropont, but he was to retain the wharf so that the Venetians would be unable to provision Negropont (ibid., 80). Cf. Norden, 439 and notes 1 and 2, who believes that by the treaty terms Venice in effect would give up Negropont to the Emperor.

[96] On the Cretan struggle see S. Xanthoudides, Ἡ Ἐνετοκρατία ἐν Κρήτῃ καὶ οἱ κατὰ τῶν Ἐνετῶν ἀγῶνες τῶν Κρητῶν (Athens, 1939) 45–48. As early as 1262 Michael had sent to Crete a Greek agent named Stengos who began to arouse the Greek population. After capturing a fortress, Stengos sought to persuade the Greeks of the island to eject their Venetian masters. Though the Greek population was eager to join Stengos, the Greek archons (including the famous Alexios Kallerges) demanded additional aid before granting overt support. After four years of inconclusive conflict, an agreement was reached in 1265 between the Greeks and Venetians of the island. See T.-Th., III, 80, for the projected treaty between Michael and Venice in 1265, by which Michael agreed to remove from Crete all of his men to be found there: "omnes homines mei Imperii, qui reperientur ibidem, meum Imperium debeat accipere."

[97] See Manfroni, Marina italiana, 18, note 2.

[98] See above, notes 14 and 16. In the treaty here under discussion Michael insisted that all the crusaders to the Holy Land using Venetian ships take an oath not to move against his Empire. See T.-Th., III, 68 and 79.

have been the uncertainty over the coming struggle, so vital for all Italy, between the forces of Charles and Manfred.

In the light of these considerations we may understand the Doge's refusal to approve the pact, which in effect would have required Venice to negate her previous policy, to bar an alliance with Charles for an attack on Byzantium, and even to recognize Michael as *de jure* Emperor of Constantinople. From the Doge's standpoint it was more advisable to maintain the status quo, while awaiting the outcome of the impending struggle in Sicily. Thus, in the failure of the negotiations between Michael and Venice, the real beneficiaries were the Genoese, who escaped the peril of being completely ousted from the Byzantine Empire.

PART III

the conflict between michael palaeologus
and the king of sicily, charles of anjou

1266-1282

9

CHARLES OF ANJOU AND MICHAEL
PALAEOLOGUS

(1266–1270)

CHARACTERS OF CHARLES AND MICHAEL

R elations between Michael Palaeologus and the Latin West entered a new and more critical phase with the defeat of Manfred at the famous battle of Benevento (26 February 1266)[1] and the subsequent enthronement of the victor, Charles of Anjou, as King of Sicily. Under this dynamic new antagonist of Michael a formidable coalition was soon to be organized — a coalition not only of the Balkan powers surrounding Constantinople but of all the hitherto disunited elements of Michael's Latin opposition, including, at last, even the papacy and Venice. In consequence, from 1266 until shortly before his death in 1282 Michael was constrained to devote almost com-

---

[1] According to the *Annales Caesenates*, *RISS*, XIV (1729) 1103, at Benevento Greeks and Cumans fought on the side of Manfred: "capta est maxima multitudo Saracenorum, Comorum, et Graecorum." This is only one example of the interesting fact that in this period we see Greek troops fighting on Italian soil under Latin commanders. See above, Chapter 3, notes 3–4, for mention of Greek forces sent by John III Vatatzes to aid the Western Emperor Frederick II. Also see below, for mention of Moreot troops (Franks and probably at least a few Greeks) fighting at the famous battle of Tagliacozzo (1268), the scene of Conradin's defeat by Charles. Note especially the *Chron. of Morea* (Greek, ll. 6291ff., and French, pars. 477ff.; also cf. Villani, I, 353), which attributes that victory to the counsel of Prince William of Achaia, who advised Charles to use cunning "after the fashion of the Greeks and Turks."

plete attention to the defeat of Charles, the fulfillment of whose ambition would have brought about the destruction of the Byzantine Empire and reimposition of Latin rule in Constantinople. In the grand conflict between the two rulers, not only were the entire resources of each state thrown into the balance, but almost the whole Mediterranean area in one way or another was involved, from Castile and Aragon in the West to Egypt and Mongol territories in the East.

As the characters of Michael and Charles exerted a decisive influence on their diplomatic and military activities, a comparison, albeit brief, seems in order. Of the sources, only Gregoras has attempted directly to contrast the two men. His analysis, valuable at the same time for its insight into the Greek attitude to their struggle, reads:

Charles, motivated not by small but great ambitions, implanted in his mind like a seed the resolution of taking Constantinople. He dreamed that if he could become master of it, he would restore the entire monarchy, so to speak, of Julius Caesar and Augustus.[2] He was very able not only in planning what he wished to do but in easily translating his thoughts into action. Clearly he far surpassed all his predecessors in the strength of his nature and intelligence. . . Nevertheless, neither his actions against the Greeks nor those of Michael Palaeologus against the Latins could be brought to a successful conclusion. For the strength of both was for a long time so evenly matched that it was well said (this was the opinion of discerning people) that if at that time such an Emperor had not been directing Greek affairs, the Empire would easily have succumbed to Charles, the King of Italy [sic]; and, conversely, if such a King had not then been at the helm of Italian affairs, the hegemony of Italy would with little difficulty have passed to Michael Palaeologus. . . During his entire life Charles never ceased to nourish plans and to carry out belligerent acts against the Greeks. But he was unsuccessful since he was checked by the counter-measures and neutralizing acts of the Emperor.[3]

---

[2] Cf. similar remarks of Sanudo, *Istoria*, 138: "aspirava alla Monarchia del Mondo," and of Thomas Tuscus, *Gesta imperatorum et pontificum, MGH SS*, XXII, 519, who quotes Charles himself as saying: "uni enim valenti viro non sufficeret totus mondus" (cf. *ibid.*, 524). Jordan, *Origines*, 407, terms Charles's ambition chimerical.

[3] For this entire quotation (culled from three passages) see Greg., 123, ll. 8–15;

As a parallel to this passage it would be instructive to quote a Latin source. But while Western accounts abound in descriptions of Charles, they have only summarily dealt with the character of Michael, limiting themselves to the usual accusations of Greek perfidy and ecclesiastical apostasy. An exception is the Venetian (or at least north Italian) *Chronicon Marchiae Tarvisinae et Lombardiae,* which, in a brief but telling phrase, terms Michael "a crafty and astute man, who knows that the labor of an able person conquers all and especially that all things obey money." [4] As for Charles, most of the Latin sources, like Gregoras, stress the vastness of his ambition, a veritable megalomania for carving out a Mediterranean Empire of both East and West by seizing Constantinople.[5] They emphasize too his restless activity, vehemence, and impatience to carry out his plans [6] — qualities clearly reflected in Charles's Sicilian rescripts, which almost invariably demand of his officials immediate action and infallible execution.[7] Of these characteristics, sovereign ambition and ability to act swiftly and decisively were possessed to a high degree, as we have seen, by Michael Palaeologus also. If we add to these a ruthlessness on the part of Michael that would hesitate at almost nothing, and equal talent on the part of both rulers for diplomacy and intrigue, we can readily understand the scope and intensity of their conflict, which in the end was to prove catastrophic for the Kingdom of Sicily and utterly exhausting to the Byzantine Empire.

144, ll. 16ff.; and 145, ll. 16–20. Gregoras, of course, refers to the Greeks as Romans.

[4] *RISS* (ed. Botteghi), VIII, 47: "sciens vir callidus et astutus quia labor probi omnia vincit, pariterque cognoscens quod pucunie obediunt omnia." Cf. Sanudo, *Istoria,* 135, who compares Palaeologus to the famous fourteenth century Ghibelline of Lucca, Castruccio Castracani.

[5] Cf. Jordan, *Origines,* 408: "c'est la grande pensée de son règne."

[6] Cf. G. Villani, *Cronica* (ed. Moutier-Dragomanni) I, 320: "[Carlo] in fare ogni grande impresa sicuro . . . covidoso d'acquistare terra e signoria . . . usava di dire, che dormendo, tanto tempo si perdea."

[7] For example, in F. Carabellese, *Carlo d'Angiò nei rapporti politici e commerciali con Venezia e l'Oriente* (Bari, 1911) — hereafter cited as Carabellese — 52, note 1: "negotium Achaye . . . dilationem non patitur."

FIRST ANGEVIN ADVANCES TOWARD THE BYZANTINE EMPIRE

When it was that Charles first contemplated the conquest of Byzantium cannot precisely be determined, though it seems certain that his ambition was affected by the geographic position of his new realm and by the Eastern aspirations of his Norman and Hohenstaufen predecessors.[8] If we are to believe the Greek historians, it was not long after the battle of Benevento (26 February 1266) that Charles began to make preparations for an attack on Constantinople.[9] That he could occupy himself with such plans even before the consolidation of his position in the Regno seems remarkable.[10] At any rate, his first overt act in the direction of the Greek East was an attempt to seize the Ionian coast opposite Italy, to which legitimate access was afforded by his claim to the possessions of Manfred in Corfu and Epirus.

These territories — originally, as we have seen, the dowry of Michael of Epirus' daughter Helen — remained, after Manfred's death at Benevento, in the hands of the Hohenstaufen governor of Corfu, Philip Chinardo. Subsequently their original grantor, Michael II, attempted to regain them. The Despot, it seems, had requested or at least seconded the mediation of the pope for the creation of an alliance against Palaeologus, to be cemented by the marriage of his widowed daughter Helen (now the prisoner of Charles)[11] to the rich adventurer and Angevin supporter Prince

---

[8] The papacy apparently feared his ambition from the start, for in the covenant of 28 June 1265 granting Sicily to Charles, the latter was explicitly forbidden to make an alliance with anyone (even the Greeks!) against the Church: "nullam etiam confoederationem . . . cum aliquo . . . Christiano vel Graeco . . . contra Romanam Ecclesiam." See del Giudice, *Cod. dipl.*, I, 25; and cf. E. Léonard, *Les Angevins de Naples* (Paris, 1954) 103. Jordan, *Origines*, 419, believes the convention of 1264 even implied a prohibition to become Greek Emperor.

[9] See Greg., 123–124, and Pach., 317. Cf. Ptolemy of Lucca, *Historia ecclesiastica*, *RISS*, XI, 1162: "Anno Domini 1269 Ecclesia Romana vacante, et Imperio similiter . . . Rex Carolus . . . incipit versus Orientem suam potentiam dilatare." Also del Giudice, *Cod. dipl.*, I, 300, note 1, who believes Charles began preparations to conquer the Orient after vanquishing the Saracens of Lucera (1269).

[10] (The term "Regno," of course, refers to the Kingdom of Sicily.) Charles still had to overcome the opposition of certain Sicilian Ghibelline barons and repel an invasion in 1268 by the Hohenstaufen Conradin, King of Germany and nephew of Manfred.

[11] On Helen's subsequent fate see del Giudice, *Cod. dipl.*, I, 123, note 2, and Dendias, *Helen, passim,* esp. 272.

Henry of Castile. Evidence for this is two letters from Pope Clement IV to Charles and Henry himself, urging such a union as of potential benefit for the restoration of the Latin Empire.[12] It was the papal hope that Henry, younger brother of King Alfonso X of Castile, would in exchange for Corfu place his arms and vast wealth at the disposal of the Emperor Baldwin, in much the same manner in which Henry had helped to finance Charles's conquest of Sicily.[13]

Like Charles of Anjou, Clement IV was a Frenchman. But, as seemed inevitable to wearers of the tiara, once ensconced on the papal throne and imbued with ideals of the Petrine tradition, Clement began to grow apprehensive over Angevin ambitions, fearing in fact lest the King covet the Epirot territories for himself. Indeed, Charles, realizing that possession of these territories would provide a key to the Greek Empire, could not, or more likely would not, persuade his prisoner Helen to marry Henry of Castile.[14] And as if to add substance to the fears of Clement, his suzerain for Sicily, Charles had been secretly negotiating with the governor of the territories, Philip Chinardo.[15] Meanwhile, to complicate the situation further, Michael II offered Chinardo the hand of his sister-in-law. The offer was accepted and the marriage performed, but soon afterwards Chinardo was murdered, probably

[12] E. Jordan, *Les registres de Clément IV* (Paris, 1893) I, 398, nos. 1164, 1165; Martène and Durand, *Thesaurus novus anecdotorum* (Paris, 1717) II, 437–438, nos. 422, 423, esp.: "huiusmodi matrimonium ̃si consummatum fuerit . . . imperatori Constantinopolitano . . . plurimum credimus fructuosum."

[13] On the relations of Charles and Henry of Castile, see the Catalan Chronicle of Bernat D'Esclot, in J. Buchon, *Chroniques étrangères relatives aux expéditions françaises pendant le XIII⁰ siècle* (Paris, 1875) 607ff. (cf. F. Critchlow trans. of D'Esclot [Princeton, 1934] 167ff.); and a letter of Charles to Henry in del Giudice, *Cod. dipl.*, I, 193ff. (= I, 29, no. 15, of R. Filangieri, *I registri della cancelleria angioina* [Naples, 1950–1951], *Testi e documenti di storia napoletana* — hereafter, Filangieri). Cf. Dendias, *Helen*, 273ff. and del Giudice, *Don Arrigo Infante di Castiglia* (Naples, 1875) (unavailable to me). Finally, for a recent account of the Henry of Castile episode see R. L. Wolff, "Mortgage," 76–78.

[14] According to Dendias, *Helen*, 271, Clement, Charles, Henry, and Michael II all agreed to the marriage, but Helen alone refused. Dade, 27, believes, with probably greater justification, that it was Charles's refusal that caused the plan to fail. Cf. a letter of Clement (ed. Jordan, IV, 392, no. 1131), indicating that the Pope saw through a plan of Charles to seize Corfu for himself by means of an alliance with the sons of Chinardo, Manfred's governor of Corfu.

[15] See Martène and Durand, *Thes. nov.*, II, col. 382.

by agents of Michael II.[16] Enraged over the crime, the son of Philip, Gazo Chinardo, now handed over the territories to Charles of Anjou, who on 16 January 1267 appointed Gazo himself captain-general of Corfu.[17] Thus in the end both Michael II and the Pope were outmaneuvered by Charles, and Henry of Castile had to indemnify himself elsewhere.[18]

Following the battle of Benevento, the Emperor Baldwin — who had fallen from papal grace because of his alliance with Manfred — lost little time in joining the side of the victor. After reconciling himself with the Pope, to whom he declared his great joy over Benevento,[19] Baldwin then approached Charles. The latter, fully cognizant of the value of Baldwin's imperial title, eagerly welcomed him and his son, Philip of Courtenay, both of whom subsequently settled at the Angevin court and received annual pensions from the Sicilian treasury.[20]

In order to strengthen his position further with respect to Constantinople, Charles at this time also established close relations with Prince William of Achaia. According to the *Chronicle of Morea* it was Charles's victory over Manfred ("a tribute to the race of Franks of which he too was one") that first attracted

---

[16] On Philip Chinardo see Pach., 508 and del Giudice, "La famiglia di Re Manfredi," *Arch. st. prov. nap.*, IV (1879) 77ff. Also P. Alexander, "A Chrysobull of the Emperor Andronicus II Palaeologus in Favor of the See of Kanina in Albania," *Byzantion*, XV (1940–1941) 199f.

[17] Pach., 508ff. and del Giudice, *Cod. dipl.*, I, no. 90, 278 (= Filangieri, I, 50, no. 97). Charles soon replaced Gazo with Garnerio Alemanno, ordering all "tam Latinis quam Grecis," to obey him (*Cod. dipl.*, I, 298; Filangieri, I, 78, no. 206). See also Charles's conciliatory letter of March 23–24 1267 instructing Alemanno to readmit to Corfu all Greeks who had fled except those responsible for the murder of Philip Chinardo (*Cod. dipl.*, I, 307–308; Filangieri, I, 82, no. 224).

[18] Angered, Henry thereupon offered his aid to the Ghibelline opponents of Charles. But he was subsequently captured at Tagliacozzo by Charles, who had him enclosed and carried around in an iron cage. See del Giudice, *Cod. dipl.*, II, 285ff.; Saba Malaspina, *Historia* (ed. Del Re), in *Cronisti . . . napoletani*, II, 280ff.

[19] See the papal response in Martène and Durand, *Thes. nov.*, II, no. 9698, col. 354E, and another letter in del Giudice, *Cod. dipl.*, I, 194. On Baldwin's previous relations with Manfred see R. L. Wolff, "Mortgage and Redemption," 65ff.

[20] See J. Buchon, *Nouvelles recherches . . . de Morée* (Paris, 1845) II, 214. On the amount of Baldwin's pension see C. Minieri-Riccio, *Il regno di Carlo I di Angiò negli anni 1271-1272* (Naples, 1875) 87; and Carabellese, 8–9.

WESTERN (above) AND GREEK PORTRAITS OF MICHAEL

CHARLES OF ANJOU

William's attention to him. Thereupon William, who from a practical point of view must have realized the futility of hoping to eject Michael Palaeologus from the Morea without external aid, proposed a marriage alliance between his daughter Isabella and Charles's young son Philip. The offer was accepted and William and his daughter sailed to Naples, where the marriage was performed.[21] Some months later the new allies journeyed together to the papal court at Viterbo, where, probably from 25 April 1267 on, pourparlers took place among Charles, William, and the titular Emperor Baldwin over the fate of Achaia and the Latin Empire.[22] These negotiations resulted in the signing of two treaties, both of the greatest importance for relations between Byzantium and the Latins. Before analyzing these documents it will be necessary briefly to review the interim actions of the Greek Emperor.

PALAEOLOGUS AND THE LATINS TO THE TREATIES OF VITERBO

The prospect of a destructive war between Charles and Manfred, which would rend Italy and keep it too occupied for an expedition to succor Latin Romania, had been understandably welcome to Palaeologus. Thus the Emperor profited from the respite afforded by the year 1265, when the storm clouds were gathering over Sicily, to perfect the defenses of his capital, strengthen his fleet, and attend to the various internal problems of his Empire. Chief among the latter was the prolonged schism within the Greek church, which had arisen in 1261 over Palaeologus' callous blinding of the rightful Emperor, young John IV Lascaris,[23] whose presence had become more and more embar-

---

[21] Greek *Chron.*, ll. 6265ff. (esp. 6270), 6285, 6346, and 6377–6468ff.

[22] The date is given in C. Minieri-Riccio, *Itinerario di Carlo I. di Angiò* (Naples, 1872) 2, and P. Durrieu, *Les archives angevines de Naples*, II, 167. F. Cerone, "La sovranità napoletana sulla Morea e sulle isole vicine," *Arch. st. prov. nap.*, XLI (1916) 21, and Zakythinos, *Despotat*, I, 45–46, believe that William did not personally appear at Viterbo. But Longnon has recently discovered a document revealing the contrary to be true. See below, text for note 27.

[23] On the blinding of John see Pach., 190ff. John was then imprisoned in the fortress of Dacibyza in Bithynia. Palaeologus meanwhile also disposed of John's

rassing to Michael in his climb to sole power in the state.

The year 1265 witnessed no further exchanges for union between Constantinople and the papacy. With Urban's death and the crystallization of the Hohenstaufen-Angevin conflict, Michael's need for papal aid had diminished. Nevertheless, the lull did not deceive him, for he was aware that once the breach in the West was closed, his Latin opponents would all too quickly redirect their attention to Constantinople. Anticipating, therefore, that the papacy could still be of use to him, Michael retained at his court in a position of honor the Bishop of Croton, whom Pope Urban had dispatched to the Bosporus just before his death. Permitting the prelate to dress in the manner of Greek bishops, Michael even arranged to give him a bishopric in the East. But, as Pachymeres relates, the Bishop soon rendered himself obnoxious and as a result was banished to Heraclea in Pontus.[24] The specific reason for his exile is unknown — possibly his bearing as a hybrid Greco-Latin ecclesiastic from south Italy was too arrogant for the Byzantine clergy, or he may perhaps have insisted prematurely on the implementation of union. Whatever the cause, his name henceforth disappears from papal-imperial correspondence,[25] and he seems to have played no further role in unionist negotiations.

What must once more have aroused Michael's anxieties was Charles's occupation of Corfu, situated uncomfortably close to imperial possessions in Macedonia and the Morea. Although it was for Michael the first tangible evidence of Angevin aggressive designs, it could not have been an unmitigated surprise, since Urban had already proclaimed that Charles's victory over Manfred would lead to re-establishment of the Latin Empire.[26]

---

sisters, the Lascarid princesses, by marrying them off to Latins: the eldest to Matthieu de Walincourt, a Frankish baron of the Morea; the second to the Count of Ventimiglia (Ventimiglia is situated near Genoa); and the third to a Bulgar prince. On these marriages see Pach., 180–181, and Greg., 92–93.

[24] Pach., 360, ll. 10ff.

[25] Except for a letter of Michael to Clement in which is mentioned the old embassy of the Bishop of Croton. See below, note 40. Cf. Norden, 449, note 2. On the Bishop see also above, Chapter 8, text and notes 66–75.

[26] A papal register of 28 March 1265, states that Charles "subsidium . . . imperii Romanie . . . dabit" (Jordan, *Reg. Clém.*, no. 224, 62).

THE TREATIES OF VITERBO (1267)

A key event affecting Michael's relations with the West was the signing in May of 1267, at the papal residence of Viterbo, of two treaties of which the aim was restoration of the Latin Empire of Romania. Of the two documents the second is the more important, but its companion-piece, signed three days before (on May 24), is of interest because of its revelation that the suzerainty secured by Charles over the Morea was to be preceded by the actual transfer of that principality. The chief provisions under which the cession was to be made are as follows:

(1) Prince William of Achaia's daughter and heiress, Isabella, was to marry Philip of Anjou, son of Charles. (2) William would retain the usufruct of Achaia during his lifetime, subject to certain restrictions regarding donations and infeudations. (3) At the death of William, the principality was to pass to Philip of Anjou or the latter's children. Failing such successors, it would go to Charles himself.[27]

The significance of the second Viterbo treaty, dated May 27, lies in the fact that it was in essence a blueprint for conquest of the Byzantine Empire. Bringing together Charles, Baldwin, William, and the Pope (except for Venice, all the Western powers from which Michael had most to fear), it defined the exact terms under which Charles would undertake to restore the Latin Empire. The general objective was enunciated in an introduction:

Michael Palaeologus, the schismatic, having usurped the name of Emperor . . . has seized the imperial city of Constantinople and the whole Empire, expelled the Emperor Baldwin and the Latins residing there, and now only a part of the principality of Achaia and Morea remains, of which he has also subjugated a considerable area . . . We, therefore, are ready with God's aid to undertake the pious task of restoring the noble limb severed by the schismatics from the body of our common mother, the Holy Roman Church.[28]

[27] For the treaty and an analysis of it see J. Longnon, "Le rattachement de la principauté de Morée au royaume de Sicile en 1267," *Jl. des savants* (1942) 134ff. It had hitherto been believed that William's chancellor, Leonard of Veroli, represented the absent Prince at the Viterbo negotiations (*ibid.*, 140).

[28] Treaty printed in del Giudice, *Cod. dipl.*, II, 30ff. (for the passage quoted

197

Following are the notable provisions embodied in the convention: (1) Charles pledged that he or his heirs would provide, within a period of six or a maximum of seven years, 2,000 cavalrymen to fight for one year in Romania.[29] (2) In return for military aid, the Latin Emperor Baldwin would cede to Charles suzerainty over the principality of Achaia. (3) The territories formerly constituting the dowry of Helen of Epirus were to be ceded to Charles but with bonds of vassalage to Baldwin.[30] (4) All islands lying outside the bay of Abydos were to be granted to Charles except for Mytilene, Samos, Kos, and Chios, all four of which would remain in the possession of Baldwin and his heirs.[31] (5) One-third of the expected conquests in Romania would be assigned to Charles in full sovereignty; the other two-thirds, including Constantinople and the four islands, would constitute the share of Baldwin. Any investitures to be granted by Baldwin would have to come from his own portion. (6) From the territory to be conquered Charles could select any part as his share. Expressly named were the Despotate of Epirus, Albania, and Serbia. (7) Charles could add to his third the Kingdom of Thessalonica if the persons to whom Baldwin had already granted it as fief should fail to fulfill their obligations.[32] (8) In the event that Baldwin and his son Philip died without legal heirs the imperial throne would devolve upon Charles and the House of Anjou. (9) Venice was guaranteed all her former rights in the Latin Empire.[33] (10) Finally, to cement the alliance between

---

see 31–33); Ducange, *Histoire de Constantinople*, I, 455ff.; and Filangieri, I, 94ff., no. 3.

[29] Del Guidice, II, 33. Included in this number would be the military contribution of William of Achaia.

[30] Del Giudice, II, 36. The cession of these territories (which included Corfu and the Epirot coast between Butrinto and Avlona) was only the regularization of a fact. See Longnon, "Rattachement," 137.

[31] Del Giudice, II, 37. In the document Kos is named Angos, though it was then generally called Langos, on which see Dade, 29, note 156. Note omission of the small isle of Nikaria (Greek, Ikaria), listed in the treaty of 1204 as a possession of Baldwin. (Cf. T.-Th., I, 476ff.) The great islands named were at this time in Greek possession.

[32] Del Giudice, II, 37–38; cf. Norden, 312; and see above, Chapter 8, note 64

[33] Del Giudice, II, 43. This clause was inserted in the hope of securing th

Baldwin and Charles, Philip of Courtenay would espouse Charles's daughter, Beatrice of Anjou, when she reached marriageable age.[33a]

It is obvious from the provisions cited that implementation of the treaty would in effect make Charles master of the Byzantine Empire. For a bare promise of aid to Baldwin, Charles would secure immediate, tangible results. His acquisition of suzerainty over, and eventual possession of, Achaia would extend his influence to the Aegean and furnish a base from which he could move by sea directly on Constantinople. Moreover, his claim to Helen's dowry, now legalized, would provide a firm foothold in the Balkans from which he could launch a land assault against the capital. This was of particular importance because the Angevin fleet was as yet incapable of attacking Constantinople successfully.

A striking negative feature of the treaty, however, was Charles's failure to secure for himself an immediate claim to the imperial title. It has been suggested that Baldwin, weak in character and impecunious as always, could not have resisted Charles's desire for the crown, had it not been for the intervention of Pope Clement.[34] But it does not seem likely that Baldwin, after undergoing long years of mendicancy in Western Europe for the sake of his Empire, would have relinquished his rights at the first glimmer of hope for the recovery of his throne. Undoubtedly Clement himself had reason to fortify Baldwin's resolution, since for the papacy it would have been a disaster, a revival of the Hohenstaufen menace, if Charles were to become Emperor of Constantinople as well as King of Sicily. In such a position Charles, as the most powerful monarch in Christendom, could easily challenge papal authority in Italy.

---

aval aid of Venice, which at the moment was apparently negotiating with 'alaeologus.

[33a] Del Giudice, II, 40–41. Charles's rescripts may well reflect a change in his ttitude to Byzantium. In a pre-Viterban diploma (of 21 March 1267) granting afe-conduct to Greek envoys, Palaeologus is termed "Magnificus princeps Palle-logus Imperator Grecorum." After Viterbo, however, Michael is generally re-erred to simply as "Palaeologus."

[34] Dade, 32.

The role of the Pope at Viterbo deserves elaboration. By his sponsorship of the treaties Clement certainly seemed to participate in Latin designs against Constantinople. Yet, on the other hand, since 1266 he had been conducting negotiations with Michael for a religious entente. Despite this seeming contradiction,[35] papal objectives remained essentially the same as under Urban: to prevent the emergence of a Latin power capable of challenging papal temporal authority in Italy, and to restore the Greek East to obedience through the achievement of religious union. With the menace of the projected invasion of Italy by another Hohenstaufen, Conradin of Swabia, nephew of Manfred, Clement would need the protective aid of Charles. But at the same time he did not wish unduly to increase Angevin power to the point that it could not be controlled. Hence he furthered unionist negotiations with Palaeologus. These Greek exchanges had the dual purpose of demonstrating papal independence of Charles and of bringing about the submission of the Greeks to Rome. In brief, it was Clement's policy to hasten the subordination of the Greek church by playing up the ambitions of Charles, and, at the same time, through union to bar Charles from Constantinople.[36]

UNIONIST NEGOTIATIONS BETWEEN POPE CLEMENT IV
AND MICHAEL PALAEOLOGUS

Although following the death of Urban IV in 1264 Michael had suspended negotiations for union, news of Charles's resounding victory over Manfred at Benevento induced him to resume pourparlers. Thus in the spring of 1266 he sent an embassy to Pope Clement, headed by Theodore Meliteniotes, Archdeacon of the court clergy.[37] Clement, on his part, showed himself receptive

[35] There is a divergence of opinion on Clement's policy. R. Sternfeld, *Ludwigs des Heiligen Kreuzzug nach Tunis 1270 und die Politik Karls I. von Sizilien* (Berlin, 1896) 35 and 56, calls it contradictory, but Norden, 445, and esp. Dade, 32, believe it consistent and well-considered. Cf. J. Haller, *Hist. Zeit.*, XCIX (1907) 29.

[36] Cf. Norden, 448.

[37] That Michael opened negotiations is assumed from Clement's letter to him dated 4 March 1267: "nostros Apocrisarios . . . novissime ad te missos . . . nobi

to advances, though in the meantime he openly declared that a Guelph victory over Manfred would be advantageous to Achaia in its struggle with the Greek Emperor.[38] Michael's first ambassadors to Clement seem to have been not official Greek envoys but trusted Italian agents, most likely monks. Men of the cloth were less vulnerable to seizure on the long and hazardous journey to the papal court, which normally traversed many miles of Angevin territory.[39]

After an initial exchange of messages, Michael sent a letter to Clement modeled apparently on an original draft by the famous Greek scholar Manuel Holobolos.[40] Stressing the political advantages of union, Michael appealed to the Pope to prevent a war between Greeks and Latins on the grounds that it would benefit only the infidel. Victory, he wrote, would be impossible for the paynim before a union of Greeks and Latins, both of whom worship the same Christ. The Greeks, he continued, honor the Pope as spiritual father and chief of all priests, and are therefore eager for reconciliation of the churches. Indeed, with Constantinople once again in Greek hands there should be nothing to hinder union: it was in fact the Pope's duty to further it. Michael closed by declaring, in accordance with traditional Greek belief, that negotiations for union should take place in a general council to be convoked in a Greek city.[41] As evidence of clerical support

---

misisti aliquid verbo, vel scripto" (in Wadding, *Ann. Min.*, IV, 304). See also an Angevin safe-conduct of 21 March 1267, in favor of Theodore Meliteniotes and the imperial envoys returning from the Holy See, which directs Charles's men to prevent the envoys from coming into contact with Angevin enemies (del Giudice, *Cod. dipl.*, I, 302).

[38] See a papal letter of 8 March 1266 to the Archbishop of Narbonne, in Martène, *Thes. nov.*, II, col. 288: "levatur Achaia."

[39] Pach., 359. The journey usually extended on land from Constantinople to Avlona, by boat to Brindisi, and thence again overland to Viterbo or Rome.

[40] Norden, 449, note 2, has reconstructed the main points of this letter from three sources: a passage of Pach., 359; the beginning of Clement's subsequent reply to Palaeologus, dated 4 March 1267 (Wadding, *Ann. Min.*, IV, 301); and, mainly, a draft of Holobolos' letter, which Michael's epistle closely followed. See V. Festa, "Lettera inedita dell' Imperatore Michele VIII Paleologo al Clemente V," *Bessarione*, VI (1899) 42ff., and also "Ancora la lettera . . . ," *Bessarione*, VI, 529ff. Worth noting is Holobolos' reference (*ibid.*, 50) to the Greeks as Γραικοί, who, in the usual Greek chancery style, were designated as Romans.

[41] From Clement's response in Wadding, *Ann. Min.*, IV, 306: "concilium in

for his policy, Michael attached to his communication a letter from the patriarch.[42]

It may be observed that the conditions suggested by Michael for union were substantially the same as those agreed upon some years before between himself and the legates of Urban. But Pope Clement, more authoritarian than his predecessor, now found the proposals, in particular those regarding a council, definitely unacceptable.[43] In an uncompromising reply to the Emperor, dated 4 March 1267,[44] Clement set forth his own requisites for union. He insisted in the first place that the confession of faith, enclosed in his epistle, be accepted without discussion, and refused Michael's request for negotiations to take place at a general council. This meant that the Greeks must automatically accept the Latin doctrine of the *filioque* (procession of the Holy Spirit from the Son as well as the Father), the Latin usage of unleavened instead of leavened bread ("azyma"), and, most important, papal primacy in matters of ecclesiastical jurisdiction — in brief, it meant relinquishment without debate of all the crucial dogmatic, liturgical, and jurisdictional points of difference between the two churches.[45] Part of Clement's epistle is worth citing for the manner in which the papal position is set forth:

---

terra tua convocari petieris." In the draft of Holobolos' letter (ed. Festa, 54) no places are specified for the council.

[42] Wadding, *Ann. Min.*, IV, 269. The Patriarch was Germanos, as Arsenios had been deposed in 1267. (See below, Chapter 11, note 62.) On the patriarchal letter see Raynaldus, a. 1267, § 80, letter of Clement to the Greek patriarch: "tua epistola dicit."

[43] See Raynaldus, a. 1267, § 72.

[44] *Ibid.*, § 79.

[45] For an analysis of the confession of faith included in Clement's letter (upon which the subsequent Union of Lyons was to be based), see J. Karmires, "Ἡ ἀποδιδομένη εἰς τὸν Μιχαὴλ Η′ Παλαιολόγον Λατινικὴ ὁμολογία πίστεως τοῦ 1274," Ἀρχεῖον Ἐκκλησιαστικοῦ καὶ Κανονικοῦ Δικαίου, II (1947) 127ff. Karmires believes that the confession is completely Latin, lacks any Greek elements, and is based on a confession embodied in an epistle of Pope Leo IX sent in 1053 to the patriarch of Antioch. Cf. Norden, 420, note 4, who believes (1) that Clement's symbol was based on the forgeries of Dominicans of Romania (who supposedly — actually falsely — based their work on the Greek fathers) and (2) that Thomas Aquinas *Contra Graecos* was based on the work of these Dominicans. But see now also A. Dondaine, " 'Contra Graecos,' Premiers écrits polémiques des Dominicains d'Orient," *Archivum fratrum praedicatorum*, XXI (1951) 320ff.

202

To Palaeologus, Illustrious Emperor of the Greeks. . . Although you seek to have a council assembled in your land, we cannot agree to convoke such a council for the discussion or definition of the faith. Not that we fear the appearance of any particular persons or that the Greeks may take precedence over the sacred Roman church, but because it would be absolutely improper — indeed it cannot be permitted, since the purity of the faith cannot be cast into doubt. We have [instead] considered sending to you nuncios expert in the law of God with whom you, your clergy, and people may confer about these matters. . . If you have any doubts or fears about professing anything in the enclosed confession of faith, send us some of your expert clergy or people and we . . . will be ready in faith and hope to explain whatever they may inquire about. . . Prepare yourself so that at the arrival of our nuncios you, your clergy, and people may humbly accept and devoutly profess the truth of the faith in order that with the help of God progress may be facilitated. After you, your clergy, and people have accepted the true faith . . . , [then] you may request the convocation of a council by this See at a place most suitable to this See . . . , a council to be strengthened by a perpetual treaty between Latins and Greeks. . . With the opportunity afforded by this letter, we proclaim that neither are we wanting in justice (as we should not be) to those who complain that they are oppressed by your Magnificence, nor shall we desist from pursuing this matter in other ways which the Lord may provide for the salvation of souls.[46]

Clement's demand — that, prior to the convocation of a general council, the Emperor, clergy, and people all accept the position of Rome in matters of faith and primacy — would of course have been extremely difficult to carry out. Even more disturbing for Michael must have been the concluding sentence of the letter, a veiled threat that if union were not speedily accepted under the conditions imposed, Clement would unleash the Angevin against Constantinople. Substance was given to the threat by Clement's public pronouncements on Angevin aspirations; and papal influence over Charles had been manifested by the latter's grant

---

[46] Letter listed though unquoted in Jordan, *Reg. Clem.*, no. 585, 199. Cited in ull in Raynaldus, a. 1267, § 72–79; and Tautu, *Acta*, no. 23, 61–69. See esp. 67: Nos tamen nullo modo proponimus concilium ad discussionem seu definitionem ujusmodi convocare . . . indecens foret, immo nec licet, nec expedit in dubium evocari praemissam verae fidei puritatem." Also 68, esp.: "concilium per Sedem)sam ad locum qui ad hoc eidem Sedi videatur idoneus, convocari petieritis, ad aritatis vinculum inter Latinos et Graecos foedere perpetuo roborandum."

of safe-conducts to Greek envoys returning to Constantinople from the Curia.[47]

The Emperor replied immediately to the Pope. But he carefully circumvented the issue of ecclesiastical primacy, offering instead to participate in a crusade to the Holy Land. As with Urban, so now in the case of Clement, this proposal produced its effect, especially since Michael promised to enlist the aid of the King of Armenia, whose realm was strategically situated with respect to the Holy Land. As Michael pointed out, if the Greeks and Latins, attacking from both sides, were joined by the King of Armenia, the defeat of Egypt would be assured. Michael took the precaution, however, of insisting that in the absence of the Greek army in the Holy Land, the Pope should guarantee imperial territories against Latin attack.[48] Still vivid in the minds of the Greeks was the crusade of 1204!

To this message, Clement replied on 17 May 1267, but a few days before the signing of the anti-Palaeologan treaties at Viterbo. The papal response ran:

That you feel sympathy for the oppressions suffered by the Holy Land, and that you deplore the injuries undergone by our dear son in Christ, the illustrious King of Armenia . . . we would more readily believe . . . if your actions would correspond to your love. . . Our very dear brother in Christ, the Illustrious King of France, . . . has assumed the Cross . . . and if he wars on the Agarenes [the Muslims] from one side and you from the other, the enemies of the Cross and the faith may expect the ruin of their destructive sect. You say that you fear an incursion of the Latins because your land would be left naked and almost completely defenseless during your absence and that of your army. For this the answer is obvious: to remove your fear by its roots return to the unity of the Roman church. . . What you have written

[47] See del Giudice, Cod. dipl., I, 299, and C. Minieri-Riccio, Alcuni fatti riguardanti Carlo I. di Angiò, 1252–1270 (Naples, 1874) 24, for an Angevin diploma of 21 March 1267 ordering a ship to be readied for an embassy returning to Constantinople from the Curia. According to del Giudice, I, 299, note 1, this safe conduct is significant because the necessity for its issuance reveals open hostility on the part of Charles toward Michael even before the Viterbo treaties.

[48] Palaeologus' letter is not preserved, but its contents are easily deducible from the response of Clement IV, dated 17 May 1267 (summarized in Jordan, Reg. Clém., no. 1201, 404; quoted in Tautu, Acta, no. 25, 71, and 72). (The Armenia referred to above is, of course, Lesser Armenia in Cilicia.)

cannot serve as an excuse, namely that your prelates and clergy should be blamed for opposing the union and not you or your people. . . Certainly you . . . , as is proper, possess by far the greater authority; therefore, you should not allow the existence of an error of this kind which is contrary to God and all justice. If you cannot coerce them, shun them as schismatics.[49]

Although it is evident that both Michael and Clement [50] had good reason to desire union, circumstances beyond their control brought about another delay.[51] Michael's need for protection sharply diminished when the ill-fated Conradin of Hohenstaufen, Duke of Swabia and young son of King Conrad IV of Germany, prepared to cross the Alps to recover his Sicilian patrimony. At this juncture Charles, threatened by invasion, could of course harbor few thoughts of aggression against Byzantium. As matters stood, therefore, Michael was only too pleased to postpone unionist negotiations. But the battle of Tagliacozzo (23 August 1268),[52] in which Charles was victorious for the second time over the Hohenstaufen and which established undisputed Angevin hegemony over Sicily, once more made Michael eager for papal protection. Before the Emperor could resume relations with Clement, however, the Pope died (28 November 1268).[53] Clement's departure from the scene, following closely upon the outcome of

[49] Martène, *Thes. nov.*, II, par. 476, 1715, esp.: "Quod si dicis te timere Latinorum incursus, si terram quam possides ducto tecum exercitu, nudam reliqueres et quasi penitus immunitam, non est longe quaerenda responsio. Nam in te est terrorem hujusmodi a radice praecidere, si ad Romanae Ecclesiae rediens unitatem. . ."

[50] For insight into the Pope's personal attitude toward the Greeks, see letter of 9 June 1267, in Jordan, *Reg. Clém.*, no. 1209, 406; quoted in Tautu, *Acta*, no. 26, 72–73, esp.: "et eorum iactantiam, quorum scientia multum est tenuis, aequanimiter tollerare. . ." Cf. the same letter, Tautu, 73, in which Clement writes that if the Greeks failed to return to unity their blood would not stain his hands, since he had performed his duty.

[51] In a passage which may refer to Clement, Pachymeres (who evidently was not too familiar with the situation in the West at this time) notes (360) that the Pope was moved by Michael's entreaties and prevented an Angevin attack: εὔοδα τὰ τῆς πρὸς τὸν πάπαν ἱκετείας καθίστα καὶ ὁ Κάρουλος ἐκωλύετο.

[52] On Conradin and Charles see esp. K. Hampe, *Geschichte Konradins von Hohenstaufen* (Leipzig, 1942) *passim*.

[53] Pope Gregory X later (1272) wrote to Michael that it was only Clement's death and the difficulty of assembling proper apocrisiarii that had prevented Clement from dispatching further envoys (Guiraud, *Reg. Grég.*, no. 194, 72).

Tagliacozzo, was a disaster for Michael. For Charles, free of Hohenstaufen interference and in a position to block the election of a new pope, was now able to exercise a completely free hand against Constantinople.

THE GENOESE SETTLEMENT AT GALATA (1267)

The emergence of Charles of Anjou as a factor in Greco-Latin affairs altered the precarious political balance that Michael had striven so hard to maintain. In order to contain this new threat Michael now felt even more impelled to establish a firm alliance with Venice or Genoa,[54] if not both. Impatient, however, over the failure of the Venetian Doge to ratify the convention of 1265, Michael turned anew to the Genoese.[55]

Probably in the summer of 1267, Michael dispatched an embassy to Genoa "pro quibusdam aliis arduis negotiis." The Genoese responded at once and sent as their envoy to Constantinople Franceschino de Camilla. Negotiations between de Camilla and Michael resulted in a treaty, of which the principal stipulation was the return of the Genoese colonists from Heraclea and the cession to them of Galata (across the Golden Horn from Constantinople) as a place of residence.[56] An important complement

[54] Genoa, racked by internal dissension and defeated by the Venetian fleet at Trapani (23 June 1266), was now less of a threat to Venice.

[55] Sanudo, *Istoria,* 146, relates that Michael first made efforts to secure the aid of individual Venetians, but "non potendo averlo, si voltò a Genovesi, e fece con loro amicitia e Confederazione." In the same year (1267) peace was effected between Genoa and Venice through the combined efforts of Pope Clement, Charles, and King Louis. On this see Raynaldus, a. 1267, § 48; and Canale, 536ff. and 536–538, who notes that Clement threatened to excommunicate Venice and Genoa if they did not make peace. See also R. Cessi, "La tregua fra Venezia e Genova nella seconda metà del sec. XIII," *Archivio veneto-tridentino,* IV (1923) 1ff., which contains hitherto unpublished documents.

[56] *Ann. Ian.,* IV, 107–108; Pach., 167–168. (The exact date of the treaty is unknown.) Cf. Canale, 637–642, who gives the credit for acquiring Galata to another Genoese legation, that of Malocello (see above, Chapter 8, note 92). C. Desimoni, "I Genovesi ed i loro quartieri in Costantinopoli," *Giornale ligustico,* III (1876) 235; Manfroni, "Relazioni," 671; and Bratianu, *Recherches,* 88, all affirm, however, that the honor belongs to de Camilla. Greg., 97, ll. 10–16, seems mistakenly to place the Genoese settlement at Galata immediately after the Greek recovery of Constantinople in 1261. Cf. A. Paspates, Βυζαντιναὶ Μελέται (Constantinople, 1877) 207, placing it in the year 1268.

to the convention of Nymphaeum, this pact [57] marks the beginning of a new period of Genoese commercial predominance in Byzantium, which was to last until after 1453.

The settlement of the Genoese at Galata (termed Pera in the Latin documents),[58] rather than in their former quarter within Constantinople, is to be attributed primarily to Michael's desire to avoid the possibility of another conspiracy such as that of Guercio. More numerous than other Constantinopolitan Latins,[59] the Genoese might well be tempted to cooperate with a potential Western aggressor. Relegation of them to an area immediately outside the capital proper obviated this danger,[60] while simultaneously reducing the Greco-Genoese and Veneto-Genoese friction within the city.[61] To a certain extent, moreover, Michael's solution would tend to guarantee Genoese aid in the capital's defense, as the colonists of the suburb would naturally be concerned over the fate of the adjacent metropolis.[62]

In the choice of Galata the Genoese themselves may have

[57] Caro, Genua, I, 195, is probably wrong in claiming that Genoa's new Greek alliance of 1267 brought an interdict upon her in that year. The cause of the interdict (which was lifted the same year) was rather differences between the Genoese podestà and archbishop. Cf. A. Ferretto, "Codice diplomatico delle relazioni fra la Liguria, la Toscana, e la Lunigiana ai tempi di Dante," Atti della soc. lig., XXI (1901) 103.

[58] For theories regarding the origin of the names Galata and Pera, see Ducange, Histoire de Constantinople (ed. Buchon) I, 362 and 364; A. Belin, Histoire de la latinité de Constantinople (Paris, 1894) 124–125; and C. Desimoni, "I Genovesi ed i loro quartieri," 247–248. While the Greek sources generally use the name Galata, the Latin prefer the term Pera (spelled Peira in Genoese documents). On Genoese usage see G. Bratianu, Actes des notaires génois de Péra et de Caffa de la fin du XIIIe siècle (Bucharest, 1927) passim.

[59] Pach., 168, notes that Venetians and Pisans were fewer than Genoese: Βενετικοὺς δὲ καὶ Πισσαίους, τὸ κατὰ πλῆθος ὀλίγον.

[60] Pach., 168: ἐντὸς μένειν τῆς πόλεως οὐκ ἐγνώκει συμφέρον . . . ὕστερον δὲ καταντικρὺ τῆς περαίας παρὰ μόνον τὸ τοῦ Γαλατᾶ φρούριον ἀσφαλὲς ἐδοκίμαξε κατοικίζειν. Also 167, ll. 5ff., and Greg., 97: οὐκ ἀσφαλὲς οὐδὲ πρὸς εἰρήνην . . . εἰσοικίζειν τῆς πόλεως. Cf. Villani, I, 291, who says of Michael's grant of Pera to the Genoese: "non fidandosi ch'eglino, nè altri Latini avessono fortezza in Costantinopoli."

[61] Pach., 167: Γεννουΐτας . . . δυσχερεῖς . . . ὑποκλίνεσθαι ῥᾳδίως 'Ρωμαίους . . . ὑπερόφρυς καὶ σοβαρούς.

[62] Cf. Lopez, Colonie, 217, who suggests that since Galata had in the past served as a residence for Jews (Ville-hardouin, Conquête de Constantinople, ed. de Wailly, 88), Michael may have intended to humble the Genoese by relegating them to a kind of ghetto. Were this true, however, Michael would have antagonized many important Genoese in imperial service.

influenced the decision of the Emperor. Not only had a number of Genoese lived there during the days of the Latin Empire,[63] but, according to the *Annales Ianuenses*, already in 1264 the Genoese government had sought permission to transfer its colony thither from Heraclea.[64] Another reason for the settlement at Galata is suggested by a modern historian, A. Paspates, who believes that the Genoese could not resume possession of their old quarter within the capital simply because the area was now occupied by the new sea walls.[65]

The possibility of Genoese aggression against Constantinople even from Galata was evidently not overlooked by Michael. For before the establishment of the Genoese in the area, he took the precaution of destroying all of its fortifications, especially the wall along the sea.[66] Moreover, to impress upon the Genoese their allegiance to him, Michael directed that their chief official, the Podestà, when received in audience, should kneel and kiss the hands and feet of the Emperor.[67] Such obeisance, it may be noted, was not required of the Venetian *bailli* or the Pisan consul, whose nationals, fewer in number than the Genoese, were permitted to reside in their old, but separate, quarters within the city.[68] As a further mark of deference, Michael ordered that all Genoese vessels sailing past the imperial palace of the Blachernae on the Golden Horn render an official salute to the Emperor.[69]

In the light of the burgeoning power of Galata in the suc-

[63] Bratianu, *Recherches*, 89–90.

[64] *Ann. Ian.*, IV, 66. Indeed, the Genoese seem to have had their eyes on Galata early. The *Liber jurium reipublicae genuensis*, I, ed. E. Ricotti (Turin, 1854) col. 185, records that in 1155 the Genoese instructed their legates to request from the Emperor an "embolum in Constantinopoli . . . et si ibi non . . . in Pera."

[65] Paspates, Βυζαντιναὶ Μελέται, 208. See Manfroni's objections to Paspates' theory, "Relazioni," 672. But Bratianu, *Recherches*, 88, does not seem particularly to oppose Paspates' view.

[66] Michael himself had been repulsed before this wall. See above, Chapter 4, section 1. The disposition of the great chain (stretching from Constantinople to Galata), so important in case of a naval attack, is not mentioned, but Michael doubtless kept it in the hands of his own men.

[67] Codinus, *De officiis* (Bonn) 75, and Ducange, *Histoire de Constantinople* (ed. Buchon) I, 361–364, who says this indicated "liege-homage."

[68] Pach., 168: Βενετικοὺς δὲ καὶ Πισσαίους, τὸ κατὰ πλῆθος ὀλίγον, μένειν ἐντὸς ἐδικαίου, ἀποκεκριμένους καὶ τούτους τῶν ἄλλων.

[69] Pach., 421, ll. 5–7.

ceeding century,[70] it may be argued that Michael failed fully to foresee, or perhaps even to concern himself with, the ultimate peril to Constantinople of a Galata in Genoese possession. Valid as this may seem with the advantage of hindsight, it cannot be denied that during his own reign, at least, Michael took every reasonable precaution to render the Constantinopolitan Genoese as powerless as possible.

WESTERN INDIVIDUALS IN IMPERIAL SERVICE: THE ZACCARIA BROTHERS AND THE LATIN CORSAIRS. FEUDALISM AND LATINS IN BYZANTIUM

In his contest with the Latins Michael did not restrict himself to alliances with powerful states, but sought to attract to his cause the services of able individuals as well. Among these were Latin adventurers, some disaffected with home conditions, others seeking in the Byzantine Empire an opportunity for acquiring easy profits. In return for military and diplomatic services Michael awarded them valuable commercial concessions, permitted them to become subjects of his Empire, or even bestowed upon them titles of nobility.[71] This naming of Latins to the Byzantine aristocracy was not an innovation of Michael's, but the renewal on a larger scale of a policy followed in the preceding century by the Comnenoi and Angeloi emperors.[72]

It was Michael's first aim, according to Sanudo, to secure the aid of individual Venetians, upon whom he intended to bestow "lavish gifts and noble Greek wives." Failing in this, the Emperor

[70] See esp. John Cantacuzene, *Historia,* III (Bonn) 212ff.

[71] See Pach., 366, ll. 3–8, describing how Palaeologus insured the fidelity of the Genoese at Galata "by making them his own men (as they would say, 'liegemen') through granting them honors" (καὶ ἰδίους ἐποίει [λυζίους εἶπεν ἄν τις ἐκείνων] ταῖς εὐμενείαις). Cf. the Treaty of Nymphaeum, Manfroni, "Relazioni," 659, 794, which forbade Genoese from becoming Greek subjects. The very fact, however, that such a stipulation had to be made implies that such cases were not unusual. See, e.g., that of a relative of the Podestà Guglielmo Guercio (see Caro, *Genua,* I, 167, note 2) and the Zaccaria brothers (Pach., vol. II, bk. VI, ch. 34).

[72] See L. Halphen, "Le rôle des 'Latins' dans l'histoire intérieure de Constantinople à la fin du XIIe siècle," *Mélanges C. Diehl,* I (Paris, 1930) 141ff.

then turned to Genoese citizens, with whom he had notable success. Among the most important of such allies were two nobles, the brothers Benedetto and Manuele Zaccaria.[73] For their services (we shall see Benedetto, for example, acting as imperial envoy to the West at critical moments),[74] the Zaccaria, in 1275 or perhaps a few years earlier,[75] were granted as imperial fief the Anatolian port of Phocaea, situated at the entrance to the gulf of Smyrna and important for its production of alum.[76] The liberality of this concession, which brought colossal profits to the Zaccaria, requires explanation. It may well be, as Lopez suggests, that Michael intended a Latin Phocaea under a vague Greek suzerainty to be a kind of imperial outpost against the Latin-held islands of the Aegean and against potential Turkish attacks from Anatolia.[77] In actual fact, to protect their alum trade from predatory Venetian and even Genoese corsairs of the Aegean, the Zaccaria did have to build a strong flotilla.[78] Some indication of their powers of resistance may be the fact that Phocaea, under hegem-

[73] On Michael's policy see Sanudo, *Istoria*, 146: "facendo larghi presenti e dando ad alcuni di loro [Venetians] Moglie delle sue Donne Greche, e non potendo averlo, si voltò a Genovesi, e fece con loro amicitia e Confederazione e ad alcuni di loro donò gran presenti e massime a due Fratelli ovver Cugini Germani, uno detto Miser Benettino Zacaria e l'altro Miser Manuel." Cf. Pach., 366, ll. 7–8.

[74] An early mention of Benedetto's relations with Michael is that of his mission as Genoese envoy to Constantinople in 1269 to secure return of the Genoese colony from Heraclea to the capital. See also below, Chapter 14, for Benedetto's important role in the Sicilian Vespers. On the brothers in general, see esp. Lopez, *Benedetto Zaccaria, passim*.

[75] Lopez, *ibid.*, 12, pushes back the date for this concession to 1267; but W. Miller, *Essays on the Latin Orient* (Cambridge, 1921) 284–285, dates the concession in 1275, and to Manuele alone. (Pach., 420, here is probably chronologically confused. Cf. also Pach., II, 558.) Sanudo, *Istoria*, 146, also seems to assign the concession to 1275, that is, right after the failure of Michael's Venetian, and the success of his Genoese, negotiations. See finally K. Hopf, "Giustiniani," in *Ersch und Gruber Encycl.*, LXVIII, 310.

[76] Alum was needed for the dyeing of cloth. On Phocaea, see Lopez, *Benedetto Zaccaria*, 26–27, and Heyd, *Histoire*, I, 438, note 1. It may be recalled that by th Treaty of Nymphaeum Genoa had secured complete jurisdiction over the nearb port of Smyrna.

[77] *Benedetto Zaccaria*, 12–13. If correct, this would help to mitigate the charg often made against Michael Palaeologus of completely neglecting his Asiati frontiers in order to concentrate on his conflict with the Latins.

[78] According to Sanudo, *Istoria*, 146, within a short time 2,000 corsairs wei killed by the Zaccaria ("morti ben do millia"). The pirate headquarters were gei erally at Negropont.

ony of the Zaccaria family, was one of the last regions of Asia Minor to succumb to the Ottoman advance.[79]

The almost continual state of war in the Morea and the Archipelago filled the Aegean with corsairs, relatively few of whom, however, were inimical to the Greeks. Many Latin free-booters, in fact, joined the Greek cause, attracted by imperial protection for their piratical acts or even the promise of an imperial dignity. By sanctioning their activities Michael was enabled not only to secure firmer control of the Aegean but to reduce the expense of maintaining a large navy. Thus the Latin corsairs, preying on Latin fleets and merchant shipping and in some cases even sharing their profits with the Emperor, played a not inconsiderable part in the success of Michael's struggle with the West.[80]

Among such allies we may mention in particular the notorious Genoese, Giovanni de lo Cavo, whose plunderous exploits against fellow-Latins — petty lords of the Archipelago or merchants — were rewarded by the Emperor, around the year 1278, with the *signoria* of the islands of Nanfio and Rhodes.[81] Lo Cavo, like his predecessor Licario, the first to be thus honored, was subsequently named Megasdukas (Grand Duke), commander of the Greek fleet,[82] after the death of the Greek admiral Alexios Philanthropenos. Command of Latin mercenaries by Greeks was of course common in the imperial army (witness the office of Grand Constable), but the appointment of Latins to direct the Greek fleet seems to have been a genuine innovation of Michael's reign.[83]

---

[79] See Lopez, *Benedetto Zaccaria*, ch. 8. Lopez also shows that the name "Zaccaria" is not to be identified with "Licario," the Lombard feudatory of Michael for Negropont; nor did Benedetto marry a sister of Michael (12–13 and 10).

[80] On piracy at this time see P. Charanis, "Piracy in the Aegean during the reign of Michael VIII Palaeologus," *Annuaire de l'institut de philologie et d'histoire orientales et slaves*, X (1950) 127ff. Also see T.-Th., III, 159–281, and Sanudo, *Istoria*, 146–147.

[81] See Sanudo, *Istoria*, 132 and 146. Also A. Ferretto, "Codice diplomatico," *Atti soc. lig. st. pat.*, XXXI [2], 146: "Ioannes de Cavo Genuensis Namphi et Rhodi nsulae dominus (1278)." Cf. Lopez, *Colonie*, 218.

[82] See Sanudo, *Istoria*, 132: "Zuan da Cavo, suo Armiraglio [of Michael]." On Licario see below, Chapter 10, section 2.

[83] For another example, that of the Genoese Andrea Gaffore, see K. Hopf,

A few words are necessary here on feudalism in Byzantium under Michael as it relates to the Latins. As Ostrogorsky has so well clarified in his recent book on Byzantine feudalism, since at least the 11th and 12th centuries the highly centralized Byzantine state had been gradually undergoing a process of decentralization, evidenced by the granting of *pronoiai* (equivalent to the Latin fiefs, except that only in Michael's reign did some of these become hereditary)[83a] with their concomitant military obligations and increasing immunities from central control. Therefore, when the Latins in 1204 occupied Greek territories, they found already developed a system similar in many ways to their own, the most important difference being the absence of subinfeudation with its accompanying feudal hierarchy so characteristic of the West. But a fundamentally feudal relationship between the Emperor and those granted a *pronoia* was now already crystallized.[84]

Thus Michael, in return for certain benefits or services, found it expedient to assign to Latins, as fiefs, various territories of the Empire. Important examples — not all exactly similar, it is true — are the bestowal of the Morea on Prince William of Achaia (1262), the grant of Negropont to Licario, and the concession of Phocaea to the Zaccaria brothers.[85] While the unwilling "vassal" William, as we have seen, immediately repudiated all obligation, Licario faithfully performed military service for the Emperor.[86]

"Urkunden und Zusätze zur Geschichte von Andros," *Sitz. Wiener Akad., phil.-hist. Kl.*, XXI (1856) 246ff. Cf. also a later Angevin diploma of 18 July 1273, on the case of a man of Perpignan, who with his family, 400 men, and two galleys, abandoned Michael's service for that of Charles of Anjou (*Arch. st. it.*, XXII, 244).

[83a] See G. Ostrogorsky, *Pour l'histoire de la féodalité byzantine*, trans. H Grégoire (Brussels, 1954), esp. 93ff. Cf. above, Chapter 4, note 62, for example.

[84] For feudal development see Ostrogorsky, *op. cit., passim*. Also the penetrating articles of P. Charanis, "Monastic Properties and the State," *Dumbarton Oak Papers No. 4* (1948) 89, 91, and "On the Social Structure and Economic Organiza tion of the Byzantine Empire in the Thirteenth Century and Later," *Byzantino slavica*, XII (1951) 94–153.

[85] See Chapter 7, section 4; Chapter 12, section 4; and Chapter 9, notes 75–76 Also Chapter 13, note 72, for Michael's use of the term "liege-homage" whe referring to certain Greek subjects; and Pach., 366, ll. 3–8.

[86] Chapter 10, notes 27–35; Chapter 12, section 4.

The case of the Zaccaria in Phocaea is rather ambiguous, as the territory, evidently under the more or less complete jurisdiction of that family, seems to have provided no direct military service to Michael.[87] Nevertheless, the Zaccaria's numerous diplomatic missions may well have been regarded not only as partial repayment for the concession of Phocaea but as a kind of fulfillment, at least in the Western sense, of the obligation of feudal service. All these considerations, then — the naming of Latins to command imperial fleets and armies, the grant to them of territories in fief (*pronoia*), and even their acceptance into the Byzantine nobility — show the great degree of penetration of Western influences in Byzantium during Michael's reign. One may be sure, however, that the fusion of Byzantine and Latin feudal usage, fostered by Michael mainly as a means of drawing Westerners into imperial service, had as its underlying aim the preservation of the Greek Empire from Western aggression.

THE GRECO-VENETIAN TREATY OF 1268 AND FURTHER DIPLOMATIC AND MILITARY ACTIVITY OF CHARLES AGAINST PALAEOLOGUS

The descent of Conradin of Hohenstaufen into Italy to recover his inheritance from Charles once more aroused the entire peninsula as it awaited the outcome of their conflict.[88] Venice was particularly affected, as the new struggle over Sicily made impossible for the present a restoration of the Latin Empire with papal and perhaps Angevin aid. Of even greater concern to Venice, however, were several other considerations. The state of semi-war existing between the Commune and Palaeologus had reduced Venetian commercial activity in the East to a minimum, a fact for which corsairs were to a considerable extent responsible.[89]

---

[87] According to Miller, *Essays on the Latin Orient*, 285, Manuele paid an annual rent to Michael for the alum mines of Phocaea. See Pach., II, 558.

[88] Rome, the Tuscan Ghibellines, and even the Sicilian barons had declared themselves for Conradin. See esp. Hampe, *Geschichte Konradins von Hohenstaufen*, 169ff.

[89] Cf. document dated 1278, in T.-Th., III, 159ff., dealing with the severe damages to Venetian trade by corsairs during the preceding years of peace. Dam-

Venice, moreover, had become increasingly alarmed by the Angevin occupation of Corfu and designs on Epirus, possession of which could challenge her sphere of influence in the Adriatic and threaten even to block her outlet to the Mediterranean. As a result the Venetians, almost in spite of themselves, were veering toward the idea of an accord with Palaeologus.

It was the Doge Raynerio Zeno who took the initiative. On 1 November 1267, he sent to the Bosporus Marco Bembo and Pietro Zeno with full powers to conclude a treaty "until such time and as may seem best to them." [90] Unfortunately for Venice, however, Michael had now abandoned the idea of an exclusive accord with the Serenissima and instead sought to reach agreements with both Venice and Genoa. Consequently, though the Venetian envoys finally succeeded in arranging a treaty (signed in Constantinople on 4 April 1268), its terms were not all that the proud Commune expected. Certain provisions of the pact of 1265 were again incorporated, it is true, but clauses considerably less advantageous to Venice were also included. The important stipulations follow:[91]

(1) A truce of five years, to take effect on 4 April 1268, was declared between the two signatories. Venice promised not to ally with any power against "the Empire of Romania." [92] (2) The

---

ages, by analogy, were probably as great if not greater in 1266–1267, a period of undeclared war between Venice and Byzantium.

[90] T.-Th., III, 89: "usque ad illud tempus, et sicut eis videbitur." Canale, 584, says that the two envoys went to Constantinople with a Greek archbishop ("aveuc li Arcevesque des Gres") and another messenger. Cf. Dandolo, 313: "dux, videns quod Balduinus a principibus Occidentis nichil favoris poterat optinere, petite treugue consensum prebuit."

[91] T.-Th., III, 93–100. Ratified in Venice 30 June. Cf. Dölger, *Regesten*, no. 1960, and Cantacuzene, III (Bonn) 189. Note how necessity may have modified the Venetian attitude toward Michael, as exemplified by the titles bestowed upon him in Venetian documents of 1265 and 1268 respectively: "fidelis imperator et moderator Graecorum" (T.-Th., 88), but then, "fidelis imperator et moderator *Romanorum*" (T.-Th., 93).

[92] T.-Th., 94, esp.: "Romaniae suo Imperio." This provision obviated the possibility of a Venetian alliance with Charles against Palaeologus. At Michael's insistence a clause was inserted that Venice would not transport troops to battle against him (T.-Th., 95: "non naulizabimus nec naulizari feciemus . . . aliquam personam, etc."). Note that Michael swore to observe the truce with Venice "super vera et veneranda cruce secundum morem Graecorum" (T.-Th., 95).

Venetians (as prescribed in the convention of 1265) would be admitted to all areas of the Empire and exempted from the payment of duties.[93] (3) Any Venetian accused of an offense against a Greek would be brought before the Venetian *bailli* or rector. In the case that a Venetian killed a Greek or Venetian within the city of Constantinople, he would be judged by the Emperor. But if a Venetian killed another Venetian outside the capital, he would be tried by the Venetian *bailli* or rector. (4) The Genoese (in contrast to the agreement of 1265), were not to be expelled from the Empire. But Venetians and Genoese were expressly forbidden to attack each other in the straits or the Black Sea. (5) No permanent commercial establishments were to be assigned to the Venetians in the Empire. For such facilities the Venetian merchants were now obliged to pay rental. (6) The Emperor pledged not to attack the Venetian possessions of Coron, Modon, Crete, and the Archipelago islands. (7) Michael promised to observe the pact signed between Venice and Prince William of Achaia regarding Negropont.[94] (8) Restitution would be made to the Emperor for damages suffered at the hands of Venetian corsairs. The Venetians promised in addition that their possessions would provide neither aid nor haven to corsairs attacking imperial territory.[95]

The situation was now reversed. Venice was in the position of petitioner, and Michael could press his advantage against the former masters of his Empire. Having concluded treaties with both Genoa and Venice, Michael could for the moment be satisfied, though he must have realized that a truce with Venice did not guarantee Venetian abandonment of the hope of recovering her old position in Constantinople by other means.

On 30 June the Doge Zeno ratified the treaty, but only a few days later he died. Fortunately for Michael, the Greek ambassa-

---

[93] T.-Th., 97; and for remaining provisions, 97–100.

[94] By that treaty, concluded 15 May 1262, Venice granted to William suzerainty over the Lombard triarchs of Negropont in exchange for commercial monopoly. See T.-Th., 46ff.

[95] T.-Th., 99. Note that damages suffered by Venice from Greek corsairs are not mentioned.

dors, George Tzimiskes and George Kalodukas, were able to secure reconfirmation from his successor, Lorenzo Tiepolo, who considered himself bound by the pact.[96] This was a great boon to Michael, as Charles of Anjou had in the meantime triumphed over Conradin at the battle of Tagliacozzo in 1268,[97] and was thus finally disencumbered of the Hohenstaufen.

With the removal of the Hohenstaufen threat, Angevin preparations against Constantinople became more ominous than ever. Of advantage to Charles at this time was the death, on 28 November 1268, of Clement IV, since papal propensity for union could no longer be used by Michael as a block to Angevin plans. Had Charles possessed sufficient strength, it is likely that he would immediately have launched an attack against Byzantium, but his military and financial resources were still inadequate for such an undertaking. Thus, in order to open an easier and less costly road to Constantinople, he spent the entire year 1269 seeking alliances with states surrounding the Greek Empire.

On 15 September 1269, Charles signed a treaty with the Hungarian King Bela IV, by the terms of which each guaranteed aid against mutual enemies "outside the faith of the church." [98] A double marriage between the two royal houses was also arranged.[99] Such close relations could be viewed only with suspicion by Venice, traditional enemy of Hungary,[100] and likewise by Palaeologus, Hungary being the most powerful state north of his possessions. Charles also contracted alliances with Stephen Uroš I of Serbia and with Tsar Constantine Tich of Bulgaria, who

[96] T.-Th., 101–102.

[97] The Greek *Chron. Mor.*, ed. Kalonaros, ll. 6946ff., attributes Charles's victory to William of Achaia, a fact unconfirmed by Villani, I, 353. Cf. Cerone, "La sovranità," 27, and Léonard, *Les Angevins de Naples*, 69. William's appearance in Italy was made possible by a one year truce with Palaeologus. See Hopf, *Griechenland*, 290, and French *Chron.*, pars. 228–235.

[98] "Conventiones amicitie . . . cum Stephano . . . Rege Ungarie . . . contra omnes . . . existentes extra fidem Ecclesie" (del Giudice, *Cod. dipl.*, III, 138). Actually Stephen V did not become King until the following year, when his father, Bela IV, died.

[99] Minieri-Riccio, *Alcuni fatti*, 55, 68, 69, and 71 (Filangieri, V, 7, 14, 24, 54, 75). Note that the documents of the Filangieri ed. as yet extend only to 1272. Also cf. Saba Malaspina, *Historia* (ed. Del Re) 298.

[100] See Sternfeld, *Ludwigs des Heiligen Kreuzzug*, 160–161.

was still excited against Palaeologus by the hatred of his wife, the sister of young John Lascaris.[101] And, in the aim of outflanking the Greek Empire from the East, Charles sought to form an alliance with the Khan of the distant Tatars of Persia.[102]

In order to provide some stamp of legality to his enterprise Charles may even have attempted to draw to his court the dethroned Greek Emperor, the blinded and imprisoned youth John IV Lascaris.[103] According to Angevin documents John actually arrived at the Angevin court and was granted a pension in order to establish residence there. But evidence of a directly contradictory nature is provided by the Greek historians Pachymeres and Gregoras, who record that sometime after the death of Michael in 1282 his son and successor Andronikos visited John in the prison at Dacybyza (Asia Minor), to which Michael had committed him.[104] In the face of this directly opposing testimony,[105] one wonders which version expresses the truth. If credence is to be given to the Angevin documents, how did Charles explain to Baldwin and young John, rival claimants for the same throne, his support of both candidates? Again, tentatively accepting the validity of the Angevin evidence, why are the Greek sources silent on John's supposed escape from prison, about which Lascarid supporters in Byzantium would certainly have created a

---

[101] Pach., 210, l. 4. Cf. Sternfeld, op. cit., 161.

[102] On Charles's negotiations with the Turks, Saracens, Mongols, and Armenians, see Cerone, "La sovranità," 201, note 2; del Giudice, Cod. dipl., III, 23, note 1; Minieri-Riccio, Alcuni fatti, 53; and Léonard, Les Angevins de Naples, 105.

[103] Cf. the somewhat analogous case of Robert Guiscard (1080), who produced a Greek in south Italy claiming to be the dethroned Greek Emperor Michael VII, escaped from his imprisonment in Constantinople. See F. Chalandon, Essai sur le règne d'Alexis Ier Comnène (Paris, 1900) 63.

[104] See Arch. st. it., XXII, 32, Charles's rescript of 9 May 1273, saying he has heard of John's escape and inviting him to his court (on the pension Buchon, Nouvelles recherches, I [1845] 215). Cf. Pach., vol. II, 103–104: [Andronikos] προσβάλλει τῇ τῶν Νικητιάτων τῆς Δακιβύζης φρουρίῳ, καὶ τῷ τυφλῷ Ἰωάννῃ συμμίξας. Also Greg., 173–174: ἧκε παρὰ τὸν τυφλωθέντα . . . Ἰωάννην τὸν Λάσκαριν, ἔν τινι πολιχνίῳ τῆς Βιθυνίας φρουρούμενον.

[105] Chapman, 85; Dade, 41; and Sternfeld, Ludwigs des Heiligen Kreuzzug, 187–188, all accept the story of young John's escape to the Angevin court but overlook the testimony of Pachymeres and Gregoras. Sternfeld believes that the success of John's presumed escape may perhaps be attributed to his sister, the Tsarina of the Bulgars.

great stir? Finally and most important, why is there nothing whatever mentioned of Charles's use of John during the preparations for his Greek undertaking? In view of this reasoning, one is strongly tempted not only to prefer the testimony of the Greek historians but to believe that the rescripts of Charles have more value as propaganda than as actual truth. Quite possibly they may refer to a false John produced by Charles to attract the support of the legitimist, pro-Lascarid Greeks of the Byzantine Empire,[106] as well as to sway the anti-Angevin sentiment of the still surviving Greek population of Charles's own territories of southern Italy and Sicily.[107]

Charles, in the meantime, had succeeded in crushing the last remaining opposition to his rule — that of the Saracens of Lucera in south Italy. Having disposed of this final pocket of resistance, he was free to draw upon Sicily's entire resources for his Greek expedition.[108] At the same time, however, he hoped to secure the naval support of both Venice and Genoa. The accord signed in 1267 between Michael and Genoa had apparently entailed no restriction against a commercial treaty between Genoa and Charles, for we find that on 12 August 1269 Charles availed himself of the cordial relations existing between his brother, King Louis of France, and Genoa to sign a treaty regulating trade between Genoa and the Regno.[109]

Charles's ally, the Latin Emperor Baldwin, was, in the interim,

---

[106] It will be recalled that Asia Minor, especially the area around Nicaea, was still pro-Lascarid and had even revolted in John's favor. See Pach., 193–201, and cf. Gardner, *Lascarids*, 260–261, for discusison of a "false" John who stirred up Asia Minor against Michael.

[107] On the Greek element remaining in the Regno see esp. R. Weiss, "The Greek Culture of South Italy in the Later Middle Ages," *Proceedings of the British Academy*, XXXVII (London, 1951) 28–29. Also Sanudo, *Istoria*, 143, and M. Scaduto, *Il monachismo basiliano nella Sicilia medievale* (Rome, 1947) *passim*. See below, Chapter 14, note 86.

[108] Del Giudice, *Cod. dipl.*, III, 127, note 1, and Saba Malaspina, *Historia* (ed. Del Re) 291–292.

[109] See *Ann. Ian.*, IV, 113ff. Cf. Caro, *Genua*, I, 227ff., and L. Belgrano, *Documenti inediti riguardanti le due crociate di san Ludovico IX* (Genoa, 1859) 378ff. According to W. Cohn, "Storia della flotta siciliana sotto . . . Carlo I d'Angiò," *Arch. stor. sic. or.*, XXV (1930) 365, ten Genoese ships were lent to Charles for three months.

continuing his own quest for allies against Michael. In March of 1269 he signed a treaty with the King of Navarre, Count Theobald of Champagne, by which Theobald, in exchange for military aid, was to be invested with one-quarter of the future conquests of the Empire of Romania.[110] The agreement, however, was in no way to prejudice the rights of Baldwin himself or agreements already made with Charles of Anjou, Hugh of Burgundy, or the Venetians [111] — an interesting proviso, for, with disposition of so much territory, it would seem that more areas had been allocated than actually had existed in the old Latin Empire. It seems likely that, in order to implement all the promises made, Greek territories of Asia Minor were also taken into consideration.[112]

Efforts on the part of Baldwin's wife, the Empress Marie of Brienne, to secure aid from her cousin, King Alfonso X of Castile, for the recovery of Constantinople failed, despite an early attempt of Marie to arrange a marriage between her son Philip and a Castilian princess.[113] Negotiations, however, of Baldwin with Ferrante Sancho, natural son of King James I of Aragon, were

---

[110] T.-Th., III, 90: "quartam partem terre dominii et honoris totius Imperii nostri Romanie." On the calculation of this date, cited *ibid.*, see Dade, 37, note 205.

[111] By the Treaty of Viterbo, it may be recalled, Charles was promised an independent seigneury in Romania, plus one-third of its conquests; Venice, her three-eighths share of the Latin Empire; Hugh of Burgundy (by special treaty with Baldwin [above, Chapter 8, note 64, and Chapter 9, text and note 32]) the Kingdom of Thessalonica; and Baldwin, Constantinople with the four great Aegean islands.

[112] Cf. Dade, 38.

[113] On this see Sanudo, *Fragmentum*, 172–173, and Canale 502. Cf. Dade, 40; and see esp. the article of R. L. Wolff, "Mortgage and Redemption of an Emperor's Son," which shows that sometime between June 1258 and May 1261, when Marie of Brienne was visiting Castile in order to secure financial aid to redeem her son Philip (held by Venetian merchants as surety for a loan to Baldwin), she at the same time negotiated with Alfonso to marry Philip to a daughter of Alfonso, hoping thereby to secure Castilian aid for her husband's tottering Latin Empire. The negotiations, however, which seem still to have been alive in 1266 (*ibid.*, 70), were nullified by the Treaty of Viterbo (1267), by the terms of which Philip in 1273 married Beatrice, daughter of Charles of Anjou. Subsequently, with Beatrice's death and a shift in the political scene, the negotiations for Philip's union with a Castilian princess were revived, in 1281, only to collapse again and lead to no result. On all this see Wolff's article, *passim*, esp. 64, 71–75, and, for bibliography on Alfonso, notes 23 and 60. For the relations between Alfonso and Michael Palaeologus in particular see below, Chapters 12–14.

somewhat more successful, culminating on 8 April 1270 in a treaty by the terms of which Ferrante, for a monetary consideration, pledged a corps of one hundred troops to fight for one year in Sicily or the Greek Empire. Ferrante himself and his troops were to appear in Trapani, Sicily, in August of 1270.[114]

It seems, on the other hand, that a proposal made by Michael to King James I of Aragon in the previous year had not resulted in the accord sought by the Emperor.[115] James himself informs us that in 1269 envoys of Michael, together with those of Abagha, Mongol ruler of Persia and son-in-law of Michael, appeared in Valencia, offering aid ("supplies by sea") to the King for his projected crusade to the Holy Land.[116] Though the motives of Michael were ostensibly to foster the crusade, it may well be that his proposal was really a pretext for seeking an Aragonese alliance so as to forestall Aragonese inclusion in an anti-Byzantine entente with Baldwin, Charles, and Castile.[117] A few years after the Greek recovery of Constantinople, Baldwin had appeared in Castile, and, as noted, the Latin Empress Marie of Brienne journeyed to Castile as well as Aragon. These visits, according to Canale and Aragonese sources, were for the purpose of securing aid against Palaeologus.[118]

---

[114] Minieri-Riccio, *Alcuni fatti*, 97 and 104–105, 110; Filangieri, III, 109; IV, 60, 130, where Charles refers to Ferrante endearingly and also becomes allied to him. Cf. Dade, 40; Sternfeld, *Ludwigs des Heiligen Kreuzzug*, 203; and esp. R. Röhricht, "Der Kreuzzug König Jacobs I. von Aragonien," *Mitt. aus d. oesterr. Gesch.*, XI (1890) 372ff. Evidently nothing of importance resulted. Similar implication in Wolff, "Mortgage and Redemption," 80, note 90.

[115] Which, however, did not hinder the establishment of Greco-Catalan commercial relations in Constantinople. See below, Chapter 10, note 90.

[116] See *The Chronicle of James I King of Aragon*, trans. J. Forster, II (London, 1883) 599–600.

[117] Cf. Sternfeld, *Ludwigs des Heiligen Kreuzzug*, 174. In the outline for the Greco-Venetian treaty of 1265, Michael had listed the "Rex Aragonum" among his potential enemies with whom Venice was not to ally against him (T.-Th., III, 79).

[118] Canale, 502: "D'ileuc (Venise) s'en alerent (Li Empereor et Marc Iustiniens) au Roi de Castele et il leur promist de doner chevaliers a plante." Sanudo, *Fragmentum*, 172–173: "imperatrix uxor eius precesserat ad petendum auxilia regum, . . . inter alios vero regis Aragoniam Jacobi ac etiam n'Anfossi generi sui regis Castelle." On this see esp. Wolff, "Mortgage and Redemption," 46, 64; also F. Soldevila, "Le voyage de Marie de Brienne en Espagne," *Atti dello VIII congresso internazionale di studi bizantini di Palermo, 1951* (Rome, 1953) 476.

In the fall of 1269 Charles made a resolute public bid to win Venice to his cause. After dispatching as envoys to the Doge the trusted Achaian knight Erard d'Aunoy and the Abbot of Monte-cassino, Charles on September 7 and 15 issued two edicts, actually declarations of war against Palaeologus, in which he appealed to the solidarity of Latin Catholicism — particularly Venetian — against the Greeks. The second and more important began:

We, Charles . . . in view of the injury committed by Palaeologus and other Greeks against the Holy Roman Church and the Christian faith, and against the magnificent Princes, Baldwin, by the grace of God Constantinopolitan Emperor of Romania, Lorenzo Tiepolo, our very dear friend the Doge of the Venetians, and William, Prince of Achaia, and against the men of Venice and other faithful Christians . . .

It went on to say that the purpose of the war was to restore to the Holy Roman Church and to Venice "the rights which they had and ought to have in the Constantinopolitan Empire." [119]

For all these grandiloquent phrases, the extended pourparlers between the Angevin envoys and the Doge failed to create an alliance. Charles's policy in north Italy and the Balkans, especially on the shores of the Adriatic, had stirred too many Venetian apprehensions. Moreover, the Venetians, for the time being, had recovered commercial privileges in the Byzantine Empire. Thus in answer to Charles's exhortations the Doge diplomatically maintained the necessity of awaiting the expiration of his treaty with Michael.[120]

Though Venice held aloof, Charles pushed ahead with his preparations. Concentrating on Achaia, he expended much effort to prepare it as his main base against Michael. He even forbade merchants to cross between the Regno and Greek territories,[121] the reason for which, evidently, was to prevent the flow of in-

---

[119] Del Giudice, *Cod. dipl.*, I, 301, note, and cf. 300. See also the excerpts from a manuscript quoted in Zakythinos, *Despotat*, I, 48, note 1.

[120] See M. Niccolini, "Sui rapporti diplomatici veneto-napoletani durante i regni di Carlo I e Carlo II d'Angiò," *Arch. st. prov. nap.*, LX (1935) 261.

[121] Del Giudice, *Cod. dipl.*, III, 51–52, edict dated 5 April 1269. Merchants could not travel "ad terram palogi." See also Carabellese, 35 and note 1.

telligence from Sicily to Constantinople as well as to block the export of provisions from Sicily to Greek territories.

Unable to secure Venetian naval support, Charles took measures to strengthen his own fleet. After Tagliacozzo there began an intense, accelerated activity in the harbors and dockyards of southern Italy, evidenced by the vast number of rescripts directed by Charles to officials of that area. The continual use in the edicts of phrases such as "pro quibusdam arduis . . . servitiis" and the constant dispatch of secret royal agents to the area attest to an increased activity that may well have been in preparation for an attack on Byzantium.[122] Of particular importance in this connection are directives ordering justiciars to accelerate preparations "for the expedition against Romania." But the wording of a number of rescripts discloses that, however demanding the directives of Charles, Angevin preparations underwent considerable difficulties and delays.[123]

The importance of the Morea in Charles's plan is indicated by the amount of provisions, money, and troops he sent there.[124] As a result of almost constant warfare, Moreot agriculture had been greatly neglected, and the resources of the principality, normally insufficient for the needs of population and army, had to be supplemented by the import of provisions from Apulia. Already in 1268, to facilitate military operations, Charles had sent to the Morea the first of a series of governors bearing the title of *bailli*.[125] In March of 1270 a fleet of twenty-five ships under the command of Ansel de Toucy was ordered to sail from Bari for the Morea. In April a new directive was issued and still another the following May, at which time the Angevin admiral was instructed to go to the aid of William of Achaia against the

---

[122] Minieri-Riccio, *Alcuni fatti*, 86–87 (esp. of 17 December 1269); also Carabellese, 15 and note 1.

[123] E.g., Charles wrote to a justiciar of southern Italy that "negotium Achaye . . . dilationem non patitur" (Carabellese, 52, note 1).

[124] On this see esp. Cerone, "La sovranità," 33–35ff. Cf. Zakythinos, *Despotat*, I, 49.

[125] First Galeran d'Ivry, then Philip de Lagonessa. See Greek *Chron.*, ll. 6536ff.; also Zakythinos, *Despotat*, I, 48–49. Cf. Ptolemy of Lucca, *Historia*, col. 1162, which probably refers to Angevin troops now sent to Achaia.

Greeks of Mistra.[126] But if these ships actually sailed,[127] their support was of little avail, a fact for which the involvement of Charles in the crusade of his brother to Tunis and the diplomatic activity of Michael Palaeologus were to be responsible.

MICHAEL'S APPEAL TO KING LOUIS IX OF FRANCE AND THE CRUSADE OF LOUIS TO TUNIS (1269–1270)

With fewer military resources at his disposal, Michael had to resort to diplomacy in order to check Charles before the latter could launch his expedition against Byzantium. For this purpose the Emperor dispatched several embassies to the West.[128] Thus, under the year 1269, the *Annales Ianuenses* state that

legates of . . . the Greek Emperor came to Genoa in order to speak to the Pope and the Kings of France and Sicily. They remained for many days, then, as is believed, departed for destinations to which they were sent. What they did or proposed, however, was not known to all.[129]

The purport of this cryptic passage, with its suggestive references to the Curia, France, and Sicily, becomes clearer as we examine the overall situation at this time.

The death of Clement IV (28 November 1268) and the success of Charles in blocking the election of a new pontiff [130] had, as we have seen, eliminated the last remaining restraint upon Charles. But Michael, searching desperately for another counter-

---

[126] Minieri-Riccio, *Alcuni fatti*, 108, 117–118, 131, and esp. 128, of 31 July. Cerone, "La sovranità," 51–52, and 48–50; and Carabellese, 14.

[127] See G. del Giudice, *Diplomi inediti di Re Carlo I su cose marittime* (Naples, 1871) 10, according to which the fleet had not yet sailed by 26 September 1270: "viginti quinque . . . vassellorum ad partes Achaye profecturorum." But cf. Sternfeld, *Ludwigs des Heiligen Kreuzzug*, 297, who writes that it sailed in August of 1270.

[128] Cf. Dölger, *Regesten*, nos. 1967, 1968, and 1971.

[129] *Ann. Ian.*, IV, 115, which also mention legates of "the sultan of Babylon and the Tatars."

[130] The election of a new pope, Gregory X, was finally forced by the podestà of Viterbo, who locked up the cardinals in conclave until a choice was made! See Berger de Xivrey, "Notice d'un manuscrit grec du 13ᵉ siècle," *Bibl. École des Chartes*, ser. V, IV (Paris, 1863) 97.

poise, was able to make shrewd appeal to the leading ruler of the West, King Louis IX of France, the elder and universally respected brother of Charles himself, whose vast prestige as arbiter between monarchs was well known.[131] Louis by now had almost completed preparations for a crusade to the Holy Land, and therefore a strong argument for French intervention in Greco-Sicilian affairs would be the adverse effect of Charles's projected expedition on Louis's own cherished plans for a crusade. Not only would Louis be deprived of Charles's support, with the Angevin troops engaged against Byzantium, but Michael too would be unable to offer military assistance. (It will be recalled that Pope Clement himself had disclosed Louis's intended crusade to Michael, in a letter discussing the Emperor's contribution to a joint Greco-Latin expedition to the Holy Land.)[132]

Louis responded to the imperial embassy [133] by dispatching envoys, who reached the Bosporus early in the following year (1270).[134] The French ruler had been deeply stirred by Michael's reference to a crusade, for, as has been astutely observed, where the question of a crusade was concerned, Louis ceased to exercise really clear judgment.[135] In the early months of 1270 Michael sent a second and more urgent message to the King of France, declaring himself, his clergy, and people ready, for the sake of union, to submit unconditionally to Louis's personal decision in the conflict with Charles. An immediate response was requested, since,

[131] Louis was asked, for example, to arbitrate between King John (Lackland) of England and his nobles.

[132] See Jordan, *Reg. Clém.*, no. 1201, 404 (= Tautu, *Acta*, no. 25, 71).

[133] On the date of the embassy see L. Bréhier, "Une ambassade Byzantine au camp de St. Louis devant Tunis," *Mélanges Iorga* (Paris, 1933) 140, note 1, who (basing his opinion on Cod. Coislianus, no. 200, in Berger de Xivrey, "Notice," 100), sets it later than do Chapman, 86, and Norden, 464, who fix it at the beginning of 1269. Cf. Dölger, *Regesten*, nos. 1967–1968. Pachymeres, incidentally, fails to mention this embassy to Louis. The famous Greek Franciscan John Parastron was an imperial envoy to Louis about this time, as indicated in a Greek New Testament presented to Louis. See Berger de Xivrey, "Notice," 97ff. On Parastron see below, Chapter 11, text and notes 39–42.

[134] See Angevin diploma of 17 December 1269 ordering horses to be prepared for the transportation of Louis's envoys to Romania "pro quibusdam servitiis" (Minieri-Riccio, *Alcuni fatti*, 86). On the texts, see Dölger, *Regesten*, no. 1968.

[135] C. Petit-Dutaillis, in *Cambr. Med. Hist.*, VI, 360.

Michael wrote pointedly, not all of his embassies to the Curia were reaching their destination.[136]

Louis was impressed by Michael's unreserved submission to his judgment, but he felt that he could not act for the church without the sanction of the Curia.[137] Accordingly, he informed the Emperor that he would advise the Cardinals of the request for union, recommending immediate consideration and the dispatch of the high-ranking Bishop of Albano to Constantinople. The reaction of the Cardinals is worthy of note: while accepting the proposals of Louis, they warned him to beware of the "insincerity and procrastination of the Greeks." [138] Before his departure for the East, the Bishop of Albano was carefully instructed by the Curia as to demands to be made of the Emperor in order to guarantee conversion of the Greek clergy. Most important was a directive for the convocation of a preliminary council in the East, at which the Emperor, his ecclesiastics, and people openly had to profess the confession of faith and Roman primacy as enclosed in the previous letter of Clement IV. Written records of these professions of faith, publicly circulated in Greek churches and monasteries, were then to be dispatched to the Holy See.[139]

Whether or not another Greek embassy reached Paris before Louis's departure on his ill-fated Tunisian crusade has been a subject of dispute.[140] We know from Pachymeres, at any rate, that

[136] See Raynaldus, a. 1270, § 3 (quoted in full in Tautu, *Acta*, no. 29, 79). The embassies exchanged by Louis and Michael are difficult to disentangle because, as Dölger points out in *Regesten*, no. 1971, we have to deal with at least three embassies for which some of the documentary evidence is lost. On these embassies see Bréhier, "Une ambassade," 139ff. For texts of the correspondence between Louis and the Curia see Tautu, *Acta*, nos. 29 and 29a, 78 and esp. 84–85.

[137] "Suum non erat tale in eodem negotio" (Tautu, *Acta*, 79).

[138] "Frustrata longae deductionis ambagibus saepefatae Sedis intentio" (Tautu, *Acta*, 84).

[139] "In Concilio de Graecis generaliter congregando . . . explicite, ac aperte . . . profiteantur, praestito juramento. . . De hujusmodi autem professionibus fient publica instrumenta . . . (et) in cathedralibus et aliis solemnibus ecclesiis et monasteriis . . . redigantur . . ." (Tautu, *Acta*, 84, 82–83, and Raynaldus, a. 1270, § 4–5.

[140] On this see Dölger, *Regesten*, no. 1971, and Bréhier, "Une ambassade," 141 and note 2. Evidence for existence of the embassy is a passage written by a later hand in the Greek New Testament ("venit alius") mentioned above. On this specifically see Berger de Xivrey, "Notice," 98–99.

about the month of June, 1270, the Emperor dispatched to Louis an impressive embassy consisting of John Bekkos, Chartophylax of Hagia Sophia, and Constantine Meliteniotes, Archdeacon of the imperial clergy, bearing many splendid gifts.[141] The Greek envoys, together with the French ambassadors still at the Greek capital,[142] journeyed from the Golden Horn to Avlona, embarked from there by boat, and then touched at Cape Passaro in Sicily. There, however, they learned that Louis had already departed for Tunis.[143] Fearful of capture, the legates crossed during a violent storm to Carthage, arriving sometime after August 3. Immediately the Greek ambassadors presented their letter to Louis, but the King, gravely ill and involved in a desperate battle with the Muslims, delayed his response. Only on the very eve of his death (24 August) could he muster sufficient strength to receive the envoys. Expressing a profound desire for peace between his brother and Michael, he promised to promote that end should he live. But his death immediately thereafter caused Michael's hopes once more to founder. And so Bekkos and Meliteniotes, "their hands empty except for promises," departed for the Bosporus at almost the very moment that Charles and his troops were debarking at Carthage to aid Louis.[144]

[141] The purpose of which was to persuade Louis to curb Charles. See Pach., 361, ll. 5–22, and 362, ll. 1–9. This is corroborated by the Primate, a contemporary French monk of the convent of Saint-Denis, who wrote that the embassy was sent "pour empetrer pais avec le roy de Secile" (M. Bouquet, Recueil des historiens des Gaules et de la France, XXIII, 73e). R. Souarn, "Tentatives d'union avec Rome: Un patriarche grec . . . ," Echos d'Orient, III (1899) 233, notes that Pachymeres does not state if the envoys were charged to renew unionist negotiations with Louis. Souarn maintains that had they been, they would have been sent instead to the Curia.

[142] See Primate, in Bouquet, Recueil, XXIII, 73d: "les messages de l'emperere des Griex vindrent, avec les messages du roy de France, de Grèce." Cf. Bréhier, "Une ambassade," 143.

[143] It is not proposed here to enter into the controversy over whether or not Charles diverted Louis's crusade from the Holy Land to Tunis in order to serve his own ends. On this see Lavisse, Histoire de France, III, 2, 101–102; Sternfeld, Ludwigs des Heiligen Kreuzzug, 206–207 and 234–235; Norden, 468; G. Monti, "Tunisia, Italia meridionale e Sicilia nel Medioevo," Nuova antologia (1939); and, recently, Léonard, Les Angevins de Naples, 106. It is difficult, however, to escape the conclusion that if Charles's great objective was Constantinople, he would have avoided his brother's crusade to Tunis were it at all possible.

[144] On the entire incident see Pach., 362–364. Also Primate, in Bouquet, Recueil,

After the death of his brother, Charles assumed command of all the French forces in place of Louis's severely ill son, Philip III, who, with the Emperor Baldwin, had accompanied his father to Tunis.[145] It is difficult to believe that with powerful French as well as Sicilian forces now at his disposal Charles did not consider the advisability of soon launching an expedition against Constantinople.[146] But whatever his intent, for the present at least he directed his attention to the achievement of a brilliant victory over the Emir of Tunis, and in November he sailed with his troops to the port of Trapani in Sicily, where, it may be recalled, Prince Ferrante of Aragon and his troops were to have arrived a few months before for service against Byzantium.[147]

With the deaths of Clement IV, then Louis, and even of the Curial representative, the Bishop of Albano (who had likewise accompanied Louis to Tunis),[148] no power remained in the West

---

XXIII, 73, who records that the death of Louis was so meaningful to the Greek envoys that they wept, "car il doubtoient . . . que le roy de Secille quant son frère . . . fu mort, ne meist aguès pour eulz prendre." Cf. Norden, 468. On the date of the embassy's arrival see Bréhier, "Une ambassade," 142; and see the same article especially for a comparison of the accounts of Pachymeres and the Primate, who alone have described the Greek embassy at Tunis. The two versions differ mainly with respect to the envoys' audience with Louis, Pachymeres recording it in detail, and the Primate not mentioning it. Bréhier, 145–146, believes in the greater reliability of Pachymeres' account, as that author drew his information from Bekkos, a protagonist in the event. The account of the Primate, on the other hand, was secured indirectly and contains contradictions.

[145] On the apparent presence of Baldwin see the peace terms made by Charles's nephew Philip with the Muslims, in Side Sacy, "Mémoire sur le traité fait entre le roi de Tunis et Philippe," Mémoires de l'academie des inscriptions et belles-lettres, N.S., IX (1831) 466. Cf. Sternfeld, op. cit., 268ff.

[146] See Sternfeld, Ludwigs des Heiligen Kreuzzug, 203–204; Dade, 41; and Previté-Orton, Cambr. Med. Hist., VI, 191. Norden, 464 (based on William de Nangis, Chronique latine, ed. H. Géraud [Paris, 1843] in Société de l'histoire de France, I, 480) believes that Charles aimed to begin a campaign in Greece in 1270. Cf. Minieri-Riccio, Il regno di Carlo, I, 92, on a complaint of one Ruggiero Maramonte of Otranto that he had been stripped by Toucy of his possessions because he had not participated in the expedition to Achaia "in the year of the elapsed thirteenth indiction," which, according to Minieri-Riccio, would extend from 1 September 1269 to 31 August 1270, i.e., at the time of the Tunisian expedition.

[147] See treaty between Ferrante and Charles in Minieri-Riccio, Alcuni fatti, 110. Cf. above, text and note 114. As mentioned, nothing seems to have come of this treaty.

[148] Primate, in Bouquet, Recueil, XXIII, 73d.

able to block Charles. Matters were becoming desperate for the Greeks when suddenly fate itself seemed to intervene. On the arrival of the Latin ships in Trapani, on November 22, so violent a storm arose that practically the entire fleet was demolished: eighteen great warships, countless smaller vessels, thousands of men and horses, and huge stocks of provisions all went to the bottom.[149] With the preparations of years destroyed, an Angevin expedition against Constantinople was now manifestly impossible. To the Greeks of Byzantium it must have seemed as if the Virgin, their protector, had saved them from disaster.[150]

[149] William of Nangis, "Gesta Philippi Tertii Francorum Regis," in Bouquet, *Recueil*, XX, 480: "perierunt . . . circa quatuor millia personarum utriusque sexus . . . et decem et octo naves fortes et magnae, cum multis minoribus, et cum equis multis et rebus infinitis." Many of these probably were Sicilian troops, since the French army had been decimated in Tunis. Also see Bartolomeo of Neocastro, *Historia Sicula*, RISS, XIII (1921) 10: "vasa periclitantur, naves franguntur, thesauri merguntur."

[150] Yet the Greek sources are surprisingly silent regarding Trapani (nor is the disaster even mentioned by Chapman). We may be sure, however, that Palaeologus, alarmed by Charles's rapid successes against Manfred, Conradin, and now the Tunisian Emir, was quickly made aware of it by his agents. On the attitude of Western chroniclers that the disaster was God's judgment, cf. Saba Malaspina, *Historia*, ed. Del Re, II, 295: "quod excessu exigente culparum;" and esp. *Annales Placentini Gibellini*, in MGH SS, XVIII, 549: "Deus qui vindex est . . . circa 60 ligna cum omnibus . . . perierunt, et fuerunt numero plus quindecim millibus."

10

CAMPAIGNS AND NEGOTIATIONS

(1270-1274)

ANGEVIN MILITARY AND DIPLOMATIC PENETRATION OF THE BALKANS:
ACHAIA, EPIRUS, ALBANIA, BULGARIA, AND SERBIA

While Charles was occupied with the Tunisian crusade, Michael took advantage of his rival's involvement to resume attacks on Achaia. His aim was to take the entire peninsula. Accordingly, in the same year (1270) he sent to Monemvasia a large army of Asiatic Greeks, Cumans, and Turks under a new commander, very possibly his nephew, the Protostrator Alexios Philanthropenos.[1] The attack of the imperial forces was met by the Frankish barons, led by William of Achaia himself. Prince William had only recently returned from Italy, where he had conferred with Charles about the defense of the Morea and presumably about the approaching marriage of his daughter, Isabella, to the second son of Charles, Philip of Anjou.[2]

For almost two years the Greek troops devastated Moreot territory, but in spite of Achaian inferiority in numbers and resources,[3] no important engagement took place.[4] It was not until

[1] Commander's name suggested by Hopf, *Geschichte*, 292. Cf. Greek *Chron. Morea*, ll. 6487–6488, and French, par. 456.

[2] The wedding took place at Trani (Apulia) in May of 1271. See Greek *Chron.*, l. 6476, and French *Chron.*, pars. 439–455. Cf. Cerone, "La sovranità," 199.

[3] See Carabellese, 18ff., for Angevin documents regarding the shipment of grain and other provisions to Achaia.

[4] According to Chapman, 88, who cites no source, the Greeks retook all parts of the Peloponnese lost after the defeat of Philes.

February of 1272 that the imperial troops were challenged by an additional force of seven hundred cavalry and infantrymen dispatched to the Morea by Charles under the command of his *bailli*, Dreux de Beaumont.[5] Such aid would undoubtedly have been provided sooner had it not been for Charles's losses at Trapani and, as eloquently attested by Sicilian diplomas, the expenses and delays that arose in preparing the troops for embarkation.[6]

Assuming control of military operations, Beaumont established his base at Nikli, near the center of the Morea and not far from the Byzantine headquarters at Mistra. He intended to engage the Greek troops in open battle and then to advance to the strongly-fortified Mistra, but the Greek commander, on direct orders from Palaeologus (who remembered the disaster at Prinitza), took care to avoid an encounter on the plains. Beaumont's inability to meet the Greek forces in pitched battle, plus the difficulty of terrain between Nikli and Mistra, persuaded him to await the enemy at his base at Nikli.[7] Meanwhile his troops engaged in pillaging Greek territory as far as the port of Monemvasia. At last, however, unable to accomplish anything of importance, both Beaumont and William departed, entrusting the security of the area to a detachment of troops under John de Nivelet.[8]

During the following two year period, from 1272 to 1274, the struggle over the Morea became progressively less violent, and the focus of the Greco-Latin conflict, diplomatic as well as military, shifted to other areas — to the Aegean islands, the central Balkans, and especially to Albania.

---

[5] Cerone, "La sovranità," 207. Cf. Longnon, *L'Empire Latin*, 241, who dates the dispatch of aid in 1271. The Greek *Chron. Mor.*, l. 6533, and French *Chron.*, pars. 468–469, both mistakenly call the commander Galeran d'Ivry. Cf. Sanudo, *Istoria*, 128: "Marescalco in Romania . . . seco 700 Huomini." Also Zakythinos, *Despotat*, I, 53, note 4, who emphasizes the inaccuracies in this part of the *Chronicle of Morea*.

[6] See Carabellese, 20 and esp. 21, an angry letter of Charles, dated 22 Augus 1271, to the justiciar of Bari, notifying him to punish Philip of Santacroce for no having the troops and transports ready to sail to Achaia on the date prescribed, delay causing him great expense: "longam moram propter quod incurrimus magn dampna in expensis dictorum militum."

[7] Greek *Chron.*, ll. 6662–6665 and 6685ff.

[8] Nivelet had lost his fief of Gueraki to Palaeologus by the treaty of Constar

In 1271 the designs of Charles in Greece seemed favored by the death of Michael II Angelos, Despot of Epirus. The Despot's considerable possessions, extending, it will be recalled, along the western coast of Greece and much of modern Albania, were divided between two of his sons. The eldest, Nikephoros, inherited old Epirus with its capital at Arta, while his half-brother, John the Bastard, secured Thessaly, of which the capital was Neopatras. Palaeologus, fearing lest both Angeloi be drawn into the Angevin orbit, formed an alliance with Nikephoros by giving him a niece in marriage. The Emperor likewise arranged another union between his nephew, Andronikos Tarchaneiotes, and the daughter of the more able Bastard, to whom he granted the title of Sebastokrator.[9] Tarchaneiotes was then appointed imperial Grand Constable and governor of Adrianople and the surrounding territory, contiguous to the Bastard's principality of Thessaly. Thus, through these two diplomatic marriages, peace was for a time preserved between the Emperor and the sons of Michael of Epirus.[10]

But ambition and perhaps dissatisfaction with his inheritance soon drove the Bastard to assume his father's role as principal Greek adversary of Palaeologus. John's pretext for taking arms was the desire to aid his son-in-law, Andronikos Tarchaneiotes, who had fled to his court, angered it seems by imperial preference for Andronikos' brother. As the Emperor prepared to punish Andronikos, the latter enlisted the aid of the Tatars, who thereupon entered the pillaged imperial territory.[11] It is at this time that we have the first evidence of contact between John the Bastard and Charles, as attested by an Angevin rescript dated 13 April 1273, in which Charles refers to John as "our very dear friend . . . the Duke of Patera."[12] Although it seems clear that a commercial agreement was then entered into, it is likely that progress was

---

inople. See Greek *Chron.*, l. 6713. Cf. Zakythinos, *Despotat*, I, 52–53, and Longnon, *L'Empire Latin*, 241. Chapman is inadequate here.

[9] Pach., 308, ll. 18–19, and Greg., 130, ll. 17–18. Nikephoros had already been named Despot by Theodore II Lascaris. See Acrop., 134, l. 5.

[10] On relations between Palaeologus and the sons of Michael II see Pach., 307–09 and 322, ll. 5–11. Also Greg., 110ff.

[11] Pach., 322ff.

[12] Carabellese, 38 and esp. 36, note 3: "Ducis Patere Karissimi amici nostri" (cf.

231

made towards the creation of a political alliance against Palaeolc gus as well.

The unexpected calamity at Trapani had forced Charles t postpone his expedition against Constantinople, but the setbac was only temporary, for he immediately began to rebuild hi shattered fleet and refurbish his alliances. His diplomacy was nov aimed at completely encircling the Greek Empire in the Balkan so as to render feasible a land expedition against the capital. Whil therefore taking care to strengthen his Achaian and Thessalia connections, Charles also sought closer relations with the Bulgar: Serbs, Hungarians, Albanians, and even the distant Mongols.[12a]

The Bulgars at first seemed drawn to the side of the Emperon The latter had tried to win them from Charles by promising to th Bulgar Tsar, Constantine Tich, the Black Sea ports of Anchialc and Mesembria, on condition that Tich marry Maria, daughter c Michael's sister Eulogia. The Tsar, fearing a new invasion of th Mongol Golden Horde, allies of Palaeologus, accepted, and i 1272 the marriage was performed. However, the promised citie were never transferred, which embittered the Bulgars and induce them to remain faithful to Charles.[13]

Charles's relations with the Serbs were even more satisfactory It was to his advantage that Michael's plan for a marriage betwee his second son, Constantine, and a daughter of the Kral, Stephe Uroš I, was not realized. The Serbs instead remained receptive t Angevin advances. So cordial did Serbo-Sicilian relations subse quently become that many Serbs enrolled in Angevin service, som even establishing colonies in southern Italy.[14]

The case of the Hungarians was somewhat more complex. A

Arch. st. it., XXII, 16–17, and 19). The Bastard was permitted the free export silk to Apulia, and the import of twenty horses from there.

[12a] On relations with the Mongols see esp. Minieri-Riccio, Alcuni fatti, 5 dated 10 June 1269, and 15 January and 3 December 1270.

[13] Pach., 342–349.

[14] On their relations see Minieri-Riccio, Saggio di codice diplomatico, I (Naple 1878) 114, no. 133; Carabellese, 38–40; and V. Makušev, "The Italian Archiv and the Materials They Contain on the History of the Slavs" (in Russian), II (S Petersburg, 1871) 67–68 (supplement to vol. XIX of Review of the Academy Sciences, no. 3).

though, as noted, they were already allied to the King of Sicily,[15] the Emperor through careful negotiations also managed to establish close relations with them. Thus in November of 1272 a Greco-Hungarian alliance was created through the marriage of Andronikos, Michael's eldest son and heir, to Anna, daughter of King Stephen V.[16] Besides the averting of the menace of an Angevin-Serb-Hungarian coalition, another consideration prompting this accord may have been the danger of an understanding between Hungary and the disaffected Lascarid party in the Byzantine Empire. Such an assumption may perhaps be made from a statement of Pachymeres that the Hungarian union was contracted by the Emperor "because of Lascarid blood in the veins of the Hungarian royal family." [17] It is interesting to note also in connection with Andronikos and his bride that when, in November of 1272, Michael conferred on his son the title of co-Emperor, he bestowed upon him and Anna privileges never before granted to a junior emperor.[18]

Charles's unceasing efforts to penetrate the Balkans resulted in the creation of a new kingdom, that of Albania. Long the pawns of the rulers of Epirus, Nicaea, and Hohenstaufen Sicily, the Albanian nobles and townsmen (especially those of Dyrrachium) had on the death of Michael II in 1271 reasserted their desire for independence. This was all the encouragement Charles needed. Taking advantage of the weakness of the new Epirot ruler, Nikephoros, and justifying his claim to parts of Albania by the convention of Viterbo (which had transferred Manfred's dowry to him by right of conquest), Charles on 21 February 1272 signed a treaty with the Albanians. In exchange for Angevin protection against the Greeks and a promise to respect Albanian "priv-

[15] See Chapter 9, notes 98–99.

[16] Pach., 317–318, and Greg., 109, ll. 7ff. Cf. also Pach., 317, ll. 6–8: "and when it became necessary to match him [Andronikos] with a proper wife, it was not easy to send embassies to the Italians [i.e., the Latins] since Charles's territory of Apulia lay between."

[17] Pach., 318, ll. 5–7. The mother of the Hungarian king, Stephen V, was a daughter of Theodore I Lascaris. On the Lascarid malcontents see above, esp. Chapter 5, note 8.

[18] Pach., 318ff., and Greg., 109, ll. 9ff. Cf. A. Heisenberg, "Aus der Geschichte und Literatur der Palaiologenzeit," *Sitzungsber. d. bayr. Akad., Phil.-Hist. Kl.* (1920) 50.

ileges,"[19] the latter elected Charles and his successors Kings of Albania.[20] Thus, with the establishment of this new kingdom, a powerful Angevin wedge was driven into the Byzantine sphere of influence in the Balkans.[21]

The gravity of this new development of course alarmed the Emperor, who had observed with growing concern the rapidity with which Charles had successively disposed of Manfred, Conradin, and the Emir of Tunis. With a resourcefulness typical of his diplomacy Michael immediately attempted to foment a revolt of the Albanians against their new ruler. This is revealed by a letter of Charles dated 1 September 1272, in which he thanked the Albanian nobles for transmitting to him letters sent them by Palaeologus. Instructing the Albanians "vigorously and powerfully to wage war against our enemy," Charles further warned them "to beware of the machinations of Palaeologus by means of which he has already deceived you in other respects."[22] Charles at once began to develop his Albanian kingdom as a northern base against Constantinople. As early as 1272 he appointed a vicar (or captain-general) for Albania with headquarters at Dyrrachium. The post

[19] In 1273, for example, Charles invested the Albanian Paul Kropa with various territories (*Acta et diplomata res Albaniae mediae aetatis illustrantia* [Vienna, 1913–1918] I, no. 300, 86). Not all the Albanian population was pro-Angevin, however. Many Albanian nobles were probably drawn to Charles because of their Catholicism and especially their desire to rid themselves of the Greeks, but others were either independent or partial to the Greeks. See Carabellese, 47ff. Cf. Norden, 479, and Hopf, *Geschichte*, 299–300.

[20] For the document see *Acta Albaniae*, I, 77, no. 269. Charles wrote that "prelati, comites, barones, milites, burgenses, universitates ac etiam singulares homines Albanie" elected him. The fact, however, that Avlona and Dyrrachium had already fallen to Charles by force of arms was doubtless important. P. Durrieu, *Les archives angevines de Naples*, I, 191, cites Charles's new title: "Dei gratia rex Sicilie et Albanie, etc." For further information on Albano-Angevin relations, see *Acta Albaniae*, nos. 269ff.; Carabellese, chs. III and IV; G. Monti, *La espansione Mediterranea del Mezzogiorno d'Italia e della Sicilia* (Bologna, 1942) 141ff.; and the same author's "La dominazione napoletana in Albania: Carlo I d'Angiò, primo re degl' Albanesi," *Rivista d'Albania*, I (1940) 1ff.

[21] Avlona was taken before 4 July 1271 (del Giudice, *La famiglia di Re Man fredi*, pp. lxxiv–lxxv, note 1). Dyrrachium fell before 20 February 1272 (*Act. Albaniae*, I, 77, no. 268), that is, in February of 1271. On the boundaries of Charles's new kingdom (which are difficult exactly to define) see Carabellese, 44 45; and M. von Sufflay, "Die Grenzen Albaniens im Mittelalter," in L. de Tha lóczy, *Illyrisch-albanische Forschungen*, I (Munich-Leipzig, 1916) 288ff.

[22] *Acta Albaniae*, I, 80, no. 282.

was first filled by Gazo Chinardo, followed in 1273 by Anselm de Cayeux.[23]

Of the various Angevin activities in the Balkans the acquisition of Albania was most fraught with danger for Palaeologus. Hitherto Achaia had been Charles's most important base. But the difficulty of land communications with Constantinople rendered it less valuable than Albania, whose strategic port of Dyrrachium marked the western terminus of the Via Egnatia, the vital trans-Balkan highway extending through Thessalonica directly to Constantinople.

LICARIO AND THE FIRST IMPERIAL CAMPAIGN IN NEGROPONT

The Latin insular possession in Greece most coveted by Michael Palaeologus was Negropont. Governed more or less jointly by three Lombard nobles (termed "triarchs") and the Venetians, and subject to the suzerainty of the Prince of Achaia, the island had considerable strategic and commercial importance. A bridge to continental Greece, it possessed at least three strong fortresses (Oreos, Negropont, and Karystos, located in the north, central, and southern parts of the island respectively). It was, since the loss of Constantinople, the seat of a Venetian *bailli* and the chief Venetian naval station in Greece.[24] And it seems to have been the principal refuge for the notorious Latin corsairs infesting the Aegean Sea.[25] In short, together with Achaia it was the main center in Greece of Latin resistance to Palaeologan designs for reconquest of the Balkans.

Greek naval forces under Alexios Philanthropenos had frequently attacked Negropont in the past,[26] but real progress to-

[23] *Ibid.*, I, 77, no. 270 and 86, no. 299.

[24] On the island's importance and history from 1205 on, see J. Bury, "The Lombards and Venetians in Euboia," *Jl. of Hellenic Studies*, VII (1886) 309ff. Each triarch had his own town center with the capital city of Negropont common to all.

[25] See, e.g., Sanudo, *Istoria*, 127 and esp. 120: "Quelli di Negroponte . . . erano potenti e givano per Mar con loro Navilij, . . . ed inferivano molti danni alle parte dell' impero."

[26] E.g., during 1270 Palaeologus, in retaliation for raids by the triarchs on the

wards subjugating the island was not made until about 1273, when the Latin adventurer Licario was entrusted with the campaign.[27] Licario, ambitious son of a humble Veronese family established in Negropont, had incurred the enmity of the Dalle Carceri, most important of the island's triarchs, because of his secret liaison or marriage to Felisa, the widow of one of them. Fleeing their wrath, he seized the castle of Anemopylae, near Karystos, from which he terrorized the surrounding area.[28] Soon, however, because of insecurity before the triarchs' superior forces or, as Sanudo remarks, in order to acquire glory for himself,[29] Licario approached the Greek admiral Alexios Philanthropenos and requested to enter Greek service. Philanthropenos led him to the Emperor, who, impressed doubtless by Licario's capabilities, his eagerness for revenge, and the possibility through him of attracting other Latins to imperial service, came to an agreement with him. Palaeologus promised imperial aid in defending his fortress, and Licario, in Western feudal style, declared himself the vassal of the Emperor.[30]

coasts of Asia Minor, attacked Oreos and captured many Latin nobles. Andrea Dandolo, 317: "Palealogus indignatus, cum potenti stolo castrum Orey obsidet, . . . et multos nobiles feudatarios captivos conduxit."

[27] Called Icarios by Pach., 410, l. 19, and Greg., 195.

[28] See Greg., 95. Sanudo, *Istoria*, 120: "detta Termopile." Cf. Pach., 410, who terms Anemopylae a great island: κατάρχοντα δὲ καὶ νήσου μεγίστης ἦν 'Ανεμοπύλας ἔθος τοῖς ἐκεῖ λέγειν. On this passage see G. Zolotas, "Γεωγραφικὰ εἰς Παχυμέρην," 'Επετηρὶς Φιλολογικοῦ Συλλόγου Παρνασσός, IX (Athens, 1906) 5ff. Also R. Guilland, "Etudes de titulature et de prosopographie byzantines. Les chefs de la marine byzantine," *Festschrift Dölger*, (*Byz. Zeit.*) XLIV (1951) 231: "Licario, archonte de la grande île Anémopyle." Cf. J. Buchon, *Nouvelles recherches historiques sur la principauté française de Morée*, II, p. lxxviii, who believes that Pachymeres' "great isle" refers to Thasos.

[29] Sanudo, *Istoria*, 120: "Licario, che non si tenesse sicuro ivi [Anemopylae] ò che non potesse patir il viver nascosamente e senza gloria." Cf. Greg., 95, and Pach., 410.

[30] See Ostrogorsky, *Pour . . . la féodalité byzantine*, 238, note 3, citing an article of Charanis, who in turn quotes Sanudo. The chronology of Licario's exploits is difficult to establish. Chapman, 90, dates his rapprochement with the Emperor between 1270 and 1274. However, K. Hopf, "Veneto-byzantinische Analekten," *Sitzungsber. d. Wiener Akad., Phil.-hist. Kl.*, XXXII (1859) 431, 463, 497–498 (an article unknown to Chapman) fixes on 1269 for his first capture of Greek islands, i.e., Kos, Seriphos, and Stampalia (see next note). But Hopf, 463, seems mistaken when he speaks of Licario as Grand Duke already in 1269, for Licario could not have received this title until after the death of Alexios Philanthropenos, who according to Guilland, "Etudes de titulature, etc.," 231, was himself named Grand

For both, the immediate aim was the capture of Negropont from the Latins.

Guerilla warfare now began in earnest on the island. In a rapid campaign Licario seized the castles of Larmena, Cuppa,[31] Clisura, and Manducho.[32] Alarmed at this success, the triarchs appealed for assistance to their liege-lord, William of Achaia, and to Dreux de Beaumont, the Sicilian commander in the area, both of whom were compelled to abandon their campaign in the Morea and march to the defense of Negropont. William was able to retake the fortress of Cuppa, but the boastful Beaumont was beaten and had to flee before Licario and the imperial troops.[33] While Beaumont was removed as *bailli* in Achaia,[34] Licario retained what he had conquered as he waited to strike the next blow with reinforcements from the Emperor.[35]

UNIONIST NEGOTIATIONS BETWEEN POPE GREGORY X AND MICHAEL PALAEOLOGUS

In September of 1271, after a prolonged interregnum of three years (the longest in the entire history of the papacy),[36] during which Charles vainly attempted to sway the papal election, an

---

Duke only ca. 1271. Cf. Greg., 95. Pach., 41, ll. 7–9, says that Michael retained Licario at first as a private citizen, entrusting him with infantry troops for the conquest of Negropont. Cf. also Sanudo, *Istoria*, 120 "[Licario] li [i.e., to Palaeologus] diede quel loco."

[31] Cuppa, with Oreos and perhaps Schiros, Zia, and Stalimene (Lemnos) had been captured by Palaeologus' navy in 1269, according to *Estratti degli Annali Veneti di Stefano Magno* (ed. Hopf), in *Chroniques gréco-romanes*, 182. Magno, a sixteenth century Venetian, had access to Venetian documents subsequently destroyed.

[32] Sanudo, *Istoria*, 123.

[33] *Ibid.*, 128, esp.: "il Principe prese il Castello della Cuppa . . . ed il Marescalco fù rotto sotto Rio [Oreos] della Gente dell' Imperatore e se ne fugì . . . e ne ebbe gran vergogna e disonore benchè nel principio . . . facesse gran bravata."

[34] Replaced apparently by William of Barre; see *Arch. st. it.*, XXII, 19.

[35] The veracity of Sanudo's account of Licario's successful Negropontine campaign in 1273 is possibly contradicted by an Angevin edict of 6 February 1274 (*Arch. st. it.*, XXIII, 39), in which Charles speaks of the success of his arms the preceding summer in Achaia: "arma . . . que fuerunt felicis estolii vassellorum nostrorum armatorum estate proxima preterita que ad partes Achaye navigarunt" (cf. Norden, 477, note 1).

[36] A. Fliche and V. Martin, *Histoire de l'église*, X (1950) 456.

Italian assumed the tiara under the name of Gregory X. Vitally interested in problems of the Holy Land, where he had hitherto been papal legate, Gregory adopted a policy of which the principal aim was the recovery of Jerusalem. To this end his ecclesiastical negotiations with Byzantium, culminating in the celebrated union of Lyons, were of central importance, not only because he saw a religious entente as genuinely beneficial to all Christendom but because he believed that only with Greek support could the Holy Land be taken and successfully maintained.[37]

A prognostication of Gregory's policy toward Constantinople was his dispatch from the Holy Land, even before his enthronement, of a systatic letter to Michael in which he announced his election and made clear his disposition for union.[38] Michael, however, did not promptly respond to this overture, a fact which seems surprising in view of his growing anxiety over the preparations of Charles. But the Emperor's conduct may have been owing to internal difficulties within his Empire. Or, aware of Gregory's advocacy of a crusade, he may have feared that Greek participation in such an expedition would compromise his own friendly relations with Baibars, the Mameluke ruler of Egypt, whose power was the chief obstacle to recovery of the Holy Land.[39] At any rate, when Gregory, in March of 1272, formally proclaimed the convocation of a general council for the year 1274,

[37] On relations between Gregory X and the Greeks, besides the works of Norden and Hefélé-Leclercq, *Histoire des conciles*, VI, pt. 1 (Paris, 1914) 153–218, see the recent, careful studies of V. Laurent, "La croisade et la question d'Orient sous le pontificat de Grégoire X," *Revue historique du sud-est européen*, XXII (1945) 105ff.; and "Grégoire X (1271–1276) et le projet d'une ligue antiturque," *Echos d'Orient*, XXXVII (1938) 257–273. For a study exclusively on the exchange of embassies, see J. Müller, "Die Legationen unter Papst Gregor X (1271–1276)," *Römische Quartalschrift*, XXXVII (1929) 57ff.

[38] Pach., 369, ll. 9–17, and 370, ll. 1–2, alone reports this. See also mention of Gregory's divinely-inspired dream regarding the crusade and the Greek union in "Cronica S. Petri Erfordensis moderna," *MGH SS*, XXX, a. 1274, 407: "ecclesia per te [Gregory] recuperat Terram Sanctam atque Grecos."

[39] See M. Canard, "Un traité entre Byzance et l'Egypte au XIIIᵉ siècle et les relations diplomatiques de Michel VIII Paléologue avec les sultans mamluks Baibars et Quala'un," *Mélanges Gaudefroy-Demombynes* (Cairo, 1937) 197–224. Canard shows that the dates of 1266 and 1263, assigned respectively by Chapman (149) and Bratianu (*Rercherches*, 206–207) for Michael's first treaty with Baibars, should be corrected to 1262.

to which Palaeologus as well as Western princes were to be invited for the purpose of organizing a crusade, the Angevin party in the Curia prevailed upon the Pope to withhold the invitation to Michael until he had responded to Gregory's original communication.[40]

Somewhat later, in the summer of 1272, John Parastron, a Constantinople-born Franciscan, brought an imperial letter to the Pope in which Michael, expressing regret that Gregory had not stopped in Constantinople on his way to Italy, assured the Pope of continued imperial solicitude for union.[41] Militating against acceptance of Michael's sentiment was the hostility of the Angevin party in the Curia, which repeatedly emphasized to Gregory that a speedier and more reliable union could be achieved through re-establishment of the Latin Empire by force.[42] In disregard of Angevin protestations, however, Gregory, on 24 October 1272, sent an embassy back to the Bosporus headed by Parastron and four Minorites, with instructions to announce to the Emperor the convocation of the forthcoming council at Lyons,

to which . . . it shall behoove you, and for which we desire and request you, to come personally if possible. . . . so that regarding the rest of the matters which are involved, we may proceed more securely with your upright counsel.

Requesting an early reply from the Emperor, Gregory enclosed the confession of faith already transmitted by Pope Clement IV. Gregory further indicated his desire to begin negotiations on

[40] See Gregory's letter to Michael dated 24 October 1272, in *Registres de Grégoire X,* ed. J. Guiraud (Paris, 1892) no. 194, 68B: "ipsorum tamen consultu suspendimus missionem anxii expectantes ut a te, etc." Charles was in Rome at this time, according to Durrieu, *Les archives angevines,* II, 174. Chapman's remark, 92, note 4, that in March of 1272 Gregory dispatched to Michael an invitation to the council, should therefore refer instead to October of that year.

[41] From Gregory's reply in Guiraud, *Reg. Grég.,* no. 194, 68B. On Parastron see below, Chapter 11, text and notes 39–42. Also see O. van der Vat, *Die Anfänge der Franziskanermissionen und ihre Weiterentwicklung im nahen Orient* (Werl in Westf., 1934) 107ff.; and, recently, in M. Roncaglia, *Les frères mineurs et l'église grecque orthodoxe au XIII° siècle* (Cairo, 1954) 149ff.

[42] Reconstructed from a later letter of Gregory to Michael. See Guiraud, *Reg. Grég.,* no. 315, 123, dated 21 November 1273. Gregory mentions the pressure of persons "magne condicionis et status."

239

secular questions immediately, so that at the council the work of peace could be made easier. The epistle ended with the admonition that if union were not quickly carried out the Pope would be forced to yield to Angevin pressure.[43] Though the final statement is reminiscent of the threat at the close of Clement's last letter, the general tenor of Gregory's epistle was more conciliatory, stressing, in contrast to that of Clement, the importance of a voluntary desire for union.[44] But the most striking difference in the attitude of the two popes lay in the degree of implementation of union to be required before the convocation of the council. Whereas Clement had demanded from the Greek clergy and also people throughout the Empire unequivocal submission to papal primacy, Gregory, as a precondition to union, seemed willing to accept from the Greek prelates alone a synodical letter containing a profession of faith and recognition of Roman primacy. Gregory, moreover, offered Michael the option of sending representatives to the council, in which case the Emperor, Patriarch, and Greek prelates had to provide written guarantees that authorized envoys would soon follow to take the oath of union.[45] Worth quoting at this point is the last part of Gregory's instructions to his Minorite apocrisiarii, in which three formulas are proposed, any one of which could be adopted by the Emperor and his clergy in making their submission to Rome:

. . . "We, coming voluntarily to obedience of this church, will recognize and accept the Roman primacy, and shortly afterwards, . . . we ourselves will repeat it personally together with the clergy and people, and we will send apocrisiarii to you as soon as possible . . ."; or if the words "we recognize" can not be secured, there may be accepted in their place the following words or their equivalent: "We therefore, the Emperor, agree with the truth of the Catholic faith. . . " But if the words "we agree" also cannot be secured, in their place may be substituted the following words or their equivalent: "We desire to recognize this faith, to assume it, profess it, and to be united with . . . the Holy Roman Church, our mother . . . in the profession of faith,

[43] For the entire letter see Guiraud, *Reg. Grég.*, no. 194, 67–73, esp. 73.
[44] *Ibid.*, 73: "fidei puritas concensum purum ac liberum exigat."
[45] *Ibid.*, 72B.

and to come to obedience of this Roman church, [and] to recognize its primacy . . ."[46]

The importance of this passage lies in its revelation that Gregory, in contrast to his predecessors, had assumed a more sensitive approach to the difficulties of union, and a tolerance of the time that would be required for its consummation. In brief, Gregory had broken with the policy that insisted that a completed union precede the establishment of secular peace.

It was, of course, Gregory's ultimate aim, after achieving a cessation of Greco-Angevin hostilities, to attack the Muslims of the Holy Land, supported by a united Christendom of East and West. But though suzerain of Charles for Sicily, Gregory was reluctant peremptorily to command the King to desist from military preparations against the Greeks. The Pope realized that Charles's support of the titular Latin Emperor Philip (who had succeeded to the claims of his father Baldwin after the latter's death in 1273) for the restoration of the Latin Empire was legitimate so long as Michael was schismatic and not a Catholic prince. And Gregory understood equally well that a premature strengthening of Michael's position by removal of the threat of Sicilian attack would render Michael less eager for union. While desisting therefore from an outright demand for Angevin disarmament, and, in particular, permitting Charles to maintain his offensive positions in Epirus and Achaia, Gregory nonetheless insisted to Charles on the absolute pre-eminence of negotiations for union.[47]

Meanwhile, Michael, fearing that delay in effecting union might enable Charles to win over the papacy, remanded to Gregory two of the four papal legates, who, along with imperial envoys, could attest to the sincerity of his efforts for union. In his letter entrusted to the nuncios Michael emphasized that on

[46] *Ibid.,* no. 195, 73–74, dated 25 October 1272.
[47] On papal intentions, see Martène, *Ampl. coll.,* VII, pars. 229–230, a letter of Gregory informing Charles of his resolution to open negotiations with Palaeologus and of the truce to be arranged. Norden, 500–501, believes that it was a diplomatic victory for Charles that Gregory did not insist on a reduction of Angevin military preparations.

behalf of union he was neglecting even pressing military and state affairs. In explanation of the delay he wrote that it was wiser not to hurry unduly, because "for the permanent establishment of union . . . much labor and time must be expended, . . . [and] in the aim of closing the old schism care should be exercised not to produce a new one."[48] Addressing Gregory in terms of the greatest filial devotion and piety[49] and at the same time requesting that his presumption be excused, Michael accused the Angevin adherents "of following their own desires, of unjustly preventing the achievement of peace . . . and of introducing enmity to the common detriment of all."[50] Michael then promised that the remaining papal nuncios, together with imperial representatives, would soon appear at the council, where they would announce the accomplishment of union. In conclusion, the Emperor asked the Pope to provide for the security of their journey,

for we greatly fear that while the envoys are bringing the fruit of such a great undertaking, perhaps that old warrior [Charles], moved by hatred of peace, may try to nullify this divine work, so that it may remain unfinished. May your divinity, however, with his great foresight repel the crafty devices of an assiduous enemy by preparing a safe way for the nuncios and brothers so that this prince may fear your ill-will; and thus their scheme [of Charles and Philip] will be annulled and the foresight of your holiness will lead to a happy conclusion.[51]

In another letter borne by Theodore and Goffridus, imperial court official and interpreter respectively accompanying the papal envoys, Michael sketched the route to be followed by his ambassadors to the council and repeated his request for safe-

---

[48] Guiraud, *Reg. Grég.*, no. 313, 120B.
[49] *Ibid.*, 119: "Sanctissimo et beatissimo domino pape veteris Rome ac univer salis ecclesie summo pontifici, et sedis apostolice successori, reverendissimo pat suo, Michael . . . sue sanctitatis obediens filius, debitam paternitati sue reveren tiam et orationum petitionem."
[50] *Ibid.*, 121B, esp.: "Hujusmodi autem presumptuose quodam modo scriber moti sumus . . . aliquos sequentes proprias voluntates et injuste pacis executioner prohibentes, . . . inimicitiam ad communem interitum omnium introduxerunt. . .
[51] *Ibid.*, 122B.

conducts. He asked, moreover, that a trusted representative of the Pope, armed with an authorization, meet his envoys on their arrival in Italy.[52] Such safeguards were necessary for Michael because failure of the imperial ambassadors to appear at the council would play directly into the hands of the Angevin supporters.

Overjoyed at Michael's letter, Gregory on 21 November 1273 dispatched a new epistle to the Emperor.[53] Though assuring Michael of his confidence in imperial intentions, Gregory nevertheless requested that the Emperor hasten the acceptance of union on the part of his clergy and people in order to disprove those critics (Charles and Philip were both personally at the papal court at this time)[54] who accused the Greek ruler of procrastination and hypocrisy and pressed for the adoption of force. Gregory directed, in addition, that the Byzantine ambassadors to the Council be granted plenary power and complete instructions. In return, he promised to provide the safe-conducts requested.[55]

Instrumental in securing safe-conducts were the Archbishop of Palermo and the papal chaplain, Nicholas Boucel, both of whom impressed upon Charles his guilt before God and man if

[52] *Ibid.*, no. 314, 122 (undated), esp.: "Theodorum curie nostre valetum et de interpretibus curie nostre Goffridum." Goffridus was probably a Latin or Gasmule in imperial service, while Theodore was doubtless the person mentioned in a later letter of Innocent V as being an envoy to Gregory: "Theodorus magnus tuae curiae dispensator" (Martène, *Ampl. coll.* VII, col. 244). Dölger (*Regesten*, no. 2002) terms Theodore Grand Constable. It is to be noted that the embassy in question carried its own interpreter, a general practice of the Greek envoys as no college of interpreters seems as yet to have existed at the papal curia.

[53] Over a year had elapsed since Gregory's first letter to Michael.

[54] Norden, 511. The previous year Gregory had left Viterbo and entered Rome, the first Pope to do so in over a decade. It is noteworthy that at Gregory's entrance the Emperor Baldwin and King Charles both acted as attendants, leading the animal he rode and holding its bridle. On the overlooked passage describing this incident see Nicholas Glassberger, "Chronica," *Analecta Franciscana*, II (Quaracchi, 1887) 84. Cf. above, Chapter 2, note 61.

[55] Guiraud, *Reg. Grég.*, no. 315, 123, esp.: "quamplures magne condicionis et status asserunt unionis predicte tractatum ex Grecorum parte diutius in figmentis verborum et simultate deductum . . . viam aliam que se videbatur offerre pre manibus potius suadentes . . . quasi non in sinceritate debita hoc tam salubre negotium prosequaris." Also, "cum potestate plenoria . . . plene . . . instructos, etc."

243

because of him Michael should withdraw from negotiations.[56] Gregory also directed another high ecclesiastic, Bernard, Abbot of Montecassino, to meet the Greek envoys on their landing in the Regno and to escort them to the Curia.[57]

With respect to the approaching general council, it should be observed that Gregory was able to secure from the reluctant Charles [58] a notable political concession. As will be recalled, the Treaty of Viterbo for the conquest of the Greek Empire was to expire in May of 1274. By repeatedly stressing to Charles the spiritual importance of the council, Gregory was finally able to induce both Charles and Baldwin to postpone the execution of their pact for one year, until 1 May 1275.[59]

Nor was this all. For the sake of union and the crusade, Gregory, just before the convocation of the council at Lyons, seems even to have pushed Charles into a truce with Palaeologus.[60] Indeed, it would appear that now, for the first and only time, the two enemies negotiated directly with each other. Unfortunately, the precise circumstances of the negotiations are un-

---

[56] Martène, *Ampl. coll.*, VII, col. 238 (Guiraud, *Reg. Grég.*, no. 318, 124, does not quote the entire document), dated 25 November, 1273 (cf. also Guiraud, *Reg. Grég.*, no. 198, 75). Gregory likewise requested safe-conducts from the Emperor Philip, other nobles, and from the Italian communes through which the imperial envoys would pass on their way to Lyons. Most of the requests are dated 25 November 1273, from Lyons (Guiraud, 124).

[57] *Ibid.*, 124, same date. The Abbot was directed to excommunicate anyone of whatever rank, who might impede the envoys (quoted in full in Martène, *Ampl. coll.*, VII, col. 236-237). On the Abbot's career see D. A. Saba, *Bernardo I Ayglerio Abate di Montecassino* (*Miscellanea Cassinense VIII*) (Montecassino, 1931) esp. 95ff.

[58] Charles's attitude is revealed in a circular letter to his officials dated 7 January 1274, in which he scoffs at the negotiations and states that the safe-conduct (which he limits to one month) was issued against his wishes ("contrariis mente nostre"). See *Arch. st. it.*, XXIII, 35, and del Giudice, *La famiglia di re Manfredi*, 232, note 1.

[59] Assumed from a papal letter to the Abbot of Montecassino in Guiraud, *Reg. Grég.*, no. 491, 209, dated 28 July 1274: "terminos eosdem usque ad kalendas primo venturi mensis maii voluntate unanimi prorogarunt." See Norden, 517-520 for details of the extension, which was signed by Philip, his father, Baldwin, having died in 1273.

[60] Reconstructed from a letter of Gregory to Charles (see Martène, *Ampl. coll.* VII, 229). Dade, 47, note 262, favors dating this one month before the Council of Lyons, i.e., in the spring of 1274.

known.[61] It may be surmised, however, that they involved a truce to hostilities in the Morea and Albania, for they seem to have had a quieting effect on the war in Romania during the first half of 1274.[62]

It is necessary at this point to stress the authority of Pope Gregory which was potent enough to exercise such a remarkable influence on Charles and Michael alike. For with the moral force of union constantly emphasized by the Pope, Charles was unable to act decisively. And as for Michael, there seems little doubt that his willingness to incur the risk of civil war by imposing union on his Empire was based on his confidence in Gregory's motives and, equally, on knowledge of the effectiveness of papal control over Charles.[63]

MICHAEL PALAEOLOGUS, THE GHIBELLINES OF LOMBARDY, AND THE GENOESE OF ITALY AND GALATA

Of direct bearing upon the struggle being waged between Michael and Charles was the political situation in northern Italy. There matters were complicated not only by the rivalry between Guelph and Ghibelline, but by the existence of opposing Genoese, Angevin, Byzantine, and Castilian interests as well. While Sicily and Genoa, in particular, had recently been on friendly terms (as evidenced by Charles's utilization of Genoese vessels for his Tunisian crusade), relations became severely strained as a result of Charles's barbaric seizure of Genoese ships and property after the destruction of his fleet at Trapani in 1270.[64] Another event which mobilized Genoese sentiment against Charles was the

[61] See Martène, op. cit., VII, 231B: "quaedam tractata dicuntur . . . quod inter mem. regem et Palaeologum hactenus sit tractatum." Cf. Norden, 518, and Haller, Historische Zeitschrift, XCIX (1907) 25. Also Dölger, Regesten, no. 2003.

[62] See Norden, 520.

[63] George Metochites, Michael's envoy to Gregory, characterizes the latter's motives as εἰς κοινωφελῆ χριστωνύμων σπουδάσματα. See M. Laurent, Le Bienheureux Innocent V (Vatican, 1947) 440. Gregory, of course, was suzerain of Charles for Sicily.

[64] See Ann. Ian., IV, 115 and W. Cohn, "Storia della flotta siciliana di Carlo I d'Angiò," Arch. stor. sicilia orien., XXV (1929) 369 and 383–384.

Genoese revolution of the same year, which brought to power in the Commune an anti-Angevin Ghibelline government.[65]

The area of most sharply conflicting interests in northern Italy was Lombardy, to the hegemony of which both Charles and King Alfonso X of Castile had personal aspirations. For Charles, control of Lombardy was an important step in his aim of dominating all Italy, whereas for Alfonso, control of Lombardy was vital for his claim to the Western imperial throne, to which he had been named in a disputed German election some years before.[66]

Charles, at the instigation of Genoese Guelph exiles who sought his aid against their home government, arrested all Genoese merchants in his kingdom and confiscated their property.[67] This unprovoked act, for which Charles was censured by the Pope,[68] drove Genoa into the arms of the anti-Angevins — the Marquis of Montferrat, vicar of Alfonso for north Italy, and the Ghibellines of Lombardy, with whom Genoa concluded an alliance on 30 October 1273.[69] Hostilities against Charles on the part of Genoa and the Ghibellines now actively broke out.

In the interim, Michael Palaeologus, perhaps uneasy over Charles's alliance with the Genoese Guelphs, made efforts to strengthen his ties with the new Ghibelline government of Genoa.

[65] Under the regime of the Captains of the People Oberto d'Oria and Oberto Spinola (1270–1285), Genoa was now to experience her golden age.

[66] Charles had been appointed by the papacy vicar of Tuscany and senator of Rome. As for Alfonso, called the Wise, see Marqués de Mondéjar, *Memorias históricas del Rei D. Alonso el Sabio* (Madrid, 1777), and, on his election, A. Busson, *Die Doppelwahl des Jahres 1257 und das römische Königthum Alfons X. von Castilien* (Münster, 1866). For fuller references see R. L. Wolff, "Mortgage and Redemption of an Emperor's Son, etc.," 59, note 27.

[67] *Ann. Ian.*, IV, 148–149; and Ferretto, "Codice diplomatico," *Atti soc. lig.*, XXXI, 279. That Charles's anger may have stemmed partially from the Genoese association with Palaeologus is perhaps revealed by an Angevin letter addressed to a justiciar of Abruzzi, in which Charles ordered that Genoese ships, together with those from territories of Palaeologus, be seized by surprise so that no property could be hidden. See Minieri-Riccio, *Il Regno di Carlo I di Angiò negli anni 1271 e 1272*, 106–107.

[68] *Ann. Ian.*, IV, p. xcvi, note 2.

[69] *Ibid.*, 167, note 1. Actually the Marquis was accorded admission to the alliance within three months. Besides furnishing a fleet Genoa provided a port of entry for Castilian troops. See also *Annales Placentini Gibellini, MGH SS*, XVIII, 553.

ITALY
under Charles of Anjou
c.1270

Natural Scale 1:8,500,000

20 10 0   20   40   60   80   100 120 Miles

REFERENCE
I. Charles' dominions and spheres of influence;
Kingdom of Sicily ....
County of Piedmont ....
Guelf League of Tuscany ....
Rome and Brescia ....
Cities otherwise in alliance with Charles underlined..... Genoa
(Piacenza and Ivrea become subject to Charles
in 1271, but he lost the alliance of Genoa etc.)
II. Boundaries of the Papal States in 1270..........
Romagna and other lands ceded by
Rudolf I. to the Papacy in 1278-79............

St Gotthard
Friuli
Brenta
R. Adda
Trent
Como
Bergamo
Novara
Cassano
Vicenza
Verona
Treviso
Istria
Milan
Cremona
Padua
Venice
LOMBARDY
Montferrat
Lodi
Mantua
Este
Adige
Turin
Vercelli
Piacenza
Alessandria
Ferrara
Alba
Tortona
Parma
Acqui
Reggio
Modena
R. Po
Savona
Lombardore
Pontremoli
Bologna
Imola
Ravenna
Genoa
Varese
Albenga
Faenza
Rimini
Pisa
Lucca
Pistoia
Florence
Sinigaglia
Ancona
R. Arno
Pucecchio
Poggbansi
Jesi
Marcha
Meloria
Volterra
Siena
Arezzo
Gubbio
Camerino
Fermo
Montepulciano
Perugia
Foligno
Ascoli
R.Tronto
CORSICA
Monte Cristo
Giglio
Radicofani
Grosseto
Orvieto
Todi
Rieti
Elba
Viterbo
Spoleto
Abruzzi
Aquila
Civita Vecchia
Tagliacozzo
Capitanata
Siponto
ROME
Campagna
Sora
Barletta
R. Tiber
Germana
Foggia
Bari
Teano
Troia
Ariano
Gaeta
Capua
Benevento
Lavello
Melfi
R. Garigliano
Naples
Nola Principato
Castellammare
Brindisi
Salerno
Taranto
Lecce
R. Sele
Otranto
Torres
Gallura
Torres
SARDINIA
Roseta
Arborea
Cagliari
Cagliari
Ustica
Lipari I.
CALABRIA
Floro
Trapani
Monreale
Palermo
Cefalù
Messina
Reggio
Val di Mazzara
S I C I L Y
Agosta
Syracuse
Tunis
Malta

Longitude   East   of   Greenwich

From three documents that have remained,[70] it appears that in about June of 1272 Michael took the initiative by dispatching to Genoa the notary Ogerius with an outline for a treaty. According to this memorandum, certain preliminary responses favorable to the imperial proposals were made by Lanfranco of Saint George, chancellor of the Commune.[71] Shortly thereafter, on August 29, Lanfranco, as plenipotentiary of the Commune, departed for the Bosporus,[72] and in the same year a treaty was concluded between the two powers. In essence a defensive-offensive alliance, the convention provided Michael with security against attack by Charles of Anjou and regulated Greek relations with the Genoese colony at Galata. The principal stipulations were the following:

(1) The Treaty of Nymphaeum would continue in effect.[73] (2) The Genoese pledged to make no alliance with enemies of Palaeologus. Any Genoese colonist disobeying this injunction and favoring the enemy by word, act, or counsel would be punished by the Genoese podestà at Pera.[74] In the event that such a person could not be apprehended he would be considered as having conspired against the Commune itself.[75] (3) The government of Genoa would be held responsible for damages committed

[70] The first document (G. Bertolotto, "Nuova serie di documenti sulle relazioni di Genova coll'impero bizantino," *Atti soc. lig. st. pat.*, XXVIII [1897] no. 19, 505–509) consists of the proposals of the Greek envoy with the preliminary responses of Lanfranco, the Genoese representative. The second (*ibid.*, no. 18, 500–504, which rightfully should follow the first) is actually the minutes of the stipulations agreed upon by Palaeologus and Lanfranco, drawn up by the latter for his own use. The third (see L. Sauli, *Della colonia dei Genovesi in Galata*, II [Turin, 1831] no. 8, 204ff.) is the treaty in its final form.

[71] Bertolotto, no. 19, 505 and 500: "ego Lanfranchus de Sancto Georgio canzellarius comunis . . . ambaxator . . . ad respondendum peticionibus sive requisitionibus ipsius domini Imperatoris." Ogerius is undoubtedly the same person as the Protonotarius of the Latin interpreters mentioned in an imperial letter to the Curia in 1278. See J. Gay, *Les registres de Nicolas III* (Paris, 1898) no. 384, 134.

[72] Bertolotto, no. 18, 500.

[73] *Ibid.*, 501.

[74] Evidently referring to this clause is the passage in Pach., 366, ll. 3–6, saying that Palaeologus insured the fidelity of the Genoese at Pera through treaties, so that they would not ally with other Latins in case Constantinople were attacked.

[75] Bertolotto, no. 18, 501–502. This clause evidently referred to Genoese corsairs or possibly to Genoese in Angevin service. In the final redaction of the treaty in 1275 (Sauli, II, 204) there was added to this clause the stipulation that if the

by corsairs who were Genoese subjects. (4) At Palaeologus' request the Genoese agreed to appoint as podestà in Galata only a person who would do honor to the Emperor as well as to the Commune.[76] (5) Genoese merchants were warned against declaring as their own the merchandise of other Latins in order that the latter might benefit from Genoese exemption from duties. Anyone guilty of such fraud would be punished by the podestà and the merchandise surrendered to the Emperor.[77] (6) To maintain secrecy with respect to movements of the Greek navy, the Emperor was permitted to hold Genoese ships in port until the sailing of his fleet.[78] (7) Severe punishments would be meted out to Genoese acting as intermediaries for enemies of the Emperor.[79] (8) Reaffirmed was the right granted to Palaeologus to commandeer Genoese merchant ships in his harbors during wartime. The fees, however, to be paid by Palaeologus for such use would be subject to arbitration if exorbitant.[80]

Despite the opinion of certain scholars,[80a] the pact was not merely a restatement of the Treaty of Nymphaeum. The most important clauses of Nymphaeum provided for war against Venice and the aid of Genoese warships for the reconquest of Constantinople. At the time of the new treaty a Greco-Venetian alliance

podestà had not prescribed a proper penalty, the Emperor could do so "secundum jura legum."

[76] Bertolotto, no. 18, 502: "homo talis juxta temporis qualitatem talis qui sit honor domini Imperatoris et comunis Ianue." This very likely alluded to the treason of the podestà Guercio.

[77] *Ibid.* See also Heyd, *Histoire*, I, 437–438.

[78] The definitive convention sets a maximum period of twenty days for retention of Genoese vessels (Bertolotto, no. 18, 503), and the final ratification amends it still further to apply only to cases where the ships would sail in the same direction as the fleet (Sauli, II, 207).

[79] Bertolotto, no. 18, 503, and no. 19, 509. An obvious allusion to Charles of Anjou, the Latin barons of Greece, and perhaps to the Angeloi princes.

[80] *Ibid.*, 503. Cf. the document of ratification in Sauli, II, 208, where it is stated that such Genoese ships would not have to participate in a war against powers friendly to Genoa. In the first document of the negotiations Michael is called "pater communis Ianue" (Bertolotto, no. 19, 508). The Emperors often referred to themselves as "father" when addressing inferiors. See Bréhier, *Institutions*, 295, and recently, A. Grabar, "God and the 'Family of Princes' Presided over by the Byzantine Emperor," *Harvard Slavic Studies, II (Festschrift Dvornik)* (Cambridge, 1954) 117ff.

[80a] G. Caro, *Genua und die Mächte am Mittelmeer*, I (Halle, 1895) 302.

249

was already in existence, and nothing was said about Genoese naval support, only merchantmen being mentioned.[81] Thus the new agreement is actually a revealing commentary on the shift in the diplomatic situation: Angevin Sicily has replaced Venice as the power against which the treaty is directed.

Though carefully negotiated, the treaty was not ratified by the Genoese government until 25 October 1275.[82] The reason for the delay may partly have been the improved relations of Michael and the Venetians, and the unionist negotiations between Constantinople and the Curia, a segment of which was outspokenly supporting the papal vassal Charles of Anjou.[83] But probably of equal or even greater importance were two events which had served in the meantime to inflame Greco-Genoese relations.

A Genoese of Galata, evidently mindful of the threat to Constantinople posed by Charles and his allies, boasted to a Greek that the capital would soon again become Latin. Stung by the taunt, the Greek struck the Genoese, who in return slew the former with his sword. When news of the killing was brought to the Emperor, he became very indignant at the Genoese colonists, and, in the words of Pachymeres, ordered an imperial official, Manuel Muzalon, "to expel the entire race and to spare none." [84] Accompanied by troops, Muzalon crossed over to Galata and surrounded their houses. The Genoese, however, pleaded with the Emperor against expulsion, promising to do whatever he directed. Michael's anger was finally mollified and the Genoese permitted to remain only after an apology and the payment of a large indemnity — a compensation, according to Pachymeres, "far more effectual than their snivelling." [85]

---

[81] Michael now depended on his own naval strength.

[82] See Sauli, II, 204ff. and esp. Manfroni, "Relazioni," 678–679.

[83] See above, note 42. Chapman, 93, note 3, says that the treaty was ratified at Genoa in 1272 and therefore cites no reasons for delay. Cf. Caro, *Genua*, I, 302, note 1, who is of the opinion that the treaty, though ratified in 1275, may actually have been in effect since 1272.

[84] Pach., 426: προστάσσει τὸ γένος ἐξαναστατοῦν ἅπαν μηδὲν μελλήσαντα.

[85] *Ibid.*: πολλῷ τῆς σφῶν κορύζης ἐκείνην ἀνυσιμωτέραν. For the entire incident see Pach., 425, ll. 12ff. and Greg., 134, ll. 1ff.

For Michael to threaten the ejection of the entire Genoese colony because of the crime of one individual may seem excessive.[86] But the reason for his harshness may well have been a desire to impress upon the Genoese that severe penalties would be immediately meted out to anyone giving comfort or support of any kind to the enemy.[87]

The second incident was even more serious. At this time the Zaccaria brothers, disturbed by competition from their Genoese countrymen, had secured from the Emperor the exclusive privilege of exporting alum from the Black Sea.[88] Although the decree was damaging to their trade, the Genoese colonists of Pera, possibly still smarting under the threat of expulsion, dared not protest. But the Genoese of the home city did not resign themselves to the edict, and a number of them, manning two galleys, sailed past the imperial palace of Blachernae on the Golden Horn without rendering the proper salute. Arriving in the Black Sea, the corsairs then seized a large ship laden with alum.[89] Meanwhile, Michael, little desirous of an imbroglio with Genoa, sought to persuade the citizens of Pera to induce the privateers to accord the appropriate imperial honors on their return. The latter, however, encouraged by a favorable wind, repeated the affront. Incensed, the Emperor sent in pursuit a flotilla manned by Gasmuloi of the marine under the Vestiarios Alexios Alyattes. The Greek sailors were able to overtake the Genoese only with the help of a huge Catalan merchant ship lying in the harbor.[90] Whereupon

---

[86] See Bertolotto, no. 18, 501, where, according to the treaty with Lanfranco, any Genoese committing a personal injury against a Greek subject could be punished by the Emperor if not already properly punished by the podestà. Cf. Greg., 134, who does not mention Michael's order for expulsion of the Genoese.

[87] Pach., 419: τοὺς Γενουΐτας παρακινουμένους ἐξ ἀναιδείας ταπεινοῦν ἐβούλετο. Also Greg., 134: ὡς ὅλης πόλεως καταστραφείσης.

[88] Pach., 420, ll. 10–12. This privilege was apparently later abolished, as is shown indirectly by an act of 1281 in G. Bratianu, Actes des notaires génois de Péra et de Caffa de la fin du treizième siècle (1281–1290) (Bucharest, 1927) 88, no. 25. See also Heyd, Histoire, I, 438.

[89] Pach., 421, ll. 12ff. See also Bertolotto, no. 21, 511, where the name of the ship's captain is given in a list of indemnities to be paid to Genoa: "Manueli de Marino . . . pro dampnis datis eisdem in nave eorum que exibat de mare majori cum alumine per Galeas . . . domini Imperatoris . . ."

[90] There was, it seems, considerable Catalan merchant activity in Constantinople.

Michael, who had been encouraging his men from the shore, ordered the guilty Genoese, in accordance with Byzantine custom, to be blinded for the insult to his honor and disobedience to his authority.[91]

PALAEOLOGUS AND KING ALFONSO X OF CASTILE

In view of the anti-Angevin alliance between Genoa and the Lombard Ghibellines on the one hand, and Genoa and Palaeologus on the other, diplomatic relations between the Ghibellines, especially their patron Alfonso X of Castile, and Michael would seem only natural. Yet so far as I have been able to discover, only a single source, the contemporary *Annales Placentini Gibellini*, explicitly couples the names of the two rulers at this time. Under the year 1271 it states that Alfonso contemplated a Byzantine alliance through the marriage of one of his daughters to a son of Michael.[92] Possible corroboration for this statement may be a

---

Already in 1268 the King of Aragon had permitted the councillors of Barcelona to designate consuls in Romania. On this see C. Marinesco, "Notes sur les Catalans dans l'empire byzantin," *Mélanges d'histoire du moyen âge offerts à M. Ferdinand Lot* (Paris, 1925) 502.

[91] Pach., 425; he does not stress Michael's reaction to the capture of the alum-laden ship. For the entire incident cf. Greg., 133ff. Also cf. Lopez, *Benedetto Zaccaria*, 35–37 (following E. Muralt, *Essai de chronographie byzantine* [Basle, 1871] 432, he dates the event ca. 1276), and Bratianu, *Recherches*, 138ff. The incident, potentially so serious for Palaeologus, must, from the Genoese point of view, have been less important, since no Genoese literary source mentions it. But see an undated letter of Michael to Genoa, published in L. Belgrano, "Cinque documenti genovesi-orientali," *Atti soc. lig.*, XVII (1885) 236–239, in which Michael may well be complaining of both incidents described above. Belgrano originally assigned the letter to ca. 1280, but Manfroni, "Relazioni," 679–680, has apparently correctly redated it within the period 1273–1275. Cf. Dölger, *Regesten*, no. 1991; Lopez, *Benedetto Zaccaria*, 36; and Bratianu, *Recherches*, 140. Chapman overlooks this letter.

[92] "Alteram vero filiam dare debet filio Palialoghi imperatoris Grecorum inimico dicti regis Karoli propter quod dictus domnus rex Karolus cambium fecit cum domno Balduino condam imperatore Grecorum qui expulsus est per dictum Palialogum de Constantinopoli et vult dictus Karolus dictum imperium Grecorum occupare" (*MGH SS*, XVIII, 553). Norden, 487, and Chapman, 96, note 6, misconstrue this passage to read that Michael Palaeologus himself was to marry Alfonso's daughter (cf. Wolff, "Mortgage," 80, note 89). The possibility that the *Annales Placentini Gibellini* have confused Palaeologus with the Latin Emperor Baldwin, whose son Philip already before 1266 (and apparently again in 1281; see above,

rather ambiguous passage in Pachymeres regarding Michael's desire to marry his son Andronikos to a Latin wife, a project not realized "because of the difficulty of exchanging embassies with the Italians [i.e., Latins], as Charles's territory of Apulia blocked the way." [93] Somewhat more satisfactory, though still not conclusive, evidence with reference to a Greco-Castilian connection is the fact that one of the two envoys dispatched by Alfonso in 1271 to negotiate with the north Italian Ghibellines was William, Count of Ventimiglia.[94] This is the same person to whom Michael had previously given in marriage a daughter of the Emperor Theodore II Lascaris, and whom Michael sent to Genoa in 1273 or 1274 as his personal envoy.[95] That a Greco-Castilian royal marriage (with Andronikos in all probability as one of the principals) failed to materialize may well have been the result of a decision of Palaeologus, by whose calculations the marriage alliance entered into with the King of Hungary was probably of greater value.[96] Not only was Castile less strategically situated than Hungary with respect to Byzantium, but the north Italian Ghibellines would

---

Chapter 9, note 113) had been under consideration as son-in-law of Alfonso, is apparently to be discarded, since the above passage would indicate that the writer of the work was clearly able to differentiate between them.

[93] Pach., 317: καὶ ἔδει συναρμόττειν αὐτὸν τῇ πρεπούσῃ συζύγῳ, τὸ μὲν πρὸς τοὺς Ἰταλοὺς πρεσβεύεσθαι εὐόδως οὐκ εἶχε τοῦ Καρούλου μεταξὺ κειμένου κατὰ τὴν Πουλίαν. Pachymeres often uses the word "Italian" to refer to Latins in general. See Pach., 21, l. 5 and 329, ll. 3–4: "the Italians who were with John [Duke John de la Roche of Athens]," whose men undoubtedly consisted more of Frenchmen and Burgundians than Italians.

[94] "Rex Castelle eius ambaxatores, scilicet comitem Guillelmum de Vinctimilliis . . . transmisit in Lombardia" (Ann. Plac. Gib., 553). Cf. also Mondéjar, Memorias históricas, 99, who quotes a Spanish chronicle saying that in 1273 the Count of Ventimiglia with other Lombards went to Castile to hasten Alfonso's military aid.

[95] See Pach., 181, ll. 1–4, and Greg., 93, ll. 2–5. Also on the embassy see Belgrano, "Cinque documenti," 227: "Guilielmum de Vintimilia karissimum generum imperii mei [i.e., of Michael], qui . . . venit ad illas partes."

[96] For Andronikos' marriage see above, note 16. That Constantine, Michael's second son, was also under consideration as a prospective husband for a Castilian princess is of course another possibility. Pach., 318, tells the story of Michael's negotiations for a diplomatic marriage between one of his sons and a daughter of Stephen Uroš I in order to draw the Serbs away from Charles's orbit. The Serb ruler insisted on Michael's eldest son, Andronikos, but was persuaded to accept Constantine until he learned that Andronikos, whom Michael falsely described to him as on the point of death, had recovered. Angry at the deception, Uroš broke off negotiations.

oppose Charles whether a Greek prince married a Castilian princess or not.

Significant, finally, in the question of the relations between Alfonso and Palaeologus is the fact that toward the middle of the year 1273 Alfonso offered his services to Pope Gregory X for convoking the Council of Lyons "in behalf of the recovery of the Holy Land and the return of the Greeks" to the church. Alfonso's precise intentions can only be surmised, since his proposal, which apparently was not accepted, is known to us solely from an uninformative letter addressed to him in reply by the Pope.[97] Nevertheless, it is not at all unlikely that Alfonso's offer was motivated by a wish to ingratiate himself with Michael as well as by his growing hostility to Charles and, most important, his desire to gain papal support for his cherished claim to the Western imperial throne.[98]

PALAEOLOGUS AND VENICE. ANGEVIN MILITARY PREPARATIONS IN THE REGNO AGAINST BYZANTIUM

In his desire to launch an expedition against Byzantium before the implementation of union, Charles sought above all to draw Venice to his side. With Venetian support it might be possible, even without papal sanction, to repeat the success of the Fourth Crusade. Particular impetus for such an accord was the fact that on 4 April 1273 the Greco-Venetian truce, signed in 1268, would expire.[99] Charles knew that Palaeologus would then attempt to secure a new treaty with Venice or an extension of the old one. In fact, Angevin and imperial envoys, both seeking an accord with the Doge, now simultaneously appeared in Venice.[100]

[97] Raynaldus, a. 1273, § 38: "pro husmodi [sic] Terrae sanctae recuperatione, ac Graecorum reditu nobis (revelare proponebas)." See also A. Busson, *Die Doppelwahl des Jahres 1257, etc.*, 101–102.

[98] See Villani, *Cronica*, I, 374, who says that Gregory was at this time angry at Charles because the latter was instrumental in breaking the peace finally effected by the Pope between the Guelphs and Ghibellines of Florence. On Alfonso's claim to the Western imperial throne see again Busson, *Die Doppelwahl*, 102.

[99] For the treaty see T.-Th., III, 92–100. Cf. Canale, 584: "iusque a V ans"; and Andrea Dandolo, 313.

[100] Canale, 648: "vint en Venise mesage de Mesire Bauduin, li Enperere de Costantinople; et mesage de Mesire Charle, li Rois de Sesile; que distrent . . .

With the Greek ambassadors came five hundred Venetian prissoners, returned by Michael to the Doge in the hope of inclining him favorably toward imperial proposals.[101]

Pope Gregory X was also interested in the contest for Venetian favor. He was opposed to an extension of the Greco-Venetian treaty because he believed that it would create dissension among the Latins, lessen the pressure on the Emperor, and thereby diminish the latter's desire for union. Therefore Gregory warned Venice no less than five times in the course of 1272 "to abstain completely from making any new treaties with Palaeologus . . . and not to extend the present one; [otherwise] you will gravely provoke all Christendom against you." [102] But the Doge Lorenzo Tiepolo preferred to disregard the papal admonitions and to leave his decision open. Subsequently, however, he sent an embassy to the Pope and advised the Angevin and Greek envoys that the question would be handled by Venetian ambassadors he would dispatch to their countries.[103]

Whether or not Venice actually renewed the treaty with Palaeologus has been a matter of discussion. While a passage in a subsequent Greco-Venetian pact, dated 19 March 1277, has been cited as evidence for an extension of the treaty,[104] the more tenable assumption would seem to be that the treaty remained tacitly in force though not officially renewed. This view is based mainly on a still later agreement, of 1278, in which Palaeologus promised to indemnify Venice for acts of piracy committed by Greek subjects. The latter agreement, comprising a huge list of

---

apareillast sa navie por entrer en sasine de l'enpire de Romanie. . . Et a celui tens . . . estoient venu mesage de Palialog." Cf. Dandolo, 320. The date is probably the last part of 1272.

[101] The prisoners apparently had been captured at Negropont. See Dandolo, 320: "VC homines Venetos, quos in galeis feudatorum Nigropontis ceperant, duci offerunt."

[102] See Guiraud, *Reg. Grég.*, nos. 845, 846, 928, 929, and esp. 927, p. 364.

[103] Canale, 650: "il feroit respundre a lor seignor par ses mesages. . ." Note that Canale, 648, says the Doge transported the Greek envoys home on Venetian galleys. Cf. Dandolo, 320.

[104] In 1275, says Norden, 540, based on text in T.-Th., III, 134: "evenit fieri et antea treuga, que conservata est Dei gratia et completa secundum pacti tempus, postea extensa fuit usque ad hodiernum diem." Ostrogorsky, *Byzantine State* (1956) 410, note 1, agrees, but evidently did not consider Dade (see next note).

Venetian complaints, includes about thirty-five cases which apparently occurred in the period 1273–1277, at the time of the supposed extension of the treaty under discussion. These Venetian claims for damages must have had some legal basis, quite probably a tacit truce. For had the piratical acts been committed in time of war, Venice could not justifiably have claimed damages.[105] Reference to such a tacit treaty (a *modus vivendi* offering considerable freedom of action to both Venice and Michael) may well be found in the following overlooked passage of the fourteenth century Emperor-historian John Cantacuzene: "The Venetians and Greeks do not have permanent treaties but only arrangements from year to year, and this dates from the time of Michael Palaeologus." [105a]

A striking fact about the Angevin documents for this period is the large number concerned with Charles's preparations for his Greek expedition. Since the destruction of his fleet at Trapani, Charles had striven energetically to build ships in Apulian ports in order to be able to fulfill his treaty obligations by 1 May 1274. And Charles now demanded that the warships and provisions be ready for sailing by 4 May 1274, under the supreme command of Philip de Toucy.[106] The diplomas in question, more numerous and imperious with the beginning of 1273, all reflect Charles's insistence on industry, security, and rigid discipline, his obsession with small details, and above all a mania for speed. Typical statements affirmed that severe penalties would be imposed and property confiscated if all were not in readiness on the date fixed, and that deserters and even high-ranking officials guilty of negligence would be punished by the loss of a foot.[107]

To secure funds for paying his mercenaries, among whom

---

[105] On this argument see Dade, 45, note 253, where the piratical acts are enumerated. Dade fixes on the years 1273–1277 from references in the text of the treaty, for example, T.-Th., III, 215, no. 2: "iam sunt quatuor anni et ultra" [i.e., before 1278].

[105a] (Bonn) III, 188, ll. 4–6.

[106] See *Arch. st. it.*, XXII, 13, dated 5 April; 15, dated 11 April; and esp. 24, dated 28 April, 1273. Also cf. *ibid.*, 13, of 5 April, and 21, of 20 April, 1273, ordering Riccardo, Saracen captain of Lucera, without fail to be at Brindisi with his men in order to sail for Romania on the date fixed.

[107] *Ibid.*, 12, of 2 April, 1273; and 20, of 19 April, 1273.

were Saracen archers and French, Provençal, and Neapolitan knights, Charles made provisions for the securing of loans.[108] Finally, to insure that all orders were faithfully carried out, Charles dispatched special inspectors to the Apulian harbors.[109] Though all these preparations "ad partes Romaniae" were intensive, they were not yet meant, it would seem, for a direct assault on Constantinople, as Charles still lacked a really strong fleet. Very probably they were directed instead to his forward bases in Achaia and Albania, where the Angevin forces, augmenting their strength in cooperation with the Latins of Greece, could await the arrival of other troops for a later attack in force.

In spite of the resolution of Charles and his massing of arms and provisions in Apulia, it appears that the expedition did not sail to the Morea at the established time.[110] No source mentions the arrival of the fleet in Achaia, nor apparently did Toucy participate in any Moreot campaign during the year. Instead he appears at this time as admiral of the Angevin naval forces operating off the Ligurian coast.[111]

The postponement of the fleet's sailing can very probably be attributed to political factors: papal pressure for an extension of the Treaty of Viterbo and a truce between Byzantium and Sicily in order to prepare the way for a union of the churches; Castilian-Ghibelline opposition to Angevin predominance in northern Italy; and especially Charles's inability to conclude a treaty with Venice so that the combination of Venetian and Sicilian fleets could assure the success of a naval expedition against Constantinople.

[108] The cost of these preparations was enormous. See, e.g., in Carabellese, 28, mention of loans, esp. one secured by Drogo de Beaumont, vicar in Achaia, from a Venetian merchant with which to pay his troops. Also Carabellese, 13, and *Arch. st. it.*, XXII, 22, under 22 April; and 25, under 30 April, 1273.

[109] *Arch. st. it.*, XXII, 23, of 27 April; cf. 28, of 5 May 1273.

[110] Carabellese, 12 and note 1, says that evidently unforeseen circumstances prevented the expedition's departure. Chapman, 97, citing for his statement only Hopf, *Griechenland*, 292 (which cites no source), affirms that "in May Charles sent to the Morea, under the command of Philip de Toucy, an army more numerous than those which had preceded it."

[111] Imperiale, *Jacopo d'Oria*, 209–210. That William of Achaia was shortly afterward named commander-in-chief of Angevin forces in Achaia (see Carabellese, 24, dated 4 April 1274, and note 4) may be further evidence that the expedition did not sail at this time.

11

THE ECCLESIASTICAL UNION OF LYONS

Theorem he Greek envoys to the Council of Lyons [1] left the Golden Horn in March of 1274. As his representatives the Emperor had selected two ecclesiastics, the former Patriarch Germanos and the Metropolitan of Nicaea Theophanes, together with three imperial officials, the Grand Logothete George Acropolites, the *Prokathemenos tou Bestiariou* Nicholas Panaretos, and the Grand Interpreter George Berrhoiotes. [2] For presentation to the Pope the envoys carried lavish gifts, including gold ikons, stoles, wrought censers, and even the magnificent altar cloth of gold and pearls which had been removed from Hagia Sophia. [3]

[1] The purpose of the council was not limited to union. Pope Gregory also proposed to reform clerical morals and, above all, to make preparations for the crusade. It is of interest that Michael himself did not appear at the Council, though certain writers of the fifteenth and sixteenth centuries affirm that at papal invitation he himself went to Lyons. On this see Vasiliev, *History* (1952) 658 and note 244.

[2] The Grand Logothete corresponds to a modern Prime Minister and Foreign Minister (see Bréhier, *Institutions,* 145). The *Prokathemenos tou Bestiariou* (though subordinate to the *protovestiarites*) was chief of the financial administration (on which see Bréhier, 149; J. Ebersolt, "Sur les fonctions et les dignités du Vestiarium byzantin," *Mélanges Diehl,* I [1930] 87 and note 5; and cf. M. Laurent, *Le Bienheureux Innocent V et son temps* [Vatican, 1947] 152, note 87, who calls Panaretos *protovestiarites*). The Grand Interpreter headed the corps of interpreters (see Bréhier, 303; and E. Stein, "Untersuchungen zur spätbyzantinischen Verfassungs- und Wirtschaftsgeschichte," *Mitt. zur osmanischen Gesch.,* II [1923–1925] 36–37).

[3] On the envoys and gifts see Pach., 384, ll. 10ff. and 385, ll. 1–8. The Em-

Unfortunately, the journey of the legates, undertaken at a time of inclement weather, was attended by disaster. At Cape Malea off the southern coast of Greece, their two ships were caught in a violent storm and the one bearing two of the nobles and all the gifts aboard was lost. The other, however, with Acropolites, Germanos, and Theophanes, along with the Franciscan John Parastron and the papal envoys Jerome of Ascoli and Bonagratia, was able to reach the port of Modon in the western Peloponnese. Upon subsequent arrival at the island of Leukas, the papal nuncios sent a communication to the Pope apprizing him of the accomplishment of union and the approaching arrival of the Greek embassy.[4] From there the envoys sailed to Italy,[5] through which, armed with papal safe-conducts and personally escorted by the Abbot Bernard of Montecassino, they travelled on to Lyons.[6]

In the meantime, in the Cathedral of St. John at Lyons, the Council was already in session. A brilliant assemblage was in attendance, including representatives of the Western rulers as well as the cardinals, the last incumbent Latin Patriarch of Constantinople Pantaleone Giustiniani, and a great number of lesser clerics. One king, James I of Aragon, came personally.[7] But conspicuously absent was the papal vassal Charles of Anjou, although

---

peror, according to Pachymeres, had originally presented the altar cloth to Hagia Sophia at the time of the withdrawal of the anathema pronounced against him for the blinding of John Lascaris; he now removed it because there was no time to have a similar one made.

[4] For the letter see Od. van der Vat, *Die Anfänge der Franziskanermissionen und ihre Weiterentwicklung im nahen Orient . . . während des 13. Jahrhunderts* (Werl in Westf., 1934), 251–252, and recently M. Roncaglia, *Les frères mineurs et l'église grecque orthodoxe au XIII⁰ siècle* (Cairo, 1954) 168–170.

[5] On the entire journey see Pach., 396–397. Neither Pachymeres nor Gregoras mentions Lyons by name. They were apparently unaware that the council was not held at Rome and that the Popes had for some time been residing in Viterbo.

[6] See Guiraud, *Reg. Grég.*, nos. 317 and 319, p. 124, for papal letters to the Abbot of Montecassino and to north Italian prelates and officials requesting safe-conducts for the Greek envoys. Also see Saba, *Bernardo I Ayglerio*, 101.

[7] Héfelé-Leclercq, *Histoire des conciles*, VI¹ (Paris, 1914) 168 (hereafter Héfelé, *Conciles*). Also see *The Chronicle of James I King of Aragon*, ed. J. Forster, II (London, 1883) 642–644. Envoys of the Kings of France, Germany, England, and Sicily were also present (see Fliche and Martin, *Histoire de l'Église*, X [1950] 494).

he had only recently been with Gregory in Florence where the latter had stopped on his way to Lyons.[8]

Of particular interest in regard to the relations of the Greek and Latin churches is the second session of the council. It was at this time that the letter of the papal nuncios announcing the approach of the Greek embassy was received and read before the assemblage. On June 24 the Greek legates themselves appeared and were solemnly escorted by the entire body of ecclesiastics to the papal palace, where Gregory and the cardinals gave them the kiss of peace. The envoys presented to the Pope a letter from the Emperor, sealed with the imperial golden bull, and two others from his son Andronikos and the Byzantine clergy. Five days later, it should be noted, without any official discussion of the dogmatic or liturgical points at issue, ceremonies preliminary to the act of union began. While Gregory himself celebrated mass before the convocation of some 1500 persons, the Epistle was read and the Evangelium chanted, first in Latin, then in Greek by a Greek deacon dressed in vestments of the Eastern church. Thereupon the famous Cardinal Bonaventura (whose prestige and learning probably kept him most frequently in touch with the Greek envoys)[8a] preached a sermon exalting the union of the churches, after which the symbol was chanted in Latin by the Western bishops, then again in Greek by the ex-Patriarch Germanos[8b] together with the Greek prelates of Calabria and two Greek-speaking papal penitentiaries. These were the Constantinopolitan Franciscan John Parastron, evidently the council's chief

---

[8] Villani, I, 372.

[8a] Significant as to the importance of the Council for the West is the fact that the great Dominican Thomas Aquinas had been commissioned by the Pope to write a work setting forth the errors of the Greek church. See A. Dondaine, " 'Contra Graecos,' Premiers écrits polémiques des dominicains d'Orient," *Archivum fratrum praedicatorum,* XXI (1951) 387ff. Thomas died on his way to Lyons and Bonaventura himself died during the closing sessions of the Council. On Bonaventura see bibliographical references in Roncaglia, *Les frères mineurs,* 175–178.

[8b] Germanos III, patriarch only for a brief time, had been displaced from his office mainly because of his inability to revoke the excommunication pronounced against Michael for the latter's blinding of young John Lascaris. See Pach., 291ff. One is struck by the fact that the highest-ranking prelate Michael could prevail upon to journey to Lyons was an ex-patriarch.

interpreter, and the Dominican William of Moerbecke, who as Bishop of Corinth was later to become noted for his translations of Aristotle. Three times the *filioque* was repeated, after which the Byzantine envoys chanted praises to Gregory in Greek and the Pope completed the celebration of mass.[9]

It was not until the fourth session, on July 6, that the formal act of union was performed. The seating arrangement of the assembly placed the Greek envoys (as at the famous Council of Florence two centuries later) at the right but *behind* the cardinals.[10] After a sermon delivered by the Cardinal-Bishop of Ostia (later Pope Innocent V), Gregory expressed joy at the "return of the Greeks to the obedience of the Roman church," an act, he said, "accomplished voluntarily and without temporal compensation." [11] Thereupon a Latin translation was read of the three letters brought by the Greek envoys. In the first, Michael, repeating the symbol prescribed by Pope Clement IV,[12] declared his acceptance of the Roman faith and primacy. He urged, however, that the Greek church be permitted to retain its symbol as recited before the schism and also its own rites, "provided they did not conflict with the ecumenical councils and patristic writings recognized by the councils." [13]

[9] On the proceedings see Mansi, *Sacrorum conciliorum nova et amplissima collectio*, XXIV (Venice) cols. 61ff. (hereafter Mansi, *Concilia*), and Héfelé, *Conciles*, 173. Also M. Laurent, *Innocent V*, 155; and, in Russian, V. Nikolsky, "The Union of Lyons. An Episode from Medieval Church History, 1261–1293," *Pravoslavnoe Obozrenie*, XXIII (1867) 5–23, and later issues (unavailable to me). It might be noted that at Bari (in 1098) the south Italian Greeks had been permitted to retain their rites, although with acceptance of the *filioque*. See P. Jaffé, *Reg. pont. rom.*, I, 694, and B. Leib, *Rome, Kiev et Byzanz à la fin du XI° siècle* (Paris, 1924) 287ff.

[10] On the seating at Lyons see Mansi, *Concilia*, col. 65: "a latere dextro post cardinales" (cf. also col. 66). On that of Florence see D. Geanakoplos, "The Council of Florence (1438–1439) and the Problem of Union between the Greek and Latin Churches," *Church History*, XXIV (1955) 330 and note 57.

[11] Mansi, *Concilia*, col. 65: "libere veniebant ad obedientiam Romanae ecclesiae, profitendo fidem, et recognoscendo primatum ipsius, nihilque temporale petendo," to which is added in Mansi, "de quo multum dubitabatur"!

[12] Including the *filioque* ("ex Patre Filioque procedentem"). For Michael's letter see Mansi, *Concilia*, cols. 67ff. Cf. Héfelé, *Conciles*, 175 and note 1.

[13] The Emperor had instructed his legates to make these declarations and requests publicly before the council (Héfelé, *Conciles*, 176).

After the reading of Andronikos' letter, probably couched in the same manner as that of his father,[14] the message of the Greek clergy was read. While testifying to imperial efforts to gain the anti-unionists, the Greek bishops[15] declared their adherence to union and informed the Pope that, if the present council were successful, the incumbent Patriarch Joseph would resign his office. The letter closed with the statement that, with papal approval of the declarations of the Greek ambassadors, the bishops would accord to the Holy See "all rights to which it had been entitled before the schism"[16] — a rather dubious concession, since papal claims had in the main burgeoned only after the conflict in 1054 between Pope Leo IX and Patriarch Michael Kerularios.[17]

At length the supreme moment arrived. As imperial plenipotentiary, George Acropolites took an oath in the name of the Emperor to abjure the schism, to profess the true, holy, and orthodox faith as expressed in the imperial letter, and, lastly, to recognize the primacy of the Roman church "to which the Emperor returned of his own volition."[18]

This solemn act completed, the Pope intoned the *Te Deum*,

[14] *Ibid.*, 176.

[15] Whose number included (titular?) Greek bishops of Latin-held cities such as Athens.

[16] Letter in Mansi, *Concilia*, cols. 74ff., esp. 77: "nihil eorum denegamus quae ante schisma praestabant patres nostri." See Pach., 392–396, who describes Michael's measures to coerce his clergy to sign this letter.

[17] See D. Geanakoplos, "The Council of Florence," 330 and note 53.

[18] "Ego Georgius Acropolita et magnus logotheta, nuncius domini imperatoris Graecorum Michaelis Ducae Angeli Comneni Palaeologi . . . ad ipsius Ecclesiae obedientiam . . . spontaneus veniens, etc." (Mansi, *Concilia*, col. 73). Héfelé, 177, is apparently wrong in saying that when Acropolites was asked for an authorization empowering him to take an oath in the Emperor's name, he could produce none. L. Delisle, "Notice sur cinq manuscrits de la Bibliothèque Nationale et sur un de Bordeaux contenant des recueils épistolaires de Bérard de Naples," *Notices et extraits des manuscrits de la Bibliothèque Nationale*, XXVII² (1879) 159, prints what is evidently a Latin translation of the authorization (cf. Dölger, *Regesten*, no. 2008). On the matter of the *filioque*, M. Jugie, *Le schisme byzantin* (Paris, 1941) 254, believes, probably correctly, that Gregory, while asking the Greeks to recognize the dogmatic truth of the *filioque*, did not oblige them actually to chant the symbol with these words. Yet the Greek envoys at Lyons (except perhaps the Archbishop of Nicaea at one point [Héfelé, *Conciles*, 173]) did chant the *filioque* (Mansi, 65–66). Also see Roncaglia, *Les frères mineurs*, 182, who says without explanation: "L'union était faite . . . sans aucune modification ni dans le symbole, ni dans le rite byzantin."

and preached a sermon expressing his jubilation on the occasion, after which the entire assemblage chanted the symbol in Latin. It was immediately repeated in Greek with the *filioque* by the ecclesiastical representatives of the Emperor, joined by the Greek bishops and abbots of the Kingdom of Sicily,[19] who, though Greek in ritual, had been united to Rome since the Council of Bari (1098). With the formal recitation of the creed the session devoted to union came to an end. It was an historic occasion, as for the first time in more than two centuries the great Eastern and Western branches of Christendom were once more in religious communion. Yet the success achieved at Lyons was more apparent than real, for though the Emperor had made personal submission to Rome, his clergy and people had not, and thus the council's significance was for centuries to remain a subject of violent controversy.[20]

A few days after the ceremony of union the Greek envoys departed from Lyons, having been presented with tiaras, mitres, and rings, "the customary ornaments of Latin prelates," as we are rather ironically informed by Pachymeres.[21] The ambassadors, according to the same author, did not immediately return to the East, but spent the summer with the Pope, possibly in Rome or at the papal palace of Viterbo.[22] It was not until the end of autumn in 1274 that, together with papal nuncios, they arrived once more in Constantinople with new letters from the Pope addressed to the Emperor, his son, and the Byzantine clergy.[23] What reception

[19] Mansi, *Concilia*, col. 66; Héfelé, *Conciles*, 178. Despite the absence of Charles, his clergy, including the Greeks of the Regno, was well represented.
[20] The Latins, considering it ecumenical, believed the union binding. To the Greek people, however, it was a "robber synod," because only representatives of the Emperor and not of all the Eastern patriarchs had participated. On the non-ecumenicity of Lyons for the Greeks see a letter of Pope Benedict XII to King Robert of Naples in 1339 (text in Raynaldus, a. 1339, § 21) and esp. a letter of Barlaam in 1339 to the pope (quoted in Geanakoplos, "The Council of Florence," 327–328).
[21] Pach., 398, ll. 1–2. Also J. Sbaralea, *Bullarium Franciscanum* (Rome, 1759) III, 215.
[22] Pach., 398, ll. 2–5. Cf. Héfelé, *Conciles*, 208–209, who states that the Greek envoys returned to Constantinople a few days after the closing of the Council.
[23] Pach., 398. For the letters see Mansi, *Concilia*, cols. 78–80 and now Tautu, *Acta*, nos. 51–53, 138–141.

they would be accorded, however, by the Greek population of the capital remained to be seen.

The establishment of union was, as already emphasized, primarily the result of Michael's conviction that only through such an accord could the menace of Charles of Anjou's invasion of the Empire be averted.[24] This sentiment of political expediency the Emperor did not attempt to conceal from his people nor particularly from his higher clergy. Indeed, the clearest expression of his views he gave in a speech to an ecclesiastical synod convoked in the imperial palace shortly before the Council of Lyons. At that time, as Pachymeres informs us, Michael stressed to his prelates that his efforts to effect union were due "only to his desire to spare the Greeks the terrible wars and effusion of blood that were threatening the Empire." Union, he declared, required concessions on only three points: (1) recognition of Roman primacy, (2) the right of appeal to Rome, and (3) commemoration of the Pope in the public prayers (diptychs).[25] None of these, he insisted, had any real importance. "For when," he exclaimed, "would the Pope appear in Constantinople to take precedence over the Greek bishops, and when would anyone trav-

[24] Pach., 370, ll. 2-4: "It was clear that the Emperor sought the union only from fear of Charles; otherwise it would never have entered his mind." Also 367, ll. 10-11. Similarly Greg., 123, ll. 3-8, and 125, ll. 2-6: "Therefore, beset by so many difficulties which drove him to desperation, the Emperor now sends an embassy to the Pope [promising] to bring about the reconciliation and union of the churches of old and new Rome, if only the Pope would avert the expedition of Charles." Cf. the Western chronicler, the Primate, in Bouquet, *Recueil des historiens des Gaules et de la France*, XXIII (Paris, 1876) 91: "aucuns furent qui crurent mieux que paour les eust plus contrainz de venir à celi concille." Also G. Villani, I, 374: "Per lo quale riconciliamento de' Greci, il detto papa confermò il detto Paglialoco imperadore dello 'mperio di Costantinopoli." See, finally, explicit mention of Michael's fear of the Latins by the Templar of Tyre in *Gestes des Chiprois*, in *Rec. hist. des croisades*, *Doc. Arméniens*, II (Paris, 1906) 789 (ed. Raynaud in *Société de l'orient latin* [Geneva, 1887] 213).

[25] Pach., 386, ll. 16-18 and 20ff. (also 395). Cf. Gregoras' version of the same speech, 125, ll. 11-16, and 126, ll. 23ff.

erse so vast a sea to carry an appeal to Rome? [26] What is there contrary to the purity of the faith in patriarchal commemoration of the Pope in the liturgical prayers?" [27] He went on to show that *oikonomia* ("considerations of self-interest" is here perhaps the best translation for this difficult word) had honorably been made use of by Greeks in the past for securing their aims.

Far from being blamed for skillfully averting the danger threatening us . . . we shall instead be praised by all wise and prudent men. Only one thing impels me to seek union, and that is the absolute necessity of averting the peril that threatens us. . . Except for that I would never have begun this affair.[28]

Though Palaeologus' aim of saving the Empire through union is clear, the tactics he employed seem at first glance inconsistent. Actually he pursued two conscious lines of action: one in his relations with the papacy, and another with his prelates. On the one hand, he emphasized the importance of religious union, attempting faithfully to carry out every demand of the papal legates.[29] (In this he was seeking particularly to silence his Angevin opponents in Italy who accused him of insincerity.)[30] On the other, he sought to minimize to his clergy the significance

---

[26] See a papal letter dated 21 July, 1266, in *Registres de Clément IV*, ed. Jordan, I, no. 346, 93, complaining that no one would make the crossing from Durazzo to Italy "propter inconstantiam maris et viarum discrimina."

[27] Pach., 387, ll. 7–8. V. Laurent, "Le serment anti-Latin du Patriarche Joseph Iᵉʳ," *Echos d'Orient*, XXVII (1927) 405, rightly believes that mention of the Pope in the public prayers was of crucial importance, as to the people it denoted communion between Latin and Greek churches (cf. Pach., 390, ll. 3–4).

[28] Pach., 387, ll. 8ff. Cf. the same sentiment in Greg., 127, ll. 9–12: "My conduct is the part of wise administration, since necessity demands that a slight damage be suffered for the sake of greater advantage." The problem of *oikonomia* involved two opposing points of view: the rigorist, which maintained that the church should be practically independent of the state, and the liberal, which insisted that when required by political necessity the church should subordinate itself to the needs of the state. On this see F. Dvornik, *The Photian Schism, History and Legend* (Cambridge, 1948) 8, 24, etc.

[29] Sanudo, *Istoria*, 135: "Tentò con ogni modo possibile aver la grazia e favor della Iclesia Romana."

[30] See the letter of Pope Gregory X to Palaeologus in Guiraud, *Reg. Grég.*, no. 315, 123, dated 21 November 1273, referring to the pressure of Angevin supporters: "qui . . . notarent quasi non in sinceritate debita hoc tam salubre negotium prosequaris."

of union, mollifying them as much as possible by insisting that union would entail no change in the symbol and only minor concessions of an insignificant nature. While to the papacy, therefore, he stressed spiritual considerations, to his clergy and people he emphasized political benefits.[31]

Michael's dual policy toward papacy and Greek clergy was in large part made possible by the sincere and tolerant attitude of Pope Gregory,[32] as well as by the distance and poor communications between Constantinople and Rome. The relatively infrequent exchange of embassies between the Holy See and the imperial court (generally at least three to four months were required for the journey) plus the extreme deference and glowing language with which Palaeologus wrote to the Curia of his zeal for union,[33] seem, at least for a time, to have limited papal awareness of Michael's real motives.[34] And, as we shall see, it was only in 1279, during the pontificate of the more realistic Pope Nicholas III, that Michael's policy threatened to break down.[34a]

Before the achievement of union at Lyons, Michael had pursued a mild policy toward his clergy,[35] striving to accustom them gradually to the idea of union. To impress upon them that nothing was to be feared from a religious accord (and especially that the Greek symbol and rites would be preserved), he encouraged the common association of Greek and Latin clerics in the divine services. Particularly welcome in the capital were Latin friars,[36]

---

[31] Cf. Norden, 504.

[32] Cf. even Pachymeres' praise of Gregory's motives, 369, ll. 9–10 and 370, ll. 1–6; also that of Palaeologus himself, 458, l. 18.

[33] Pach., 359, l. 8, emphasizes Palaeologus' flattery of the Popes. Cf. the extravagant terms of an imperial letter addressed to Gregory, published in *Reg. Grég.*, no. 313, 11. Also see the important article of M. Viller, "La question de l'union des églises entre Grecs et Latins," *Revue d'histoire ecclésiastique*, XVI (1921) 263, who believes that Palaeologus was a complete hypocrite regarding union.

[34] Gregory's successors were not free of suspicion of imperial motives, since twice within a few years after Lyons they required Michael to reiterate his oath of fidelity to Rome. See V. Grumel, "Les ambassades pontificales à Byzance après le II° Concile de Lyon," *Echos d'Orient*, XXIII (1924) 442, note 2.

[34a] See Chapter 13, text and notes 58–60.

[35] In contrast to his severity after Lyons. See H. Evert-Kapessova, "La société byzantine et l'union de Lyon," *Byzantinoslavica*, X (1949) 28ff.

[36] Pach., 360, ll. 5–7 and 17–18. Also 368, l. 12.

including Greeks of southern Italy who were of the Latin faith.[37] In the words of Pachymeres, the Emperor sought

to establish and preinsure the union, which was still in a state of negotiation, by receiving and sending to the bishops and patriarch at Hagia Sophia a great number of friars, with a view to their participating with the Greek clergy in the psalms, in the entrance to the sanctuaries and the stations, in common partaking of the blessed bread called *antidoron*, and indeed in all other Greek usages except the Holy Communion (which they did not request).[38]

Among the Greco-Latin clergy who came to Constantinople was the bilingual Bishop of Croton, from whom Michael himself, as we have seen, learned the essentials of the Latin faith. He was permitted by the patriarch to dress in the fashion of the Greek clergy and it was even arranged to give him a church.[38a] More important was the Constantinople-born Franciscan, John Parastron, who had been sent to the Emperor as a papal legate.[39] He was a zealous advocate of union and it was owing in no small degree to his efforts that union was finally pronounced at Lyons. Favorable to the Greek rites, Parastron minimized the controversy over the double procession of the Holy Spirit. He was in the habit of entering into the sanctuary of Constantinopolitan churches, and, standing at the side of the Greek celebrants, he would join in the reading of the offices.[40] Of modest demeanor and conciliatory attitude, he was popular among the Greek clergy,

[37] The subsequent influence of these events on the south Italian Greeks is mentioned by Sanudo, *Istoria*, 143. Referring presumably to the early fourteenth century, he says: "Sonovi anco molti Greci in Calabria ed in Terra d'Otranto che ubbidiscono alla Santa Chiesa Romana, mà forse non così devotamente come farianno, se l'imperatore Sior Michele Paleologo e il Patriarca . . . fossero . . . ubbidienti."

[38] Pach., 360, l. 19 and 361, ll. 1–4. Doubtless there is reference here to the difference between Greek and Latin practices of communion in one or two kinds. Partaking of the Greek communion would probably have indicated premature acceptance of union on the part of the Latin friars.

[38a] On the Bishop see Guiraud, *Reg. Urbain*, I, no. 748, 357, and no. 848, 406. Also Pach., 360, ll. 8–16. For reasons not entirely clear, but which Pach. attributes to ill-feeling, the Bishop was later exiled to Heraclea in Pontus.

[39] Guiraud, *Reg. Grég.*, no. 194, 68B. According to the same letter Palaeologus had previously dispatched Parastron to the Pope as his envoy.

[40] Pach., 371–372.

who, at his death shortly after the Council of Lyons, sought his canonization from the Pope.[41] His tolerance and understanding of the Greek mentality thus played an important part in persuading certain of the Greek clergy that communion with Rome was not reprehensible and might even be beneficial.[42]

Despite the frank appeals of the Emperor, only a section of the high clergy was convinced that the political situation demanded union with Rome.[43] The remainder of the prelates, practically all the lower clergy, the monks, and the vast majority of the people remained firm in their opposition, believing that union would bring not only imposition of the hated *filioque* but adoption of Latin usages as well.[44]

There seems little doubt, to judge from the accounts of the contemporary historians, that had Charles of Anjou been permitted by the papacy to launch a full-scale expedition, Constantinople would almost surely have fallen.[45] How then to explain the intransigence of the anti-unionist Greek clergy, the people, and even of many state officials [46] — an attitude apparently oblivious of political realities?

It is possible, of course, that the peril may have seemed more threatening to Palaeologus than to some of his subjects, who may not have been so acutely aware of the political situation. Moreover, the adherents of the young Emperor, John IV Lascaris, were understandably less concerned than Michael over the possible

[41] See Nicholas Glassberger, *Chronica,* in *Analecta Franciscana,* II (Quaracchi, 1887) 88: "pro eius canonizatione Imperator Graecorum et Praelati Graeciae instanter apud dominum Papam laborabant." Cf. G. Golubovich, "Cenni storici su Fra Giovanni Parastron," *Bessarione,* X (1906) 295ff.

[42] Pach., 372, ll. 7ff. Viller, "La question de l'union," 282, believes that the chief cause for the failure of union was lack of understanding on both sides. Cf. A. Fliche, "Le problème oriental au second concile oecuménique de Lyon," *Orientalia christiana periodica (Miscellanea Jerphanion),* XIII (1947) 483, who emphasizes that at Lyons the papacy and Emperor alone reached an understanding.

[43] Pach., 386, ll. 12–13; 387, ll. 17–18.

[44] See e.g., Pach., 389, ll. 13–14: "We must maintain for our descendants what [i.e., the practices] we have received from our fathers."

[45] Pach., 358, ll. 16–17. Greg., 123, ll. 3–8. Cf. Villani, I, 389: "Paglialoco non avea podere nè in mare nè in terra di risistere alla potenzia e apparecchiamento del re Carlo."

[46] Pach., 390, ll. 8–9; 391; 399ff.; 484; and 505, ll. 14–15. Also see note 44, above

loss of the latter's throne.[47] But these observations would have been applicable only to a small minority of Greeks; the widespread opposition to union was rooted rather in certain basic attitudes and fears of the Greek people.

From the viewpoint of the Byzantine clergy the opposition was based mainly on a conflict between two basic conceptions of the church. To the monarchical claims of the papacy was opposed the Byzantine concept of the pentarchy, according to which the Eastern patriarchs, while acknowledging the honorary primacy of Rome, rejected papal assertions of universal disciplinary jurisdiction which would have made of the Eastern bishops mere satellites of the Holy See.[48] While for the West, in accordance with Latin canonistic development, supreme ecclesiastical jurisdiction was vested in the Pope alone, for the Eastern church the highest religious authority resided in the ecumenical councils representing all the patriarchs.[49]

As for the attitude of the Byzantine populace, they, like other peoples in history, had a mystical view of their Empire. They believed that its territories were held together by the person of

[47] See Pach., 393, ll. 12–16, and 485, ll. 19–20, for mention of pro-Lascarid, anti-Palaeologan sentiment. Cf. J. Troitskiĭ, *Arsenius and the Arsenites* (in Russian) (St. Petersburg, 1873) 99–101.

[48] On pentarchic theory see esp. F. Dvornik, *The Photian Schism, History and Legend* (Cambridge, 1948) 150 and note 2; M. Jugie, *Le schisme byzantin*, 37–38; 222–223, 232. J. Karmires, "The Schism of the Roman Church," Θεολογία, XXI (1950) 30–31, 65–66; and more recently D. Geanakoplos, "The Council of Florence," 325 and notes 8–10.

[49] Complicating the difference in ecclesiastical polity on the Byzantine side was the traditional authority of the Emperor over the Greek church — the so-called Caesaropapism — according to which the Emperor in time of political stress (as in the case of the efforts of Palaeologus) would seek to accommodate the Greek church to the needs of the state. The role of Caesaropapism (a not altogether satisfactory term) has been the cause of sharp controversy: e.g., the Roman Catholic M. Jugie, *Le schisme byzantin*, 3–9, esp. 10, believes that it was chiefly responsible for preparing the schism, while, on the other hand, the typically modern Greek attitude (see Ch. Papadopoulos, *The Primacy of the Bishop of Rome* [in Greek] [Athens, 1930], esp. 207ff.) ascribes the basic cause of the schism to papal attempts to impose Roman primacy of jurisdiction over the Greek church. It is significant in connection with Caesaropapism that the papacy in general believed that Michael had practically absolute authority over the Greek church and thus refused to accept his protestations of the difficulties involved in persuading his clergy and people to accept union. See especially Chapter 9, text and note 49, on Clement IV's letter to Michael.

the Emperor but that the efficacy of his office depended on his adherence to the purity of the Orthodox faith. He was the living symbol of the continuity and fortune (*tyche*) of the Empire, and to the Greek mentality an attack on the faith was therefore an attack on the destiny of the Empire itself.[50]

Since the foundation of the capital, the Byzantines had believed that the city was under the special protection of the Virgin. Indeed, her protection had often saved the city in the past.[51] Constantinople had fallen to the Latins in 1204, but that event, as the Greek historians repeatedly affirm, had been owing to the loss of God's grace as a result of the sins of the Greek people. By the same token, the reconquest of the capital in 1261 by Michael Palaeologus was due to the recovery of Divine favor.[52] The Greek people must have reasoned, therefore, that the Empire would certainly crumble if the purity of the faith were altered through adoption of the Latin confession. To the great mass of the people, *oikonomia* had no application where the safety of Constantinople, "the city guarded by God," was concerned. Divine power would save the city even from the Angevin peril. This, it would seem, is the meaning of a prelate's reply to Michael at a synod in which the Emperor had stressed political considerations: "If danger threatens, the bishops' duty is only to pray; it is the task of the Emperor to find a way to repel the enemy." [53]

Probably a more conscious explanation for the resistance to union was the popular sentiment that it was the prelude to Latin-

[50] See Previale, "Un panegyrico inedito per Michele VIII Paleologo," 10, note 4. Also H. Gelzer, *Byzantinische Kulturgeschichte* (Tübingen, 1909) 29; and O. Treitinger, *Die öströmische Kaiser- und Reichsidee nach ihrer Gestaltung im höfischen Zeremoniell* (Jena, 1938) 159.

[51] E.g., in 626 during the reign of Heraclius. On the Virgin-protector see A. Grabar, "Un graffite slave sur la façade d'une église de Bukovine," *Revue des études slaves*, XXIII (1947) 89ff.; R. L. Wolff, "Footnote to an Incident of the Latin Occupation of Constantinople: The Church and the Icon of the Hodegetria," *Traditio*, VI (1948) 319ff.; and A. Frolow, "La dédicace de Constantinople dans la tradition byzantine," *Revue de l'histoire des religions* (1944) 61ff.

[52] See Chapter 6, text and note 5.

[53] Pach., 389, ll. 14–17. Cf. the anti-Latin polemic of the contemporary George Moschabar, in A. Demetracopoulos, *Graecia orthodoxa* (Leipzig, 1872) 62: "The true Orthodox are by Him [Christ] preserved from every visible and invisible attack of the enemy."

ization of the Greek church and people.[54] Though the existence of a Greek ethnic consciousness at this time may not always be explicit, it cannot be denied that the Greeks, as a people, regarded themselves as very distinct from the Westerners. In general, the Latins were considered not only heretical [55] but smugly supercilious [56] and culturally inferior.[57] This antagonism had been deepened by the crusades and, above all, by the fifty-seven years of subjugation to, and enforced union with, the Latin church resulting directly from the Fourth Crusade.[58] It is no wonder, then, that a Greek supporter of the union was looked upon with horror as a traitor. No more striking corroboration for this feeling is possible than the taunt flung at the imperial envoy, Archdeacon George Metochites, who had espoused the union: "Fraggos kathestekas!" ("You have become a Frank!").[59] In this vein wrote the unionist Patriarch Bekkos: "Men, women, the old and young . . . consider the peace a war and the union a separation." [60]

In the light of this explanation it would appear that the question of the *filioque*, so bitterly resented by the Greeks, actually masked the vital underlying problem of the hostility between Greeks and Latins. Thus, to the anti-unionist Orthodox, union with submission to papal authority meant not only ecclesiastical apostasy but betrayal of the Greek sense of national pride.

These powerful anti-Latin sentiments were propagated among

[54] See the remarkable speech of Palaeologus in Greg., 127, ll. 1–7, warning his subjects that conquest of Constantinople by Charles would completely Latinize them. For a more extended treatment of the Greek fear of Latinization see esp. my article, "The Council of Florence," 10–12.

[55] Demetracopoulos, *Graecia orthodoxa*, 47–48, and Pach., 376, ll. 9–10.

[56] On this see the orations of Michael's court orator, Holobolos (*Manuelis Holoboli Orationes*, 39).

[57] See *Typikon for St. Michael*, 771, for Palaeologus' description of the Latins as a "half-barbarian people."

[58] Note Holobolos' excoriation of the Latin oppressors in his orations (ed. Treu) 44 and 70. Also *Typikon for St. Michael*, 790, where Michael writes of "the haughty Latins who tyrannized over Constantinople."

[59] From the report of Metochites as printed in M. Laurent, *Innocent V*, 424, note 23. To the Greeks of the period the term "Frank" was synonymous with "Latin." Cf. the disparaging modern Greek term ἐφράγκεψες ("You have become a Frank," i.e., "a Catholic."). Cf. also Pach., 401, ll. 15–16: "They avoided their own brothers [the unionists] as execrable."

[60] Migne, *PG*, vol. 141, col. 952D.

the people by monks, always the most fervent supporters of Orthodoxy — the nucleus of whom were the Arsenites,[61] adherents of the deposed Patriarch Arsenios, who had originally opposed Michael's usurpation of the throne.[62] And to the people who only too easily recalled the days of the Latin occupation, the words of the monks fell on fertile soil.[63]

Palaeologus has been contemptuously termed *Latinophron* ("pro-Latin") by Greek writers.[64] His relations with the Latins were, to be sure, closer than were those of his predecessors, yet in each instance what may have appeared to anti-Latin Greek contemporaries and to Orthodox scholars of more recent times as softness toward the hated enemy, now appears rather to be part of a shrewdly calculated, pro-Greek policy, which cannot properly, or at least without qualification, be called *Latinophron*. Even in the face of the severe punishments Palaeologus inflicted on anti-unionist Greek prelates and monks in order to enforce union, it would seem unwarranted to say that he was more partial to the Latin faith than to the Greek.[65] Questions of dogma were of less concern to him than was survival of the Empire.

[61] On the Arsenites see Pach., 277 and 382. The most recent study is that of V. Laurent, "Les grandes crises religieuses à Byzance: la fin du schisme Arsénite," *Académie Roumaine Bulletin de la section historique*, XXVI, 2 (1945) 1ff. See further J. Sykoutres, "Περὶ τὸ σχίσμα τῶν Ἀρσενιατῶν," Ἑλληνικά, II (1929) 257ff. and later issues.

[62] Arsenios had been deposed by a Byzantine synod in 1267 when Michael threatened to appeal to Rome for absolution from patriarchal excommunication, previously imposed for his blinding of John Lascaris.

[63] On this see H. Evert-Kapessova, "La société byzantine et l'union de Lyon," *Byzantinoslavica*, X (1949) 29–31 and 33–34.

[64] For example, by the Greek historian of the Council of Florence (1438–1439), S. Syropoulos, *Historia vera unionis non verae . . . Concilii Florentini* (Hague, 1660) 238. Regarding Michael's unionist Patriarch, John Bekkos, who was also called *Latinophron* by his contemporaries, see the interesting article of G. Hofmann, "Patriarch Johann Bekkos und die lateinische Kultur," *Orientalia christiana periodica*, XI (1945), esp. 140 and 161, who shows that for one stigmatized as *Latinophron* Bekkos had surprisingly little knowledge of Latin culture and Latin theological writings — none, for example, of the works of his great contemporary Thomas Aquinas.

[65] On Michael's treatment of the monks see Pach., 488–491 and Greg., 127ff. For an argument that Michael was "far from practicing a general policy of hostility to the monasteries," see G. Rouillard, "La politique de Michel VIII Paléologue à l'égard des monastères," *Etudes byzantines*, I (1943) 83ff. As to the false legends regarding Michael's personal chastisement of monks on Mount Athos,

It seems improbable that Michael underestimated the popular Greek antipathy to the Latins. An Emperor who had reached the throne primarily through demagoguery, and through artful manipulation of the Greek army, nobility, people, and particularly the clergy,[66] would hardly have lost touch with public feeling sufficiently to misconstrue the reaction to so important an issue. Negotiations almost culminating in union had in fact been conducted some years before by the Emperor John III Vatatzes, and Michael had then had ample opportunity to observe popular sentiment.[67] It is much more probable that Michael's policy was a calculated risk, the difficulties of which, with respect both to the papacy and to his own clergy and people, he thought he could surmount through skillful diplomacy. From this standpoint, therefore, his unionist program may be considered simply an extension on the religious plane of his diplomatic policy toward the Latins for the preservation of his throne and Empire.

FERMENT IN CONSTANTINOPLE AFTER THE COUNCIL OF LYONS

While the Greek envoys to Lyons were in the West the opponents of union, though quietly gaining strength in Constantinople,[68] bided their time, and with the return of the ambassadors and ratification of the union by the Emperor, anti-unionist agitation began to assume major proportions. On 16 January 1275, in the imperial palace, before the Emperor, papal nuncios, and

---

see S. Binon, *Les origines légendaires et l'histoire de Xeropotamou et de Saint-Paul, de l'Athos* (Louvain, 1942) 110ff. In addition to what has been said about Michael's policy toward the Greek church, there should also be mentioned his extreme solicitude for rebuilding churches and monasteries immediately after the reconquest of Constantinople (see above, Chapter 6, section 2) as well as his numerous rescripts in favor of Greek monasteries, for two of which he himself wrote *regulae* (his Autobiography and the *Typikon for St. Michael*).

[66] See above, Chapter 2, text and notes 59–64.

[67] See Pach., 366, ll. 13ff. Also Greg., 129, ll. 13–19, who relates that during Vatatzes' reign, the famous scholar N. Blemmydes was forced to write his pro-unionist works in secret because of popular feeling. On the negotiations between Vatatzes and the papacy with a view to restoring to the Greeks Constantinople, then in Latin possession, see F. Schillman, "Zur byzantinischen Politik Alexanders IV," *Römische Quartalschrift*, XXII (1908) 108ff.

[68] Pach., 386, ll. 5–6.

imperial envoys, the ceremony of Lyons was repeated with the chanting of the epistle in Greek and Latin and commemoration of Gregory in the diptychs as "highest pontiff of the apostolic church and ecumenical Pope." [69] Despite this ceremony, however, the people and most of the clergy did not at this time make their submission to Rome. Such indeed was the eruption of anti-unionist feeling following these rites that the Emperor was forced to postpone for over two years the official ceremony of acceptance on the part of the Greek populace.[70]

When Michael elevated the unionist John Bekkos to the Patriarchal throne, schism within the Greek church became as acute as that separating Rome and Byzantium.[71] Anti-unionist sentiment now penetrated all classes of Byzantine society, involving members of the imperial family itself. One of the chief antiunionist leaders was Eulogia, Michael's own sister,[72] who in the past had strongly encouraged her brother's ambitions. With such fanaticism did she oppose his policy that she is reported to have preferred the destruction of her brother's reign to any alteration in the purity of the faith.[73] Together with her daughter Maria, Tsarina of the Bulgars, to whom she soon fled for refuge, Eulogia conceived the daring plan of creating an alliance between the Bulgars and the Mamelukes of Egypt in order to crush Michael between them.[74] But the scheme produced no important results.

[69] Pach., 399, ll. 7–17.

[70] See below, Chapter 13, sections 1 and 2. Greg., 130, ll. 11–15, notes that the liturgy with the papists present was performed only once in the Blachernae palace.

[71] Pach., 401, ll. 12–16, esp.: ὁπόσον ἦν χθὲς τὸ πρὸς τοὺς Ἰταλούς . . . τοσοῦτον καὶ πρὸς τοὺς ἰδίους. On Bekkos, at first an anti-unionist, see Pach., 374–382; Greg., 123, ll. 5–8; also cf. R. Souarn, "Tentatives d'union avec Rome: Un patriarche grec catholique au XIIIᵉ siècle," Echos d'Orient, III (1900) 229–237; and the inadequate work of A. Zotos, Ἰωάννης ὁ Βέκκος Πατριάρχης Κωνσταντινουπόλεως Νέας Ῥώμης ὁ Λατινόφρων (Munich, 1920).

[72] On Eulogia see Pach., 379, ll. 16–18. Because of her anti-unionist activities (it will be recalled that she was a nun) Michael exiled her to the fortress of St. George (Pach., vol. II, p. 15). Apparently, however, she escaped from there to Bulgaria.

[73] George Metochites, Historia dogmatica, in A. Mai, Patrum nova bibliotheca, VIII (Rome, 1871) 38.

[74] Pach., 427–429. Also G. Vernadsky, "Relations between the Golden Horde

More serious was the opposition of the Angeloi princes, Nikephoros of Epirus and his brother, John the Bastard of Thessaly. Posing as pious defenders of Orthodoxy against the heretic Latins (they were at the same time in contact with Charles of Anjou!), the Angeloi made their territories a refuge for anti-unionist malcontents fleeing Constantinople. On 1 May 1277, at Neopatras, the Bastard even convoked a synod, composed mainly of refugee monks, which anathematized Emperor, Pope, and Patriarch as heretics.[75]

With the monks constantly haranguing the people, *libelli* openly being published against the Emperor,[76] and even state officials in opposition, Michael was extremely hard put to maintain his policy. At first he was comparatively lenient toward the foes of union, hoping to win them by persuasion, but the intransigence of his opponents induced him, after Lyons, to resort to sheer force. Thus he cruelly exiled or blinded many anti-unionists and confiscated their property.[77] Turning harshly on the monks, whom he considered the chief instigators of the opposition, the Emperor meted out particularly severe punishments to two, Meletios and Ignatios, removing the tongue of the first and blinding the latter. (Ignatios' only crime apparently consisted in reporting to friends that he had seen Michael conforming to Latin ecclesiastical usages!)[78] A number of imperial officials were similarly treated, and, finally, the death penalty was decreed even for such acts as reading or possessing *libelli* directed against the Emperor.[79]

Egypt, and Byzantium under . . . Michael Palaeologus" (in Russian), *Seminarium Kondakovianum*, I (1927) 73ff.

[75] On this see below Chapter 13, text and notes 17–20.

[76] See A. Vassilief, *Anecdota graeco-byzantina*, pt. 1 (Moscow, 1893) 179–188, for a *libellus* entitled "Panagiotae cum azymita disputatio." Holding the Latin beliefs, especially that of the azymes, up to ridicule, the *libellus* reproduces a (hypothetical) discussion between the patriarch and an "azymite." Cf. Pach., 491–492.

[77] Pach., 482ff.

[78] On these two monks — who were sent to Rome in 1279 to be chastened by the Pope and who were benevolently returned only to be punished by Michael — see Pach., 489ff. On the torture of Holobolos, see also Pach., 192–193.

[79] Pach., 459 and 483ff. Also cf. Sanudo, *Istoria*, 135: "E fece battar, ferir e

Particularly disquieting to the Basileus were the plots that were, or that he believed were, being organized against the regime. Goaded by his suspicions, Michael permitted his old friend Kotys, accused perhaps falsely of treason, to die of torture after being handed over to the imperial Latin troops (evidently the Varangians) in order that a confession might be extracted from him.[80] Makarios, a man universally admired for his piety, was also put to death on the report that he had conspired with "the states of the west," a phrase referring apparently to the rulers of Epirus and Thessaly.[81] Once before, in 1267, Michael had been justifiably aroused by discovering a serious plot organized against him by a certain Frangopoulos[82] and twelve others. (That conspiracy, it is interesting to observe, had been betrayed to the Emperor by the Latin Charles, whose murder of the Protovestiarios Muzalon in 1258 had paved the way for Michael's accession to the throne.)[83]

From the intensity of these disorders, tantamount almost to civil war, it might appear that too great a price had been paid for the sake of union. But the ruthless persistence of the Emperor in his policy leaves little doubt that in his eyes the political advantages derived from union compensated for all the internal turmoil, however severe.[84]

distrugger molti suoi Calogeri Grechi e Prelati." Other important officials punished were the *Logothetes ton Genikon* Theodore Muzalon and even the son of Acropolites. On this see Pach., 495f.

[80] On Kotys see Pach., 485 and 486, esp. l. 17. He is the same person who, years before, had warned Michael that his life was endangered. See above, Chapter 1, text for note 51.

[81] On Makarios see Pach., 489, ll. 9–11. On the use of the term "west" (meaning Epirus) see I. Ševčenko, "Imprisonment of Manuel Moschopulos in the year 1305 or 1306," *Speculum*, XXVII (1952) 156, note 95.

[82] On Frangopoulos (literally "son of Franks"), a not uncommon name in Byzantium and one which was often used derisively by the Greeks, see V. Laurent, "Légendes sigillographiques et familles byzantines," *Échos d'Orient*, XXX (1931) 469.

[83] On the Frangopoulos plot (in which the Patriarch Arsenios was also implicated), see Pach., 284, ll. 16ff. Also cf. Sykoutres, *op. cit.*, II, 292; and Troitskiĭ, *Arsenios and the Arsenites* (in Russian) 940ff.

[84] See Pach., 390, ll. 5–9, who recounts that the Grand Oikonomos, Xiphilin, just before Lyons, had implored the Emperor not to incite a civil war for the sake of avoiding a foreign conflict.

12

THE AFTERMATH OF LYONS

(1274–1277)

IMMEDIATE POLITICAL RESULTS OF UNION

For Michael Palaeologus the proclamation of union at Lyons was a veritable diplomatic triumph. It saved his capital from the danger of an imminent Latin invasion and gained him the support not only of the Pope but of a general council as well. Henceforth, an expedition by Charles, theoretically at least, would be regarded by Western Christendom not as a crusade but as a fratricidal war between two Catholic princes.[1] Union, in effect, had made Byzantium a kind of papal protectorate.

Beyond this, it would seem that through religious accord Michael had even obtained tacit papal approval for his attempt to recover the remainder of Latin Romania.[2] Restoration of the

[1] Pach., 410, ll. 14–16, quotes the Pope as saying, "We cannot permit Christians to fight Christians lest we provoke the wrath of God against us." See also 384, ll. 12–13. Cf. Delisle, "Notice," no. 8, 164, a letter of Michael to Gregory, dated July or August of 1274, expressing the policy he hoped the papacy would adopt in Byzantine affairs: "Debet autem in Grecorum imperio dominari ille quem elegerunt Greci regnare super eos, et ipse debet reddere ad apostolicam sedem honorem debitum; non enim vult noster imperator propter parentelam suam effusionem fieri sanguinis Christianorum."

[2] For such tacit approval the best evidence is the lack of any real papal opposition to the violent new offensive of Palaeologus in Romania. It may be significant also that Michael's letters alluded to the surrender of Romania as the "*peace* between Greeks and Latins." See, e.g., Guiraud, *Reg. Urbain,* II, no. 295, 135. Cf. also an important tract of Humbert de Romans, *Opus Tripartitum,* in Mansi, *Concilia,* XXIV, cols. 109–136 (which was written for the Council of Lyons and may

old imperial frontiers in Greece[3] was, of course, a difficult matter, and a tolerant papal attitude in this connection might prove of no little value. But the price demanded for such sanction was still to be paid — personal submission of the Greek clergy and people to the Holy See, and imperial cooperation with the West in a crusade to the Holy Land.

As for King Charles and the titular Latin Emperor, Philip of Courtenay, though outmaneuvered by Michael, they now proclaimed that, union notwithstanding, Palaeologus could not be excused for usurping Romania from its rightful Latin rulers.[4] Sharing their view was Venice, whose representatives at Lyons had solemnly declared that she did not intend to renounce her claims to Romania.[5] In spite of this attitude, however, the conviction seems to have prevailed in the West that by effecting union with the Greeks Pope Gregory had recognized the legitimacy of Michael's possession of Constantinople.[6]

Probably indicative of the determination of Philip to persist in his claims was his cession, on 10 March 1274, of the Kingdom of Thessalonica to his brother-in-law, Philip of Anjou, second son of King Charles, on the occasion of Philip of Anjou's marriage to Isabella, daughter of Prince William of Achaia.[7] The grant of this

---

well reflect the sentiments of Pope Gregory), which suggests specific, *peaceful* ways for Michael to secure Latin Romania: "quod vel per pecuniam a Latino principe acquiratur . . . vel . . . per pacta aut matrimonia."

[3] See in Delisle, "Notice," 164: "ad recuperandum imperiale dominium." That Michael intended to restore even Bulgaria and Serbia to the Empire seems revealed by his bull of August 1272, renewing the old Patriarchate of Ochrida with jurisdiction over Serbia and Bulgaria. See H. Gelzer, "Ungedruckte und wenig bekannte Bistümerverzeichnisse der orientalischen Kirche," *Byz. Zeit.*, II (1893) 42–46.

[4] Pach., 410, l. 9. Also see below, note 72, for what are doubtless Charles's views as expressed in a letter of Pope Innocent V to Michael.

[5] Canale, 678; and Dandolo, 321: "ibi ambaxatores Veneti, pro conservacione suorum iurium in imperio Romanie . . . publice protestati sunt."

[6] See, e.g., Villani, I, 374: "Per lo quale riconciliamento de' Greci, il detto papa confermò al detto Paglialoco imperadore dello 'mperio di Costantinopoli." Also the epistle of Urban IV to Michael, in Guiraud, *Reg. Urbain*, II, no. 295, 138A, expressing readiness to recognize Michael as legitimate Emperor and even to protect his heirs, if he accepted union and thus became a Catholic prince (ed. Tautu, *Acta*, 21). Cf. also Delisle, "Notice," no. 8, 164, as quoted in the first note of this chapter.

[7] The old edition of Ducange, *Histoire de Constantinople* (Venice, 1729) 17, has printed more of this document than have later editions.

empty title (for which the Emperor Philip had not even awaited the renunciation of Duke Hugh of Burgundy!)[8] may well have been motivated by the aim of maintaining and further stimulating the interest of King Charles.[9] For through the cession of Thessalonica the encirclement of Constantinople, in theory at least, would be practically complete.[10] And to Charles the moral balm of legality was always of vital concern in justifying any offensive action to be undertaken.

IMPERIAL OFFENSIVES AGAINST CHARLES IN ALBANIA AND JOHN THE BASTARD IN THESSALY: THE BATTLES OF NEOPATRAS AND DEMETRIAS

Religious peace between East and West was officially established, but the military conflict between Greeks and Latins remained as pronounced as ever. It was not coincidental that Michael made his most determined effort to drive the Latins from Romania at almost the very moment that union was being solemnized at Lyons. Having restrained his attacks in Achaia during the period preceding the Council, now in 1274 and 1275 he launched against Albania and Thessaly powerful new offensives.

In the spring of 1274 Michael's troops had occupied two important Albanian towns, the port of Butrinto and the fortress of Berat, which was strategically situated in the center of the country. The defending Angevin forces, suffering great losses, were thrown back to Dyrrachium and Avlona on the Adriatic.[11] Greek troops, joined by sympathetic Albanians from the interior, now assailed Dyrrachium, besieging it several times during the same year. Occupied as Charles was with Genoa and the Ghibellines throughout 1274 and the first part of 1275, he nevertheless

[8] See Chapter 9, note 111.
[9] Cf. Chapman, 126, who believes Philip's action was motivated by discouragement. Shortly before this, Philip had offered Thessalonica also to the Prince of Achaia. See G. Monti, "Da Carlo I a Roberto di Angiò," *Arch. stor. prov. nap.*, LX (1935) 161–162.
[10] *Ibid.*, 162. Monti's opinion disagrees with that of Cerone, "La sovranità napoletana," *Arch. stor. prov. nap.*, XLI (1916) 235, who believes that Charles did not take the grant seriously.
[11] *Arch. st. it.*, XXIII, 240, letter of Charles dated 24 August 1274.

dispatched reinforcements, provisions, and munitions to succor the two towns.[12] His anxiety over their fate is revealed by two letters addressed to his officials in Albania. In the first Charles disclosed that the Greek fleet, aided by pirates in imperial service, had almost succeeded in cutting Angevin communications between Italy and Greece. Charles censured one of his officials because he did not "on the approach of Palaeologus' ships, order his vessels and others of our subjects to be drawn on to land for security." [13] In the other communication, dated 29 September 1275, Charles wrote of hearing that "the army of Palaeologus has penetrated to the vineyards of the city of Dyrrachium." The situation became so threatening that Charles had to issue special orders to his commander Narjot de Toucy, whom he was replacing, not to leave the city and thus further stimulate enemy attacks.[14] Despite his concern, Charles could only remain on the defensive, since he was still preoccupied with difficulties in Italy. During this period the Genoese were sacking Sicilian coastal areas,[15] while Ghibellines, fleeing in large numbers to Corfu or elsewhere in Romania, added strength to the anti-Angevin cause.[16] Meanwhile, though the Greek threat to the two Albanian ports continued throughout 1275 and 1276, the Angevin forces were able to retain a precarious hold upon them.[17]

[12] *Ibid.*, 433–438, and Carabellese, 67–68.

[13] "Per vasa Paliologi quinque Barce hominum Durrachii et una de Ydronto more piratico capta fuerunt . . . adventu galearum Paliologi debueris Barcas et alia vasa fidelium nostrorum in terram duci facere" (*Arch. st. it.*, XXIV, 381–382, dated 30 September 1275). From 1274 to 1279 the entire coastline of the Regno, from Otranto to Croton, remained in a state of war, with an Angevin fleet patrolling continually between Albania and Italy. See Carabellese, 31 and note 1.

[14] *Acta Albaniae*, I, no. 348, 101. Possibly revealing Charles's need for attracting the favor of Greeks and Albanians of Albania (and perhaps also of southern Italy) is a rescript dated 6 December 1274 to the justiciar of Bari, ordering that all Albanian and Greek slaves must be freed immediately or severe penalties would be incurred. See *Acta Albaniae*, no. 334, 97.

[15] *Ann. Ian.*, IV, 167–168, and *Arch. st. it.*, XXIII, 228. Cf. Caro, *Genua*, I, 357–359. Charles so feared Genoese and Greek piratical attacks that in 1277 he ordered a steel chain to be stretched across the harbor of Brindisi. See W. Cohn, "Storia della flotta siciliana sotto Carlo I d'Angiò," *Arch. st. sic. orientale*, XXVIII (1932) 59.

[16] See Carabellese, 58 and esp. note 2, Angevin rescript referring to "manifestis proditoribus regni nostri" now in Corfu.

[17] *Acta Albaniae*, nos. 356–359, 103–104. At this time, Charles, on the de-

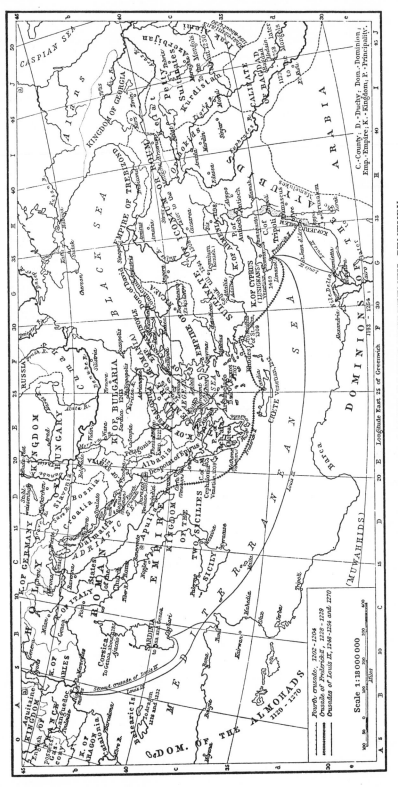

THE MEDITERRANEAN LANDS IN THE THIRTEENTH CENTURY

Palaeologus' ablest Greek opponent was John the Bastard of Thessaly, much of whose strength lay in his appeal to dissenters within imperial territories as well as in his connections with Michael's Latin enemies. In order to deprive the Bastard of the aid of Charles and the Latin lords of Romania, Michael asked the Pope to excommunicate him. Such a request was certainly justifiable in Michael's eyes, as the Bastard was, after all, a disloyal subject whose territory had formerly constituted part of the Byzantine Empire. It was Michael, in fact, who had granted him the rank of Sebastokrator. And was not the Bastard in the eyes of Rome a schismatic? Though Michael emphasized these points,[18] Pope Gregory did not grant his request. The reason for the refusal is not stated, but it may be ascribed to Gregory's desire to maintain the balance between Charles and Michael until the latter had made it clear by more than words that the Greek people would fully accept the union and join in the crusade to the Holy Land.[19]

Despite the papal rebuff, Michael made a vigorous effort to crush the Bastard by military means. In 1275, concurrent with his Albanian offensive, he dispatched to Thessaly a great army of more than thirty thousand mercenaries under the joint command of his brother, the Despot John Palaeologus, and Alexios Kaballarios.[20] In addition, the Emperor ordered a fleet of seventy-three vessels under the Protostrator Alexios Philanthropenos to attack the Latin lords of Greece, thereby preventing the dispatch of aid to the Bastard.[21]

fensive in Albania, dispatched an embassy to the Bulgar Constantine Tich. See M. Laurent, *Innocent V*, 260.

[18] See the memorandum presented to Gregory at Lyons by Michael's envoys, esp.: "Non recipiat . . . papa hominem qui fuerit infidelis imperio Grecorum et habeat terras et castra, et quod non permittat dominus papa aliquem Latinorum principum suscipere eum" (Delisle, "Notice," no. 8, 163). In the report of Ogerius, Protonotarius of the Emperor (see below, Chapter 13, text and notes 72–73), dated 1279, the Bastard and Nikephoros are referred to as "servi, et submanuales Imperii [qui] sacramentum. . . Imperatori fidelitatis et ligii homagii multotiens presti-terunt."

[19] See Norden, 550, note 1.

[20] Cf. Sanudo, *Istoria*, 121: "Trenta mila a Cavallo." Pach., 324, ll. 9–10, lists 40,000 men including naval forces.

[21] Pach., 325, ll. 4–8. Since the nominal head of the fleet, the Grand Duke

So swift was the advance of the imperial army that the Bastard was caught off guard and besieged in his lofty fortress of Neopatras. But in spite of the fewness of troops at his disposal and the gravity of his situation, the Bastard was able to save himself by resourcefulness and daring. Descending the city walls by rope, he successfully traversed the entire enemy camp, posing as a lowly groom seeking a stray horse. Three days later he appeared at Thebes,[22] where he made an alliance with the Megas Kyr, Sire John de la Roche, from whom he secured three hundred horsemen.[23] Returning quickly to Neopatras at the head of his new troops, the Bastard attacked the Greek army still surrounding his capital.[24] Taken completely by surprise at the onslaught of the disciplined Latin troops, the imperial forces (whose unity was already impaired by a heterogeneity of races) became demoralized and took to flight despite efforts of the Despot to restrain them.[25]

At the news of this remarkable victory the Latin lords of the Archipelago became greatly encouraged [26] and sent a fleet of ships, largely Venetian ones from Crete and Negropont, to attack the imperial fleet anchored at Demetrias on the Gulf of Volos.[27] The assault of the large Latin ships, upon whose prows wooden

---

Michael Lascaris, was too old, Philanthropenos, though only Protostrator, exercised the effective naval command. On this R. Guilland, "Le Protostrator," *Revue des études byzantines*, VII (1950) 165, who, however, appears to date this event as "ca. 1271."

[22] Strictly speaking, in Attica, according to Greg., 114, ll. 5–6, but the court's main residence was at Thebes.

[23] Pach., 328, ll. 5–16; according to Greg., 114, l. 9, 500 horsemen.

[24] Sanudo, *Istoria*, 121, relates that when Duke John de la Roche saw the imperial army, he said in Greek: "Poli laos oligo atropi [sic]" ("many people but few men!").

[25] Pach., 329, ll. 7–18. Greg., 115, ll. 17–19, attributes the Greek debacle to divine punishment for the sacrilegious conduct of their Cuman mercenaries.

[26] Pach., 332, ll. 1–4, and Sanudo, *Istoria*, 121: "andorono presuntuosamente."

[27] As to the relative strength of the Greek and Latin fleets in the following naval battle (referred to as that of Volo by J. Bury, "The Lombards and Venetians in Euboia," *Jl. of Hellenic Studies*, VII [1886] 336), Pach., 332, l. 4, speaks of the Latins as having only half or a third as many ships as the Greeks. Greg., 117, ll. 18–19, writes of over 50 Greek vessels, and (ll. 20–24) more than 30 Cretan and Euboian (Negropontine) ships. Sanudo, *Istoria*, 121, reports 62 Latin and 80 Greek ships: "XII trà Galee e Tarrette e 50 altri Legni da Remo . . . incontrando l'Armata dell' Imperatore ch'era di 80 Gallee."

towers had been erected,[28] was so violent that many Greeks on the more numerous imperial vessels were thrown into the sea or wounded. But as the battle reached its climax and defeat seemed imminent for the Greeks, the Despot John Palaeologus suddenly appeared with reinforcements. While escaping from Neopatras, he had heard rumors of the naval battle raging nearby,[29] and with men gathered from the surrounding area he rode in one night the forty mile distance to Demetrias. As John appeared and caught sight of his desperate countrymen, he cried out to them in a loud voice not to surrender. Enheartened, the Greeks began to rally, the more so as the Despot began to replace the tired and wounded with his own men who had found boats on shore. The conflict raged throughout the day until at last the Latins were utterly defeated.[30] All but two of their ships were captured; Guglielmo II dalle Carceri, triarch of Negropont, was killed and many Latin nobles taken prisoner, including Guglielmo's brother, Francesco, and Fillippo Sanudo, possibly captain of the entire Latin forces.[31] It is to be noted that the Venetians of Negropont, perhaps in observance of their truce with Michael, took no official part in the battle, the Venetian Sanudo apparently participating only as a private citizen.

The Emperor's concern over the collapse of his army at

---

[28] Greg., 117, ll. 24–25. His description of the battle (which he terms "a wall [i.e., land] not a sea battle," 118, ll. 18–19) is especially dramatic.

[29] Pach., 332, ll. 10ff. According to Greg., 119, ll. 11–12, when the Despot, on arrival, saw how the battle was going, he knelt on the shore, crying aloud to God for aid as he poured sand on his head. A description of such conduct may have been a commonplace in Byzantine historical writing. Cf. a similar passage on the Emperor Theodosius I in Rufinus, *Historia Ecclesiastica* (in *Eusebius Werke*, ed. Schwartz-Mommsen, II [Leipzig, 1908] Bk. XI, 33).

[30] Greg., 120, ll. 12–14, whose account, with that of Sanudo, provides the key to the remarkable victory: καὶ ἀεὶ τοὺς τραυματίας ἀναλαμβάνων ἄλλους ἀμοιβαδὸν εἰσῆγε νεαροὺς καὶ ἀκμάζοντας. Sanudo, 122: "Facea montar sopra dette delli suoi soldati ben armati . . . contra Nemici, li quali stanchi ed assaltati de Gente perita di Guerra, e frescha, facilmente furono vinti." Cf. Pach., 333–335.

[31] See Sanudo, 122, who lists the Latin prisoners: Gaetano, Sestier of Negropont, Butarello (who was blinded by the Emperor), Francesco da Verona, Filippo Sanudo Capitano, Zuan Sanudo, and his son and son-in-law, Guglielmo de Scora, and others. The triarch Giberto of Verona escaped to the city of Negropont, which he would have lost to Greek troops who then came to attack, had it not been for the aid of the Venetian bail and the Duke of Athens.

Neopatras was exceeded only by his joy at the news of the victory at Demetrias. So encouraged was Michael by the latter that, in the words of Sanudo, "he believed he was about to expel the Latins completely from Greece either by war or through pacts, and for this purpose he neglected every other care." [32] As we shall see, Demetrias was, in truth, to mark the beginning of a great new campaign for the restoration of Negropont and the islands of the Archipelago to the Empire.

RELATIONS OF POPES GREGORY X AND INNOCENT V WITH PALAEOLOGUS (1274–1277): GRECO-ANGEVIN TRUCES, THE EMBASSY OF GEORGE METOCHITES FOR A CRUSADE THROUGH ASIA MINOR, AND THE NEW DEMANDS OF INNOCENT V

In a memorandum delivered to Pope Gregory probably immediately after the Council of Lyons, the Greek envoys stated:

Inasmuch as our lord, the holy Emperor, should with all his resources render service to the Holy Land, we seek that he may have peace with all Latin princes and kings as shall seem best to our most holy lord, the Pope. [33]

In response to this appeal, and more especially because of the papal aim for the pacification of Christendom prior to the crusade, Pope Gregory set about to arrange a truce between Charles and Michael.

Accordingly, sometime before September or October of 1274, [34] Gregory sent the Abbot Bernard of Montecassino to Constantinople in company with the imperial envoys who had ap-

---

[32] Pach., 336–337 and esp. Sanudo, 122: "scazzar al tutto li Latini dalla Grecia ò con Guerra ò con patti, e rimmesso ogn' altro trattato, ch'avesse, e ogn' altra cura, si mise a questa sola." Cf. above, note 3. Bury, in "Lombards and Venetians, etc.," 337, states (plausibly) that Licario was probably present at this battle.

[33] Delisle, "Notice," no. 8, 163, dated July or August.

[34] The date is known from a donation of 20 September 1274, made by Bernard (who mentions his forthcoming departure from Italy) to his personal doctor Stephen of Montezario. See A. Caplet, *Regesti Bernardi I Abbatis Casinensis* (Rome, 1890) 191 and 193, nos. 437 and 439. On Bernard consult (with caution) D. Saba, *Bernardo I Ayglerio* (Montecassino, 1931) 98ff.

peared at Lyons.[35] The letters carried by Bernard expressed the joy of Gregory and the West over the achievement of union [36] and contained instructions for a Greco-Angevin truce to extend to 1 May 1276.[37] Such an agreement was impossible for Charles, however, because of the Treaty of Viterbo, the execution of which had already been extended for a year, as we have seen, to 1 May 1275. To remove this difficulty Gregory now directed the Abbot on his way to the Greek capital to stop first in Naples and to obtain from Charles and Philip a second extension on the grounds that it was necessary "for a more complete consummation of union." [38] With the success of his negotiations in Naples, Bernard was subsequently able to complete his mission to Constantinople, and thus a Greco-Angevin truce was arranged to last until 1 May 1276.[39] It must be noted, however, that acceptance of the armistice was dictated on both sides by expediency: Charles, still on the defensive in Italy, needed a respite in the East, while Michael, about to undertake his offensive against John the Bastard, was only too glad to deprive the Prince of Angevin support.

On his return to Italy Bernard announced to the Pope that an imperial embassy would soon follow to discuss the crusade.[40] To this Greek embassy we must direct particular attention because

[35] Delisle, "Notice," no. 8, 163. Cf. letter of Pope Innocent V, dated 23 May 1276 (in Martène, *Ampl. coll.*, VII, no. 28, 244). Also see M. Laurent, *Innocent V*, 263 and esp. 268.

[36] Of the papal letters (all dated 28 July 1274 in Guiraud, *Reg. Grég.*, 207–209), that to Palaeologus (207B) expresses the wish that he could personally have come to Lyons, thereby clearly disproving the statements of certain sources that Michael had appeared at the Council (see above, Chapter 11, note 1). Others are addressed to Andronikos and the Greek clergy, urging them to eradicate the remnants of schism and support the Emperor.

[37] Guiraud, *Reg. Grég.*, no. 490, 208: "ut inter te ac carissimos in Christo filios nostros Philippum . . . et Carolum . . . treuge sufficientis temporis ineantur."

[38] *Ibid.*, no. 491, 209, same date, instructions to Abbot Bernard: "ad pleniorem consummationem ipsius treuge . . . taliter prorogationem ulteriorem."

[39] This date of termination (cf. Potthast, *Regesta*, no. 20949) has been established by Delisle, "Notice," 134. That a truce existed in 1276 is proved also by a passage in T.-Th., III, 182, which records that in January of 1276 a Greek captain debarked at Corfu "quia erant in treugua dominus Imperator. . . Rege Karolo." Cf. also on the treaty E. Léonard, *Les Angevins de Naples*, 532, note to p. 117.

[40] Caplet, *Regesti*, p. ciii. Cf. M. Laurent, *Inn. V*, 269 and note 62. Also Léonard, *Les Angevins*, 116.

of its extraordinary proposal that Latin crusaders be used to re-conquer Anatolia from the Turks for the Greek Empire. The two imperial ambassadors, George Metochites, pro-unionist Arch-deacon of Constantinople, and the Grand Intendant Theodore, who served as interpreter,[41] met with Gregory in the summer of 1276, probably in the town of Beaucaire in southern France. But the Pope — absorbed with the problems attendant upon the elec-tion of Rudolf of Hapsburg to the Western imperial throne and the rejection of the claim of Alfonso X of Castile [42] — was at first unable to devote much attention to the envoys. The latter ac-companied him, therefore, to Lausanne, where the numerous matters relating to the crusade were discussed.[43] Already at the Council of Lyons Gregory had declared that the arms of both Eastern and Western Emperors would crush resurgent Islam,[44] while Michael in his epistle read at the Council had promised troops, money, provisions, and whatever else was necessary for the passage to the Holy Land.[45] But now at Lausanne Metochites, in the name of the Emperor, made a striking proposal: namely, that the Latin crusaders, instead of making the crossing by sea,

[41] See M. Laurent, *Inn.* V, 269, who includes C. Gianelli's ed. (419ff.) of the report of Metochites himself; for another edition see V. Laurent, "Le rapport de Georges le Métochite, Apocrisiaire de Michel VIII Paléologue auprès du Pape Gregoire X," *Revue historique du sud-est européen*, XXIII (1946) 240ff. On Metochites (for whom safe-conducts were again obtained from Charles) see V. Grumel in *Dict. théol. cath.*, VI, col. 1238. On the Grand Intendant (μέγας διοικητής), who acted as interpreter, see M. Laurent, *Inn.* V, 270, note 69. On the Roman Curia's apparent lack of a college of interpreters at this time see B. Altaner, "Sprachkenntnisse u. Dolmetscherwesen . . . im 13. u. 14. Jahrh.," *Zeitsch. f. Kirchengesch.*, LV (1936) 85ff., and cf. E. van Moé, "L'envoi de nonces à Constantinople par les papes Innocent V et Jean XII," *Mél. d'arch. et d'histoire*, XLVII (1930) 53.

[42] On the imperial election see M. Laurent, *Inn.* V, 270 and A. Zisterer, *Gregor X. und Rudolf von Hapsburg* (Fribourg-en-Brisgau, 1891) (unavailable to me).

[43] This is known from Innocent's first letter to Palaeologus, dated 23 May 1276 (in Martène, *Ampl. coll.*, VII, col. 244, no. 28; cf. M. Laurent, *Inn.* V, 478). At Lausanne Metochites saw the Western Emperor, Rudolf of Hapsburg, take the cross. See *Annales Basileenses*, in *MGH SS*, XVII, 198.

[44] Statement repeated in report of Metochites, in Laurent, *Inn.* V, 440.

[45] Delisle, "Notice," no. 7, 162: "per exercitum, et per pecuniam, et per victualia, et per omnimodam aliam providenciam." Michael promised this on con-dition that there would be peace with his Latin neighbors: "solum modo si habuerit pacem cum vicinis suis Latinis."

proceed on land across the Balkans to Constantinople, march through Asia Minor, and, finally, before invading Syria, rest in the territory of Michael's son-in-law Abagha, the Mongol Khan of Persia. Such a land route (actually the classic passage of the first crusades) would, of course, necessitate the reconquest from the Turks of former Byzantine territory in Asia Minor.[46]

According to a report left us by Metochites, Pope Gregory was favorable to the plan. Impressed especially by Metochites' plea for recovery of the ancient and glorious Christian cities of Anatolia, Gregory was persuaded as well that the land route would avoid the hardships of a long sea voyage.[47] It was also believed that Anatolia would provide an excellent base of operations from which to conquer and maintain possession of Jerusalem. Most important, such a route would obviate the difficulty of finding sufficient ships to transport the Western armies.[48]

The advantages of the plan for Michael were compelling. No doubt he thought that thereby an otherwise unavoidable and dangerous crusade — which would bring powerful Latin armies to Greek soil — could in the end be turned to the profit of the Greeks. Had not his predecessor Alexios I Comnenos in similar fashion

[46] ὡς ἵν' ἡ δίοδος γένηται τῶν κινηθησομένων διὰ ξηρᾶς ἡ πρὸς τὸν ἅγιον τόπον ἀπάγουσα, καὶ μὴ διὰ θαλάσσης . . . καὶ ὡς οἰκονομήσει βασιλεὺς διαμηνύσεσι ταῖς πρὸς τὸν οἰκεῖον γαμβρόν, τὸν τῶν Ἀτταρίων δεσπόζοντα, διὰ Τουρκίας ὑποκειμένης . . . εἰς τὴν προτέραν ἐπαναδραμεῖν δεσποτείαν καὶ τὴν ἀρχαίαν ἀποκατάστασιν τὴν χριστώνυμον. From Metochites' report in M. Laurent, Inn. V, 436–437. The occupation of Asia Minor was to take place either before or after the conquest of Jerusalem (ibid., 437: εἴτε πρὸ τῆς ἀναρρύσεως γῆς ἁγίας εἴτε μετέπειτα). Cf. V. Laurent, "Grégoire X et le projet d'une ligue antiturque," Echos d'Orient, XXXVII (1938) 272. On the political situation in Asia Minor at this time see P. Wittek, Das Fürstentum Mentesche: Studien zur Geschichte Westkleinasiens im 13.-15. Jh. (Istanbul, 1934) 1–31, and Arnakis, Οἱ Πρῶτοι Ὀθωμανοί, 37ff.; Ostrogorsky, Byzantine State (1956) 438.

[47] Metochites, 436–437, esp.: πολλὴν τὴν δυσχέρειαν ἐχούσης λογικοῖς τε ζῴοις καὶ τοῖς ἀλόγοις τῷ τοσούτῳ μήκει τοῦ διαστήματος.

[48] On the attitude of the Pope and his theoreticians regarding the land route, see V. Laurent, "La croisade et la question d'orient sous le pontificat de Grégoire X," Revue historique du sud-est européen, XXII (1945) 133; and esp. the same author's "Grégoire X," 265–267. Cf. also the work of the 14th century theoretician Fidence of Padua, Liber recuperationis Terrae Sanctae, in G. Golubovich, Biblioteca bio-bibliografica della Terra Santa e dell' Oriente Francescano, II (1913) 51 and 57. M. Laurent, Inn. V, 273, does not think that Gregory was well-informed as to the risks involved.

utilized the Latin armies of the First Crusade to help reconquer much of Asia Minor for Byzantium?[49] Execution of Michael's plan would at the same time thwart the menace to the Greek Empire of Mameluke Egypt, whose forces had already penetrated Armenia.[50]

To insure complete accord on the proposal, the Pope and the imperial envoys agreed that a cardinal should be sent to the Bosporus. Of greater interest is the fact that Gregory was to meet personally with Michael in Brindisi, shortly after Easter of 1276, or, if this rendezvous in the Regno were considered unsafe, the Pope would instead cross over to Avlona.[51] Unfortunately, the meeting was prevented by the death of Gregory, in January of 1276.[52] Had the conference in Brindisi materialized, it would have anticipated by almost a century the famous journey to the West in 1369 of the Emperor John V Palaeologus.[53]

With the death of Gregory there disappeared a real opportunity for a united Christendom to oppose the Turkish advance in Asia Minor. That a restoration of Anatolia to the Greeks through Latin arms could have been successfully accomplished is, however, questionable: the mutual distrust of Latins and Greeks, the probable unwillingness of the Latin leaders (as in the First Crusade) to relinquish territory conquered by their arms, the opposition of the Seldjuks, of independent Turkish Emirs, and possibly of recalcitrant Mongols,[54] and, not least, the temptation for the Latins to seize Constantinople during the

---

[49] *Alexiade* (ed. Leib) II, 231. Cf. P. Charanis, "Byzantium, the West, and the Origin of the First Crusade," *Byzantion,* XIX (1949) 17ff.

[50] On this see Guilland, in *L'Europe orientale,* 212.

[51] See Metochites' report, in *Inn.* V, 440. Also *ibid.,* 439: αὐτὸς δὲ μετὰ τὴν λαμπροφόρον ἡμέραν τῆς σωτηριώδους κυριακῆς ἀναστάσεως ἐξελθὼν ἐλεύσεται πρὸς Βρεντήσιον, ὅ τε βασιλεὺς ἀφίξεται πρὸς Αὐλῶνα . . . ἢ τὸ παράπαν ὑπόνοιά τις εἰ λογισθείη. . .

[52] M. Laurent, *Inn.* V, 271.

[53] See O. Halecki, *Un empereur de Byzance à Rome* (Warsaw, 1930).

[54] Abagha, Mongol Khan of Persia, with possessions in Anatolia, had sanctioned the passage through Asia Minor at the request of his father-in-law, Michael. He had also sent a representative to the Council of Lyons. But it seems difficult to believe that Abagha really would have approved a Greco-Latin military occupation of Anatolia and a Latin feudal regime in Syria. Cf. V. Laurent, "Grégoire X," 271.

campaign — all these were serious drawbacks.[55] Nevertheless, it is a fact of capital importance for the diplomacy of Michael (and one often overlooked when he is condemned for the neglect of his Turkish borders) that, though fully occupied by the Angevin menace in the West, he was able to take advantage of the situation and to propose measures for repelling the Turkish danger in the East.

The new Pope, Innocent V,[56] continued negotiations with Metochites, but the specific plan for a land expedition through Anatolia was apparently abandoned.[57] The Basileus, it seems, had confidence only in Gregory, or perhaps Innocent himself may have refused to undertake a campaign which would mainly have benefited the Greeks. At any rate, the crusade was still the principal matter for discussion, and through his envoys Michael emphasized his continuing desire to cooperate. The Greek ambassadors pressed questions about the participation of the Western rulers in, and their attitude toward, the crusade, and also about plans for the capitulation of Egypt. In addition they insisted on papal excommunication of the Bastard and dissolution of the latter's alliance with Charles and Philip,[58] both of whom, despite their recent truce with the Emperor, continued to send troops and arms to the Albanian coast.

The projected crusade to Egypt posed an acute problem for

[55] As V. Laurent, "Grégoire X," 264, emphasizes, the Greek population itself probably opposed a crusade through the Byzantine Empire (Pachymeres and Gregoras, in fact, make no mention of Michael's plan for the land crusade) because they feared a repetition of 1204. After all, Charles's son had taken the cross (see below, note 69), and Charles himself might come. Michael, however, as Laurent (268 and note 3) points out, probably based his confidence on the influence of Pope Gregory, who planned personally to lead the crusade. On this see Andrea Dandolo, 320, and a letter of Gregory to Philip III of France dated 3 July 1274, in C. Langlois, *Le règne de Philippe III, Le Hardi* (Paris, 1887) 419–420, no. 3. Cf. Norden, 472.

[56] On relations of Innocent V and Palaeologus see M. Laurent, *Inn. V*, 256–286, esp. pertinent letters listed in the catalogue in the appendix.

[57] There is no mention of the plan in Innocent's first letter to Michael, in which the Pope replies to the Emperor's questions about a crusade. See M. Laurent, *Inn. V*, 274 and 478, no. 146.

[58] See Innocent's letter in Martène, *Ampl. coll.*, VII, no. 28, par. 244: "Quos apostatos appellarunt, excommunicationis sententia per sedem proferretur eamdem."

Michael. Already allied by treaty to Baibars, the Mameluke ruler of Egypt, he was now committing himself to a crusade against him.[59] If the expedition failed, as had often happened to such Western campaigns in the past, Constantinople would remain alone against a strong Egypt.

During the negotiations between Innocent and Metochites,[60] Charles seems to have been almost continuously at the papal court, pressing the Pope to reply unfavorably to Michael's proposals and insisting on an Angevin expedition against Byzantium. The conduct of Charles has been vividly described by Pachymeres, who records that

every day the Greek envoys saw Charles throw himself at the feet of the Pope. Indeed, to such a rage was he driven that he furiously bit the sceptre which he held in his hands and which Italian princes are in the habit of carrying.[61]

Pachymeres might be suspected of exaggeration were it not for a similar passage in the chronicle of the contemporary Sicilian Bartolomeo of Neocastro.[62] Charles, of course, had reason to be angry when he saw his careful and elaborate plans repeatedly postponed and himself constantly thwarted in his greatest ambition. Outmaneuvered by Michael at Lyons, he undoubtedly thought that with Innocent V, a fellow Frenchman, now elected to the papal throne, he would at long last achieve his aim. But success was again to elude him.

[59] Their treaty dated from 1261. A period of coolness followed in 1264, then a renewal of the treaty in 1267. See M. Canard, "Un traité entre Byzance et l'Egypte au XIII e siècle," *Mél. Gaudefroy-Demombynes* (Cairo, 1937) 220–222, where Canard also voices suspicions of an anti-Latin conspiracy between Michael and Baibars. See also his "Le traité de 1281 entre Michel Paléologue et le Sultan Qualâ'un," *Byzantion*, X (1935) 669–670. According to Pach., 427–429, Maria, Palaeologus' anti-unionist niece and wife of the Bulgar Tsar, informed the Egyptian ruler Baibars of Michael's dealings with the Latins. But it should be noted that the West had also made advances to Baibars. See M. Laurent, *Inn.* V, 276.

[60] See M. Laurent, *Inn.* V, catalog of letters, nos. 146ff.

[61] Pach., 410: Ἑώρων οὖν ἐκεῖνον ὁσημέραι τῶν ποδῶν τοῦ πάπα προκυλινδούμενον, καὶ ἐς τοσοῦτον ταῖς μανίαις συνισχημένον ὥστε καὶ τὸ ἀνὰ χεῖρας σκῆπτρον, ὃ σύνηθες κρατεῖν τοῖς τῶν Ἰταλῶν μεγιστᾶσιν, ὀδοῦσιν ἐκ μανίας καταφαγεῖν. This passage suggests that in dealing with Charles Innocent lacked the quiet firmness of Gregory.

[62] *Historia Sicula, RISS*, XIII, pt. 3 (1921) 22; "iracundia fervidus, dentibus frendet, rodens robur, quod in manu tenebat." Cf. Villani, I, 374: "per lo riconciliamento col Paglialoco. . . Re Carlo fu molto cruccioso."

It was Innocent himself who wrote to Michael of Charles's attitude. Using Angevin aspirations as a threat, he informed the Emperor of Charles's insistence that this was a favorable opportunity for an expedition against Constantinople.[63] (Evidently this was a reference to the recent conclusion of Charles's war with Genoa, in the spring of 1276, for which Innocent himself had mediated the peace.) [64]

Unlike Gregory, Innocent did not favor a personal meeting with Michael to discuss the crusade and the completion of union.[64a] Instead he prepared to send to the Greek capital an embassy of three Franciscans and their Greek-speaking Minister-General, Jerome of Ascoli.[65] Metochites and Theodore were to accompany the Franciscans, together with four members of another Greek embassy more recently arrived from the East, the Metropolitan of Serres, Theodore Monomachos, Calada, and John Pagano.[66] We can only speculate upon the purpose of this last imperial embassy to the Curia. Very probably it sought to hasten the return of Metochites and to secure another extension of Michael's truce with Charles, which was to end on 1 May 1276.[67]

---

[63] Martène, *Ampl. coll.*, VII, col. 248, second letter of Innocent to Michael.

[64] See A. Ferretto, "Codice diplomatico delle relazioni fra la Liguria la Toscana e la Lunigiana ai tempi di Dante," *Atti soc. lig. st. pat.*, XXXI, pt. 2 (1901) 80, no. 178. Cf. Caro, *Genua*, I, 371ff.

[64a] Cf. Metochites' impression of Innocent, in M. Laurent, *Inn.* V, 441: "He was eager for union but not in the same manner as Gregory." Also Norden, 563.

[65] Martène, *Ampl. coll.*, VII, no. 30, col. 248; and Delisle, "Notice," no. 9, 165. M. Laurent, *Inn.* V, 280 and note 102, lists the Franciscan chronicles mentioning the embassy. The usual safe-conducts were granted by Charles (*Arch. st. it.*, XXV, 38). It is of interest that the party seems to have included an Italian doctor, Stephen (friend to Abbot Bernard), who, at papal request, was to minister to a sick son of Palaeologus (*Arch. st. it.*, XXV, 37). Cf. M. Laurent, *Inn.* V, 478, no. 144, who says that Andronikos is here referred to. The Byzantine court had its own physicians, the chief medical officer from the thirteenth century on being called *aktouarios* (Bréhier, *Institutions*, 150).

[66] The Archbishop is known only from the initial "L" listed in a safe-conduct issued by Charles. For the entire document see M. Laurent, *Inn.* V, 411; also on the Archbishop, 281, note 106 (cf. *Arch. st. it.*, XXV, 37). Pagano was probably a Latin in Greek service, while "Calada" may be a corruption of the Greek Κλαδᾶς.

[67] See *Arch. st. it.*, XXV, 38, document mentioning negotiations for a further one-year truce. Cf. M. Laurent, *Inn.* V, 281.

Innocent's attitude at this time is known from a dossier of letters emanating from the Curia between 23 and 26 May 1276.[68] One epistle to Michael lists the Western participants in the forthcoming crusade (including, significantly, the eldest son of King Charles) and, in typical papal fashion, conveniently releases Michael from his treaty obligations to Baibars of Egypt.[69] With respect to Michael's demand for excommunication of the Bastard, however, Innocent wrote suggestively that it was not advisable "because of the opposition of certain Latin princes." [70] A large number of other letters regarding union and politico-military affairs were also dispatched to Michael as well as to Andronikos and the Greek clergy.[71] Particularly worthy of note is one letter in which Innocent informed Michael that Philip claimed no longer merely the title of Emperor but possession of Constantinople, "the city of which Baldwin had been violently despoiled." Also mentioning Charles's claims on the Empire, the Pope emphasized the intention of both princes to take the city by force.[72]

The tone of Innocent's letter is at first glance surprising. Hardly two years after the Council of Lyons a Pope was discussing the legitimacy of Latin claims on the Greek capital! Objectively, however, these statements of Innocent should be regarded in the context of papal insistence on complete implementation of union. Thus Innocent stressed two points: Michael and the Greek clergy, in the presence of papal envoys, were to take personal oral oaths accepting the Latin confession and papal primacy. The symbol, moreover, was to be chanted with the addition of the *filioque*. This demand for personal oaths was, from the point of view of the Curia, justifiable, since, as Innocent wrote to Michael,

---

[68] On these letters, formerly attributed to Pope John XXI, see Delisle, "Notice," 136–138; and Van Moé, "L'envoi de nonces," 43–48 and 57.

[69] Martène, *Ampl. coll.*, VII, no. 28, col. 244, esp.: "Primogenitus regis Siciliae . . . non obstante juramento." Also see M. Laurent, *Inn. V*, 282.

[70] See Norden, 552, note 1. Michael's forces were then still menacing Angevin Albania (*Acta Albaniae*, I, no. 359, 104).

[71] For a summary of these letters (ten in all), which are printed in Martène, VII, see M. Laurent, *Inn. V*, 282–283.

[72] Martène, VII, cols. 247–248, dated 23 May 1276, where Innocent also insists that Michael conform to the terms of a truce (probably for Albania and Greece).

Acropolites at Lyons had presented no written authorization from the Emperor, nor had the Greek clergy's letter contained a profession of faith but only vague mention of papal primacy.[73] It was logical therefore to demand assurances. But to the Greek clergy, who had been solemnly promised by the Emperor that under no circumstances would insertion of the *filioque* into the symbol be permitted,[74] the demand would come as a severe humiliation and indication of bad faith. Evidently foreseeing such a reaction, Innocent in another letter modified his demands, declaring that retention of the Greek rites would be permitted provided there was no infringement of papal beliefs and canons. Moreover, Innocent instructed his legates "if absolutely necessary, and then under protest, to accept whatever concessions you are able to secure from the Greek clergy." Finally, to insure execution of his instructions by the Greek prelates, the Pope directed his envoys to visit the principal cities of the Empire and to excommunicate anyone interfering with the union.[75]

Fortified with this detailed mandate, the embassy left Rome at the end of May 1276. Apparently to avoid traversing the Regno, the nuncios embarked at Ancona in northern Italy. There, however, before sailing, they learned of the death of the Pope. The Franciscans returned to the Curia while the Greek envoys continued on to the Golden Horn.[76] Innocent's death had intervened at a moment when the union signed at Lyons might have been seriously jeopardized by pointed papal references to Western claims on Constantinople.

[73] Martène, VII, col. 254. But cf. the letter (Latin translation from Greek original) in Delisle, "Notice," 159, which certainly seems to be a blanket imperial authorization to Acropolites and the Greek envoys to Lyons. Possibly the papacy wanted an authorization referring specifically to the signing of union. On this matter of imperial authorization see Héfelé, *Conciles*, 210; Grumel, in *Dict. théol. cath.*, IX, col. 1394; and Dölger, *Regesten*, no. 2008.

[74] Shortly before Lyons Michael had issued golden bulls in favor of his clergy, stating that not one iota of the creed would be changed. See Pach., 395, ll. 8ff.

[75] From letters of Innocent to Michael (in Martène, VII, 248–249); to the Greek clerics (249–251); to Andronikos (251–252); and from instructions to the papal envoys (253–256). See especially 257, the letter modifying these instructions. Cf. Grumel, *loc. cit.*, col. 1394.

[76] See M. Laurent, *Inn. V*, 285, esp. note 129.

SECOND PHASE OF THE CAMPAIGN IN NEGROPONT
AND THE ARCHIPELAGO: THE TRIUMPH OF LICARIO

Inspired by the imperial victory at Demetrias where the finest of the Latin nobility had been captured or slain, Michael Palaeologus embarked on an offensive to expel the Latins entirely from the Greek islands.[77] The campaign was entrusted to the Latin Licario, John Palaeologus having retired to private life disappointed over his failure at Neopatras.[78] At the head of Greek and Latin troops, including Negropontine islanders who flocked to his standard,[79] Licario first attacked Karystos, capital of the southern triarchy of Negropont, which he won after a long siege on land and sea. For this victory Michael invested Licario with the entire island as an imperial fief (Sanudo attributes the gesture to Michael's desire to insure Licario's loyalty), in return for which Licario was to serve the Emperor with two hundred knights. At the same time Palaeologus bestowed upon Licario a noble Greek wife and a rich dowry.[80]

These marks of imperial favor spurred Licario to futher conquests. Gradually the Latin made himself master of almost the entire island of Negropont, seizing the fortresses of Cuppa, Larmena, Clisura, and Manducho. Only the capital city of Negropont remained to the triarchs.

Nor did Licario overlook the other Latin-held islands of the Archipelago. Investing neighboring Skopelos, whose inhabitants believed it impregnable, he forced its capitulation when its supply

[77] See above, note 32.
[78] Philanthropenos, appointed Grand Admiral, was apparently recovering from his wounds at this time. Pach., 337, ll. 1–13.
[79] Sanudo, *Istoria*, 122: "fatto un Grande essercito de le Genti sue de Levante e de Ponente, fece suo Mega Duca Miser Licario [Sanudo is probably mistaken in attributing this title to Licario so early] . . . il quale avea presso di se molti dell' isola di Negroponte." The Latin Rosso Matafora and his sons supported Licario (*ibid.*), as, evidently, did discontented Greeks (Greg., 95, l. 23).
[80] Sanudo, *Istoria*, 123, esp.: "l'Imperator, acciò il detto Mega Duca li fusse più leal e lo servisse più fedelmente, li fece dono di tutta l'isola di Negroponte pigliandosi . . . con obbligazion di servirlo con 200 Cavallieri; li diede ancora per Moglie una Nobile dell' Imperio con Grandi entrate [presumably, rich revenues] e ricchezza."

of water became exhausted. The Venetian lord of Skopelos, Filippo Ghisi, whose other island possessions of Skyros, Skiathos, and Amorgos were also taken, was sent to Constantinople in chains. Continuing his campaign, Licario seized Cerigo and Cerigotto off the southern coast of the Morea, as well as Keos, Seriphos, Astypalos, Santorin, and Therasia. He had greater difficulty with Stalimene (Lemnos), one of whose feudal lords, Paolo Navagaioso, and his wife between them withstood a three year siege before surrendering.[81] Thus most of the islands of the Archipelago, with the notable exception of Naxos, returned to Greek possession.

Encouraged by his success, Licario at last determined to take the capital city of Negropont. Assembling his forces, which included Spanish and Catalan mercenaries and even former Sicilian partisans of Manfred,[82] he landed (ca. 1275) at Oreos in the northern part of the island.[83] Moving against the capital, he prepared an ambuscade outside its walls. Sure enough, the proud Latins, among them the gouty Duke John I de la Roche of Athens-Thebes and the triarch Giberto da Verona, brother of Felisa, rode disdainfully through the town gate to meet the Greek forces. In the' battle that followed both triarch and Duke were captured along with the brother of Licario.[84] Negropont now seemed to be at the mercy of Licario, but he did not advance to take it. His decision was the result of other developments.[85]

[81] On Licario's campaign in Negropont and the Archipelago see Sanudo, *Istoria*, 123–124 and 127; also Greg., 98, ll. 15–17, and Hopf, *Geschichte*, 304ff. Cf. J. Rennell Rodd, *The Princes of Achaia and the Chronicles of Morea* (London, 1907) I, 293–294.

[82] Sanudo, *Istoria*, 125: "Gente d'Armi Spagnola e Catalana e del Reame di Scicilia, ch'era stata del Re Manfredi." This is evidently the first appearance of the Catalans in Greece. Noteworthy also is the presence of adherents of Manfred, some of whom had already fled to Corfu (see above, text and note 16).

[83] For date see R. Guilland, "Etudes de titulature et de prosopographie byzantines: Les chefs de la marine byzantine," *Byz. Zeit.*, XLIV (1951) 231. On Oreos see Pach., 411, l. 10.

[84] Sanudo, *Istoria*, 125 and esp. 126: "Miser Gilberto fù morto e Miser Giovanni dalla Rozia preso." (Sanudo states wrongly that Giberto was killed.) On Licario's brother see Pach., 411, l. 18.

[85] Sanudo, *Istoria*, 126: "dicesi da alcuni, che Miser Licario Mega Duca non volse proceder più oltre."

At the same time that Michael had dispatched a fleet to Negropont, he also had sent to Thessaly against the Bastard an army under John Synadenos, Grand Stratopedarch, and Michael Kaballarios,[86] Grand Constable. On the famous plain of Pharsalos, the imperial forces, deceived by the Bastard's strategy of ambushes and daunted by the impetuous attack of the Prince's Italian mercenaries, suffered a crushing defeat. Synadenos was captured, while Kaballarios, though able to escape, died soon afterwards of his wounds.[87]

In the meantime, news of the imperiled capital of Negropont reached Jacques de la Roche, governor of Nauplia in the Morea. By forced marches de la Roche quickly reached the city — though Sanudo's statement that he made it in one day is to be doubted. The capital was saved. Faced with new troops and with the defeat of the imperial army, and opposed by a determined Venetian *bailli*, Licario lifted the siege. But before leaving the island he established garrisons in various fortresses.[88] Then he set out for Constantinople with his Latin prisoners. There he was accorded another honor by the Emperor, who elevated him to the Byzantine nobility as Grand Constable, commander of the Empire's Latin mercenaries, a post formerly held by Michael himself and now fallen vacant with the death of Kaballarios. Shortly afterwards, at the death of Alexios Philanthropenos, Licario was again advanced, acquiring the title of Grand Duke (Megas Dukas), commander of the Greek fleet.[88a]

[86] On the derivation of the word "Kaballarios" from the Western term "chevalier," see E. Stein, "Untersuchungen zur spätbyzantinischen Verfassungs- und Wirtschaftgeschichte," *Mitteil. zur osmanischen Gesch.*, II (1923–1925) 31 and note 5. (On the Kaballarios family see Pach., 65, l. 9, and 324, l. 13.) As "Kaballarios" is a proper name, it is possible that it is not necessarily derived from "chevalier."

[87] Pach., 411 and 412, esp. l. 5: ὁ ὑπ' ἐκείνῳ λαὸς Ἰταλός. Also Greg., 145, ll. 23–24. The Bastard's Latin auxiliaries were probably secured from Duke John of Athens or possibly even from Charles, both of whom were allied with him.

[88] Sanudo, *Istoria*, 126–127.

[88a] Pach., 413, ll. 7 and 15–18 and II, 546. K. Hopf, "Veneto-byzantinische Analekten," in *Sitzunsb. der Akademie der Wiss.*, Phil.-hist. Kl., XXXII (Vienna, 1859) 479, says that the Genoese pirate, Giovanni de lo Cavo, succeeded Licario as Grand Admiral. According to an unused passage in T.-Th., III, 273, however, lo Cavo is listed as *comes* ("derobatis . . . per Johannem de lo Cavo, comitum un-

The scene of Licario's triumph before the Emperor and the humiliation of the captive Giberto, who had spurned Licario as brother-in-law, has been dramatically described by Gregoras. When the haughty Giberto was led into the imperial presence, he was horrified to see Licario, the former humble knight, splendidly dressed in official robes ("he who only yesterday had been his servant!") not only consorting familiarly with the Emperor but even whispering in the imperial ear. It was too much for Giberto's Latin pride to bear, and, already weakened by his wound, he fell dead to the ground.[89]

After this revenge Licario returned to Negropont, presumably to await a suitable opportunity for seizing the capital city. Establishing headquarters at the castle of Filla nearby, he continued his depredations against the Latins, maintaining such a reign of terror that travel in the area became hazardous. During this time he also carried on attacks against the islands of the Archipelago, ravaging and capturing Seriphos and Syphnos and making raids with the imperial fleet on the Duchy of Athens-Thebes.[90]

At the height of his romantic career, however, Licario suddenly and inexplicably vanishes from history. There seems to be no mention of his death or even of the children reportedly born to him by his Greek wife.[91] Had Licario been disgraced by the Emperor or captured or killed by the Latins of Romania, the circumstances doubtless would have been recorded by the historians. In view of their silence it is possible that he may have died quietly in Constantinople in imperial service. This theory is at least suggested by an overlooked remark of Pachymeres, isolated and completely out of context, that during the struggle over religious union in Constantinople, Licario was entrusted by Palaeologus with the arrest of a high Byzantine official.[92]

---

decim lignorum armatorum"), *i.e.*, a subordinate official in the Greek navy (cf. Codinus, *De officiis*, 28). See also Guilland, "Etudes de titulature et de prosopographie byzantines: Les chefs de la marine," 212ff., who does not list lo Cavo among the Grand Dukes. But again cf. Sanudo, *Istoria*, 132 and note 4.

[89] Greg., 97, ll. 1–10.

[90] Sanudo, *Istoria*, 127 and Pach., 413, ll. 15–18.

[91] Sanudo, *Istoria*, 123: "della qual Miser Licario ebbe figli."

[92] Pach., 489: ἐπαγγείλας τῷ 'Ικαρίῳ τὴν τοῦ μεγάλου δουκὸς περιεζωσμένῳ τιμήν

The story of Licario's activities fills an important and illuminating page in the record of Byzantine-Latin relations. Indeed, his campaigns caused greater damage to the Latins of Romania than those of any other commander in imperial service except for Michael's own brother, John Palaeologus. Thus Licario's career provides additional proof that Michael's policy of utilizing Latins in Greek service and granting them high office yielded not inconsiderable returns.

With respect to Duke John I de la Roche of Athens-Thebes, whom Licario had brought a prisoner to Constantinople, the Emperor did not, as in the case of William of Achaia in 1262, extort territory as the price of freedom. In the present instance Michael at first considered the advantage of allying with the Duke by giving him one of his daughters in marriage.[93] But instead he released de la Roche for a ransom of thirty thousand *solidi*.[94] That the marriage did not materialize was probably due to Michael's fear of opposition on the part of the Duke's Theban vassals as well as to the severity of the Duke's gout.[95] Furthermore, as had happened with respect to William of Achaia, it was

εἰς χεῖρας ποιεῖται. Another possible clue to his end may be found in Sanudo, *Istoria*, 144, which mentions a victory achieved by Licario in Paphlagonia, evidently against the Turks: "Ivi già Miser Licario Mega Duca detto avea avuto una gran Vittoria. . . Elevato d'indi Miser Licario lò mandò . . . contra li Latini ch'erano in le parti de Romania." But this event, it seems indicated, may have occurred before his Archipelago campaigns. The correlation of dates and events in Licario's short but remarkable career is difficult because of the differences and inexactitudes of the sources. Probable references to Licario (hitherto apparently overlooked) are also to be found in T.-Th., III, 190 ("detentos a Menga Ducha de Stalimine"); 220; 237 ("Lichari"); 259 ("dominus exercitus Lemenga comestabele. . . Delochari et Amiragius"); and possibly 277. On Licario cf., finally, L. de Mas Latrie, "Les Seigneurs Tierciers de Négropont," *Revue de l'Orient latin*, I (1893) 413ff.

[93] Sanudo, *Istoria*, 136: "tentò il detto Imperator dar sua Figlia per Moglie a Miser Giovanni dalla Roccia per retaggio legitimo." The last words suggest that Michael had hopes of eventually securing the Duchy. Also Pach., 413: δοκιμάσας λαμβάνειν γαμβρόν. Pachymeres adds that oaths were exchanged at the Duke's release: ὑφ' ὅρκοις ἀσφαλέσιν. According to Miller, *Latins in Levant*, 140, it would have been logical for Michael to demand the Athenian possessions of Argos and Nauplia in order to round out the Byzantine province of the Morea.

[94] Sanudo, *Istoria*, 136: "lo fece libero per trenta mila soldi di grossi, ed insieme on un Pisano" (note mention of a Pisan). Cf. Pach., 413. Also see *Arch. st. it.*, er. IV, III (1879) 162.

[95] Sanudo, *Istoria*, 136: "vedendolo tanto aggravato di indisposizione del corpo, he parea fuori di se e ch'avesse a vivere poco, non volse far le nozze."

too easy for an unfriendly pope — and at this time pontiffs were succeeding each other rapidly — to declare the alliance dissolved. As if to corroborate Michael's judgment, John did not long survive his captivity, dying in 1280, only one year after his release.[96] He was succeeded by his brother William, son-in-law of John the Bastard and a declared enemy of Palaeologus.[97]

As a result of the imperial campaigns in Romania Michael had achieved a signal triumph. Indeed, he had succeeded in capturing the rulers of the three strongest states of Latin Greece: William, Prince of Achaia, Giberto dalle Carceri, triarch of Negropont, and Duke John of Athens-Thebes. Despite this success, however, Michael knew that he could not hope to recover all of Latin Greece or even to insure his present position until he had smashed the power of Charles of Anjou, the real force behind the Latin princes of Romania.[98]

THE GRECO-VENETIAN TREATY OF 19 MARCH 1277

The grand expedition of Charles to restore Constantinople to the Latins, so long in preparation and so long postponed, seemed after Lyons more distant than ever. This the always practical-minded government of Venice was not slow to recognize. Further dismayed by the spectacular success of Licario in the Aegean and the severe damage to Venetian trade in Greek waters at the hands of corsairs,[99] the Commune resolved to come to an

[96] *Ibid.*: "Il detto Duca ritornato alla patria sua Attene, morse poco dappoi." See also *ibid.*, note 1, where the date of 1280 is cited by the editor, Hopf.

[97] According to Pach., 413, ll. 15–18, Licario ravaged the Duchy's coasts during William's reign: τοῦ μεγάλου δουκὸς ἀξίαν τοῦ Ἰκαρίου καὶ τὸν στόλον ἄγοντος.

[98] See C. De Lellis, *Gli atti perduti della cancelleria angioina*, B. Mazzoleni ed., in *Regesta chartarum italiae*, I¹ (Rome, 1939) no. 216, 400, dated 1278, order of Charles to William de la Roche of Athens-Thebes to look after the territory of the latter's brother "qui per Paleologum detinetur in carcere." Shortly before this, on 26 August 1278 (a few months after the death of William of Achaia on 1 May 1278), Charles ordered his Vicar General for Achaia to inform the Latin barons of Romania, including John de la Roche, to take an oath of fealty (*Arch. st. it.*, ser. IV, I [1878] 433). This was in accordance with the provisions of the Treaty of Viterbo. All the Achaian feudatories, both Latin and Greek, including women, were to swear homage and fealty. Cf. Longnon, *L'Empire Latin*, 249–250.

[99] See below, text and notes 108–112.

agreement with the Emperor. Several embassies were exchanged, but it was not until 2 September 1276 that Marco Bembo and Matteo Gradenigo, envoys of the Doge Jacob Contarini, were authorized to reach a settlement. During the ensuing negotiations which took place in the Greek capital, Gradenigo died and the pact was concluded, on 19 March 1277,[100] by Bembo alone. In essence the accord was a two year truce to hostilities. Provision was made for an automatic six months extension at the time of expiration, on condition that during the two year period neither party gave notice of intention to terminate the agreement.[101] Other significant clauses were as follows:

(1) The Venetians would be granted a quarter in Constantinople but within well-restricted limits. Permanent houses and two churches would be provided at the Emperor's expense for the use of the Venetian *bailli*, councillors, and merchants. Similar provision would be made for the Commune's merchants in Thessalonica and other areas of the Empire.[102] (2) Venetians could trade in any part of the Empire without the payment of duties. (3) The validity of the convention signed in 1268 between Genoa and the Emperor would be recognized. Thus the Genoese would not be expelled from the Empire, and the Venetians in addition agreed to maintain peace with Genoa in the Black Sea and the Sea of Marmora. Any quarrels between the two Italian powers would be adjudicated by the Emperor, who would impose whatever damages were necessary for payment to the injured party. (4) Venice agreed neither to make alliances with, nor to transport

[100] According to Norden, 540, note 1, a new Greco-Venetian treaty had been signed in 1275. There seems, however, to be no trace of it in the sources. Dade, 50, on the basis of certain words in this treaty of 1277 (T.-Th., III, 134: "ex alio principio renovaretur"), believes it to be a new agreement rather than an extension of a previous treaty.

[101] On the circumstances leading to the signing of the treaty see the Latin text in T.-Th., III, 135–137, esp.: "usque ad complementum duorum annorum [et] voluntate utriusque partis . . . ultra dictum terminum teneatur per sex menses." Cf. Andrea Dandolo, 324.

[102] T.-Th., III, 139–141. Cf. Heyd, *Histoire*, I, 435. (For the limits of the Venetian quarter in Constantinople see T.-Th., 139. Cf. H. Brown, "The Venetians and the Venetian Quarter in Constantinople to the Close of the 12th Century," *Jl. of Hell. Studies*, XL (1920) 75ff.; and C. Diehl, "La colonie Vénitienne à Constantinople," *Etudes byzantines* (1905) 245ff.

the troops of, Michael's enemies for the duration of the treaty.[103] (5) Both Venice and the Emperor were guaranteed a free hand in Negropont, even to the extent of conquering it. (6) The Emperor confirmed the remaining territorial possessions of the Venetian Lords Marco II Sanudo, Duke of the Archipelago (i.e., of Naxos) and Bartolomeo Ghisi, ruler of several Aegean islands. In return, the two nobles promised not to support enemies of the Emperor, particularly corsairs unfriendly to him.[104] (7) The Emperor agreed to respect the Venetian possession of Coron, Modon, and Crete and to withdraw from the latter island "the men whom he had there." [105] (8) Palaeologus pledged restitution to Venetians who had suffered loss of property at the hands of imperial subjects, while Venice was to indemnify citizens of the Empire plundered by Venetian pirates. This stipulation was made retroactive to 1265, the year of the first Greco-Venetian treaty. (9) If either signatory committed an act contrary to the terms of the treaty, the other pledged not to begin hostilities but to renegotiate.[106]

[103] T.-Th., III, 142 and 148.

[104] T.-Th., III, 138. On Sanudo and Ghisi see Miller, *Latins in Levant*, 578. The Ghisi family (vassals and at the same time rivals of the Sanudi) were lords of Skiathos, Skopelos, Skyros, Keos, Seriphos, and Amorgos, which had been seized by Licario (see above, text and note 81). Cf. Andrea Dandolo, 324; also Dölger, *Regesten*, no. 2026.

[105] T.-Th., III, 137–138, esp.: "homines, quos habet Imperium nostrum ad ipsam insulam extrahet eos inde." Crete had been stirred by uprisings of the Greek population. The very next year (1278) the Cretan brothers Chortatzes, during a rebellion resulting in the death of the Venetian Duke of Crete (see Canale, 664ff.), fled to Constantinople, where they were cordially received by the Emperor and given lands in Asia Minor. (In this connection it is to be noted that according to a clause in the treaty of 1277 under consideration, all Venetian and Greek prisoners, including those of Crete, were to be released. See T.-Th., III, 145.) This fact, plus the clause cited in the text regarding imperial agents in Crete, clearly reveals Michael's encouragement of the Cretan revolts — unofficial, of course, so as not unduly to provoke Venice. For a summary of these events see S. Xanthoudides, Ἡ Ἐνετοκρατία ἐν Κρήτῃ καὶ οἱ κατὰ τῶν Ἐνετῶν ἀγῶνες τῶν Κρητῶν (Athens, 1939) 49–55.

[106] T.-Th., III, 143 and 146, esp.: "ymo pocius significabit . . . ut emendetur, quicquid contra ipsam treugam fuerit attemptatum." Additional clauses, similar to those in previous Greco-Venetian treaties, concerned the punishment of malefactors in Constantinople, piracy, the export of money and grain, and, interestingly enough, the trade of Greek merchants in Venice (*ibid.*, 146). For the Greek text of the treaty see Miklosich and Müller, *Acta et diplomata*, III, 84–96. George Acropolites

Although the treaty incorporated many earlier Greco-Venetian compromises and agreements, Venice was not content — a fact revealed by her termination of it after the passing of only two years.[107] Evidently the Venetians still could not forget that the development of events — in particular the election of a sympathetic pontiff — might someday permit the long-awaited crusade against Constantinople with restoration of Venetian supremacy in the East.

From the Greek point of view the treaty was much more satisfactory. Though finally forced to grant the Venetians a quarter in the capital and immunity from duties, the Emperor, for the time being at least, had achieved his objective of decisively splitting Venice from Sicily as well as finding a counterpoise to the Genoese in Constantinople. Moreover, he had even managed to include in the truce favorable reference to Negropont and the Venetian princes of the Greek islands. Despite this considerable diplomatic achievement, Michael, too, realized that his success was only temporary and that once Charles secured papal blessing for a Greek crusade, Venice would hardly hesitate to rejoin the ranks of his enemies.

To be considered in connection with this treaty is an illuminating and suggestive Venetian document dated the following March, 1278. Actually it is a procès-verbal of claims for damages suffered by Venetian merchants at the hands of corsairs — many in the service of Michael — during the period preceding the treaty of 1277.[108] The list, which was submitted by the Doge to the Em-

---

signed both Greek and Latin copies for the Emperor, while Ogerius, the imperial notary (perhaps a Gasmule or Genoese), signed only the Latin copy (T.-Th., III, 149 and Miklosich and Müller, III, 96). Specifically on the question of Venetian export of Greek grain and its connection with Michael's depreciation of the *hyperpyron*, see F. Dölger, *Byz. Zeit.*, XLIX (1956) 429, criticism of R. Lopez and I. Raymond, *Medieval Trade in the Mediterranean World: Illustrative Documents* (New York, 1955) 429.

[107] See Chapter 14, section 1.

[108] T.-Th., III, 159–281. (Note that the list occupies over 120 pages!) The document was apparently justified by an article in the treaty of 1277 (see the last of the nine clauses mentioned above). On piracy at this time see P. Charanis, "Piracy in the Aegean during the reign of Michael VIII Palaeologus," *Annuaire de l'institut de philologie et d'histoire orientales et slaves*, X (1950) 127ff.

peror, is huge and enumerates in detail no less than two hundred and seventy-one individual cases of piracy. Besides providing an occasional bit of information on chronology and the identification of various little-known persons[109] (especially non-Venetian and non-Genoese merchants in Romania),[110] the document enables us to observe the remarkable extent to which Michael utilized Latins as freebooters in his service.[111] Indeed, the large number of such cases, especially those in which Venetian goods were seized expressly by imperial command,[112] strongly substantiates the thesis that piracy was purposely encouraged by the Emperor in order to force the Venetians to reach an accord with him.

[109] For example, the words "quia erant in treugua" (T.-Th., 182) indicate that a treaty may have existed in 1267 between Charles and Palaeologus. Note also useful references to the battle of Demetrias (200) and to either Philanthropenos or to Licario (190, 220, and 277).

[110] See references to Pisan merchants (*ibid.*, 228, 264) and to Catalans (225).

[111] As Latin corsairs in Greek service, the document lists, among others, Giovanni de le Cavo (179, 252, 273, etc.); John Senzaraxon (216, 273, etc.); and the Genoese Andrea Gaforus (241, 265, etc.) Cf. K. Hopf, "Urkunden und Zusätze zur Geschichte von Andros," *Sitz. Wiener Akad. phil.-hist. Kl.*, XXI (1856) 246ff. Also Hopf, *Griechenland*, LXXXV, 310, note 73.

[112] Note the names of Greek officials — even of Michael himself — listed as responsible for damaging Venetian property (170, 174, 190, 200, and esp. 172: "dampnificaverit ipsum dictus dominus Imperator de ipso frumento"). See also 231, where it is noted that Greeks looted Venetian houses in Constantinople. The possibility should not be overlooked, however, that the list may have been padded by the Venetian authorities.

13

PAPAL DEMANDS AND ANGEVIN OFFENSIVES

(1277–1281)

RELATIONS BETWEEN PALAEOLOGUS AND POPE JOHN XXI

As might be expected, the popes succeeding Innocent V became increasingly insistent toward the Emperor in their demands for the consummation of union. After the brief pontificate of Hadrian V, a Portuguese under the name of John XXI put on the triple crown (20 September 1276). One of John's first acts was to dispatch to Constantinople letters already prepared by Innocent V.[1] The personnel of Innocent's embassy was now changed, however, the original legates being replaced by two Bishops, Jacob Ferentino and Godfried of Turin, and two Dominicans. Worthy of note is the substitution of prelates for priests in the delicate task of insuring implementation of union.[2]

Among the letters entrusted to the nuncios was one drawn up by John XXI, which included a request to the Emperor for a fresh profession of faith, to be subscribed to orally, and for renewed

[1] On John's pontificate and the identification of letters in this embassy see E. Van Moé, "L'envoi de nonces à Constantinople par les papes Innocent V et Jean XXI," *Mél. d'arch. et d'hist.*, XLVII (1930) 48ff.

[2] See Van Moé, "L'envoi," 49. The substitution was in part also due to the inability of the Greek-speaking Franciscan Jerome of Ascoli, leader of the previous embassy, to return to Constantinople. Cf. Ptolemy of Lucca, *Historia ecclesiastica*, *RISS*, XI (1727) cols. 1176–1177. On this embassy also see Chapman, 131, whose occasionally false chronology (following Pachymeres) has been corrected by V. Grumel, "Les ambassades pontificales à Byzance," 437ff. E. Cadier, *Le registre de Jean XXI* (Paris, 1898), omits letters relating to Greek affairs.

recognition of Roman primacy.[3] Another document, in effect the passport of the nuncios, was addressed to all civil and ecclesiastical authorities to be encountered en route, and, in the name of the Pope, requested safe passage for the envoys and their party.[4] On their journey to the Bosporus the papal ambassadors were to be accompanied by the Greek envoys then at the Curia, for whom Charles once again had to issue safe conducts.[5]

Events transpiring in Constantinople after the arrival of the papal embassy are known from letters subsequently dispatched to the Curia by the Greek authorities. In one epistle the Emperor, after the most extravagant phrases in praise of mutual efforts to achieve union, declared that the Greek clerics in synod had affixed their signatures and seals to newly-made confessions.[6] These documents were being brought to the Curia by a mission consisting of the Metropolitan of Cyzicus Theodore Scutariotes, the Chartophylax and Archdeacon Constantine Meliteniotes, and the Archdeacon and *Epi ton deeseon* George Metochites.[7]

Probably most important to the Pope was the information transmitted by the Emperor and Patriarch regarding the ceremonies in the capital, which publicly confirmed the Union of Lyons in accordance with the demands of Popes Innocent V and John XXI.[8] At the Blachernae palace in April of 1277, almost

[3] Van Moé, "L'envoi," 52 and 59. Worth noting is the fact (60f.) that the envoys were authorized by the Pope to select any available interpreters for both Greek and Latin — further proof of the lack of official Curial interpreters at this time.

[4] *Ibid.*, 61–62.

[5] *Arch. st. it.*, XXV (1877) 411–412, dated 26 November 1276. Also edict of 28 November listing as the imperial envoys Andronikos Margida (Masgodos?), the cleric George Aulinus, and two men named John.

[6] J. Gay, *Les registres de Nicolas III* (Paris, 1898) 76B, no. 220 (undated): "que in ipsis apertius continentur sunt vallata et etiam roborata propriis subscriptionibus et sigillis." Cf. Dölger, *Regesten*, nos. 2028–2029.

[7] Gay, *Reg. Nic.*, 77A. Angelos Johannes and Andronikos Masgodos, the Emperor's personal secretaries, also accompanied the envoys (possibly as interpreters). They are probably to be identified, at least in part, with those mentioned in note 5, above. In another letter Andronikos stressed Michael's preoccupation with incursions of Turks and even Christians (probably John the Bastard and his brother Nikephoros). See Gay, *Reg. Nic.*, 77, no. 221.

[8] *Ibid.*, 83, no. 228, esp.: "papa . . . Johannes XXI[us] petiit . . . ut affirmet, ratificet per corporale sacramentum imperium nostrum ea que dictus magnus Logotheta juravit."

three full years after Lyons, Michael and Andronikos, before a large gathering of Greek clergy, officials, and the papal nuncios, took oral oaths recognizing Roman primacy and the Latin profession of faith, thus publicly ratifying the oath taken by Acropolites at Lyons. Documents were then drawn up in Latin, signed by the Emperors in Greek, and sealed with a golden bull.[9]

In his profession of faith enclosed with these documents, Michael, conforming to papal instructions, accepted the *filioque*, the Roman doctrine of purgatory, the seven sacraments as held by Rome, the Latin teaching on the azymes, and, once again, papal primacy with the right of appeal to the Holy See and submission of all churches to Rome.[10] Though Michael's declarations seem to have added nothing really new to previous imperial avowals, his statements were now more explicit than ever before. The demands of Innocent V and John XXI had produced at least this effect! But protestations of obedience notwithstanding, the Emperor once more beseeched the Pope to permit the Greek church to retain its own rites and symbol "as it was recited before the schism until now." "For your holiness," he added, "this is neither an important nor unusual request, but for us it is a difficult matter because of the vast number of people involved." [11]

Even more significant was the synodical letter addressed to the Pope at this time by the Patriarch John Bekkos and his

[9] *Ibid.*, 83. Cf. Raynaldus, a. 1277, § 27ff. Also see the short monograph of R. Stapper, *Papst Johannes XXI.* (Münster, 1898) 86. That the matter of an oral oath was a real stumbling block is attested in a letter from a papal envoy in Constantinople to Pope Gregory just before the Council of Lyons: "Iuramentum autem noluit facere imperator, asserens hoc non esse consuetudinis apud eos et subscriptio habetur pro firmitate etiam iuramenti" (quoted in O. Van der Vat, *Die Anfänge der Franziskanermissionen . . . im nahen Orient . . . während des 13. Jahrhunderts* [Werl in Westf., 1934] 252). An oral oath, of course, necessitated some sort of public ceremony.

[10] Gay, *Reg. Nic.*, 82, esp.: "Spiritum Sanctum . . . ex Patre et Filio procedentem" and "septem esse . . . sacramenta . . . Sacramentum Eucharistie ex azimo."

[11] *Ibid.*, 83: "ut nostra ecclesia dicat secundum symbolum prout dicebat hos ante sysma et usque ad hodiernum diem, et quod permaneamus in nostris ritibus. . . Hoc ante igitur non grave est vestre sanctitati et non inconsuetum et nobis nunc difficile propter populi immensam multitudinem." Note also the similar tenor of Andronikos' letter, 84, no. 229.

307

clergy.[12] It appears that at the public ceremony at Blachernae the Greek clerics had refused to take the personal oral oath demanded by the papal legates. Yet meeting in synod they authorized Bekkos to draw up a document recognizing Roman primacy and enclosing a profession of faith. But while in effect recognizing the *filioque*, the profession avoided specific reference to the Greek equivalent, *ekporeuesthai*, so desired by the papacy.[1] Furthermore, in the letter Bekkos tried to reconcile the Greek and Latin positions on the *filioque* by emphasizing the absence of any real difference between the two beliefs. In still another passage Bekkos, discussing the Greek and Roman attitudes toward the sacraments and the question of azymes, accepted the positions of both churches as equally admissible. Like the Emperor Bekkos also pleaded for retention of the Greek rites on the ground that they had "prevailed in the Greek church from the very beginning." [14] Included in the letter, lastly, was an elaborately worded statement of obedience to the Pope, with a promise to render to Rome all prerogatives possessed before the schism [1] and with recognition of the right of appeal to Rome. With these promises, declared the Greek prelates, the work of union was now fully completed. As Bekkos wrote in conclusion, obviously to soften the papal demand for individual oral oaths, the Greek clergy had confirmed the act of union by affixing to the document their signatures, "which among us have the strength of an oath." [1]

[12] See Greek text in Stapper, *Papst Johannes XXI.*, 115ff., and Latin version in Gay, *Reg. Nic.*, 84, no. 230. Cf. Dölger, *Regesten*, no. 2028, and S. Lampros "Αὐτοκρατόρων τοῦ Βυζαντίου χρυσόβουλλα καὶ χρυσᾶ γράμματα," Νέος Ἑλληνομνήμων XI (1914) 120.

[13] Gay, *Reg. Nic.*, 86, no. 230. On this see V. Grumel, *Dict. théol. cath.*, IX pt. 1, col. 1395. Cf. A. Demski, *Papst Nikolaus III.*, 216, who says that their statement of the *filioque* was precise.

[14] Gay, *Reg. Nic.*, 86: "a fonte Deo et Patre, profunditur autem et ab ipse Filio quemadmodum a fonte . . . non tamen duo fontes Spiritus sunt Pater e Filius." Also "credentes . . . azimum panem . . . ex fermentato confectum pane sanctum etiam illud cognoscimus." Also, 87: "sic debemus nos permanere incommutabiliter in ritibus qui a principio obtenti sunt in ecclesia nostra."

[15] *Ibid.*, 85B: "omnes prerogativas et privilegia que ante schisma."

[16] *Ibid.*, 85A: "ab universitate magne synodi, que apud nos paulo ante fuera celebrata . . . unionis . . . consumata est." Also "humilitas nostra cum toto sacre ipsius conventu firmavit et roboravit subscriptionibus manualibus, que apud no vigorem obtinent juramenti." On other papal letters to the Roman nuncios, seem

The acts of the Council of Blachernae publicly proclaiming the union to the Byzantine population were sent by the Emperor to Nikephoros of Epirus and John the Bastard of Thessaly, with an order that they conform to the council's decisions. The two refused, however, and this necessitated the convocation of another synod at Hagia Sophia on 16 July 1277, at which time both Princes, at imperial insistence, were anathematized. (It is notable that the papal nuncios, despite the discretionary authority with which they were empowered, refused to join in this act.)[17] Five months later, in December of 1277, the Bastard in retaliation convoked at Neopatras an anti-unionist council[18] of eight bishops, a few abbots, and one hundred monks — mainly refugees from imperial territory — which proceeded to anathematize Pope, Emperor, and Patriarch as enemies of Orthodoxy.[19]

In an effort to check the growth of organized opposition, the Emperor thereupon dispatched an army against the Bastard, but a number of Michael's own generals, themselves antipathetic to union, deserted to the enemy. Victory, nevertheless, fell to the imperial forces, the renegades being returned to Constantinople in chains.[20]

THE PONTIFICATE OF NICHOLAS III AND THE NEW
DEMANDS ON MICHAEL PALAEOLOGUS

When the ambassadors of Palaeologus bearing the results of the Blachernae council arrived in Italy, they found that Pope

---

ingly mitigating the papal demands with respect to the Greek rites and the *filioque*, see Grumel, "Les ambassades," 438; Van Moé, "L'envoi," 53; and cf. also Grumel, *Dict. théol. cath.*, IX, pt. 1, cols. 1401–1402.

[17] See letter of Nicholas III to the Emperor (in Martène, *Ampl. coll.*, VII, col. 260) mentioning his refusal and that of his predecessors to excommunicate the Angeloi. Cf. Stapper, *Papst Johannes XXI.*, 88.

[18] On the place and date of this council see V. Grumel, "En Orient après le II° Concile de Lyon," *Echos d'Orient*, XXIV (1925) 322–323. Chapman, 122, wrongly dates it in May of 1277.

[19] See Raynaldus, a. 1278, § 13–14, for details of tortures inflicted on pro-unionist Greek bishops during the council. A second anti-unionist council met in 1278 with the main objective, however, of supporting the Arsenite party at Constantinople; see Grumel, "En Orient," 322.

[20] See below, text and notes 72–74. Also Pach., Bk. 6, ch. 24, and Raynaldus, a. 1277, § 42.

John XXI had already died.[21] Once again the fate of religious union depended on the election of a new pontiff. Immediately a severe struggle broke out in the Curia. More determined than ever, Charles redoubled his efforts to secure the election of a favorable candidate, and the danger increased that control of the papacy would fall into his hands. But the anti-Angevin party eventually triumphed, and six months later, on 25 November 1277, Nicholas III, an Italian of the Orsini family, was elevated to the throne.[22]

With the election of Nicholas the series of pontiffs in some degree sympathetic to the Angevin cause came to an end. Only a short time after his accession, in fact, Nicholas induced Charles to renounce both the imperial vicariate of Tuscany and the senatorship of Rome.[23] Thus the power of Charles was, temporarily, curtailed, and for the first time he was relegated to the role in Italian politics that had originally been intended when the Sicilian crown had been bestowed upon him.

Not only did Nicholas curb Charles's ambitions in Italy, he absolutely forbade an Angevin attack on Constantinople. In this way, of course, Nicholas performed a valuable service for Michael. But such was not the Pope's ultimate aim. What Nicholas envisaged was no less than papal world hegemony in which the Holy See, acting as arbiter between Charles and Michael, would itself hold the balance between East and West.[24] At the same time, while seeking to favor neither Charles nor Michael, Nicholas insisted upon a more rigorous consummation of religious union than had any of his predecessors. Unfortunately, however, he did not reveal the sage tolerance and patience of Gregory X, instead

[21] Known from the first letter of John's successor, Nicholas, to Michael, in Gay, *Reg. Nic.*, 124, no. 367: "moram apocrisariorum tuorum apud sedem eandem, quam ipsius Sedis vacatio."

[22] On Charles's presence at the Curia see R. Sternfeld, *Der Kardinal Johann Gaëtan Orsini* (Berlin, 1905) 283.

[23] Ptolemy of Lucca, *Hist. eccl.*, RISS, XI (1727) col. 1183. Nicholas also persuaded the Emperor Rudolph of Hapsburg to renounce the Romagna in favor of the Holy See.

[24] On the policy of Nicholas see A. Demski, *Papst Nikolaus III.* (Münster, 1903) 212–226; also Greg., 144, ll. 18ff., for his statement on the balance between Charles and Michael. Cf. Dante's opinion of Nicholas, *Inferno*, canto 19, 52ff.

demanding complete unity of dogmatic beliefs and liturgical custom.

In the meantime Michael, as usual fully informed by his agents of Charles's manipulations in the Curia, had awaited the election with apprehension. Accordingly, his response to an embassy officially announcing the enthronement of the new pontiff was even more enthusiastic than usual.[25]

On the papal side, it was not until October of 1278, almost a whole year after Nicholas' election, that a new embassy was organized in answer to the elaborate mission headed by the Metropolitan (historian) Theodore Scutariotes.[25a] The refusal of the Greek clergy to take personal oaths, and especially Michael's failure to authorize or even to mention in his last communications a political settlement with Charles, must have rendered Nicholas wary and not a little suspicious of imperial motives.[26] Consequently, Nicholas took care to prepare very full and explicit directives for his plenipotentiaries.

Four letters were sent to Constantinople. In the first the Pope, after the usual expressions of praise for the Emperor's decision openly to repudiate the schism, enjoined even greater zeal so that "what was begun by you may easily be finished by the Greek clergy." Nicholas stressed pointedly that implementation of union and papal requests depended entirely on the Emperor.[27] But to help Michael in his task, he wrote that he was sending to Constantinople the Bishop of Grosseto, Bartholomew, and three Minorites, Bartholomew of Sens, Philip of Perugia, and Angelo of Urbino. Nicholas closed with a refusal to accede to Michael's request for excommunication of Charles's Greek allies, explaining

---

[25] See Gay, *Reg. Nic.*, 132–134, nos. 382–383. Cf. Dölger, *Regesten*, no. 2038.

[25a] It is notable that in an imperial document concerning Theodore's ecclesiastical rank (see Zachariä von Lingenthal, *Jus Graecoromanum*, ed. Zepos, I [Athens, 1931] 503), Michael makes reference to the Donation of Constantine (see F. Dölger, *Byzanz und die europäische Staatenwelt* [Speyer am Rhein, 1953] 109, note 64).

[26] Cf. Demski, *Papst Nikolaus*, 218.

[27] Gay, *Reg. Nic.*, 123–124, no. 367: "quod totaliter a te hujusmodi negotium ejusque dependet consummata perfectio." In affairs of union the popes were always inclined to attribute too much coercive power to the Emperors.

that no change in policy was warranted since the previous deci sion of Innocent V.[28]

In a second letter to the Emperor, papal suspicions were more clearly revealed. Touching directly on the dissension be tween Michael and "our dearest sons in Christ, the illustrious Emperor (Philip) of Constantinople and Charles, King of Sicily," Nicholas rebuked Michael for sending to him envoys unauthorized to discuss the "temporalia" (i.e., peace with Charles), and for stressing the "spiritualia" so much as to seem to be hoping thereby to gloss over the "temporalia." [29] (Strange indeed for a Pope to complain that a ruler was sacrificing temporal for spiritual con siderations!) Nicholas then directed Michael within five months after receipt of his letter to send plenipotentiaries to the Curia fully authorized to negotiate a settlement with Charles. Michael in the meantime, was to conduct preliminary discussions with papal envoys regarding a truce.[30]

In another letter, directed to Andronikos, little of importance was added, but in that addressed to the Patriarch and Greek clergy Nicholas expressed dissatisfaction "that those things re quested by this church . . . for the further consummation . . . of union were not fulfilled." [31] He was referring obviously to the Greek clerics' equivocation regarding the *filioque* and to the omission of a personal oral oath.

Important as these letters are, they do not reveal all aspects of Nicholas' policy. Much more informative is a long and elab orate confidential memorandum in which Nicholas directed his nuncios specifically as to their conduct and the demands to be made on the Greeks. For its view of the internal workings o

[28] *Ibid.*, 124: "quia nulla postmodum novitas immutavit nec nos ad eas re sponsionem putavimus immutandam."

[29] *Ibid.*, no. 368, 124B, esp.: "nec ad illud scripto seu verbo respondens . . licet ejusdem ecclesie circumspecta provisio non indigne a spiritualibus elegeri initium assumendum," and "tua instans et repetita petitio, quod ad Latinos e Grecos in caritate mutue solidandos tractatus erat temporalium premittendus."

[30] *Ibid.*, 125A, esp.: "infra quinque menses . . . circa treugas certi tempori cum dictis principibus ineundas eorundem nuntiorum nostrorum persuasionibu acquiescas."

[31] *Ibid.*, no. 370, 126: "illa que ad ipsum consumandum plenius . . . ex ejus dem ecclesie parte requisita, nec adimpleta fuerunt."

papal diplomacy, this document is perhaps one of the most illuminating in the entire history of the schism, and as such deserves careful attention.

The directive begins:

Upon arrival you may bless benignly and lovingly on our part our
very dear son in Christ, our Michael Palaeologus, illustrious Emperor
of the Greeks and his dear son, noble Andronikos. Likewise, you may
carefully inform them how joyfully, how sympathetically we and our
brothers received their letters containing their professions of faith,
recognition of Roman primacy, and voluntary obedience to Rome.[32]

In a succeeding passage, however, Nicholas, despite his remark
upon the reception of the imperial confessions, directs that another profession of faith and statement of adherence to Rome
be secured from the Emperor and his son, and especially from
the patriarch and prelates, inasmuch as the original professions
were not composed according to the exact form prescribed by
the papacy.[33]

The memorandum continues by instructing the envoys to say,
in reply to the Emperor's request for preservation of the Greek
rites, that "unity of faith does not permit diversity in its confessors
or in confession . . . especially in the chanting of the symbol." [34]
Referred to in particular here, of course, is the Greek refusal to
accept the addition of the *filioque* to the creed. Expatiating on
this matter, the document declares explicitly that "the Roman
church, after due deliberation, desires that the symbol be chanted
uniformly with addition of the *filioque* by both Latins and
Greeks." As for the rest of the Greek rites, the Pope, like his
predecessors, would permit the Greeks to retain "only those which
seem to the Apostolic See . . . not to impair the integrity of the
Catholic faith or . . . of the sacred canons." [35]

---

[32] *Ibid.,* 127B.
[33] *Ibid.,* 128, esp.: "nondum . . . juxta formam ab eadem ecclesia traditam."
[34] *Ibid.,* 128B: "unitas fidei non patitur diversitatem in professoribus suis sive
in professione . . . maxime in decantatione symboli."
[35] *Ibid.,* 128B. Most important of the rites involved was the Greek use of
leavened instead of the Latin unleavened bread (azymes). At this point reference
is made by Nicholas to a truce to be entered into between Palaeologus and Charles

Turning to the important matter of papal supremacy, the Pope instructs that "the patriarch and rest of the clergy of every fortress, village, or any other place, all and each singly, recognize, accept, and confess with a sworn oath the truth of the faith and primacy of the Roman church . . . without any condition or addition." Nicholas then prescribes for his legates the oath to be taken by the clerics, emphasizing at the same time that none of the Greek ecclesiastics must be permitted to evade this personal oath.[36] The Greek clergy had previously objected to the practice on the grounds that such oath-taking was contrary to their custom.[37]

Mindful that in the last analysis it was the Greek populace that had to be won over to union, Nicholas directed his envoys to make sure that "those who exercise the office of preachers publicly and carefully instruct their congregations in the true faith and chant the creed with addition of the *filioque*." [38] Moreover, the Pope prescribed that his legates personally visit all the principal centers of the Empire and, in cathedrals, churches, and monasteries, collect from the people duly witnessed, individual professions of faith and attestations to papal primacy. Of these statements signed copies were to be sent to Rome. It was only after deposition of these guarantees as well as an admission of schism on the part of the Greek clergy that the patriarch and his

---

(129A). And in a subsequent passage Nicholas, though requested by Palaeologus, refuses to excommunicate the Angeloi princes of Epirus and Neopatras (131A).

[36] *Ibid.*, 129A, esp.: "que petenda sunt a patriarcha, prelatis, et clero civitatis, cujuslibet castri, vici seu loci . . . prestito juramento." The oath was evidently similar to that taken in 1274 at Lyons by the imperial envoy George Acropolites. See 129A, and cf. Héfelé, *Conciles,* 177, note 2.

[37] *Reg. Nic.*, 129A: "nullam decet patriarcham, prelatos predictos aut clerum consuetudinem quod jurare non consueverint allegare. . ." Compare this refusal of the Greek ecclesiastics to take an oath to the pope with similar conduct on their part during the Latin occupation. At that time the oath required for the acceptance of papal authority included the clasping of their hands within those of a papal legate according to Western feudal custom. On this see L. Bréhier, "Attempts at Reunion of the Greek and Latin Churches," ch. XIX, *Camb. Med. Hist.*, IV, 606.

[38] *Reg. Nic.*, 129B: "illi qui officium predicationis exercent publice predicent et exponant fideliter suis populis eandem fidei veritatem et cantent etiam simbolum cum additione illa . . . filioque."

314

prelates could request from the papal envoys confirmation of their clerical offices.[39] Nicholas' insistence on papal sanction of Greek clerical offices, though particularly inadmissible to the Greeks, was, from the papal point of view, perhaps only to be expected, since all appointments made by a "schismatic" clergy would be considered *ipso facto* uncanonical.

Severe as were these demands, a further directive was at this point inserted which was certain to anger and humiliate the Greeks. This was in regard to the dispatch of a permanent cardinal-legate to the Greek capital. Anticipating strong opposition to such a proposal, the Pope, in a revealing passage, charged his envoys "cautiously and diligently to study a way to prepare his [the legate's] arrival, planting the seed in colloquies with the Emperor by affirming that the presence in Constantinople of a cardinal with full authority would be very useful . . . and suggesting that the Emperor himself make the request for a cardinal-legate." [40]

To expedite matters the nuncios were to inquire if the Emperor possessed a record of such a legate in the past, or if anyone could recall the kind of reception previously accorded resident legates, or had information regarding their place of residence, size of retinue, and especially the nature of their jurisdiction.[41] Doubtless Nicholas here had in mind the residence of a cardinal-legate in Constantinople for a period during the Latin occupation,[42] for in the years between 1054 and the conquest (1204)

[39] *Ibid.*, 129B, esp.: "in cathedralibus et aliis sollempnibus ecclesiis et monasteriis locorum, in quibus professiones et recognitiones hujusmodi facte fuerint et . . . redigantur in scriptis." Also "super confirmatione status sui . . . petere curaverunt."

[40] *Ibid.*, 130A, esp.: "caute et diligenter studeatis viam ejus adventum preparare . . . et suggerendo eidem imperatorem quod ipse legatum peteret cardinalem."

[41] *Ibid.*, 130A: "qualiter ibi legati sedis apostolice sunt admissi, qualiter honorati, qualiter exhibiti, ubi specialius consueverant conservari, quomodo prelati et alii veniebant ad vocationem ipsorum, qualiter parebatur eis in judiciis contentiosis et aliis etiam. . ."

[42] In the early years of the Latin Empire, the Pope, in order to keep the Latin patriarch of Constantinople weak, had maintained a cardinal-legate in the capital. But in later years, with the Empire's decline, the patriarch himself had assumed the function of legate. See Wolff, "Latin Empire," 818, and his "Politics in the Latin Patriarchate," 288.

there seems to have been no permanent papal legate in the capital.

This directive regarding the dispatch of a legate is probably the most striking part of the entire document, and indeed constituted a new and more severe demand on the Greek church. To Nicholas, accustomed as the papacy had become to the appointment of legates to the Latin nations, such a procedure would be more or less normal [43] and would at the same time be a real test of Michael's sincerity. But to the Greeks, unwilling to recognize the remarkable development of papal claims during the eleventh and twelfth centuries, this could mean only that their church had now lost its independence of action and had in fact fallen to the same level as a subservient church of the West [44] — a circumstance all too reminiscent of Latin domination. Finally, the admission of a legate would directly contravene Michael's assurances to his clergy that no pope or permanent papal representatives would set foot in the capital.[45]

Nicholas, despite the general firmness of his tone, seems to have felt a certain insecurity about the Greek reaction to his demands, as is evidenced by his issuance of supplementary memoranda in which he instructed his envoys to be prudent and cautious, to gloss over the oral clerical oath if it could not immediately be secured, and, in his own words, "to progress circumspectly lest something be said or done by you whereby the union might be broken." [46] Nevertheless, in order not to inhibit the efforts of his legates unduly, Nicholas drew up yet another

---

[43] The practice of sending legates with full authority began early in the Roman church, and by the thirteenth century was standard practice. See *Catholic Encyclopedia*, IX (1910) 118–119.

[44] In line with this reasoning, the patriarchal title of οἰκουμενικός, to which the papacy had in the past often objected, would now become meaningless and perhaps have to be discarded. For the significance of this title, especially from the Western point of view, see V. Laurent, "Le titre de Patriarche Oecuménique et Michel Cérulaire à propos de deux de ses sceaux inédits," *Miscellanea G. Mercati*, III (Vatican, 1946) esp. 385–386.

[45] Pach., 387, ll. 2ff.

[46] Also in *Reg. Nic.*, no. 377, 131: "si id omnino haberi non possit, dimictatur sub cauta et colorata dilatione." Also no. 376, 131: "ne per vos aliquid dicatur vel fiat, per quod negotium rumpatur." Cf. Demski, *Papst Nikolaus*, 220, who does not think that Nicholas mitigated his demands.

directive in which he ordered his instructions to be carried out completely, "lest through some crafty astuteness the union might suffer damage." [47] The Pope, it appears, wanted all of his demands fulfilled if at all possible, but without at the same time so alienating the Greek people that further attempts at union would be futile.[47a]

To summarize our analysis of the significance of this document: in explicitly demanding acceptance of the *filioque*, permitting at best only a partial retention of Greek rites, imposing a personal oath on all Greek clerics together even with a demand for confirmation of their offices, and proposing, finally, the appointment of a permanent legate to the Golden Horn, the directive reveals that what Pope Nicholas sought through union was nothing less than complete submission of the Greek church to Rome. In addition, the memorandum provides insight into the diplomacy as well as the mentality of a pope significant in the history of the schism, thus helping us to understand, from the confidential words of Pope Nicholas himself, to what extent the underlying Greek distrust of papal motivations and fear of the possible consequences of Michael's unionist policy were justifiable.

Armed with the papal directives and accompanied by the imperial envoys still at the Curia, the papal legates left for Constantinople in the first part of 1279.[48] In the meantime, however, the situation in the Greek capital had deteriorated as a result of the public ceremony of union at Blachernae and a new incident involving the Patriarch John Bekkos. Surprisingly enough, Bekkos, Michael's chief supporter in his conflict with the clergy, had incurred imperial displeasure, as a result, it seems, of too active intervention in behalf of anti-unionist Greek exiles.[49] Conse-

---

[47] *Reg. Nic.*, no. 372, 127: "ne per alicujus dolosam astutiam dispendia turbationis incurrat." This document, incidentally, is attributed by Martène, *Ampl. coll.*, VII, col. 257, to Pope Innocent V.

[47a] In another accompanying memorandum, *Reg. Nic.*, no. 371, 126, the legates were given authority to hear confessions, excommunicate, and impose the interdict on the Greeks.

[48] The date is known from an Angevin safe-conduct issued to them on 7 January (*Arch. st. it.*, ser. IV [1878] II, 193).

[49] Héfelé, *Conciles*, VI, 213; and Chapman, 123.

quently, at an inquest in which accusations were made against him, Bekkos offered his resignation and on 2 March 1279 retired to a monastery.[50] But his withdrawal served only to provide the masses with a new martyr and thus to increase still further the hatred against the Emperor. Such was the situation when the papal embassy met the Emperor near Adrianople, some distance from Constantinople, where Michael had been called by state affairs.[51]

Michael's position was, to say the least, difficult. The disgrace of the Patriarch and the expected violent opposition of his prelates to the new papal demands would not be easy to explain to the envoys. This was another instance in Michael's career in which the challenge before him demanded the exercise of all his resourcefulness.

First of all, with regard to the Patriarch's retirement, Michael declared to the envoys that the prelate was in need of a short rest. Instructing Bekkos to remain silent about the incident, Michael then prevailed upon him to receive the envoys at his retreat in the monastery of the Mangana.[52] The trouble with the Patriarch was thus for the moment satisfactorily concealed; but it would be more difficult to justify to the Greek clergy the fresh papal demands.[53] Realizing that the explosion of indignation which would result must at any cost be prevented or at least concealed from the legates, Michael, before permitting a meeting of the ambassadors and his prelates, convoked the latter in

---

[50] Pach., 449ff.

[51] Pach., 455, l. 14.

[52] Pach., 455, ll. 15–19ff.

[53] Pach., 456, ll. 4–17. Pachymeres' passage is significant because he describes the Greek attitude to union and to this embassy in particular, saying that the papal envoys came to declare that "not by words but by acts is peace to be achieved, and that if we sincerely desire union with them, we ought to make public confession of the same faith. What caused them to be more demanding was the railleries of the schismatics (as they called us), who, conversing with many of their friars [in Pera], affirmed that the union was only a farce and that the real test would be reciting the symbol with the *filioque*. They [the anti-unionists] thought thereby to embarrass the Emperor and to force him to break the peace or openly to renounce the ancient doctrine, and thus to authorize their resistance to the separation."

synod. In a frank speech before them he completely cast aside any remaining pretence at moral justification for union and, more openly than ever before, exposed his policy of pure expediency. According to Pachymeres, he said:

You know very well with how much difficulty the present accord was achieved . . . I realize that I have used force against many of you and have given offense to many friends, even grieving my own family . . . I thought that the affair would now be ended and that the Latins would demand nothing more, as I promised you in my golden bulls in the church. But some of us, who, I am convinced, are attempting to create differences (I do not know why unless they spoke thus in order to test us and to stir up trouble), when conversing with friars in Pera, called the union a farce and a fraud. They declared that further proof of union should be demanded. This then is the purpose of the present embassy. I wished to speak to you first and to inform you of this so that upon hearing them [the papal envoys] you will not suddenly become disturbed and accuse me of bad faith when you observe my conduct towards them. God is my witness that I will not alter one accent or one iota of the faith. I promise to hold aloft as a standard this divine symbol of our fathers and to combat not only the Latins but any people that would dispute this matter. If I receive the envoys warmly it will do you no harm. It is my belief that we should receive them cordially and treat them kindly, lest . . . we stir up new game, since there is now a new Pope who is not so well-disposed to us as was Gregory.[54]

As a result of this masterful speech the sting was removed in advance from the papal demands, and all went as the Emperor desired: the synod listened calmly to the envoys and no manifestation of discontent was provoked. To convince the envoys completely of his sincerity, the Basileus had them conducted to the imperial prisons, where they could see with their own eyes anti-unionist clerics and even close relatives of the Emperor in irons.[55] It was at this time that Palaeologus handed over to the nuncios for punishment by the Pope the anti-unionist monks, Ignatios and

---

[54] Pach., 457–459. The words "stir up new game" in the last sentence refer undoubtedly to Charles of Anjou. This speech as reported by Pachymeres, like others in his work, is probably stylized and influenced by the tradition of Greek historical writing.

[55] Pach., 459, ll. 10ff.

Meletios. (But they were received benevolently by Nicholas, who returned them to Michael with a request for clemency.)[56]

Though Palaeologus had reason to be satisfied with his handling of a difficult situation, the task of executing the demands of Pope Nicholas still remained. After the subsequent return of Bekkos to the patriarchal throne on 6 August 1279 [57] (doubtless the presence of the nuncios and public opinion helped to force his recall), a council, as directed by the Pope, was convoked. There the clergy were again asked to take an individual oral oath with the *filioque* as prescribed by Nicholas, but once more they remained firm in their refusal.[58] Unable to induce his prelates to comply,[59] Michael could secure only another declaration in writing similar to that of April 1277. This time, however, few prelates would sign. If we can believe Pachymeres, the Emperor, in his desperate need to impress the Pope with a long list of signatures, even had a notary forge the signatures of non-existent bishops.[60]

The clerical declaration contained a fresh profession of faith including the teaching of the *filioque*. But instead of the unequivocal Latin confession demanded by Nicholas, the prelates' declaration again carefully avoided the Greek expression (*ekporeuesthai*) for the *filioque*, employing ambiguous circumlocutions in its place.[61]

[56] Pach., 462, ll. 15ff.; also 463, ll. 7–9, noting that the imperial as well as the papal action was intended as flattery.

[57] Pach., 461, ll. 8–10.

[58] On this see the letter of Andronikos to the Pope in Raynaldus, a. 1280, § 19–22; also reference to it in George Metochites, *Historia dogmatica* (ed. Mai) *Patrum nova bibl.*, VIII, Bk. I, no. 79, p. 104. Cf. Grumel, *Dict. théol. cath.*, IX, pt. 1, col. 1398.

[59] At this point Pach., 461, l. 11, mistakenly calls the pope Urban. Possinus, who did the glossary section for the Bonn ed. of Pachymeres, believes (764) that Pachymeres has confused "Urban" with "Orsini," the family name of Nicholas.

[60] Pach., 461, esp.: πολλαῖς μὲν ὑπογραφαῖς μήτ' ὄντων ἐπισκόπων μήτ' ἐπισκοπῶν οὐσῶν, μιᾷ καὶ τῇ αὐτῇ χειρὶ τοῦ γραφέως. Pachymeres says that Michael hoped his list would not appear inferior to that of a Latin synod, which generally contained more than 100 episcopal signatures; he is uncertain of Bekkos' involvement in the forgery.

[61] Pach., 462, ll. 4ff. See also a letter of Andronikos sent to the Pope as a result of the papal embassy, in Raynaldus, a. 1280, § 19–22. The letter, devoted almost exclusively to repeating professions of faith, has been omitted in Gay,

In conformity with Nicholas' demands, and for the second time since Lyons,[62] Michael and Andronikos, on 1 September 1279, at the Blachernae palace in Constantinople, renewed their oaths to the Holy See before the papal legates.[63] A signed copy of the imperial oaths with the letter and signatures of the clergy was then sent to the Pope.[64] These two documents, it should be noted, were the sole accomplishment of the elaborate embassy of the Bishop of Grosseto and his companions. At the departure of the embassy, the anti-unionist agitation in the capital reached its climax.[64a] To combat the increasing opposition to his policy the Emperor was forced to mete out graver punishments. Imprisonment, torture, and exile became commonplace, and it was at this time that the penalty of death was decreed for the reading or possession of *libelli* against the regime.[65]

While the papal legates were in the East, Pope Nicholas informed Charles of his wish to begin negotiations for a truce and eventual peace between Sicily and Byzantium. Thus on 18 October 1278 Nicholas wrote to Charles that he would renew political negotiations with the Emperor, while, simultaneously, Charles and Philip should prepare envoys properly empowered to open negotiations with Palaeologus at the Angevin court.[66] Evidently the Pope was prepared, if necessary, to have the pourparlers carried on in Rome before the papal Curia itself.[67]

Reg. Nic. Cf. also George Metochites, *Historia dogmatica,* VIII, 104 and Bekkos, *Apologia, no.* 2, in Migne, *PG,* vol. CXLI, col. 1011.

[62] Contrary to general opinion (e.g., Viller, "La question de l'union," *Rev. d'hist. éccl.,* XVII, 264), it was not three times but twice after Lyons that Michael was required to take an oath to Rome, first under John XXI (April 1277) and now under Nicholas III. On this see Grumel, "Les ambassades," 442, note 2.

[63] See Raynaldus, a. 1280, § 19–22, where the date is wrongly given as September of 1280. Cf. Dölger, *Regesten,* no. 2041, and Grumel, "Les ambassades," 447.

[64] For the letter see A. Theiner and F. Miklosich, *Monumenta spectantia ad unionem ecclesiarum Graecae et Romanae* (Vienna, 1872) 14, l. 18. Also cf. Dölger, *Regesten,* no. 2041.

[64a] See V. Grumel, "Le II⁰ concile de Lyon et la réunion de l'église grecque," *Dict. théol. cath.,* IX, col. 1391. Also Evert-Kapessova, "La société byzantine, etc.," 39, note 97.

[65] See above, Chapter 11, text and notes 79–84.

[66] Gay, *Reg. Nic.,* 131, no. 378: "inibi opportuno tempore."

[67] *Ibid.,* 132: "vel si ipsi imperatori et tibi non videtur hoc posse in partibus

It was probably in the first part of 1280 that the Bishop of Grosseto and his companions returned to Italy with the imperial documents and the synodical letter of the Greek clergy. No doubt from a political standpoint Nicholas was far from pleased with the results accomplished, since Michael made no reply to his suggestions for a Greco-Angevin peace. Manifestly the Emperor did not desire this, as success in the continuing undeclared war in Romania favored his designs. Cognizant of this fact, Charles meanwhile redoubled his efforts to alter papal policy by emphasizing Michael's use of union as a cover for war on the Latins of Romania. Yet, though Charles personally remained for long periods at the Curia,[68] his efforts were in vain. Nicholas was determined to establish a firm union, but not at the price of an Angevin Constantinople.

Nicholas now sent a new mission to the Greek capital, inquiring severely why his demands had not been fulfilled. The bearers of the letters, Marchus and Marchetus,[69] were granted a lengthy audience by the Emperor, who ordered that a detailed summary of their discussion be drawn up in Latin by the protonotarios of the imperial Latin interpreters, Ogerius.[70] This document was then delivered to the papal messengers as an *aide-mémoire* in reporting to the Pope.

In the report composed by Ogerius, it is explained that the

---

illis de facili fieri, aut securitatibus debitis roborari, cum apocrisarios ejusdem Paleologi . . . ad hoc concurrentibus coram nobis, etc." Printed thus also in Wadding, *Ann. Min.*, V, 51. This passage does not appear in Chapman, who instead (135 and note 4) quotes another passage from Martène (*Ampl. coll.*, VII, cols. 275–276) which does not appear in the letter as published by Gay. Chapman's passage includes the phrase "ita quod ei vel tibi sedationis ipsius impedimentum non valeat imputari," which Chapman translates as "the present occupation [Greek] of Constantinople was not an obstacle to negotiations." It should be rendered "[Carry out our request] so that you or he may not be accused of impeding a settlement of this matter." An important difference in meaning! See also Potthast, *Regesta*, no. 21478.

[68] Sternfeld, *Der Kardinal Johann Gaëtan Orsini*, 283. Also see Chapman, 134, note 2, who refers to Pope Nicholas a quotation of Sanudo that applies instead to Charles.

[69] On the ambassadors see Norden, 593, note 1, and Grumel, "Les ambassades," 444. Cf. Dölger, *Regesten*, no. 2044.

[70] For document (the only surviving record of the embassy) see Gay, *Reg.*

Emperor is "unable at present to fulfill his business as he has done before"[71] because of grave external and internal difficulties in the Empire. As evidence Ogerius declares that immediately after the imperial pledge of fidelity to the Pope, two subjects of the Empire, the Bastard John and his brother Nikephoros, began to create disturbances.[72] When the Basileus requested the two Princes' adherence to the union, they refused, whereupon the Emperor had them excommunicated by nuncios of the Holy See (!) and the Greek church.[73] The Emperor, continues Ogerius, then sent an army against the "heretics," but its commanders, among them close relatives of the Emperor, deserted to the enemy. Another disturber of the union, the report complains, is the Greek ruler of Trebizond (situated on the southeast coast of the Black Sea). Seeking to replace the "heretical" Michael, this ruler has even usurped the imperial title,[74] an act to which he was pushed by anti-unionist Greeks and Latins from Constantinople.[75]

Nic., 134, no. 384, undated. Raynaldus evidently wrongly lists it under a. 1278, § 13. Cf. Grumel, "Les ambassades," 442, who places it during the first three months of 1280.

[71] Gay, Reg. Nic., 135, no. 384: "quod non potest . . . sanctus imperator complere ad presens negotia sua, etc."

[72] Ibid., 135A, esp.: "Servi et submanuales imperii sacramentum . . . fidelitatis et ligii homagii." Note the mention of the Western concept of liege homage in this imperial letter, written originally in Latin.

[73] Ibid., 135A, esp.: "expositam excommunicationem a nuntiis sancte apostolice sedis, etc." This assertion of excommunication by papal nuncios seems directly contrary to Nicholas' statement of refusal.

[74] Ibid., 136A. Cf. Pach., 519–520. Also J. Fallmerayer, Geschichte des Kaiserthums von Trapezunt (Munich, 1827) 139ff.; W. Miller, Trebizond, the Last Greek Empire (London, 1926) 28–29; and esp. A. Vasiliev, "The Foundation of the Empire of Trebizond," Speculum, XI (1936) 32–34, who shows that (contrary to the meaning implied in Ogerius' report) the Trapezuntine rulers had assumed the imperial title already before this time. Michael justifiably looked upon the orthodox "Emperor" of Trebizond, who himself had aspirations to Constantinople (see Vasiliev, 33), as a potential rival for the allegiance of Constantinopolitan anti-unionists. Moreover, it was even possible that Trebizond might join Charles's grand coalition against him. (See del Giudice, Cod. dipl., I, 219, mentioning the appearance of Provençal merchants with letters from Charles at the Trapezuntine court in 1266 and 1267.) In 1282 Michael finally succeeded in arranging an alliance with John, ruler of Trebizond, by giving him one of his daughters in marriage.

[75] Gay, Reg. Nic., 136, no. 384: "ad eundem principem Trapesunde homines

As disrupters of union Ogerius also lists female relatives of the Emperor, in particular Michael's sisters and their families, who, however, have been imprisoned and their property confiscated. He expatiates once more on the threat to union of the Bastard of Thessaly, who has given refuge to anti-unionist Greeks. And he complains also of the unremitting aid provided by the Latin lords of Thebes, Athens, Negropont, and the Morea to the Bastard and Nikephoros against the Emperor. The report concludes with the claim that in a recent battle against the Negropontine Latins, an inferior imperial fleet and army was able to emerge victorious only with Divine aid.[76]

This detailed account with its mass of evidence was, of course, an eloquent plea for greater papal understanding of the complexities of the imperial position, and in particular another, but more subtle, request for excommunication of the Angeloi princes and their Latin allies. Above all, Michael's enumeration of internal and external pressures — even his mention of the divinely inspired victory against the Latins — was an attempt to emphasize the precariousness of the imperial position in the face of the combined force of Charles and his Latin coalition, the Angeloi, Trebizond, and Greek traitors within the Empire. The inevitable result of this formidable opposition, it is implied, would be complete destruction of union and the fall of Constantinople to Charles unless Nicholas would mitigate his demands and continue to oppose an Angevin attack on Byzantium.

About this time Michael dispatched another envoy to the Curia, Mandas (also called Merkurios), Domestic of Hagia Sophia. Although the precise purpose of this embassy is obscure, we do know that while traversing the Regno (perhaps in the company of Marchus and Marchetus), Mandas was seized by Angevin agents and subsequently released only at papal intervention. Significantly, this marked the first occasion that Charles

---

cum ipsis intimationibus, erant et Latini simul cum eisdem transmissis, cooperantes ipsam legationem ipsorum."
[76] *Ibid.*, 134 and 136B.

had actually dared to seize an imperial ambassador to the Holy See.[77]

Whether Marchus and Marchetus reached the Curia before or after Nicholas' death on 22 August 1280 is not certain. In any event, the death of the Pope before he could frame a reply to Palaeologus permits us only to speculate on Nicholas' reaction to the report of Ogerius.[77a]

THE WAR IN ACHAIA AND ALBANIA

On 1 May 1278 Prince William Villehardouin of Achaia died, one year after the decease of his son-in-law and heir-designate, Philip of Anjou.[78] At William's death Philip's father Charles, in accordance with the treaty of Viterbo signed in 1267 by William, Baldwin, and Charles, became direct seigneur of Achaia and liege-lord of all Romania.[79] This development seemed menacing for Michael Palaeologus, but in reality it was to prove favorable. For in place of a native-born prince solicitous of Achaia's welfare, the territory now acquired a foreign, absentee ruler, already burdened by the administration of numerous realms and deeply absorbed in his projected conquest of the Greek Empire.

---

[77] Pach., 475, ll. 16ff., esp.: περιπεσὼν τοῖς τοῦ ῥηγὸς ἀλίσκεται . . . καὶ προσταχθὲν αὐτίκα παρὰ τοῦ πάπα, φυλακῆς ἀπολύεται. Cf. Dölger Regesten, nos. 2044–2045.

[77a] In the opinion of Grumel, "Les ambassades," 447, and Dict. théol. cath., IX, pt. 1, cols. 1401–1402, Michael "formally disobeyed" a papal warning carried by Marchus and Marchetus, and this "disobedience" suffices to explain Michael's subsequent excommunication and the end of the union. (But cf. L. Bréhier, ch. XIX, Cambridge Med. Hist., IV, 613: "Palaeologus struggled to the end to uphold the union." Even Pach., 476, ll. 3–4, says, "The Emperor did all he could to uphold the superficial union.") The thesis of Michael's disobedience, however, besides being uncorroborated (there is, unfortunately, a dearth of documents for these particular years), must also be considered — as it has not been — in the light of the important diplomatic activity being carried on at this time in Constantinople, Aragon, Sicily, and the Curia. On this see Chapter 14, esp. section 3, and text and note 67.

[78] On William's death see Greek Chron. Morea, ll. 7753ff. and French Chron., par. 534. On Philip see Longnon, L'Empire Latin, 249.

[79] On 26 and 27 August 1278 Charles sent to Achaia as his vicar-general Galeran d'Ivry (not Rosso de Sully as stated in the French Chron., par. 539) to receive oaths of fidelity from the lords of Romania, "tam Latinis tam Grecis." See Arch. st. it., ser. IV (1878) I, 433.

The inadequacy of the Angevin administration of Achaia is attested by the frequency with which the *baillis* whom Charles appointed to govern the principality replaced each other.[80] Still more revealing is the fact that the Greek population and even the Frankish feudatories (the former possibly affected by Charles's exactions for a war against fellow-Greeks) resisted the rapacity of the royal officials and not infrequently rose in rebellion.[81]

The internal disorders which pervaded the principality after the death of William enabled the imperial troops of Mistra and Monemvasia successfully to wage almost continuous war against the *baillis* of Achaia.[82] Indeed, after the failure of the last important Achaian expedition against the Greeks at Scorta in 1276 [83] and the disastrous defeat later in Arcadia of the Latins under the command of Gautier de Sumeroso,[84] the *baillis* had to remain almost entirely on the defensive. Palaeologus' forces, accordingly, were able to extend their conquests along the coasts of the Peloponnese and into Arcadia. As a consequence, Charles was forced to maintain troops in Achaia and deprive himself of strength he was massing for the campaign against Constantinople.[85]

It was probably this lack of success against the Greeks of Mistra and Monemvasia, together with the costly flow of troops and money to Achaia after 1278,[86] that convinced Charles how

[80] For their names see Zakythinos, *Despotat*, I, 57.

[81] Cerone, "La sovranità napoletana," *Arch. st. prov. nap.*, XLII (1917) 60–61, 67.

[82] Except for a short truce in 1281 for the exchange of prisoners. See Rennell Rodd, *The Princes of Achaia and the Chronicles of Morea* (London, 1907) I, 267 and Zakythinos, *Despotat*, I, 57–59.

[83] Greek *Chron.*, ll. 7165–7243, and French *Chron.*, par. 497.

[84] See *Historiae Sabae Malaspinae continuatio* in R. Gregorio, *Bibliotheca scriptorum qui res in Sicilia gestas sub Aragonum imperio retulere*, II (Palermo, 1792) 336: "Gualterius de Sumeroso per Graecos interemptus in conflictu extitit, et gens tota periit." On a putative relative of Sumeroso, held prisoner by the Greeks, see Mazzoleni ed. of De Lellis, *Gli atti perduti*, I[1], 573, no. 57.

[85] *Historiae Sabae Malaspinae continuatio*, etc., II, 336–337: "Erat enim Regis intentio, ut terra . . . manuteneri tantum, et defendi valeret [et] milites tantum . . . ad defensionem . . . destinabat."

[86] It was probably an aim of Charles's reorganization of the Achaian mint at Clarenza in 1279 to produce coins with which to pay his troops in Achaia and Albania. See G. Monti, "La Zecca di Clarenza sotto Carlo I," *Nuovi studi angioini*

GREECE IN 1278

little could be accomplished against Constantinople in an expedition via the Morea. Moreover, a direct naval attack on the metropolis was still not feasible because of papal opposition and especially the failure of his attempts to conclude an alliance with Venice. Abandoning Achaia, therefore, as his main base, Charles directed his attention to strengthening his positions in Albania and Epirus. From there he could easily move against nearby Macedonia, whence, with the aid of his Balkan allies, he could launch a land expedition directly against the capital.[87]

Charles's concentration on Albania and Epirus was further necessitated by Palaeologus' penetration of this area, a fact also of concern to the Despot Nikephoros, who particularly feared imperial corsairs operating off the Epirot coast.[88] There is a record of negotiations for a treaty between Charles and Nikephoros as early as 1276–1277,[89] and we may believe that in 1278, at Clarentza in the Morea, Ludovico de Roheriis, a knight of Charles, received the homage of Nikephoros for his sovereign.[90] But it was apparently not until 10 April 1279 that Charles was able to make a formal alliance with Nikephoros, whereby, presumably in exchange for military aid against Palaeologus, the Greek prince declared himself the vassal of Charles, evidently gave up his son as security, and even ceded to the King important areas of Epirus. These consisted of the castles of Panormum, Butrinto, Syboto, and Vonitza, all of which had formerly constituted part of the

---

(Trani, 1937) 597ff. To maintain such mercenaries Charles often had products of Apulia sold in the Orient, especially in Negropont and Clarenza (see Carabellese, 41).

[87] On Charles's policy see also Saba Malaspina, "Rerum Sicularum historia," in *Cronisti e scrittori sincroni napoletani*, ed. Del Re, II (Naples, 1868) 314.

[88] On these Greek pirates see *Arch. st. it.*, ser. IV, I, 247. Also *ibid.*, 12, Angevin order of 19 March 1278 regarding a chain to protect the harbor of Brindisi, possibly from Greek corsairs.

[89] *Arch. st. it.*, ser. III, XXV, 181, Angevin rescript dated 12 June 1276 concerning an oath of Nikephoros to William of Achaia, in behalf of Charles, regarding certain Achaian territory to be received. See also Carabellese, 43 and note 2, Angevin safe-conduct for "Stomatos et Focinos nuncios magnifici viri Nichifori despoti." Cf. 105, note 4. On the relations between the Bastard John and Charles at this time, cf. Carabellese, 43 and note 1, and 36, mentioning a concession of Charles to Thessalian silk dealers.

[90] See Carabellese, 42. Cf. Hopf, *Geschichte*, 301A, according to whom Nikephoros had sworn homage to Charles in July of 1276.

dowry of Nikephoros' sister, Helen, at the time of her marriage to Manfred.[91] Most significant of these concessions was Butrinto, a port for the imperial-held fortress of Berat, which, strategically situated in the mountain fastness of central Albania, was the gateway to Macedonia.

THE ANGEVIN LAND OFFENSIVE AGAINST PALAEOLOGUS: THE BATTLE OF BERAT (1280–1281)

In conformity with his strategy of attacking the Emperor by land via Albania and Epirus,[92] Charles sent to those areas on 13 August 1279 a new vicar-general, the famous Hugo le Rousseau de Sully.[93] Sully, an energetic, headstrong, haughty Frenchman,[94] received a steady influx of troops and supplies from the Regno throughout 1279 and the first part of 1280 with which to fortify the Angevin fortresses in Albania.[95] Provisions and siege engines, artisans and Saracen archers were all sent across the Adriatic.[96] And in the latter part of 1280 an increasing number of ships laden with technical specialists — masons, engineers, and carpenters — in addition to money and horses were also dispatched.[97] All this

[91] See *Acta Albaniae*, 113, no. 390, letter of Charles concerning "magnifico viro domino Nichiforo despoto Comnino duce castrum Bothroton [*sic*] et alia omnia castra, casalia et terras, que de terris . . . quas tenuerunt olim Manfredus . . . et Philippus Chinardus, ad manus ipsius despoti devenerunt, etc." Cf. *Arch. st. it.*, ser. IV, II, 199; *ibid.*, IV, 17; and a suggestive passage of Pach., 508, esp.: τῷ ῥηγὶ δὲ Καρούλῳ . . . φιλίως εἶχον καὶ κατὰ συνθήκας εἰρήνευον. On the complicated history of this dowry, parts of which at one time belonged to Michael II, Manfred, Philip Chinardo, Charles of Anjou, Palaeologus, and Nikephoros, see especially Chapters 3 and 9 above.
[92] See Greg., 146, ll. 4–5: "Having equipped many naval forces, he prepared more land forces."
[93] *Arch. st. it.*, ser. IV, II, 355.
[94] See Pach., 509, ll. 14–19, who calls him "Ros Solymas" and attributes the name "Ros" to the resemblance of Sully's red hair to that of the (Varangian) Russians! On Sully see also Greg., 146, l. 6 and Sanudo, *Istoria*, 129 ("Rosso de Solino"). Cf. further Buchon, *Nouvelles recherches*, II, 231, and G. Typaldos, "'Ο 'Ρὼς Σολυμᾶς τῶν Βυζαντινῶν, etc.", 'Επετηρὶς 'Εταιρείας Βυζαντινῶν Σπουδῶν, II (1925) 316ff.
[95] Carabellese, 103–104 and *Acta Albaniae*, 123, no. 410.
[96] *Acta Albaniae*, 125, no. 413. Cf. Cohn, "Storia della flotta," *Arch. st. sic. orien.*, XXIX, 40.
[97] See *Arch. st. it.*, ser. IV, III, 20 and esp. *Acta Albaniae*, 125–133. Even

was in preparation for an expedition, which, according to the threefold testimony of Pachymeres, Gregoras, and Sanudo, was to move across Greece to Thessalonica and ultimately against Constantinople itself.[98]

During the last part of 1280 [99] an army of about two thousand Angevin knights and Saracen archers together with six thousand infantrymen,[100] all under the command of Sully, suddenly moved across Albania, seized Kanina, and laid siege to the strongly fortified imperial town of Berat, the key to the Via Egnatia and all of Macedonia.[101] As Sully moved up his siege machines to invest the mountain fortress, its Greek governor relayed an urgent request to Constantinople for reinforcements. The Emperor, ap-

materials for making Greek fire ("de igne greco") were sent to Sully, ibid., 127, no. 422.

[98] Pach., 509: μέχρι καὶ πόλεως Θεσσαλονίκης, ἔτι δὲ καὶ πόλεως αὐτῆς πεζῇ συμβαλεῖν. Greg., 146, ll. 7-9: "And he planned nothing else than to take the fortress of Bellegrada and the principal fortresses of Macedonia and then to march unhindered to Byzantium." Sanudo, Istoria, 129: "[Charles] intendendo acquistar l'Imperio di Romania mandò Miser Rosso de Solino"; and 131, where Sanudo records that after his defeat at Berat Charles "rimase molto fallito del suo disegno, ch'era d'andar con l'essercito suo in sin in Costantinopoli." Cf. Norden, 622, according to whom Charles hoped to establish at Berat a base of operations for a land expedition against Constantinople.

[99] The exact date of the beginning of the siege is uncertain. Hopf, Geschichte, 324, and Chapman, 140, refer to what must be the start of the siege as August and September, respectively, of 1280; Longnon, L'Empire Latin, 259, also speaks of the summer of that year (cf. Norden, 622). One of the chief sources, Sanudo, Istoria, 132, writes thus of the defeat itself: "la rotta di Belgrado fù nel principio dell' anno secondo del Ducato de Miser Zuan Dandolo da S. Moisè" — which would be at the beginning of 1281. Since we know that the siege of Berat was of considerable duration (see Sanudo, Istoria, 129: "andando l'ossidione in longo") and that the Greek army probably approached Berat in March of 1281 (see below, note 111), the final defeat of Sully would therefore seem to have taken place in early April of 1281 (Hopf, 325).

[100] Sanudo, Istoria, 129: "circa due mila e più Uomini d'arme e circa sei mila Pedoni, trà quali eran molti Saraceni." Cf. Pach., 509, who records that 3,000 men crossed the Adriatic. According to him Sully and his commanders were so confident of victory that already in advance they divided up the Greek territories to be conquered. See above, Chapter 3, text of note 54, for a similar passage regarding the battle of Pelagonia.

[101] Berat (Greek, Bellegrada) had been recovered by Palaeologus from Charles in 1274. With Avlona and Kanina it formed the southern belt of fortresses in Albania. On this see P. Alexander, "A Chrysobull of Emperor Andronicus II," Byzantion, XV (1940-1941) 189. Chapman, 140, note 4, refers to Berat as "the capital of Albania."

parently surprised at the speed with which troops and siege engines had been transported across the Adriatic, now became apprehensive lest the possible fall of Berat permit the army to cross as easily to Thessalonica and even to the capital.[102] For, as already mentioned, Constantinople's defenses had been prepared mainly for an attack by sea rather than a land assault.[103] To add to the Emperor's alarm, the unionist struggle was now at its very height, and he had reason to fear that Charles's coalition with the Latins of Romania and the Angeloi princes might attract anti-Palaeologan Greeks as well as Venetians of the capital. In this connection we may note that the Greco-Venetian treaty had already expired in March of 1279. It was thus for the Emperor an extremely critical situation.

Quickly assembling an army of his best troops, Palaeologus put in charge his most trusted and capable generals: as commander the Grand Domestic Michael Tarchaneiotes, with subordinates the Emperor's son-in-law Michael Angelos,[104] the Grand Stratopedarch John Synadenos, and the Tatas of the Court, the eunuch Andronikos Enopolites.[105] In order to encourage his troops and subjects (to all of whom Charles's ultimate objective and his intense hatred of the Greeks were by now, of course, well known) [106] the Emperor ordered the recitation of public prayers for the security of the Empire. There is a striking passage in Pachymeres relating that after a night-long supplication to God for victory and performance of the *euchelaion* (annointing with holy oil), the Patriarch and all the prelates of the capital blessed and distributed to the troops pieces of papyrus sprinkled with holy oil (*phakelloi*), which, it would seem, were to be carried into battle as a kind of phylaktery.[107] It is a curious irony that in

[102] Pach., 510, ll. 15ff.

[103] See above, Chapter 6, section 4.

[104] Though brother to Nikephoros and John the Bastard, Michael Angelos had become pro-imperial through marriage to a daughter of Palaeologus. See Pach., 510, ll. 1–2; 439, l. 19; and 440, ll. 9–10. Cf. Dölger, *Regesten*, no. 2032.

[105] Pach., 512, ll. 1–8.

[106] See Autobiography of Palaeologus, IX, 7: "Charles had declared that no one hated anyone as he hated us." Cf. also Pach., 512, l. 7.

[107] Pach., 511–512, esp. 511: φακέλλους δὲ παπύρων ποιήσαντας τῷ καθαγνισθέντι ἐλαίῳ βάπτειν. Also Greg., 147, l. 1.

this moment of grave external peril, Michael, like so many of his predecessors, turned to what alone could provide unity and moral support for his people — the Byzantine church!

The siege of Berat continued. Along with heavy reinforcements and provisions,[108] Charles took care to send letters to Sully directing the conduct of the siege and emphasizing his intense personal interest in the campaign.[109] On 6 December 1280, while joyously commending Sully for his capture of the suburbs surrounding Berat, Charles ordered him to take the town by storm.[110] This was doubtless in anticipation of the arrival of Greek reinforcements.

It was probably in March of 1281 that the Greek army approached Berat.[111] Advancing cautiously in obedience to imperial instructions to avoid an open battle and to rely instead on ambushes and raids, the Grand Domestic Tarchaneiotes sought first to provide provisions for the town's starving people. This he did by loading rafts during the night on the Asounes River which ran by the citadel and floating them down to the besieged inhabitants.[112] But the maneuver was soon discovered by the Latin leaders, who determined to prevent further provisioning of the fortress.

At this juncture it appears that Sully decided to survey the situation personally.[113] Accompanied by a small party of twenty-five picked men, the audacious commander approached the imperial troops on guard at the river. But suddenly imperial Turkish auxiliaries, waiting in ambush nearby (evidently they had warn-

[108] *Acta Albaniae*, 129, no. 431; and 131, nos. 438 and 440, esp. mention of 300 slingers; 128, no. 425, reference to carpenters, engineers, and *petraroli* (should be *petraboli*, rock throwers?).

[109] *Acta Albaniae*, 131, letter no. 438. Charles wrote to Sully "ad captionem castri Belligradi, que ultra quam dici valeat cordi nostro residet." Cf. 129, no. 431. These are perhaps additional evidence that Berat was the prelude to greater conquests.

[110] *Ibid.*, 131, no. 441. In a letter of 26 December 1280 (132, no. 443), Achillas Straquagatus (!), apparently a Greek in Angevin service, is mentioned.

[111] See Pach., 512. Greg., 147; also Léonard, *Les Angevins de Naples*, 134, who says it was April.

[112] Pach., 512, ll. 11ff. Cf. Sanudo, *Istoria*, 129: "con ingenio fornissero quel luogo di Vittuarie." The Asounes (modern Lioum) is not to be confused with the Booses River which was situated on the other side of Berat; see Pach., 510.

[113] Sanudo, *loc. cit.*: "volea andar a soraveder l'essercito de Nemici."

ing of Sully's approach), wheeled out, isolated the Latins, and seized Sully, whose horse was shot from under him.[114] While Sully's entourage tried to escape, the rest of the Angevin troops became so panic-stricken by the capture of their leader that they too took to flight. Encouraged by this success, the entire imperial army — including even troops from within the besieged town — followed in hot pursuit, with the Greek archers, as formerly at Pelagonia, aiming at the horses of the heavily-armed Latin knights. Most of the Latin troops and generals together with an enormous booty fell into Greek hands. Only those Latins escaped who were able to cross the river Booses on the other side of the town and outride their pursuers to Kanina.[115]

The prisoners, among them Sully,[116] were taken to Constantinople, where they had to take part in an imperial triumph. In chains, on foot or on horseback, they were paraded through the streets of the capital to the taunts and jeers of the Greeks, whose emotions, already inflamed against the Latins by the enforced union, were now raised to an even higher pitch of excitement by this manifest attempt to begin the conquest of the Greek Empire.[117]

[114] Sanudo, *loc. cit.*: "s'incontrò con l'imboscata, che Turchi, ch'eran con li Greci, aveano fatto; e fù preso da loro." Cf. Greg., 147, l. 17, who writes of "ambushes and machinations" on the part of the Greeks; and Pach., 513, l. 14.

[115] Pach., 515, and Sanudo, *Istoria*, 129: "l'essercito s'impaurì talmente, che si mise in fuga, fuggendo il giorno e la notte sequente continuamente, etc." The description presented here has been drawn mainly from Sanudo and partly from Pachymeres and Gregoras. Actually Pachymeres offers a few additional details, for instance, that the capture of the huge Sully was made possible by the stumbling of his horse. According to Pachymeres, 514, ll. 11–12, at dawn of the next morning the Greek soldiers attacked the Latin army, "holding their shields together, each one grasping the piece of papyrus" which had been blessed by the Greek clergy. Also, Pachymeres notes that the onslaught of the Greeks created such panic among the enemy that the Latin cavalry in its precipitous flight cut down many of its own men (Pach., 513–514).

[116] On the fate of Sully see esp. Pach., 519, l. 9, who records that he was incarcerated with the others in the prison of Zeuxippos. Sanudo, *Istoria*, 129, states that after many years he was released and returned to Apulia. Cf. Buchon, *Nouvelles recherches*, II, 231; and Typaldos, " Ὁ Ῥὼς Σολυμᾶς," 316, note 2. Andronikos II, Michael's successor, probably exchanged Sully in 1284 or 1285 for Greek prisoners held in Sicily.

[117] See the very long and dramatic description of the triumph in Pach., 515–519.

For Palaeologus Berat was a spectacular victory.[118] Such was his personal satisfaction that to commemorate the battle he ordered scenes from it, together with other victories "with which God had favored him," to be painted on the walls of the imperial palace of Blachernae.[119]

Despite its importance, the significance of the battle of Berat has not been fully appreciated by most scholars. This is not surprising, as it was overshadowed by the more dramatic Sicilian Vespers which soon followed. In reality, however, after Pelagonia and the reconquest of Constantinople, Berat was probably the most important military encounter of Palaeologus with the Latins during his entire reign. Not only were the vast Angevin preparations of twenty months destroyed and Berat saved, but all of Epirus dominated by Berat and Ioannina soon again fell into imperial hands, a circumstance which enabled Michael's troops to advance on Dyrrachium and Avlona.[120] More important, the victory marked the complete failure of the attempt to launch a land expedition against the capital. Thus, as a result of his defeat at Berat, Charles had to shift his strategy to a sea attack against Constantinople,[121] a fact which now made indispensable the support of the Venetian fleet.

[118] See, e.g., Greg., 148, ll. 6–9: "The Greeks achieved a very great victory without great effort, one which easily surpassed all their hopes." The battle of Berat is, incidentally, not mentioned in Guilland, *L'Europe orientale*, or Vasiliev, *History of the Byzantine Empire* (1952). But the amount of attention and emphasis given to it by *all* the principal sources, including Palaeologus' own Autobiography, IX, 9, attests unquestionably to its importance.

[119] Pach., 517, ll. 2–5. Cf. Cinnamus, *Historia* (Bonn, 1836) 267, who tells of paintings similarly made for the Emperor Manuel I Comnenos (12th century).

[120] See Sanudo, *Istoria*, 129: "alla fine il detto Castello della Gianina, che è in la Vallona, e Duraccio fù restituito all' Imperator de Greci predetto." Actually Dyrrachium remained Angevin to 1284, though the victory at Berat enabled imperial troops to advance to the town. On this see Alexander, "Chrysobull of Andronicus II," 195–196. Also *Acta Albaniae*, 135, no. 457; 137, no. 460; and 138, nos. 461–462, the last, dated January of 1282, being one in which Charles makes provision for the defense of Dyrrachium at the approach of Palaeologus' son. Cf. Dade, 56.

[121] Cf. Greg., 148, ll. 9–12.

334

14

MICHAEL'S TRIUMPH: THE SICILIAN VESPERS

(1282)

however disastrous for Charles, the debacle of the Angevin forces at Berat was not displeasing to Venice, whose lifeline through the Adriatic was seriously threatened by Angevin control of the Straits of Otranto. Thus, while Charles more than ever realized the necessity of securing Venetian aid against Constantinople,[1] there remained the task of allaying the deep-rooted apprehensions of the Commune.

In the meantime, however, conditions in the East had themselves gradually been effecting a change in the Venetian attitude. More than a decade of unsatisfactory truces and accords with Palaeologus had taught the citizens of the Serenissima that not they but the Emperor usually profited from such arrangements. Venetian trade in the Greek Empire had been crippled, Venetian merchants shabbily treated and their privileges all too frequently curtailed. In spite of claims of the Doge for damages, Greek pirates did not cease predatory attacks on the Commune's shipping, and, as time went on, Venice's Aegean island possessions

---

[1] Sanudo, *Istoria*, 132: "per questo (la rotta di Belgrado) il Rè invitò Veneziani a confederazione."

one by one were being stripped from her. Worst of all, Venetian jealousy rankled the more as the prosperity of the rival Genoese continued to increase. Disillusioned therefore in so many respects, Venice at last was ready to disregard traditional anxieties and enter into an alliance with Charles for a joint expedition against Palaeologus.[2]

Preliminary negotiations between the two powers had already commenced, it appears, with the expiration of the Greco-Venetian accord on 19 March 1279. (Indeed, if we are to believe Sanudo, Venetian agents had been in Apulia for four years prior to 1281 conducting pourparlers.) [3] Perhaps as a result, Venice and Charles undertook joint naval operations in the waters of Romania, the main purpose of which was to protect Negropont from Greek corsairs. But their efforts produced few beneficial results. For, as Sanudo reports, on three occasions when Charles dispatched ships to the East, quarrels broke out between the allied forces, a fact which enabled the Greeks to advance upon and devastate the capital city of Negropont.[4]

Eloquent testimony to the inadequacy of Angevin naval strength at this time is provided by an incident in July of 1281, when eight warships were boldly dispatched by the Emperor against the Regno itself: the unexpected appearance of Greek

[2] See, e.g., *Deliberazioni del Maggior Consiglio di Venezia*, ed. R. Cessi, II (Bologna, 1931) 134, no. XXX, dated 7 February 1281, order of the Venetian Grand Council to its consul in Apulia to report carefully on Charles's preparations against Palaeologus and to await further instructions.

[3] *Istoria*, 131: "per questo li Abitatori nostri Veneziani e trattatori stettero in Puglia ben circa quatro anni trattenuti in Puglia con parole dal Rè."

[4] *Ibid.*, 129–130: "Mandò il Rè Carlo trenta Gallee . . . Ma questa Armata non fece danno alcuno all' Imperatore . . . Indi mandò . . . un' altra fiata quindici Gallee, gli Uomini delle quali vennero in controversia con Veneziani et per questo volsero danneggiar e devastar la Campagna di Negroponte. E un altra fiata ne mandò sei . . . li Esserciti e le Armate del Rè Carlo non giovorono punto alla Romania." Actually this passage of Sanudo may come in the wrong place chronologically and could perhaps refer to the supplementary pact signed at Orvieto between Venice and Charles (see below, text for note 14, and cf. Dade, 54). The passage must refer to Michael's reign, however, since succeeding passages of Sanudo doubtless refer to that of Andronikos. On these events in general cf. Bury, "Lombards and Venetians in Euboia," *Jl. Hell. Studies*, VII (1886) 342, who believes that the Negropontine fortresses of Clisura and Argalia were taken by the Latins in ca. 1281 and 1282 respectively.

vessels and their harrying of the Apulian coast near Otranto [5] seem to have provoked near-panic among the Sicilian officials.[6] A more decisive development conducing to the conclusion of a Veneto-Angevin accord was the death on 22 August 1280 of Pope Nicholas III, whose powerful influence had restrained Charles from attacking Constantinople. With his passing and the election to the papal throne of an Angevin adherent (Martin IV), the last remaining political and moral obstacle to a expedition against the Greek capital was removed.

Negotiations now led quickly to a formal alliance, which was signed on 3 July 1281 at the papal city of Orvieto, by Venice, Charles, and the latter's son-in-law, the titular Latin Emperor Philip of Courtenay. The principal articles of this important treaty are the following: [7]

(1) The alliance was to be directed against those powers whose hostility to the Emperor Philip, King Charles, or Venice dated from the period of the Latin occupation of Constantinople.[8] (2) All earlier agreements, rights, and privileges drawn up or possessed in the past by the parties concerned were recognized as valid.[9] Specifically guaranteed was the former Venetian position on the Golden Horn. (3) The Doge, Philip, and Charles, or the latter's eldest son (likewise named Charles), were to partic-

---

[5] See *Arch. st. it.*, ser. IV, IV, 14, order of Charles, dated 25 July 1281, to justiciar of Capitanata to attend personally to the defense of the coastline because "Paleologo mandava quattro grosse navi e quattro galere per infestare quelle marine" (summary of Minieri-Riccio). Cf. also *ibid.*, IV, 9, edict of 30 May 1281, in which Charles speaks of "galee inimicorum per maritimas Apulie discurrunt." Cf. W. Cohn, "Storia della flotta siciliana sotto il governo di Carlo I d'Angiò," *Arch. st. per sic. or.*, XXIX (1933) 46.

[6] See Cohn, *loc. cit.*: "non nisi Galee quatuor piratarum Ydronti venerant et nulla ibi mora protracta ad partes alias diverterunt." On the reaction of the officials, *ibid.*, 47.

[7] For the entire treaty see T.-Th., III, 287–295. For a summary of its terms cf. N. Nicollini, "Sui rapporti diplomatici veneto-napoletani," *Arch. st. prov. nap.*, LX (1935) 264 ff. Léonard, *Les Angevins*, 134, wrongly cites 1282 as the treaty date.

[8] T.-Th., III, 290.

[9] T.-Th., III, 289–290. By this stipulation, the Viterbo treaties, the investiture of territories on the part of Baldwin II, and the rights of the papacy in Constantinople were all recognized ("nec non et pacta omnia, facta cum Imperatoribus precedentibus, tam in spiritualibus, quam in temporalibus").

ipate personally in the expedition to Romania.[10] (4) Approximately eight thousand cavalrymen and horses would be provided for the campaign by Charles and Philip. The Doge on his part would supply forty or more armed galleys "to secure control of the sea," while Charles and Philip would furnish the transports for carrying men, horses, and provisions.[11] (5) The date for the *passagium* to Constantinople was fixed as not later than April of 1283.[12] The Venetians promised to dispatch their fleet from home by the first of April in order to make contact with the forces of Charles and Philip at Brindisi by the 15th of that month, at which time joint operations would begin against Byzantium.[13]

[10] T.-Th., III, 290: "in proprijs personis in Romaniam, . . . aut filius suus primogenitus." That the Doge wished to go personally (to insure the Venetian share in the conquest) is also observed by Sanudo, *Istoria*, 132: "Miser Zuan Dandolo Doge di Vinegia, che volesse andar seco in persona a questa espedizione del riaquisto di Costantinopoli."

[11] T.-Th., III, 290: "circa octo milia equorum . . . quadraginta galeas, etc."

[12] And *not* 1282 as a number of scholars believe (e.g., Hopf, *Geschichte*, 326B; and Heyd, *Histoire*, I, 435). Since the date of this main expedition is vital, I insert here a translation of the pertinent passage (T.-Th., 290): "the terminus for initiating the *passagium* should be the month of April in the second year (*sit mensis Aprilis secundo venturus*), in manner that the Doge with his maritime army or fleet should set sail from Venice on the first day of the said month of April at the latest. The Emperor and the King, or his son, with their army should sail from the port of Brindisi at the latest in the middle of the said month of April, in order that in the middle of that month all ships may make contact in the sea at Brindisi." If this passage is read in the light of another, supplementary treaty signed on the same day (see below, text and notes 14–15), the date of the main expedition to Constantinople must be 1283 and not 1282. For according to the supplementary pact a campaign was to be carried on in the East for seven months a year "until such time as the *passagium* to Romania shall be made by them against Palaeologus" ("usque ad illud tempus, quo fiet per ipsos passagium in Romaniam contra Paleologum") — clear reference to a preliminary campaign, to begin in May of 1282, a fact which would therefore render impossible the sailing of the main expedition in *April* of 1282. For further proof of 1283 for the main expedition see also *Arch. st. it.*, ser. IV, IV, 174, an edict of Charles dated 5 April 1282, ordering that 4,000 iron stakes being constructed in Venice for the expedition against Michael (*ibid.*, note 7) be transported to Trani (southern Italy) by 30 September *next*. The date prescribed is obviously too late for the preliminary campaign and must therefore refer to the main expedition of April 1283. (Nicollini, "Sui rapporti ven.-nap.," 265; Dade, 56; Norden, 626, note 2; and O. Cartellieri, *Peter von Aragon und die sizilianische Vesper* [Heidelberg, 1904] 711ff., accept 1283 but with little explanation). The dating of the main expedition against Constantinople as 1283 rather than 1282 is of considerable significance, as will be noted below, for determining the role of Michael in the conspiracy leading up to the outbreak of the anti-Angevin revolution of the Vespers in Sicily.

[13] T.-Th., III, 290.

On the same day that this treaty was signed, a shorter supplementary pact was also drawn up and approved by the allies. Its purpose, evidently, was to set in motion a preliminary campaign, or at least to maintain the Latin positions in Romania until the launching of the principal attack. For these subordinate operations the Doge, for seven months of the year until departure of the main expedition, was to provide fifteen galleys, while Charles and Philip would supply an equal number of ships plus ten cargo vessels (*teride*), the latter to carry about three hundred armed cavalrymen.[14] These forces were to assemble at the island of Corfu not later than 1 May 1282 for the opening of preliminary hostilities against Palaeologus.[15]

Whether the three principals were joined in their coalition by Charles's Greek allies is not clear from the sources. While the Despot Nikephoros of Epirus was not actually a signatory to the treaties in question, he does appear to have entered into another, possibly secret, accord with the three parties. This fact is disclosed by a communication of Charles, dated 25 September 1281, to the marshal of the Regno and vicar of Achaia, Philip of Lagonessa, informing the latter of a treaty concluded on his part with "the Despot Nikephoros Comnenos . . . , the Emperor [Philip] of Constantinople, and the Doge, for the purpose of combating Michael Palaeologus." [16] As for the participation, formal or otherwise, of John the Bastard in the Orvieto agreements, evidence is

---

[14] T.-Th., III, 296–297: "in mari per septem menses in anno usque ad illud tempus, quo fiet per ipsos passagium in Romaniam contra Paleologum et alios. . ." It is possible that one or even all of the joint Angevin-Venetian expeditions to Negropont mentioned by Sanudo (see above, note 4, and cf. also Sanudo, *Istoria*, 132) may instead have been a result of this agreement.

[15] T.-Th., III, 296–297: "apud insulam Corphou in Kalendis mensis Maii primo futuri." See note 12 above. Final official ratification of the pacts by the Doge, Philip's chancellor, and Charles's ambassador took place in Venice on 2 August 1281. See *ibid.*, 298–308. Cf. Sanudo, *Istoria*, 132.

[16] *Arch. st. it.*, ser. IV, IV, 17, where an Italian translation is printed: "Re Carlo avendo conchiuso un trattato col despota Nichiforo Comneno Duca, coll' imperadore di Costantinopoli e col Doge . . . per combattere il Paleologo, etc." Dade, 58, believes that this document refers instead to John the Bastard (cf. Norden, 628). However, the letter seems clearly to indicate Nikephoros, because Charles at the same time also ordered that Michael, son of the "same Despot Nikephoros," then held a hostage by Charles's *bailli*, Philip of Lagonessa, be released and that Philip prepare for the expedition against the Emperor.

lacking. His cooperation, however, may have been considered less important than that of Nikephoros, whose territory could offer several ports of debarkation to the allied fleets in an advance on the Greek capital.[17]

THE ANTI-BYZANTINE POLICY OF POPE MARTIN IV
AND THE DISRUPTION OF UNION

At the death of Pope Nicholas III (22 August 1280) a bitter struggle had broken out between the Orsini and pro-Angevin cardinals over the election of a successor. The issue, in effect, was freedom of the papacy from Angevin control. Charles, prevented by illness from appearing personally at Viterbo, was nevertheless in constant communication with his supporters in the Curia. Six months later the intrigues of Charles were finally successful, and on 22 February 1281 a Frenchman, Martin IV, was elected Pope.[18] Blindly subservient to Charles, Martin proceeded to submit the church to Angevin domination, thereby nullifying his predecessors' careful work of maintaining the papacy independent of Sicily.[19]

Under Charles's influence Martin now altered papal policy with respect to Michael, lending the church's prestige to the forthcoming expedition against Constantinople by sanctioning it as a pious crusade against schismatics and usurpers. In the words of the Orvieto treaty, the expedition was intended for

[17] Charles, of course, was already friendly, if not formally allied, to the Bastard. See above, Chapter 10, text and note 12.

[18] On this important conclave, one of the longest in the medieval period, see R. Sternfeld, "Das Konklav von 1280 und die Wahl Martins IV. (1281)," *Mitteilungen für österreichische Geschichtsforschung*, XXXI (1910) 1ff. (an article overlooked by Chapman and Dade and appearing after the publication of Norden's book). Sternfeld, 14, shows in particular that contrary to Villani, I, 391, Charles, after the death of Nicholas III, could not have appeared personally at the conclave because he was at the time sick at Lagopesole in the Regno. Nevertheless, as Sternfeld emphasizes, Charles was in constant communication with the pro-Angevin cardinals, and their efforts, together with pressure from the anti-Orsini government of Viterbo, overcame the influence of the numerous Orsini cardinals and thus secured the election of Martin.

[19] Martin restored to Charles the senatorship of Rome, previously removed by Nicholas III. On this see Saba Malaspina, *Historia* (ed. Del Re), 329.

340

the exaltation of the Orthodox [i.e., Catholic] faith and the reintegration of the Apostolic power, which, through the loss of the Empire of Romania (removed from obedience by the now ancient schism), has experienced severe maiming in the mystic body of church unity . . . [and, also,] for the recovery of the Empire of Romania, which is held by Palaeologus and other occupiers and possessors of the Empire.[20]

Martin's name does not appear in the document as a signatory. Yet the facts that the signing took place in the Curia at the papal residence of Orvieto,[21] that one of the witnesses was the faithful Abbot of Montecassino, Bernard Ayglier,[22] and, lastly, that John of Capua (probably a papal notary) drew up the document,[23] indicate unmistakably that Pope Martin had at the very least assumed an approving and protective attitude toward the entire proceedings.

On 18 October 1281, only a few weeks after final Venetian ratification of the Orvieto pact and without any preliminary warning, the Pope took the extreme step of excommunicating the Emperor,[24] thus disrupting the union signed at Lyons. The bull reads:

[20] T.-Th., III, 289. This same sentiment of a crusade is reflected by the *Gesta Philippi Tertii Francorum Regis* of the contemporary Guillaume de Nangis, in Bouquet *Rec. hist. des Gaules*, XX, 516, which speaks of "Christianissimus Rex Siciliae Karolus cruce signatus." But cf. the *Historia Sicula* of the Sicilian Bartolomeo of Neocastro *RISS*, XIII, pt. 3 (1921) 11, which describes Charles as assuming "latronis crucem."

[21] Both the Curia and Orvieto are explicitly mentioned in the Venetian document of confirmation. See T.-Th., III, 298, no. 375: "in Romana curia apud Urbem Veterem." Shortly after the election of Martin IV the Curia had abandoned Viterbo as its place of residence and moved to Orvieto. See *Encicl. ital.*, XXXV (1937) 489.

[22] T.-Th., III, 295. Bernard, like Martin, was French. On Bernard see Chapter 12, section 3. Note that another witness was Bernard (Bérard) of Naples, whose important collection of papal documents is cited as "Notice" in Chapters 11 and 12.

[23] T.-Th., 295: "et ego Johannes de Capua, publicus Apostolica auctoritate notarius, etc." On this point see J. Haller's review of Norden's work in *Hist. Zeit.*, XCIX (1907) 10. Also cf. Norden, 625.

[24] On the date of this first excommunication (overlooked by most scholars) see Chapman, 142, and esp. G. La Mantia, "Studi sulla rivoluzione siciliana del 1282," *Arch. st. sic.*, VI (1940) 99–100. Cf. R. Sternfeld, "Der Vertrag zwischen dem Paläologen Michael VIII. und Peter von Aragon im Jahre 1281," *Arkiv für Urkundenforschung*, VI (1918) 277, who dates it 17 April 1281, on the basis of *Ann. Ian.*, V, 16. However, the *Ann. Ian.* list only the year (1281) but no month.

We declare that Michael Palaeologus, who is called Emperor of the Greeks, has incurred sentence of excommunication as supporter of the ancient Greek schismatics and therefore heretics . . . Moreover, we absolutely forbid all individual kings, princes, dukes, marquises, counts, barons, and all others of whatever pre-eminence, condition, or status, all cities, fortresses, and other places from contracting with this Michael Palaeologus any alliance or association of any sort or nature that may be proposed while he is excommunicate . . . If anyone contravenes this order, that person . . . *ipso facto* shall be excommunicated. Moreover, his lands . . . shall undergo ecclesiastical interdict, and he shall be deprived of all property he holds from any churches whatever, and he shall suffer other spiritual penalties as we think best; and any such alliances contracted . . . we declare to be null and void.[25]

That the excommunication — renewed by Martin on 7 May and again on 18 November 1282 [26] — was an unprovoked political act in behalf of Charles is well attested by numerous sources including the Venetian Marino Sanudo and the *Annales Ianuenses*. While Sanudo writes, "I affirm as reverently as I am able [that the excommunication] was ill-advised, because this affair of King Charles completely upset the union of Greek and Roman churches which was on the way to being completed," the *Annales* note even more critically that through his act Martin showed himself "remarkably partial to Charles." [27]

Cf. Dade, 55. It should be noted that Norden's treatment of the Vespers and the role of Palaeologus therein is entirely inadequate.

[25] Text printed in Raynaldus, a. 1281, § 25, but omitted from M. Olivier-Martin, *Les registres de Martin IV* (Paris, 1901). See also *Annales Altahenses* (*Continuatio*) *MGH SS*, XVII, 409, the editor of which seems wrongly to date the first excommunication of Michael as 18 November 1281.

[26] See Olivier-Martin, *Reg. Martin*, 100, no. 269; and 115, no. 278. The bull of 7 May forbids Western powers to send military aid or provisions to Palaeologus. (This bull was issued after the outbreak of the Sicilian revolt.) The second bull, of 18 November, declares Michael deposed from his throne if he does not return to the church and render full satisfaction to Charles by 1 May 1283. A similar demand was made for the submission of Peter of Aragon (Olivier-Martin, *Reg. Martin*, 107, no. 276). For complete texts see also Raynaldus, a. 1282, § 8–10. Cf. Dade, 58, and Grumel, *Dict. théol. cath.*, col. 1402, who wrongly gives as the dates 26 March and 18 October. See also Potthast, *Regesta, nos.* 21896 and 21948.

[27] Sanudo, *Istoria*, 138: "(Il che dico tuttavia con emendazione e riverenza quanto posso esser stato mal fatto), perche essendosi in Via d'unir la Chiesa Greca con la Romana, questa cosa di Rè Carlo la disturbò del tutto." Also *Ann. Ian.*, V, 16: "favorabilis dicto regi mirabiliter existens."

As for Michael Palaeologus, one can well imagine his reaction to the excommunication.[28] After striving to the very end to fulfill papal demands,[29] even to the point of risking civil war in his Empire, Michael, in one brief moment, found the work of twenty years destroyed and himself left practically alone to face the massed power of Charles, Venice, and now the papacy!

In his anger at the papal action, Michael seriously considered measures to destroy all traces of the union among his people. But, realistic even in this terrible crisis, he decided that such a course, by condemning all previous accomplishments, would irrevocably deprive him of Rome's support in the event of future need.[30] (Martin, after all, might soon be succeeded by an anti-Angevin pope!) Fortifying Michael's decision was the recent severe defeat of the Greeks at the hands of the Turks on the Sangarios River, with its grave implications for Byzantine control of Asia Minor.[31] Thus the Emperor did not formally denounce the union. Nevertheless, he expressed his resentment by forbidding the mention of Martin's name in the public prayers recited during the liturgy (diptychs), and by attempting to reconcile himself with the

[28] According to Pach., 505, ll. 18ff., Michael was informed of the excommunication by his envoy to the Curia, the Bishop of Nicaea, whose colleague of Heraclea had died on the trip home.

[29] Sanudo, *Istoria*, 137, affirms (in an unnoticed passage) that Michael did more than any other Greek Emperor for the Roman church and even built a tower in Acre (the Holy Land) at his own expense: "alcun' Imperator Greco non hà fatto tanto per la Chiesa, e per ben della Cristianità, quanto . . . Sior Michieli, il qual anco fece fabricar in Acri una bella e Gran Torre a sue proprie spese." Note the following words, which show Sanudo's sympathy for Michael: "per il chè a mio giudicio il Signor Iddio li fù in ajuto suo e di suo Fiol e de suoi Eredi fin' ora." See even the opinion of the 14th century papal supporter, the Dominican missionary to the East, Guillaume d'Adam, *De modo Sarracenos extirpandi*, in *Rec. des hist. des crois., Doc. Armén.*, II (Paris, 1906) 545, that Michael, though a usurper, defended the Roman church to the end of his life: "licet imperium violenti et infideli usurpacione habuerit, tamen Romane Ecclesie humilis et devotus ejus suscepit obedienciam et fidem, quam et tenuit viriliter et defendit usque ad terminum vite sue." On Michael's fidelity to the union see also Norden, 631; Dade, 58; and esp. Bréhier, *Camb. Med. Hist.*, IV, 613: "Michael Palaeologus struggled to the end to uphold the union."

[30] Pach., 506, ll. 1–14, esp.: ἐπιστάντος καὶ αὖθις καιροῦ τοῦ ταῦτα ζητήσοντος.

[31] Pach., 506, ll. 14–17. Cf. Sanudo, *Istoria*, 144, who comments thus on the same sequence of events: "Paleologo . . . come disperato lassò la Custodia d'un sua Provincia ottima . . . Paflagonia, tolta da Turchi."

Greek church, the support of which was so necessary in the approaching climax of his struggle against the West.[32]

THE ALLIANCE BETWEEN MICHAEL PALAEOLOGUS
AND KING PETER III OF ARAGON

Events from the siege of Berat, beginning in the latter half of 1280, to the celebrated revolt of the Sicilians against Charles (30 March 1282) in which Angevin plans against the Greeks were completely disrupted, are recounted in fragmentary, even conflicting, fashion by the various chroniclers of East and West. Nevertheless, in order to indicate what role, if any, Michael played in the preparation of this catastrophe for Charles, an attempt must be made to examine the evidence, often circumstantial to be sure, and thus to reconstruct the pattern of Byzantine diplomacy during this crucial period.

Though angered at the development of events, Michael could not have been unduly surprised at the formation of the Angevin-Venetian alliance. Reports on the Italian situation from his agents, the failure of the offensive at Berat, and especially the election of Martin IV to the papal throne were clear indications of the direction of Angevin policy. Martin's attitude to Michael was in fact revealed at the very outset of his pontificate by his disdainful reception of two imperial envoys, Leo and Theophanes, Bishops of Heraclea and Nicaea. These prelates, apparently dispatched to the Curia before the death of Nicholas to explain the situation in Constantinople and assure Nicholas of Michael's undiminished desire for union,[33] had been captured by Angevin agents and were now conducted to the new Pope at Charles's command.[34]

---

[32] Pach., 506, esp. ll. 1–3, and 507, l. 5.

[33] See Pach., 505, ll. 9ff., who attributes the rude reception of the envoys to the growing Latin awareness that the union was a fraud for all except the Emperor, the Patriarch, and those around them: χλεύην τὸ γεγονὸς καὶ οὐκ ἀλήθειαν ἄντικρυς. Cf. Grumel, *Dict. théol. cath.*, IX, pt. 1, col. 1402, who believes that Michael had sent Leo and Theophanes to the Curia immediately after hearing of Martin's election.

[34] *Arch. st. it.*, ser. IV, IV, 3, dated 9 January 1281. On the identification of

Shortly after the conclusion of the Orvieto pact, Michael was explicitly warned of danger by the Genoese, who had already been approached by Angevin envoys seeking their participation in the projected expedition. It was evidently Charles's aim to invite a refusal on the part of the Genoese (who, of course, had everything to lose and nothing to gain by the venture), and thus to justify their exclusion from Constantinople after the seizure of the capital. Protesting engrossment in other matters, the Genoese immediately dispatched an envoy to the Bosporus.[35]

Whatever Michael's immediate reaction to Charles's diplomatic coup, he must meanwhile, following the usual pattern of his diplomacy, have been seeking other alliances with which to neutralize the mortal danger of a successful Angevin-Venetian-papal coalition. But in the face of such a combination, what possibilities of alliance in the West remained? The German Emperor Rudolph of Hapsburg seemed aloof; France was under the rule of Charles's faithful nephew Philip III; and Pisa, with its still powerful fleet, was too bitter an enemy of Genoa actively to support the latter's Greek ally.[36] Thus the only remaining states of importance, besides friendly Genoa, were distant Aragon and Castile.

The ruler of Aragon at this time was King Peter III, who, fortunately for Michael, had his own reasons for hatred of Charles. Constance, his wife, was the daughter of Manfred, and for this reason Peter considered the Angevin a usurper and Sicily the rightful inheritance of Constance. Therefore, while eagerly welcoming pro-Hohenstaufen refugees from Sicily (the famous John of Procida, for example, became his trusted adviser and secre-

---

this embassy (in *Arch. st. it.* the names Philip and Constantine are listed) with that of Leo and Theophanes, see Dölger, *Regesten*, no. 2049. Possibly referring to the same embassy is a passage in Salimbene, *Cronica* (Bernini ed.) II, 214, but listed under the date 1282: "coram papa et cardinalibus in consistorio lecte fuerunt littere, quod Palialogus in Constantinopolitana urbe ex Grecis papam fecerat et cardinales."

[35] *Ann. Ian.*, V, 16–17. Cf. Imperiale, *Jacopo d'Oria*, 231.

[36] On Pisan policy see below, text and notes 81 and 82. Sanudo's remark in *Istoria*, 137, "(Carlo) fattosi tributario . . . il Commun di Pisa," thus seems to refer to the period immediately before the Vespers.

tary), Peter as early, it appears, as 1269 began to nourish designs against Sicily [37] and in 1280 even began the construction of a fleet, presumably to invade the island.[38]

Peter's resentment and probable intentions against Charles may well have been disclosed to Michael by Sicilian Ghibellines fleeing Angevin tyranny or by Catalan merchants who were voyaging in increasing numbers to the Bosporus.[39] But the precise time at which negotiations for a secret understanding were actually entered into by the two rulers is not clear from the sources.[40] According to the contemporary Dominican chronicler, Ptolemy of Lucca (later secretary to the papal curia), a Greco-Aragonese treaty of alliance was concluded after Martin's excommunication of Palaeologus. And this treaty, of which Ptolemy claims to have seen documentary proof, was contracted for the express purpose of "stripping the Regno from King Charles." [41]

Ptolemy's affirmation of a Greco-Aragonese alliance is corroborated more or less emphatically by several important contemporary sources of opposing political sympathies. First, the

[37] On this see O. Cartellieri, *Peter von Aragon und die sizilianische Vesper* (Heidelberg, 1904) 14–15.

[38] Saba Malaspina, *Rerum Sicularum historia* (ed. Del Re) 320ff., a generally accurate contemporary writer and later member of the papal court, says Peter's preparations began *before* the death of Nicholas, i.e., already in 1280. Cf. Sternfeld, "Der Vertrag," 282. The policy of Peter of Aragon is revealed by documents published by I. Carini, *Gli archivi e le biblioteche di Spagna in rapporto alla storia d'Italia*, II (Palermo, 1884–1897); and by the already cited book of Cartellieri, *Peter von Aragon*. Cartellieri's work, supported by an article of H. Wieruszowski, "Conjuraciones y alianzas políticas del rey Pedro de Aragón contra Carlos de Anjou antes de la Visperas Sicilianas," *Boletín de la Academia de la Historia*, 107 (Madrid, 1935) 549–560, removes any doubt that Peter had relations with the Sicilian Ghibellines before the outbreak of the Sicilian Vespers (end of March, 1282). M. Amari, of course, in his celebrated *La guerra del Vespro Siciliano* (Milan, 1886), insisted on interpreting the Vespers principally as a nationalist Sicilian uprising.

[39] See C. Marinesco, "Notes sur les Catalans dans l'empire byzantin," *Mélanges F. Lot* (Paris, 1925) 501ff.

[40] On this cf. Sternfeld, "Der Vertrag," 283. Dade, 61, believes that Palaeologus probably first approached Peter. Legend has it, however, that John of Procida began the negotiations on his own initiative. On Procida see below, text and notes 62–66.

[41] *Historia ecclesiastica, RISS*, XI (1727) cols. 1186–1187: "inter Palaeologum, et Regem Aragonum qui vocabatur Petrus . . . de auferendo Regnum Regi Carolo: quem tractatum ego vidi."

Gestes des Chiprois, written by the Templar of Tyre, a generally reliable, well-informed observer of the period, reports that when Michael heard of the armament under preparation by King Peter "he sent to him as messenger . . . a citizen of Genoa named Benedetto Zaccaria, who negotiated and brought about an accord between them for an amount of money that the Emperor had sent to the King of Aragon." [42] Secondly, the Ghibelline *Annales Placentini* of north Italy state, under the month of April 1282, that "it is believed that Peter constructed a great fleet with the aid and counsel of the Kings of Castile and England [!] and with the aid and money of Palaeologus, King and Emperor of the Greeks." [43] A third contemporary chronicle, that of the Guelph Franciscan, Salimbene of Parma, records that when Peter landed in Sicily shortly after the Vespers, "he had as confederates the King of Castile and Palaeologus." [44]

Doubtless of greater significance is the often neglected testimony of Pope Martin himself as quoted in his bull of excommunication (18 November 1282) against Michael and Peter. In the document Martin explicitly mentions "counsel, aid, and favor, together with pacts and confederations entered into [by Peter] with him [Michael] against us, the church, and King Charles." [45]

[42] *Les gestes des Chiprois*, ed. G. Raynaud, in *Soc. de l'or. latin* (Geneva, 1887) 213: "si manda de par luy.j. mesage au roy d'Aragon . . . j. bourgois de Jene quy ot nom s[ire] Benet Zaquerie, et traita et pourchasa l'acort entr'iaus pour une cantité d'aver que le dit empereor manda au roy d'Aragon." On Zaccaria see below, section 4.

[43] *Ann. Plac. Gib.*, MGH SS, XVIII, 574: "De mense Aprilis rex Aragonis fecit magnum apparatum navigii, et creditur quod ipse fecit tam magnum apparatum cum auxilio et conscilio regis Castelle et regis Anglie et cum auxilio et avere Palialoghi regis et imperatoris Grecorum." No specific treaty is mentioned here, but a close connection is certainly implied. For relations between Peter and England see F. Kern, "Eduard I. von England u. Peter von Aragon," *Mitteil. d. Inst. für oesterr. Geschichtsfor.*, XXX (1909) 412ff., and esp. 421, a letter from Edward to Peter, dated 23 January 1282, regarding many negotiations for a marriage between the two houses, which never was realized. Also see C. Langlois, *Le règne de Philippe III le Hardi* (Paris, 1887) 142. Finally, see A. Bozzola, "Guglielmo VII Marchese di Monferrato e Carlo I," *Arch. st. prov. nap.*, XXXVII, 12, note 5, who believes that Castile was allied to Michael before the Sicilian Vespers.

[44] *Cronica*, ed. Bernini, II (Bari, 1942) 213: "Petrus rex Aragonie . . . qui adiutores habebat regem Castelle et Palialogum." On Castile see preceding note and below, text and notes 78–80; also Appendix A.

[45] G. La Mantia, "Studi sulla rivoluzione siciliana del 1282," *Arch. st. per la*

347

Asserting that popular opinion regarded Michael as an author of the secret Sicilian conspiracy preceding the Vespers, Martin lists the names of a large number of men involved, including, besides Michael, Peter of Aragon, John of Procida, and Benedetto Zaccaria.[46] This document, termed by several important modern scholars as of such capital significance that it should end all controversy about a conspiracy anterior to the Vespers, reveals that before the Vespers so widespread a conspiratorial movement had been organized against Angevin rule in Sicily that not only the Greek and Aragonese rulers but Italian Ghibellines and various Sicilian nobles, including John of Procida, were involved.[47]

Most important of all, however, is the testimony of an almost entirely overlooked document emanating from the chancery of Peter of Aragon himself, which emphatically affirms a close connection between Peter and Michael. In a letter of January 1282 (i.e., *before* the Vespers) addressed to Pisa and requesting the Commune's aid against Charles, Peter writes:

You know, of course, that that wicked and impious Charles intends shortly to attack the Emperor of Constantinople, united to me by a bond of recent friendship (*nove amicitie linea nobis unitum*). I have decided in my heart of hearts to oppose the presumptuous daring of this King with firm disposition and with all my power. For I intend . . . to enter the Kingdom of Sicily and there to establish myself . . . with a large force of my men. And thus, while that King will believe fictitiously (*sub fabula*) that he has conquered the Greeks, the Sicilians will find themselves irrevocably subject to my rule.[48]

---

sic., VI (1940) 104 and note 1: "contra nos et praefatam Ecclesiam ac regem Carolum consilio, auxilio vel favore, nec non pactis et confederationibus initis cum eodem ex tunc argumenta verisimilia deferebantur; vox praeterea publica et communis accusationis quasi continuo incessabat." Cf. Olivier-Martin, *Reg. Martin*, no. 276, 112.

[46] La Mantia, *loc. cit.*

[47] *Ibid.*, 106–114, esp. 111, and note 2. La Mantia quotes the opinion of Carini, *Gli archivi e le bibl.*, II (1884) 46. La Mantia's carefully documented article seems conclusively to prove the vastness of the conspiracy against Charles.

[48] See F. Kern, *Acta Imperii Angliae et Franciae 1267–1313* (Tübingen, 1911), no. 28, 17: "Intellecto siquidem, quod ipse Karolus Constantinopolitanum imperatorem nove amicitie linea nobis unitum velud nequam et inpius presentialiter intendit invadere, in armario cordis nostri firma dispositione concepimus eiusdem

The phrase "united to me by a bond of recent friendship" may, of course, signify nothing more than a vague understanding with no specific commitments, but in view of the separate involvement of each of the two rulers in plans against their common enemy, Charles, it seems quite unlikely that this was anything less than a genuine alliance for mutual aid.

Despite the evidence adduced — some of which, as noted, has hitherto not been taken into consideration — certain scholars have doubted the existence of a Greco-Aragonese alliance on the grounds that both Pachymeres and Gregoras fail to mention such an accord.[49] But it is not at all unusual for Pachymeres to omit events which occurred outside the Byzantine orbit or which might seriously detract from Greek prestige. Thus even more glaring examples of such omissions are his silence on the site of the Council of Lyons and especially on the existence of the Treaty of Nymphaeum (1261), so vital, as we have seen, for Palaeologus' retention of Constantinople.[50] As for Gregoras, it is necessary only to cite a passage of his, again hardly appreciated, which certainly suggests at least close Greco-Aragonese cooperation before the Vespers:

First of all [the Emperor], after sending riches of all kinds, incited to war against Charles, King Frederick [!] of Sicily so that he [Michael] might at least prevent the departure of his [Charles's] fleet and turn Charles's main attention to cares within his own territories, so to speak, rather than to foreign areas. And the Emperor considered this his greatest and most effective accomplishment, more remarkable in fact than any of his others. Thus the shrewdness of the Emperor rendered

---

regis ad posse presumptuosis ausibus obviare. Intendimus namque . . . rengnum introire Sicilie ibique residentiam facere . . . cum exfortio gentis nostre. Itaque cum rex ipse credet sub fabula sibi subdidisse Romeos, invenient Siculi nostro dominio infallibiliter se subiectos." This extremely important document has apparently escaped the notice of almost all modern scholars including Chapman, Lopez (see Appendix A), Wieruszowski, Cartellieri, Léonard, and, finally, V. Laurent (see his communication, "Les Vêpres Siciliennes et les dessous de la politique byzantine," *Atti dello VIII congresso bizantino di Palermo*, I [Rome, 1953] 409–412). Only Dade, 59, cites it. Cf. with this document the testimony of Michael below, text and note 112.

[49] E.g., Lopez, *Benedetto Zaccaria*, 71–73.
[50] See Chapter 4, text and note 44.

the naval forces of Charles ineffectual, since he had diverted them to wars in Charles's own neighborhood.[51]

Those denying the existence of a Greco-Aragonese alliance point likewise to the silence of the Catalan chroniclers, Bernat D'Esclot and Ramon Muntaner.[52] But, as with Pachymeres, it must be recognized that it was to the interest of both men, patriotic chroniclers writing in the critical period after the Vespers, to deny any credit for the Aragonese conquest of Sicily to an excommunicated Greek Emperor. For it would certainly prejudice the claim of Aragon to Sicily were it publicly known that the Aragonese occupation was the result of partnership with heretical enemies of the Papacy.

If only as a gesture to tradition, we should finally mention an anonymous but controversial Sicilian chronicle, the famous *Rebellamentu de Sichilia*. Supporting in considerable detail the existence of a Greco-Aragonese accord, it deals mainly with the Sicilian patriot John of Procida (actually by birth a Salernitan from the mainland) and his alleged series of voyages to Constantinople, Sicily, Aragon, and the papal court before the Vespers to organize a huge anti-Angevin conspiracy involving not only

[51] Greg., 146, ll. 16–24: πρῶτον μὲν οὖν χρήματα πέμψας παντοδαπὰ τὸν Σικελίας ἐξεπολέμωσε ῥῆγα Φερδέριχον κατὰ τοῦ Καρούλου, ἵν' εἰ μή τι ἄλλο, τῶν γοῦν ναυτικῶν δυνάμεων ἐκείνου κωλύῃ τὸν ἔκπλουν καὶ ἀντιπερισπᾷ τὰς καιριωτέρας φροντίδας πρὸς τοὺς ἐκ πλευρᾶς ὡς εἰπεῖν πόνους μᾶλλον ἢ τοὺς ὑπερορίους· ὃ δὴ καὶ μέγιστον ἔδοξεν ἔργον καὶ τελεσιουργόν, εἴπερ τι τῶν πάντων ἕτερον. τὰς μὲν οὖν ναυτικὰς τοῦ Καρούλου δυνάμεις οὕτως ἀπράκτους ἀπέδειξεν ἡ τοῦ βασιλέως σύνεσις, πρὸς τοὺς ἐγγύθεν πολέμους ἀντιπερισπάσας αὐτάς. The mention here of Frederick's name, it is true, seems at first glance contradictory. But it may well be explained as an anachronism: Gregoras, writing in the fourteenth century, very likely simply confused the name of Peter's son as ruler of Sicily with that of Peter (cf. Greg., 124, ll. 16–17, where the same kind of mistake seems to be made). It is clear, moreover, that the context of events described, while unquestionably referring to Michael, could hardly relate to Frederick, since Michael died at the end of 1282, Peter and Charles of Anjou both in 1285 (at which time the latter's son Charles II the Lame succeeded Charles), and Frederick did not come to the throne until much later, in 1295–1296. Charles the Lame (d. 1309), fully involved in war with Aragon over the island of Sicily, had no time for ambitious designs against Constantinople. See A. De Stefano, *Federico III d'Aragona re di Sicilia* (Palermo, 1937) *passim*.

[52] Again Lopez, *Benedetto Zaccaria*, 73. For these chronicles see Bernat D'Esclot, *Crónica del Rey en Pere*, in *Chroniques étrangères* (Buchon ed.) 565ff., esp. 612. Also Ramon Muntaner, *Chronik des edlen en Ramon Muntaner*, ed. K. Lanz (Stuttgart, 1844) 1ff.

Michael and Peter but discontented Sicilian nobles and other parties as well. Though the work may well preserve certain characteristics of Sicilian tradition, a great many discrepancies (not to mention the impossible portrayal of Michael as a spineless, snivelling ruler easily manipulated by Procida) have been pointed out in it by such scholars as O. Cartellieri, R. Lopez, and the famous Michele Amari. Hence, despite the valiant attempt of its most recent editor, Sicardi, to re-establish the chronicle's authenticity, until more solid evidence of its veracity has been adduced to balance its many obviously fanciful elements, we must continue to look upon it as a later, pro-Sicilian fabrication.[53]

THE ROLE OF POPE NICHOLAS III AND THE MISSIONS OF BENEDETTO ZACCARIA

Certain contemporary sources affirm that not only was there an alliance between Peter and Michael but that even Pope Nicholas III himself was involved. Now at first glance one would expect that Peter would not have dared to prepare war against the papal vassal, Charles, while this strong-willed Pope was alive.[54] Nonetheless, there is some reason to suspect that not only

[53] For the chronicle and Sicardi's analysis see *Lu Rebellamentu di Sichilia*, *RISS*, XXXIV, pt. 1 (1917) and introduction. Also the strong remarks of Cartellieri, *Peter von Aragon*, 235; Amari, *La guerra del Vespro Siciliano*, I, 52; and Lopez, *Benedetto Zaccaria*, 69–70, all believing it spurious. Among those favoring its authenticity besides Sicardi are Chapman (who gives no arguments whatever) and La Mantia, "Studi sulla rivoluzione," 117. Cf. also N. Buscemi, *La vita di Giovanni da Procida* (Palermo, 1836) (inaccessible to me); and the perceptive work of I. Sanesi, "Giovanni da Procida e il Vespro Siciliano," *Rivista storica italiana*, VII (1890) 489–519. Two other later anonymous chronicles, *Liber Jani de Procida et Palioloco*, and *Leggenda di messer Gianni di Procida* (also in *RISS*, XXXIV), which support the central role of Procida before the Vespers, are very probably based on the *Rebellamentu*, or possibly all three may stem from a common source now lost.

[54] It is the opinion of Sternfeld, "Der Vertrag," 281, and Wieruszowski, "Conjuraciones," 560, that negotiations between Peter and Michael began *before* Nicholas' death on 22 August 1280. Michael may well have suspected a Veneto-Angevin alliance from the joint dispatch of ships to Negropont in March of 1280. See Sanudo, *Istoria*, 129–130. Cf. statement of *Rebellamentu* (Sicardi ed.) 5, that it was 1279 when Procida sailed to Constantinople and Aragon to arrange the conspiracy (Buchon ed., 737). But cf. Cartellieri, *Peter von Aragon*, 76ff. and Bozzola, "Guglielmo VII di Monferrato e Carlo I," 26.

was Nicholas aware of Peter's aims and preparations, but that he may even have actively encouraged him.

In the first place, as is well-known, the Orsini cardinals in the Curia — Pope Nicholas, it will be recalled, was an Orsini — were violently anti-Angevin and openly favorable to Peter. Dreaming of establishing a kingdom for themselves in north Italy, they knew that Angevin hegemony over Constantinople as well as Rome and most of Italy meant abandonment of their schemes and relegation of the papacy to a role of dependence upon Angevin wishes.[55] Through the conquest of Constantinople a preponderance of power would fall into the hands of Charles, thus producing a politico-diplomatic revolution not only in the East but also in Italy. Such a situation, in effect the attainment of the grand Mediterranean monarchy to which Charles aspired,[56] would have been impossible for the Papacy as well as other Italian states to tolerate.

On this basis it would not seem unreasonable for Nicholas to oppose the schemes of Charles and even seek his expulsion from Sicily. It was the papacy that had summoned Charles to Italy to oust Manfred: why should Pope Nicholas not replace his recalcitrant vassal with Aragon? This, in substance, is stated by the contemporary Franciscan Minister-general, Salimbene of Parma, who avers that "Pope Nicholas had given it [Sicily] to him [Peter] in hatred of King Charles with the consent of certain cardinals then in the Curia." [57]

[55] On the Orsini cardinals see Sternfeld, "Das Konklav von 1280," 20, and the same author's Der Kardinal Johann Gaëtan Orsini (Berlin, 1905), passim. Cf. Previté-Orton, ch. VI, Cambridge Med. Hist., V, 194. It may be significant that the Roman Orsini, in 1283, after the outbreak of the Vespers, actually supported the excommunicated Peter against Charles.

[56] See below, text and note 100.

[57] Salimbene, II, 225: "papa Nicholaus III dederat eam sibi in odium regis Karuli cum consensu aliquorum cardinalium, qui tunc erant in curia." On this action of Nicholas see Cartellieri, Peter von Aragon, 56ff., who has collected the sources mentioning it. Also cf. Sternfeld, "Der Vertrag," 282 and note 2, who believes that Salimbene's statement is more than mere rumor. (It is to be noted that here Sternfeld changed the opinion he expressed in a previous article, "Das Konklav von 1280," in which he had denied Nicholas' involvement in the conspiracy. In "Der Vertrag" Sternfeld suggests that this transfer of Sicily to Peter was one reason for the extreme bitterness of the conclave of 1280 following Nicholas'

The divergence of interests between Nicholas and his vassal Charles had been evident almost from the beginning. As previously noted, Nicholas, shortly after his enthronement, had removed Charles from the senatorship of Rome and vicariate of Tuscany — that is, from virtual control of these important areas [58] — and seems to have taken an unfavorable view of his ambitions in the Balkans. But with Charles chafing at such restrictions, guilty of subverting papal policy in his attack on Berat and, finally, if we may believe Sanudo, negotiating with Venice for an expedition against Constantinople itself,[58a] it would appear that the energetic Nicholas could not but have taken measures to protect papal interests and especially the union with Michael.[59]

Confirmation of the thesis of Nicholas' involvement in secret Greco-Aragonese negotiations may or may not be provided by several documents recently discovered by H. Wieruszowski bearing the signature of John of Procida, secretary of the Aragonese chancery. According to one, dated 4 August 1278 and worded in the guarded language befitting a conspirator, King Peter sent as his envoy "to the Roman Curia and to the Lord Emperor regarding certain of our affairs" Taberner, judge of the Aragonese court. A similar document, dated 31 August 1279, refers, once more in cryptic terms, to the mission of Taberner. In the latter document in particular, Peter commends Taberner for his work in the business at hand — negotiations over the crusading tithe —

death.) Cf. F. Savio, *Arch. st. sic.*, XXVI, 358ff. Norden, 643, believes, however, that Nicholas would not have dared to strike at Charles.

[58] See Chapter 13, text and notes 23–24 and cf. below, note 62.

[58a] Nicholas' death occurred on 22 August 1280, but Charles had acutely threatened Greco-Albanian territory since 1279, with the siege of Berat beginning probably in summer or early fall of 1280 (immediately after Nicholas' death?). In any case, as shown, it was certainly against papal policy for Charles to attack Constantinople. See also Sternfeld, "Das Konklav von 1280," 18–19. For Sanudo's statement see *Istoria*, 131.

[59] Further evidence ostensibly supporting Nicholas' involvement is given in the next few pages. (It should be noted that the question here is not Nicholas' possible role in instigating the revolt of the Sicilian people, but his involvement in the secret negotiations between Peter and Michael.) Another indication of the bad relations between Nicholas and Charles is provided by a passage in Villani, I, 384, who attributes Nicholas' enmity to Charles to the refusal of the latter to permit the marriage of his nephew to a niece of the Pope.

and directs him to proceed diligently "in other matters with which we have instructed you." [60] The Emperor here referred to, according to Wieruszowski, is not the Western Rudolph of Hapsburg but the Byzantine Michael Palaeologus.[60a] That Taberner's mission is not mentioned in the papal registers on Aragonese tithes is for Wieruszowski proof that Taberner must have been charged with a mission different from that of the tithe — probably therefore the conquest of Sicily.[61]

Details of the supposed negotiations between Peter, Michael, and Pope Nicholas are provided by the famous but controversial fourteenth century chronicle of the Florentine Guelph, Giovanni Villani. Villani writes that Nicholas

was greatly opposed to all of Charles's enterprises, and with money it is said he had from Palaeologus, agreed and gave aid and favor to the treaty and rebellion that was being organized against King Charles in the island of Sicily.[62]

Then Procida (whom Villani — evidently following the customary simplification effected by tradition — portrays as the master organizer of the negotiations) showed Nicholas a document from Michael, in which the Emperor recommended him to the Pope and gave to Procida and "messer Orso" (Pope Nicholas Orsini) freely of his treasure, "thus pushing him [Nicholas] with this money secretly against King Charles." [63] Having secured papal

[60] "In aliis que vobis commissimus." Quoted in Wieruszowski, "Conjuraciones," 591, document no. 5, addressed to a Pistoian merchant and friend of Peter, asking for aid for Taberner on his mission "pro quibusdam nostris negociis ad Curiam Romanam et ad dominum imperatorem" (see also document no. 5, and ibid., 562, for discussion).

[60a] Wieruszowski also refers to Michael in "Der Anteil Johanns von Procida an der Verschwörung gegen Karl von Anjou," Gesammelte Aufsätze zur Kulturgeschichte Spaniens, V (1935) 237. Wolff, "Mortgage of an Emperor's son," 75, note 72, suggests a possible reference to Philip of Courtenay.

[61] Wieruszowski, "Conjuraciones," 562. Cartellieri, Peter von Aragon, 235, demonstrates that the anonymous chronicles which remain concerning Procida (see RISS, XXXIV, pt. I, ed. Sicardi) are "novellistische Bearbeitungen der Erzählung, wie sie Villanis Chronik bietet," and, for the historian, are "völlig wertlos." On the reliability of Cartellieri's work see Sternfeld, "Der Vertrag," 276.

[62] Villani, I, 384: "fugli molto contra in tutte sue imprese, e per moneta che si disse ch'ebbe dal Paglialoco, acconsentì e diede aiuto e favore al trattato e rubellazione ch'al re Carlo fu fatto dell' isola di Cicilia."

[63] Ibid., 390: "presentò a lui e a messer Orso . . . commovendolo segretamente

support for his plan, Procida, continues Villani, sailed to Catalonia where he prevailed upon King Peter to join in the conspiracy with Michael, Nicholas, and the Sicilian barons. Peter then sent Procida to Constantinople to secure subsidies for constructing his fleet. In the meantime, Nicholas died, but the conspiracy, according to Villani, continued without him.[64]

In the light of documents recently discovered by Wieruszowski and of others already known from the earlier work of Saint-Priest,[65] it seems likely, however, that Procida did not play the central role of negotiator attributed to him by Villani. For the documents bearing Procida's signature disclose that at the time that he was purportedly at Constantinople, Sicily, and the papal Curia, he was actually signing official papers in Aragon. Wieruszowski, to be sure, allows that Procida might have made a voyage or two during this period, but she concludes, probably correctly, that his role in the preparation of the Sicilian Vespers was more limited and consisted primarily in negotiations with the Sicilian nobles.[66] Thus, though we may accept with a reasonable degree of assurance the existence of an alliance between Michael and Peter prior to the Vespers, until more persuasive evidence is forthcoming, the adhesion of Nicholas to this accord must be looked upon as only a tantalizing hypothesis and considerably less than established fact.

That Michael Palaeologus did, however, provide "Greek gold" to Peter and the anti-Angevin cardinals of the Curia (if not to

---

colla detta moneta contro al re Carlo." It has been suggested that Villani's source of information is also the *Rebellamentu de Sichilia*; see *RISS*, XXXIV, 45.

[64] Villani, I, 390.

[65] See Saint-Priest's appendices in his *Histoire de la Conquête de Naples*, IV (Paris, 1849) 197ff. On their importance see Wieruszowski, "Conjuraciones," 562, and also her "Der Anteil Johanns von Procida an der Verschwörung gegen Karl von Anjou," 230ff.

[66] Wieruszowski, "Conjuraciones," 560 and 563, suggests that the treaty between Peter and Michael was probably concluded with the Greek envoys at Peter's court, and in Procida's presence. Cartellieri, *Peter von Aragon*, 229, enumerates and shows the impossibility of the eight voyages of Procida as listed by the *Rebellamentu*. A brother of John of Procida, it may be noted, acted as negotiator for William of Montferrat between Aragon and the Ghibellines of northern Italy; see Cartellieri, 90.

Pope Nicholas III) is attested by several Greek and Latin sources. According to Pachymeres, Michael was constantly sending gold to the Italians, "especially to the cardinals," [67] and, in the supplementary, more specific expression of Gregoras already quoted in full above, "first of all, by sending great amounts of money Michael incited King Frederick [sic] to war against Charles." [68]

As for Western sources, besides the evidence of the contemporary Gestes des Chiprois previously mentioned, there is the statement of Sanudo (for which he cites as his source Roger Loria, the famous Sicilian admiral commanding the Aragonese navy) that "the Emperor [Michael] had promised to give each year to the King of Aragon 60,000 hyperpyra until the end of the war." [68a] We may add to this also the less important testimony of the Dominican Brocardus, an early fourteenth century French crusader theorist (the provenience of whose information is obscure), who records that "with great subsidies of money and promises [Palaeologus] persuaded Lord Peter, then King of Aragon . . . to occupy Sicily so that he might in this manner prevent Charles from invading his Empire. And this was done." [69]

---

[67] Pach., 360: ταῦτά τε συχνάκις διεμήνυε, καὶ χρυσὸν πέμπων καδδηναλίοις [sic]. This seems to refer to 1269 or 1270, but Michael undoubtedly continued this tactic. On Nicholas' reputed avariciousness, see Dante, Divine Comedy, Inferno, canto 29, ll. 69–72.

[68] Greg., 146: πρῶτον μὲν οὖν χρήματα πέμψας παντοδαπὰ τὸν Σικελίας ἐξεπολέμωσε ῥῆγα Φερδέριχον κατὰ τοῦ Καρούλου; and l. 13: ἀνθίστασθαι καὶ ὅπλοις καὶ χρήμασι. On the mention of Frederick see above, note 51. Again in regard to subsidies it should be noted that Ptolemy of Lucca, XI, col. 1187, in his mention of the Greco-Aragonese treaty (which he claims to have seen) makes no explicit mention of money given to Peter by Michael. Yet since Ptolemy does not quote verbatim from the treaty, he could well be referring to Greek subsidies with the words "cum suo adjutorio (Petrus) facit armatam in mari." On this see Sternfeld, "Der Vertrag," 278.

[68a] Istoria, 133: "il detto imperatore (Michael) avea promesso dar al Rè d'Aragona ogn' anno 60 mila Lipperi insino a guerra finita." This subsidy, to judge from Sanudo, was evidently not continued after the Vespers.

[69] Brocardus, Directorium ad passagium faciendum, in Rec. des hist. des crois., Doc. Armén., II (1906) 433 (a work perhaps rather to be attributed to Guillaume d'Adam; see Bibliography): "dominum Petrum, regem tunc Aragonie, [Paleologus] induxit magnis exhibitis pecuniis et promissis quod, predicto Karolo rebellante, Siciliam occuparet, ut sic ipsum Karolum ab invasione imperii removeret; quod et factum est." Cf. Villani, I, 393, who mentions 30,000 ounces of gold given Peter by Michael.

Granted, then, the probability of an alliance between Michael and Peter before the Vespers and the dispatch of gold from Byzantium to Aragon, it may fairly be asked who was entrusted with the delicate matter of negotiations between the two powers, if we set aside Procida's voyages to Constantinople as historically unsubstantiated. The function of intermediary — or at least of principal Greek ambassador — was fulfilled by Michael's faithful friend, the Genoese noble Benedetto Zaccaria. Witness the passage quoted earlier from the *Gestes des Chiprois*:

> When Michael heard of the armament under preparation by King Peter he sent a messenger to him, . . . a citizen of Genoa named Benedetto Zaccaria, who negotiated and brought about an accord between them for an amount of money that the Emperor had sent to the King of Aragon.[70]

There is also the passage, already cited in part, from Ptolemy of Lucca, which states that among the mediators between Michael and Peter was "Lord Benedetto Zaccaria of Genoa with certain other Genoese who were lords in the territory of Palaeologus." [71] Even Martin IV's bull of excommunication, it will be recalled, explicitly names Zaccaria among the conspirators engaged in the Sicilian sedition.[72] Collateral evidence of Zaccaria's activity is a letter subsequently sent by King Peter, then in Sicily, to Constance, widow of the Emperor John III Vatatzes and sister of Manfred (she was living at the time in Catalonia), revealing that she had entrusted to Zaccaria money to be given to Peter for the Aragonese expedition against Sicily.[73] In conclusion, and by no means least in importance, there is the personal interest of Zac-

---

[70] *Gestes des Chiprois* (ed. Raynaud) V, § 415.

[71] *RISS*, XI, col. 1186: "Dominus Benedictus Zacharias de Janua cum quibusdam aliis Januensibus, qui Domini erant in terra Palaeologi." Cf. Sanudo, *Istoria*, 172-173. Note also mention in *Rebellamentu*, 15ff., of one "Accardu Latinu" (= Zaccaria? cf. Dölger, *Regesten*, no. 2059). Ostrogorsky, *Byzantine State* (1956) 413, also stresses Genoese mediation.

[72] See above, text and note 46.

[73] For the document see *Ricordi e documenti del Vespro Siciliano*, II, 33. Also see Lopez, *Benedetto Zaccaria*, 90; and esp. below, Appendix A, where Zaccaria is mentioned as Palaeologus' ambassador to Aragon just after the Vespers (May 1282).

caria himself. With his family the vassals of Michael and lords of the rich alum-producing territory of Phocaea in Asia Minor, Zaccaria must have realized that an Angevin-Venetian victory in the approaching struggle would pose a grave danger to their territories. His efforts to aid Palaeologus are therefore understandable.

MICHAEL'S RELATIONS WITH GENOA, CASTILE,

MONTFERRAT, AND PISA

A successful Angevin-Venetian invasion of Constantinople would not only threaten the Zaccarian possessions in the East but no doubt entail the economic ruin of Genoa. In the interest of survival, therefore, the Commune sought to maintain close rapport with Michael during this period. Thus in 1278, according to the *Annales Ianuenses*, the Genoese emissary, Guglielmo da Savignone, was dispatched to the Greek capital; in 1280, Manuele di Negro with four ships; and, in February of the same year, Pietro Arcanto.[74] There is reason to believe, moreover, that it was the Genoese who in August of 1280 sent to Michael a ship laden with troops from the West — a vessel which Charles, it seems, tried vainly to intercept.[75]

Though it is clear that Genoa, with vital interests of her own at stake, was of no little aid to Michael, she did not, it appears, officially and openly offer assistance.[76] This reticence is doubtless attributable to fear of strong Angevin and Venetian reprisals in Italy as well as of papal excommunication. (One may recall the previous Genoese experience with papal censure after the Treaty of Nymphaeum.)

Close ties also seem to have existed at this time between

---

[74] On Savignone, esp. see Bratianu, *Recherches*, 307; on di Negro see *Ann. Ian.*, V, 9; and for Arcanto see Ferretto, *Codice diplomatico*, XXXI², 346, note.

[75] See Charles's rescript in *Arch. st. it.*, ser. IV, III, 165: "quedam vassella onerata gente, que vadit in auxilium Paliologi." Cf. Norden, 624.

[76] On this see Manfroni, "Relazioni," 681. Also Belgrano, "Cinque documenti," *Atti soc. lig.*, XVII, 241, a letter, dated 1283, of Andronikos to the Genoese notifying them of his father's death and promising to preserve their traditional friendship. Apparently, therefore, Greco-Genoese relations had not been broken.

Genoa, King Alfonso X of Castile, and the latter's chief ally in northern Italy, the Marquis William VII of Montferrat.[77] While the marriages of William and his son to daughters of Alfonso served to bring together Castile and Montferrat,[78] William in 1281 prevailed upon Genoa to send two galleys to Catalonia.[79] Material for the relations of Alfonso of Castile, Aragon, and northern Italy during this period has not, it is true, been exhaustively studied. But what is already known seems to indicate that Alfonso, Peter of Aragon, William of Montferrat and Genoa were each, in various degrees, diplomatically involved with Palaeologus.[80]

Before leaving this discussion of events prior to the Vespers, mention must be made, though briefly, of Pisa, the third great Italian naval power. Documents inform us that Pisa, traditionally Ghibelline, was thanked by Palaeologus at the end of 1281 or beginning of 1282 for refusing to put at Charles's disposal ten galleys requested by the Angevin for his Greek expedition.[81] As a result, however, of pressures exerted by Pope Martin IV and probably the Venetians (with whom Pisa was then allied), the Pisans were compelled to associate themselves, however reluctantly, with the Angevin coalition and thus to refuse an invitation of Peter of Aragon to join in an anti-Angevin alliance.[82]

[77] For a good summary of their relations see Lopez, *Benedetto Zaccaria*, 78ff. and A. Bozzola, "Un capitano di guerra e signore subalpino," *Miscellanea di storia italiana*, R. Dep. di st. patria per le antiche prov., ser. 3, XIX (Turin, 1922) 386–394.

[78] Lopez, *Zaccaria*, 82.

[79] See *Ann. Ian.*, V, 14–15. Cf. Imperiale, *Jacopo d'Oria*, 232, and Amari, *La guerra del Vespro Siciliano*, I, 155–162, Finally, cf. Salimbene's mention of Michael, Peter, and Castile, above, note 44. In 1285, Andronikos married a daughter of the Marquis of Montferrat. See Pach., vol. II, 87, and *Ann. Ian.*, V, 61.

[80] On relations of Castile and Aragon see Cartellieri, *Peter von Aragon*, 65; Bozzola, "Un capitano di guerra," 386ff., and his "Guglielmo VII Marchese di Monferrato e Carlo I," 26. Cf. above, Chapter 10, text and notes 66, 92–98; and see Appendix A, text and note 3.

[81] See F. Kern, *Acta Imperii Angliae et Franciae*, no. 25, 15, Charles's letter asking Pope Martin to forbid Pisa to give help to Palaeologus and instead to provide him with aid. Also no. 26, 16, Palaeologus' thanks to Pisa for refusing aid to Charles ("postulata navigia denegastis").

[82] *Ibid.*, no. 27, Pisa declares to Pope Martin she will support Charles only at the wish of the Pope. (Note Pisa's friendly words here for Palaeologus.) Also no.

FINAL ANGEVIN PREPARATIONS AGAINST CONSTANTINOPLE

While Michael was engrossed with plans to protect himself from the expected Latin assault, Charles in Italy was assiduously organizing the expedition against Constantinople. His preparations were on a grand scale.

In order to raise money he levied crushing imposts on his subjects, ordering his justiciars in particular to collect a great tax for the Greek war.[83] Added to this, was the collection of the tithe for the crusade, authorized by Pope Martin in the Treaty of Orvieto.[84] Such fiscal abuses exploiting Charles's subjects for a foreign war were, of course, extremely unpopular among the *Regnicoli* and further increased their hatred for their French masters, who had displaced the popular Hohenstaufen dynasty. The attitude of the Sicilians toward a conflict with Byzantium is vividly described by the contemporary chronicler Bartolomeo of Neocastro, who writes that the Sicilians opposed a war with "our friends the Danaeans [i.e., the Greeks] of Romania, against whom he [Charles] assumed the cross of a robber, under the guise of which he was accustomed to shed innocent blood." [85] Bartolomeo's observation is of particular interest because it may well reflect the

---

28, dated 18 January (?), 1282, Peter's letter to Pisa and the reply of the Commune: "nolentes sancte matris ecclesie et ipsius regis indingnationem incurrere, respondere petitioni, quam facitis, non audemus." On the role of Pisa in these events, there is an inadequate account in D. Winter, *Die Politik Pisas während der Jahre 1268–1282* (Halle, 1906) esp. 67 and 70. But see now S. Borsari, "I rapporti tra Pisa e gli stati di Romania nel duecento," *Riv. stor. ital.*, LXVII (1955) 486–488.

[83] *Arch. st. it.*, ser. IV, IV, 3 and 174ff. Regarding financial exploitation on the part of Angevin officials, see Bartolomeo of Neocastro, *RISS* (1921) XIII, 10, and Saba Malaspina (ed. Del Re) 330–331. Cf. E. Sthamer, "Aus der Vorgeschichte der sizilischen vesper," *Quellen und Forsch. aus italien Archiven und Bibl.*, XIX (1927) esp. 266ff. and 306ff.; G. La Mantia, "Studi sulla riv.," 132.

[84] Potthast, *Regesta*, no. 21873; text in Raynaldus, a. 1282, § 5–6.

[85] Bartolomeo of Neocastro, 10: "jam hebet conditio intolerabilis servitutis; quidquid enim laboriosis studiis popularis cura satagebat acquirere, applicari fisco suo censuerat insatiabilis ingluvies Galli hujus. Ista sibi satis non fuerant; jam contra amicos nostros Danaos, videlicet Romaniae, contra quos latronis crucem assumpsit, sub cujus specie consuevit effundere sanguinem innocentum."

influence of the still numerous population of Greek descent in southern Italy and Sicily.[86]

Charles's naval and military preparations exceeded even those specified by the Orvieto treaty. According to Sanudo, Charles equipped one hundred ships on the island of Sicily and three hundred others in Naples, Provence, and Romania, which were to carry a total of eight thousand or more cavalrymen.[87] Sanudo also gives some indication of the tactics to be employed in the investment of Constantinople. Evidently Charles intended to range his ships in a solid line "extending from one sea to the other" (probably from the Bosporus to the Golden Horn) and thus to prevent the arrival by sea of reinforcements, especially of the much-feared Tatars, Michael's most faithful allies.[88] Sanudo, in addition, mentions huge iron stakes, perhaps to be used in storming the seaward walls of the capital. Supplementing Sanudo's remarks [89] is an Angevin rescript dated 28 October 1281 listing a huge collection of tools to be gathered for the expedition, including two thousand iron mattocks, three thousand iron stakes,

[86] On these Italo-Greeks see Chapter 11, note 37; and esp. R. Weiss, "The Greek Culture of South Italy in the Later Middle Ages," *Proceedings of British Academy*, XXXVII (1951) 25–29, who shows that the sentimental ties of these Greeks to Byzantium were still strong, and that this attitude was heightened by the policy of Charles, who, in contrast to the Hohenstaufens, "now regarded the Basilian [Greek] monks with suspicion as heretics and as subjects of the Greek patriarchate" — hence the many attempts in the Angevin period to suppress the Greek rite.

[87] *Istoria*, 138. Cf. Villani, I, 388, who writes of more than 100 galleys, 20 great cargo ships, 200 others for transporting horses, and other (presumably smaller) vessels. The same figures are quoted in *Rebellamentu*, 738. Cf. also Saba Malaspina (ed. Del Re) 329–330 and 314 for Charles's naval preparations in the Regno. It is to be noted also that on 7 April 1282 Charles ordered the preparation of a fleet of 22 galleys and 8 transports to fight Michael under John Chauderon. See *Arch. st. it.*, ser. IV, IV, 174. That these ships were ready to sail on short notice is indicated by a passage in *Ann. Ian.*, V, 18, recording that right after the Vespers Charles sailed to besiege rebellious Messina with 90 ships and *uscerios*, 22,000 cavalry, and 60,000 footmen.

[88] Sanudo, *Istoria*, 138: "disegnava andar ad assediar la Città di Costantinopoli da parte da Mar, e da un Mar all' altro . . . e massime Tartari, de quali più temeva, che di altri."

[89] *Ibid.*: "e fortificarsi talmente ivi con stecadi e altri modi." Sanudo's statement that the stakes were to be used to ward off Greek darts ("che Costantinopolitani non potessero offender la sua Gente pur con Veretoni ò dardi") is unclear. It

sledges for smashing rocks, ropes, iron shovels, axes, and kettles for boiling pitch. In still another document Charles directs the transportation to Trani of the "four thousand iron stakes that are under construction in Venice." [90]

Charles issued explicit orders, even to the smallest details, for the armament of his ships. With the same meticulous care he provided for the armor of his knights, as attested by directives to a Pisan merchant for the manufacture of 2,500 shields of different sizes, all of white, covered with leather, and having emblazoned in the center of each the royal emblem of lilies. [91]

Charles anticipated, no doubt, that Michael would seek to create dissension among his Sicilian subjects as he himself was doing in Epirus, Thessaly, Trebizond, and very probably among Lascarid malcontents in Constantinople. Possibly in fear of a Sicilian revolt, therefore, Charles as early as 1278 proscribed the carrying of arms by his subjects and forbade the exportation of provisions to Greek territories. [92] Doubtless his apprehensions were aggravated by incursions of Greco-Genoese pirates, whose daring led them to ravage even the coasts of Sicily. [93] Finally, as additional evidence of his suspicions, there may be cited his rigorous instructions for holding Greek prisoners incommunicado. [94]

But most disturbing to Charles must have been the discontent of the numerous noble supporters of the Hohenstaufen on the island of Sicily. Whatever may be the accuracy of certain chronicles making the Regno noble Giovanni Procida the principal architect of revolt, it seems clear from the recent, careful investigations of La Mantia, Wieruszowski, and Pontieri that the Sicilian barons, in contact with anti-Angevin elements in other parts of Italy, and in particular with Michael Palaeologus, had

---

will be recalled that Palaeologus had already heightened the seaward walls. See above, Chapter 6, section 4.

[90] *Arch. st. it.*, ser. IV, IV, 17–18 and Sanudo, *Istoria*, 174.

[91] *Ibid.*, 174–175, dated 7 April 1282 (but explicitly "for the expedition against Palaeologus"); and 174, of 26 March 1282.

[92] La Mantia, "Studi sulla riv.," 133–134. Cf. Carabellese, 128–131.

[93] See Cohn, "Storia della flotta siciliana," *Arch. st. sic. orien.*, XXIX, 46.

[94] *Arch. st. it.*, ser. IV, IV, 13.

cooperated to organize a great conspiracy against Charles.[95] And to the arguments of these scholars may be added a neglected but significant statement of the generally well-informed Sanudo that the Sicilians revolted "as the result of a treaty with the Emperor Sir Michael and his followers." [95a]

With the completion of his vast web of alliances, Charles had now succeeded almost entirely in encircling Constantinople, and his prestige, if not actual authority, was unrivaled in Europe.[96] The mere enumeration of his titles is impressive: he was King of Sicily, Arles, and Albania,[97] and, at least in name, of Jerusalem. He was ruler of Provence, Anjou, Forcalquier, and the Morea, and had the Emir of Tunis and, if we are to believe Sanudo, even the Commune of Pisa as tributaries.[98] Moreover, besides having ties of kinship with the Kings of France and Hungary, he was allied to the rulers of the Serbs and Bulgars[99] as well as the Greek princes of Epirus and dissidents of the Byzantine Empire. His newest and most powerful ally was Venice, the leading naval power of Europe, and, most important of all, he had at last secured the sanction of the papacy to lead a crusade against Byzantium. Against this enormous coalition Michael stood almost alone. So desperate was his position that it may well have been more critical than that of any other ruler in the entire period of the Middle Ages. It is no wonder that the destruction of the Greek Empire seemed imminent and that the Venetian Sanudo, the Byzantine Gregoras, and a distant troubadour of Provence could

[95] La Mantia, "Studi sulla riv.," 133–134.

[95a] *Istoria*, 147: "L'isola di Scicilia ribellò al Rè Carlo, come ho detto, e fu per trattato dell' imperator Sior Michiel e suoi seguaci." Cf. Villani, I, 389 and Amari, *La guerra del Vespro Siciliano*, I, 131. The principal Sicilian conspirators were Palmiero Abbate, Alaimo da Lentino, and Gualtieri di Caltagirone.

[96] Villani, I, 388: "era il più possente re . . . che nullo re de' cristiani."

[97] Albania, it is true, was almost lost since 1274. On Arles see Léonard, *Les Angevins de Naples*, 133.

[98] *Istoria*, 137: "(Carlo) fece il detto Regno di Tunisi tributario . . . (e) il Commun di Pisa" (passage hitherto overlooked). But see above, notes 81–82; Dölger, 489–490, *Regesten*, no. 2054; and esp. Borsari, "Rapporti tra Pisa, etc.," which collectively seem rather to indicate Pisa's neutrality just before the Vespers.

[99] Already the Serbian King Stephen Uroš II, by agreement with Charles, had opened the attack against Michael. The new Bulgar Tsar, George I Terter, had taken steps in 1281 to conclude an Angevin alliance. See *Arch. st. it.*, ser. IV, IV, 10.

all record that Charles at this moment stood on the threshold of world hegemony! [100]

THE REVOLUTION OF THE SICILIAN VESPERS AND
THE ROLE OF MICHAEL PALAEOLOGUS

But before Charles's grandiose project could be set in motion an event took place which completely ruined his carefully laid plans — the outbreak of the celebrated Sicilian Vespers. In the capital city of Palermo on Easter Monday, 30 March 1282,[101] during a religious festival, a French soldier molested a young Sicilian married woman before the church of Santo Spirito. Attacked by her outraged relatives and friends, he was at once struck down and the cry "death to the French" quickly arose on all sides. In the massacre that followed some two to three thousand Frenchmen (80,000 according to one source!) were put to death and the remainder expelled from Sicily.[102] Exiled Sicilian barons, supporters of the Hohenstaufen, at once returned to Palermo and the uprising soon became a revolution which spread rapidly throughout the island.

When Charles first heard of the Palermitan uprising he be-

[100] Sanudo, *Istoria*, 138: "aspirava alla Monarchia del Mondo." Greg., 123, ll. 10–12: "He dreamed of the entire Empire of Julius Caesar and Augustus, if only he could become master of Constantinople." For the remarks of the troubadour, Peire de Chastelnau, see G. Monti, *Nuovi studi angioini*, 415: "il re Carlo sarà signore . . . della maggior parte del mondo." It should be noted that Charles apparently intended, after taking Constantinople, to continue on to Jerusalem, of which he was already titular ruler (on which see Villani, I, 388). Léonard, *Les Angevins de Naples*, 74, says that Charles's adherents suggested to him that he follow the great example of Charlemagne!

[101] Date (Monday, 30 March) cited by Bartolomeo of Neocastro, 11, who is probably our principal contemporary source and an eyewitness to the event. The leading modern Italian scholar of the Vespers, E. Pontieri, has come to the conclusion (as he graciously wrote this author recently) that Bartolomeo's date (followed also by Cartellieri, *Peter von Aragon*, especially 210) is the most accurate "because he is best informed and closest to the events." Previously Pontieri, in the older edition of his important *Ricerche sulla crisi della monarchia siciliana nel secolo XIII* (Naples, 1950) 178 (in company with Amari, *La guerra del Vespro Siciliano*, I, 193, note 1; Chapman, 144; and Ostrogorsky, *Byzantine State* [1956] 413) had leaned toward 31 March.

[102] D'Esclot, *Cronica* (ed. Buchon), 629, says 80,000. Cf. also Sanudo, *Istoria*, 147–149, esp. 148; Bartolomeo of Neocastro, 17; Amari, *Vespro Siciliano*, I, 172.

came infuriated at the disturbance to his plans and immediately ordered ships to set out for Sicily.[103] But with the graver news that the key port of Messina was also disloyal, Charles (biting his sceptre in wrath, to quote the chronicler), ordered the entire armament prepared for the Greek expedition diverted to besiege Messina.[104] It is of no little significance that just before the city's investment (in which its inhabitants valiantly opposed two hundred ships and twenty-seven thousand cavalry),[105] the people bethought themselves of aid from Byzantium and for this purpose dispatched to Palaeologus a Genoese named Alafrancus Cassanus.[106] Meanwhile seventy Angevin ships lying in the arsenal of Messina were burned [107] — an action in which agents of the allies and the Greek colony of Messina may possibly have had a hand.[108] Ultimately the siege failed, and in August of 1282 Peter of Aragon (who meantime sailed with his fleet to Tunis, there ostensibly to engage in battle with the Muslims) landed in Sicily. Before his arrival, however, he had prudently awaited a summons from the Sicilians.[109] Thus Charles's forces were completely expelled from the island and the Hohenstaufen avenged.

[103] Four ships according to Bartolomeo of Neocastro, 22. Cf. D'Esclot, 629.

[104] Bartolomeo of Neocastro, 22: "Iracundia fervidus dentibus frendet, rodens robur, quod in manu tenebat." Charles ordered his men: "Ite . . . classes paratas cum toto exfortio quas in Graecos paraveram, vobiscum ducite."

[105] Figures found in Sanudo, *Istoria*, 148–149; this now included all the strength Charles could muster from throughout all of Italy. Cf. *Ann. Ian.*, V, 18, which says 22,000 cavalry and 60,000 footmen.

[106] Bartolomeo of Neocastro, 36–37: "Oportebat populum Pharium in principio guerrae hujus ad notitiam Palaeologi Romaeorum Imperatoris notos facere motus suos, etc." Note that Bartolomeo terms Palaeologus Emperor of the "Romans."

[107] D'Esclot, 632; Bartolomeo of Neocastro, 36–37. Cf. Saba Malaspina (ed. Del Re) 352.

[108] Dade, 63, suggests that Michael's agents may have participated in the burning of the ships.

[109] Bartolomeo of Neocastro, 42; D'Esclot, 632; Villani, I, 402–403. It may seem strange, in the light of the evidence of collusion before the Vespers, that Peter delayed so long before moving to Sicily. But several important reasons may be adduced in explanation: first, Peter was himself probably taken by surprise at the suddenness of the Vespers revolt, and thus may well have desired to see how successful the uprising would prove before taking action. Second, rather than completely prejudicing his claim to Sicily in the eyes of Catholic Europe, especially the papacy, by overtly helping to foment rebellion against the Sicilian high suzerain, the pope, he may have preferred to await an appeal from the Sicilians.

The insult of the French soldier to the girl of Palermo, which resulted in the immediate slaughter of her offender, was, of course, only a fortuitous incident.[110] But it was the occasion for an explosion of popular Sicilian resentment against the foreign oppressor sufficient to bring to a head the probably still incomplete conspiratorial preparations and, in a remarkably short time, to inflame the entire island into rebellion. The speed of this development serves as a measure not only of the intensity of national feeling against the French, but also, it would appear, of the progress that had already been made in the conspiratorial plans.

That Michael Palaeologus, on his part, had nothing whatever to do with the incident at the church of Santo Spirito is beyond question. Yet it seems justifiable to assume that, had he not already actively been supporting the conspiratorial movement with liberal financial aid and encouragement, its intrigues would have been less effective, and, at the supreme moment, would have lacked the capacity to grasp the opportunity that presented itself and to transform anti-Angevin sentiment into an overt revolution.[111]

Thus, through his role in the preparations leading to the Vespers as well as his crushing victory over Charles at Berat, Michael could celebrate the crowning diplomatic and military triumph of his career. For with Charles's own Kingdom of Sicily

---

More concretely, we know that he feared an attack from the King of France, the nephew of Charles of Anjou, Philip III, who already in May of 1282 had warned Peter (Cartellieri, *Peter von Aragon*, 169, 187, cites the sources) that any attack on Angevin Sicily by Peter's fleet, then being massed in Aragon, would be followed by a French invasion of Peter's realm. Not to be discounted, finally, is the attitude of the Sicilians themselves. Having overthrown one foreign master, they did not immediately desire a second, and it was only after an unsuccessful appeal to the Pope and realization of their inability to combat Charles alone that they formally summoned Peter to become their ruler.

[110] On this see E. Pontieri, "Un capitano della guerra dell' vespro Pietro II Ruffo di Calabria," *Arch. st. Calabria e Lucania*, I (1931) 471, and the same author's article on the Vespers in *Encicl. it.*, XXXV (1937) 224.

[111] In this connection see also the work, in Greek, of the fourteenth century Byzantine writer, Nikephoros Chumnos, "Encomium to the Emperor Andronikos Palaeologus" (J. Boissonade, *Anecdota graeca*, II [Paris, 1830] 31), in which he says that the Byzantines believed that their military success at Berat in 1281 was a contributory cause of the Sicilian uprising.

in the throes of revolution, an Angevin expedition against Constantinople was now manifestly impossible. Having saved both throne and Empire, shortly afterwards Michael himself could write in his Autobiography, with a considerable degree of truth if not complete modesty:

The Sicilians, who had only scorn for the forces remaining to the barbarian King [Charles], dared to take arms and deliver themselves from servitude, and, in fact, if I dare to say that God prepared their liberty and that he did it by my own hands, I would be telling only the truth.[112]

[112] Autobiography, 9, IX: σικελοὶ δὲ τῆς λοιπῆς ἰσχύος ἐκείνου ὡς οὐδὲν οὔσης καταφρονήσαντες, αἴρειν ἐτόλμησαν ὅπλα καὶ τῆς δουλείας ἑαυτοὺς ἀνεῖναι· ὥστ' εἰ λέγοιμι καὶ τὴν νῦν ἐκείνων ἐλευθερίαν θεὸν μὲν παρασκευάσαι, δι' ἡμῶν δὲ παρασκευάσαι, τῇ ἀληθείᾳ συμβαίνοντα λέγοιμι.

Epilogue

THE END OF ANGEVIN DESIGNS ON
BYZANTIUM AND THE DEATH OF
MICHAEL PALAEOLOGUS

Oespite the revolt of the Sicilians, Charles does not seem at once to have abandoned his plans to conquer Byzantium. Angevin chancery documents, in fact, reveal that on 4 May 1282 he sent military reinforcements and money to Avlona in Albania.[1] But the complete occupation of Sicily by the Aragonese forced Charles to realize that reconquest of the island would require his undivided attention.[2] Thus, on 3 November 1282, he sent an embassy to the Doge requesting for use against Sicily what were doubtless the forty Venetian ships promised at Orvieto for the Greek campaign.[3]

Venice, however, did not desire to be drawn into an unprofitable Angevin-Aragonese conflict. On the contrary, the Grand Council ordered all Venetian citizens to quit Sicily within one

[1] *Arch. st. it.*, ser. IV, IV, 176; also 174, edict of 7 April 1282. Cf. Cartellieri, *Peter von Aragon*, 149.

[2] On Charles's attitude note esp. Sanudo, *Istoria*, 133: "Rè Carlo predetto ebbe assai da far' a ricuperar la Scicilia." Also *Ann. Ian.*, V, 18: "Karolus . . . graviter perturbatus et motus, dimisso proposito quod erat contra Grecos in eadem estate proficisci, omnino cum toto dicto apparatu ad obsidionem Messane celeriter properavit." Also see *Arch. st. it.*, ser. IV, IV, 350 (9 September 1282), and V, 361 (3 December 1283), documents mentioning exchanges of prisoners with Michael and his son Andronikos respectively — further evidence, probably, of Charles's renunciation of his designs.

[3] *Arch. st. prov. nap.*, I (1876) 96, and cf. Nicollini, "Sui rapporti Veneto-napoletani," *Arch. stor. prov. nap.*, n.s., LX (1935) 266. See also letter (cited *ibid.*) of Charles's son to the Doge, dated 7 January 1283, seeking the same ships.

month.[4] Moreover, as the Sicilian war progressed adversely for Charles (the conflict was to continue for twenty years!) and Angevin plans to conquer Byzantium began to appear completely illusory, Venice instead entered into negotiations with Constantinople, and in 1285 concluded a ten-year truce with Michael's son and successor, Andronikos.[5] Consequently, any aggressive designs Charles still entertained against the Greek capital were finally dissipated, and in the few years before his death in 1285, he occupied himself exclusively with unsuccessful diplomatic and military endeavors to recover Sicily and to protect his territorial possessions in Romania.[6]

Charles's reign extended three years beyond that of Michael,[7] who himself lived only some nine months after the outbreak of the Vespers. During the last months of his reign, the Emperor, freed at last from the menace of the Latins, was able to direct his attention to the grave Turkish threat on his Asiatic frontiers.[8] His endeavors in this respect, important as they were for subsequent Byzantine history, are outside the scope of this book. Nevertheless, it should be pointed out that his failure adequately to protect his Anatolian borders was essentially due to his preoccupation with his deadly rival in the West.[9]

Having no more than returned to Constantinople from his Anatolian campaigns, the Emperor in November of 1282 was obliged once more to march against the rebellious John the Bastard of Thessaly. With the death of his best generals (particularly his brother John), Michael, though exhausted from his

[4] *Deliberazioni del Maggior Consiglio di Venezia*, ed. R. Cessi, II (Bologna, 1931) 139, nos. XLVIII and XLIX.

[5] For the truce see T.-Th., III, 322ff.

[6] See a letter of Charles, dated 5 December 1283, to Nikephoros of Epirus regarding aid from Angevin Achaia for the latter against Andronikos Palaeologus. In C. De Lellis, *Gli atti perduti della cancelleria Angioina*, Mazzoleni ed., in *Regesta chartarum italiae* (Rome, 1939) I, pt. I, no. 58, 573.

[7] Charles died in 1285, Michael in 1282.

[8] See Pach., 502ff. and Greg., 142ff.

[9] For modern works on the Turkish problem see esp. G. Arnakis, Οἱ Πρῶτοι Ὀθωμανοί (Athens, 1947) 37ff., and the meagre treatment of Chapman, 146ff. It was after publication of these works that material was made available revealing Michael's aim to use Western crusading armies to recover Anatolia for the Empire. See Chapter 12, text and notes 46–55.

labors and suffering from an acute disease of the intestines, took personal command of his troops. Against the wishes of the Empress he crossed the Sea of Marmora during a violent storm, debarking at Rodosto, from which he rode with difficulty to the village of Pachomios in Thrace. There, unable to rise from his bed, he received the auxiliary Tatar troops sent by his faithful ally, Nogai.[10]

Michael's malady rapidly became worse, and on Friday, 11 December 1282, at the age of fifty-eight, he died. Present during his last moments was his son and successor Andronikos. More orthodox than pious, and fearful lest his father's body be mutilated by wild beasts or desecrated by Latins or fanatical anti-unionist Greeks, Andronikos immediately had the corpse carried under cover of night to the nearby town of Selymbria.[11] There, without ceremony of any kind, the body was later placed in a coffin in the obscure monastery of Christ the Saviour.[12]

Thus, after an eventful reign of twenty-four years, during which Constantinople was restored to the Greeks and the Empire once more played an influential, if less decisive, role in European affairs, Michael VIII Palaeologus was laid to rest, without imperial ceremony or, evidently, even the rites of the church.[13] Nevertheless, he could die with the satisfaction that his diplo-

---

[10] On all this see Pach., 524–528.

[11] Pach., 528–532; II, 107 (where he says Andronikos feared that Tatars would seize the corpse). Greg., 149–155 (esp. 153, ll. 1–14) and 159, ll. 21–22.

[12] Pach., II, 107. Also Greg., 159. Cf. Sphrantzes, 24. Cf. next note.

[13] The Western sources even more than the Greek have stressed the lack of ecclesiastical rites, because of his unionist activities. See, for example, the remarkable, doubtless exaggerated statement in Ann. Ian., V, 16, that he was not buried by 1300! ("non fuit traditus sepulture, immo in . . . 1300"). There is a 14th century Greek source unused in this respect which gives what purports to be the exact date of his burial — Sunday, 17 April 1283, at the monastery of the Saviour in Selymbria. Text recently published in Vizantiskii Vremennik, II (XXVII) (1949) 281–282, ed. B. Goryanov, and reading: καὶ ἐτάφη εἰς τὴν συλημβρίαν ἐν τῇ μονῇ τοῦ Χριστοῦ ἀπριλλίῳ ιζ' ἡμέρᾳ κυριακῇ. Cf. the testimony of Pachymeres, II, 55, 107, indicating that Michael's body was placed in a coffin (ἐν αὐτῷ τῷ ναῷ αὐτῇ λάρνακι) in the Selymbrian monastery evidently much later, in what seems to have been the month of April. On the typical attitude to Michael of the anti-unionists who triumphed in Byzantium with the accession of Michael's son, Andronikos, see M. Calecas, Adversus Graecos, in Migne, PG, vol. 152, col. 211, which says (reminiscent of the Annales Ianuenses) that Michael's cadaver remained intact as proof of his soul's perversity!

macy and arms had saved Byzantium from the peril of a new Latin invasion and that he had securely established a dynasty on the imperial throne. At the same time his arch-enemy Charles of Anjou, in his determination to restore the island of Sicily to the dismembered Regno, was doomed to spend the remaining years of his life in a bitter, fruitless struggle against opponents encouraged by Palaeologus.[14]

No more fitting tribute to the arduous labors of Michael against the Latins has been pronounced than these succinct words of Gregoras: "The Empire would easily have fallen under the domination of Charles, King of Italy [sic] had such an Emperor not then been at the helm of Greek affairs." [15] But it must not be overlooked that his undeniable successes were dearly bought. For in the long and difficult process of saving the Empire from the West, Michael so weakened its religious unity and drained its financial and military strength that, by a remarkable irony of history, he helped to pave the way for Byzantium's ultimate conquest by the Turks.

[14] See Greg., 148, ll. 16–18: "Soon afterwards Charles died, unable to the end to bear his sorrow [over the loss of Sicily and failure of his Greek expedition] which was deep and hard to endure."

[15] Greg., 144: εἰ μὴ τηνικαῦτα τοιοῦτος βασιλεὺς τοῖς Ῥωμαίων ἐπεστάτει πράγμασι, ῥᾳδίως ἂν ὑπὸ τῷ ῥηγὶ τῆς Ἰταλίας Καρούλῳ ἡ Ῥωμαίων ἡγεμονία ἐγεγόνει. The fact that Gregoras calls Charles King of Italy is a sure indication of the great impression Charles's power had made on the Greeks.

appendices

appenдix a

FURTHER ARGUMENTS ON THE EXISTENCE OF A GRECO-ARAGONESE ALLIANCE PREVIOUS TO THE SICILIAN VESPERS

In a valuable study on the career of Benedetto Zaccaria, R. Lopez maintains that no alliance existed between Michael and Peter of Aragon prior to the outbreak of the Sicilian Vespers (30 March 1282). His proof rests primarily on the conduct of a Greek embassy which reached Catalonia at the end of May 1282. The imperial envoys, Benedetto Zaccaria and the Archbishop of Sardis, told Peter upon arrival at his court that they would inform him of their mission after returning from Castile, to which they were about to journey. Owing to the existence of a Castilian civil war, however, the envoys returned to Aragon apparently without meeting King Alfonso. Nor did they see Peter, as he had already sailed with his fleet to Africa and then Sicily. Thus the envoys were not able to meet with the Aragonese ruler until September of 1282 in Palermo. At that time discussions took place over a projected marriage between Michael's son Andronikos (whose Hungarian wife, Anna, had recently died) and a daughter of Peter. But the Greek envoys, complaining of the advanced age of the Aragonese princess as well as the inadequacy of their own authority, suggested instead that Aragonese envoys be sent to Constantinople for further discussion.[1]

The evidence cited by Lopez is, in the first place, *ex post facto*. He argues that there could have been no alliance before the Vespers because two, then six months *after* the Vespers Zaccaria and the Archbishop of Sardis treated Peter as "an occasional ally," not as one with whom an alliance had previously been formed. The supposed reticence of the envoys to reveal the purpose of their embassy until they had seen Alfonso, and moreover, their hesitancy over a marriage between the Greek and Aragonese ruling families are for Lopez convincing

---

[1] On Lopez' arguments see his *Benedetto Zaccaria*, 66–69 and 78. For the document in question see Lopez, 256–257; *Ricordi e documenti del Vespro Siciliano*, II (Palermo, 1882) 4; and A. de Saint-Priest, *Histoire de la conquête de Naples*, IV, 213–214.

disproof of the previous formation of an accord.[2] It is possible, however, to interpret these data in a different manner.

When the envoys subsequently encountered Peter in Palermo conditions had completely changed. With the outbreak of the Vespers and the expulsion of Angevin forces from Sicily, the danger of an Angevin invasion of Constantinople had practically disappeared. Thus the Greek envoys were in a far better bargaining position regarding marriage proposals between the two royal houses, a fact presumably manifested by their allusion to the age of the Aragonese princess and by the suggestion for further negotiations in Constantinople.

Nor does the unwillingness of the Greek envoys to divulge the purpose of their embassy until their return from Castile necessarily indicate, as Lopez maintains, that no alliance existed. It may well be that Michael, quite possibly already allied to both King Alfonso of Castile and Peter of Aragon, had instructed his envoys to give consideration to the daughter of Alfonso as well as to Peter's before committing him to so important a matter as the marriage of his eldest son and heir. It is noteworthy that Lopez himself strongly supports the existence at this time of close Greco-Castilian relations, if not of an actual alliance,[3] and the testimony of the *Annales Placentini* may be recalled to the effect that already in 1273 Alfonso had proposed a union between one of his daughters and a son of Michael.[4]

In further support of his thesis Lopez adduces a letter of King Peter to his minister John of Procida dated 29 July 1283 (again after the Vespers), in which Peter emphasizes his refusal of a marriage with the Greeks and, moreover, his lack of confidence in a plan to secure Greek subsidies for the continuing war with Charles over Sicily. Peter's attitude may very well have stemmed from a desire to appear dissociated from the "Greek schismatics" in order not to damage his claim to the possession of Sicily vis-à-vis the Papacy and Catholic Europe. If this interpretation is correct, it would be only natural for Peter to write (as he did) disapprovingly of a dynastic union, "especially at this time, with the Greeks who are in open rupture with the church." [5] As for

[2] Lopez, *Benedetto Zaccaria*, 78.
[3] *Ibid.* Cf. Chapter 10, section 5, above, and Chapter 14, note 43. The seventeenth century historian G. Zurita, *Los cinco libros, etc.* (Saragossa, 1610) Bk. III, ch. 13, records that in 1281 a marriage was proposed between a Castilian princess and the titular Latin Emperor, Philip of Courtenay. Lopez (91, note 52) suggests that as Philip was already married, his name may well have been mistaken for that of Andronikos, son of Michael. But, actually, Philip's wife had already died. See Chapter 9, note 113, and Chapter 10, note 92.
[4] *Ann. Plac. Gib., MGH SS*, XVIII, 553. See Chapter 10, text and notes 92–96.
[5] Lopez, *Benedetto Zaccaria*, 71–72. For the letter see Saint-Priest, *Histoire de*

Peter's phrase regarding Greek subsidies, this may instead reflect Peter's realization that, with the end of the Angevin threat to Constantinople as a result of the Vespers, the Byzantine Emperor (now Michael's son Andronikos) would feel there was no need for further financial aid to Aragon.[5a]

Lopez' final argument is to demonstrate, on the basis of two Genoese documents indicating Zaccaria's residence in Pera (Galata) during July and August of 1281, that Zaccaria could not possibly have been in Catalonia during this period.[6] One must question, however, why negotiations with Peter necessarily had to be confined to these two months of 1281. Evidence, on the contrary, indicates that negotiations between the two rulers may have taken place in the period before 1281 — that is, in 1278–1279 if we are to believe Wieruszowski[7] — or in any case at the end of 1280 or early 1281, at which time any doubts Michael might have had about the timing of an Angevin attack and the necessity of securing aid apart from the papacy were erased by Charles's siege of Berat and certainly by news of the ominous conflict in the Curia following the death of Pope Nicholas III. The arguments delineated here, together with the documentary evidence contained in Chapter 14 (especially the testimony of Peter himself),[8] would seem, therefore, to corroborate the existence of a Greco-Aragonese alliance before the Vespers.

---

la conquête de Naples, IV, 232ff., and C. Carucci, *La guerra del Vespro*, II (Subiaco, 1931) 123, esp.: "maxime isto tempore quo Greci sunt taliter cum Ecclesia."

[5a] See Chapter 14, text and note 68a, statement of Sanudo on Greek subsidies to Aragon.

[6] Documents in G. Bratianu, *Actes des notaires génois de Pera et de Caffa* (1927) 80 and 126. See Lopez, *Benedetto Zaccaria*, 84.

[7] See Chapter 14, text and notes 60–61.

[8] See Chapter 14, text and note 48.

appenδix B

SIX UNPUBLISHED DOCUMENTS ILLUSTRATING BYZANTINE-LATIN RELATIONS DURING THE REIGN OF MICHAEL PALAEOLOGUS

1.

The following document should be considered in connection with a similar one printed in Tafel and Thomas, *Urkunden*, III, 24, no. 338, by the terms of which Venetian officials of Constantinople were, in 1259, authorized to raise loans for the needs, especially defensive, of the Latin Empire of Constantinople. According to the present document, the Venetian Podestà of Constantinople, Marco Gradenigo (on whom see Chapter 5, note 22), and his councillors, Gerardino Longo and Ermolao Giusto, in 1260 borrowed 200 *hyperpyra* from Giovanni Gussoni (doubtless a Venetian) for "servicio nella guerra," a phrase evidently referring to the Greek threat to Constantinople posed by Michael Palaeologus. (On this see Chapter 4, section 1, and esp. text and notes 22–26.) The document describes the difficulties experienced by the same Gussoni, some thirty years later, in attempting to collect his original loan from the Venetian government, in view of the fact that he had, so it appears, already sold the articles of merchandise granted to him by the government as security.

Apart from its historical value, the document may be of interest to the economist as an example of Venetian commercial practice. Written in Italian, it was certainly drawn up after 1301, the latest date cited in the text. But to judge from the absence of official Venetian seals, etc., it may be a copy of an earlier document.

1260. 5 Agosto Indizione terza. Marco Gradenigo Podestà in Constantinopoli e despota dell' impero de Romania Gerardino Longo e Ermolao Giusto Consiglieri
Avendo havuto facolta dal Doge Renier Zen per lettere de 1259 indizione seconda 4 Decembre di poter pigliare sopra il nome suo et del comun di Venezia yperperi doro 3000 per negotii del Comun et havendone essi presi 200 da Giovanni Gussoni quali furono impiegarsi nel servicio della guerra, fano al dicto Gussoni una carta d'obligazione acció essi yperperi gli siino restituiti in Venezia et gli consignano due sacci bollati l'uno con sette catine compre per 13 yperperi la dozena et un altro con opere de varii compre per

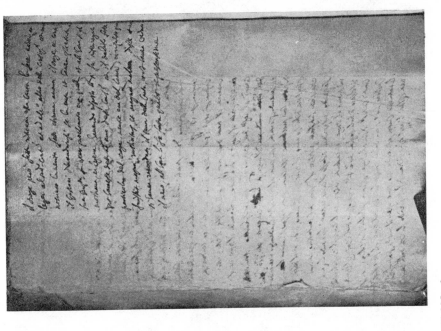

DOCUMENT NO. 1

DOCUMENT NO. 6

yperperi 140 da esser portati in Venezia et vendute per cavarne il tasso di essi 200 yperperi per la soddisfazione d'esso Gussoni da esser fatto il pagamento in due ratte obligando il doge et il commun al pagamento del doppio quando non cosi facessero. Hora essendo del 1290 del mese 6 di luglio comparse esse Giovanni Gussoni et havendo presentata essa carta al Doge Pietro Gradenigo ricercando di poter far procedere essa carta perche s'approssimavanno la preterizione delli 30 anni, il Doge prese in mano, vide che il debito era stato sodisfatto, riprese il Gussoni del tentativo, et non sapendo rispondere abasso il capo, et parti lasciando la carta in mano al Doge, et conferita la cosa con li consiglerii consultamente risalsero di farla togliar della quarantia. Doppo del 1301 ser Joanne Contarini conseglier disse al Doge presente gli altri suoi collegi, et il Gussoni sudetto si era doluto con esso lui che dal Doge gli fosse stata levata essa carta asserendo esso Doge esser il debitore perche gli avea prestati li yperperi a suo Padre di falsificando la cosa dalla verita il Doge però fatta ritrovar essa carta, la fece veder et leger al sudetto Contarini et al alcuno altro delli consiglieri et conosciuta la verita fatto chiamar avanti il Doge et consiglieri il Gussoni dimandatogli se la carta, che havea presentata a sua Serenita per esser proclamata era quella che allora si gli mostrava, et legeva havendo risposto che si fu interogato perche havesse detto ad uno delli consiglieri che il debito fosse particolare del Doge mentre era del Comun, et rispose quod fuisset magna rusticitas et magnum malum disse et non se haver recordato il tenor della carta, et che havea creduto dir il vero, allora li fu fatta qualche reprezenzione.

Biblioteca Marciana, Venice;
Lat. class. 14, no. 37, fol.
20r-v.

2.

This document, drawn up in Negropont, 11 February 1262, is a record of a business transaction between two former Latin inhabitants of Constantinople, Stephanus de Niola and Petro de La Calcina, both of whom had probably fled Constantinople seven months earlier when troops of Michael Palaeologus had captured the city (see above, Chapter 5, text and note 75). I am grateful to the Archivist Morozzo della Rocca for pointing out this document to me in Venice.

In nomine Dei eterni amen. Anno ab incarnacione Domini Ihesu Christi millesimo ducentesimo sexagesimo primo, mense februarii, die undecimo intrante, indicione quinta, Nigroponte. Manifestum facio ego quidem Stephanus de Niola olim habitator in Constantinopoli, nunc habitator in Nigroponte cum meis heredibus tibi namque Petro de La Calcina quondam habitatori in Constantinopoli, nunc habitatore Nigroponte et tuis heredibus, quoniam de omnibus commendacionibus quas feci aput . . . Bernardum Garra et eius fratrem Arnaldum de Civitate Argense que fuerunt de libre

379

denarorum Arnaldensium centum sexaginta quattuor et solidos qui[ndecim atque aput] Gyrardum Fornerium habitatorem Castri Penneque fuerunt libre [sexa]ginta quinque [dictorum denarione?] et aput Bernardum Fornerium habitatorem dicti castri que fuerunt [libre per omnia?] viginti quinque predictorum denariorum et de omni proficiio quod de ipsis tempore aliquo abebitur medietatem habes cum michi soli de dictis denariis cartule facte fuerint. Quam quidem medietatem tuam suprascriptorum omnium denariorum et lucri quod habebitur a modo tibi sit licitum disponere, committere et facere quicquid tibi placuerit et melius videbitur nullo tibi contradicente. Quod si unquam contra hanc manifestationis cartulam ire temptavero, tunc emendare debeam cum meis heredibus tibi et tuis heredibus totam predictam tuam medietatem in duplum et hec manifestationis cartula in sua permaneat firmitate. Signum suprascripti Stephani de Niola qui hec rogavit fieri.† Ego Iacobus de Niola testis subscripsi. Ego Arnaudus de Niolas testis subscripsi. S. T. Ego Iohannes Beltraymo presbiter et notarius complevi et roboravi.

> *Arch. di Stato, Venice; Manimorti Pergamene del convento di San Stefano, Venice.*

3.

(Documents 3, 4, and 5 illustrate Greco-Venetian-Jewish relations in Crete during the reign of Michael VIII.)

Document drawn up in Candia, Crete, 8 February 1282. Sambathinus, a Jew, promises to indemnify Constantine Curocha for losses the latter might suffer under certain conditions.

Die octavo intrante. Promictens promicto ego Sambathinus iudeus habitator in Candida eum meis heredibus vobis Constantino Curocha villano Iohannis Cornaro lo Sclavo et Iacobine eius uxori ambobus habitatoribus in casali nomine Cudeci et vestris heredibus et successoribus, quod si aliquod dampnum vobis accideret de aliqua carta seu cartis, quam vel quas habuerit Helyas Allamannus iudeus socer meus ab initio usque modo, totum illud dampnum vobis debeam de meis bonis propriis emendare, sub pena totius illius dampni in duplum, et insuper auri libras quinque. Testes Iacobus Dandulo et Bartholomeus Grimaldi, Dominicus Poppo vicedominus. Complere et dare.

> *Arch. di Stato, Venice; Notai del Regno di Candia, Notarial documents of Crescenzio of Alexandria, fol. 13r.*

4.

Drawn up in Candia, Crete, 22 May 1282. Alexios Kallerges, presumably a Greek, promises to repay grain borrowed from the Venetian Iohannes Gradonico. (On the famous Kallerges family, which was involved with Michael Palaeologus in anti-Venetian revolutionary activities, see Chapter 8, text and esp. note 96.)

Manifestum facio ego Alexius Kalergius habitator in Candida quia recepi cum meis heredibus alte Iohanne Gradonico olim de confinio Sancti Pauli de Veneciis nunc habitatori Chanee mensuras boni frumenti Cretensis trecentas quod michi prestitisti causa amoris. Et debeo tibi ipsum reddere hic in Candida de frumento Milipote, conductum ad domum tuam meis expensis, salvum in terra, sub pena dupli. Et inde in antea. Testes Bartholomeus Grimaldi notarius et Nicolaus Belli. Complere et dare.

Arch. di Stato, Venice; Notai
del Regno di Candia, Crescenzio
of Alexandria, fol. 31v.

5.

Drawn up in Candia, Crete, 11 January 1282. Business transaction.

Iacobus Albertus et Clemens Lando rogavit me ut facerem commissionem nomine eorum Marco Barastro, generalem et spetialem super omnibus eorum negotiis, unam vel plures, quot oportuerint. Presbiter Michael et Iacobellus Grimaldi. Testis. Complere et dare.

Arch. di Stato, Venice; Notai
del Regno di Candia, Crescenzio
of Alexandria, fol. 8v.

6.

Three anonymous epigrams in political verse (Venice, Bibl. Marciana, greco 464, fol. 1r), eulogizing Michael VIII Palaeologus, or, very possibly, his grandson, Michael IX (d. 1320). Written presumably in Constantinople during the late 13th or first quarter of the 14th century, these verses are cited by Chapman (182) and others as referring to Michael VIII and as being an autograph of the famous Byzantine scholar, Demetrios Triklinios. But I am informed by my good friend, the learned scholar Professor A. Turyn, that on palaeographical grounds this attribution to Triklinios is erroneous, since the leaf containing the epigrams is written in an entirely different hand and is actually only an extraneous insert bound with the Triklinian ms. of Hesiod (Venice, Marciana, greco 464), the latter of which is subscribed in 1316 and 1319.

The verses, of conventional panegyric style and wording, offer no new material of particular historical importance. It is of possible interest, however (since Michael VIII, among the late 13th and 14th century Byzantines, was generally execrated as Latinophile and a heretic), that the Michael here referred to is called "the great leader of the Ausones, the pride of the Romans" (ll. 27–28, τὸν μέγαν Αὐσονάρχην, τὸ τῶν Ῥωμαίων καύχημα). (Such terms are, on the other hand, common to Byzantine encomia.) In view of the fact that K. Krumbacher years ago recorded the existence of these verses, along with an announcement of imminent publication by M. Treu — a publication which never materialized, possibly because of the poor legibility of the leaf — the verses deserve to be published. (A few wrong spellings and accents have been corrected below.) See Krumbacher, *Gesch. der byz. Litt.* 780, 555; and S. Lampros, Νέος Ἑλληνομνήμων, XIII (1916) 30, who discusses one Manuel Phakrases, to whom several other epigrams in the same leaf are dedicated. (Both Krumbacher and Lampros wrongly believe all the epigrams to be an organic part of the Triklinian Hesiod volume.) Lastly, see esp. the recent book *The Byzantine Manuscript Tradition of the Tragedies of Euripides* (Urbana, 1957) 26, note 43 by A. Turyn, to whom I am indebted for helping me to read these epigrams.

The above remarks, it is hoped, by removing the confusion resulting from the wrong association of the leaf in question with Triklinios, may help to clarify the circumstances of the composition of the epigrams and thus lead to a positive identification of the person referred to therein.

(Each epigram is marked by a large initial capital projected to the left of the page column, with the text of each epigram written continuously in the MS.)

Εἰς τὸν θάνατον τοῦ βασιλέως κυρ(οῦ) Μιχαὴλ τοῦ Παλαιολόγου:

I

Δεῦτε φυλαὶ πάσης τῆς γῆς ἀρχαί τε πᾶσαι δεῦτε,
καὶ γένη τὰ πολύσπορα πάντων ἀνθρώπων ἅμα,
χορὸν συστήσασθε κοινὸν καὶ κλαύσατε συντόνως.
ἰδοὺ γὰρ καταλέλοιπεν ὡς ὄναρ ὁμοῦ πάντα
5 πάντων ἡμῶν ὁ βασιλεύς, ὁ φοβερὸς τοῖς ἔργοις,
ὁ τῶν πενήτων πλουτιστής, ὑπομονῆς ὁ στῦλος·
τὸ στέφος, τὸ διάδημα, σὺν ἀλουργίδι ξίφος,
καὶ πᾶσαν ἄλλην ἀρχικὴν δορυφορίαν κράτους,
καὶ πρὸς τὸν τάφον ἔδραμεν, ὦ συμφορᾶς, ὦ πάθους: †††

II

10 Ἥλιε, κρύψον σου τὸ φῶς καὶ σύστειλον ἀκτῖνας·
νεφέλαι, συγκαλύψατε τὸ πλάτος τὸ τοῦ πόλου,

καὶ πᾶσα κτίσις πένθησον ἀνθρώπων τε καὶ ζῴων.

ὁ Μιχαὴλ γὰρ ὁ φαιδρός, ὁ μέγας ἄναξ πέλων,
Παλαιολόγων ὁ βλαστός, ἀνδρικωτάτη φύσις,
15 ὃν ἔφριξαν οἱ βάρβαροι τούτους μονομαχοῦντα,
ἐφθάρη, φεῦ τῆς συμφορᾶς, καὶ τάφῳ συνεσχέθη,
καὶ σκότ(ος) ὡς ἱμάτιον δεινῶς περιεβλήθη·
ὢ τῆς ζημίας τῆς κοινῆς, οἷος φωστὴρ ἐκρύβη: †††

III †Τοῦ αὐτοῦ:

Θάνατε, τίς ἡ μάχη σου, καὶ τί τὰ βέλη, φράσον,
20 ἅπερ ἐκφέρεις καθ' ἡμῶν καὶ φθείρεις πάντ(ας) ἄρδην·
καὶ οὐκ αἰδεῖ τοὺς ἄρχοντας, οὐ βασιλέας τρέμεις,
οὔτε μικρὸν οὔτε πτωχόν, οὐδ' αὖ γε ξένων φείδει.
ἀπόλοιτό σου τῆς ἀρχῆς ἡ δρακοντεία ῥίζα,
ἥτις εἰς φῶς προήνεγκε βλάστην σωματοφθόρον,
25 σὲ τὸν δεινόν, σὲ τὸν κακόν, σὲ τὸν φθορέα πάντων,
σὲ τὸν ἁρπάσαντα καὶ νῦν ἡμῶν ἐκ μέσου, φεῦ μοι,
τὸν Μιχαὴλ τὸν φοβερόν, τὸν μέγαν Αὐσονάρχην,
τὸ τῶν Ῥωμαίων καύχημα, τὸ τῶν ἀνδρείων κλέος:

383

BIBLIOGRAPhy

GLOSSARY

INDEX

annotateδ bibliogRaphy[1]

An attempt has been made to provide a complete bibliography of the subject treated in this book. However, works of a popular nature and those cited in the footnotes only in passing have been omitted.

PRIMARY SOURCES

I. Documentary Sources

A. Greek

Cotelier, J. *Ecclesiae graecae monumenta*, 3 vols. (Paris, 1677–1686).

Dmitrievskij, A. "Τυπικὸν τῆς ἐν τῷ περιωνύμῳ βουνῷ τοῦ Αὐξεντίου . . . μονῆς τοῦ Ἀρχιστρατήγου Μιχαήλ, in *Opisanie liturgičeskih rukopisej*, vol. I, pt. 1, Τυπικά (Kiev, 1895) 769–794. Important, apologetic work by Michael. Cited here as *Typikon for St. Michael*; see Ch. 1, note 1.

Dölger, F. *Regesten der Kaiserurkunden des oströmischen Reiches*, pt. 3 (1204–1282) in *Corpus der griechischen Urkunden des Mittelalters und der neueren Zeit* (Munich-Berlin, 1932). Indispensable bibliographical aid.

Drinov, M. "O nekotorych trudach Demetriya Chomatiana kak istoricheskom materialye," *Vizantiiski Vremennik*, II (1895) 1–23.

Festa, N. "Lettera inedita dell' imperatore Michele VIII Paleologo al Clemente IV," *Bessarione*, VI (1899) 42ff. Also "Ancora la lettera di Michele Paleologo," *ibid.*, 529ff.

—— *Theodori Ducae Lascaris Epistulae CCXVII* (Florence, 1898).

Gedeon, M. Τυπικὸν τῆς ἐπὶ τοῦ βουνοῦ τοῦ Αὐξεντίου σεβασμίας μονῆς Μιχαὴλ τοῦ Ἀρχιστρατήγου (Constantinople, 1895). Same *typikon* as Dmitrievskij's but from another MS.

Heisenberg, A. "Aus der Geschichte und Literatur der Palaiologenzeit," *Sitzungsb. d. bayer. Akad. Wissen.* (1920) 10. Abh., 33ff. Contains Michael's *prostagma* of Nov., 1272; cf. Dölger, *Regesten*, no. 1994.

Meyer, Ph. *Die Haupturkunde für die Geschichte der Athos-Klöster* (Leipzig, 1894).

Miklosich, F. and J. Müller. *Acta et diplomata res graecas italasque illustrantia* (Vienna, 1860–1890) esp. vols. 1–3. Fundamental documents.

---

[1] While this volume was in press S. Runciman's *The Sicilian Vespers* (Cambridge, 1958) was published in England. This well-written book focusing on the political history of Sicily and Charles of Anjou appeared too late to be consulted for this work. The reader is referred to it for differences in the use of sources and in points of interpretation on the episode of the Vespers, which figures prominently in both works.

Papageorgiu, P. "Zum Typikon des Michael Palaiologos," in *Byz. Zeit.*, X (1901) 530–539. On typikon published by M. Gedeon; see also Papageorgiu's "Zwei iambische Gedichte saec. XIV–XIII," *Byz. Zeit.*, VIII (1899) 674ff.

Pitra, J. *Analecta sacra et classica Spicilegio solesmensi parata*, VI (Paris-Rome, 1891). For letters of Demetrios Chomatianos.

Sathas, C.[or K.] Μνημεῖα Ἑλληνικῆς Ἱστορίας, *Documents inédits relatifs à l'histoire de la Grèce*, 9 vols. (Paris, 1880–1890).

Spata, G. *Le pergamene greche* (Palermo, 1862). Also *Le pergamene greche existenti nel grande archivio di Palermo* (Palermo, 1864).

Troitskii, J. *Imperatoris Michaelis Palaeologi de vita sua opusculum necnon regulae quam ipse monasterio S. Demetrii praescripsit fragmentum* (St. Petersburg, 1885). Important source on Michael's life, by himself; cited as Autobiography: see Ch. 1, note 1 and, for additional information, Dölger, *Regesten*, no. 2061.

Vasilevskij, V. "Epirotica saeculi XIII," *Viz. Vremennik*, III (1896) 233–299.

B. Latin

Belgrano, L. "Cinque documenti genovesi-orientali," *Atti della società ligure di storia patria*, XVII (1885) 223ff. Documents unused by Chapman.

—— *Documenti inediti riguardanti le due crociate di san Ludovico IX* (Genoa, 1859).

—— "Prima serie di documenti riguardanti la colonia di Pera," *Atti soc. lig. stor. patria*, XIII (1877–1884) 97–336. Useful.

Bertolotto, G. "Nuova serie di documenti sulle relazioni di Genova col impero bizantino," *Atti soc. lig. stor. patria*, XXVIII (1898) 339–573. Important: single edition of some texts.

Borgo, F. dal. *Raccolta di scelti diplomi pisani* (Pisa, 1765).

Bourel de la Roncière, C. *Les registres d'Alexandre IV*, 2 vols. (Paris, 1902).

Bratianu, G. *Actes des notaires génois de Péra et de Caffa de la fin du treizième siècle* (Bucharest, 1927). Contains several important documents.

Cadier, E. *Le registre de Jean XXI* (Paris, 1898).

Capasso, B. *Le fonti della storia delle provincie napolitane dal 568 al 1500* (Naples, 1902). Basic.

—— *Historia diplomatica Regni Siciliae 1250–1266* (Naples, 1874). Important.

—— *Monumenta ad Neapolitani ducatus historiam pertinentia*, 2 vols. (Naples, 1881–1892).

Caplet, A. *Regesti Bernardi I Abbatis Casinensis* (Rome, 1890).

Carini, I. *Gli archivi e le biblioteche di Spagna in rapporto alla storia d'Italia*, 2 vols. (Palermo, 1884ff.). Important for Vespers.

Carucci, C. *Codice diplomatico Salernitano del secolo XIII*, 2 vols. (Subiaco, 1931–1934). Useful for Vespers.

Cessi, R. *Deliberazioni del Maggior Consiglio di Venezia*, II (Bologna, 1931).

BIBLIOGRAPHY

Ciampi, I. *Chronache e statuti della città di Viterbo* (1872).

Delisle, L. *Notice sur cinq manuscrits de la Bibliothèque Nationale et sur un manuscrit de la Bibliothèque de Bordeaux contenant les recueils épistolaires de Bérard de Naples*, in *Notices et extraits de la Bibliothèque Nationale*, XXVII² (Paris, 1879) 87–167. Important; contains documentary texts.

Durrieu, P. *Les archives angevines de Naples*, 2 vols. (Paris, 1886–1887).

Ferretto, A. "Codice diplomatico delle relazioni fra la Liguria la Toscana e la Lunigiana ai tempi di Dante," *Atti della soc. lig. st. patria*, XXXI, pts. 1–2 (1901–1903). Basic documents.

Festa, N. "Le lettere greche di Federigo II," *Archivio stor. ital.*, XIII (1894) 1–34.

Filangieri, R. *I registri della cancelleria angioina*, in *Testi e documenti di storia napoletana* (Naples, 1950ff.) vols. I–VIIff. Basic; vast project to republish Angevin archives almost entirely destroyed in Second World War. Cited as *Registri*; see Introduction.

Gay, J. *Les registres de Nicolas III* (Paris, 1898–1938). Basic.

Ghetti, B. *I patti tra Venezia e Ferrara dall' 1191 al 1313* (Rome, 1907).

Giudice, G. del. *Codice diplomatico del regno di Carlo I e II d'Angiò*, 3 vols. (Naples, 1863–1902). Indispensable.

———— *Diplomi inediti di Re Carlo I d'Angiò su cose marittime* (Naples, 1871). Brief.

———— "La famiglia di re Manfredi," *Archivio storico per le province napoletane*, III–IV (1878–1880). New ed. (1896) unavailable to me. Important.

Golubovich, G. *Biblioteca bio-bibliografica della Terra Santa e dell' Oriente francescano*, II (Quaracchi, 1913). Important for Franciscans and the East.

Guiraud, J. *Les registres de Grégoire X* (Paris, 1892–1906). Basic.

———— *Les registres d'Urbain IV* (Paris, 1901–1929). Basic.

Héfelé, C. *Histoire des conciles*, ed. H. Leclercq, VI, pt. 1 (Paris, 1914). Standard work.

Hopf, K. "Urkunden und Zusätze zur geschichte der Insel Andros," *Sitzungsb. der Wiener Akademie der Wissens.*, XXI (1856) 221–262.

Huillard-Bréholles, J. *Historia diplomatica Friderici Secundi*, 6 vols. (Paris, 1859–1861). Fundamental.

Jamison, E. "Documents from the Angevin Registers of Naples: Charles I," *Papers of the British School at Rome*, XVII (1949) 87–180. Useful.

Jordan, E. *Les registres de Clément IV* (Paris, 1893–1945). Basic.

Kern, F. *Acta Imperii Angliae et Franciae, 1267–1313* (Tübingen, 1911). With several documents important for Vespers.

Lombardo, A. *Documenti della colonia veneziana di Creta, I: Imbreviature di Pietro Scardon (1271)*, Documenti e Studi per la Storia del Commercio e del Diritto Commerciale Italiano, XXI (Turin, 1942).

Lombardo, A. and R. M. Della Rocca. *Documenti del commercio Veneziano nei secoli XI–XIII*, 2 vols. (Turin, 1940). Contains several documents of interest.

—————— *Nuovi documenti del commercio Veneto dei sec. XI–XIII* (Venice, 1953). Useful new documents esp. for period of Latin Empire.

Manfroni, C. "Le relazioni fra Genova l'impero bizantino e i Turchi," *Atti della società ligure di storia patria*, XXVIII (Genoa, 1896) 1ff. Contains basic documents, esp. best ed. of Treaty of Nymphaeum.

Mansi, J. *Sacrorum conciliorum nova et amplissima collectio* (Venice, 1770). Standard work for councils.

Martène, E. and U. Durand. *Thesaurus novus anecdotorum* (Paris, 1717) esp. vols. I–II. Contains important texts.

—————— *Veterum scriptorum . . . amplissima collectio*, esp. vol. VII (Paris, 1733). Important texts.

Mazzoleni, B. *Gli atti perduti della cancelleria angioina transuntati da Carlo De Lellis*, pt. 1, *Il Regno di Carlo I*, 2 vols. (Rome, 1939–1943) in *Regesta chartarum italiae*. Summaries made by De Lellis ca. 1701, after which some documents were destroyed; contains documents unused by Norden, Chapman, or Dade.

Minieri-Riccio, C. *Alcuni fatti riguardanti Carlo I. di Angiò, 1252–1270* (Naples, 1874). Important documents; the editions of Minieri-Riccio, a book collector with little knowledge of Latin and Greek, are very valuable, drawn as they are from Angevin archives, but they are not always truly critical, the Latin texts being sometimes paraphrased incorrectly in Italian.

—————— *Alcuni studii storici intorno a Manfredi e Corradino della imperiale casa di Hohenstaufen* (Naples, 1850).

—————— *Brevi notizie intorno all' archivio angioino di Napoli* (Naples, 1862).

—————— *Cenni storici intorno i grandi uffizii del regno di Sicilia durante il regno di Carlo I. d'Angiò* (Naples, 1872).

—————— *Diario angioino dal 4 gennaio 1284 al 7 gennaio 1285* (Naples, 1873).

—————— *Della dominazione angioina nel reame di Sicilia* (Naples, 1876).

—————— *Genealogia di Carlo I. di Angiò* (Naples, 1857).

—————— *Genealogia di Carlo II. di Angiò* (Naples, 1882).

—————— *Itinerario di Carlo I. di Angiò* (Naples, 1872).

—————— *I notamenti di Matteo Spinelli da Giovenazzo difesi ed illustrati* (Naples, 1870). Also *I notamenti di Matteo Spinelli novellamente difesi* (Naples, 1874).

—————— *Notizie storiche tratte da 62 registri angioini* (Naples, 1877).

—————— *Nuovi studii riguardanti la dominazione angioina nel regno di Sicilia* (Naples, 1876).

—————— *Il regno di Carlo I. di Angiò negli anni 1271 e 1272* (Naples, 1875). Fundamental; cited as *Regno*.

—————— "Il regno di Carlo I. d'Angiò dal 2 gennaio 1273 al 31 dicembre 1283," *Arch. stor. ital.*, ser. III, vol. XXII (1875) 3–32, 235–263). Also subsequent issues, cited *passim* as *Arch. st. it.*

—————— "Il regno di Carlo I. d'Angiò dal 4 gennaio 1284 al 7 dicembre 1285," *Arch. st. it.*, ser. IV, VII (1881) 3–24; 304–312.

—————— *Saggio di codice diplomatico* (Naples, 1878–1883).

——— *Studii storici fatti sopra 84 registri angioini* (Naples, 1876).
——— *Ultima confutazione agli oppositori di Matteo Spinelli* (Naples, 1875).
Müller, G. *Documenti sulle relazioni delle città toscane coll' oriente cristiano e coi turchi* (Florence, 1879). Basic.
Nitti di Vito, F. *Le pergamene di S. Nicola di Bari (1266–1309)* (Trani, 1936) in *Codice diplomatico barese*, XIII.
Noiret, H. *Documents inédits pour servir à l'histoire de la domination vénitienne en Crète* (Paris, 1892).
Olivier-Martin, M. *Les registres de Martin IV* (Paris, 1901).
Potthast, A. *Regesta pontificum romanorum . . . MCXCVIII ad a. MCCCIV*, 2 vols. (Berlin, 1873–1875).
Raynaldus, O. *Caesaris Baronii O. Raynaldi . . . Annales ecclesiastici denuo excusi . . . ab A. Theiner* (Barri-Ducis, 1870) esp. vol. XXII. Cited as Raynaldus. Originally published in Rome, 1646–1727. Gives important letters on unionist negotiations, largely reprinted elsewhere.
Riant, P. *Exuviae sacrae Constantinopolitanae*, 3 vols. (Geneva, 1877–1878; also Paris, 1904).
Ricotti, E. *Liber jurium reipublicae genuensis*, I (Turin, 1854) in *Historiae patriae monumenta*, VII. Basic.
Ripoll, T. *Bullarium Ordinis Fratrum Praedicatorum*, I (Rome, 1729).
Rubió I Lluch, A. *Diplomatari de l'orient català (1301–1409)* (Barcelona, 1947). With several documents on Constance of Hohenstaufen.
Saint-Priest, A. de. *Histoire de la conquête de Naples*, 4 vols. (Paris, 1847–1849). Old but valuable for appended documents.
Sanudo, Marino (Torsello). *Epistulae*, in J. Bongars, *Gesta Dei per Francos* (Hanover, 1611). Unused letters of Sanudo to Andronikos II.
Sbaralea, J. *Bullarium Franciscanum* (Rome, 1759) vol. I.
Schillman, F. "Zur byzantinischen Politik Alexanders IV," *Römische Quartalschrift*, XXII (1908) 108–131. Contains letters omitted from published papal registers.
Società Siciliana per la storia patria. *Ricordi e documenti del Vespro Siciliano*, 2 vols. (Palermo, 1882). Contains documents and accounts of importance.
Tafel, G. and G. Thomas. *Urkunden zur älteren Handels- und Staatsgeschichte der Republik Venedig*, pts. 2 and 3 (Vienna, 1856–1857), in *Fontes rerum austriacarum*, II, *Diplomataria et acta,* XIII–XIV. Fundamental collection of Venetian documents; cited as T.-Th.
Tautu, A. *Acta Urbani IV, Clementis IV, Gregorii X (1261–1276) e registri Vaticani (. . . juris canonicis orientalis, Fontes)* Ser. III, vol. V, 1 (Vatican, 1953). Reliable new ed. of texts regarding Union of Lyons; see G. Hofmann's review in *Orient. chr. per.* (1954) 203–204.
Terlizzi, S. *Documenti delle relazioni tra Carlo I d'Angiò e la Toscana*, in *Documenti di storia italiana*, XII (Florence-Rome, 1914). Unimportant for this book.
Teulet, A. *Layettes du trésor des chartes* (Paris, 1866) II, III, *Archives de l'empire inventaires et documents*. Important.

Thallóczy, L. de, C. Jireček, and E. de Sufflay. *Acta et diplomata res Albaniae mediae aetatis illustrantia,* 2 vols. (Vienna, 1913–1918). Fundamental collection of documents for Albania; cited as *Acta Albaniae.*
Wadding, L. *Annales Minorum* (Quaracchi, 1931–1934) esp. vols. IV–V. Important.

C. Vernacular

Boüard, A. de. *Documents en français des archives angevines de Naples* (*règne de Charles Ier*) (Paris, 1933–1935).
Recoura, G. *Les assises de Romanie* (Paris, 1930).
Topping, P. *Liber consuetudinum Imperii Romaniae. Feudal institutions as revealed in the Assizes of Romania* (Philadelphia, 1949). Useful English translation.

II. Literary Sources

A. Greek

Acropolites, George. *Opera,* ed. A. Heisenberg (Leipzig, 1903) 2 vols., vol. I containing the *Historia,* cited here as Acrop. Earlier ed. by I. Bekker, *Annales* (Bonn, 1837). The basic source for Nicene Empire.
Andréeva, M. "A propos de l'éloge de l'Empereur Jean III Vatatzes," *Seminarium Kondakovianum,* X (1938) 133–145.
Anna Comnena. *Alexiade,* ed. B. Leib, 3 vols. (Paris, 1937). *Alexias,* ed. A. Reifferscheid, 2 vols. (Leipzig, 1884).
Arsenios, Autorianos. *Testamentum* (of Patriarch Arsenios) in Migne, *PG,* vol. 140, cols. 947–958.
Bekkos, John. Treatises on church union, etc., in Migne, *PG,* vol. 141.
Calecas, Manuel. *Adversus Graecos,* Migne, *PG,* vol. 152, cols. 11ff.
Cantacuzene, John. *Historia,* ed. L. Schopen, 3 vols. (Bonn, 1828). 14th century source.
Chronicle of Morea. Τὸ Χρονικὸν τοῦ Μορέως, Greek version ed. by J. Schmitt (London, 1904); also recent ed. by P. Kalonaros (Athens, 1940), which is used here; French version, ed. by J. Longnon, *Livre de la conqueste: Chronique de Morée* (Paris, 1911); the less important Italian, *Cronaca di Morea,* ed. by K. Hopf in *Chron. gréco-romanes* (Berlin, 1873); and the Aragonese, *Libro de los Fechos,* ed. by A. Morel-Fatio (Geneva, 1885). On the various versions and the bias of this important 14th century source for Moreot history, see Longnon, *Chron. de Morée,* pp. liff.
Codinus Curopalata. *De officialibus palatii Constantinopolitani et de officiis magnae ecclesiae liber,* ed. I. Bekker (Bonn, 1839).
Dorotheos of Monemvasia. Βιβλίον ἱστορικὸν περιέχον ἐν συνόψει διαφόρους καὶ ἐξόχους ἱστορίας (Joannina, 1750).

BIBLIOGRAPHY

Ephraem. *Chronographia*, ed. I. Bekker (Bonn, 1840).

George (= Gregory) of Cyprus. *Laudatio Michaelis Palaeologi*, Migne, *PG*, vol. 142, cols. 346–386. Also ed. J. Boissonade, in *Anecdota Graeca*, I (Paris, 1829) 313–393. Panegyrics of Michael and his son Andronikos.

Gigante, M. *Poeti Italobizantini del secolo XIII* (Naples, 1953).

Gregoras, Nikephoros. *Bizantina historia*, ed. L. Schopen, I. Bekker, 3 vols. (Bonn, 1830–1845). Important, though a 14th century source; vol. I cited as Greg.

Holobolos, Manuel. *Orationes*, ed. M. Treu (Potsdam, 1906–7). Important, neglected source on events of 1259–1261.

———— Hymn honoring Michael (unpublished by Boissonade) in M. Treu, "Manuel Holobolos," *Byz. Zeit.*, V (1896) 546f.

Metochites, George. *Historia dogmatica*, in A. Mai, *Patrum nova bibliotheca*, VIII (Rome, 1871) 38ff. With useful details.

Müller, J. Anonymous Poem, in "Byzantinische Analekten," *Sitz.-Ber. Akad. Wien., Phil.-hist. Kl.*, IX (1852) 366–389. See ch. 5.

Nikephoros Blemmydes. *Curriculum vitae et carmina*, ed. A. Heisenberg (Leipzig, 1896).

Nikephoros Chumnos. " Ἐγκώμιον εἰς τὸν Αὐτοκράτορα Κυρὸν Ἀνδρόνικον τὸν Παλαιολόγον," in J. Boissonade, *Anecdota Graeca*, II (Paris, 1830) 1ff.

Niketas Choniates. *Historia*, ed. I. Bekker (Bonn, 1835). Basic Greek source on Latin conquest of 1204.

Pachymeres, George. *De Michaele et Andronico Palaeologis*, 2 vols., ed. I. Bekker (Bonn, 1835). Vol. I cited simply as Pach.; the basic contemporary source for Michael's reign. As a high ecclesiastical and state official, he gives an eyewitness account.

Philes, Manuel. *Manuelis Philae Carmina*, ed. E. Miller (Paris, 1855). Poems, some concerning Michael's reign.

Previale, L. "Un panegyrico inedito per Michele VIII Paleologo," *Byz. Zeit.*, XLII (1942) 1ff.

Sathas, K. " Ἀσίζαι τοῦ Βασιλείου τῶν Ἱεροσολύμων καὶ τῆς Κύπρου," in *Bibliotheca Graeca Medii Aevi*, VI (Paris, 1877) 1ff.

Scutariotes, Theodore. Ἀνωνύμου Σύνοψις Χρονική, in K. Sathas, *Bibliotheca Graeca Medii Aevi*, VII (Paris, 1894). Unpublished elsewhere except for excerpts in Heisenberg ed. of Acropolites. A contemporary source extending to 1261, largely drawn from Acrop. but with some additions; actually compiled after 1282.

Sphrantzes (formerly Phrantzes), George. *Chronicon* (Bonn, 1838). 15th century source; J. Pappadopoulos ed. of 1935 inaccessible to me. On this work's authenticity see Ostrogorsky, *Byz. State* (1956) 417.

Siderides, X. "Μανουὴλ Ὁλοβώλου, Ἐγκώμιον εἰς Μιχαὴλ Η΄ Παλαιολόγον," Ἐπετηρὶς Ἑτ. Βυζαντινῶν Σπουδῶν, III (1926) 174–191.

Vassilief, A. *Anecdota graeco-byzantina*, pt. 1 (Moscow, 1893) 179–188, document entitled "Panagiotae cum azymita disputatio." A contemporary dispute over azymes.

B. Latin

d'Adam, Guillaume. *De modo Sarracenos extirpandi*, in *Recueil des historiens des croisades. Documents Arméniens*, II (Paris, 1906) 521ff.

—— *Annales Altahenses (Continuatio)*, *MGH SS*, XVII (1861) 408ff.

—— *Annales Cavenses*, *MGH SS*, III, 185–197.

—— *Annales Parmenses Maiores*, *MGH SS*, XVIII 664ff.

—— *Annales Placentini Gibellini*, in *MGH SS*, ed. Pertz, XVIII (1863) 457ff. Important, contemporary Ghibelline source for northern Italy.

—— *Annales Urbevetani*, in *Muratori, RISS*, XV, pt. 5 (on Viterbo).

—— *Annales Caesenates*, in *Muratori, RISS*, XIV (1729).

—— *Annali Genovesi di Caffaro e de' suoi continuatori* (= *Annales Ianuenses*), ed. L. Belgrano and C. Imperiale de Sant' Angelo, esp. vols. IV–V (Genoa–Rome, 1890–1929), in *Fonti per la storia d'Italia*, 11–14 *bis*. The basic Genoese source; cited as *Ann. Ian.*

Bartolomeo of Neocastro. *Historia Sicula*, ed. G. Paladino, in *Muratori, RISS*, XIII, pt. 3 (1921) 1ff. Contemporary Sicilian source.

Brocardus. *Directorium ad passagium faciendum*, in *Recueil des historiens des croisades, Documents Arméniens*, II (1906) 367ff. 14th century Dominican source. According to L. Bréhier, *Dict. d'hist. géog. ecclés.*, X, 792–793, this source should be ascribed to Guillaume d'Adam.

—— *Chronicon Marchiae Tarvisinae et Lombardiae*, ed. L. Botteghi, in *Muratori, RISS*, VIII, pt. 3, new ed. (1916) 1ff. Otherwise known as *Annales S. Justinae Patavini, MGH SS*, XIX (1866) 148–193. Important contemporary source for north Italy.

—— *Cronica S. Petri Erfordensis moderna*, *MGH SS*, XXX.

—— *Corpus Chronicorum Bononensium*, ed. A. Sorbelli, in *RISS* (1913) II, 1, 159ff.

Dandolo, Andrea. *Chronica*, ed. E. Pastorello, in *Muratori, RISS*, XII, pt. 1 (Bologna, 1941–49). Covers most of Michael's reign; generally reliable though written in early 14th century.

Glassberger, Nicholas. *Chronica*, in *Analecta Franciscana*, II (Quaracchi, 1887). Moravian Franciscan, d. early 16th century.

Gregorio, R. *Historiae Sabae Malaspinae continuatio*, in *Bibliotheca scriptorum qui res in Sicilia gestas sub Aragonum imperio retulere*, II (Palermo, 1792).

Humbert de Romans. "De his quae tractanda videbantur in concilio generali Lugduni, opus tripartitum," in Mansi, *Sacrorum conciliorum . . . collectio*, XXIV, cols. 109–136. Important, contemporary Dominican source for problems of union, esp. Lyons Council.

Jamsilla, Niccolò. *Historia de rebus gestis Frederici II. Imperatoris ejusque filiorum Conradi et Manfredi, 1210–1258*, in *Cronisti e scrittori sincroni napoletani*, ed. G. Del Re, II (Naples, 1868) 105ff. Contemporary source, esp. for Manfred.

Malaspina, Saba. *Rerum Sicularum historia (1250–1285)*, in G. Del Re, *Cronisti e scrittori sincroni napoletani*, II (Naples, 1868) 205ff. Contemporary chronicler attached to papal court; important for Manfred's and Charles's reigns.

Manenti, Luca di Domenico. *Cronica*, in Muratori, *RISS*, XV, pt. 5. 15th century historian of Orvieto.

Matthew Paris. *Chronica Majora*, ed. H. Luard (London, 1874) in *Rolls Series*, II–V. 13th century English historian.

Nangis, Guillaume de. *Chronique latine*, ed. H. Géraud (Paris, 1843) in *Soc. l'hist. de France*; also in Bouquet, *Rec. des hist. des Gaules et de la France*, XX, esp. *Gesta Philippi III*, 466ff. Contemporary French monk of St. Denis; some interesting details.

Pipinus, F. *Chronicon*, in Muratori, *RISS*, IX, 587ff.

Primate. *Chronicon*, trans. into French by J. du Vignay, in Bouquet, *Recueil des historiens des Gaules et de la France*, XXIII (Paris, 1876) 5–106. Contemporary French monk of St. Denis who wrote in Latin.

Ptolemy of Lucca. *Historia ecclesiastica*, in Muratori, *RISS*, XI (1727) col. 753ff. Contemporary Italian Dominican; later had access to papal archives at Avignon.

Riant, P. *Exuviae sacrae Constantinopolitanae*, II (Geneva, 1878).

Salimbene de Adam. *Cronica*, new ed., F. Bernini, 2 vols. (Bari, 1942). Famous work by contemporary Franciscan of Parma.

Sanudo, Marino (Torsello). *Fragmentum*, ed. C. Hopf, in *Chroniques gréco-romanes* (Berlin, 1873); also new ed. of R. L. Wolff, "Hopf's So-called 'Fragmentum' of Sanudo," *J. Starr Memorial Volume* (1953) 149ff. See Ch. 5.

———— *Istoria del regno di Romania*, ed. C. Hopf in *Chroniques gréco-romanes* (Berlin, 1873) 99–170. Extremely important 14th century Venetian source, originally in Latin but Italian version alone survives; based on eye-witness reports and documentary material; see Introduction.

———— *Secreta fidelium crucis*, in J. Bongars, *Gesta Dei per Francos* (Hanover, 1611) II, 1–281. Sanudo's major work, though of little value here.

Stefano Magno. *Estratti degli Annali Veneti di Stefano Magno*, ed. Hopf, in *Chron. gréco-romanes* (Berlin, 1873) 179ff. Occasionally contains information unavailable elsewhere.

Templar of Tyre. *Chronique du Templier de Tyr, Les gestes des Chiprois*, in G. Raynaud, *Soc. de l'or. latin* (1887) 139ff. Important Cypriote chronicle, contemporary with Vespers.

Thomas Tuscus. *Gesta imperatorum et pontificum*, in *MGH SS*, XXII (1872) 483ff. Contemporary Franciscan source.

Vincent of Beauvais. *Bibliotheca mundi* (Douai, 1624). Dominican, d. 1264.

C. Vernacular and Oriental

Abulfeda. *Annales Moslemici*, ed. J. Reiskii and J. Adler (Hafniae, 1789) IV–V.

Anonymous of Trani. Anonymous South Italian Chronicle of 13th century, of disputed authenticity, published in F. Davanzati, *Dissertazione sulla seconda moglie del re Manfredi e su' loro figliuoli* (Naples, 1791).

Bar Hebraeus. *The Chronography of Abû'l Faraj* . . . , ed. E. Budge, I (London, 1932). Contemporary Arab-Christian source, interesting details but to be used with caution; see esp. Ch. 5.

Bertoni, G. *I trovatori d'Italia* (Modena, 1915). A poem or two on Charles and Michael.

Buchon, J. *Chroniques étrangères relatives aux expéditions françaises pendant le XIIIᵉ siècle* (Paris, 1875). Important, contains D'Esclot, etc.

Canale, Martino da. *La Chronique des Veniciens de maistre Martin da Canal,* ed. Polidori-Galvani, in *Archivio storico italiano*, VIII (1845) 229–798. Very important contemporary Venetian source, written in French; cited as Canale.

Chronicle of Morea. For Greek, French, Italian, and Aragonese versions see Greek Literary Sources under *Chronicle of Morea.*

Chronicon Altinate, in *Arch. st. it.*, VIII (1845) ed. A. Rossi.

Collenuccio, P. *Compendio de le istorie del Regno di Napoli*, ed. Saviotti, I (Bari, 1929). 15th century Italian humanist source; a few useful details.

D'Esclot, Bernat. *Crónica del Rey en Pere*, in J. Buchon, *Chroniques étrangères relatives aux expéditions françaises pendant le XIIIᵉ siècle* (Paris, 1840) 565ff. Also English trans., *Chronicle of the Reign of King Pedro III of Aragon by Bernat Esclot*, by F. Critchlow (Princeton, 1934). Important for Vespers.

Forster, J. *The Chronicle of James I King of Aragon*, trans. from Catalan, 2 vols. (London, 1883).

Joinville, Sire de. *Histoire de Saint Louis*, ed. N. de Wailly (Paris, 1874).

Muntaner, Ramon. *Chronik des edlen en Ramon Muntaner*, ed. K. Lanz (Stuttgart, 1844); also *Crónica*, ed. E. B. (Barcelona, 1927); and *The Chronicle of Muntaner*, tr. by Lady Goodenough (London, 1920).

Pipino, Francesco. *Chronicon*, in *Muratori, RISS*, IX. Contemporary Dominican source of Bologna, of no real importance.

Lu Rebellamentu di Sichilia, ed. E. Sicardi, in *Muratori, RISS*, XXXIV, pt. 1, new ed. (1917) 5ff.; also contains *Liber Jani de Procida et Palialoco*, 49ff. and *Leggenda di messer Gianni di Procida*, 65ff. Cf. old ed. of *Rebellamentu*, in J. Buchon, *Chroniques étrangères relatives aux expeditions françaises* (Paris, 1840). On the disputed authenticity of these works see Ch. 14, sections 3 and 4, text and notes.

Rosell, C. y López. *Crónicas de los reyes de Castilia, desde don Alfonso el Sabio hasta . . . don Fernando y doña Isabel* (Madrid, 1919–1930).

Rutebeuf. "La complainte de Constantinople," in *Onze poèmes de Rutebeuf*, ed. J. Bastin and E. Faral (Paris, 1946) 35–42. Probably a Western propaganda effort against Michael composed soon after 1261.

Spandugnino, Theodoro. *De la origine degli imperatori ottomani*, etc., in K. Sathas, *Documents inédits relatifs à l'histoire de la Grèce*, IX (Paris, 1890) 135ff. A later work but with some interesting material.

BIBLIOGRAPHY

Speciale, Niccolò. *Historia Sicula, Muratori, RISS,* X, 917ff. Near-contemporary Franciscan source.
Spinello (or Spinelli), Matteo da Giovenazzo. *Annali,* ed. G. Vigo and G. Dura (Naples, 1872); also ed. G. Del Re, in *Cronisti e scrittori sincroni napoletani,* II (Naples, 1868).
Villani, Giovanni. *Cronica,* ed. I. Moutier and F. Dragomanni esp. vol. I (Florence, 1844). Florentine writer, d. 1348; to be used with caution.
Ville-hardouin, G. de. *Conquête de Constantinople,* ed. N. de Wailly (Paris, 1882). For 4th Crusade.
Zurita, G. *Los cinco libros primeros de la primera parte de los Anales de la Corona de Aragón* (Saragossa, 1552–1610). 16th century Spanish writer who used good sources.

SECONDARY WORKS

Alexander, P. "A Chrysobull of the Emperor Andronicus II Palaeologus," *Byzantion,* XV (1940–1941) 167ff. Very useful.
Allatius, L. *Graeciae Orthodoxae,* 2 vols. (Rome, 1652).
Altaner, B. *Die Dominikanermissionen des 13. Jahrhunderts* (Halberschwerdt, 1924). Useful.
———— "Sprachkentnisse u. Dolmetscherwesen . . . im 13. u. 14. Jahrh.," *Zeitsch. für Kirchengesch.,* LV (1936) 85ff.
Amantos, K. "Βολερόν," Ἑλληνικά, II (1929) 124–126.
———— "Σάλωνα-Τσάκωνες," Ἑλληνικά, X (1938) 210–212.
Amari, M. *La guerra del Vespro Siciliano* (Milan, 1886). Celebrated though somewhat biased work on the Vespers.
Arabantinos, P. Χρονογραφία τῆς Ἠπείρου (Athens, 1856).
Armingaud, J. *Venise et le Bas-Empire* (Paris, 1868).
Arnakis, G. Οἱ Πρῶτοι Ὀθωμανοί (Athens, 1947). New insights.
Arndt, H. *Die innere Politik Manfreds von Sizilien* (Heidelberg, 1910) 42 pp.
Atiya, A. *The Crusade in the Later Middle Ages* (London, 1938).
Babinger, F. "Rum," *Encyc. of Islam,* III (London–Leyden, 1936) 1174–1175.
Balaschev, G. *The Emperor Michael VIII Palaeologus and the Establishment of the Turk-Oguz on the Black Sea,* transl. from Russian into Rumanian by N. Banescu (Jassi, 1940). Inaccessible to me.
Barthold, W. *Zwölf Vorlesungen über die Geschichte der türken Mittelasiens* (Berlin, 1935).
Baynes, N. "The Supernatural Defenders of Constantinople," *Analecta Bollandiana, Mél. Peeters,* I (1949) 165–177. Also in Baynes, *Byzantine Studies and Other Essays* (London, 1955) 248–260.
Begleres, G. "Μιχαὴλ τοῦ Παλαιολόγου Αὐτοβιογραφία," Δελτίον Ἱστορικῆς καὶ Ἐθνολογικῆς Ἑταιρείας, II (1895) 520ff. Review of Troitskiǐ's ed. of Michael's Autobiography.

397

Belin, A. *Histoire de la latinité de Constantinople* (Paris, 1894). Of little value.

Berger de Xivrey. *Notice d'un manuscrit grec du XIIIe siècle, Bibliothèque de l'Ecole des Chartes*, sér. V, IV (1863) 97–118. Contains a text.

Bernhardi, W. *Matteo di Giovenazzo, eine Fälschung des XVI. Jahrhunderts* (Berlin, 1868).

Bertaux, E. "Les Français d'outre mer en Apulie et en Epire au temps des Hohenstaufen d'Italie," *Revue historique*, LXXXV (1904) 16ff.

Bertelè, T. *L'imperatore alato nella numismatica bizantina* (Rome, 1951). Useful new material.

——— *Il palazzo degli ambasciatori di Venezia a Costantinopoli* (Bologna, 1932).

Besta, E. *La cattura dei Veneziani in Oriente* (Feltre, 1920).

Binon, S. *Les origines légendaires et l'histoire de Xeropotamou et de Saint-Paul, de l'Athos* (Louvain, 1942).

Borsari, S. "Federico II e l'Oriente bizantino," *Rivista stor. italiana*, LXIII (1951) 279ff.

——— "La politica bizantina di Carlo d'Angiò dal 1266 al 1271," *Archivio storico per le province napoletane*, n.s., XXXV (1956) 319–349. Helpful; with references.

——— "I rapporti tra Pisa e gli stati di Romania nel duecento," *Rivista stor. ital.*, LXVII (1955) 477–492. One of the few studies on Pisan history of the 13th century.

Bozzola, A. "Un capitano di guerra e signore subalpino," in *Miscellanea, R. Deputazione di storia patria per le antiche provincie*, ser. 3, XIX (Turin, 1922) 388–394.

——— "Guglielmo VII Marchese di Monferrato e Carlo I d'Angiò," *Arch. stor. prov. nap.*, XXXVI (1911) 289–328, 451–474; XXXVII (1912) 1–28. Important.

Bratianu, G. *Études byzantines d'histoire économique et sociale* (Paris, 1938).

——— "L'hyperpère byzantin et la monnaie d'or," *Mélanges C. Diehl*, I (Paris, 1930) 37ff.

——— *Recherches sur le commerce génois dans la Mer Noire au XIIIe siècle* (Paris, 1929). Thorough and sound.

Bréhier, L. "Une ambassade Byzantine au camp de St. Louis devant Tunis," *Mélanges Iorga* (Paris, 1933) 139ff. Useful.

——— "Attempts at Reunion of the Greek and Latin Churches," ch. XIX, in *Cambridge Medieval History*, IV (1927) 594ff. Accurate survey.

——— *L'église et l'Orient au moyen-âge. Les croisades* (Paris, 1928). Somewhat dated.

——— *Les institutions de l'empire byzantin* (Paris, 1949). Useful survey.

Brightman, F. *Liturgies Eastern and Western* (Oxford, 1896).

Brown, H. "The Venetians and the Venetian Quarter in Constantinople to the Close of the Twelfth Century," *Jl. of Hellenic Studies*, XL (1920) 68–88.

Buchon, J. *Histoire des conquêtes et de l'établissement des français dans les états de l'ancienne Grèce sous les Ville-Hardouin* (Paris, 1846). Superseded.

—— *Nouvelles recherches historiques sur la principauté française de Morée*, 2 vols. (Paris, 1843–1845). Important.

—— *Recherches et matériaux pour servir à une histoire de la domination française*, 2 vols. (Paris, 1840). Important.

—— *Recherches historiques sur la principauté française de Morée*, 2 vols. (Paris, 1845). In certain respects superseded.

Bury, J. "The Lombards and Venetians in Euboia," *Jl. of Hellenic Studies*, VII (1886) 309–352. Useful.

Bussi, F. *Istoria della città di Viterbo*, II (Rome, 1743). Contains a text; see ch. 1.

Busson, A. *Die Doppelwahl des Jahres 1257 und das römische Königthum Alfons X. von Castilien* (Münster, 1866).

Byrne, E. *Genoese Shipping in the Twelfth and Thirteenth Centuries* (Cambridge, 1930).

Caddeo, R., etc. *Storia maritimma dell' Italia dall' evo antico ai nostri giorni*, vol. I (Milan, 1942).

Cadier, L. *Essai sur l'administration du royaume de Sicile sous Charles Ier et Charles II d'Anjou* (Paris, 1891).

Cahen, C. "Quelques textes négligés concernant les Turcomans de Rûm au moment de l'invasion Mongole," *Byzantion*, XIV (1939) 131–139.

Cais de Pierlas, E. *I conti di Ventimiglia* (Turin, 1884).

Capmany, A. de *Memorias históricas sobre la marina, comercio y artes de la antigua ciudad de Barcelona*, II (Madrid, 1779).

Canard, M. "Le traité de 1281 entre Michel Paléologue et le Sultan Qalâ'ûn," *Byzantion*, X (1935) 669–680.

—— "Un traité entre Byzance et l'Egypte au XIIIe siècle et les relations diplomatiques de Michel VIII Paléologue avec les sultans Mamlûks Baibars et Qualâ'ûn," *Mélanges Gaudefroy-Demombynes* (Cairo, 1937) 197–224.

Capasso, B. *Ancora i diurnali di Matteo da Giovenazzo* (Florence, 1896).

Carabellese, F. *Carlo d'Angiò nei rapporti politici e commerciali con Venezia e l'Oriente* (Bari, 1911). Contains excerpts from Angevin documents, though, despite the title, with little material on Byzantium.

Caro, G. *Genua und die Mächte am Mittelmeer*, 2 vols. (Halle, 1895) Still valuable.

Cartellieri, O. *Peter von Aragon und die sizilianische Vesper* (Heidelberg, 1904). An important work on the Vespers from the Aragonese point of view but inadequate for the Greek side.

Carucci, Carlo. *La guerra del Vespro nella frontiera del Principato (Codice diplomatico Salernitano*, II) (Subiaco, 1931). Useful.

Cerone, F. "La sovranità napoletana sulla Morea e sulle isole vicine," *Arch. stor. prov. napoletane*, XLI (1916) 5–64 and 193–226; XLII (1917) 5–67. Accurate work with quotation of documents.

Cessi, R. "La tregua fra Venezia e Genova nella seconda metà del sec. XIII,"

Archivio Veneto-Tridentino, IV (1923) 1ff. Contains documentary texts.

Chalandon, F. *Essai sur le règne d'Alexis Ier Comnène* (Paris, 1900).

———— *Histoire de la domination Normande en Italie et Sicile* (Paris, 1907) 2 vols. Excellent work.

———— *Jean II et Manuel I Comnène* (Paris, 1912).

Chapman, C. *Michel Paléologue restaurateur de l'empire byzantin (1261–1282)* (Paris, 1926). See Introduction and *passim.*

Charanis, P. "The Aristocracy of Byzantium in the 13th Century," *Studies in Roman Economic and Social History for A. C. Johnson,* ed. R. Coleman-Norton (Princeton, 1951) 336–355. Valuable.

———— "Byzantium, The West and The Origin of the First Crusade," *Byzantion,* XIX (1949) 17ff.

———— "An Important Short Chronicle of the Fourteenth Century," *Byzantion,* XIII (1938) 335–362. Useful.

———— "Monastic Properties and the State in the Byzantine Empire," *Dumbarton Oaks Papers, No. 4* (Cambridge, 1948) 53ff. Very important study.

———— "A Note on the Population and the Cities of the Byzantine Empire in the Thirteenth Century," *Joshua Starr Memorial Volume* (New York, 1953) 135–148. Useful.

———— "On the Ethnic Composition of Byzantine Asia Minor," Προσφορὰ εἰς Σ. Κυριακίδην (Thessalonica, 1953).

———— "On the Social Structure and Economic Organization of the Byzantine Empire in the Thirteenth Century and Later," *Byzantinoslavica,* XII (1951) 94–153. Very important.

———— "Piracy in the Aegean during the reign of Michael VIII Palaeologus," *Annuaire de l'institut de philologie et d'histoire Orientales et Slaves,* X (1950) 127–136.

Cohn, W. "Die Geschichte der sizilischen Flotte unter der Regierung Konrads IV. und Manfreds," *Abhandlungen zur Verkehrs-und Seegeschichte,* IX (1920) 22ff.

———— "Storia della flotta siciliana sotto il governo di Carlo I d'Angiò," *Archivio storico per la Sicilia orientale,* XXV (1929–1930) and later issues. Important; contains references and quotations from Angevin documents.

Czebe, G. "Studien zum Hochverratsprozesse des M. Paläologos im Jahr 1252," *Byzantinisch-neugriechische Jahrbucher,* VIII (1931) 59–98. Useful.

Dade, E. *Versuche zur Wiedererrichtung der lateinischen Herrschaft in Konstantinopel* (Jena, 1938). See Introduction and *passim.*

Dalleggio d'Alessio, E. "Les sanctuaires urbains et suburbains de Byzance sous la domination latine, 1204–1261," *Revue des études byzantines,* XII (1953) 50–61.

Darkó, E. *Byzantinisch-ungarische Beziehungen in der zweiten Hälfte des 13. Jahrhunderts* (Weimar, 1933). Useful, but to be used with caution.

Davanzati, D. *Dissertazione sulla seconda moglie di re Manfredi e su loro figliuoli* (Naples, 1791). Contains passages from the Anonymous of Trani; copy available at Archivio di Stato of Naples.

Dawkins, R. "Greeks and Northmen," *Essays Presented to R. R. Marett* (London, 1936) 35ff.

———— "The Later History of the Varangian Guard: Some Notes," *Jl. of Roman Studies*, XXXVII (1947) 39ff.

DeFrancesco, R. *Michele II° Angelo Comneno d'Epiro e la sua discendenza* (Rome, 1951) 49 pp. Of little value.

Demetracopoulos, A. *Graecia orthodoxa* (Leipzig, 1872). Contains excerpts from important texts.

———— *Historia schismatis quod intercedit inter ecclesiam occidentalem et orientalem* (Leipzig, 1867). In Greek.

Demski, A. *Papst Nikolaus III.* (Münster, 1903). Disappointing.

Dendias, M. " Ἑλένη Ἀγγελῖνα Δούκαινα Βασίλισσα Σικελίας καὶ Νεαπόλεως," Ἠπειρωτικὰ Χρονικά, I (1926). Cited as *Helen*. Useful.

———— "Le Roi Manfred di Sicile et la battaile de Pelagonie," *Mélanges C. Diehl*, I (Paris, 1930) 55ff.

Desimoni, C. "I Genovesi ed i loro quartieri in Costantinopoli nel secolo XIII," *Giornale ligustico di archeologia, storia, e delle arti*, III (1876) 217–274. Valuable; to be checked against Bratianu.

Diehl, C. "La colonie Vénitienne à Constantinople," *Études byzantines* (Paris, 1905) 245ff.

———— "The Fourth Crusade and the Latin Empire," ch. 14 in *Cambr. Med. Hist.* (1936) IV, 415ff.

Di Giovanni, V. *Di alcuni cronache siciliane dei secoli XIII–XV* (Bologna, 1865). Of little value.

Dölger, F. *Beiträge zur Geschichte der byzantinischen Finanzverwaltung* (Leipzig-Berlin, 1927). Important.

———— "Chronologisches und Prosopographisches zur byzantinischen Geschichte des 13. Jahrhunderts," *Byz. Zeit.*, XXVII (1927) 291ff. Useful.

———— "Die dynastische Familienpolitik des Kaisers Michael Palaiologos (1258–1282)," *Festschrift E. Eichmann* (Paderborn, 1940) 179ff. Valuable.

———— "Rom in der Gedankenwelt der Byzantiner," in *Byzanz und die europäische Staatenwelt* (1953). Very important.

———— "Der Vertrag des Sultans Qualâ'ūn von Ägypten mit dem Kaiser Michael VIII. Palaiologos (1281)," *Serta Monacensia, Festschrift Babinger* (Leiden, 1952) 60–79. Important.

Dondaine, A. " 'Contra Graecos' Premiers écrits polémiques des Dominicains d'Orient," *Archivum fratr. praed.*, XXI (1951) 320–446. Useful.

———— "Nicolas de Cotrone et les sources du 'Contra errores Graecorum' de Saint Thomas," *Divus Thomas*, XXVIII (1950) 313–340. Unavailable to me.

Dragoumis, E. Χρονικῶν Μορέως Τοπωνυμικά. . . (Athens, 1921). Unavailable to me.

Dräseke, J. "Der Kircheneinigungsversuch des Kaisers Michaele Palae-
ologus," *Zeitschrift für wissenschaf. Theologie,* XXXIV, 325ff.
────── "Theodoros Laskaris," *Byz. Zeit.,* III (1894) 498–515.
Ducange, C. *Familiae Augustae Byzantinae* (Venice, 1729). Old but still
useful.
────── *Histoire de l'empire de Constantinople sous les empereurs français*
(Paris, 1657); ed. J. Buchon, 2 vols. (Paris, 1826). Very important;
includes an account, the first, of the reign of Michael Palaeologus; super-
seded but containing insights of value.
Dudan, D. *Il dominio Veneziano di Levante* (Bologna, 1938). Fair, general
work.
Durrieu, P. *Les archives angevines de Naples,* 2 vols. (Paris, 1886–1887).
Dvornik, F. *The Photian Schism, History and Legend* (Cambridge, 1948).
Excellent; esp. useful for role of Photius in later tradition.
Ebersolt, J. *Orient et occident, recherches sur les influences byzantines et
orientales en France pendant les croisades* (Paris, 1929).
────── "Sur les fonctions et les dignités du Vestiarium byzantin," *Mélanges
C. Diehl,* I (1930) 81ff.
Egidi, P. *La Communitas Siciliae del 1282* (Messina, 1915).
Episkop Arsenij. *Pŏslanie s ispovĕdaniem vĕry, poslannoe ot ŭsĕh Svjatogor-
cev k carju Mihailu Paleologu, kogda etot vseusilno spĕšil nerazsuditelno
soedinit s nami Italiancev, etc.* (Moscow, 1895). Relations of Athonite
monks and Michael concerning union; unavailable to me.
Evert-Kappesova, H. "La société byzantine et l'union de Lyon," *Byzantino-
slavica,* X (Prague, 1949) 28ff. Useful.
────── "Une page des relations byzantino-latines. Le clergé byzantin et
l'union de Lyon (1274–1282)," *Byzantinoslavica,* XIII (1952–53) 68–
92.
────── "Une page. . . Byzance et le St. Siège à l'époque de l'union de
Lyon," *Byzantinoslavica,* XVI (1955) 297–317.
────── "Une page. . . La fin de l'union de Lyon," *Byzantinoslavica,* XVII
(1956) 1–18.
Fallmerayer, J. *Geschichte des Kaiserthums von Trapezunt* (Munich, 1827).
Ficker, J. "Manfreds zweite Heirath und der Anonymus von Trani," *Mit-
teilungen des Instituts für oesterreichische Geschichtsforschung,* III
(1882) 358–368.
Finke, H. *Konzilienstudien zur Geschichte des 13. Jahrhunderts* (Münster,
i.w., 1891).
Finlay, G. *History of Greece,* 7 vols. (Oxford, 1877) esp. III. Old but some-
times still useful.
Fliche, A. "Le problème oriental au second concile oecuménique de Lyon,"
Orientalia christiana periodica, XIII (1947) 483ff. Nothing new.
Fliche, A. and V. Martin. *Histoire de l'église,* X (1950) 76–85; 446–460;
487–497. On the Lyons Council and its negotiations.
Fortescue, A. *The Uniate Eastern Churches; The Byzantine Rite in Italy,
Sicily, Syria, and Egypt* (London, 1923).

Fotheringham, J. "Genoa and the Fourth Crusade," *English Historical Review*, XXV (1910) 20–57.

———— *Marco Sanudo* (Oxford, 1915). Important.

Fournier, P. *Le royaume d'Arles et de Vienne* (Paris, 1891).

Frolow, A. "La dédicace de Constantinople dans la tradition byzantine," *Revue de l'histoire de religions* (1944) 61ff.

Gardner, A. *The Lascarids of Nicaea: The Story of an Empire in Exile* (London, 1912). Cited as *Lascarids*; useful, solid work though with few references to sources; after Meliarakes, standard on Nicaea.

Gay, J. *L'Italie meridionale et l'empire byzantin (867–1071)* (Paris, 1904). Fundamental.

———— "Notes sur le second royaume français de Sicile," in *Mélanges Jorga* (1933) 309ff.

Geanakoplos, D. "The Council of Florence (1438–1439) and the Problem of Union between the Greek and Latin Churches," *Church History*, XXIV (1955) 324–346. Helps to rehabilitate Syropoulos; also contains full bibliography on unionist negotiations of later Middle Ages.

———— "Emperor Michael VIII Palaeologos and the Latins: A study in Greco-Latin Relations (1258–1282)," unpublished doctoral dissertation (Harvard University, 1953) 800pp.; the present work is a total revision of this.

———— "Greco-Latin Relations on the Eve of the Byzantine Restoration: The Battle of Pelagonia–1259," *Dumbarton Oaks Papers No. 7* (1953) 99–141; with two appendices: "Pelagonia or Kastoria,"; and "Ansel de Toucy or Ansel de Cayeux? An Attempt to Identify Acropolites' Disputed 'Asel.' "

———— "Michael VIII Palaeologus and the Union of Lyons (1274)," *Harvard Theological Review*, XLVI (1953) 79–89.

———— "The Nicene Revolution of 1258 and the Usurpation of Michael VIII Palaeologos," *Traditio*, IX (1953) 420–430.

———— "On the Schism of the Greek and Roman Churches. A Confidential Papal Directive for the Implementation of Union (1278)," *Greek Orthodox Theological Review*, I (1954)- 16–24.

Gelzer, H. "Der Patriarcat von Achrida," *Abhandl. sachsischen Gesellschaft der Wissen.*, XX (1902) 231ff.

Gerola, G. "L'aquila bizantina e l'aquila imperiale a due teste," *Felix Ravenna*, new ser., a. IV, fasc. 1 (XLIII, 1934) 7–36.

Giunta, F. *Bizantini e bizantinismo nella Sicilia Normanna* (Palermo, 1950). Useful for Greek influences in south Italy; documented.

Glotz, G. *L'ordalie dans la Grèce primitive* (Paris, 1904).

Golubovich, G. *Biblioteca bio-bibliografica della Terra Santa e dell' Oriente francescano*, II (1913). Valuable.

———— "Cenni storici su Fra Giovanni Parastron," *Bessarione*, X (1906) 295ff.

Grabar, A. "God and the 'Family of Princes' Presided over by the Byzantine Emperor," *Harvard Slavic Studies*, II (*Festschrift Dvornik*) (Cambridge, Mass., 1954).

———— "Un Graffite Slave sur la façade d'une église de Bukovine," *Revue des études slaves*, XXIII (1947) 89ff.

Gregorovius, F. *Geschichte der Stadt Athen im Mittelalter*, 2 vols. (Stuttgart, 1889).

Grumel, V. "Les ambassades pontificales à Byzance après le II° concile de Lyon," *Échos d'Orient*, XXIII (1924) 437–447. Important.

———— "Le II° concile de Lyon et la réunion de l'église grecque," *Dict. de théol. cath.*, IX, pt. 1, cols. 1391–1410. Important.

———— "En Orient après le II° concile de Lyon," *Echos d'Orient*, XXIV (1925) 321ff.

Guardione, F. *Sul dominio dei ducati di Atene e Neopatria dei re di Sicilia* (Palermo, 1895). Unavailable to me.

Guilland, R. "La destinée des empereurs de Byzance," 'Επ. 'Ετ. Βυζ. Σπ. (1954) 37ff. Esp. for blinding of John.

———— *Essai sur Nicéphore Grégoras l'homme et l'oeuvre* (Paris, 1926).

———— "Études de titulature et de prosopographie byzantines. Les chefs de la marine byzantine," *Byz. Zeit.*, XLIV (1951) 212–240.

———— "Études de titulature et de prosopographie byzantines. Le protostrator," *Revue des études byzantines*, VII (1950) 156ff.

———— "Le Grand Connétable," *Byzantion*, XIX (1949) 99ff.

———— "Les ports de Byzance sur la Propontide," *Byzantion*, XXIII (1953) 181–204 and 205–338. Useful.

———— "Sur quelques grands dignitaires byzantins du XIV° siècle," *Mélanges Harmenopoulos* (1951) 179ff.

———— Section on Michael VIII's reign in Diehl, Guilland, etc., *L'Europe orientale de 1081 à 1453* (Paris, 1945) 177–221. Very useful.

Guldencrone, D. *L'Achaie Féodale* (Paris, 1886). Unsatisfactory.

Halecki, O. *Un Empereur de Byzance à Rome* (Warsaw, 1930). Fine work.

Haller, J. Review article of Norden in *Historische Zeitschrift*, XCIX (1907) 1–34. Unduly harsh.

Halphen, L. "Le rôle des 'Latins' dans l'histoire intérieure de Constantinople à la fin du XII° siècle," *Mélanges C. Diehl* (Paris, 1930), I, 141ff.

Hampe, K. *Geschichte Konradins von Hohenstaufen* (Innsbruck, 1894, and new ed. Leipzig, 1942). Important.

———— *Urban IV. und Manfred* (Heidelberg, 1905).

Hazlitt, W. *The Venetian Republic: Its Rise, Growth, and Fall* (London, 1900), esp. vol. I.

Héfelé-Leclercq. *Histoire des conciles*, VI¹ (Paris, 1914). Standard work on church councils.

Heiler, F. *Urkirche und Ostkirche* (Munich, 1937). Excellent modern work on Greek church.

Heisenberg, A. "Aus der Geschichte und Literatur der Palaiologenzeit," *Sitzungsb. d. bayerischen Akademie der Wissens. zu München*, 10. *Abhandlung* (1920) 1–144. Important.

———— "Kaiser Johannes Batatzes der Barmherzige," *Byz. Zeit.*, XIV (1905) 160–235.

404

——— "Studien zu Georgios Akropolites," *Sitzungsber. bayer. Akad. Wissen.* (1899) II, 463–558.

Heyd, W. *Histoire du commerce du Levant au Moyen-Age*, 2 vols. (Leipzig, 1885–1886) (reprinted 1936). Standard work; cited as *Histoire*.

Hofmann, G. "Patriarch Johann Bekkos und die lateinische Kultur," *Orientalia christiana periodica*, XI (1945) 141–164. Instructive.

Hopf, K. *Geschichte des Insel Andros und ihrer Beherrscher in dem Zeitraume von 1207–1566*, in *Sitzungsb. der Wiener Akademie der Wissens., Phil.-hist. Kl.*, XVI (1855) 23–131.

——— *Geschichte Griechenlands vom Beginn des Mittelalters bis auf unsere Zeit*, in *Allgemeine Enzyklopädie der Wissenschaften und Kunste*, ed. Ersch und Gruber, LXXXV (Leipzig, 1867). A basic work, wretchedly organized and frequently inaccurate, yet still extremely useful because of its enormous amount of detail; includes a section, now largely outdated, on Michael Palaeologus.

——— *Storia di Carlo d'Angiò e della guerra del Vespro Siciliano* (Naples, 1862). Material later republished in Sanudo, *Istoria*, ed. K. Hopf, in *Chron. gréco-romanes* (Berlin, 1873) 99ff.

——— "Urkunden und Zusätze zur Geschichte von Andros," *Sitz. Wiener Akad., phil.-hist. Kl.*, XXI (1856) 246ff.

——— "Veneto-byzantinische Analekten," *Sitzungsb. Wiener Akademie der Wissens., Phil.-hist. Kl.*, XXXII (1859) 365–528. Still useful.

Imperiale, C. *Jacopo d'Oria e i suoi Annali* (Venice, 1930). Good survey.

Iorga, N. *Histoire de la vie byzantine*, 3 vols. (Bucharest, 1934). Valuable bibliographical data.

——— "Notes et extraits pour servir à l'histoire des croisades au XVe siècle," *Revue de l'orient latin*, IV (1896).

Janin, R. *Constantinople byzantine développement urbain et répertoire topographique* (Paris, 1950).

——— *La géographie ecclésiastique de l'empire byzantin*, pt. 1, vol. III: *Les églises et les monastères* (Paris, 1953).

——— "Les sanctuaires de Byzance sous là domination latine," *Études byzantines*, II (Bucharest, 1944–1945) 134–184. Useful.

——— "Les sanctuaires des colonies latines à Constantinople," *Revue des études byzantines*, IV (Bucharest, 1946) 163–178. Useful.

Jerphanion, G. de. "Les inscriptions Cappadociens et l'histoire de l'empire grec de Nicée," *Orientalia chr. periodica*, I (1935) 239–256.

Jireček, C. *Geschichte der Bulgaren* (Prague, 1876).

——— *Geschichte der Serben* (Gotha, 1911) I.

——— *Die Heerstrasse von Belgrad nach Constantinopel* (Prague, 1877).

——— "Staat und Gesellschaft im Mittelalterlichen Serbien: Studien zur Kulturgeschichte des 13.–15. Jahrhunderts," *Denkschriften der kaiserlichen Akademie der Wissenschaften in Wien., Phil.-hist. Kl.*, vol. 56, 2 (Vienna, 1912) 1–76.

——— "Valona im Mittelalter," *Illyrisch-Albanische Forschungen*, ed. L. von Thallóczy (Munich–Leipzig, 1916) I.

405

Jordan, E. *L'Allemagne et l'Italie aux XII° et XIII° siècles* (Paris, 1939).

——— *Les origines de la domination angevine en Italie* (Paris, 1909). Standard work covering period to 1268.

Jordan, H. *Topographie der Stadt Rom in Alterthum* (Berlin, 1871). Containing esp. *Mirabilia*, 619ff.

Jugie, M. *Le schisme byzantin. Aperçu historique et doctrinal* (Paris, 1941). Important.

Kahane, H. "Italo-byzantinische Etymologien, Scala," *Byz.-neugr. Jahrb.*, XVI (1939–40) 33ff.

Kalligas, P. Μελέται Βυζαντινῆς Ἱστορίας (Athens, 1894). With a short survey on Michael's reign.

Kalomenopoulos, N. Article on Voluntaries in Μεγάλη Ἑλληνικὴ Ἐγκυκλοπαιδεία, XII (Athens, 1931) 487–488.

Kambourouglos, D. Note on Γασμοῦλοι in Πρακτικὰ τῆς Ἀκαδημίας Ἀθηνῶν, IV (Athens, 1929) 24.

Kantorowicz, E. *Kaiser Friedrich II* (Berlin, 1927).

——— "The 'King's Advent' and the Enigmatic Panels in the doors of Santa Sabina," *Art Bulletin*, XXVI (New York, 1944) 207ff. Useful.

Karmires, J. "The Schism of the Roman Church," (Eng. trans.) Θεολογία, XXI (1950) 37–67.

——— "Ἡ ἀποδιδομένη εἰς τὸν Μιχαὴλ Η' Παλαιολόγον Λατινικὴ ὁμολογία πίστεως τοῦ 1274," Ἀρχεῖον Ἐκκλησιαστικοῦ καὶ κανονικοῦ Δικαίου, II (Athens, 1947) 127ff.

Karst, A. *Geschichte Manfreds* (Berlin, 1897).

Kern, F. "Eduard I. von England u. Peter von Aragon," *Mitteil. d. Inst. für oesterr. Geschichtsfor.*, XXX (1909) 412ff.

Kougeas, S. "Ὁ Γεώργιος Ἀκροπολίτης Κτήτωρ τοῦ Παρισινοῦ κώδικος τοῦ Σουΐδα," *Byzantina Metabyzantina*, I (New York, 1949) 61–74.

Koukoules, Ph. Βυζαντινῶν βίος καὶ πολιτισμός, III (Athens, 1949). Valuable.

Krause, J. *Die Eroberungen von Constantinopel im dreizehnten und fünfzehnten Jahrhundert* (Halle, 1870).

Kretschmayr, H. *Geschichte von Venedig*, 3 vols. (Gotha, 1905–1934). Standard.

Krischen, F. *Die Landmauer von Konstantinopel* (Berlin, 1938).

Krumbacher, K. *Geschichte der byzantinischen Litteratur*, 2nd. ed. (Munich, 1897). Fundamental.

Kyrou, A. "Les Byzantins à Venise," *Ekloge*, III (1947) 702–707. Popular; in Greek.

La Mantia, G. "Studi sulla rivoluzione siciliana del 1282," *Archivio storico per la sicilia*, VI (1940) 97–135. Important; the most recent work on the Vespers.

La Monte, J. "Some Problems in Crusading Historiography," *Speculum*, XV (1940) 57–75. Useful bibliography.

——— "Three Questions concerning the Assizes of Jerusalem," *Byzantina Metabyzantina*, I (1946) 201–211.

Lampros, S. "Αὐτοκρατόρων τοῦ Βυζαντίου χρυσόβουλλα καὶ χρυσᾶ γράμματα," Νέος Ἑλληνομνήμων, XI (1914) 94–128 and 241–254.

―――― "Τὸ Βενετικὸν προξενεῖον ἐν Θεσσαλονίκῃ," Νέος Ἑλληνομνήμων, VIII (1911) 206–228. Nothing new.

―――― "Σημείωσις περὶ τοῦ τάφου τῆς βασιλίσσης τῆς Νικαίας ἐν Valentia," Νέος Ἑλληνομνήμων, XVIII (1924) 13–17.

―――― "Unedirte Münze Michaels Paläologos," Zeit. für Numismatik, IX (1882) 44–46.

Langlois, C. Le règne de Philippe III le Hardi (Paris, 1887).

Lappa-Zizikas, E. "Un traité de Théodore II Lascaris," Actes, VIᵉ congrès intern. d'études byzantines (Paris, 1948–1950) 119–126.

Lascaris, M. "Vagenitia," Revue historique du sud-est européen, XIX (1942) 423–437.

Laurent, M. H. Le bienheureux Innocent V (Pierre de Tarentaise) et son temps (Vatican, 1947). Thorough.

―――― "Georges le Métochite ambassadeur de Michel VIII Paléologue auprès d'Innocent V," Studi e testi, 123, Miscellanea G. Mercati (Vatican, 1946) 136ff.

Laurent, V. "Le cas de Photius dans l'apologétique du Patriarche Johan XI Beccos (1274–82) au lendemain du deuxième concile de Lyon," Echos d'Orient, XXIX (1930) 396–407.

―――― "La chronique anonyme du Cod. Mosquensis Gr. 426 et la pénétration turque en Bithynie . . . ," Rev. Etudes byz., VII (1950) 207ff. References to Michael.

―――― "La croisade et la question d'orient sous le pontificat de Grégoire X," Revue historique du sud-est européen, XXII (1945) 106–137. Important.

―――― "La date du premier couronnement de Michel VIII Paléologue," Échos d'Orient, XXXVI (1937) 165–169.

―――― "La domination byzantine aux bouches du Danube sous Michel VIII Paléologue," Revue historique du sud-est européen, XXII (1945) 184–198.

―――― "Une famille turque au service de Byzance: Les Mélikès," Byz. Zeit., XLIX (1956) 349–368.

―――― "La généalogie des premiers Paléologues," Byzantion, VIII (1933) 125–149. Useful.

―――― "Les grandes crises religieuses à Byzance. La fin du schisme Arsénite," Academie Roumaine, Bulletin de la section historique, XXVI, 2 (Bucharest, 1945) 1ff. Fine work.

―――― "Grégoire X et le projet d'une ligue antiturque," Échos d'Orient, XXXVII (1938) 257–273. Important.

―――― "Légendes sigillographiques et familles byzantines," Échos d'Orient, XXX (1931) 466ff.; XXXI (1932) 327ff.

―――― "Les manuscrits de l'histoire byzantine de Georges Pachymère," Byzantion, V (1929) 129ff.

―――― "Notes de chronographie et d'histoire byzantine," Échos d'Orient, XXXVI (1937) 162–165.

―――― "Le Pape Alexandre IV (1254–1261) et l'Empire de Nicée," Échos d'Orient, XXXIV (1935) 26–55. Unfinished but important.

———— "Le rapport de Georges le Métochite Apocrisiaire de Michel VIII Paléologue auprès du Pape Gregoire X (1275–76)," *Revue historique du sud-est européen*, XXIII (1946) 233–247.

———— "Le serment anti-Latin du Patriarche Joseph I," *Échos d'Orient*, XXVII (1927) 396ff.

———— Communication: "Les Vêpres Siciliennes et les dessous de la politique byzantine," *Atti dello VIII congresso internazionale di studi bizantini di Palermo, 1951*, I (Rome, 1953) 409–412.

Lea, H. C. *Superstition and Force* (Philadelphia, 1892).

Lehman-Haupt, C. "Τζάκωνες," Εἰς μνήμην Σπυρίδωνος Λάμπρου (Athens, 1935) 353ff.

Lehmann, B. *Die Nachrichten des Nik. Chon. G. Akrop. u. Pachym. über die Selcugen in der Zeit von 1180-bis 1280* (Leipzig, 1939).

Lemerle, P. *Philippes et la Macédoine orientale* (Paris, 1945).

Lenormant, F. *La Grande-Grèce*, 3 vols. (Paris, 1881).

Lentz, E. *Das Verhältnis Venedigs zu Byzanz, nach dem Fall des Exarchats bis zum Ausgang des neunten Jahrhunderts* (Berlin, 1891).

Léonard, E. *Les Angevins de Naples* (Paris, 1954). Recent; accurate.

Lequien, M. *Oriens Christianus*, 3 vols. (Paris, 1740).

Loenertz, R. "Autour du Chronicon Maius attribué à G. Phrantzes," *Miscellanea G. Mercati*, III (1946) 273–311. Important.

———— "Les établissements dominicains de Pera-Constantinople," *Échos d'Orient*, XXXIV (1933) 334ff.

Longnon, J. *L'Empire Latin de Constantinople* (Paris, 1949). Solid and with full references.

———— *Les Français d'outre-mer au moyen-âge* (Paris, 1929).

———— "Le Patriarcat Latin de Constantinople," *Jl. des savants* (1941) 174ff. Review of Santifaller with additional documents.

———— "Le rattachement de la principauté de Morée au royaume de Sicile en 1267," *Jl. des savants* (1942) 134ff. Important.

———— "La reprise de Salonique par les Grecs en 1224," *Actes du VI° congrès inter. d'études byzantines*, I (Paris, 1950) 141–146. Important.

Lopez, R. "Alfonso el Sabio y el primer Almirante Genovés de Castilla," *Cuadernos de historia de España*, XIV (1950) 5–16.

———— *Genova marinara nel duecento: Benedetto Zaccaria, ammiraglio e mercante* (Messina-Milan, 1933). Thorough and stimulating.

———— *Storia delle colonie genovesi nel Mediterraneo* (Bologna, 1938). One of the very best surveys of Genoese history.

Lopez, R. and I. Raymond. *Medieval Trade in the Mediterranean World Illustrative Documents . . .* (New York, 1955).

Magnocavallo, A. "Di alcuni codici del Liber Secretorum Fidelium Crucis di Marino Sanudo (il Vecchio)," *Nuovo archivio veneto*, VI (1903) 174–180.

———— *Marin Sanudo il Vecchio e il suo projetto di crociata* (Bergamo, 1901). Best work on Sanudo.

Makušev, V. *Monumenta historica slavorum meridionalium vicinorumque populorum e tabulariis et bibliothecis italicis deprompta*, I (Warsaw, 1874–1882).

Malavolti, O. *Dell' historia di Siena* (Venice, 1599).

Manfroni, C. *Storia della marina italiana dalle invasioni barbariche al trattato di Ninfeo* (Livorno, 1899). Useful.

—— "Sulla battaglia dei Sette Pozzi e le sue consequenze," *Rivista marittima* (Rome, 1900) 229ff. Useful.

Marinesco, C. "Du nouveau sur Constance de Hohenstaufen," *Byzantion*, I (1924) 451–468.

—— "Notes sur les Catalans dans l'empire byzantin," *Mélanges F. Lot* (Paris, 1925) 501ff. Useful.

Mas-Latrie, L. de. *Commerce et expéditions militaires de la France et de Venise au moyen âge* (Paris, 1880).

—— "Généalogie des Rois de Chypre de la famille de Lusignan," *Archivio Veneto*, XXI (1881) 309–360.

—— *Histoire de l'île de Chypre*, 3 vols. (Paris, 1852–1861).

—— "Les seigneurs Tierciers de Négrepont," *Revue de l'Orient Latin*, I (1893) 413ff.

Meliarakes, A. Ἱστορία τοῦ Βασιλείου τῆς Νικαίας καὶ τοῦ Δεσποτάτου τῆς Ἠπείρου (Athens-Leipzig, 1898). Old but still valuable for its insights and documentation; together with Gardner the old standard works on Nicaea and the Despotate of Epirus. Cited as *Nicaea*.

Mercati, A. "Note archivistiche, bibliografiche, paleografiche, storiche su un documento dell' anno 1277 di Giovanni Bekkos patriarca di Costantinopoli," *Orientalia christiana periodica* (*Miscellanea G. Hofmann*), XXI (1955) 256–264.

Mercati, S. G. "Giambi di ringraziamento per la conquista di Costantinopoli (1261)," *Byz. Zeit.*, XXXVI (1936) 289ff.

—— "Sulla vita e sulle opere di Giacomo di Bulgaria," *Actes du IVͦ congrès international des études byzantines*, IX (1935) 165–176.

Merkel, C. "La dominazione di Carlo I d'Angiò in Piemonte e in Lombardia e i suoi rapporti colle guerre contro re Manfredi e Corradino," *Memorie della Reale Accademia delle Scienze di Torino*, ser. II, XLI (1891).

—— "L'opinione dei contemporanei sull' impresa Italiana di Carlo I d'Angiò," *Memorie della R. Accademia dei Lincei* (1889) ser. IVa, IV, pt. 1, 313ff.

—— "Il Piemonte e Carlo I d'Angiò prima del 1259," *Memorie della Reale Accademia delle Scienze di Torino*, XL, ser. 2 (Turin, 1890) 3–98.

Merores, M. "Der Venezianische Adel," *Vierteljahrschrift für Sozial- und Wirtschaftsgeschichte*, XIX (1936) 137–237.

Meyer-Plath, B. and A. M. Schneider. *Die Landmauer von Konstantinopel* (Berlin, 1943). Important.

Michalopoulos, P. Κωνσταντῖνος Σάθας *1842–1914* (Athens, 1949). Brief commemorative article.

Michel, K. *Das Opus tripartitum des Humbertus de Romans O.P.* (Graz, 1926). Unavailable to me.

Miller, K. *Itineraria Romana* (Stuttgart, 1916). Useful.

Miller, W. "The Empire of Nicaea and the Recovery of Constantinople," ch. 16 in *Cambridge Medieval History*, IV (1936) 478–516.

———— *Essays on the Latin Orient* (Cambridge, 1921). Valuable.

———— "Greece and the Aegean under Frank and Venetian Domination," ch. 15 in *Cambridge Med. History*, IV (1923) 432ff.

———— *The Latins in the Levant* (New York, 1908). Best general work on Latin rule in Greece, many views of which are undergoing revision through new researches; with brief treatment of Michael's reign.

———— "Salonika," *English Historical Review*, XXXII (1917) 161–174.

———— *Trebizond the Last Greek Empire* (New York, 1926). Useful.

Miret y Sans, J. "La princesa Griega Lascaris," *Revue hispanique*, X (1903) 455ff.

———— "Tres princesas griegas," *Revue hispanique*, XV (1906) 668–716.

———— "Nuevos documentos de la tres princesas Griegas," *Revue hispanique*, XIX (1908) 112ff.

Monacis, Laurentius de. *Chronicon de rebus Venetis* (Venice, 1758).

Mondéjar, Marqués de G. I. *Memorias históricas del rei D. Alonso el Sabio i observaciones a su chronica* (Madrid, 1777). Contains important material.

Monti, G. "Da Carlo I a Roberto di Angiò," *Archivio storico per le province napoletane*, LX (1935) 154ff.

———— *La dominazione angioina in Piemonte* (Turin, 1930).

———— "La dominazione napoletana in Albania: Carlo I d'Angiò, primo re degli Albanesi," *Rivista d'Albania*, I (1940) 1ff.

———— *La espansione mediterranea del Mezzogiorno d'Italia e della Sicilia* (Bologna, 1942). Rarely cites sources.

———— *Il Mezzogiorno d'Italia nel Medioevo* (Bari, 1930). With references.

———— *Nuovi studi angioini* (Trani, 1937). Excellent bibliographies.

Moravcsik, G. *Byzantinoturcica: Die byzantinischen Quellen der Geschichte der Türkvölker*, 2 vols. (Budapest, 1942). A basic guide to Byzantine literature.

Müller, J. "Die Legationen unter Papst Gregor X (1271–1276)," *Römische Quartalschrift*, XXXVII (1929) 57ff.

Nicol, D. "The Date of the Battle of Pelagonia," *Byz. Zeit.*, 49 (1956) 68–71. Useful.

———— *The Despotate of Epirus* (Oxford, 1957). Recent, solid work, parts of which supersede Meliarakes.

———— "Ecclesiastical Relations between the Despotate of Epirus and the Kingdom of Nicaea, 1215–1230," *Byzantion*, XXII (1930) 207–228.

Nicollini, N. "Sui rapporti diplomatici veneto-napoletani durante i regni di Carlo I e Carlo II d'Angiò," *Arch. st. prov. nap.*, LX (1935) 229–286. Useful.

Nikolsky, V. "The Union of Lyons. An Episode from Medieval Church History, 1261–1293," *Pravoslavnoe Obozrenie*, XXIII (1867) 5–23 and later issues. Unavailable to me.

Nomides, M. Ἡ Ζωοδόχος Πηγή (Istanbul, 1937).

Norden, W. *Das Papsttum und Byzanz* (Berlin, 1903). Very valuable; see Introduction.

Ortoleva, G. *San Bonaventura e il secondo concilio di Lione* (Rome, 1874). Unavailable to me.

Ostrogorsky, G. "Agrarian conditions in the Byzantine Empire in the Middle Ages," *Cambridge Economic History*, I (1941) 194–223. Useful.

—— *History of the Byzantine State*, transl. by J. Hussey (Oxford, 1956); also German ed., *Geschichte des byzantinischen Staates* (Munich, 1952). Best general history of Byzantium.

—— *Pour l'histoire de la féodalité byzantine*, trans. H. Grégoire (Brussels, 1954). Excellent, detailed analysis.

—— "Zum Stratordienst der Herrschers in der byzantinischen-slavischen Welt," *Seminarium Kondakovianum*, VII (1935) 189ff. Important.

Palmieri, A. "I vicarii patriarcali de Costantinopoli," *Bessarione*, VII (1904) 41–53.

Papademetriou, S. " Ὁ ἐπιθαλάμιος Ἀνδρονίκου II τοῦ Παλαιολόγου," *Byz. Zeit.*, XI (1902) 452–460.

Papadopulos, A. *Versuch einer Genealogie der Palaiologen 1259–1453* (Munich, 1938). Cited as *Genealogie*; very helpful; see Introduction.

Pappadopoulos, J. "Phrantzes est-il réellement l'auteur de la grande chronique qui porte son nom?" *Actes du IV' congrès international des études byzantines*, I (Sofia, 1935) 176ff.

—— *Théodore II Lascaris, Empereur de Nicée* (Paris, 1908). Rather inadequate.

Paspates, A. Βυζαντινὰ Ἀνάκτορα (Athens, 1885).

—— Βυζαντιναὶ Μελέται (Constantinople, 1877).

Pelliot, P. "Les Mongols et la papauté," *Revue de l'orient chrétien*, XXIII (1922–1923) 3ff.; XXIV (1924) 225ff.; XXVIII (1931–1932) 3ff.

Pichler, A. *Geschichte der kirchlichen Trennung zwischen dem Orient und Occident*, 2 vols. (Munich, 1864–1865).

Pinzi, C. *Storia della città di Viterbo*, II (Rome, 1889.

Pontieri, E. "Un capitano della guerra dell' Vespro Pietro II Ruffo di Calabria," *Archivio storico per la Calabria e la Lucania*, I (1931) 269ff. Included as part 2 of next listed work.

—— *Ricerche sulla crisi della monarchia siciliana nel secolo XIII* (Naples, 1942; new ed. 1950). Very important. Also article on the Vespers in *Enciclopedia Italiana*, XXXV (1937) 224.

Previale, L. "Un Panegyrico inedito per Michele VIII Paleologo," *Byz. Zeit.*, XXXXII (1942) 1ff. Good analysis of Holobolos' encomium.

Previté-Orton, C. *Shorter Cambridge Medieval History*, vol. II, esp. on Sicilian Vespers, 765–766 (Cambridge, 1952).

Proctor, E. "Materials for the reign of Alfonso X of Castile, 1252–1284," *Transactions of the Royal Historical Society* (London, 1931) 39ff.

Ramsay, W. *Historical Geography of Asia Minor* (London, 1890). Standard.

411

Rasovskii, D. "Polovtsy," *Seminarium Kondakovianum*, VII (1935) 245–262; VIII (1936) 161–182, and later issues. Best work on the subject.

Rennell Rodd, J. *The Princes of Achaia and the Chronicles of Morea*, 2 vols. (London, 1907). Outdated but not worthless.

Riant, P. "Les dépouilles religieuses enlevées à Constantinople au XIIIᵉ siècle," *Mémoires de la société nationale des antiquaires de France*, IV, ser. 6 (1875) 1–214.

Rodotà, P. *Dell' origine progresso, e stato presente del rito greco in Italia.* 3 vols. (Rome, 1758–1763). Still useful.

Rodriguez, F. "Origine, cronologia e successione degli imperatori Paleologi," *Rivista di araldica e genealogia*, I (Naples, 1933) fasc. 4–5. Useful; see Ch. 1.

Röhricht, R. "Der Kreuzzug König Jacobs I. von Aragonien (1269)," *Mitteilungen des österreichischen Instituts für Geschichtsforschung*, XI (1890) 372–395.

Romanin, S. *Storia documentata di Venezia*, 10 vols., esp. vol. II (Venice, 1853–1861; reprinting, 1925). Famous work with important documents.

Romano, G. "Messina nel Vespro Siciliano," *Atti dell' Accad. Peloritana*, XIV (1900) 185ff.

Romanos, J. Περὶ τοῦ Δεσποτάτου τῆς Ἠπείρου (Corfu, 1895). Reliable, extends to end of Despotate; superseded in part by Meliarakes and Gardner, and now Nicol.

Roncaglia, M. *Les frères mineurs et l'église grecque orthodoxe au XIIIᵉ siècle (1221–1274)* (Cairo, 1954). Useful survey; see review of V. Laurent in *Byz. Zeit.*, XLIX (1956) 137–139.

Rossi, G. *Storia della città di Ventimiglia* (Oneglia, 1886).

Rouillard, G. "La politique de Michel VIII Paléologue à l'égard des monastères," *Études byzantines*, I (1943) 73–84. Useful.

Ruano, E. "Huéspedes del impero de oriente en la corte de Alfonso X el Sabio," *Estudios dedic. a M. Pidal*, VI (1956) 631–645.

Rubió i Lluch, A. *Paquimeres i Muntaner*, in *Memòries de la secció historico arqueol. del Institut d'Estudis Catalans*, I, (Barcelona, 1927).

Runciman, S. "Byzantine Trade and Industry," *Cambridge Economic History*, II (1952) 86–118. Useful.

—— *The Eastern Schism* (Oxford, 1955). Useful.

—— *History of the Crusades*, vol. III (Cambridge, 1954). Very fine work, esp. on 4th Crusade.

Saba, D. *Bernardo I Ayglerio Abate di Montecassino*, in *Miscellanea Cassinense*, no. 8 (Montecassino, 1931) 95ff. Rather popular.

Sabatini, G. Rossi. *L'espansione di Pisa nel Mediterraneo fino alla Meloria* (Florence, 1935).

Sabellico, M. *Historia rerum Venetarum, degl' istorici delle cose Veneziane* (Venice, 1718).

Sambin, P. *Il vescovo Cotronese Niccolò da Durazzo e un inventario di suoi codici latini e greci (1276)* (Rome, 1954). Unavailable to me.

412

Sanesi, I. "Giovanni di Procida e il Vespro Siciliano," *Rivista storica italiana*, VII (1890) 489–519. On the problem of Procida and the Vespers.

Santifaller, L. *Beiträge zur Geschichte des lateinischen Patriarchats von Konstantinopel* (Weimar, 1938). Good study.

Sathas, C. [or K.] *La tradition hellénique et la légende de Phidias de Praxitèle et de la fille d'Hippocrate du moyen âge* (Paris, 1883) 1–28. Interesting.

Saulger, R. *Histoire nouvelle des anciens Ducs de l'Archipel* (Paris, 1698). Rare, interesting work.

Sauli, L. *Della colonia dei Genovesi in Galata* (Turin, 1831), 2 vols. Though superseded, contains a few documents unprinted elsewhere.

Savio, F. *Studi storici sul Marchese Guglielmo III di Monferrato ed i suoi figli* (Turin, 1885).

Scaduto, M. *Il. monachismo basiliano nella Sicilia Medievale: Rinascita e decadenza* (Rome, 1947). Fine, recent survey, also covering Angevin period.

Schirrmacher, F. *Die letzten Hohenstaufen* (Göttingen, 1871).

Schlumberger, G. "Le tombeau d'une impératrice byzantine à Valence en Espagne," *Byzance et croisades* (Paris, 1927) 57ff.

Schneider, A. M. "Mauern und Tore am Goldenen Horn zu Konstantinopel" (Göttingen, 1951), *Nachrichten d. Akad. d. Wiss. in Gott. l. Philol.-hist. Kl.*, 1950, no. 4. Unavailable to me.

Schneider, A. M. and M. Nomides. *Galata topographisch-archäologischer Plan* (Istanbul, 1944).

Schneider, F. "Beiträge zur Geschichte Friedrichs II. und Manfreds," *Quellen und Forschungen aus italienischen Archiven und Bibliotheken*, XV (1912).

———— "Eine Quelle für Manfreds Orientpolitik," *Quellen und Forschungen aus italienischen Archiven und Bibliotheken*, XXIV (1952–1953) 112ff. Useful.

Serra, G. *La storia della antica Liguria e di Genova*, 4 vols. (Turin, 1834). Old but not worthless.

Setton, K. "The Byzantine Background to the Italian Renaissance," *Proceedings of the American Philosophical Society*, C, no. 1 (1956) 1ff. Very valuable survey, esp. for 14th and 15th centuries.

———— "On the importance of Land Tenure and Agrarian Taxation in the Byzantine Empire, from the Fourth Century to the Fourth Crusade," *Amer. Jl. of Philology* (1953) 225–259. Useful survey.

Ševčenko, I. "Imprisonment of Manuel Moschopulos in the year 1305 or 1306," *Speculum*, XXVII (1952) 133–157.

Siatos, A. Μία Ποινικὴ Δίκη κατὰ Μιχαὴλ Παλαιολόγου, μέ θεοκρισίαν (Athens, 1938). Popular but useful.

Siderides, X. "Μανουὴλ Ὁλοβώλου Ἐγκώμιον εἰς Μιχαὴλ Η´ Παλαιολόγον," Ἐπετηρὶς Ἑτ. Βυζ. Σπουδῶν, III (1926) 168ff.

———— "Ὁ ἐν Γενούῃ Βυζαντινὸς Πέπλος," Ἐπετηρὶς Ἑτ. Βυζαντινῶν Σπουδῶν, V (1928) 376–378.

Simonsfeld, H. *Andreas Dandolo und seine Geschichtswerke* (Munich, 1876).

——— "Studien zu Marino Sanudo dem Aelteren," *Neues Archiv der Gesellschaft für ältere deutsche Geschichtskunde,* VII (1882), 45–72. Partly superseded by Magnocavallo.

Sinogowitz, B. "Zur Eroberung Thessalonikes im Herbst 1224," *Byz. Zeit.,* XLV (1952) 28.

Skržinskaja, E. "The Genoese in Constantinople in the 14th Century" (in Russian), *Vizantiskii Vremennik,* I (26) (1947) 215ff.

Sobernheim, M. Article on Baibars, in *Encyclopedia of Islam* (1913).

Soldevilla, F. "Le voyage de Marie de Brienne en Espagne," *Atti dello VIII congresso intern. di studi bizantini di Palermo 1951,* I (Rome, 1953) 476. Very brief.

Soranzo, G. *Il papato, l' Europa cristiana, e i Tartari* (Milan, 1930). Useful synthesis.

Sotomayor, M. El patriarca Beccos, según J. Paquimeres, *Estudios Eclesiást.,* XXXI (1957) 327ff. Unavailable to me.

Souarn, R. "Tentatives d'union avec Rome: Un patriarche grec catholique au XIII° siècle," *Echos d'Orient,* III (1899–1900) 229–237; 351–361. Outdated.

Spuler, B. *Die Mongolen in Iran* (Leipzig, 1939). Important.

Stählen, F. *Pagasai und Demetrias* (Berlin, 1934).

Stapper, R. *Papst Johannes XXI* (Münster, 1898). Fairly useful.

Stefano, A. De. *Federico III d'Aragona re di Sicilia* (Palermo, 1937).

Stein, E. "Untersuchungen zur spätbyzantinischen Verfassungs- und Wirtschaftgeschichte," *Mitteil. zur osmanischen Geschichte,* II (1923–1925) 1–62.

Stephanides, B. Ἐκκλησιαστικὴ Ἱστορία (Athens, 1948). Esp. section on unionist attempts, pp. 315–364.

Sternfeld, R. *Der Kardinal Johann Gaëtan Orsini* (Berlin, 1905).

——— "Das Konklav von 1280 und die Wahl Martins IV. (1281)," *Mitteilungen für österreichische Geschichtsforschung,* XXXI (1910) 1ff. Useful; unused by scholars of the Vespers.

——— *Ludwigs des Heiligen Kreuzzug nach Tunis 1270 und die Politik Karls I. von Sizilien* (Berlin, 1896). Important though old.

——— "Der Vertrag zwischen dem Paläologen Michael VIII. und Peter von Aragon im Jahre 1281," *Arkiv für Urkundenforschung,* VI (1918) 276ff. Important; unused by many scholars of the Vespers.

Sthamer, E. "Aus der Vorgeschichte der sizilischen Vesper." *Quellen und Forschungen aus italienischen Archiven und Bibliotheken,* XIX (1927) 262ff.

Sufflay, M. von. "Die Grenzen Albaniens im Mittelalter," in L. de Thallóczy, *Illyrisch-Albanische Forschungen,* I (Munich-Leipzig, 1916) 288ff.

Svoronos, J. Πῶς ἐγεννήθη καὶ τί σημαίνει ὁ δικέφαλος ἀετὸς τοῦ Βυζαντίου (Athens, 1914).

Swift, E. "The Latins at Hagia Sophia," *American Jl. of Archaeology,* 2nd ser., XXXIX (1935) 458–474.

414

Sykoutres, J. "Περὶ τὸ σχίσμα τῶν 'Αρσενιατῶν," Ἑλληνικά, II (1929) 257ff. and later issues. Penetrating.

────── "Συνοδικὸς τόμος τῆς ἐκλογῆς τοῦ Πατριάρχου Γερμανοῦ τοῦ Γ' (1265–6)," 'Επετηρὶς 'Ετ. Βυζαντινῶν Σπουδῶν (1932) 178–212.

Syropoulos, S. Historia vera unionis non verae . . . Concilii Florentini (Hague, 1660). Controversial Greek account of Florence Council; see Ch. 11.

Tafel, T. De Thessalonica eiusque agro (Berlin, 1839).

────── Via militaris Romanorum Egnatia (Tübingen, 1841).

Tafrali, O. Thessalonique au quatorzième siècle (Paris, 1913).

────── Thessalonique des origines au XIV° siècle (Paris, 1919). Moderately useful synthesis.

Throop, P. Criticism of the Crusade: A Study of Public Opinion and Crusade Propaganda (Amsterdam, 1940). Focuses mainly on Western side of crusades; see esp. ch. 6 on Humbert of Romans.

Tosti, D. Storia della badia di Montecassino (Rome, 1888) esp. vol. III. Standard.

Treitinger, O. Die öströmische Kaiser- und Reichsidee nach ihrer Gestaltung im höfischen Zeremoniell (Jena, 1938).

Troitskiï, J. Arsenius and the Arsenites (in Russian) (St. Petersburg, 1873).

Typaldos, G. "Οἱ ἀπόγονοι τῶν Παλαιολόγων μετὰ τὴν ἅλωσιν," Δελτίον τῆς 'Ιστορικῆς καὶ 'Εθνολογικῆς 'Εταιρείας τῆς 'Ελλάδος, VIII (1923) 129ff. Interesting but to be used with caution.

────── " 'Ο 'Ρὼς Σολυμᾶς τῶν Βυζαντινῶν," 'Επετηρὶς 'Ετ. Βυζαντινῶν Σπουδῶν, II (1925) 316ff.

Uspenskij, F. "Vizantijskie istoriki o mongolach i egipetskich mamljukach," Viz. Vrem., XXIV (1923–1926) 1ff.

Usseglio. "Il regno di Tessaglia," Rivista di storia, arte, archeol. della prov. di Allessandria, VII (1899) 111ff. Unavailable to me.

Valenti, G. "Vestigia di Manfredi Hohenstaufen Re di Sicilia e Signore di 'Romania,' " Numismatica (1939) 1ff.

Van der Vat, O. Die Anfänge der Franziskanermissionen und ihre Weiterentwicklung im nahen Orient und in den Mohammedanischen Ländern während des 13. Jahrhunderts (Werl in Westf., 1934). Useful.

Van Millingen, A. Byzantine Constantinople. The Walls of the City and Adjoining Historical Sites (London, 1899). Still very valuable.

Van Moé, E. "L'envoi de nonces à Constantinople par les papes Innocent V et Jean XXI," in Mélanges d'archéologie et d'histoire, XLVII (1930) 39–62. Useful.

Vasiliev, A. "Foundation of the Empire of Trebizond," Speculum, XI (1936) 3–37.

────── Histoire de l'empire byzantine, 2 vols. (Paris, 1932). New ed. in English, History of the Byzantine Empire (Madison, 1952). Useful general history.

────── "On the Question of Byzantine Feudalism," Byzantion, VIII (1933) 584–604. Superseded by Ostrogorsky and Charanis.

────── "The opening stages of the Anglo-Saxon Immigration to Byzantium in the Eleventh Century," *Seminarium Kondakovianum*, IX (1937) 39–70.

Vasiljevsky, V. "Varjago-russkaja i varjago-angliiskaja v konstantinople XI i XII vekov," *Trudy* (St. Petersburg, 1908) vol. I, 176ff.

Vassilief, A. *Anecdota graeco-byzantina* (Moscow, 1893).

Verlinden, Ch. *Les empereurs belges de Constantinople* (Brussels, 1945).

Vernadsky, G. "Relations between the Golden Horde, Egypt, and Byzantium under . . . Michael Palaeologus" (in Russian), *Seminarium Kondakovianum*, I (1927) 73ff.

Vernet, F. Article on Lyons Council in *Dict. théol. catholique*, IX pt. 1, cols. 1374–1391.

Viller, M. "La question de l'union des églises entre Grecs et Latins. . ." *Revue d'histoire écclésiastique*, XVI (1921) 260–305; 515–532; XVIII (1920) 20–60. Penetrating; best study on the subject.

Walter, F. *Die Politik der Kurie unter Gregor X.* (Berlin, 1894).

Weiss, R. "The Greek Culture of South Italy in the Later Middle Ages," *Proceedings of British Academy*, XXXVII (1951) 23–50. Important new insights.

——— "The Translators from the Greek of the Angevin Court of Naples," *Rinascimento*, III–IV (1950) 195–226. Useful.

White, L. *Latin Monasticism in Norman Sicily* (Cambridge, 1938). Good ch. on Greek monasticism.

Wieruszowski, H. "Der Anteil Johanns von Procida an der Verschwörung gegen Karl von Anjou," *Gesammelte Aufsätze zur Kulturgeschichte Spaniens*, V (Münster, 1935) 230–239. Useful.

——— "La corte di Pietro d'Aragona e i precedenti dell' impresa Siciliana," *Arch. stor. it.*, I (1938) 141–162; and II (1938) 200–217. Useful.

——— "Conjuraciones y alianzas politicas del rey Pedro de Aragón contra Carlos de Anjou antes de la Visperas Sicilianas," *Boletín de la Academia de la Historia*," 107 (Madrid, 1935) 547–602. Contains several new documents. Important.

Winter, D. *Die Politik Pisas während der Jahre 1268–1282* (Halle, 1906). Nothing on Greek relations.

Wittek, P. *Das Fürstentum Mentesche: Studien zur Geschichte Westkleinasiens im 13.–15. Jh.* (Istanbul, 1934).

Wolff, R. L. "Baldwin of Flanders and Hainaut, First Latin Emperor of Constantinople: His Life, Death, and Resurrection, 1172–1225," *Speculum*, XXVII (1952) 281–322. Valuable.

——— "Footnote to an Incident of the Latin Occupation of Constantinople: The Church and the Icon of the Hodegetria," *Traditio*, VI (1948) 319–328.

——— "Hopf's So-Called 'Fragmentum' of Marino Sanudo Torsello," *The Joshua Starr Memorial Volume* (New York, 1953) 149–159. New ed. of *Fragmentum*. See p. 95.

——— "The Latin Empire of Constantinople 1204–1261," unpublished doctoral dissertation, Harvard University (1947) 4 vols. Exhaustive; see Introduction.

—— "The Latin Empire of Constantinople and the Franciscans," *Traditio*, II (1944) 213–237.

—— "Mortgage and Redemption of an Emperor's Son: Castile and the Latin Empire of Constantinople," *Speculum*, XXIX (1954) 45–84. Very important.

—— "A New Document from the Period of the Latin Empire of Constantinople: The Oath of the Venetian Podestà," *Annuaire inst. phil. et d'hist. or.-sl. (Mél. Grégoire)*, XII (1952) 539–573. Contains document.

—— "The Organization of the Latin Patriarchate of Constantinople, 1204–1261. Social and Administrative Consequences of the Latin Conquest," *Traditio*, VI (1948) 33–60. Useful.

—— "Politics in the Latin Patriarchate of Constantinople," *Dumbarton Oaks Papers No. 8* (Cambridge, 1954) 225–303. Valuable.

—— "Romania: The Latin Empire of Constantinople," *Speculum*, XXIII (1948).

Wittek, P. *The Rise of the Ottoman Empire* (London, 1938). Good.

Wroth, W. *Catalogue of Imperial Byzantine Coins in the British Museum* (London, 1908).

Xanthoudides, S. Ἡ Ἐνετοκρατία ἐν Κρήτῃ καὶ οἱ κατὰ τῶν Ἐνετῶν ἀγῶνες τῶν Κρητῶν (Athens, 1939). Standard work.

Yver, G. *Le commerce et les marchands dans l'Italie meridionale au XIIIᵉ et XIVᵉ siècles* (Paris, 1903).

Zakythinos, D. "Crise monétaire et crise économique à Byzance du XIIIᵉ au XVᵉ siècle," *L'Hellénisme contemporain*, I² (1947) 169ff.; II² (1948) 150ff. Important.

—— *Le Despotat grec de Morée 1262–1460*, I (Paris, 1932); II (Athens, 1953). Thorough; standard work on Morea of Palaeologoi.

—— "Μελέται περὶ τῆς διοικητικῆς διαιρέσεως καὶ τῆς ἐπαρχιακῆς διοικήσεως ἐν τῷ Βυζαντινῷ κράτει," Ἐπετηρὶς Ἑταιρείας Βυζαντινῶν Σπουδῶν, XVII (1941) 209–214; XVIII (1948) 71–91.

—— "La population de la Morée byzantine," *L'Hellénisme contemporain*, III (1949) 7ff.

Zepos, R. "Τὸ Δίκαιον εἰς τὸ Χρονικὸν τοῦ Μορέως," Ἐπετηρὶς Ἑταιρείας Βυζαντινῶν Σπουδῶν, XVIII (1948) 202–220.

Zerlentes, P. Φεοδαλικὴ Πολιτεία ἐν τῇ Νήσῳ Νάξῳ (Hermenoupolis, 1925). Inaccessible to me.

Zisterer, A. *Gregor X. und Rudolf von Hapsburg* (Fribourg-en-Brisgau, 1891).

Zolotas, G. "Γεωγραφικὰ εἰς Παχυμέρην," Ἐπετηρὶς Φιλολογικοῦ Συλλόγου Παρνασσός, IX (Athens, 1906) 5ff.

Zotos, A. Ἰωάννης ὁ Βέκκος Πατριάρχης Κωνσταντινουπόλεως Νέας Ῥώμης ὁ Λατινόφρων (Munich, 1920). Of little value; see criticism in *Echos d'Orient*, XXIV [1925] 26–32.

417

GLOSSARY OF BYZANTINE TITLES

Certain of the titles below are simply honorary and entail the performance of no specific duties. Moreover, some titles in this period were undergoing transformation, with a corresponding shift of position in the hierarchy of ranks. Hence the difficulty of establishing precise meanings for the terms in Michael's reign. For further information see Diehl, Guilland, *et al.*, *L'Europe orientale de 1081 à 1453*, esp. 379–392; Bréhier, *Les institutions de l'empire byzantin*, esp. 136–153; and E. Stein, "Untersuchungen zur spätbyzantinischen Verfassungs- und Wirtschaftsgeschichte," *Mitt. zur osmanischen Gesch.*, II (1924) 1–62. Also see (Pseudo) Codinus, *De officialibus palatii Cpolitani et de officiis magnae ecclesiae Liber* (Bonn, 1839).

Basileus
> The Emperor, title often coupled with *Autokrator.*

Caesar
> Title ranking below *Sebastokrator.* Reserved usually for imperial family or granted to outsiders for important services to the state.

Chartophylax
> Secretary of the episcopal chancery. The *Grand Chartophylax* was an important dignitary of the patriarch.

Despot
> Highest-ranking official after the Emperor. Title sometimes implying a limited kind of sovereignty or even right of succession to the throne. Usually granted to princes-of-the-blood but on rare occasions to foreigners.

Domestic of Hagia Sophia
> Ecclesiastical official ranking immediately after the two heads of the antiphonal choirs in Hagia Sophia.

Epi ton deeseon
> Receiver of petitions addressed to the Emperor. Important because of his proximity to the throne.

Grand Constable
> Commander of the Latin mercenaries of the Empire, ranking next to the *Protostrator* and *Grand Stratopedarch.* Title created in imitation of the Norman Constable.

Grand Domestic
> Commander-in-chief of the imperial army. High-ranking title generally reserved for close relatives of the Emperor.

Grand Logothete
> Highest-ranking minister of the Empire. Handled various aspects of administration, notably foreign affairs.

Grand Primikerios
> Master of ceremonies in the imperial palace.

Grand Stratopedarch
> High official in charge of armaments and provisions for the troops.

419

Megas Dukas (Grand Duke)
> Commander of the imperial fleet, sometimes with only nominal command.

Megas Kyr (The Great Lord)
> Title by which the Burgundian Duke of Athens-Thebes was known to his Greek subjects.

Pansevastos
> Title of honor, highest of a hierarchy of such titles.

Parakoimomenos
> Originally the chief eunuch of the imperial chamber. In Michael's period this official also performed other important duties of state.

Prokathemenos tou Vestiariou
> Minister of finance who had replaced the *Logothete of the Treasury*.

Protokynegos
> Court official who held the imperial stirrup while the Emperor mounted and was in charge of the hunt.

Protostrator
> Commander of the vanguard and light-cavalry troops.

Protovestiarites
> Official originally connected with the imperial chamber, now an important personage exercising military command.

Protovestiarios
> In this period head of the treasury administration. One of the highest Byzantine titles, ranking above the *Grand Domestic*.

Sebastokrator
> High official ranking just below the *Despot*. Title reserved for imperial family.

Tatas of the Court
> Tutor of the heir-apparent.

Vestiarios
> Title of honor, in this period usually connected with the treasury administration. Originally, official in charge of the imperial wardrobe.

inδεx

Abagha, Khan of Mongols, 101n, 220, 288, 289n
Abbate, Palmiero, 363n
Abydos, Bay of, 198
Achaia, Principality of, 14, 41, 55, 64, 80, 140, 154, 157, 166, 169, 176, 195, 221, 232, 235, 237, 241, 257, 279, 325, 326, 328, 339; Michael's campaigns in, 1263-66, 171-75; in treaties of Viterbo, 197, 198, 199, 201, 221; Michael's campaigns in, 1270-72, 229-30. See also Morea
Acre, 82; Michael's tower at, 343n
Acropolites, George, Grand Logothete and historian, 8, 10, 28, 30n, 37-38, 42, 71, 76, 77, 79, 85, 93, 107, 112, 276n, 302n; at Michael's treason trial, 24; character of, 28; hatred of Muzalons, 35n, 37-38; mission to Bulgars, 81; reads prayers of thanksgiving, 121; at Lyons, 258, 259, 262, 294, 307, 314n
d'Adam, Guillaume, 343n, 356n
Adramyttion, 88
Adrianople, 231, 318
Aenos, 88
Agridi Kounoupitza, 159
Albania, 47, 51, 53, 198, 230, 231, 235, 245, 257, 279, 280, 290, 326n, 329, 330, 353n, 363, 368; Charles made King of, 233-34
Albano, Bishop of, 225, 227
Alemanno, Garnerio, 194n
Alexander III, Pope, 44
Alexander IV, Pope, 61, 157
Alexios I Comnenos, Byzantine Emperor, 43n, 288
Alexios III Angelos, Byzantine Emperor, 18, 28n, 34
Alexios Palaeologus, 18
Alexios Strategopoulos, 62, 68, 92-94, 145; recovers Constantinople, 97-115, 119; prepares capital, 120-21, 123

Alfonso X, King of Castile, 193, 219, 246, 252, 254, 287, 359, 375-76
Allatius, Leo, 94
Alubardes, 132, 140-41
Alum, 210, 251, 358
Alyattes, Alexios, 251
Alyattes, Nikephoros, 60
Amalfi, 82; merchants of, 133
Amari, M., 346n, 351
Amorgos, 296, 302n
Anatolia (Asia Minor), 81, 90, 126, 210, 217, 219, 236n, 302n, 343, 358, 369; Greek proposal to use Latin crusading armies in, 287-90
Anchialos, 181, 232
Ancona, 133, 183, 294
Andravida, 158, 173
Andronikos II Palaeologus, Emperor and son of Michael, 121, 175, 260, 262, 263, 292n, 293, 307, 312, 313, 320n, 321, 336n, 358n, 359n, 368n, 369, 375-77; and John Lascaris, 217-18; marriage of, 233, 253; and burial of Michael, 370
Andronikos Palaeologus, father of Michael, 18, 21
Anemopylae, 236
Angelo of Urbino, 311
Angeloi, 17n, 314n, 331
Angelos, Michael, 331
Anjou, County of, 363
Anna, daughter of Frederick II. See Constance
Anna, daughter of Michael II of Epirus, 57
Anna, Hungarian wife of Andronikos II, 233, 375
Annales Ianuenses, 84, 85, 148, 152, 153, 162-63, 208, 342, 358
Annales Placentini Gibellini, 252, 347, 376
Anonymous of Trani, 50n
Anonymous Poem, 107, 108n
Ansaldo d'Oria, 148

421